HOSEA, JOEL, AND AMOS

In this commentary, Graham R. Hamborg offers a timely and up-to-date assessment of the books of Hosea, Joel, and Amos. Recognising that each had a compositional history leading to the final forms by which we know them, he brings a literary approach to the texts and connects them to other parts of the Hebrew Bible/Old Testament. Hamborg also draws attention to topics where there are a range of scholarly views. 'Closer Look' sections explore significant themes and terms in greater depth, and 'Bridging the Horizons' sections indicate how the texts are of continuing significance in today's world. Conveying the meaning and importance of Hosea, Joel, and Amos in non-technical language and in an accessible style, this volume will be a valuable commentary for biblical scholars, students, and non-specialists for years to come.

Graham R. Hamborg earned his doctorate from the University of Nottingham. The author of *Still Selling the Righteous: A Redaction-Critical Investigation into Reasons for Judgment in Amos 2:6–16* (2012), he is an ordained minister in the Church of England.

NEW CAMBRIDGE BIBLE COMMENTARY

GENERAL EDITOR: Ben Witherington III

HEBREW BIBLE/OLD TESTAMENT EDITOR: Bill T. Arnold

EDITORIAL BOARD
Bill T. Arnold, *Asbury Theological Seminary*
James D. G. Dunn, *University of Durham*
Michael V. Fox, *University of Wisconsin-Madison*
Robert P. Gordon, *University of Cambridge*
Judith M. Gundry, *Yale University*
Ben Witherington III, *Asbury Theological Seminary*

The New Cambridge Bible Commentary (NCBC) aims to elucidate the Hebrew and Christian Scriptures for a wide range of intellectually curious individuals. While building on the work and reputation of the Cambridge Bible Commentary popular in the 1960s and 1970s, the NCBC takes advantage of many of the rewards provided by scholarly research over the last four decades. Volumes utilize recent gains in rhetorical criticism, social scientific study of the Scriptures, narrative criticism, and other developing disciplines to exploit the growing advances in biblical studies. Accessible jargon-free commentary, an annotated "Suggested Readings" list, and the entire New Revised Standard Version (NRSV) text under discussion are the hallmarks of all volumes in the series.

PUBLISHED VOLUMES IN THE SERIES
1 Peter, Ruth Anne Reese
Ephesians, David A. deSilva
Philippians, Michael F. Bird and Nijay K. Gupta
Acts, Craig S. Keener
The Gospel of Luke, Amy-Jill Levine and Ben Witherington III
Galatians, Craig S. Keener
Mark, Darrell Bock
Psalms, Walter Brueggemann and William H. Bellinger, Jr.
Matthew, Craig A. Evans
Genesis, Bill T. Arnold
The Gospel of John, Jerome H. Neyrey
Exodus, Carol Meyers
1–2 Corinthians, Craig S. Keener
James and Jude, William F. Brosend II
Judges and Ruth, Victor H. Matthews
Revelation, Ben Witherington III

Hosea, Joel, and Amos

Graham R. Hamborg
University of Nottingham

CAMBRIDGE
UNIVERSITY PRESS

University Printing House, Cambridge CB2 8BS, United Kingdom

One Liberty Plaza, 20th Floor, New York, NY 10006, USA

477 Williamstown Road, Port Melbourne, VIC 3207, Australia

314–321, 3rd Floor, Plot 3, Splendor Forum, Jasola District Centre, New Delhi – 110025, India

103 Penang Road, #05–06/07, Visioncrest Commercial, Singapore 238467

Cambridge University Press is part of the University of Cambridge.

It furthers the University's mission by disseminating knowledge in the pursuit of education, learning, and research at the highest international levels of excellence.

www.cambridge.org
Information on this title: www.cambridge.org/9781108482387
DOI: 10.1017/9781108687362

© Graham R. Hamborg 2023

This publication is in copyright. Subject to statutory exception and to the provisions of relevant collective licensing agreements, no reproduction of any part may take place without the written permission of Cambridge University Press.

First published 2023

A catalogue record for this publication is available from the British Library.

Library of Congress Cataloging-in-Publication Data
NAMES: Hamborg, Graham R., author.
TITLE: Hosea, Joel, and Amos / Graham R. Hamborg, University of Nottingham.
DESCRIPTION: First edition. | Cambridge, United Kingdom ; New York, NY, USA: Cambridge University Press, 2023. | Series: New Cambridge Bible commentary | Includes bibliographical references and index.
IDENTIFIERS: LCCN 2022025428 | ISBN 9781108482387 (hardback) | ISBN 9781108687362 (ebook)
SUBJECTS: LCSH: Bible Hosea – Commentaries. | Bible Joel – Commentaries. | Bible Amos – Commentaries.
CLASSIFICATION: LCC BS1565.53 .H36 2023 | DDC 224–dc23/eng/20220615
LC record available at https://lccn.loc.gov/2022025428

ISBN 978-1-108-48238-7 Hardback
ISBN 978-1-108-71215-6 Paperback

Cambridge University Press has no responsibility for the persistence or accuracy of URLs for external or third-party internet websites referred to in this publication and does not guarantee that any content on such websites is, or will remain, accurate or appropriate.

Contents

List of Supplementary Sections	page xi
Preface	xiii
A Word about Citations	xv
List of Abbreviations	xvii

I **VOLUME INTRODUCTION** ... 1
  Prophets and Prophetic Texts ... 2
  The Book of the Twelve ... 6
  Suggested Readings ... 12

II **BOOK OF HOSEA** ... 16
  A Introduction to Hosea ... 16
    Hosea as Literary Text ... 18
    The Composition History of the Book of Hosea ... 20
    Key Themes in the Book of Hosea ... 27
  B Suggested Readings on Hosea ... 30
  C Commentary on Hosea ... 34
    1 Hosea's Marriage – Hosea 1–3 ... 34
      Hosea 1:1 – Heading ... 34
      Hosea 1:2–2:1 [3] – Hosea's Wife and Children ... 37
      Hosea 2:2–15 [4–17] – A Wife and Mother Condemned ... 50
      Hosea 2:16–23 [18–25] – People and Land Restored ... 59
      Hosea 3 – 'The Lord Loves the People of Israel' ... 64
    2 Prophetic Words of Judgement and Restoration – Hosea 4:1–11:11 ... 71
      Hosea 4 – YHWH's Contention with Priest and People Alike ... 71
      Hosea 5:1–7 – Judgement on Priests, People, and King ... 94
      Hosea 5:8–7:16 – Ephraim's Sickness ... 98
      Hosea 8 – Israel Has Forgotten His Maker ... 119

vii

viii   *Contents*

Hosea 9:1–9 – 'Do Not Rejoice, O Israel'	128
Hosea 9:10–10:15 – Agricultural Similes and Metaphors of Israel	134
Hosea 11:1–11 – Israel, YHWH's Child	146
3 Guilt and Healing – Hosea 11:12–14:9 [12–14]	157
Hosea 11:12–12:14 [12:1–15] – Ephraim, Judah, and Jacob	157
Hosea 13 [13:1–14:1] – Ephraim's End	171
Hosea 14 [14:2–10] – 'I Will Heal Their Disloyalty'	180

III BOOK OF JOEL	189
A Introduction to Joel	189
Joel as Literary Text	190
The Composition History of the Book of Joel	191
Key Themes in the Book of Joel	197
B Suggested Readings on Joel	200
C Commentary on Joel	202
1 A Disastrous Plague of Locusts – Joel 1:1–2:27	202
Joel 1:1 – Heading	202
Joel 1:2–4 – Hear and Tell	203
Joel 1:5–14 – Calls to Lament	206
Joel 1:15–20 – The Day of YHWH is Near	214
Joel 2:1–11 – Proclamation of the Day of YHWH	219
Joel 2:12–14 – A Summons to Turn to YHWH	224
Joel 2:15–17 – Let Everyone Assemble and Let the Priests Weep	228
Joel 2:18–27 – YHWH's Promise of Restoration	230
2 YHWH's Spirit Poured Out on All Who Call Upon His Name – Joel 2:28–32 [3:1–5]	237
Joel 2:28–29 [3:1–2] – YHWH's Spirit Poured Out	237
Joel 2:30–32 [3:3–5] – Everyone Who Calls Upon the Name of YHWH Shall Be Saved	239
3 Judgement on the Nations and Blessing on Judah – Joel 3 [4]	244
Joel 3:1–3 [4:1–3] – Announcement of Judgement on the Nations	244
Joel 3:4–8 [4:4–8] – Tyre and Sidon and the Regions of Philistia	246
Joel 3:9–15 [4:9–15] – Judgement Executed	248
Joel 3:16–17 [4:16–17] – YHWH Dwells in Zion	251
Joel 3:18–21 [4:18–21] – Judah, Edom, and Egypt	253

IV BOOK OF AMOS	260
A Introduction to Amos	260
Amos as Literary Text	261

The Composition History of the Book of Amos	264
Key Themes in the Book of Amos	268
B Suggested Readings on Amos	272
C Commentary on Amos	276
1 A Series of Oracles against the Nations – Amos 1–2	276
Amos 1:1 – Heading	276
Amos 1:2 – YHWH Roars from Zion	277
Amos 1:3–2:3 – Oracles against Foreign Nations	279
Amos 2:4–16 – Oracles against Judah and Israel	297
2 Words of YHWH to Israel – Amos 3–4	308
Amos 3:1–2 – 'You Only Have I Known'	308
Amos 3:3–8 – YHWH Has Spoken: Who Can But Prophesy?	310
Amos 3:9–11 – Summon the Witnesses	314
Amos 3:12–15 – Warn the Wealthy	316
Amos 4:1–3 – The Cows of Bashan	318
Amos 4:4–5 – 'Come – and Transgress'	320
Amos 4:6–12 – 'Yet You Did Not Return to Me' ·	322
Amos 4:13 – The One Who Forms the Mountains and Creates the Winds	326
3 Words of Amos to Israel – Amos 5–6	327
Amos 5:1–17 – Lament for a Fallen Nation	327
Amos 5:18–20 – 'Alas for You Who Desire the Day of YHWH'	337
Amos 5:21–27 – 'Let Justice Roll Down like Waters'	339
Amos 6:1–14 – 'Alas to Those Who Live in Luxury But Are Not Grieved over the Ruin of Joseph'	344
4 A Series of Visions – Amos 7:1–9:6	350
Amos 7:1–9 – 'This is What the Lord YHWH Showed Me'	350
Amos 7:10–17 – 'O Seer, Go, Flee'	356
Amos 8:1–3 – The Basket of Summer Fruit	362
Amos 8:4–7 – Cheating the Poor and Needy	363
Amos 8:8–14 – The Time of Judgement is Coming	365
Amos 9:1–6 – Judgement Executed	368
5 The Future: Judgement and Blessing – Amos 9:7–15	371
Amos 9:7–10 – The Future: Judgement – But Not on All	371
Amos 9:11–15 – Blessing and Security	374
Author Index	377
Scripture Index	381
Subject Index	405

Supplementary Sections

A Closer Look: A Wife of Prostitution	*page* 41
A Closer Look: Baalism, Canaanite Religion, and Ancient Ugarit	55
Bridging the Horizons: The Metaphor of the Unfaithful Wife	69
A Closer Look: Knowledge of and by YHWH	76
A Closer Look: Hosea and the Ten Commandments	78
Bridging the Horizons: Priestly Responsibility	85
A Closer Look: 'Ephraim' in Hosea	92
Bridging the Horizons: Israel's Alliances with Foreign Nations	118
A Closer Look: The Covenant Concept in Scholarly Research	121
Bridging the Horizons: The Judgement and Mercy of YHWH	156
A Closer Look: Jacob in Hosea 12	162
A Closer Look: Fasting	213
A Closer Look: The Day of YHWH	215
Bridging the Horizons: Joel 2:28–32 in the New Testament	243
A Closer Look: The Destiny of the Nations	256
A Closer Look: Zion	279
Bridging the Horizons: Atrocities and War Crimes	294
A Closer Look: Oracles against the Nations	295
A Closer Look: The Nazirites	306
A Closer Look: Justice in the Gate	333
A Closer Look: Justice and Righteousness	335
A Closer Look: Woe Oracles	338
A Closer Look: The Prophets, the Cult, and Sacrifice	341
Bridging the Horizons: Martin Luther King Jr.	343
A Closer Look: The Prophets as Intercessors	354
A Closer Look: Seers and Prophets	361

Preface

When I first came to study the Hebrew Bible it was the book of Amos that most stimulated me, and I have remained engaged with Amos scholarship over many years. My in-depth engagement with the books of Hosea and Joel is more recent, but I have found that they too have much to offer. It has been a pleasure and a privilege to write this volume, and my thanks are due to Bill Arnold as editor for his invitation to write it, and for his prompt communications across the Atlantic which have helped to bring it to fruition. My thanks also to Professor Graham Davies, whose suggestion it was that I offer to write a volume for the NCBC series, and who was among those who fostered in me a love of the Hebrew Bible.

I see the purpose of commentary as being elucidation of the text in the light of the best available current scholarship. This volume aims to be accessible to non-specialists, such as undergraduate students, ordinands and seminarians, preachers, and teachers in faith communities, and interested laypeople. It also aims to be of value within scholarly circles, by contributing to scholarly discussion of contested issues, and by making a few original proposals at some points. To fulfil these diverse aims is challenging, and the reader must judge the degree to which I have been successful.

The volume is in four parts: a 'Volume Introduction', in which methodological considerations are addressed, and one part covering each of Hosea, Joel, and Amos. The latter parts are based on the NRSV, the text of which is set out in the commentaries within each part. A revision of NRSV was brought out in 2021, and is the version followed. Recognising that, for some time, many readers may still be using the previous edition, I have noted its different translation when the difference seems significant, referring to the previous edition as the 'pre-2021 NRSV'. I have sometimes referred to the New International Version (NIV) for comparison where the Hebrew text is unclear or admits of more than one possible translation. The books of

Hosea and Joel both contain sections of variance in numbering between the Hebrew text and English translations. In these sections I have cited the English references, with the Hebrew reference following in square brackets: hence 'Hosea 1:10–2:1 [2:1–3]'. I have referred to the Greek (Septuagint) text or other ancient versions only when they aid translation or understanding of the Hebrew text.

In citing secondary literature I have given priority to works in English wherever possible, in the expectation that the majority of readers will be English-speaking. Where works in German are cited it is because they are important works that have not been translated and have no equivalent in English, or because they have been seminal in the history of scholarship. Where I have quoted from an article, I have put the page number of the quotation in brackets after those of the article: hence *BTB* 13 (1993): 54–63 (60).

The draft of this volume was substantially complete prior to the publication of recent commentaries by M. D. Carroll R. on Amos, J. Goldingay on Hosea–Micah, T. S. Hadjiev on Joel and Amos, and R. Routledge on Hosea. I have consulted them all, and have made some changes to my text in the light of them; but undoubtedly there would have been more references to them had they been available earlier in my preparation. The redaction-critical method that this volume employs distinguishes it from them, making it in no way superfluous to them.

My doctorate on the book of Amos and subsequent study and writings have been undertaken on a part-time basis, alongside holding full-time ministerial posts in the Church of England. Throughout these years my wife and family have been a constant support and joy. I therefore dedicate this book to my wife Ruth, and to my children Jo, Pete, Chloë, Rosie, and Rob, and their families, all of whom have enriched my life beyond measure.

A Word about Citations

All volumes in the NCBC include footnotes, with full bibliographical citations included in the note when a source is first mentioned. Subsequent citations include the author's initial or initials, full last name, abbreviated title for the work, and date of publication. Most readers prefer this citation system to endnotes that require searching through pages at the back of the book. In this volume treating three books, the full bibliographical citation is given on its first occurrence in each of the separate parts on Hosea, Joel, and Amos. Similarly, footnote numbering begins afresh in each part.

The Suggested Reading lists, also included in all NCBC volumes after the introductions, are not part of this citation apparatus. Annotated and organised by publication type, the self-contained Suggested Reading lists are intended to introduce and briefly review some of the most well-known and helpful literature on the biblical text under discussion.

Abbreviations

AB	Anchor Bible
ABD	*The Anchor Bible Dictionary* (6 vols.), ed. D. N. Freedman (New York: Doubleday, 1992)
ANEM	Ancient Near Eastern Monographs
ANET	*Ancient Near Eastern Texts Relating to the Old Testament*, ed. J. B. Pritchard (3rd ed., with supplement; Princeton: Princeton Press, 1969)
AOAT	Alter Orient und Altes Testament
AYB	Anchor Yale Bible
BASOR	*Bulletin of the American Schools of Oriental Research*
BCE	Before Common Era
BCOT	Baker Commentary on the Old Testament
BDB	F. Brown, S. R. Driver, and C. A. Briggs, *Hebrew and English Lexicon of the Old Testament* (3rd printing; Oxford: Clarendon Press, 1976)
BEATAJ	Beiträge zur Erforschung des Alten Testaments und des antiken Judentum
BHS	*Biblia Hebraica Stuttgartensia*, ed. K. Elliger and W. Rudolph (Stuttgart: Deutsche Bibelgesellschaft, 1976–1977)
BRT	*Baptist Review of Theology*
BTB	*Biblical Theology Bulletin*
BZAW	Beihefte zur Zeitschrift für die alttestamentliche Wissenschaft
CB	Coniectanea Biblica
CBC	Cambridge Bible Commentary
CBQ	*Catholic Biblical Quarterly*
CBR	*Currents in Biblical Research*
CE	Common Era

CUP	Cambridge University Press
DLT	Darton, Longman and Todd
ET	*Expository Times*
EvT	*Evangelische Theologie*
EVV	English Versions
FAT	Forschungen zum Alten Testament
FCB	Feminist Companion to the Bible
FOTL	Forms of Old Testament Literature
FRLANT	Forschungen zur Religion und Literatur des Alten und Neuen Testaments
IB	*Interpreter's Bible*, ed. G. Buttrick (New York: Abingdon Press, 1952)
ICC	International Critical Commentary
ICJ	International Court of Justice
JBL	*Journal of Biblical Literature*
JBQ	*Jewish Biblical Quarterly*
JHS	*Journal of Hebrew Scriptures*
JNES	*Journal of Near Eastern Studies*
JSOT	*Journal for the Study of the Old Testament*
JSOTSup	Journal for the Study of the Old Testament Supplement Series
JSS	*Journal of Semitic Studies*
KAT	Kommentar zum Alten Testament
KJV	King James Version
LHBOTS	Library of Hebrew Bible/Old Testament Studies
LXX	Septuagint
MSS	Manuscripts
MT	Masoretic text
NCB	New Century Bible
NCBC	New Cambridge Bible Commentary
NIB	*The New Interpreter's Bible* (12 vols.), ed. L. E. Keck (Nashville: Abingdon Press, 1994–1998)
NICOT	New International Commentary on the Old Testament
NIDB	*The New Interpreter's Dictionary of the Bible* (5 vols.), ed. K. Doob Sakenfeld (Nashville: Abingdon Press, 2006–2009)
NIV	New International Version
NKZ	*Neue kirchliche Zeitschrift*
NRSV	New Revised Standard Version
OAN	Oracles against the Nations

List of Abbreviations

OTE	*Old Testament Essays*
OTG	Old Testament Guides
OTL	Old Testament Library
OTS	*Oudtestamentische Studiën*
OUP	Oxford University Press
PEQ	*Palestine Exploration Quarterly*
SBL	Society of Biblical Literature
SBLAB	Society of Biblical Literature Academia Biblica
SBLDS	Society of Biblical Literature Dissertation Series
SBLSymS	Society of Biblical Literature Symposium Series
SBTS	Sources for Biblical and Theological Study
SJOT	*Scandinavian Journal of Theology*
SOTSMS	Society for Old Testament Study Monograph Series
SWBA	Social World of Biblical Antiquity
TB	*Tyndale Bulletin*
TDOT	*Theological Dictionary of the Old Testament* (15 vols.), ed. G. J. Botterweck and H. Ringgren (Grand Rapids: Eerdmans 1974–1995)
TOTC	Tyndale Old Testament Commentary
VT	*Vetus Testamentum*
VTSup	Vetus Testamentum Supplement Series
WMANT	Wissenschaftliche Monographien zum Alten und Neuen Testament
ZAW	*Zeitschrift für die alttestamentliche Wissenschaft*

I Volume Introduction

The books of Hosea, Joel, and Amos are the first three books of the Book of the Twelve Prophets, as Jewish tradition refers to them, or the Minor Prophets as they are known in Christian tradition. The term 'minor' may be taken to refer to their length rather than to their importance.

Hosea 1:1 indicates to the reader that they can expect to find prophetic words of the Lord that came to Hosea in the eighth century BCE, during the reigns of various kings of Judah and of King Jeroboam II of Israel.[1] Many sections of the book describe and warn of impending judgement and destruction of the people, principally for their idolatry and offering of sacrifices to Baal. However, such words are interspersed with others which portray the tender mercy of YHWH, and the concluding chapter contains a promise that 'I will heal their disloyalty; I will love them freely' (Hos. 14:4).

Amos 1:1, similarly, indicates that the book to follow contains words of Amos from the same century, in the days of Uzziah king of Judah and Jeroboam II king of Israel. Again, the words of this book describe and warn of impending judgement and destruction, with few words of mercy and hope. Indeed, most of the book is unrelenting in its message of judgement. The dominant reasons for judgement in this text are the unjust treatment of the poor and their exploitation by their rich fellow Israelites, rather than the unfaithfulness to YHWH described in the book of Hosea. However, similarly to Hosea, the book ends with words of promised blessing.

---

[1] The name 'Israel' refers variously in the Hebrew Bible to (1) the northern of the two kingdoms formed when the united monarchy came to an end after the death of Solomon (as recounted in 1 Kgs 12); (2) to the united monarchy, or to refer to the two kingdoms of Israel and Judah as an entity; and (3) from the Babylonian Exile onwards, to refer to the community of faith. In Hos. 1:1 and Amos 1:1 it refers to the northern kingdom.

2   *Volume Introduction*

Between these two books comes the book of Joel.[2] There is no chrono-logical information given in the opening verse, and there is no internal evidence to indicate that the compilers of the book intended it to be read against any particular historical background. The first two chapters describe the devastation of a plague of locusts, with an invitation to return to YHWH and proclaim a fast in order to seek an end to the disaster. This is followed by promises of blessing on the people, and announcement of a universal judgement of the nations.

PROPHETS AND PROPHETIC TEXTS

Much scholarship of the nineteenth and early twentieth centuries, influenced by scholars such as Julius Wellhausen, held the eighth-century prophets – Amos, Hosea, Isaiah, Micah – in high regard, seeing them as the pinnacle of Israelite ethical religion. This led to great interest in the figures of the prophets themselves, and many studies and commentaries approached the texts with the aim of stripping away any material deemed not to derive from the prophet in order to unearth the original, pure message delivered by the prophet. As Childs wrote with regard to Amos, 'Great effort was expended throughout the literary critical period of the late nineteenth and early twentieth centuries by such commentators as Wellhausen and Harper to recover the *ipsissima verba* of Amos who was held in high esteem as the earliest written prophet and exponent of ethical monotheism.'[3] A consequence was a tendency to denigrate material deemed to be 'secondary' or 'inauthentic', and to see less interpretative and theological significance in such material than in that deemed to be 'original'.[4]

In the later part of the twentieth century, however, and on into the twenty-first century, literary approaches have come to the fore that value the texts as much as the people and events that the texts describe. This development reflects, partly, frustration that texts were being viewed more as a window to be looked through rather than as something to be studied and appreciated in their own right. It also reflects trends in modern literary

---

[2]   This is the order in MT: the place of Joel in LXX is mentioned later.

[3]   B. S. Childs, *Introduction to the Old Testament as Scripture* (London: SCM, 1979): 397.

[4]   See, for example, W. R. Harper, *A Critical and Exegetical Commentary on Amos and Hosea* (ICC; Edinburgh: T & T Clark, 1905): cxxxi–xxxiv (with regard to Amos) and clix–cxlii (with regard to Hosea). His use of the terms 'glosses' and 'interpolations' also feels pejorative. Surprisingly the vocabulary of original/secondary and authentic/inauthentic resurfaces in M. D. Carroll R., *The Book of Amos* (NICOT; Grand Rapids: Eerdmans, 2020).

studies more widely.[5] Some recent studies take a 'final form' approach, in which the composition history of the text is of less concern than the final form itself.[6] Others seek to investigate the composition history of the text, considering that each purported stage in its composition can have interpretative significance. The method employed to discern the composition history of the text is redaction criticism, and it is a method and approach that this commentary will use. It has the merit that it takes seriously the final form of the text as being a key focus of interpretation, but is also ready to find interpretative significance in earlier compositional layers where they can be identified with reasonable confidence; and it does not rule out the possibility of reaching behind the text to the spoken words of an historical prophet, even though this is not the key focus of the method. Due humility is necessary in recognising that the further back in time and in numbers of compositional layers proposed, the more provisional scholarly reconstructions become. Yet for some texts there is a reasonable scholarly consensus regarding the main outlines of their composition history, despite the inevitable variation in detail between the proposals of different scholars.

Sweeney describes redaction-critical work as being 'concerned with reconstructing the compositional and editorial process by which earlier texts are taken up to be reread, reinterpreted, edited, and rewritten in relation to the concerns of later times'.[7] Barton notes that

> respect for the original sources did not mean that the redactors *never* changed their raw materials. In prophetic texts, for example, it is common to find comments updating the original prophetic oracles (e.g. Isa 16:13–14), and it is probable that the desire to apply the prophet's words to the editor's own situation led to frequent changes in the wording of the original oracles.[8]

Such processes imply that those working with, copying, expanding, and developing prophetic texts held what they received as continuing to convey a divine message for their generation. But they did not regard the inherited tradition as so fixed that it could not be re-applied, with new material added, or with existing material placed in a new literary context. In these

---

[5] As noted by C. Meyers with regard to a parallel move in Pentateuchal scholarship in her *Exodus* (NCBC; New York: Cambridge University Press): 2.

[6] Childs's *Introduction to the Old Testament as Scripture* was significant and influential for the impetus towards final-form studies.

[7] M. A. Sweeney, *The Twelve Prophets*, vol. 1 (Berit Olam Studies in Hebrew Narrative and Poetry; Collegeville, MN: Liturgical Press, 2000): xx.

[8] J. Barton, 'Redaction Criticism', *ABD* 5:644–7 (646–7, italics original).

4 *Volume Introduction*

quotations Sweeney speaks of a 'compositional and editorial process', and Barton refers within a few lines both to 'redactors' and 'editors', and these and other terms are used by redaction critics. The choice of terminology is of less importance than the recognition that in the periods in which the texts were formed, there was both respect for what was inherited, and freedom to develop it.[9] As Schart notes, 'the ongoing rewriting of the prophetic heritage certifies that the prophetic collections were successful in mediating the word of God into different historical situations'.[10] While some are critical of the redaction-critical method for dealing in probabilities and possibilities rather than in the supposed certitude of the final form of the text,[11] the riposte to be made is that a focus on only the final form is restrictive compared to what I have called elsewhere the 'promising array of exegetical opportunities'[12] that redaction criticism opens up.

The identification of earlier compositional layers underlying the final form of the text is made on the basis of various kinds of indicator. Structural markers such as headings and endings to units of text, literary style and presentation, particular vocabulary which may be characteristic of texts widely dated to particular periods, historical references to particular times or circumstances, and thematic considerations all play a part. While there is always a danger of circular argument ('Composition A contains particular vocabulary or themes, therefore material containing such vocabulary or themes belongs to Composition A'), a cumulative case built on a combination of these indicators can lead to a high degree of probability and plausibility that the compositional layer identified did indeed exist at a point in the history of the text's development.[13] In this commentary the introductions to each of Hosea, Joel, and Amos will explore what compositional layers may be plausibly identified in the case of each book.

---

[9] This is in contrast to later centuries in which the Canon was deemed to be closed, and the text to be unalterable. At this point application to new contexts and generations is achieved by commentary on the text.

[10] A. Schart, 'Reconstructing the Redaction History of the Twelve Prophets: Problems and Models', in J. D. Nogalski and M. A. Sweeney (eds.), *Reading and Hearing in the Book of the Twelve* (SBLSymS, 15; Atlanta: SBL, 2000): 34–48 (46).

[11] This certitude is itself not absolute, once textual difficulties and the difficulty of determining structural patterns in the final form of some texts are taken into account.

[12] G. R. Hamborg, 'The Post-722 and Late Pre-exilic Redactional Compositions Underlying the Amos-Text', in R. P. Gordon and H. M. Barstad (eds.), *'Thus Speaks Ishtar of Arbela': Prophecy in Israel, Assyria, and Egypt in the Neo-Assyrian Period* (Winona Lake: Eisenbrauns, 2013): 143–59 (159).

[13] See further G. R. Hamborg, *Still Selling the Righteous: A Redaction-Critical Investigation into Reasons for Judgment in Amos 2:6–16* (LHBOTS, 555; London: T&T Clark, 2012): 4–22.

Prophets and Prophetic Texts

The means by which sayings presumably spoken by the prophets such as Hosea and Amos became literary text is the part of the process about which we know least. P. R. Davies refers to 'a deep chasm of ignorance' to which scholars should own up in this respect.[14] Elsewhere, however, he notes that while prophetic literary texts akin to those of the Hebrew Bible are not found in the ancient Near East, transcribing and retaining of prophetic oracles and similar material is. He writes of Amos:

> That a number of oracles were written or uttered and transcribed, then placed in the local palace or temple archive (in this case, presumably at Bethel) is quite probable. This is a process attested elsewhere in the ancient Near East. But there are no parallels to scrolls as *edited* literary products, only a collection of texts from the same source, written, bound or stored together (and in this case, perhaps labelled 'Words of Amos of Tekoa: What He Saw about Israel Two Years before the Earthquake'). But later, and for a presumably good reason, it was thought that the words of Amos had a new purpose and that they should be rearranged and supplemented to fulfil that purpose.[15]

Similarly, Edelman writes that 'the temple complex at Bethel would have been a likely source for the materials in Hosea, Amos, and some of the Elijah and Elisha traditions'.[16] Thus we may imagine that prophetic words were recorded and stored in places such as Bethel and Samaria, and that with the fall of the northern kingdom they were taken to Jerusalem for safe keeping.

The commentaries in this book will focus primarily on the text itself, seeking to find interpretative meaning in all the significant stages of composition which can plausibly be identified. Linville comments that ancient writers would have struck 'a suitable balance between tradition, adaptation and innovation. There would always be circumstances that required new ideas and ways of thinking about tradition. Inherited stories and oracles attributed to the great prophets of old would have been given a new emphasis

---

[14] P. R. Davies, 'Amos, Man and Book', in B. E. Kelle and M. B. Moore (eds.), *Israel's Prophets and Israel's Past: Essays on the Relationship of Prophetic Texts and Israelite History in Honor of John H. Hayes* (LHBOTS, 446; New York: T & T Clark International, 2006): 113–31 (117).

[15] P. R. Davies, 'Why Do We Know about Amos?' in D. V. Edelman and E. Ben Zvi (eds.), *The Production of Prophecy: Constructing Prophecy and Prophets in Yehud* (London: Equinox Publishing Ltd, 2009): 55–72 (63–4, italics original).

[16] D. V. Edelman, 'From Prophets to Prophetic Books: The Fixing of the Divine Word' in D. V. Edelman and E. Ben Zvi (eds.), *Production of Prophecy*: 29–54 (41).

6 Volume Introduction

and meaning as circumstances changed.'[17] The task of commentary today is to continue to explore how words from ancient times hold meaning and significance for much later, contemporary times.

THE BOOK OF THE TWELVE

In introducing and commenting on Hosea, Joel, and Amos as three separate texts, this commentary is following what has been usual and widespread practice. However, since the early 1990s several scholars have argued that ancient tradition, both Jewish and Christian, provides evidence that the twelve books of Hosea–Malachi were read as one 'Book of the Twelve' or 'Minor Prophets'. That all were generally written on one scroll is indisputable. These scholars argue that this was not merely a technical convenience, however, arising from the fact that the individual texts would not warrant a whole scroll each. Rather, they suggest, we should endeavour to read and interpret the Book of the Twelve as one book, not as twelve books which happen to share a scroll.[18]

An early reference to the 'Twelve Prophets' is found in the apocryphal book of Sirach, which derives from the second century BCE.[19] Chapters 44–49 are headed a 'Hymn in Honour of Our Ancestors'. They laud figures from Enoch, Noah, and Abraham onwards, including Elijah, Isaiah, and Ezekiel as prophets. Then 49:10 says: 'May the bones of the Twelve Prophets send forth new life from where they lie, for they comforted the people of Jacob and delivered them with confident hope.' This, it is argued, provides evidence that there was a collection of twelve texts named after twelve prophets, which were seen as one book.

In the Babylonian Talmud, Baba Batra (section 14b) states: 'Our Rabbis taught: The order of the Prophets is, Joshua, Judges, Samuel, Kings, Jeremiah, Ezekiel, Isaiah and the Twelve Minor Prophets.'[20] This is taken

---

[17] J. R. Linville, *Amos and the Cosmic Imagination* (SOTSMS; Aldershot: Ashgate Publishing Company, 2008): 9.

[18] Significant proponents of this view include P. R. House, A. Schart, J. D. Nogalski, M. A. Sweeney, R. Albertz, J. Wöhrle. See the 'Suggested Readings'.

[19] The text can be reliably dated to the first quarter of the second century BCE on the basis of the information given in the book's own prologue. See J. J. Collins, 'Ecclesiasticus, or the Wisdom of Jesus Son of Sirach', in J. Barton and J. Muddiman (eds.), *The Oxford Bible Commentary* (Oxford: Oxford University Press, 2000): 667–98 (667).

[20] I. Epstein (ed.) *The Babylonian Talmud. Seder Nezikin III. Baba Bathra. Tr. into English with Notes, Glossary and Indices*, vol. 1 (London: Soncino Press, 1935): 70.

The Book of the Twelve

7

as evidence that the 'Twelve Minor Prophets' were seen as one work in the same way that Jeremiah, Ezekiel, and Isaiah were. The preceding section of Baba Batra (13b) also states that 'Between each book of the Torah there should be left a space of four lines, and so between one Prophet and the next. In the twelve Minor Prophets, however, the space should only be three lines.'[21] Nogalski draws attention, too, to Jerome's Prologue to the Twelve Prophets, in which he states that 'the Twelve is one book', and from his review of external sources he concludes that 'Jewish and Christian traditions from 200 BCE to the Middle Ages indicate that the Twelve Prophets were counted as a single book.'[22]

Alongside such external evidence, advocates of interpreting the Book of the Twelve as one book seek to establish internal connections. Literary, structural, and thematic considerations are all brought into play. In literary terms, Nogalski has demonstrated the importance of 'catchwords' which link different texts within the Book of the Twelve. There are occurrences of these in Hosea, Joel, and Amos. For example, Joel 3:16a [4:16a] says: 'YHWH roars from Zion, and utters his voice from Jerusalem.' A few lines of Hebrew text later, Amos 1:2a is identical. Again, Joel 3:18 [4:18] says 'the mountains shall drip with sweet wine', and the almost identical phrase is found in Amos 9:13. Such catchwords seem to be strategically placed to link the different texts together.

Structural considerations are less convincing across the twelve texts as a whole, but may indicate some earlier groupings of texts at a prior stage of development. Thus Hosea, Amos, Micah, and Zephaniah all begin with superscriptions which include chronological references to kings of Judah, and in the cases of Hosea and Amos to kings of Judah and Israel. Further on in the Book of the Twelve, the headings to the texts of Haggai and Zechariah both contain a chronological reference to the reign of the Persian king Darius.

Thematically, Nogalski identifies four recurrent themes. First is the 'Day of YHWH', which, with regard to the books with which this volume is concerned, is strongly present in the book of Joel, and also in Amos 5:18–20. It recurs in Zephaniah 1, and is alluded to in other parts of the Book of the Twelve. The second recurring theme that he identifies is strongly present in Hosea and Joel, namely the fertility of the land. Hosea 2:8 refers to

---

[21] *Babylonian Talmud*: 66.
[22] J. D. Nogalski, *The Book of the Twelve: Hosea–Jonah* (Smyth & Helwys Bible Commentary; Macon, GA: Smyth & Helwys, 2011): 2–3 (3).

8   *Volume Introduction*

YHWH as the giver of grain, wine, and oil, and as punishment for Israel's unfaithfulness he threatens to take it back (2:9) and to lay waste the vines and fig trees (2:12); however, at a future time of restoration the earth will provide grain, wine, and oil once more (2:22). At the end of Hosea is the promise that Israel shall grow grain, and blossom like the vine (14:7 [8]). The opening section of Joel then describes a devastation of the land caused by a plague of locusts, leading to a call to repentance and the proclamation of a fast (2:12–17), which in turn leads to a promise of renewed blessing, as part of which 'You shall eat in plenty and be satisfied' (2:26). A third recurrent theme is exploration of the fate of God's people: put very broadly, Hosea and Amos deal with the punishment and restoration of Israel, and Micah and Zephaniah do the same with regard to Judah; Haggai and Zechariah 1–8 describe the people responding to the call to turn to YHWH, and the consequent re-building of the Temple and promise of restoration of Jerusalem; the remaining six texts and Zechariah 9–14 then continue to deal in various ways with the fate of the people. The fourth recurrent theme is that of theodicy, a theme which Nogalski sees as occurring principally within the first seven texts. Specifically, themes of YHWH's compassion and judgement are explored through quotations of Exodus 34:6–7, variously adjusted in Joel 2:13; 3.21 [4:21]; Jonah 4:2; Micah 7:18–20; Nahum 1:3.[23] Other thematic proposals have been put forward. For example, House sees themes of sin in the texts of Hosea–Micah, punishment in Nahum–Zephaniah, and restoration in Haggai–Malachi.[24] It is generally accepted that this is too simplistic: to make an obvious point, the books of Hosea–Micah contain many passages which promise restoration and blessing.

Not all scholars are persuaded, however, that there ever was such an intention that the Book of the Twelve should be read as one book. The external evidence admits of more than one possible interpretation. With regard to the much quoted Sirach 49:10, it may be noted that the verse refers to the twelve prophets as people rather than as texts (texts don't have bones!). While Baba Batra section 14b does indeed say that only three lines should be left between the twelve texts of the Minor Prophets, as opposed to four lines between other books, it also states that the reason why Hosea is not placed

---

[23]   Nogalski presents a concise summary of these in his introduction in *Hosea–Jonah*: 11–16. His earlier article 'Book of the Twelve', *NIDB* 1:488–9 gives three of these same themes, but does not include the 'fate of God's people'.

[24]   P. R. House, *The Unity of the Twelve* (JSOTSup 97; Sheffield: Sheffield Academic Press, 1990).

The Book of the Twelve

ahead of Isaiah, whom he preceded chronologically: 'Since his book is so small, it might be lost.'[25] This suggests that the reason why the twelve texts were written on one scroll was precisely because of their short length, rather than because it was being suggested that they should be interpreted as one book. Furthermore, there is no superscription to the Book of the Twelve to suggest that it should be read or interpreted as one book.

With regard to internal evidence, the 'catchwords' to which Nogalski draws attention are, in some cases, noteworthy. However, the order in which the texts appear in different manuscript traditions varies. In the Hebrew, Masoretic text (MT), the order is Hosea, Joel, Amos, Obadiah, Jonah, Micah, Nahum, Habakkuk, Zephaniah, Haggai, Zechariah, and Malachi. Contrastingly, the Greek Septuagint (LXX) order is Hosea, Amos, Micah, Joel, Obadiah, Jonah, Nahum, Habakkuk, Zephaniah, Haggai, Zechariah, and Malachi.[26] Some of the strongest apparent catchword links of adjacent books only hold good with the MT order, and Nogalski's whole approach depends on his argument that the MT order is original, and that LXX has changed the order in the direction of making it more chronological. This change of order by LXX is, he argues, an understandable one, whereas there is no ready explanation of why MT would have changed the LXX order, were it older. The two significant commentaries to date on the Book of the Twelve as a single work take different approaches to the differing order of the books in MT and LXX. Nogalski, in accordance with his approach, treats solely the MT, while Sweeney sets out to interpret both the MT Book of the Twelve and the LXX Book of the Twelve synchronically.[27] Then even if Nogalski's case on the precedence of the MT order is accepted, it remains true that some of the catchwords that he identifies as linking different texts may be more readily granted as being of significance than others.

---

[25]   *Babylonian Talmud*: 70.
[26]   A third variant is apparent in the Qumran scroll 4QXII^a, in which it appears that Jonah followed Malachi at the end of the collection.
[27]   The terms 'synchronic' and 'diachronic' have become part of regular scholarly usage. Synchronic interpretation seeks to focus on the text as a whole, and to draw attention to commonalities rather than differences and discrepancies, while diachronic approaches seek to point up those features which suggest differences of origin and varying literary layers within a text. The two are not complete opposites, and many studies will draw on both approaches. Thus Sweeney writes that his commentary 'necessarily includes diachronic considerations in order for the synchronic analysis to make sense' (xxxix). See further C. M. Tuckett, 'Synchronic Exegesis', in R. J. Coggins and J. L. Houlden (eds.), *A Dictionary of Biblical Interpretation* (London: SCM, 1990): 657–8.

There are also considerations of structure which count against the view that the Book of the Twelve should be read as one book. As Cuffey notes, 'there are no clear markers (such as a superscription) which direct us to read it as a unified piece';[28] and as Ben Zvi notes, the twelve books have never been assigned a common title.[29] Additionally, as Barton notes, later rabbinic or Christian texts never say 'as it was written in the Book of the Twelve'; rather, if the source is identified it is by the name of the individual prophetic text.[30] In terms of thematic unity, the four 'recurrent themes' that Nogalski suggests can indeed be identified, but they are broad themes, which means that their identification has less value as an argument for the unity of the twelve texts than if they were more specific and focused.

Some scholars who work with the Book of the Twelve as a whole recognise earlier collections within it. Schart, Nogalski, Albertz, and Wöhrle all posit or accept the likelihood that there was a sixth-century collection, widely referred to as a 'Book of the Four', produced in the exilic or early post-exilic period, and comprising Hosea, Amos, Micah, and Zephaniah. The common elements in the superscriptions of each of these four texts, the themes of sin, punishment, and restoration within them all, the fact that the four of them together provide an explanation of the destruction of the kingdoms of Israel and Judah, and some possible common editing of them as a group of texts combine to make this plausible.

Pushing further back still, many scholars think it likely that the texts of Hosea and Amos were read together and influenced each other. Jeremias argues that this process began early on, soon after the destruction of the northern kingdom in 722.[31] Various verses in the Hosea-text appear to have been taken or adapted from the Amos-text: for example, Hosea 4:15b takes from Amos 4:4, and possibly also from Amos 8:14; Hosea 8:14 with its 'I will send fire upon' is derived from the refrain in the punishment announced

---

[28] K. H. Cuffey, 'Remnant, Redactor, and Biblical Theologian: A Comparative Study of Coherence in Micah and the Twelve', in J. D. Nogalski and M. A. Sweeney (eds.), *Reading and Hearing* (2000): 185–208 (201).

[29] E. Ben Zvi, 'Twelve Prophetic Books or "The Twelve": A Few Preliminary Considerations', in J. D. Watts and P. R. House (eds.), *Forming Prophetic Literature: Essays on Isaiah and the Twelve in Honor of John D. W. Watts* (JSOTSup, 235; Sheffield: Sheffield Academic Press, 1996): 125–57 (137).

[30] J. Barton, *The Theology of the Book of Amos* (Cambridge: Cambridge University Press, 2012): 37.

[31] J. Jeremias, 'The Interrelationship between Amos and Hosea', in J. D. Watts and P. R. House (eds.), *Forming Prophetic Literature* (1996): 171–86.

on foreign nations in Amos 1–2. Jeremias sees these 'Amos-like' verses in Hosea as redactional, added to an already existing, at least partly written, Hosea-text. He also sees an influence in the opposite direction, from Hoseanic tradition to Amos. However, this is of a different kind: he writes that 'I am deeply convinced that there was never a book of Amos without a clearly discernible effect from Hoseanic texts.'[32] Amos 3:2 and 7:9 are seen as particularly clear examples of the influence of Hoseanic material, with there being other, more fleeting but still significant, examples elsewhere. Jeremias's proposal is well argued, and the likely mutual influence of the two texts upon one another evident in a number of passages will be noted and considered in the relevant sections of the commentaries in this volume.

Scholarly debate will continue as to whether the Book of the Twelve should be read and interpreted as one book or as twelve. In large measure it will be the interpreter's choice and preferred method that determines the outcome. Proponents of reading and interpreting the Book of the Twelve as one book can be said to have succeeded in demonstrating that their intention to do so is justified, and is a valid interpretative approach. However, to read and interpret each text as a book in its own right remains an equally valid approach. As Albertz, an advocate of seeing the Book of the Twelve as one book, notes: 'We must remember that the book of the Twelve Prophets wants to be read not only as a unit (definitely polyphonic!) but also as a collection of individual documents.'[33] The book of Joel has become a particular focus of study within Book of the Twelve studies;[34] nevertheless, as Seitz observes, 'The Book of Joel, given its discrete character as a book, must not be allowed to vanish behind a complex reconstruction of the history of the development of a twelve book collection. It must stand on its own, and yet speak within its specific literary context as well.'[35]

The approach of this volume will be to comment on and interpret the texts of Hosea, Joel, and Amos as three separate books. Where intertextual links, catchwords, and themes appear to be clear and significant, these will be noted,

---

[32] J. Jeremias 'Interrelationship' (1996): 177.

[33] R. Albertz, *Israel in Exile: The History and Literature of the Sixth Century BCE* (trans. G. Green; SBL Studies in Biblical Literature, 3; Atlanta: SBL, 2003): 207.

[34] See, for example, J. D. Nogalski, 'Joel as Literary Anchor in the Book of the Twelve', in J. D. Nogalski and M. A. Sweeney (eds.), *Reading and Hearing* (2000): 91–109; J. Jeremias, 'The Function of the Book of Joel for Reading the Twelve', in R. Albertz, J. D. Nogalski, and J. Wöhrle (eds.), *Perspectives on the Formation of the Book of the Twelve* (BZAW, 433; Berlin: W. de Gruyter, 2012): 77–88.

[35] C. R. Seitz, *Joel* (International Theological Commentary on the Holy Scripture of Old and New Testaments; London/New York: Bloomsbury/T&T Clark, 2016): 6.

and comments as to their interpretative significance will be included as a contribution to the understanding and interpreting of each separate book.

The composition history of each book will be explored in each introduction, using redaction-critical methodology. This will enable the commentaries themselves to explore and explain how these books were read, interpreted, re-applied, and understood at each stage of their composition, in the belief that readers, interpreters, preachers, and scholars today continue the process of appropriation and interpretation in each generation. Barton cites approvingly the words of Laurin from the 1970s: 'The canonizing process ... teaches us to accept each stage in the developing canon as having authority in witnessing to how each generation heard God's will for themselves.... The people of God in each generation must engage the canonizing process, that is, must hear the spirit convincing it of God's word for itself in its own situation.'[36] This commentary aspires to these worthy aims.

SUGGESTED READINGS

Suggestions for further reading on the separate books of Hosea, Joel, and Amos are made following the introduction to each book. The two sections here reflect questions of methodology raised in the 'Volume Introduction'.

Redaction Criticism

Barton J., 'Redaction Criticism', *ABD* 5:644–7.

Barton J., *Reading the Old Testament: Method in Biblical Study* (2nd ed.; London: DLT, 2003).

Ben Zvi E. and M. H. Floyd (eds.), *Writings and Speech in Israelite and Ancient Near Eastern Prophecy* (SBLSymS, 10; Atlanta, GA: SBL, 2000).

Clements R. E., 'The Prophet and His Editors', in D. J. A. Clines, S. E. Ford, and S. E. Porter (eds.), *The Bible in Three Dimension* (JSOTSup, 87; Sheffield: Sheffield Academic Press, 1990): 203–20; repr. R. E. Clements, Old Testament Prophecy: From Oracles to Canon (Louisville: Westminster John Knox Press, 1996): 217–29.

---

[36] J. Barton, 'The Canonical Meaning of the Book of the Twelve', in J. Barton and D. J. Reimer (eds.), *After the Exile: Essays in Honor of Rex Mason* (Macon, GA: Mercer University Press, 1996): 59–73 (64–5). The quotation is from R. B. Laurin, 'Tradition and Canon', in D. A. Knight (ed.), *Tradition and Theology in the Old Testament* (London: SPCK, 1977): 261–74 (272).

Collins T., *'The Mantle of Elijah': The Redaction Criticism of the Prophetical Books* (Sheffield: JSOT Press, 1993).

Leveen A., 'Reading the Seams', *JSOT* 29 (2005): 259–87.

Melugin R. F., 'Prophetic Books and the Problem of Historical Reconstruction', in S. B. Reid (ed.), *Prophets and Paradigms: Essays in Honor of G. M. Tucker* (JSOTSup, 229; Sheffield: Sheffield Academic Press, 1996): 63–78.

Stone L. G., 'Redaction Criticism: Whence, Whither, and Why? Or, Going Beyond Source and Form Criticism without Leaving Them Behind', in E. E. Carpenter (ed.), *A Biblical Itinerary: In Search of Method, Form and Content* (JSOTSup, 240; Sheffield: Sheffield Academic Press, 1997): 77–90.

Sweeney M. A., 'Formation and Form in Prophetic Literature', in J. L. Mays, D. L. Petersen, and K. H. Richards (eds.), *Old Testament Interpretation: Past, Present and Future, Essays in Honor of Gene M. Tucker* (Nashville: Abingdon Press, 1995): 113–26.

De Vries S. J., *From Old Revelation to New: A Traditio-Historical and Redaction-Critical Study of Temporal Transitions in Prophetic Predication* (Grand Rapids, MI: Eerdmans, 1995).

The Book of the Twelve

In this more recent area of scholarship, key volumes which set out particular understandings of the Book of the Twelve (and, in some cases, of a proposed Book of the Four) include:

Albertz R., *Israel in Exile: The History and Literature of the Sixth Century BCE* (trans. D. Green; SBL Studies in Biblical Literature, 3; Atlanta, GA: SBL, 2003): 204–37.

House P., *The Unity of the Twelve* (JSOTSup, 97; Sheffield: Sheffield Academic Press, 1990).

Jones B. A., *The Formulation of the Book of the Twelve* (SBLDS, 149; Atlanta, GA: Scholars Press, 1995).

Nogalski J. D., *Literary Precursors to the Book of the Twelve* (BZAW, 217; Berlin: W. de Gruyter, 1993).

Nogalski J. D., *Redactional Processes in the Book of the Twelve* (BZAW, 218; Berlin: W. de Gruyter, 1993).

Schart A., *Die Entstehung des Zwölfprophetenbuchs: Neubearbeitungen von Amos im Rahmen schriftenübergreifender Redaktionsprozesse* (BZAW, 260; Berlin: W. de Gruyter, 1998).

Werse N. R., *Reconsidering the Book of the Four: The Shaping of Hosea, Amos, Micah, and Zephaniah as an Early Prophetic Collection* (BZAW, 517; Berlin: W. de Gruyter, 2019).

Wöhrle J., *Die frühen Sammlungen des Zwölfprophetenbuches: Entstehung und Komposition* (BZAW, 360; Berlin: W. de Gruyter, 2006).

Wöhrle J., *Der Abschluss des Zwölfprophetenbuches: Buchübergreifende Redaktionsprozesse in der späten Sammlungen* (BZAW, 389; Berlin: W. de Gruyter, 2008).

The following collections of essays are all useful. I have not listed separately the titles of the many valuable contributions within them, and encourage readers interested in this area of research to obtain the relevant volumes:

Albertz R., J. D. Nogalski, and J. Wöhrle (eds.), *Perspectives on the Formation of the Book of the Twelve: Methodological Foundations – Redactional Processes – Historical Insights* (BZAW, 433; Berlin/Boston, MA: W. de Gruyter, 2012).

Ben Zvi E., J. D. Nogalski, and T. Römer (eds.), *Two Sides of a Coin: Juxtaposing Views on Interpreting the Book of the Twelve/The Twelve Prophetic Books* (Piscataway: Gorgias Press, 2009).

Nogalski J. D. and M. A. Sweeney (eds.), *Reading and Hearing in the Book of the Twelve* (SBLSymS, 15; Atlanta, GA: SBL, 2000).

Pede D. E. and D. Scaiola (eds.), *The Book of the Twelve – One Book or Many? Metz Conference Proceedings, 5–7 November 2015* (FAT, 2/91; Tübingen: Mohr Siebeck, 2016).

Redditt P. L. and A. Schart (eds.), *Thematic Threads in the Book of the Twelve* (BZAW, 325; Berlin: W. de Gruyter, 2003).

Watts J. W. and P. R. House (eds.), *Forming Prophetic Literature: Essays on Isaiah and the Twelve in Honor of John D. W. Watts* (JSOTSup, 235; Sheffield: Sheffield Academic Press, 1996).

Two commentaries are:

Nogalski J. D., *The Book of the Twelve: Hosea–Jonah* (Smyth & Helwys Bible Commentary; Macon, GA: Smyth & Helwys, 2011).

Sweeney M. A., *The Twelve Prophets*, vol. 1: *Hosea, Joel, Amos, Obadiah, Jonah* (Berit Olam Studies in Hebrew Narrative and Poetry; Collegeville, MN: Liturgical Press, 2000).

Suggested Readings

Further articles and books:

Barton J., 'The Day of Yahweh in the Minor Prophets', in C. McCarthy (ed.), *Biblical and Near Eastern Studies in Honour of Kevin J. Cathcart* (JSOTSup, 375; London: T&T Clark International, 2004): 68–79.

Coggins R. J., 'The Minor Prophets: One Book or Twelve?' in S. Porter et al. (eds.), *Crossing the Boundaries: Essays in Biblical Interpretation in Honour of Michael D. Goulder* (Leiden: E. J. Brill, 1987): 57–68.

LeCureux J., 'Restored Hope? The Function of the Temple, Priest, and Cult as Restoration in the Book of the Twelve', *JSOT* 41 (2017): 493–510.

Nogalski J. D., 'Book of the Twelve', in *NIDB* 1:488–9.

Nogalski J. D., *The Book of the Twelve and Beyond: Collected Essays of James D. Nogalski* (Ancient Israel and Its Literature, 29; Atlanta, GA: SBL, 2017).

Schart A., 'The First Section of the Book of the Twelve Prophets: Hosea – Joel – Amos', *Interpretation* 61 (2007): 138–52.

Sweeney M. A., 'The Place and Function of Joel in the Book of the Twelve', *Society of Biblical Literature 1999 Seminar Papers* (Atlanta, GA: Scholars Press, 1999): 570–95.

Wöhrle J., '"No Future for the Proud Exultant Ones": The Exilic Book of the Four Prophets (Hos., Am., Mic., Zeph.,) as a Concept Opposed to the Deuteronomistic History', *VT* 58 (2008): 608–27.

Wöhrle J., 'Joel and the Formation of the Book of the Twelve', *BTB* 40 (2010): 127–37.

Wolfe R. E., 'The Editing of the Book of the Twelve', *ZAW* 35 (1935): 90–129.

II Book of Hosea

A INTRODUCTION TO HOSEA

The book of Hosea explores the relationship that YHWH has with his people. It portrays YHWH as closely involved with his people, because 'YHWH loves the people of Israel' (3:1). A wide range of images and metaphors is employed in the service of this exploration, the most famous of which is the analogy with the unsatisfactory marriage of the prophet to 'a wife of prostitution'[1] (1:2) described in chapters 1–3. Elsewhere YHWH speaks as Israel's parent: 'When Israel was a child, I loved him, and out of Egypt I called my son' (11:1). In other parts of the text further images abound:

> In his help to Israel Yahweh is physician (14:4; 7:1; 11:3) and shepherd (13:5). In his judgment he is hunter (7:12), carnivore (5:14; 13:7f.), wound and infection (5:12). As Saviour he is like dew (14:5) and fruitful tree (14:8). Yahweh looks on Israel as herd (13:5–8), heifer (10:11), vine (10:1), grapes and early fig (9:10). In her sin and suffering Israel is like the sick (5:13); a fickle bird (7:11f.); a stubborn cow (4:16); an unborn child (13:13); a cake of bread (7:8); morning mist (6:4); chaff, smoke and dew (13:3). In restoration Israel is compared to the flourishing plant life of Lebanon (14:5–7) and sown ground (2:21ff.).[2]

The book of Hosea has been the object of much scholarly interest over the years. Hosea 1:1 sets the prophet's ministry in the eighth century BCE. An earlier period of scholarship, from Wellhausen onwards, set particular store on the eighth-century prophets, who were seen as the originators

---

[1] Throughout the Hosea-text (specifically, in 1:2; 2:2, 4, 5; 3:3; 4:10, 11, 12, 13, 14, 15; 5:3, 4; 6:10; 9:1), the translation of the nominal and verbal forms of the root *znh* were translated in the pre-2021 NRSV as whoredom/whore/whoring/playing the whore. The most recent revision, on which this commentary is based, has preferred the translation of prostitution/prostitute/prostituting.

[2] J. L. Mays, *Hosea* (OTL; London: SCM, 1969): 9–10.

A Introduction to Hosea

of an ethical monotheism which became a basic tenet of Israelite religion. Additionally there has been a scholarly fascination with the first three chapters, which concern Hosea's marriage(s): the accrued scholarly literature on these chapters is vast. Furthermore, Hosea is of interest in being the only prophetic text in the Hebrew Bible describing a prophet of the northern kingdom of Israel. Amos 1:1 indicates that his contemporary, Amos, while addressing the northern kingdom, was himself from Tekoa, in the southern kingdom of Judah (see the commentary *ad loc*).

Most of the Hosea-text contains words concerning the northern kingdom of Israel. The books of Kings describe the history of this kingdom from its breakaway from the southern kingdom of Judah and rule of the house of David (1 Kgs 12) through to its destruction at the hands of the Assyrians in 722 BCE (2 Kgs 17). Hosea 1:1 dates Hosea's prophetic ministry to the reigns of Kings Uzziah, Jotham, Ahaz and Hezekiah of Judah and of King Jeroboam II of Israel. The particular list of kings gives some surprise, since several parts of the text appear to concern happenings in Israel later than the reign of Jeroboam, after whose reign a series of coups led to a succession of short reigns. 2 Kings 15 tells that his son Zechariah ruled for just six months before being murdered by Shallum; that Shallum ruled for just one month before being killed by Menahem; that Menahem ruled for ten years, and was succeeded by his son Pekahiah, who after two years was assassinated by his captain Pekah; and that Pekah was assassinated by Hoshea, who became the last king before the destruction of the kingdom by the Assyrians.[3] There is also surprise in the inclusion of Hezekiah: while there is uncertainty as to the date of his accession, at most the fall of Samaria in 722 was only some three years into his reign. The inclusion of Judean kings alerts us, however, to the fact that within the text there are several passages referring to Judah (1:7; 1:11 [2:2]; 4:15; 5:5, 12–14; 6:4, 11; 8:14; 10:11; 11:12 [12:1]; 12:2 [3]). Some of these are condemnatory of Judah (5:5, 12–14; 6:4, 11; 8:14; 10:11; 12:2 [3]), while others contrast condemnation of Israel with blessing for Judah (1:7; 11:12 [12:1]), and one (1:11 [2:2]) sees blessing for Israel and Judah together. Some older commentators who saw all the positive and hopeful units as additions to the prophet's original message viewed all references to Judah in like manner.[4] In more recent scholarship these references have been important in the

---

3   Accounts of these events are given in G. I. Davies, *Hosea* (OTG; Sheffield: Sheffield Academic Press, 1993): 14–19; A. A. Macintosh, *A Critical and Exegetical Commentary on Hosea* (ICC; Edinburgh: T&T Clark, 1997): lxxxiii–lxxxvii.

4   E.g. W. R. Harper, *A Critical and Exegetical Commentary on Amos and Hosea* (ICC: Edinburgh, T&T Clark, 1905): clix–clxi.

discernment of literary layers which constitute part of the composition history of the text. An important recognition is that, even though the greater part of the text concerns Israel, the preservation and development of the text took place in Judah after 722. As a literary work, the text belongs not to the eighth-century kingdom of Israel, but in its earliest substantive form to the southern kingdom of Judah in the late eighth century, and in its final form to the post-exilic community of the late sixth or early fifth century. Some commentators seek to match particular units of text to particular historical events or settings. However, Ben Zvi is right to observe that '[t]he fact that many possible scenarios could fit the world portrayed in the book is proof positive that the text is written in such a way that is not strongly anchored into any particular historical event'.

Hosea as Literary Text

All commentators acknowledge that the Hosea-text presents many textual challenges. Andersen and Freedman comment that 'the text of Hosea competes with Job for the distinction of containing more unintelligible passages than any other book of the Hebrew Bible'.[5] Older commentators tended to attribute the apparently unintelligible nature of several passages to textual corruption. Thus, for example, Harper considered that the text was 'one of the most corrupt in the O. T., the number of passages which almost defy interpretation being extremely large'. He went on to indicate that while some help could be obtained from the ancient versions 'in many cases resort must be made to critical conjecture'.[6] An alternative explanation which gained ground during the second half of the twentieth century is that, since Hosea was from the northern kingdom of Israel, the language reflects a northern-kingdom dialect of Hebrew.[7] We have virtually no extant writings in such a dialect, and consequently some scholars urge caution in accepting this.[8] Despite some cautionary warnings, the theory remains attractive, and is described by Kelle as having achieved a 'consensus status'.[9] This commentary is on the NRSV text, which takes the Hebrew MT as its basis, while

---

[5] F. I. Andersen and D. N. Freedman, *Hosea* (AB, 24; New York: Doubleday, 1980): 66. A similar comment is made by C. L. Seow, 'Hosea, Book of', ABD 3: 292.

[6] W. R. Harper *Amos and Hosea* (1905): clxxiii–clxxiv.

[7] J. L. Mays *Hosea* (1969): 5; C. L. Seow 'Hosea, Book of': 292.

[8] Thus F. I. Andersen and D. N. Freedman *Hosea* (1980): 67 write that the 'supposition that Hosea is writing in a distinctive dialect of Hebrew has not been confirmed'.

[9] B. E. Kelle, 'Hosea 4–14 in Twentieth-Century Scholarship', CBR 8 (2010): 314–75 (319).

A Introduction to Hosea 19

making use of other ancient versions where the sense of MT is unclear. Textual issues are addressed insofar as they need to be to aid exegesis, but for more detailed textual comments the reader is referred to the commentaries of Macintosh and Wolff.[10]

The text in its final form has three main sections: chapters 1–3, chapters 4–11 [4:1–11:11], and chapters 12–14 [11:12–14:10].[11] Each section concludes with positive words of hope (3:5; 11:8–11; 14:4–9 [5–10]). Within chapters 1–3 we find prose narratives told in the third person in 1:2–2:1 [1:2–2:3] and in the first person (3:1–5). Between them 2:2–15 [4–17] comprises prophetic words of divine speech, followed by two sets of words introduced by 'On that day' (2:16–20, 21–23 [18–22, 23–25]). Within chapters 4–14 a feature of the text is that it is not comprised of neat, structured units of which the beginnings and ends are clear. Structural markers are few. A comparison with the Amos-text is in order: there we find many units with a clear 'Thus says YHWH' or 'Hear this' or 'Woe to' or 'This is what the Lord God showed me' at their head, and in many cases a concluding 'says YHWH' at the end. Many have the clear form-critical structure of a judgement-oracle.[12] The Hosea-text, in contrast, has few opening and concluding formulae, and its sayings do not follow a consistent structure. Nevertheless, there are indicators of when a new unit is beginning. Hosea 4:1 begins 'Hear the word of the Lord', and 5:1 begins 'Hear this' (cf. Amos 3:1; 4:1; 5:1). Each of these imperatives opens a new section, and subsequent imperatives may also be taken to do so: 'Blow the horn' (5:8); 'Set the trumpet to your lips' (8:1); 'Do not rejoice, O Israel' (9:1). Thereafter it is by thematic content that we may identify progression into new sections. Hosea 9:10 begins a section (9:10–10:15) which contains three consecutive similes or metaphors: Israel is like grapes

---

[10] A. A. Macintosh *Hosea* (1997); H. W. Wolff, *Hosea* (trans. G. Stansell; Hermeneia; Philadelphia: Fortress Press, 1974).

[11] So H. W. Wolff *Hosea* (1974): xxix–xxxii, who refers to the three sections as 'transmission complexes'. A majority of scholars recognises this threefold division: *inter alia*, M. J. Buss, *The Prophetic Word of Hosea: A Morphological Study* (BZAW, 111; Berlin: Verlag Alfred Töpelman, 1969); G. I. Davies *Hosea* (1992); J. A. Dearman, *The Book of Hosea* (NICOT; Grand Rapids, MI: Eerdmans, 2010). Some prefer to see just two sections (chapters 1–3 and 4–14): so G. Eidevall, *Grapes in the Desert. Metaphors, Models and Themes in Hosea 4–14* (CB Old Testament Series, 43; Stockholm: Almqvist & Wiksell, 1996): 9; J. L. Mays *Hosea* (1969): 15–17. J. Goldingay, 'Hosea 4 and 11, and the Structure of Hosea', *TB* 71 (2020): 181–90 suggests four sections (after the superscription): 1–3; 4:1–9:9; 9:10–13:16 [14:1]; 14:1–8 [2–9].

[12] See C. Westermann, *Basic Forms of Prophetic Speech* (Louisville, KY: Westminster/John Knox Press, 1991).

in the wilderness that YHWH found (9:10); Israel is a luxuriant vine (10:1); Israel was a trained heifer (10:11). The content of 11:1–11 (or certainly 11:1–9) is such that it may readily be read as a unit. The third main section (11:12–14:9 [12–14]) contains reference to the patriarch Jacob (12:2–12 [3–13]) and to the exodus from Egypt (12:13 [14]–13:6). The references to past traditions fade, but the section continues on to 13:16 [14:1]. The imperative 'Return, O Israel, to YHWH your God' (14:1 [2]) inaugurates the final section 14:1–9 [2–10].

Unsurprisingly, the difficulty of the text has led to a wide range of scholarly views concerning the composition history of the text in both past and current scholarship. Kelle is correct in writing that 'nearly all of the long-standing scholarly disputes concerning chs. 4–14 remain alive in the current critical conversation'.[13] This remains the case despite some significant studies of Hosea since the 1970s. Before setting out the approach of this commentary it is therefore necessary to consider, albeit briefly, the approaches of at least some of these studies.[14]

The Composition History of the Book of Hosea

The commentary of Wolff, with its form-critical method and its attention to the book's transmission history, provides a point of reference for subsequent studies.[15] As noted, Wolff identified chapters 1–3, chapters 4–11 [4:1–11:11], and chapters 12–14 [11:12–14:10] as three separate transmission complexes. He considered that all three complexes 'are parallel to each other in that they move from accusation to threat, and then to proclamation of salvation. Each may stem from different writers, but they all belong to the same circle of Hosea's contemporary followers.' These transmission complexes were, he considers, 'already fixed in writing during the prophet's lifetime'. Subsequently a 'relatively early Judaic redaction supplemented Hosea's prophecy with a Judaic salvation eschatology' evident in 1:7 and in the expansion of 3:5, and possibly also in the final line of 9:4. In due course there was a 'later Judaic redaction which took Hosea's accusations and threats against the Northern Kingdom and applied them in like manner to Judah'. It is not possible to know when the three transmission complexes were combined into one text, but this 'was probably accomplished with the

---

[13]   B. E. Kelle 'Hosea 4–14' (2010): 316.
[14]   For fuller reviews of scholarly approaches to the book of Hosea, see B. E. Kelle, 'Hosea 1–3 in Twentieth-Century Scholarship', *CBR* 72 (2009): 179–216; B. E. Kelle, 'Hosea 4–14' (2010).
[15]   H. W. Wolff *Hosea* (1974).

A Introduction to Hosea

final redaction, when the superscription 1:1 was added'. The closing 14:9 [10] was also added at this point, in the exilic or early post-exilic period. The process of redaction notwithstanding, Wolff considers that 'for the most part ... Hosea's own speech is unmistakeable'.[16]

Wolff's readiness to see actual words of the prophet Hosea within most sections of the text, and to see the prophet's hand in the early compilation of his words, and then also to see evidence of some Judean editing of the text, is seen in the subsequent works of, *inter alia*, Emmerson, Macintosh, and Dearman. Emmerson acknowledges her following of Wolff in his structural analysis of the text,[17] and makes explicit her assumption that the words of the text should be seen as being authentic to the prophet Hosea himself 'where no compelling reasons can be urged against their authenticity'.[18] But, as the title to her book indicates, she recognises that the text shows the influence of Judean preservation and transmission. Her work takes seriously that the development of the text is worthy of investigation and interpretation.

Macintosh sees the book as primarily the work of Hosea himself, with some subsequent redactional changes and additions:

> If then, the book of Hosea represents what is fundamentally a literary composition, forged from a blend of the latter of his public oracles, of his personal amplifications and of his meditations upon them, there can be no doubt that Hosea himself was the author and composer. That does not preclude the possibility that, like Jeremiah, he was assisted by a personal scribe or that his endeavour was promoted by some redactional activity.[19]

Dearman notes that if older scholarship saw the prophets primarily as speakers rather than authors, nevertheless 'in the case of Hosea this presupposition is being reassessed', and he refers approvingly to Macintosh's comments. However, in contrast to Wolff and Macintosh, Dearman is cautious about the possible formation of any literary text of Hosea prior to the destruction of Samaria by the Assyrians in 722. We should consider, he suggests,

> the possibility that the book (as opposed to the earlier [oral?] presentations by the prophet) originated in the aftermath of Samaria's fall and was produced in Judah by refugees from the Assyrian onslaught. Public dissemination of

---

[16]   H. W. Wolff *Hosea* (1974): xxix–xxxii.

[17]   G. I. Emmerson, *Hosea: An Israelite Prophet in Judean Perspective* (JSOTSup, 28; Sheffield: JSOT Press, 1984): 169 n. 2.

[18]   G. I. Emmerson *Hosea* (1984): 8.

[19]   A. A. Macintosh *Hosea* (1997): lxix.

Hosea's prophecies would provide confirmation that Israel's political demise was an act of YHWH's judgment. It is certainly to Judah that we should look for an early written collection of Hosea's prophecies, even if not the first one, and in Judah also for the subsequent preserving of them.[20]

This view has much to commend it.

Other scholars are dubious about the likelihood of the text preserving primarily words of an eighth-century prophet. Yee's study is of the literary text and its stages of composition. She starts with the latest, final form of the text and works backwards into earlier stages. She finds two principal redactional layers: the final one was Deuteronomistic and was formed in the Babylonian exile of the sixth century. It is this final redaction which gave the book its present shape. It was preceded by a previous Deuteronomistic redaction to be dated to the time of Josiah in the seventh century. Prior to this, a small first collection of material was made in the late eighth century, shortly after the fall of the northern kingdom in 722, the contents of which are all to be found within chapters 1–3. She identifies words attributable to the prophet Hosea in each of chapters 1–3, 4–11, and 12–14, but they do not constitute the majority of the text.[21] Among more recent redaction-critical studies, Rudnig-Zelt finds the oldest material to be a series of sayings concerning Israel's folly, to be found within chapters 5–7. These are taken to be from the late eighth century, after 722. They were expanded by additional sayings in a process which continued into the sixth century. The main literary work, however, is a product of the Second Temple period, after the building of the Temple in the late sixth century, and revisions were made to this on into the Hellenistic period.[22] The study of Vielhauer proposes that there was a series of stages of development from an original nucleus to be found within chapters 4–9: this original nucleus recorded the prophet Hosea's concern with political matters, while the later developments widened the focus to include cultic matters.[23]

---

[20] J. A. Dearman *Hosea* (2010): 4–5.

[21] G. A. Yee, *Composition and History in the Book of Hosea: A Redaction Critical Investigation* (SBLDS, 102; Atlanta, GA: Scholars Press, 1987).

[22] S. Rudnig-Zelt, *Hoseastudien: Redaktionskritische Untersuchungen zur Genese des Hoseabuches* (FRLANT, 213: Göttingen: Vandenhoeck & Ruprecht, 2006).

[23] R. Vielhauer, *Das Werden des Buches Hosea: Eine redaktiongeschichtliche Untersuchung* (BZAW, 349; Berlin: de Gruyter, 2007); R. Vielhauer, 'Hosea in the Book of the Twelve', in R. Albertz, J. D. Nogalski, and J. Wöhrle (eds.), *Perspectives on the Formation of the Book of the Twelve: Methodological Foundations – Redactional Processes – Historical Insights* (Berlin: de Gruyter, 2012): 55–76.

A Introduction to Hosea 23

Finally, we may note the contribution of those who work with the final form of the text. The commentary of Ben Zvi reads the text as a product of late monarchic or, more likely, post-monarchic Judah.[24] In a society in which only a small minority had the ability to read and write 'both the authorship and readership are to be found among literati who were the few bearers of high literacy in their society'.[25] The text therefore reveals to us the late sixth or fifth rather than the eighth century BCE. The purported eighth-century monarchic setting 'shaped and to some extent reflected an already existing image of the past among the readership of the book'.[26] More recently Bos has produced a detailed study which builds on Ben Zvi's approach, but takes it further.[27] He agrees that the work belongs to post-monarchic Yehud, and may be taken to derive from circles of literati; and while it is likely that the author(s) used some older literary sources, it is this main, final composition which should be the object of our interest and study. Bos considers that Ben Zvi has paid insufficient attention to the status in the Persian period of places which loom large in the text, namely Bethel, Mizpah, and Samaria, all of which, he argues, should be seen as being in competition with Jerusalem in that period. He also takes the anti-kingship units of the text to point to this period. Bos sees his work as part of a wider movement of scholarship towards a 'new paradigm' in the study of prophetic texts, which is itself part of a wider movement in Hebrew Bible scholarship which is sceptical of much to which scholarship has hitherto held. Thus he holds that Deuteronomy is a late sixth-century or fifth-century composition, and that there never was a Deuteronomic reform in the time of Josiah, that tradition itself being a product of the Persian period. He considers that the Hosea-text post-dates this Persian period Deuteronomy. This late dating of Hosea has, he recognises, implications for other areas of study. For example, the 'Yahweh alone' and aniconic emphases of the Hebrew Bible can no longer be seen as pre-exilic on the evidence of an eighth-century dating of Hosea: rather these must themselves be seen as Persian period developments in Israelite–Judahite religion. The concluding sentence of his study expresses the 'hope that this monograph provides more support for the newer paradigm'.[28]

---

[24] E. Ben Zvi, *Hosea* (FOTL; Grand Rapids: Eerdmans, 2005).
[25] E. Ben Zvi *Hosea* (2005): 12.
[26] E. Ben Zvi *Hosea* (2005): 18.
[27] J. M. Bos, *Reconsidering the Date and Provenance of the Book of Hosea: The Case for Persian-Period Yehud* (LHBOTS, 580; London/New York: Bloomsbury/ T&T Clark, 2013).
[28] J. M. Bos *Reconsidering* (2013): 170. There remains a gulf within Hebrew Bible scholarship between those who, like Bos, take what is sometimes termed (mainly by opponents) a

Several considerations point against the book as a whole being an exilic or post-exilic creation. Following John Day, it may be noted that much of the text presupposes the recent existence of the northern monarchy; that condemnation of Baal worship, and the people's worship of God as a bull-calf, makes most sense in a pre-exilic setting; that worship takes place under trees and on mountain tops, with a multiplication of local altars and sacred pillars; that there is criticism of cult activity at Bethel and Gilgal for reasons other than it not taking place in Jerusalem.[29] Furthermore, as noted, the judgements threatened are various, and not simply of exile. The most likely setting for a first edition of the text is in the late eighth century, in the years following the fall of Samaria and the end of the northern kingdom of Israel at the hands of the Assyrians. Northern refugees and Jerusalem scribes would have worked together in Jerusalem. However, some parts of the text originated in later times. This commentary employs a redaction-critical methodology. However, the difficulty of the text, in terms of translation and its resistance to form-critical analysis, and the wide range of current scholarly views concerning its dating and composition history, must lead to caution and humility in its exercise. I consider that the Amos-text, for example, yields more assured results, to the degree that it is possible to speak of a consensus among a considerable number of scholars.[30] The same is not true of Hosea, for which the lack of clear literary forms and of well-defined units necessitates a greater reliance on thematic considerations, with the increased danger of circular argument.[31] Nevertheless, tentative proposals may be made. A starting point is Wolff's recognition that the three

'minimalist' approach and those who hold to longer established views on Old Testament history and the dating of texts. Consideration of this debate lies beyond the scope of this commentary. Suffice it to say that I find myself unconvinced by the scepticism of the proponents of the 'new paradigm' towards the biblical accounts of pre-exilic Israel and Judah, and I make the observation that the hypothesis of it being circles of literati who composed, read, and re-read prophetic text is itself no more than a hypothesis, about which equal doubts might be expressed. The studies of Ben Zvi and Bos nevertheless yield valuable insights, on which I have drawn.

[29] J. Day 'Hosea and the Baal Cult', in J. Day (ed.), *Prophecy and the Prophets in Ancient Israel: Proceedings of the Oxford Old Testament Seminar* (New York: T&T Clark, 2010): 202–24 (202–3). See also H. M. Barstad, 'Hosea and the Assyrians', in R. P. Gordon and H. M. Barstad (eds.), *Thus Speaks Ishtar of Arbela: Prophecy in Israel, Assyria, and Egypt in the Neo-Assyrian Period* (Winona Lake, IN: Eisenbrauns, 2013): 91–110; M. Leuchter, 'Hosea's Exodus Mythology and the Book of the Twelve', in L.-S. Tiemeyer (ed.), *Priests and Cults in the Book of the Twelve* (ANEM, 14; Atlanta, GA: SBL Press, 2016): 31–50 (33 n. 6).

[30] See the 'Introduction to Amos'.

[31] See the comments on circular argument in the 'Volume Introduction'.

A Introduction to Hosea

transmission complexes that he identifies (chapters 1–3, 4–11, 12–14) were not combined until the final redaction. His views need modification in the light of subsequent studies, but he is surely correct that chapters 1–3 were not joined to chapters 4–14 until the final stage of redaction. Wolff considers that redactional processes continued 'down to the Deuteronomistic circles of the exilic period'.[32] More likely, however, is that they continued beyond this time, into the early decades of the Second Temple period, and that it was at this late stage that chapters 1–3 were added as a prefix to chapters 4–14. We need, therefore, to consider the composition history of the two separately. The arguments for what is proposed here are set out in the relevant sections of the commentary.

Within chapters 4–14, the concluding verses 14:4–9 [5–10], with the superscription in 1:1, are the sum of those added in the final redaction (with 14:9 [10] being the latest addition of all). Words of bounteous blessing in a final section are characteristic of a number of prophetic texts whose final form was shaped in this period (cf. Amos 9:11–15; Mic. 7:18–20; Zeph. 3:14–21).

These were added to a form of the text that had been developed in the exilic period, in which 11:12–14:3 [12:1–14:4] was added as a block. The arguments for this view include its use of themes and language in Amos and Deuteronomy, its reference to earlier prophets (12:10 [11]), its understanding of Moses as a prophet (12:13 [14]), and its references to patriarchal traditions, which would have been better known in the sixth than in the eighth century. The preceding 11:10–11 are an exilic (or possibly later) addition to the original 11:1–9. Hosea 8 contains three additions: 8:14 is dependent on Amos 1–2; 8:6a reflects exilic polemic such as is found more extensively in a passage like Isaiah 44:9–20; and 8:1b includes a familiarity with the concept of YHWH's covenant with Israel which many scholars see as only emerging in the late pre-exilic or exilic period. The covenant concept is also found in 6:7, and the commentary suggests that the whole of 6:7–10 is exilic, possibly incorporating earlier material in 6:8–9. Preceding these, 6:5, with its developed understanding of 'the prophets', is probably also exilic. Exilic application to Judah's exile is made in 6:11a and 9:4b.

Additions had also been made a century further back, in the seventh century. The reference in 4:5 to the stumbling of the prophets may reflect verses such as Jeremiah 2:8, 26; 6:13; and the use of the same verb 'stumbles' with reference to Judah in 5:5 indicates that this line, too, is a seventh-century

---

[32]   H. W. Wolff *Hosea* (1974): xxxi.

entry into the text. Hosea 4:15 is an adaptation of Amos 4:4; 5:5. The sequence of imperatives in 10:12 is similar to that of 4:15, and 10:12 also draws from the Amos-text in using the verb 'seek' (*dāraš*) (cf. Amos 5:4–6, 14–15); it belongs to the same set of redactional changes, as does the reference to Judah in the preceding 10:11b. Finally, the theme of the rejection of the prophetic message as a reason for judgement is found in 9:7–9: this theme seems to have come into prominence from the seventh century onwards.

Hence by far the greater part of Hosea 4–11 goes back to the earliest, late eighth-century text, composed in Jerusalem following the fall of Samaria. Its shape is not a strongly structured one, but some features may be noted. Chapter 4 and 5:1–7 contain words of accusation against and judgement on people, priests, and kings. The section 5:8–7:16 introduces themes of Israel's relationships with foreign powers, and of the nation's sickness. It includes an extended passage (6:4–7:10) in which YHWH's love for his people and his desire to heal them wrestle with his wrath against their wrongdoing, the latter in the end prevailing. Chapter 8 and 9:1–9 continue words of accusation and judgement. The section 9:10–10:15 uses images of Israel to develop further the accusations and announcements of judgement. Chapter 11 employs the image of Israel as YHWH's child, concluding with final verses in which YHWH's love and mercy are set against his previously expressed anger (11:8–9). Whether wrath or mercy will triumph is left unresolved.

The essential shape of Hosea 4–11 is unchanged by the relatively few subsequent additions made to it. After some additions in the seventh century, an exilic redaction added further material and the whole of 11:12–14:3 [12:1–14:4]. A post-exilic redaction was formed by the addition of 14:4–9 [5–10], at which point Hosea 1–3 was joined to it.

It is scarcely possible to outline such a scheme within Hosea 1–3. In the commentary I accept the arguments of those who see 1:10–2:1 [2:1–3] as post-exilic on the basis of its echo of the promise in the patriarchal narratives of the number of the people of Israel being like the sand of the sea, and of the future promise of the peoples of Judah and Israel being gathered in repossessing of the land. It is also evident to me that 2:16–23 [18–25] comprises two post-exilic additions. Both begin with future-looking chronological formula, and that future is one of positive hope. The covenant with the wild animals in 2:18 [20] reflects dependence on late priestly material (cf. Gen. 9:9–10; Ezek. 34:25–28). The pairing of righteousness and justice in 2:19 [21] reflects the influence of texts such as Amos 5:7; 6:12; Isaiah 1:21. YHWH's answering in 2:21–22 [23–24] connects it to his answering in the post-exilic 14:8 [9]. The issues surrounding Hosea 3 are multifarious, but

A Introduction to Hosea

in the commentary I accept the arguments of those who view the chapter as a unity; that the vocabulary in 3:1 of 'love' and 'other gods' presupposes Deuteronomy; that 3:4 is most naturally read as referring to the time of exile in the sixth-century exile; and that the hope expressed in 3:5 is characteristic more of the post-exilic period more than of any other. I therefore take the whole chapter to be a post-exilic composition.

Key Themes in the Book of Hosea

The dominant theme of the earliest, late eighth-century composition is that Israel will be judged for her unfaithfulness to YHWH. In the context of the marriage metaphor this is described as her 'prostitution' or 'prostituting' herself (1:2; 2:2–13 [4–15]; 4:10–14; 5:3; 6:10). The same imagery is used in 2:2–13 [4–15] in describing Israel's punishment: she will be publicly disgraced and humiliated as an unfaithful wife.[33] Other judgements threatened are that YHWH will put an end to the kingdom of Israel (1:4), no longer having pity on them (1:6); the land will mourn, and its inhabitants who live in it will languish (4:3); priest and people have all gone astray, as a result of which they will eat, but not be satisfied (4:4–10); the people will seek YHWH but not find him, and they will be devoured (5:6–7); Ephraim will become a desolation (5:9); they will be destroyed (7:13); an enemy will pursue Israel (8:3); they will be swallowed up (8:8); YHWH will not accept the people's sacrifices, but rather will punish their sins by returning them to Egypt and Assyria (8:13; 9:3; 11:5), and in Assyria they will eat unclean food (9:3); there will be a lack of grain and wine (9:2); YHWH will bereave them of their children (9:12); he will drive them out of his house (9:15), and they will become wanderers among the nations (9:17); their altars and pillars will be broken down (10:1–2); there will be no king, the calf-god of Bethel will be carried off to Assyria, and the high places will be destroyed (10:3–8); their fortresses will be destroyed in war (10:14); the sword will rage in their cities, consuming the oracle-priests (11:6).

The people's unfaithfulness – prostitution – is seen in their worship of Baal (2:8, 13; 9:10; 11:2) and in the offering of sacrifices to the calf-god of Bethel (8:5–6; 10:5). It is seen, too, in their going to Egypt or Assyria for help instead of turning to YHWH (5:13; 7:10–16; 8:9). Other sins condemned are that there is no faithfulness, loyalty, or knowledge of God in the land (4:1);

---

[33] The text betrays the perspective of a male-dominated society: the commentary will draw attention to some important feminist critiques of the difficult imagery employed here.

instead, there is swearing, lying, murder, adultery, and bloodshed (4:2), wickedness and injustice (10:13–15); the priests have failed to instruct the people (4:4–6) and have fed on the sin of the people (4:8); wine and new wine take away understanding (4:11); the people practice idolatry and divination, offering sacrifice on mountain tops and under trees (4:12–13) and multiplying altars (8:11; 10:1); there is adultery and prostitution (4:13b–14); Israel's pride testifies against him (5:5; 7:10); Israel's love and loyalty evaporate as quickly as the morning mist (6:4–6); there is corruption and treachery (7:1–4) in which kings play a major part (7:5–7); the people have spurned the good, despite YHWH's many instructions (8:3, 12); they have set up kings and princes without reference to YHWH (8:4); Israel has trusted in his own power (10:13), and is bent on turning away from YHWH (11:7).

Both 1:2–2:15 [17] and 4:1–11:9 conclude, however, with words expressing YHWH's love, mercy, and tenderness towards his people. In 2:14–15 [16–17] YHWH declares that he will lure his people back into the wilderness to woo her afresh, and predicts that there they will respond to his love. In 11:8–9 YHWH's tenderness bursts out: 'How can I give you up, O Ephraim? ... my compassion grows warm and tender. I will not execute my fierce anger.' Some older commentators saw all these positive, hopeful words as additions to the original message of the prophet Hosea,[34] but from the second half of the twentieth century most have taken them to be original to the prophet or to an older layer of literary text,[35] as does this commentary. No attempt is made to resolve the tension between these words and the dominant motifs of accusation and judgement. In the post-722 historical setting of this first composition, the words of judgement served to provide an explanation of why YHWH had allowed the kingdom of Israel to be destroyed. The concluding brief words concerning YHWH's continuing tenderness towards his people expressed, perhaps, a fleeting confidence that this was not the end of the story.

The seventh-century additions served to warn the current generation of Judeans not to make the same mistakes that had led to the end of the northern kingdom (4:15; 5:5; 10:11b, 12), and that to reject prophetic warnings would itself constitute iniquity and warrant punishment (9:7–9). The Judean redactors were, presumably, concerned that their generation were in danger of incurring YHWH's wrath as had the Israelites.

---

[34] E.g. W. R. Harper *Amos and Hosea* (1905): clix–clxi.
[35] So, *inter alia*, F. I. Andersen and D. N. Freedman *Hosea* (1980); G. I. Davies *Hosea* (1992); A. A. Macintosh *Hosea* (1997); J. L. Mays *Hosea* (1969); H. W. Wolff *Hosea* (1974).

A Introduction to Hosea 29

The exilic redaction was formed in the wake of the destruction of Judah and Jerusalem in 587. This was seen as the result of YHWH's judgement on Judah. Consequently both the accusations and the announcements of judgement are now applied to the people of sixth-century Judah. As Ben Zvi notes, from a post-monarchic perspective there is a 'merging of conceptual horizons' and 'Judah is conceptually subsumed under Jacob/Israel.' A result is that 'divine complaints against Ephraim become relevant to Israel/Jacob, and therefore to Judah'.[36] Further expressions of judgement are added, still naming Ephraim and Samaria, but pointing in reality to Judah: YHWH will send fire upon their cities (8:14); he will be a dangerous animal to them (13:7–8); he will take away their king (13:10–11); YHWH will send an east wind and dry up springs (13:15); Samaria shall fall by the sword, and their little ones will be dashed in pieces and their pregnant women ripped open (13:16 [14:1]). Additional accusations are made: the people have broken YHWH's covenant and transgressed his law/instruction (Torah) (8:1); they have made idols of silver and gold (8:4b); there have been lies and deceit (11:12 [12:1]), falsehood and violence (12:1 [2]), use of false balances to oppress and gain wealth (12:7–8 [8–9]); Israel has failed to respond to YHWH's love (13:4–6), but instead has rebelled against him (13:16 [14:1]). Chapter 12 introduces references to the patriarch Jacob, suggesting that the people's tendency to act deceitfully can be traced back to their ancestors. The redaction concludes with a summons to return to YHWH (14:1–3). While a different kind of conclusion to those of the first composition (2:14–15 [16–17]; 11:8–9), it functions in like manner in providing hope that the present calamities may not be the end.

A final redaction in the post-exilic period added promises of future blessing (14:4–8 [5–9]). These entailed YHWH's healing of the people's disloyalty, loving them freely, and turning from his anger towards them (14:4 [5]). Chapters 1–3 were joined to chapters 4–14, with additions within chapters 1–3 promising that YHWH will take his people as his wife for ever in righteousness, justice, steadfast love, mercy, and faithfulness (2:19–20 [21–22]); that he will establish a covenant with the created world on the people's behalf, and will abolish war and insecurity from the land (2:18 [20]); that the earth will yield its produce (2:22 [24]); and that the peoples of Israel and Judah will be united together as YHWH's children and people, under one head, returning to David their king, and as recipients of YHWH's mercy (1:10–2:1 [2:1–3]; 2:23 [25]; 3:5). The final verse 14:9 [10] urges readers to pay attention to the whole preceding, final-form text.

---

[36]   E. Ben Zvi *Hosea* (2005): 247–8.

30   *Book of Hosea*

The commentary will seek to interpret the text in the literary contexts out-lined above, upholding the view expressed in the 'Volume Introduction' that each stage of composition yields interpretative meaning and significance. Despite the tentative nature of the results of redaction-critical investigation in respect of the Hosea-text, the rewards of its approach are rich, and the benefits outweigh those of approaches that insist on restricting interpreta-tion to one literary layer only, be it the supposed 'original' text or the final form thereof.

B SUGGESTED READINGS ON HOSEA

Introductory Works

There is no recent short guide to the book of Hosea. G. I. Davies's 1973 vol-ume remains useful, as is Birch's article in *The New Interpreter's Dictionary of the Bible* (*NIDB*). Kelle's two review articles give a good assessment of current scholarly research.

Birch B., 'Hosea, Book of', *NIDB* 2: 894–900.
Davies G. I., *Hosea* (OTG; Sheffield: Sheffield Academic Press, 1993).
Kelle B. E., 'Hosea 1–3 in Twentieth-Century Scholarship', *CBR* 72 (2009): 179–216.
Kelle B. E., 'Hosea 4–14 in Twentieth-Century Scholarship', *CBR* 8 (2010): 314–75.

Commentaries

Most of the commentaries locate the origin of much of the text in the min-istry of the prophet Hosea, accepting also compositional development subsequent to an initial written work. That of Ben Zvi comments on the final form.

Andersen F. I. and D. N. Freedman, *Hosea* (AB, 24; New York: Doubleday, 1980).
Ben Zvi E., *Hosea* (FOTL, 21A/1; Grand Rapids, MI: Eerdmans, 2005).
Davies G. I., *Hosea* (NCB; London: Marshall Pickering, 1992).
Dearman J. A. *The Book of Hosea* (NICOT; Grand Rapids, MI: Eerdmans, 2010).
Goldingay J., *Hosea–Micah* (BCOT; Grand Rapids, MI: Baker Academic, 2020).

Harper W. R., *A Critical and Exegetical Commentary on Amos and Hosea* (ICC; Edinburgh: T&T Clark, 1905).

Jeremias J., *Der Prophet Hosea* (Das Alte Testament Deutsch; Göttingen: Vandenhoeck & Ruprecht, 1983).

Macintosh A. A., *Hosea* (ICC; Edinburgh: T&T Clark, 1997).

Mays J. L., *Hosea* (OLT; London: SCM, 1969).

Nogalski J. D., *The Book of the Twelve: Hosea–Jonah* (Smyth & Helwys Bible Commentary; Macon, GA: Smyth & Helwys, 2011).

Routledge R., *Hosea* (TOTC, 24; London: IVP, 2021).

Rudolph W., *Hosea* (KAT, 13/1; Gütersloh: Gütersloher Verlaghaus Gerd Mohn, 1966).

Sweeney M.A., *The Twelve Prophets, vol 1: Hosea, Joel, Amos, Obadiah, Jonah* (Berit Olam Studies in Hebrew Narrative and Poetry; Collegeville, MN: Liturgical Press, 2000).

Wolff H. W., *Hosea* (trans. G. Stansell; Hermeneia; Philadelphia: Fortress Press, 1974).

Special Studies

The studies of Bos, Buss, Chalmers, Chung, Daniels, Eidevall, Holt, and Kakkanattu are all substantive and useful. In German, the works of Nissinen, Rudnig-Zelt, and Vielhauer all bring a redaction-critical approach to the text. A separate section below notes studies related to Hosea 1–3.

Alt A., 'Hosea 5:8–6:6: Ein Krieg und seine Folgen in prophetischer Beleuchtung', *NKZ* 30 (1919): 537–68 (repr. A. Alt, *Kleine Schriften zur Geschichte des Volkes Israel* 2 (Munich: Beck, 1953): 163–87).

Barstad H. M., 'Hosea and the Assyrians', in R. P. Gordon and H. M. Barstad (eds.), *Thus Speaks Ishtar of Arbela: Prophecy in Israel, Assyria, and Egypt in the Neo-Assyrian Period* (Winona Lake, IN: Eisenbrauns, 2013): 91–110.

Bos J. M., *Reconsidering the Date and Provenance of the Book of Hosea: The Case for Persian-Period Yehud* (LHBOTS, 580; London/New York: Bloomsbury/T&T Clark, 2013).

Buss M. J., *The Prophetic Word of Hosea: A Morphological Study* (BZAW, 111; Berlin: A. Töpelman, 1969).

Chalmers R. S., *The Struggle of Yahweh and El for Hosea's Israel* (Sheffield: Phoenix Press, 2008).

Chung Y. H., *The Sin of the Calf: The Rise of the Bible's Negative Attitude toward the Golden Calf* (LHBOTS, 523; London/New York: Bloomsbury/T&T Clark, 2010).

Daniels D. R., *Hosea and Salvation History: The Early Traditions of Israel in the Prophecy of Hosea* (BZAW, 19; Berlin: de Gruyter, 1990).

Day J., 'Pre-Deuteronomic Allusions to the Covenant in Hosea and Psalm LXXVII', *VT* 36 (1986): 1–12.

Day J., 'Hosea and the Baal Cult', in J. Day (ed.), *Prophecy and the Prophets in Ancient Israel: Proceedings of the Oxford Old Testament Seminar* (New York: T&T Clark International, 2010): 202–24.

Day P., 'A Prostitute Unlike Women: Whoring as Metaphoric Vehicle for Foreign Alliances', in B. E. Kelle and M. B. Moore (eds.), *Israel's Prophets and Israel's Past: Essays on the Relationship of Prophetic Texts and Israelite History in Honor of John H. Hayes* (LHBOTS, 446; London: T&T Clark, 2006): 167–73.

Eidevall G., *Grapes in the Desert: Metaphors, Models and Themes in Hosea 4–14* (CB Old Testament Series, 43; Stockholm: Almqvist & Wiksell, 1996).

Emmerson G. I., *Hosea: An Israelite Prophet in Judean Perspective* (JSOTSup, 28; Sheffield: JSOT Press, 1984).

Goldingay J., 'Hosea 4 and 11, and the Structure of Hosea', *TB* 71 (2020): 181–90.

Holt E. K., *Prophesying the Past: The Use of Israel's History in the Book of Hosea* (JSOTSup, 194; Sheffield: Sheffield Academic Press, 1995).

Jeremias J., *Hosea und Amos: Studien zur den Anfängen des Dodekapropheton* (FAT, 13; Tübingen: J. C. B. Mohr, 1995).

Jeremias J., 'The Interrelationship between Amos and Hosea', in J. W. Watts and P. R. House (eds.), *Forming Prophetic Literature: Essays on Isaiah and the Twelve in Honor of John D. W. Watts* (JSOTSup, 235; Sheffield: Sheffield Academic Press, 1996): 171–86.

Jeremias J., 'Hosea in the Book of the Twelve', in L.-S. Tiemeyer, and J. Wöhrle (eds.), *The Book of the Twelve: Composition, Reception, and Interpretation* (VTSup, 184; Leiden: Brill, 2020): 111–23.

Kakkanattu J. P., *God's Enduring Love in Hosea: A Synchronic and Diachronic Analysis of Hosea 11:1–11* (Tübingen: Mohr Siebeck, 2006).

Krispenz J, 'Idolatry, Apostasy, Prostitution: Hosea's Struggle against the Cult', in L.-S. Tiemeyer (ed.), *Priests and Cults in the Book of the Twelve* (ANEM, 14; Atlanta, GA: SBL Press, 2016): 9–30.

B Suggested Readings on Hosea

Leuchter M., 'Hosea's Exodus Mythology and the Book of the Twelve', in L.-S. Tiemeyer (ed.), *Priests and Cults* (2016): 31–50.

Machinist P., 'Hosea and the Ambiguity of Kingship in Ancient Israel', in J. T. Strong and S. V. Tuell (eds.), *Constituting the Community: Studies on the Polity of Ancient Israel in Honor of S. Dean McBride Jr.* (Winona Lake, IN: Eisenbrauns, 2005): 153–81.

Nissinen M., *Prophetie Redaktion und Forschreibung im Hosea-buch: Studien zum Werdegang eines Prophetenbuches im Lichte von Hos 4 und 11* (AOAT, 231; Vevalear/Neukirchen-Vluyn: Butzon & Bercker/Neukirchener Verlag, 1991).

O'Kennedy D. F., 'Healing as/or Forgiveness? The Use of the Term אפר in the Book of Hosea', *OTE* 14 (2001): 458–74.

Rudnig-Zelt S., *Hoseastudien: Redaktionskritische Untersuchungen zur Genese des Hoseabuches* (FRLANT, 213: Göttingen: Vandenhoeck & Ruprecht, 2006).

Sweeney M. A., 'A Form Critical Rereading of Hosea', *JHS* 2, https://doi .org/10.5508/jhs.1998.v2.a1.

Trotter J. M., *Reading Hosea in Achaemenid Yehud* (JSOTSup, 328; Sheffield: Sheffield Academic Press, 2001).

Vielhauer R., *Das Werden des Buches Hosea: Eine redaktiongeschichtliche Untersuchung* (BZAW, 349; Berlin: de Gruyter, 2007).

Vielhauer R., 'Hosea in the Book of the Twelve', in R. Albertz, J. D. Nogalski, and J. Wöhrle (eds.), *Perspectives on the Formation of the Book of the Twelve: Methodological Foundations – Redactional Processes – Historical Insights* (Berlin: W. de Gruyter, 2012): 55–76.

Yee G. A., *Composition and Tradition in the Book of Hosea: A Redaction Critical Investigation* (SBL Dissertation Series, 102; Atlanta, GA: Scholars Press, 1987).

Special Studies on Hosea 1–3

Angel H., '*Rebuke your Mother*: But Who is She? The Identity of the Mother and Children in Hosea 2:4–7', *JBQ* 44 (2016): 13–20.

Bird P., '"To Play the Harlot": An Inquiry into an Old Testament Metaphor', in P. L. Day (ed.), *Gender and Difference in Ancient Israel* (Minneapolis: Fortress Press, 1989): 75–94.

Boshoff W., 'The Female Imagery in the Book of Hosea: Considering the Marriage Metaphor in Hosea 1–2 by Listening to Female Voices', *OTE* 15 (2002): 23–41.

Clines D. J. A., 'Hosea 2: Structure and Interpretation', in E. A. Livingstone (ed.), *Studia Biblica 1978, vol. 1: Papers on Old Testament and Related Themes* (JSOTSup, 11; Sheffield: JSOT Press, 1979): 83–103.

Fontaine C. R., 'A Response to Hosea', in A. Brenner (ed.), *A Feminist Companion to the Latter Prophets* (FCB, 8; Sheffield: Sheffield Academic Press, 1995): 60–9.

Graetz N., 'God Is to Israel as Husband Is to Wife: The Metaphoric Battering of Hosea's Wife', in A. Brenner (ed.), *A Feminist Companion to the Latter Prophets* (1995): 126–45.

Hadjiev T. S., 'Adultery, Shame, and Sexual Pollution in Ancient Israel and in Hosea: A Response to Joshua Moon', *JSOT* 41 (2016): 221–36.

Keefe A., 'The Female Body, the Body Politic and the Land: A Sociopolitical Reading of Hosea 1–2', in A. Brenner (ed.), *A Feminist Companion to the Latter Prophets* (1995): 70–100

Kelle B. E. *Hosea 2: Metaphor and Rhetoric in Historical Perspective* (SBLAB, 20; Atlanta, GA: SBL Press, 2005).

Moon J., 'Honor and Shame in Hosea's Marriages', *JSOT* 39 (2015): 335–51.

Routledge R., 'Hosea's Marriage Reconsidered', *TB* 69.1 (2018): 25–42.

Setel T. D., 'Prophets and Pornography: Female Sexual Imagery in Hosea', in L. Russell (ed.), *Feminist Interpretation of the Bible* (Oxford: Blackwell, 1985): 86–95.

Sherwood Y., *The Prophet and the Prostitute: Hosea's Marriage in Literary-Theoretical Perspective* (JSOTSup, 212; Sheffield: Sheffield Academic Press, 1996).

Thelle R. I., 'Self as *Other*: Israel's Self-Designation as Adulterous Wife, a Self-Reflective Perspective on a Prophetic Metaphor', in R. I. Thelle, T. Stordalen, and M. E. J. Richardson (eds.), *New Perspectives on Old Testament Prophecy and History: Essays in Honour of Hans M. Barstad* (VTSup, 168; Leiden: Brill, 2015): 104–20.

C COMMENTARY ON HOSEA

1 Hosea's Marriage – Hosea 1–3

Hosea 1:1 – Heading

> 1 The word of the LORD that came to Hosea son of Beeri, in the days of Kings Uzziah, Jotham, Ahaz, and Hezekiah of Judah, and in the days of King Jeroboam son of Joash of Israel.

C Commentary on Hosea

The editorial heading to Hosea invites the reader to see all that follows as the 'word of YHWH'. It is not only divine speech, in which YHWH speaks in the first person, that is to be acknowledged as such, but the whole text, including words attributed to the prophet, words of repentance to be expressed by the people (6:1–3; 14:2b–3 [3b–4]), and, in chapters 1–3, brief elements of narrative. The expression 'the word of YHWH came to' – woodenly, 'the word of YHWH which was to' – is found in narrative texts concerning prophets (e.g. 1 Sam. 15:10; 2 Sam. 7:4; 1 Kgs 17:2), and became a standard literary heading to prophetic texts. The closest parallels to the opening 'The word of YHWH that came to [Personal Name]' are in Joel 1:1; Micah 1:1; Zephaniah 1:1,[37] but the formula is found with only minor variation in Ezekiel, Jonah, Haggai, Zechariah, and Malachi. The naming of a prophet's father is found in the openings of the books of Isaiah, Jeremiah, Ezekiel, Hosea, Joel, Jonah, Zephaniah, and Zechariah. Chronological dating by reference to the reign of kings is present in Isaiah, Jeremiah, Ezekiel (with a primary chronological reference to the years of exile), Hosea, Amos, Micah, and Zephaniah. In the case of Hosea and Amos, whose words are addressed primarily to the northern kingdom of Israel, kings of both Judah and Israel are given. Scholars examining the similarities and discrepancies in such headings have drawn various and varying conclusions. As noted in the 'Volume Introduction', some have seen the similarities of the headings in Hosea, Amos, Micah, and Zephaniah as contributing to their belief that one stage of compositional development in the Book of the Twelve was the existence of a 'Book of the Four' comprising these texts. Many have noted that the chronological references are akin to those of the books of Kings, and deduce that they reflect Deuteronomistic influence.[38] Not all agree with this latter argument,[39] but what is widely agreed is that these headings, in their present, final forms, derive from the exilic period or, more probably, from the post-exilic period, in which it may be assumed that mutual influencing took place and common literary conventions emerged.[40] These headings therefore give us a view into the world of post-monarchic Judah,

---

[37] The LXX of Jer. 1:1 has: 'The word of God which came to Jeremiah.'

[38] In the case of Hosea, so *inter alia* J. L. Mays *Hosea* (1969): 17; A. A. Macintosh *Hosea* (1997): 2–3.

[39] Declining to see specific Deuteronomistic influence are *inter alia* F. I. Andersen and D. N. Freedman *Hosea* (1980): 147; J. M. Bos *Reconsidering* (2013): 138–9.

[40] A. A. Macintosh *Hosea* (1997): 2–3 considers that the date of present superscription of Hos. 1:1 falls at some time between the mid-sixth and mid-fourth centuries.

in which these texts were preserved and edited, and were viewed as holding YHWH's authority. While a prophet's words are portrayed as addressing a particular historical time – and we have little reason to doubt that they did so, and that the earliest literary layers were formed not too far after that time – the texts were seen in post-monarchic Judah as relevant to and addressing people of their own day. The headings were important in the work of preservation, and in indicating to readers how they were being invited to read the text. The chronologies of both Hosea 1:1 and Amos 1:1 name Judean kings first and Israelite kings second, despite the texts being primarily addressed to the northern kingdom, reinforcing the point that these are Judean texts.

As noted in the 'Introduction to Hosea', the list of kings given is surprising. The stretch of Judean kings, from Uzziah to Hezekiah, indicates the belief that, in contrast to the short period in which Amos was active (see 'Amos 1:1: Heading'), Hosea's ministry continued over many years. Uzziah reigned in Judah until 742, and Jeroboam reigned in Israel until 746. The chronology of Hezekiah's reign is disputed, but the earliest likely year is 725. So even if Hosea began his ministry just three years, say, before the end of Jeroboam's reign and continued, say, three years into the earliest dating of Hezekiah's reign, that gives a span of 749–722, a nearly thirty-year period leading up to the fall of the northern kingdom. The question then arises: Why were none of the kings of northern Israel after Jeroboam included? The years 746–722 saw a series of coups in Israel, with a series of short reigns following Jeroboam's long and stable reign (see 2 Kgs 15 and the 'Introduction to Hosea'). It has been suggested that no king of Israel after Jeroboam is mentioned because he was viewed as the last legitimate king. However, this suggestion fails to address the non-inclusion of his son Zechariah who, if his father was legitimate, must be so himself. Did the post-exilic editors, then, not know their history? Did they not bother, or not have the means, to ascertain the names and dates of the Israelite kings of the final years of the kingdom? We can only surmise. But what does seem to be true is that a preoccupation with dates and occasions has been of greater interest to modern scholars than to the ancient editors. That the northern kingdom was allowed to come to an end was most certainly viewed as the consequence of YHWH's actions in judgement, and readers of later centuries were being invited to understand and learn from this. But the details of history were of less importance than this overarching perspective. 'Remembering Hosea was remembering that the North fell to the Assyrians … and that Northern Israel's fall was both an unheeded warning to Judah and a direct

C Commentary on Hosea

pre-figuration of fallen Judah.'[41] It may be that the duplication of the same list of Judean kings in Isaiah 1:1 indicates that the editors took the two prophets to be contemporaries[42]; and that the parallel with Amos 1:1's naming of Uzziah king of Judah and of Jeroboam king of Israel may have been intended to indicate their contemporariness also. All these prophets had spoken words from which later generations might learn.

It is important to recognise that the superscription gives us an exilic or post-exilic perspective. However, that does not mean that our reading of the text must be restricted to interpreting it solely from such a perspective.[43] The redaction-critical method employed by this commentary recognises that behind the final form of the text lay earlier literary layers. It is my view that much of chapters 1–3 and 4–11 belong to the earliest, Post-722 Composition of the text, and that further material was brought in during the seventh century and in the sixth-century exilic period, as well as in the post-exilic period in which the final form was completed. The text can, therefore, be interpreted in the variety of literary contexts formed at the various stages of its composition history.

The name 'Hosea' is, more properly, 'Hoshea'. By longstanding convention, he is called 'Hosea' in English translations to avoid confusion with others named Hoshea, notably the last king of Israel. The name means 'Salvation'. According to Numbers 13:8, 16, it was Joshua's original name, which Moses changed. Hosea 1:1 names him as the son of Beeri. Nothing is known to us of who Beeri was, and the purpose of including his father's name was, presumably to distinguish him from others named Hoshea, just as the reference to Jeroboam 'son of Joash' distinguishes him as Jeroboam II, and not Jeroboam I, who is 'Jeroboam son of Nebat' (1 Kgs 11:26; 12:2 and *passim*).

Hosea 1:2–2:1 [3] – Hosea's Wife and Children

> [2] When the LORD first spoke through Hosea, the LORD said to Hosea, 'Go, take for yourself a wife of prostitution and have children of prostitution, for the land commits great prostitution by forsaking the LORD.'[3] So he

---

[41] E. Ben Zvi, 'Remembering Hosea: The Prophet Hosea as a Site of Memory in Persian Period Yehud', in E. Ben Zvi, C. V. Camp, D. M. Gunn, and A. W. Hughes (eds.), *Poets, Prophets, and Texts in Play: Studies in Biblical Poetry and Prophecy in Honour of Francis Landy* (LHBOTS, 597; London/New York: Bloomsbury/T&T Clark, 2015): 37–57 (43).

[42] The suggestion of F. I. Andersen and D. N. Freedman *Hosea* (1980): 149 that possibly 'the editor inadvertently used the same list of Judean kings as for Isaiah' is implausible.

[43] As is done in, for example, E. Ben Zvi *Hosea* (2005); J. M. Bos *Reconsidering* (2013).

38 *Book of Hosea*

went and took Gomer daughter of Diblaim, and she conceived and bore
him a son.

[4] And the LORD said to him, 'Name him Jezreel; for in a little while I will
punish the house of Jehu for the blood of Jezreel, and I will put an end to
the kingdom of the house of Israel. [5] On that day I will break the bow of
Israel in the valley of Jezreel.'

[6] She conceived again and bore a daughter. Then the LORD said to him,
'Name her Lo-ruhamah, for I will no longer have pity on the house of
Israel or forgive them. [7] But I will have pity on the house of Judah, and I
will save them by the LORD their God; I will not save them by bow, or by
sword, or by war, or by horses, or by horsemen.'

[8] When she had weaned Lo-ruhamah, she conceived and bore a son. [9] Then
the LORD said, 'Name him Lo-ammi, for you are not my people and I am
not your God.'

[10] Yet the number of the people of Israel shall be like the sand of the sea,
which can be neither measured nor numbered; and in the place where
it was said to them, 'You are not my people', it shall be said to them,
'Children of the living God.' [11] The people of Judah and the people of
Israel shall be gathered together, and they shall appoint for themselves
one head; and they shall rise up from the land, for great shall be the day
of Jezreel.

2 Say to your brothers, Ammi, and to your sisters, Ruhamah.

As noted in the 'Introduction', Hosea 1–3 has drawn considerable scholarly
interest. This reflects the potency of the imagery of Hosea's marriage. It also
reflects the multiple interpretative challenges that commentators recognise.[44] There is the challenge of genre: What kind of writing are we dealing
with? Is it allegory, as older Jewish and Christian interpreters preferred to
treat it? Or are parts of it biographical (1:2–8; 2:1 [3]) and autobiographical
(3:1–5), or do they at least contain some biographical information, as commentators of the late nineteenth century and much of the twentieth century
preferred to think?[45] If so, what is to be made ethically of divine commands
to 'take a wife of prostitution and have children of prostitution'[46] (1:2) and

---

[44] For a selection of comments from different periods on the various challenges of the text
see Y. Sherwood, *The Prostitute and the Prophet: Hosea's Marriage in Literary-Theoretical
Perspective* (JSOTSup, 212; Sheffield: Sheffield Academic Press, 1996): 11–12.

[45] So several of the commentaries which I have consulted in preparation of this volume,
including F. I. Andersen and D. N. Freedman *Hosea* (1980); G. I. Davies *Hosea* (1992); J.
A. Dearman *Hosea* (2010); A. A. Macintosh *Hosea* (1997); J. L. Mays *Hosea* (1969); H. W.
Wolff *Hosea* (1974).

[46] For the translation see note 1 in Section II.

to 'Go, love a woman who has a lover and is an adulteress' (3:1)? Is it a work of rhetorical literary fiction told to convey religious and theological truths in order to help the Israelites understand YHWH's relationship to them in judgement and restoration? Such a view might relieve the ethical difficulties somewhat – but not greatly, since the offensive divine commands remain in the story. This leads to the challenge of what kinds of reaction and response are aroused in the reader. Feminist commentators rightly draw attention to the maleness of the telling, and of much interpretation over the years, right up to and into the twenty-first century. Thoughtless male interpretation can fail to note and comment on the sexual violence towards a woman and the cruelty to children expressed not by someone portrayed as evil, but in divine pronouncements such as 2:3–4 [5–6], no less.[47] Then there are interpretative challenges: Of what did the accusation of faithlessness comprise? Was it cultic, concerning Israel's involvement in Baal worship? And if so, of what did such Baal worship consist in the eighth-century BCE? And how was this understood in subsequent centuries in which the text was formed and developed, and to what issues then current did it relate? Or did the faithlessness signify political rather than cultic misdemeanours? Then there are literary and redaction-critical challenges. Are there earlier and later literary layers within these chapters? How are different sections within them related to one another? How do chapters 1–3 relate to chapters 4–14? Do they hold significance not just as the opening chapters of the Hosea-text but of the Book of the Twelve?[48] Finally, there is the question of how – indeed whether – the imagery of a 'wife of prostitution' (1:2) can have contemporary theological value.

---

[47] Among a large and growing volume of feminist approaches to Hos. 1–3 may be mentioned: G. Baumann, *Love and Violence: Marriage as a Metaphor for the Relationship between YHWH and Israel in the Prophetic Books* (Collegeville, MN: Liturgical Press, 2003); P. Bird, '"To Play the Harlot": An Inquiry into an Old Testament Metaphor', in P. L. Day (ed.), *Gender and Difference in Ancient Israel* (Minneapolis: Fortress Press, 1989): 75–94; W. Boshoff, 'The Female Imagery in the Book of Hosea: Considering the Marriage Metaphor in Hosea 1–2 by Listening to Female Voices', *OTE* 15 (2002): 23–41; C. R. Fontaine, 'A Response to Hosea', in A. Brenner (ed.), *A Feminist Companion to the Latter Prophets* (FCB, 8; Sheffield: Sheffield Academic Press, 1995): 60–9; N. Graetz, 'God Is to Israel as Husband Is to Wife: The Metaphoric Battering of Hosea's Wife', in A. Brenner (ed.), *A Feminist Companion to the Latter Prophets* (1995): 126–45; T. D. Setel, 'Prophets and Pornography: Female Sexual Imagery in Hosea', in L. Russell (ed.), *Feminist Interpretation of the Bible* (Oxford: Blackwell, 1985): 86–95; Y. Sherwood *The Prostitute and the Prophet* (1996).
[48] C. D. Bowman, 'Reading the Twelve as One: Hosea 1–3 as an Introduction to the Book of the Twelve (the Minor Prophets)', *Stone-Campbell Journal* 9 (2006): 41–59.

40   *Book of Hosea*

My approach will be – in line with the redaction-critical method that this commentary adopts[49] – to set out my understanding of the composition history of these chapters. I shall then proceed to comment on each section of text within chapters 1–3. Engagement with some of the interpretative challenges will follow the comments on chapter 3 in the 'Bridging the Horizons: The Metaphor of the Unfaithful Wife' section.

That Hosea 1–3 is a transmission complex separate from chapters 4–14 is widely recognised. It seems that only late on in the transmission process were the two joined. The effect of the joining is that chapters 1–3 function as an introduction to the book as a whole. The primary thematic overlap is the accusation of prostitution (1:2; 2:2–13 [4–15]; 4:10–15; 5:3–4; 6:10; 9:1). At some points this is related to Baal worship (2:8, 13, 16–17 [2:10, 15, 18–19]; 9:10; 11:2; 13:1). The effect of joining 1–3 to 4–14 is that readers read 4–14 with the powerful imagery of 1–3 ringing in their ears, and accusations of Israel's unfaithfulness to YHWH in 4–14 are read within a mental framework of the marriage metaphor from 1–3. Another thematic overlap is that of the wilderness as a place where YHWH had been and could again be close to his people (2:14–15 [16–17]; 9:10; 13:5). There are also differences between 1–3 and 4–14. In contrast to 1–3 there is no narrative material in 4–14. Moreover, in 4–14 northern Israel is most frequently referred to as 'Ephraim', but this name does not occur at all in 1–3.

It is evident that 1–3 had its own composition history. The relationship between the narrative material in chapters 1 and 3 has been much debated (see the commentary on Hosea 3). The relationship between chapters 1 and 2 also warrants comment. The principal focus of 1:2–8 is the naming of Hosea's children. The taking a wife of prostitution introduced into 1:2 seems unrelated, and is not picked up on again until chapter 2. It is probable that the present form of 1:2 was shaped when once separate material in chapters 1 and 2 was brought together into the first written composition. This was subsequently enlarged by the addition of 1:2–2:1 [3] and by sections beginning 'On that day' in 2:16–20 [18–22] and 2:21–23 [23–25] (see the commentary on Hosea 2: 16–23).

The opening line of 1:2 constituted the heading to this section of text prior to its incorporation with chapters 4–14 and the addition of 1:1. Wolff translates it as 'How Yahweh began to speak through Hosea.'[50] There follows immediately YHWH's command to Hosea to 'take a wife of prostitution'.

---

[49]   See the 'Volume Introduction'.
[50]   H. W. Wolff *Hosea* (1974): 8.

C Commentary on Hosea   41

The verb 'take' (*laqaḥ*) is that used generally for taking a wife (Gen. 4:19; Exod. 34:16; 1 Sam. 25:40). It can also be used for a man taking a woman for intercourse (Lev. 20:14, 17, 21), allowing Davies to propose that the command is for Hosea not to marry, but rather to take a prostitute (the word 'wife' also means simply 'woman').[51] However the linking of prostitution and adultery elsewhere in Hosea (4:13–14) and the working out of the extended metaphor of YHWH's relationship with his people make the usual understanding more probable.

A Closer Look: A Wife of Prostitution

The root *znh* in its verbal form 'prostitute oneself' or nominal form 'prostitution' is found four times within 1:2, then in 2:2, 4, 5 [4, 6, 7]; 3:3 and in 4:10–15, 18; 5:3, 4; 6:10; 9:1. Of eighty-four occurrences in the Hebrew Bible, twenty are in Hosea.[52] The root *n'p*, in verbal form 'commit adultery' or in nominal form 'adultery', is found in 2:2 [4]; 4:2, 13–14, as well as the nominal form 'adulteress' in 3:1. The two terms are found together in 2:2 [4]; 4:13–14. Krispenz comments that they 'are actually used in Hosea as if they were synonymous'.[53] While this is true, it is helpful to remember the differences between the two. On the one hand, *znh* signifies acts of promiscuity, including prostitution (pre-2021 NRSV: whoredom). While shameful, such acts were not illegal. On the other hand, marriage was a legal matter, and the wife belonged to her husband. To commit adultery was an offence against a woman's husband. For the prophet knowingly to marry a 'wife of prostitution' would be to marry a shameful woman, in the knowledge that his legal rights as husband would be violated.

The prophet's marriage to Gomer in response to YHWH's command is akin to prophetic symbolic actions found elsewhere in the prophetic corpus. In some cases it is perfectly possible to believe that they were carried out as described. On the one hand, Jeremiah's buying and smashing of an earthenware jug to symbolise that YHWH 'will break this people and this city, as one breaks a potter's vessel' (Jer. 19:1–13) is entirely plausible. On the other hand, did Isaiah really walk naked and barefoot for

---

[51] G. I. Davies *Hosea* (1992): 50.
[52] T. D. Setel 'Prophets and Pornography' (1985): 91.
[53] J. Krispenz, 'Idolatry, Apostasy, Prostitution: Hosea's Struggle against the Cult', in L.-S. Tiemeyer (ed.), *Priests and Cults* (2016): 9–30 (10 n. 6).

three years (Isa. 20:2–4)? Did Ezekiel really lie on his left side for three hundred and ninety days, followed by forty days lying on his right side (Ezek. 4:4–8)? While not impossible, the reader's credulity is stretched if these are taken as historical, biographical accounts. The account of Hosea's marriage to Gomer stretches the reader's credulity in a different way. There is no physical impossibility about the action. The incredulity is, rather, born of moral outrage – or at least, of moral surprise. The text tarnishes the reputation of Gomer: she is characterised from the outset as a prostitute. It tarnishes the reputation of Hosea, who proceeds to marry Gomer despite her character. And it tarnishes the ethical reputation of YHWH: he it is who commands this marriage in which promiscuity and adultery will be evident.

Unsurprisingly, commentators both ancient and modern have endeavoured to find explanations which make YHWH's command in 1:2 more palatable than the bare reading of the text suggests.[54] Several so-called pre-critical scholars interpreted Hosea 1–3 as an allegory, in Jewish tradition of YHWH and his people, and in Christian tradition of Christ and the Church. Modern commentators who see them as containing historical, biographical content come up with a variety of strategies. Wolff attempts to defend Gomer's reputation (and thereby Hosea's also) by arguing that many young women of the time took part in 'bridal rites of initiation then current in Israel', such rites entailing intercourse. The term 'wife of prostitution' referred to any young woman who had submitted to these rites. She was 'therefore not an especially wicked exception; she is simply representative of her contemporaries'.[55] The evidence for the practice of such rites in Israel is weak, and the majority of commentators do not follow Wolff. Andersen and Freedman are representative of a number of scholars who hold that the wording of 1:2 reflects not what was known at the time of the marriage, but what subsequently proved to be the case. 'Gomer was not promiscuous when Hosea married her … what she was when he married her is not the main point of interest.… It is what she became in marriage that makes the oracles.'[56] Such an interpretation defends Hosea's honour, while Gomer's promiscuity

---

[54] Y. Sherwood *The Prostitute and the Prophet* (1996): 19–82 surveys an extensive range of writings from various periods which seek to explain and defend the biblical text in various ways.

[55] H. W. Wolff *Hosea* (1974): 15.

[56] F. I. Andersen and D. N. Freedman *Hosea* (1980): 165–6.

C Commentary on Hosea

is assumed to have begun or emerged at a time later than the marriage. However, this interpretation comes from the interpreter, not from the text. If the text is read as biography there is no escaping the difficulties that scholars strive to explain and excuse.

While there may be actual happenings behind the text, the precise nature of these eludes us. It is more profitable to investigate the literary text itself. The text is best read as a metaphor in which Hosea's marriage to Gomer represents the relationship between YHWH and Israel. It is not allegory, which would require that each element of the story represents some reality in that relationship, and within which there should be consistency. The metaphor engages the reader, rather, at the level of emotion. Logical consistency is neither evident nor required. Hence Israel's representation as Hosea's wife, but also as his children, need not lead us to ask: well, which is it?[57] Schmitt notes that in the Hebrew Bible 'Israel' is generally male. Cities, in contrast, are generally female. He concludes that it must be 'Samaria' that is seen as YHWH's wife rather than 'Israel'.[58] Within the emotion of the metaphorical language, however, such logical precision is unnecessary: Israel, Samaria, the land – the distinctions become less important than the strength of feelings that the text conveys. The metaphor leaves the reader with the unarguable knowledge that YHWH sees his people as faithless. The roots *znh* and *n'p* both convey this faithlessness. In chapters 4–14 Israel's faithlessness is seen in both the cultic realm (e.g. 4:12–13, 17–18; 13:1–2) and in the political realm (e.g. 5:13; 7:11, 16; 12:1 [2]). In chapters 1–3 the focus is on the cultic realm, with Baal specifically mentioned (2:8, 13, 16–17 [10, 15, 18–19]). The metaphor entails the attributing of strong emotion to YHWH, 'emotions such as jealousy and honor which are not captured as fully by the more generic language of an angry god who punishes his people by sword, famine and pestilence'.[59] These emotions attributed to YHWH extend to the desire

---

[57] Koch suggests that '[t]he land is seen as God's unfaithful wife, and the people are her sons', a suggestion found among other commentators also. But the distinction is hard to maintain. See K. Koch, *The Prophets, vol. 1* (trans. M. Kohl; London: SCM, 1982): 76–93 (89).

[58] J. J. Schmitt, 'Gender Correctness and Biblical Metaphors: The Case of God's Relation to Israel', *BTB* 26 (1996): 96–106; J. J. Schmitt, 'Yahweh's Divorce in Hosea 2 – Who Is That Woman?' *SJOT* 9 (1995): 119–32.

[59] R. I. Thelle, 'Self as *Other*: Israel's Self-Designation as Adulterous Wife, a Self-Reflective Perspective on a Prophetic Metaphor', in R. I. Thelle, T. Stordalen, and M. E. J. Richardson (eds.), *New Perspectives on Old Testament Prophecy and History: Essays in Honour of Hans M. Barstad* (VTSup, 168; Leiden: Brill, 2015):104–20 (106). On YHWH's

44   Book of Hosea

to publicly disgrace and humiliate the unfaithful mother (2:3–13 [4–15]), images which later readers would have seen as pointing to the destruction of Samaria in 722 and Jerusalem in 587. These were judgements sent by YHWH not merely as the cool sentencing of a judge but, in the light of Hosea 1–3, as an outworking of his jealous anger. Built into the text, however, is the recognition that 'YHWH loves the people of Israel, though they turn to other gods' (3:1 cf. 1:10–2:1 [2:1–3]; 3:5). As the sections Hosea 4–11 and 12–14 end with words of hope, so too does Hosea 1–3. The metaphor encompasses emotions not only of hurt and jealous anger, but also of continuing love despite it.[60]

The first instruction to Hosea to 'take a wife of prostitution' is followed immediately by a second: to have children of prostitution. Some consider that the children were 'children of prostitution' because of the prostitution of their mother,[61] others because they themselves would grow up to be equally promiscuous.[62] The former seems more probable if, indeed, the question even needs to be asked. Some suggest that in view of Gomer's promiscuity, the phrase indicates that Hosea was not the father; however this seems dubious, and nothing in the text supports it. More important is the explanation for the metaphor: 'for the land commits great prostitution by forsaking YHWH'. The land may be taken as synonymous with its people;[63] it is a feminine noun, so fits well into the chapter's metaphor.

Hosea 1:3 names Hosea's wife for the first and only time: she is Gomer, son of Diblaim. In contrast to the names of the children in 1:4, 6, 9, neither name is given any particular significance or meaning. This concise verse leads into the central motif of Hosea 1, the naming of Hosea's and Gomer's children. The first son is named 'Jezreel' (1:4), a name admitting of multifarious significance. The name means 'God sows', a meaning picked up in 2:22–23 [24–25]. As a place name it denotes a wide plain between the highlands of

---

honour, see J. Moon, 'Honor and Shame in Hosea's Marriages', *JSOT* 39 (2015): 335–51; T. S. Hadjiev, 'Adultery, Shame, and Sexual Pollution in Ancient Israel and in Hosea: A Response to Joshua Moon', *JSOT* 41 (2016): 221–36.

[60]   The question of the offensiveness of some of the language of the metaphor to which feminist interpreters draw justifiable attention will be addressed in the Bridging the Horizons section 'The Metaphor of the Unfaithful Wife'.

[61]   J. L. Mays *Hosea* (1969): 26.

[62]   H. Angel, '*Rebuke your Mother*: But Who is She? The Identity of the Mother and Children in Hosea 2:4–7', *JBQ* 44 (2016): 13–20.

[63]   G. I. Davies *Hosea* (1992): 52; A. A. Macintosh *Hosea* (1997): 7–8.

C Commentary on Hosea

Samaria and Galilee. Various traditions tell of battles fought in it (e.g. Judg. 6:33; 1 Sam. 29:1, 11). King Ahab had a palace there (1 Kgs 21:1), and there his wife Queen Jezebel arranged for the murder of Naboth so that Ahab could acquire the adjacent vineyard (1 Kgs 21:1–16). Finally, it was at Jezreel that Ahab's son King Joram, his wife Jezebel, his seventy sons, and the many staff of Ahab's and Joram's court were slaughtered in the revolt of Jehu which brought down the house of Omri and put the house of Jehu on the throne (2 Kgs 9–10). Jeroboam II and his son Zechariah belonged to the line of Jehu. It is this last significance that 1:4 picks up on: YHWH will punish the house of Jehu for the blood of Jezreel. The verb 'punish' is frequent in Hosea (1:4; 2:13 [15]; 4:9, 14; 8:13; 9:9; 12:2 [3]) and in Jeremiah (e.g. 11:22; 21:14). The word 'blood' is plural ('bloods'), indicating not a single act of killing, but the mass extermination that 2 Kings 9–10 depicts. The declaration of 1:4 is in tension with the narrative of 2 Kings 9:1–13, in which Jehu's revolt is initiated by Elisha. If YHWH sanctioned it through his prophet Elisha, how is it that he now condemns it through his prophet Hosea? Wolff suggests that Hosea 1:4 belonged to the earliest period of Hosea's ministry, in which 'there was yet no connection with the prophetic traditions of the ninth century'.[64] This is dubious; and even if so, the problem remains for readers of a later time. A possible reconciliation might be achieved by a comparison with Isaiah 10:5–19, in which Assyria is first declared to be the rod of YHWH's anger in punishing his people, but is then itself condemned for its actions carried out in arrogant defiance of YHWH. Similarly, perhaps, the actions of Jehu grew out of a prophetic word, but were then taken too far in the level of slaughter that was undertaken. The reader may bring such a possibility to the text. Alternatively, as Macintosh suggests, the Hosea-text considers simply that murder is murder (and, in 4:2, one of the marks of the nation's lack of loyalty to YHWH), and the account of Jehu's commissioning in 2 Kings 9 does not change that.[65] Certainly the contemporary reader is likely to find the slaughter of 2 Kings 9–10 abhorrent, and therefore to be amenable to such bloodshed being condemned in Hosea 1:4. The punishment decreed is that YHWH will put an end to 'the kingdom of the house of Israel'. This could mean either the end of the line of the house of Jehu or the end of the nation. In the literary context of the first written composition after the destruction of the kingdom in 722 the latter is the more natural understanding.

---

[64] H. W. Wolff *Hosea* (1974): 18.
[65] A. A. Macintosh *Hosea* (1997): 17.

46   *Book of Hosea*

Hosea 1:5 then uses the name 'Jezreel' in a different sense. It is the place of frequent battle where, it is said, the bow of Israel will be broken. The bow represents a nation's might (cf. Jer. 49:35), and there YHWH will break Israel's might. With the opening formula ('On that day'), it is likely that this verse was added to 1:4 on the basis of Jezreel being a catchword. This addition was made within the first, late eighth-century composition from the oral material or isolated literary sayings from which it was compiled.[66] Thematically it confirms the message that Israel's doom is writ.

The narrative resumes in 1:6 with the birth of Gomer's second child, a daughter, to whom YHWH tells Hosea to give the name Lo-ruhamah, meaning 'Not pitied'. This naming, and that in 1:9, is akin to the naming of Isaiah's children in Isaiah 7:3; 8:3–4 in that the name itself signifies a message: no longer will YHWH pity and spare his people. YHWH's compassionate pity for his people was (as we would say today) part of Israel's DNA (cf. Exod. 34:6; Ps. 103:13), so Hosea 1:6 constitutes a stark reversal of a belief presumably dearly held. The translation of the final line by NRSV as 'or forgive them' is a valid one; but it could be translated as 'I will withdraw it (*sc.* pity) from them' (Wolff) or 'I will certainly carry them off' (Bos).[67] NRSV's translation is satisfactory, but the Hebrew has the verb repeated to give a stronger force, which Dearman's 'I will certainly not forgive them' reflects.[68]

It is widely agreed that 1:7, which has the nature of an aside referring positively to Judah rather than negatively to Israel, disturbs the flow of the text and represents an addition to its original formulation. Several commentators see in it a contrast between the destruction of Samaria by the Assyrians in 722 and the deliverance of Jerusalem from the Assyrians in 701, and therefore attribute it to the period subsequent to 701 but prior to the destruction of Jerusalem by the Babylonians in 587.[69] This is plausible. However it is more likely that it is part of the re-working of the text by the post-exilic redactors of the text,[70] who also introduced 1:10–2:1 [2:1–3]. The presence of bow, sword, and war link it to 2:18 [20], also from these post-exilic redactors. The portrayal of YHWH saving, but not by weapons of war,

---

[66]   In his examination of such connecting formulae De Vries includes Hos. 1:5 as an example of a 'move from one event or situation to another within the proximate future': S. J. De Vries, *From Old Revelation to New* (Grand Rapids, MI: Eerdmans, 1995): 52–3.

[67]   H. W. Wolff *Hosea* (1974): 8; J. M. Bos *Reconsidering* (2013): 104–5.

[68]   J. A. Dearman *Hosea* (2010): 89.

[69]   So *inter alia* J. A. Dearman *Hosea* (2010): 98; A. A. Macintosh *Hosea* (1997): 25; J. L. Mays *Hosea* (1969): 29.

[70]   The verse is read as a natural part of the Persian period text by E. Ben Zvi *Hosea* (2005): 48; J. M. Bos *Reconsidering* (2013): 58–61.

C Commentary on Hosea 47

echoes Joshua 24:12, part of a chapter containing Deuteronomistic features which suggest that much, if not all, of it derives from the exilic period.[71]

The narrative resumes in 1:8–9 with the birth of Gomer's third child, a son, to whom YHWH tells Hosea to give the name Lo-ammi, meaning 'Not my people'. A sense of a progression of time is given by the chronological note saying that only after Lo-ruhamah was weaned was Lo-ammi conceived. The time from birth to weaning was at least two, probably three, years; so time is passing with Israel still under YHWH's judgement. For the first time the text moves into divine speech in which YHWH addresses the people in the second person as he explains the significance of the name: 'for you are not my people and I am not your God'. The translation of the last clause as 'I am not your God' is usual, but entails an emendation:[72] it literally reads 'I am not yours.' However, some prefer to avoid making the emendation by seeing an allusion to the explanation of the divine name given in Exodus 3:14, and translating 'I am not I AM to you.'[73] Whatever the preferred translation, the import is clear. Just as YHWH's compassionate pity for his people was, in all probability, assumed (1:6), so too was the assumption that Israel was YHWH's people and he was their God (e.g. Exod. 6:7). But now the naming of Hosea's and Gomer's third child signifies the opposite: YHWH, in his judgement, will no longer treat them as his people and will no longer be their God.

The naming of all three children thus signifies YHWH's intended complete judgement on Israel. From within 1:4–9 the only reason for judgement given is the 'blood of Jezreel' (1:4); but over it all stands 1:2's metaphor of Israel's faithlessness as the explanation. That theme will be explored further in chapter 2, which in the earliest, eighth-century, text followed 1:2–9 directly. The post-exilic redactors, however, added 1:10–2:1 [2:1–3] as a short unit expressing future hope. Hosea 2:1 [3] functions as a transition from 1:10–11 [2:1–2] to 2:2–13 [4–15]. This is evident in its direct, second-person address which mirrors that of 2:2 [4] rather than 1:10–11 [2:1–2]. Davies considers that 1:10 [2:1] and 1:11 [2:2] were originally separate sayings in view of the differing use of the name 'Israel': in 1:10 [2:1] it refers

---

[71] E. W. Nicholson, *God and His People: Covenant and Theology in the Old Testament* (Oxford: Clarendon Press, 1986): 160–3.

[72] Reading *lō' 'ĕlōhêkem* for *lō' 'ehyeh lākem*.

[73] So *inter alia* J. A. Dearman *Hosea* (2010): 89, 99–100; J. L. Mays *Hosea* (1969): 22, 29. The verbal form *'ehyeh* (I am) is identical in Exod. 3:14 and Hos. 1:9. On this verbal form and the divine name see C. Meyers, *Exodus* (NCBC; Cambridge: Cambridge University Press, 2005): 57–9.

48 *Book of Hosea*

to the whole people, that is, both nations, while in 1:11 [2:2] it refers to the northern kingdom.[74] While this may be so, it is not a problem that the usage changes: by the late sixth century both uses were established, and the change would not have jarred. That these verses move from judgement to hope is not an argument in favour of them being later than the preceding text, since the eighth-century composition contains verses within it expressing hope (2:14–15 [16–17]; 11:8–9). But that they are exilic or post-exilic is indicated (1) by their casual familiarity with the promise from the patriarchal narratives that the people of Israel shall be like the sand of the sea: while this could have been known from oral tradition, it probably reflects the later written account; and (2) by the hope of the reunification of Judah and Israel: other passages in which this hope is expressed (Isa. 11:12–13; Jer. 3:18; 31:27–34; Ezek. 37:15–23) all belong to the sixth century.[75] The insertion is consistent with the pattern in the final form of the text: as the major sections, chapters 4–11 and 12–14, end with hope (11:8–11; 14:4–9 [5–10]), so within chapters 1–3 each chapter also ends with hope (1:10–2:1 [2:1–3]; 2:14–23 [16–25]; 3:5). The verses draw from 1:2–9 and were composed for this literary context. Their purpose is not to undermine or contradict 1:2–9, but to accept that the history of those now in exile and of returnees to the homeland included the faithlessness of their own people (among whom they included Israelites of the northern kingdom), and that YHWH's promised blessing was granted only after his judgement had taken effect.

The promise that the number of the people of Israel shall be like the sand of the sea (1:10 [2:1]) is expressed in Genesis 22:17; 32:12. In the early post-exilic period the Judean population in the land was low: this promise held out the hope that it would increase.[76] The promise also reverses the judgement expressed in the naming of Hosea's and Gomer's third child. Where it was said to the people 'You are not my people (= Lo-ammi)',[77] it is now said that they shall be 'Children of the living God' – and not children of prostitution. Continuing into 1:11 [2:2], the promise has three elements. Firstly, the peoples of Judah and Israel shall be gathered together.

---

[74]   G. I. Davies *Hosea* (1992): 62.

[75]   So, *inter alia*, G. I. Davies *Hosea* (1992): 62.

[76]   Isaiah 51:2 offers a similar hope based on the story of the patriarch Abraham.

[77]   The location of the 'place where' is not specified. Mays suggests that in view of the closing phrase of 1:11 [2:2] it could be Jezreel. Alternatively it could be the place where Lo-ammi was named. The word 'place' (*māqôm*) is also used of a sanctuary. The matter has no great interpretative significance. See further F. I. Andersen and D. N. Freedman *Hosea* (1980): 203; J. L. Mays *Hosea* (1969): 32.

C Commentary on Hosea

The verb can be used of gathering for an assembly or for battle (cf. 1 Sam. 7:6–7), but is also used of gathering the people to bring them back from the places to which they have been exiled (Ezek. 37:21). Secondly, the gathered, reunited people of Judah and Israel shall appoint 'one head (*rōš*)'. The term can be used of a military leader or chief (Num. 14:4; Judg. 11:8) or of a king (1 Sam. 15:17–18). Thirdly, under this leader they shall rise up from the land.[78] The land from which they shall rise up is not specified. If the verse was taken to derive from the prophet Hosea or from the eighth century it would be necessary to postulate that it might be Egypt or Assyria that is meant. Better, however, is the longstanding recognition that the reference is to a return from exile in Babylon, from where the people will be gathered. A further possible interpretation proposed by some is that there is a play on the meaning of the name Jezreel, 'God sows', and that the reference is to Israel sprouting up from the earth. This would then be a positive use of the name, reversing its negative significance in 1:4, just as 2:1 [3] reverses the names of his siblings. It would also anticipate 2:23 [25], as does 2:1 [3]. Perhaps the ambiguity is deliberate: the reader may see one or other significance, or more than one layer of meaning, in the text. It would also match the ambiguity (again, perhaps deliberate) of the term 'head'. Who is it that is meant? – the text does not specify. It is possible that it is a post-monarchic avoidance of the word 'king'. However, in the literary context of Hosea 1–3 one cannot avoid the comparison with 3:5, in which the people will seek 'David their king', that is, a royal descendant of King David.[79]

As noted, 2:1 [3] effects a transition to chapter 2 by its formal similarity with 2:2 [4] of second-person address. Its content, however, is one with 1:10–11 [2:1–2]. After the time of judgement the names Lo-ruhamah (Not pitied) and Lo-ammi (Not my people) become Ruhamah (Pitied) and Ammi (My people). Logically it must be the elder brother Jezreel who is addressed. However, the imperative verb and those addressed are in plural form: 'Say [pl.] to your brothers, Ammi, and to your sisters, Ruhamah.' The imagery of the individual family becomes the nation for which the family is the metaphor. In its anticipation of 2:23 [25] the verse forms an *inclusio* around the words of chapter 2 that follow.

---

[78] The pre-2021 NRSV had the less probable 'take possession of the land'.

[79] E. Ben Zvi *Hosea* (2005): 48 comments that the post-monarchic readership 'cannot but contextually relate it to 3:5'.

Hosea 2:2–15 [4–17] – A Wife and Mother Condemned

² Plead with your mother, plead –
 for she is not my wife,
 and I am not her husband –
that she put away her prostitution from her face,
 and her adultery from between her breasts,
³ or I will strip her naked
 and expose her as in the day she was born,
 and make her like a wilderness,
 and turn her into a parched land,
 and kill her with thirst.
⁴ Upon her children also I will have no pity,
 because they are children of prostitution.
⁵ For their mother has prostituted herself;
 she who conceived them has acted shamefully.
For she said, 'I will go after my lovers;
 they give me my bread and my water,
 my wool and my flax, my oil and my drink.'
⁶ Therefore I will hedge up her way with thorns;
 and I will build a wall against her,
 so that she cannot find her paths.
⁷ She shall pursue her lovers,
 but not overtake them;
and she shall seek them,
 but shall not find them.
Then she shall say, 'I will go
 and return to my first husband,
 for it was better with me then than now.'
⁸ She did not know
 that it was I who gave her
 the grain, the wine, and the oil,
and who lavished upon her silver
 and gold that they used for Baal.
⁹ Therefore I will take back
 my grain in its time,
 and my wine in its season;
and I will take away my wool and my flax,
 which were to cover her nakedness.
¹⁰ Now I will uncover her shame
 in the sight of her lovers,
 and no one shall rescue her out of my hand.

C Commentary on Hosea

[11] I will put an end to all her mirth,
  her festivals, her new moons, her Sabbaths,
  and all her appointed festivals.
[12] I will lay waste her vines and her fig trees,
  of which she said,
 'These are my pay,
  which my lovers have given me.'
I will make them a forest,
  and the wild animals shall devour them.
[13] I will punish her for the festival days of the Baals,
  to whom she offered incense
and decked herself with her ring and jewellery,
  and went after her lovers,
  and forgot me, says the Lord.
[14] Therefore, I will now allure her,
  and bring her into the wilderness,
  and speak tenderly to her.
[15] From there I will give her her vineyards,
  and make the Valley of Achor a door of hope.
There she shall respond as in the days of her youth,
  as at the time when she came out of the land of Egypt.

Throughout 2:2–15 [4–17] is found a clearly deliberate moving back and forth between sentences which appear to relate to Hosea's marriage and others which appear to relate to YHWH's relationship to Israel and the land. For example, the punishment of 2:3a [5a] appears to be on the prophet's wife, but that of 2:3b [5b] on the land. We do well to avoid any suggestion that different materials have been brought together, creating awkwardness. As Sweeney comments, the ambiguity between Hosea–Gomer and YHWH–Israel 'is part of the rhetorical strategy of the passage, which establishes Hosea's marriage to Gomer as the paradigm for YHWH's relationship with Israel and draws the reader into the paradigm'.[80]

The opening imperative of 2:2 [4] immediately raises a question: who is being instructed: 'Plead with your mother'? Sweeney takes it closely with the preceding verse and suggests that the older brother Jezreel addresses his siblings Ammi and Ruhamah.[81] Most commentators, however, take it

---

[80] M. A. Sweeney, *The Twelve Prophets*, vol. 1 (Berit Olam Studies in Hebrew Narrative and Poetry; Collegeville, MN: Liturgical Press, 2000): 25.

[81] M. A. Sweeney *Twelve Prophets* 1 (2000): 11–12. In 2:1 [3] he takes the names (without the commas that NRSV supplies after them) as being in apposition to 'brother' and

to be all the children who are addressed. There is a tension if the passage is read too literally, or too strictly allegorically, in that both mother and children represent Israel. Hence Wolff wonders 'whether Hosea summons the people of Israel against the land of Israel; the youth against the leaders; the morally superior against those chiefly responsible for Israel's guilt', noting that the 'allegory contains many possibilities of interpretation'.[82] Macintosh construes it as 'an invitation to individual Israelites to rise in condemnation of the idolatry and corruption of the nations as a whole'.[83] Dearman sees the key throughout Hosea as being that Israel is YHWH's household. This allows for her being simultaneously spouse and children.[84] The metaphorical language does not, in fact, require logical precision, the portrayal of a breakdown of relationship being evident regardless. NRSV's 'Plead' translates the verb *rîb*, which, along with the related noun *rîb* ('indictment') will be found again in chapter 4. It carries legal connotations, and could be translated 'Accuse'. But it is also used in other settings, including that of a family dispute. The translation 'Remonstrate' fits the context well. The declaration that 'she is not my wife and I am not her husband' is seen by some as a formal divorce formula.[85] There is barely evidence to support this. However, the statements do reveal a total breakdown of relationship – both that of husband and wife and of YHWH and Israel. The putting away of 'prostitution from her face' and 'adultery from between her breasts' is taken by some to mean the removal of jewellery from the face and between the breasts which would have signified that a woman was a prostitute. Wolff comments that these 'were probably certain marks or emblems, e.g., headbands, belts, rings, necklaces, or similar jewelry'.[86] Again, there is hardly evidence of this. On the one hand, Jeremiah 3:3 refers to Israel having the 'forehead of a prostitute (pre-2021 NRSV: whore)', and there are occasional references to faithless Israel beautifying herself with painted face or eyes and ornaments (Jer. 4:30; Ezek. 23:40). On the other hand, when Tamar acts as a prostitute she put on a veil, and is thought by Judah to be a prostitute because her face was covered (Gen. 38:14–15). Furthermore, in the metaphor of Ezekiel 16:8–14 jewellery is given to Israel by YHWH as a sign of his love.

'sister' giving the sense: 'Say to your brother Ammi and to your sister Ruhamah, "Plead with your mother ..."'

[82] H. W. Wolff *Hosea* (1974): 33.
[83] A. A. Macintosh *Hosea* (1997): 41–2.
[84] J. A. Dearman *Hosea* (2010): 44–9 and *passim*.
[85] H. W. Wolff *Hosea* (1974): 33.
[86] H. W. Wolff *Hosea* (1974): 33–4.

C Commentary on Hosea

53

Macintosh is correct that the abstract nouns 'prostitution/whoredom' and 'adultery' are best taken to denote behaviour rather than alleged physical symbols of that behaviour.[87]

If the wife/Israel does not respond to such remonstration, the husband/YHWH will strip her, expose her, make her like a wilderness and kill her with thirst (2:3 [5]). As noted, the actions of the first half of the verse are against the wife, while those of the second half are against the land: within the metaphorical language of the chapter the two are to be read as one. The stripping naked of the wife is sometimes taken as the consequence of the cessation of the husband's obligation to provide clothing for his wife (Exod. 21:10). However the focus is not on the withdrawal of provision, but on public humiliation of the woman (cf. 2:10 [12]). The land will become a parched desert: fertility is YHWH's gift, not Baal's (cf. 2:8, 13 [10, 15]), and he can withdraw it at will. Within the metaphor, both mother and children suffer the same fate (2:4 [6]). The public shaming of the wife is justified, according to the text, because she has acted shamefully (2:5a [7a]). As a prostitute, she has not even waited for clients to come to her, but has gone after lovers who will provide her with gifts as payment (2:5b [7b]). The 'lovers' signify the Baals, and the gifts described prepare the ground for the forthcoming application of the imagery to the land/nation in 2:8–13 [10–15]. The mother's lovers will provide bread and water (foods basic to life), wool and flax (basic to clothing), oil and drink. The term 'drink' is rare, found elsewhere only in Psalm 102:9 [10] and in Proverbs 3:8. Since water has already been included, it may be taken as drinks, perhaps alcoholic, more pleasurable than essential.

But before the imagery is applied to the people of the land in 2:8 [10] there comes the first of three sayings introduced by 'Therefore' (2:6, 9, 14 [8, 11, 16]). In prophetic judgement oracles *lākēn* marks the transition from accusation to announcement of judgement.[88] In 2:6–7 [8–9]), however, what is announced are actions designed not to destroy, but to prevent the wife/Israel from achieving successful pursuit of her lovers and thereby to bring her back to her husband/YHWH. The wall to be built signifies a stone rampart, about a metre high, often built at the edge of a vineyard (cf. Isa. 5:5). With this and the growth of thorn bushes, she will be unable to find her lovers, and so will return to her husband. This does not represent any change

---

[87] A. A. Macintosh *Hosea* (1997): 40.

[88] The connective is rarely used in Hosea (only in these verses and 13:3) compared to its frequent occurrence in Isaiah, Jeremiah, Ezekiel, and Amos. In 2:6 [8] the Hebrew has *lākēn hinanî*, and in 2:14 [16] *lākēn hinnēh*, both of which are emphatic: 'Therefore behold'.

54   *Book of Hosea*

of heart on her part, but a restriction of her movements. The verb 'seek' (*bāqaš*) is used in 5:6, 15 of seeking YHWH: because the seeking of lovers – the Baals – will now fail, the hope is that Israel might now seek YHWH. Its use here anticipates its later occurrences. Similarly the verb 'return' (*šûb*) anticipates its twenty further occurrences in the Hosea-text (see the commentary on 6:1).

Hosea 2:8 [10] resumes the focus of 2:5 [7] on who it is that provides the produce of the land. Grain, wine, and oil constituted staple elements of food and drink, the three being frequently found together (e.g. Deut. 7:13; 11:14; 28:51; Joel 1:10; 2:19; in Ps. 104:15 with 'bread' rather than 'grain'). Silver and gold, however, were not staples: these costly items were needed, the text suggests, for Baal worship. The verse encapsulates a crucial question for Israel's beliefs: Who provided the fertility of the land – Baal or YHWH? The next verse (2:9 [11]) makes matters clear as YHWH speaks: 'I will take back *my* grain … *my* wine … *my* wool … *my* flax' (italics added). The list draws from both 2:5 [7] and 2:8 [10]. The ambiguity between wife–husband and YHWH–Israel/land continues with the withdrawal of provisions leading to exposure of the wife's nakedness. As in 2:3 [5], this represents not merely the removal of clothing as a provision, but a deliberate and conscious shaming, as 2:10 [12] makes explicit. NRSV's 'shame' (2:10 [12]) translates *nablût*, a noun found only here. The most common translations are 'shame' or 'lewdness'. The verbal root from which it is derived means 'be senseless/foolish', and Dearman's translation as 'folly' is entirely in order.[89] The wife's folly and shame become that of the people, for whom mirth will be put to an end, along with the festivals that were part of it (2:11 [13]). The word 'festivals' is singular in the Hebrew text: we might translate that her 'round of festivals' is ended, that is, it encompasses the annual cycle of festivals rather than any particular one. New Moon and Sabbath are found together also in 2 Kings 4:23, Isaiah 1:13, and Amos 8:5, indicating that the pairing is at home in the pre-exilic period. The festivals are referred to as 'her' festivals: they are not YHWH's! Similar is Amos 5:21–23, which refers to the keeping of 'your' festivals and assemblies. The withdrawal of grain, wine, and oil would make the celebration of festivals impossible. But more than that, the husband/YHWH purposes that all mirth and celebration for the wife/Israel be ended. Vines and fig trees will be laid waste (2:12 [14]). A mark of blessing would be that people might 'sit under their own vines and their own fig

---

[89]   J. A. Dearman *Hosea* (2010): 108.

C Commentary on Hosea 55

trees' (2 Kgs 18:31 = Isa. 36:16; Mic. 4:4), but in Hosea 2:12 [14] any such hope is denied. If Israel insists on seeing these as provisions of the Baals – her lovers' pay[90] – then YHWH's removal of them will reveal his overruling of such a belief. His actions will be punishment for the keeping of the festival days of the Baals (2:13 [15]). We have few contemporary extra-biblical sources to aid our understanding of what took place on such festival days, and in the past some scholars have indulged in fanciful descriptions of what might have gone on in fertility rites associated with them, often entailing supposed sacred prostitution (see the Closer Look section on 'Baalism, Canaanite Religion, and Ancient Ugarit').

The final reason that 2:13 [15] gives for YHWH's actions is that in going after the Baals, they 'forgot me'. The verb is used as the antonym of knowing YHWH in 4:6, and signifies the ignoring of YHWH. Deuteronomy 6:12–14; 8:19 similarly link forgetting YHWH and following other gods. The verse ends with the concluding formula 'oracle of YHWH' (NRSV: says YHWH). The same formula ends the whole of chapters 4–11 (11:11). Here it marks not the end of a whole section, but a pause before the change of tone in 2:14–15 [16–17].

A Closer Look: Baalism, Canaanite Religion, and Ancient Ugarit

In the Hosea-text 'Baal' appears both in the singular (2:8, 16 [10, 18]; 13:1) and in the plural 'Baals' (2:13, 17 [15, 19]; 11:2), as well as in the place name 'Baal-peor' (9:10). Worship of and sacrifice to Baal is the focus of sustained opposition in the books of the so-called Deuteronomistic History, Joshua–2 Kings (e.g. Judg. 2:11–13; 3:7; 1 Kgs 18:17–40) and in Jeremiah (e.g. 2:8, 23; 7:9). While Deuteronomy does not contain the name 'Baal' the strong criticism of the religion of the Canaanites, viewed as the former inhabitants of the land (Deut. 7:1–6; 12:2–7), encompasses it. The biblical descriptions refer to hilltop shrines, altars, standing stones or pillars, wooden poles, and images of deities.[91] Further light was shed on the nature of Canaanite religion with the publication of the Ras Shamra texts in 1929. These cuneiform tablets from the coastal town of Ugarit in the thirteenth and twelfth centuries reveal that '[a]lthough El is the chief god in the Canaanite pantheon ... Baal is clearly the most active. He is the

---

[90] The Hebrew word *'etnâ* occurs only here, but may be taken as equivalent to *'etnan*, which is used in 9:1 of a prostitute's pay.

[91] J. A. Dearman, 'Canaan, Canaanites', *NIDB* 1: 532–5.

bringer of rain, on which the fertility of the soil depends.'[92] John Day has argued that the Baal of the biblical texts 'is essentially the same as the god Baal known from the Ugaritic texts'.[93] The texts show Baal as responsible for bringing joy to farmers who faced the loss of bread, wine, and oil, and refer to Baal as the one who brings rain and on whom fertility depends. The implication of Hosea 2:8, 13 [10, 15] that the Israelites had looked to Baal as the source of fertility rather than to YHWH is thus entirely likely. The degree to which Baal religion comprised fertility rites entailing sexual activity, however, is something concerning which scholarly debate continues. Dearman describes the situation fairly:

> There was once a strong tendency among scholars to conclude that Canaanite religion was heavily influenced by fertility concerns and thus sexually charged and immoral. This assumption takes polemical references in the OT as blanket descriptions of Israel's opposition and tends to universalize from the occasional text or scattered remains of material culture that are attributed to the Canaanites. Among many current scholars, however, the tendency is in the other direction, namely, to deny such things as sacred prostitution or other sexual rites as part of Canaanite religion. The degree to which concerns for fertility also influenced various Canaanite cultic practices is a complex question, for which there are no easy answers.[94]

The Ugaritic texts indicate, further, that the one god Baal was known in various locations. Consequently scholars now accept that the variously named Baal gods of the Hebrew Bible such as Baal of Peor (Num. 25:3), Baal-hermon (Judg. 3:3), Baal-berith (Judg. 8:33), are different expressions of the one god Baal rather than different gods. Day and Van der Toorn both make comparison with local naming of the Virgin Mary in Roman Catholicism.[95]

In the books of Kings the mark of a religiously successful reign is that the king opposed Baalism and turned to YHWH, while that of a religiously unsuccessful reign is that he served and worshipped Baal (e.g. 1 Kgs 16:31–33; 22:51–53; 2 Kgs 3:2; 23:4–5). Does such a narrative assume that where a king leads, his people follow? That may be so in

---

[92]   J. Day, 'Canaan, Religion of', in *ABD* 1: 831–7 (831).
[93]   J. Day 'Hosea and the Baal Cult' (2010): 202–24 (205).
[94]   J. A. Dearman 'Canaan, Canaanites': 534–5.
[95]   J. Day 'Hosea and the Baal Cult' (2010): 206; K. Van der Toorn, 'Baals', in *NIDB* 1: 369–70.

C Commentary on Hosea

terms of the official religion of the land. But it is likely that popular, local family religion remained largely unaffected. Archaeology indicates that polytheism continued to characterise the land certainly up to the sixth-century Babylonian exile, and this is confirmed by a text such as Jeremiah 44:15–22. Indeed, the Deuteronomi(sti)c polemic against Baalism would not have been necessary were it otherwise. Albertz finds that '[t]hrough-out the pre-exilic period the Israelite family largely preserved its cultic independence', and that it was the aim of the Deuteronomistic theologians to counter any such polytheistic independence and bring it into line with official Yahwism.[96]

Many older commentators took the whole or much of 2:14–23 [16–25] to be later, optimistic additions to an original wholly condemnatory text.[97] More recent scholars, however, recognise that at least some of the book's expressions of YHWH's love and tenderness (generally including that in 2:14–15 [16–17]) were present in the earliest form of the text. They constitute an essential part of the portrayal of YHWH as holding an internal dialogue between his anger and his mercy. This internal dialogue is clearest in 6:4–7:10 (see the commentary *ad loc*) and in 11:8–9, but is evidenced also in 2:14–15 [16–17] being an integral part of 2:2–15 [4–17].

A third 'Therefore' (*lākēn*) opens 2:14 [16] (see the commentary on 2:6 [8]), linking it with what has gone before. However, what follows on from the accusation made against the wife/Israel is now not an announcement of judgement, but an attempt by the husband/YHWH to restore a damaged relationship. Clines calls this 'a delightful reversal of the expected'.[98] He will not punish her, but allure (pre-2021 NRSV: persuade) her. The translation 'allure' is well made, correctly conveying the sense of 'entice' or, as Dearman translates, 'woo'.[99] It is the verb used in Exodus 22:16 [15] of a man seducing a virgin. It is used of Samson being seduced by his Philistine wife (Judg. 14:15) and by Delilah (Judg. 16:5). Jeremiah 20:7 complains that YHWH has enticed the prophet to speak YHWH's word, and so incur derision. Here YHWH/the husband entices Israel/the wife to come with him into the

---

[96] R. Albertz, *A History of Israelite Religion in the Old Testament Period, vol. 1: From the Beginnings to the End of the Exile* (London: SCM, 1994): 103.

[97] So, for example, W. R. Harper *Amos and Hosea* (1905): clx, 236–45.

[98] D. J. A. Clines, 'Hosea 2: Structure and Interpretation', in E. A. Livingstone (ed.), *Studia Biblica 1978*, vol. 1 (JSOTSup, 11; Sheffield: JSOT Press, 1979): 83–103 (86).

[99] J. A. Dearman *Hosea* (2010): 120–1.

wilderness. In 2:3 [5] the land was to be made like a wilderness as punishment. In 2:14 [16], in contrast, it is to be a place in which YHWH and Israel/the husband and wife can become close to one another. With the next verse referring to 'the time when she came out of the land of Egypt', the wilderness in 2:14 [16] undoubtedly points to the time of Israel's origins, and to a presumed precious time in the wilderness which YHWH hopes to resurrect. Such a positive view of the wilderness period is in contrast to the dominant Pentateuchal portrayal of it as a time when the people consistently complained against both YHWH and Moses. But it is at one with the imagery of Hosea 9:10, in which YHWH 'found' Israel 'like grapes in the wilderness'.[100] There in the wilderness, YHWH/the husband will 'speak tenderly to her': literally, 'I will speak to her heart.' There she will be given her vineyards (2:15 [17]): a restoration after the previous laying waste of her vines and fig trees (2:12 [14]). There is, perhaps, a fleeting reminder that vineyards and their fertility are in YHWH's gift, not that of the Baals. A further promise is made that the Valley of Achor will be made a door of hope. The location of the Valley of Achor is disputed, but is, anyway, immaterial: it is the word's literary impact that is of significance. The name means 'trouble', and the promise is that the valley of trouble will become the door of hope. There is a probable allusion to the story of Achan's sin in Joshua 7: the names Achan and Achor sound similar and share two of their three consonants. In that narrative Achan is brought to the Valley of Achor to be stoned: Joshua puns on the name Achor in using the verb from which the name is formed to declare 'Why did you bring trouble on us? YHWH is bringing trouble on you today' (Josh. 7:25). In the Achan narrative YHWH turns from his anger only after Achan has been stoned (Josh. 7:26). Contrastingly, in Hosea 2:14–15 [16–17] YHWH's actions in speaking tenderly to Israel, and in restoring her vineyards to her, aim to avoid such punishment. That avoidance is premised on the expectation that Israel/the wife will respond 'as in the days of her youth'. The word 'youth' is derived from the same verbal root as 'child/boy' (na'ar) in 11:1, which also refers to exodus from Egypt: that the two verses echo one another is surely deliberate. In the first, eighth-century composition, 2:14–16 [16–17] concluded what became chapters 1–3, and 11:1–9 concluded chapters 4–11. Both passages convey the tug of war within the heart of YHWH: Which will prove stronger, his anger or his pity and mercy? While on a verse count it is anger and punishment which win out, in

---

[100] The only other texts which view the wilderness time positively are Deut. 32:10 and Jer. 2:2.

C Commentary on Hosea 59

terms of the strategic literary placing of the words of hope, it is mercy. The tension between the two, however, is left unresolved.

These comments have interpreted these verses within the eighth-century literary layer to which they originally belonged. It is likely, however, that Judean readers in the post-monarchic period will have taken the wilderness time to be their period of exile after 587, and the exodus from Egypt to express the hope of return from exile. As Trotter notes, 'The Persian period reader ... would associate such imagery with the "exile and return", the most striking and historically immediate event involving absence from and return to the ancestral homeland.'[101] It is unsurprising, therefore, that there follows a section best taken as deriving from this later period.

Hosea 2:16–23 [18–25] – People and Land Restored

[16] On that day, says the LORD, you will call me 'my husband', and no longer will you call me 'My Baal'.[17] For I will remove the names of the Baals from her mouth, and they shall be mentioned by name no more.[18] I will make for you a covenant on that day with the wild animals, the birds of the air, and the creeping things of the ground, and I will abolish the bow, the sword, and war from the land, and I will make you lie down in safety.[19] And I will take you for my wife for ever; I will take you for my wife in righteousness and in justice, in steadfast love and in mercy.[20] I will take you for my wife in faithfulness, and you shall know the LORD.
[21] On that day I will answer, says the LORD,
    I will answer the heavens
    and they shall answer the earth,
[22] and the earth shall answer the grain, the wine, and the oil,
    and they shall answer Jezreel;
[23] and I will sow him for myself in the land.
And I will have pity on Lo-ruhamah,
    and I will say to Lo-ammi, 'You are my people',
    and he shall say, 'You are my God.'

These verses comprise two sections beginning 'On that day'. Within 2:16–20 [18–22] the wife/Israel is referred to in the second-person feminine singular (2:16, 19–20 [18, 21–22]), third-person feminine singular (2:17 [19]), and third-person masculine plural (2:18 [20]). The arrangement is most probably

---

[101]   J. M. Trotter, *Reading Hosea in Achaemenid Yehud* (JSOTSup, 328; Sheffield: Sheffield Academic Press, 2001): 192–3.

redactional, bringing together a possibly older saying (2:16 [18]) with sayings formed for this literary context. The whole is best read as belonging to the early post-exilic (Persian) period. The grounds for taking it as such are largely thematic. The animals mentioned in 2:18a [20a], and the idea of a covenant with them, reflect priestly material in Genesis and passages in Ezekiel to be dated no earlier than the sixth century. Similarly the picture of peace in 2:18b [20b] reflects material elsewhere to be similarly dated. Additionally, the formula 'On that day' very often indicates an addition.[102] The final verse forms an *inclusio* with 2:1 [3] which, as has been argued, belongs to the post-exilic redaction of the text. These sections were formed specifically for this literary context, and are carefully integrated with what precedes. Thus 2:16–17 [18–19] continue the theme of the Baals (2:8, 13 [10, 15]). The 'bow, sword, and war' of 2:18 pick up on 1:7. The quality of mercy (*raḥămîm*) in 2:19 [21] picks up on the names Lo-ruhamah (1:6) and Ruhamah (2:1 [3]) and on the related verb 'pity' (1:6, 7; 2:4 [6]). The grain, wine, and oil of 2:22 [24] pick up on 2:8 [10]. The name Jezreel in 2:22 [24] relates back to 1:4, 5, 11 [2:2]. The marriage metaphor of chapters 1–2 is continued in 2:16, 19–20 [18, 21–22]. The qualities of steadfast love and faithfulness in 2:19–20 [21–22] anticipate their appearance in 4:1.[103] There is also thematic overlap with 14:4–8 [5–9]: it is YHWH who effects change, and who provides for and protects Israel, bringing peace, stability, and abundant fertility[104]; these verses also belong to the post-exilic redaction. Hosea 2:16–23 [18–25] function as commentary on chapters 1–2. With chapter 3, they serve to relate the metaphors of chapters 1–2 to a later generation. As Ben Zvi writes:

> It is worth emphasizing that both the mother and the children are Israel and so are the readers of the book. Of course, they are Israel in the theological/ideological, trans-temporal sense of the term. From their perspective, Israel has sinned, was punished, reads and learns about its past from which its perspective is a reflection of the status of its relation with YHWH. This Israel encompasses the people who lived in northern and southern monarchical polities ... that is, 'all Israel'. This Israel ... can read about itself, can be called

---

[102] In 1:5 the addition was an early one, within the first, eighth-century composition of the text. In the Hebrew Bible as a whole it is most prevalent, however, within later periods.

[103] The Hebrew *ḥesed* (steadfast love) is used in both verses. In 4:1 NRSV's 'faithfulness' translates *ʾĕmet*, while in 2:20 [22] it translates *ʾĕmûnâ*. The two are from the same verbal root. See the commentary on 4:1 ('YHWH's Contention with Priest and People Alike') for comments on these two terms.

[104] E. Ben Zvi *Hosea* (2005): 308.

C Commentary on Hosea   61

to remonstrate with itself, and can imagine itself as both 'she-is-pitied' and 'she-is-not-pitied', as YHWH's people.[105]

The marriage metaphor is resumed in 2:16 with the announcement of a day when Israel will call YHWH 'husband' (*'îš*) rather than 'master' (*ba'al*). The text exploits the ambiguity of the term *ba'al*. Both *'îš* and *ba'al* are terms for 'husband', the former being more intimate, and the latter more frequently used in the legal sense of the wife belonging to her husband, and emphasising the husband's rights (Exod. 21:22; Deut. 24:4). This verse suggests that YHWH himself could be addressed as 'Baal', that is, 'Master' or 'Lord'. Presumably some had seen this as a valid and proper way of addressing him. However, the dangers of confusion and syncretism were not far away in such a form of address, and the verse looks forward to the term *ba'al* being used no longer. The next verse, most likely the redactor's comment on 2:16, makes explicit that in the coming day of salvation, no mention of the Baals would be heard on Israel's lips. The plural 'Baals' is here a generic term for other gods.[106]

In 2:18 [20] YHWH promises to make a covenant, not with Israel, but on Israel's behalf.[107] The covenant will be with the wild animals, the birds of the air, and the creeping things of the ground. Both people and crops could be harmed by these, so in the coming day of salvation YHWH will restrain them. The list of creatures is similar to those in Genesis 1:30; 9:2, which belong to the priestly strand of the Pentateuch, and to Ezekiel 38:20. In Genesis 9:9–10 YHWH establishes a covenant with Israel and with the animals. Ezekiel 34:25–28 envisages a covenant of peace in which wild animals will not harm Israel. 'As a prophetic eschatological idea it seems mainly to belong to the 6th century.'[108] The promise continues with the establishing of peace in the land. The word *'ereṣ* can mean either the land (of Israel) or the earth in its entirety: the context implies the former. NRSV's 'abolish' is more literally a breaking of the bow, sword, and war, the same verb as is used in 1:5 of breaking the bow of Israel. Bow, sword, and war occur also in 1:7, a verse which also entered the text in the post-exilic redaction (see the commentary *ad loc*). As a result of the security promised, Israel will lie down in safety. In the light of the taking of a wife in the following verses, Sweeney sees a sexual

---

[105]   E. Ben Zvi *Hosea* (2005): 63.
[106]   J. A. Dearman *Hosea* (2010): 124–5; H. W. Wolff *Hosea* (1974): 39, 50.
[107]   NRSV seeks to smooth the text by changing MT's 'for them' to 'for you'. However, MT makes perfectly good sense, and the change is unnecessary.
[108]   G. I. Davies *Hosea* (1992): 84.

62   *Book of Hosea*

innuendo in Israel being made to lie down.[109] While possible, the language of lying down in safety does not require such an understanding.

In 2:19–20 [21–22] YHWH promises to 'take' (NIV 'betroth') Israel as his wife. This betrothal signifies the final step towards marriage, with the obligations of marriage already applying (Deut. 22:23–24). YHWH's taking will be 'for ever' (*lə'ôlām*), that is, lifelong (cf. Exod. 21:6, where NRSV translates 'for life'). The repetition of the verb reinforces the promise. With the reprise of the marriage metaphor it is tempting to see these verses as older than the post-exilic literary context in which they are now set, and as belonging with the older parts of chapters 1–2. However, the promise of a future new, permanent marriage fits most naturally in the post-exilic setting, and these verses were probably composed for this literary context. As bride-price YHWH promises gifts of righteousness, justice, steadfast love, and mercy. Each word is found elsewhere in the text. 'Righteousness' (*ṣedeq*) occurs in 10:12 as something that YHWH will rain upon the people if they seek him. 'Justice' (*mišpāṭ*) is found in 12:6 [7] as a quality to which the people are urged to hold fast (*mišpāṭ* is also found in 5:1; 6:5 with the meaning 'judgement' and in 10:4 with the meaning 'litigation'). These two terms, therefore, anticipate verses in Hosea 4–14. However, one must wonder whether a stronger resonance is not in the pairing of justice and righteousness in texts such as Amos 5:7; 6:12 and Isaiah 1:21, 27; 5:7; 9:7 [6]; 33:5 (cf. Prov. 21:3). These verses indicate that justice and righteousness are qualities for which YHWH looks in his people, and which he bestows upon them (see 'A Closer Look: Justice and Righteousness'). The post-exilic redactors and their readers had, we may assume, some familiarity with these texts. More characteristic of the Hosea-text is the quality of 'steadfast love' (*ḥesed*): it is found in 4:1; 6:4, 6; 10:12; 12:6 [7], translated variously as 'loyalty', 'love', and 'steadfast love'. Again, it is a quality which YHWH bestows, and which he looks to find in his people. The quality of 'mercy/pity' (*raḥămîm*) is at home in chapters 1–2 in respect of the name of Gomer's second child (1:6; 2:1 [3]; 2:23 [25]), but is found also in the reversal of YHWH's anger in 11:8–9. The post-exilic redactors' choice of words to describe how YHWH would bless his future wife/Israel drew, therefore, from a range of pertinent texts. Following the repetition of 'I will take/betroth you' in 2:20 there comes a final gift, that of faithfulness. As noted, the Hebrew word used (*'ĕmûnâ*) is not the same word translated 'faithfulness' in 4:1, but is from the same root. Yet again, it can be a divine attribute or a human quality. It implies

---

[109]   M. A. Sweeney *Twelve Prophets* 1 (2000): 36.

C Commentary on Hosea 63

reliability and trustworthiness. The people in the land in the late sixth or fifth century, following the years of exile, thus hear words of reassurance that after the vicissitudes of earlier years symbolised by the marriage metaphor of chapters 1–2, there is now the promise of a new marriage in which YHWH will not fail them, and in which they will receive and hold on to the gifts of righteousness, justice, steadfast love, mercy, and faithfulness that he gives. The verses conclude with the assurance that they will 'know YHWH'. The verb *yāda'* (know) or noun *da'at* (knowledge) are found in reference to the relationship between YHWH and Israel in 4:1, 6; 5:3; 6:6; 8:2; 13:4, and are, therefore, terminology characteristic of the text as a whole: see further 'A Closer Look: Knowledge of and by YHWH'.[110]

The second 'On that day' introduces a sequential saying based on the verb 'answer' (2:21–22 [23–24]). Thematically it connects to 14:8 [9], where YHWH assures the people that he will answer them. The earth answering the grain, wine, and oil connects to 2:9, 12 [11, 14], reversing the removal and laying waste of the produce of the land. The answering presumes an intercession or a calling to YHWH (cf. 1 Sam. 7:9; 1 Kgs 18:37; Pss. 3:4 [5]; 34:4 [5]; 118:5, 21). It could be taken as a response to the calling on YHWH of 2:16 [18] (cf. the same verb 'call' in Pss. 3:4 [5]; 118:5); but no specific point of reference is required to this quite general promise. The sequence ends with the answering of Jezreel. The name functions as a synonym for Israel, the two names sounding similar (*yizr'e'l* and *yiśrā'ēl*). The name also provides the link to the final verse. The name 'Jezreel' means 'God sows' (see 'Hosea 1:2–2:1 [2:3] – Hosea's Wife and Children'), and YHWH promises that he will sow Israel in the land.[111] In 1:4 the name was a sign of YHWH's punishment to come: in 2:23 [25] it becomes a sign of his blessing to come. Similarly, and as in 2:1 [3], the negative significance of the names of Lo-ruhamah and Lo-ammi (1:6, 9) no longer stands: YHWH will have pity on 'Not pitied', and to 'Not my people' will say 'You are my people.' As noted, 2:1 [3] and 2:23 [25] frame the chapter. The final sentence in which Israel professes 'You are my God' links to 14:3 [4], in which Israel is urged to 'say no more, "Our God", to the work of our hands'. Thus YHWH answers Israel, sows him in the land, and Israel acknowledges YHWH as his God.

---

[110] I am aware that, in these comments on 2:19–20, I have several times referred the reader to comments elsewhere. I have done so on the basis that 2:19–20, despite coming earlier on in the text, are chronologically later verses which inherit understandings from the passages to which the reader is referred.

[111] MT has 'sow her', which NRSV changes to 'sow him' in order to refer to Jezreel. However, the feminine is perfectly appropriate in referring to Israel more generally.

64   *Book of Hosea*

The section 2:16–23 [18–25] concludes chapters 1–2, with Israel taken as YHWH's wife in faithfulness (2:20 [22]) and as his children sown in the land, who receive his mercy and are declared to be his people (2:23 [25]). The marriage metaphor and the parent–child metaphor, which provided such devastating critique of Israel in 1:2–9; 2:2–13 [4–15], now provide the basis of YHWH's promises for a hopeful future.

Hosea 3 – 'The Lord Loves the People of Israel'

> 3 The LORD said to me again, 'Go, love a woman who has a lover and is an adulteress, just as the LORD loves the people of Israel, though they turn to other gods and love raisin cakes.'² So I bought her for fifteen shekels of silver and a homer of barley and a measure of wine.³ And I said to her, 'You must remain as mine for many days; you shall not prostitute yourself, you shall not have intercourse with a man, nor I with you.'⁴ For the Israelites shall remain many days without king or prince, without sacrifice or pillar, without ephod or teraphim.⁵ Afterwards the Israelites shall return and seek the LORD their God and David their king; they shall come in awe to the LORD and to his goodness in the latter days.

A biographical reading of Hosea 1–3 poses various questions concerning the relationship between chapter 3 and chapters 1–2. Is the woman that the prophet is to love (3:1) the same woman, Gomer (1:3)? If so, is chapter 3 a parallel, complementary account of the events of chapters 1–2, or a different episode in the relationship between the prophet and his wife? If a parallel account, does the first-person, autobiographical presentation indicate that chapter 3 was the earlier written account? If a different episode of events, is it subsequent to or prior to those recorded in chapter 1? The questions have been variously answered.[112] The variety of answers given suggests that the

---

[112] See the discussions in the commentaries. That chapter 3 might be a parallel account to chapter 1 is rejected by most, on the basis that chapter 1 focuses principally on the birth and naming of the children (e.g. Wolff, Andersen and Freedman, Dearman). Chapter 3 is taken by some to be a first-person account of the prophet, who was not familiar with the account in chapter 1, which is taken as a composition of the editor who brought together material in chapters 2 and 3 (e.g. Wolff, Macintosh). The majority holds that the wife of chapter 3 is the same woman as in chapter 1 (Wolff, Mays, Macintosh, Dearman); however, some consider that the woman of chapter 3 is not Gomer (e.g. Davies, Sweeney, Nogalski; of these Davies suggests that in chapter 1 the prophet did not marry Gomer, and that chapter 3 concerns his marriage, while Sweeney considers that '[t]he text suggests that Hosea bought himself a prostitute for marriage in the aftermath of his failed marriage to Gomer'). Virtually all take chapter 3 to describe a later episode in the

C Commentary on Hosea

65

questions were not of major importance to those who compiled and edited the text,[113] and that it is more helpful to approach it from a literary perspective. As Ben Zvi notes, '[t]he details of Hosea's life are important only as metaphors and imagery'.[114]

A literary approach must address the question of whether the text is an original unity, or whether there have been additions to an original core. Among those who read it biographically in an eighth-century setting, there is widespread agreement that the phrases 'and David their king' and 'in the latter days' in 3:5 were added, either in the exilic or post-exilic period.[115] Some take the whole of 3:5 as an addition (with varying opinions, and sometimes some vagueness, as to when this was made), arguing that, while 3:4 naturally follows 3:3 as its interpretation, 3:5 is an interpretation without a preceding action or words that it interprets. Others respond that if it is an addition, it is simply one that makes explicit the ultimate purpose of 3:3–4, namely Israel's restoration after a time of cleansing; and that it links to the statement in 3:1 that YHWH loves the people of Israel.[116] Arguments in favour of reading the chapter as a unity are, firstly, that the actions of 3:1–2 and their explanation in 3:3–4 belong together as a prophetic sign; and, secondly, that 3:4 would make an unsatisfactory, incomplete ending, without the positive hope for the future expressed in 3:5. 'Without v. 4 the report has no real interpretation.... Without v.5 Hosea's conception of the strategy of Yahweh's love is abridged.'[117] Werse describes 3:5 as 'inseparable from vv. 1–4'.[118] The question then arises as to the period in which chapter 3 was formed as literary text. Pointers to the early post-exilic period as the most

---

prophet's life. See F. I. Andersen and D. N. Freedman *Hosea* (1980): 291–4; G. I. Davies *Hosea* (1992): 105–9; J. A. Dearman *Hosea* (2010): 131–2; A. A. Macintosh *Hosea* (1997): 96–8; J. L. Mays *Hosea* (1969): 54–6; J. D. Nogalski, *The Book of the Twelve: Hosea-Jonah* (Smyth & Helwys Bible Commentary; Macon, GA: Smyth & Helwys, 2011): 65–6; M. A. Sweeney *Twelve Prophets* 1 (2000): 38–40, 39; H. W. Wolff *Hosea* (1974): xxii, 59.

[113] J. L. Mays *Hosea* (1969): 55 refers to the text having an 'oblique indifference' to biographical questions.

[114] E. Ben Zvi *Hosea* (2005): 80.

[115] So *inter alia* H. W. Wolff *Hosea* (1974): 57, 63.

[116] See the discussions in the commentaries. Those who see just the phrases 'and David their king' and 'in the latter days' as additions include: J. L. Mays *Hosea* (1969): 60; H. W. Wolff *Hosea* (1974): xxxi, 57, 63. Those who see the whole of 3:5 as an addition include: W. R. Harper *Amos and Hosea* (1905): clx–clxi, 223–4; A. A. Macintosh *Hosea* (1997): 109–12 (Macintosh holds that 3:5 derives from Hosea, but was added here by an editor).

[117] J. L. Mays *Hosea* (1969): 55. The unity of the chapter is argued, too, by G. I. Emmerson *Hosea* (1984): 12–13.

[118] N. R. Werse, *Reconsidering the Book of the Four: The Shaping of Hosea, Amos, Micah and Zephaniah as an Early Prophetic Collection* (BZAW, 517; Berlin: de Gruyter, 2019): 58.

likely setting are found in its thematic parallels with other exilic and post-exilic prophetic texts to which the commentary will draw attention. There may be older material which has been incorporated into the chapter, but if so it is insufficiently complete to allow meaningful interpretation apart from the later literary context in which it is now set. It was composed for this literary context, with thematic links to chapter 2 which the commentary will note.

The word 'again' ('ôd) in 3:1 connects Hosea 3 to Hosea 1–2. Grammatically it can be taken with 'YHWH said to me' (as NRSV) or with 'Go, love' (as NIV).[119] Hosea 3:1 contains both a commanded action and its interpretation. The 'Go, love' parallels the 'Go, take' of 1:2. The prophet is commanded to 'love a woman who has a lover': the word 'lover' more usually means simply 'companion', but in Jeremiah 3:20 it signifies 'husband', and in Song of Songs 5:16 is in parallel with 'lover'. The translation here as 'lover' is therefore justified. The woman is described, also, as an adulteress. The word links to 2:2 [4]. The interpretation of YHWH's command follows immediately. The prophet is to love an adulterous woman just as YHWH loves the people of Israel despite their turning to other gods. Hosea 11:1 refers to YHWH loving Israel, and 9:15 declares that he will love Ephraim no more because of the wickedness of their deeds. Thematically closest to 3:1, however, is 14:4 [5], which belongs to the post-exilic literary layer of the text: it declares that YHWH will 'love them freely'. Echoing behind these post-exilic texts is Deuteronomy's use of the verb 'āhēb (love) as an election term (e.g. Deut. 7:8, 13; 10:15; 23:5 [6]). Israel's turning to other gods also echoes Deuteronomistic terminology (Deut. 31:18, 20). Yet, as Vielhauer notes, while in Deuteronomy Israel's turning to other gods leads to punishment, here in Hosea 3:1 YHWH's love continues despite it.[120] Linked to their turning to other gods is the people's love of raisin cakes. That these could be an innocent part of Israelite cultic activity is evident from 2 Samuel 6:19. More pertinent, however, is the link with devotion to the queen of heaven condemned in Jeremiah 7:18 (cf. 44:15–19). Again, while in the Jeremiah texts this leads to the pouring out of YHWH's anger and wrath (Jer. 7:20; 44:24–30), in Hosea 3:1 YHWH's love persists despite the people's actions.

Responding to YHWH's command, the prophet buys the woman (3:2). The verb can signify that there was some element of bargaining over the

---

[119] The more usual positioning of the word favours NRSV's translation. Those who take it as NIV cite Zech. 1:17; 11:15 as illustrative of its positioning as the first word in a clause, giving it emphasis.

[120] R. Vielhauer 'Hosea in the Book of the Twelve' (2012): 60–1.

C Commentary on Hosea

sum paid. To whom the price was paid is not indicated. She may have been someone's slave; or some suggest that she was a temple prostitute being bought. Presumably the transaction represented a bride-price.[121] LXX appears to preserve a genuine variant reading, followed by NRSV, in including a measure of wine as part of the price: MT has it as a homer of barley and a lethech of barley. The variation cannot be explained by any possible misreading. The term 'lethech' is found only here. It is traditionally thought to have been half a homer. Wolff suggests that the entire price paid was equivalent to about thirty shekels, the value of a female slave according to Exodus 21:32 and Leviticus 27:4.[122] The narrative, however, is not greatly interested in the precise purpose or value of the transaction: it is YHWH's taking of Israel that is signified, and the point is his readiness to do so. The imagery used is both strange and offensive to contemporary readers. Modern slavery is a live issue in the twenty-first century CE, and those who teach and preach in faith community settings will wish to make clear that Hosea 3:2 does not give license to its practice.

The narrative of 3:3 and its interpretation in 3:4 belong closely together. As in 2:6 [8] the husband restricts the woman's movements, so in 3:3 he enforces a ban so that his wife cannot prostitute herself (cf. 2:2 [4]). The final phrase (NRSV 'nor I with you') is literally 'and I also with you', which can be variously understood. NRSV reflects the understanding of most commentators that the words indicate abstinence from sexual intercourse. Andersen and Freedman, however, translate as 'Then indeed I will be yours',[123] indicating the resumption of normal marital relations after a period of time, so that it looks to the interpretation in 3:5 as well as that in 3:4. Sherwood sees the words as expressing mutual contract: as the prophet enforces exclusive commitment to him, so he promises exclusive commitment to her.[124] The restrictive measures are to be in place 'for many days', that is, a substantial but temporary period of time. The interpretation in 3:4 makes clear that it is primarily YHWH's actions in respect of Israel that are in view. For many days, also, the Israelites will lack things that had been a normal part of their existence. The list of lacks includes political and administrative leadership (king or prince), cultic practice (sacrifice and pillar), and means of knowing God's will (ephod and teraphim). Davies notes that the

---

[121] See further J. D. Nogalski *Hosea–Jonah* (2011): 67; H. W. Wolff *Hosea* (1974): 61.
[122] H. W. Wolff *Hosea* (1974): 61.
[123] F. I. Andersen and D. N. Freedman *Hosea* (1980): 291, 304–5.
[124] Y. Sherwood *The Prostitute and the Prophet* (1996): 128–9 n. 155; 132.

content of this verse draws from other parts of the Hosea-text in respect of the first four of these.[125] Kings and princes/officials (*śārîm*) are condemned together in 7:3–7; 8:4, and their removal is announced in 7:16; 13:10. As will be noted in the comments on 8:4, it is uncertain whether the Hosea-text as a whole is anti-monarchical in principle. But from the post-exilic perspective of 3:4, the pre-exilic monarchy had already failed. The term *śārîm*, which may be used of military leaders or administrative court officials (cf. 2 Sam. 3:38; 1 Kgs 4:2), is found in 3:4; 5:10; 7:3, 5, 16; 8:4, 10; 9:15; 13:10: they are viewed consistently negatively. The political mechanisms of state had failed the people, and 3:4 declares that the people must survive a period with no such mechanisms in place. Sacrifice is referred to in 4:13–14; 6:6; 8:13; 9:4; 12: 11 [12]; 13:2, being seen as of no value to the people or to YHWH, who desires steadfast love (*ḥesed*) rather than sacrifice (6:6). Hosea 10:1–2 condemns Israel's pillars (*maṣṣēbôt*). As will be noted in the commentary on 10:1–2, these are sometimes mentioned neutrally rather than negatively in the Pentateuch; however, Hosea 3:4 picks up the negative associations of 10:1–2. The final pair of words – ephod and teraphim – were means of making enquiry of YHWH. 1 Samuel 23:8–12 contains an account of David asking the priest Abiathar to bring the ephod so that he may ascertain Saul's intentions. YHWH gives yes/no answers to questions, suggesting that consulting the ephod may have entailed the casting of lots. In priestly texts it is part of the priest's attire (Exod. 28:4, 12, 15, 25–28). In Judges 8:27 Gideon made an ephod out of gifts given to him by the people in gratitude for his victorious leadership. However 'all Israel prostituted themselves to it there'. Consultation of teraphim could also assist in making decisions (Ezek. 21:21 [26]; Zech. 10:2). In Genesis 31:19, 34–35 they are household gods that Rachel takes with her when she accompanies Jacob in leaving Laban. Disapproval of them is expressed in 1 Samuel 15:23 (where NRSV translates as 'idolatry') and 2 Kings 23:24. Ephod and teraphim are found together in Judges 17:5; 18:14, 17–18, 20. Hosea 3:4 accepts them as means of consulting YHWH that Israel will be denied for this 'many days' period.

At the end of this period, 'the Israelites shall return and seek YHWH their God' (3:5). The two verbs are used together also in 7:10 as something that they failed to do, but the promise of 3:5 is that they will. They will seek 'YHWH their God and David their king': the exact same words are used in Jeremiah 30:9, the literary context of which concerns both Israel and Judah (Jer. 30:4) and which, like Hosea 3:5, looks to the time beyond the

---

[125]   G. I. Davies *Hosea* (1992): 102–3.

C Commentary on Hosea

69

sixth-century period of exile in Babylon. The linking of YHWH and David in the promised future after exile is found also in Ezekiel 34:23–24; 37:24–25. Trotter notes that these texts (including Hos. 3:5) are not worded in such a way as to promote any attempt to restore a Davidic monarchy.[126] The future hopes expressed in this period come in various forms, as is the case even within the Hosea-text: 1:11 [2:2] and 3:5 both look to a brighter future after exile, and should be read as complementary rather than contradictory.

The period of Israel's restriction (3:4), symbolised by Hosea's restriction of his wife (3:3), thus leads to the promise of Israel's future positive relationship with YHWH (3:5), when they will come to him in awe and experience his goodness. Mays asks regarding 3:4: 'Does it point to a deprived existence in their own land (2:6), or to life in the wilderness (2:14), or to exile (9:3; 11:5)?'[127] From an exilic and post-exilic perspective, there can be no doubt that it was the period of exile itself which is so interpreted (cf. Deut. 30:1–10; 1 Kgs 8:46–50). This time of exile was to be viewed as neither a time of YHWH's defeat, nor a purposeless time of meaningless hardship, but as preparatory to Israel's future blessing. Bos points out that the verb 'return' (3:5) can carry the simultaneous associations of physical return from exile and spiritual return to YHWH.[128] Albertz summarises matters well: Hosea 3 challenges the Israel of the late sixth century 'to understand the loss of the monarchy, the elite, military power, festal worship, and professional oracles, superficially a bitter experience, as an ultimately wise and loving pedagogical lesson of their God, by means of which everything that disrupted the relationship between Yahweh and his people was purged to make possible a new beginning'.[129] The metaphor of Hosea's marriage is appropriated in the service of this intention.

Bridging the Horizons: The Metaphor of the Unfaithful Wife

The metaphor of marriage to symbolise YHWH's relationship with his people has, in principle, great potential. The portrayal of a positive marriage characterised by love and faithfulness allows for a positive understanding of YHWH's relationship with his people as one of mutual

---

[126] J. M. Trotter *Reading Hosea* (2001): 110–11.
[127] J. L. Mays *Hosea* (1969): 59.
[128] J. M. Bos *Reconsidering* (2013): 111–12.
[129] R. Albertz, *Israel in Exile: The History and Literature of the Sixth Century BCE* (trans. D. Green; SBL Studies in Biblical Literature, 3; Atlanta, GA: SBL, 2003): 236.

love, closeness, and intimacy. Hosea 1–3, however, offers the metaphor of a marriage characterised by adultery and promiscuity. Feminist biblical scholars have drawn attention to several problematic features of this metaphor.[130] That the text, written (presumably) by males and for a male readership, adopts an entirely male perspective is unarguable. Biblical commentary of the nineteenth and much of the twentieth century was also predominately a male enterprise, and many a male commentator appears to identify with Hosea more readily than with Gomer. This is somewhat ironic: Hosea stands for YHWH, and it is Gomer who stands for the people of God, among whom are scholars who write commentaries.[131] Feminist writers rightly invite both female and male readers to hear the text from a female perspective. To do so raises many questions. Chief among them are the apparent condoning of sexual violence against the wife, and the husband's controlling behaviour towards her. The punishment of the wife entails stripping her naked in public humiliation (2:3, 9–10 [2:5, 11–12]), threatening to kill her (2:3 [5]), and punishing her children (2:4 [6]). The necessity for such actions is blamed on the wife (2:2, 5, 8, 12–13 [2:4, 10, 14–15]). The husband exercises total control and restriction of the wife's freedom (2:6–7, 9, 11–12 [2:8–9, 11, 13–14]; 3:3). The wife is denied the opportunity to name her children (1:4, 6, 9). Thelle comments that the marriage metaphor 'allows for a portrayal of violence that is "up close and personal", expressing emotions such as jealousy and honor which are not captured as fully by the more generic language of an angry god who punishes his people by sword, famine and pestilence'[132]; and therein lies the metaphor's potency. But Yee is correct in warning that 'Hosea's metaphor makes its monotheistic point at the expense of real women and children who were and still are victims of sexual violence.'[133] In Hosea 3 the woman is objectified to the point that she is not even named. She is 'bought', that is, treated completely as a slave. The language of the husband expressing love (3:1) while in practice controlling her and restricting her movements (3:3) sounds, to modern

---

[130] See some of the literature cited at note 47 in Section II, 'Hosea's Marriage – Hosea 1–3'.

[131] Y. Sherwood *The Prostitute and the Prophet* (1996) comments that 'commentators enter into the consciousness of the prophet' (261), and that '[i]n resisting identification with the woman, androcentric commentators support the ideology of the text but resist its symbolic roles' (264).

[132] R. I. Thelle 'Self as *Other*' (2015): 104–20 (106).

[133] G. A. Yee, 'Hosea: Introduction, Commentary and Reflection', *NIB* 7: 197–297 (198).

C *Commentary on Hosea* 71

ears, classic abusive behaviour. Furthermore, Hosea 1–3 reinforces the perspective that male equates to 'good' and female equates to 'bad'. The text portrays the prophet's concern 'to contrast Yahweh's positive (male) fidelity with Israel's negative (female) harlotry ... we may note indications of an objectified view of female experience as separate from and negative in relationship to male experience'.[134]

There are, of course, significant cultural differences between marriage in the ancient Near East and contemporary western societies. 'Women were married through arrangements between families, and the idea of marriage as a partnership of equals was not part of the equation.'[135] Lawcodes sentenced adulterers to death (Lev. 20:10; Deut. 22:22). Nevertheless, the use of the marriage metaphor of Hosea 1–3 in today's world remains fraught with difficulty, and runs the risk of seeming to affirm behaviour which faith communities, along with others, must challenge uncompromisingly. Those for whom these words are 'Holy Scripture' will not wish to abandon them, but to appropriate the metaphor only with the utmost care.

The potency of the metaphor and its placing at the beginning of the text may result in it dominating the reader's mind as they embark on reading chapters 4–14. Certainly language of Israel's prostitution and adultery is found there.[136] But so, too, is a plethora of other images (see the Introduction to Hosea), which each shed their own light on the relationship between YHWH and Israel. A rounded reading of the text will acknowledge the marriage metaphor as a dominant, but not the only, image that contributes to the text's understanding of YHWH's relationship with Israel.

2 Prophetic Words of Judgement and Restoration – Hosea 4:1–11:11

Hosea 4 – YHWH's Contention with Priest and People Alike

> 4 Hear the word of the Lord, O people of Israel;
>   for the Lord has an indictment against the inhabitants of the land.
> There is no faithfulness or loyalty,
>   and no knowledge of God in the land.

---

[134] T. D. Setel 'Prophets and Pornography' (1985): 93–4.
[135] J. D. Nogalski *Hosea–Jonah* (2011): 59.
[136] In 4:10–15; 5:3–4; 6:10; 7:4; 9:1. It is not found in chapters 12–14.

² Swearing, lying, and murder,
and stealing and adultery break out;
bloodshed follows bloodshed.
³ Therefore the land mourns,
and all who live in it languish;
together with the wild animals
and the birds of the air,
even the fish of the sea are perishing.

⁴ Yet let no one contend,
and let none accuse,
for with you is my contention, O priest.
⁵ You shall stumble by day;
the prophet also shall stumble with you by night,
and I will destroy your mother.
⁶ My people are destroyed for lack of knowledge!
Because you have rejected knowledge,
I reject you from being a priest to me;
and since you have forgotten the law of your God,
I also will forget your children.

⁷ The more they increased,
the more they sinned against me;
they changed their glory into shame.
⁸ They feed on the sin of my people;
they are greedy for their iniquity.
⁹ And it shall be like people, like priest;
I will punish them for their ways
and repay them for their deeds.
¹⁰ They shall eat, but not be satisfied;
they shall prostitute themselves but not multiply,
because they have forsaken the Lord
to devote themselves to 11 prostitution.

Wine and new wine
take away the understanding.
¹² My people consult a piece of wood,
and their divining rod gives them oracles.
For a spirit of prostitution has led them astray,
and they have prostituted themselves, forsaking their God.
¹³ They sacrifice on the tops of the mountains,
and make offerings upon the hills,
under oak, poplar, and terebinth
because their shade is good.

C Commentary on Hosea

Therefore your daughters prostitute themselves,
and your daughters-in-law commit adultery.
^{14} I will not punish your daughters when they prostitute themselves
nor your daughters-in-law when they commit adultery;
for the men themselves go aside with prostitutes,
and sacrifice with temple female attendants;
thus a people without understanding comes to ruin.

^{15} Though you prostitute yourself, O Israel,
do not let Judah become guilty.
Do not enter into Gilgal
or go up to Beth-aven,
and do not swear, 'As the Lord lives.'
^{16} Like a stubborn heifer,
Israel is stubborn;
can the Lord now feed them
like a lamb in a broad pasture?

^{17} Ephraim is joined to idols –
let him alone.
^{18} When their drinking is ended, they indulge in sexual orgies;
they love lewdness more than their glory.
^{19} A wind has wrapped them in its wings,
and they shall be ashamed because of their altars.

The opening 'Hear the word of YHWH' operates at three levels: it introduces the immediate unit 4:1–3; it introduces chapter 4, with the 'Hear this' of 5:1 marking the beginning of the section following; and it introduces the whole block 4:1–11:11, which is rounded off with the formula 'says YHWH'. While there are elements of compositional development within chapters 4–11, the essential shape of the block was evident in the earliest literary composition of the text in the late eighth century, in the years after the destruction of the northern kingdom in 722. Within chapter 4, verses 1–9 link the failure, sin, and consequent punishment of the priests with that of the people as a whole. The remainder of the chapter contains various accusations against the people and priests, with no clear markers indicating the beginning or end of individual sayings: rather they flow into one another, a feature characteristic feature of the Hosea-text. The frequent shifts between second- and third-person address may indicate differing origins of the material within the chapter in a pre-literary stage, but do not undermine a sense of thematic unity in the text.

Chapter 4 sets out accusations against the people as a whole and, within them, the priests. The wrongdoings concerning which accusation is made bring judgement in their wake. In the literary context of late eighth-century Judah this served both to explain the disaster of 722, and also to act as a warning to the nation of Judah. The chapter is introduced by a call to the people of Israel to 'Hear', an injunction which also introduces the following section (5:1) and, indeed, sections of the Amos-text (3:1; 4:1; 5:1; 8:4).[137] What will be heard is that YHWH has an indictment (*rîb*) against the people, the inhabitants of the land.[138] NRSV's translation of *rîb* as 'indictment' captures well the legal sense of the term. The root from which it derives can refer to a dispute between individuals (e.g. Gen. 13:7–8; 26:20–22; Prov. 15:18; 17:14), and to strife which can lead to military conflict (Judg. 11:25; 12:2). In Exodus 17:2 it is used of the people's complaint against Moses, leading to the place at which the people complained being given the name *Mərîbâ* (17:7). In the book of Job it is used of Job's complaints against YHWH (Job 9:3; 13:19; 23:6; 40:2). Its dominant usage, however, is in a legal setting (Exod. 23:2–3, 6; Deut. 19:17; 21:5; 2 Sam. 15: 2–4).[139] Several prophetic texts take up the legal analogy in employing what is often referred to as a 'prophetic lawsuit'. Westermann's classic treatment of prophetic speech forms includes this as a variant of the prophetic judgement speech.[140] As the *rîb* unfolds, YHWH is both plaintiff and judge, while those accused and sentenced are the inhabitants of the land.

The initial accusations against the people are set out in 4:1–2. In 4:1 they comprise the absence of positive qualities which the text considers should have characterised the people's way of life, while in 4:2 they comprise the presence of negative practices. The first charge is that there is no faithfulness (*'ĕmet*) and loyalty (*ḥesed*). The term *'ĕmet* implies total reliability and trustworthiness. In Exodus 18:21 Moses's father-in-law Jethro uses it in urging Moses to look for able and trustworthy men to assist him in the arbitration

---

[137] J. D. Nogalski *Hosea–Jonah* (2011): 74 notes that the command to 'hear the word' occurs fourteen times in the Book of the Twelve: twice in Hosea (4:1; 5:1), five times in Amos (3:1, 13; 4:1; 5:1; 8:4), six times in Micah (1:2; 3:1, 9; 6:1, 2, 9) and once in Joel (1:2). All introduce words of judgment.

[138] The word 'land' can be translated 'earth', and Goldingay translates thus in order to propose that 4:1–3 tell the people of Israel to see what is going on throughout the earth; but if complacent about their own behaviour, 4:4–19 will awaken them with a shock, just as Amos 2:6–16 does at the end of the series of oracles against the nations in Amos 1:3–2:16 (see the commentary *ad loc*). See J. Goldingay, 'Hosea 4 and 11' (2020): 181–90; J. Goldingay, *Hosea–Micah* (Baker Commentary on the Old Testament Prophetic Books; Grand Rapids: Baker Academic, 2020): 73–4, 77–80. While an interesting reading, the usual more straightforward reading is to be preferred.

[139] H. Ringgren, '*rîb*', *TDOT* 13: 473–9.

[140] C. Westermann *Basic Forms* (1991): 199–200.

C Commentary on Hosea

of disputes and the administration of justice. In Joshua 2:12 Rahab asks the Israelite spies for a sign of their *'ĕmet* (NRSV 'good faith'). Hezekiah reminds YHWH that that he has walked before him in *'ĕmet* (2 Kgs 20:3; NRSV 'faithfulness'). In Psalm 19:9 [10] YHWH's ordinances are *'ĕmet* (NRSV 'true'). This is its only occurrence in Hosea (although a related word is used in 2:20 [22]). The term *ḥesed* is variously translated in different contexts and in different English Versions (EVV): 'loyalty', 'love', 'steadfast love', 'loving kindness', and 'mercy' are all translations which are found. The fourteen chapters of Hosea contain six occurrences of it which, in comparison to its occurrence in other prophetic texts, is sufficient to justify seeing it as a characteristic Hosean term. Sweeney writes that it 'conveys fidelity in and to a relationship, whether between human beings ... or between human beings and YHWH'.[141] In 1 Samuel 20:8 it is linked to the making of a sacred covenant of friendship between David and Jonathan. But it can also be used more informally, as when Joseph asks Pharaoh's butler to do him the kindness (*ḥesed*) of mentioning him to Pharaoh (Gen. 40:14). The *ḥesed* that YHWH looks for in his people is loyalty to him, expressed in their actions towards one another: hence the perceived lack of *ḥesed* expressed in 4:1 leads to the kinds of wrong actions towards one another that 4:2 will describe. It has sometimes been argued that *ḥesed* is specifically a covenantal term, and certainly it is likely that once the concept of a covenant between YHWH and Israel became established and widespread it was understood in this way.[142] However it is not the case that it is only and always so used. What is evident is that, when used of YHWH's attitude and actions towards Israel (e.g. Exod. 15:13) or of Israel's desired attitude to YHWH (e.g. Jer. 2:2), it is a strongly relational term.[143] The two terms *'ĕmet* and *ḥesed* are often found together (e.g. Gen. 47:29; Josh. 2:12; Ps. 85:10 [11]). In the ancient credal formula of Exodus 34:6–7 they are characteristics of YHWH, who is 'a God merciful and gracious, slow to anger, and abounding in steadfast love (*ḥesed*) and faithfulness (*'ĕmet*)'. In Hosea 4:1 their absence on Israel's part signifies that the relationship between YHWH and his people is under threat.

The final accusation of 4:1 is that there is no 'knowledge of God' in the land. Hosea 4:4–6 indicate that the people's lack of knowledge results from the priests having 'rejected knowledge', and so failing to instruct the people. This knowledge of God clearly comprises, therefore, YHWH's teaching and

---

[141] M. A. Sweeney *Twelve Prophets* 1 (2000): 44.

[142] See 'A Closer Look: The Covenant Concept in Scholarly Research'.

[143] See further H.-J. Zobel, '*ḥesed*', in *TDOT* 5: 44–64; and the excursus on *ḥesed* in G. I. Davies *Hosea* (1992): 94–9.

76   *Book of Hosea*

instruction. However, to know YHWH and for YHWH to know Israel also carries relational overtones appropriate to this book in which the images of husband–wife (1–3) and parent–child (11:1–9) play a significant role.

A Closer Look: Knowledge of and by YHWH

It is a characteristic of the book of Hosea that the verb *yāda'* (know) and noun *da'at* (knowledge) are used to describe the relationship between YHWH and Israel: YHWH 'knows' Israel/Ephraim (5:3; 13:5), and Israel is expected to 'know' or have 'knowledge' of God/YHWH (2:20 [22]; 4:1, 6; 6:6; 8:2; 13:4). In commenting on 2:20 [22] in the original Cambridge Bible Commentary on Amos, Hosea, and Micah (1971), McKeating wrote that 'the verb "to know" in Hebrew is rich in overtones. It can in some contexts mean "to have sexual intercourse with". No gross meaning is intended here, but the prophet ... may be referring obliquely to the next stage; promises, betrothal, and now consummation.'[144] In writing thus McKeating is representative of scholarship at the time in making much of the fact that the verb is often used as a euphemism for sexual inter-course. So, for example, in Genesis 4 Adam 'knew his wife Eve, and she conceived and bore a son' (4:1); Cain 'knew his wife, and she conceived and bore Enoch' (4:17); and 'Adam knew his wife again, and she bore a son' (4:25). This opens the way to describing the relationship between YHWH and Israel as one of deep, personal intimacy. This understanding is based on older studies such as that of Baumann (1908).[145] But rival interpretations existed. Some, such as Huffmon (1966), connected the vocabulary with that of ancient Near Eastern vassal treaties, and argued that this was technical language for legal recognition of sovereign and vassal by one another.[146] This leads to a different, more technically defined, understanding of the relationship between YHWH and Israel. Yet another view, put forward by McKenzie (1955), focuses on *da'at* as priestly instruction. He notes that in both Hosea 4:6 and Malachi 2:6–9 *da'at* is in parallel with *torah*, translated as 'instruction'. Priestly knowledge, McKenzie argued, is concerned not with purely ritual matters, but

---

[144] H. McKeating, *Amos, Hosea, Micah* (CBC; Cambridge: Cambridge University Press, 1971): 88.

[145] G. Baumann, 'עדי und seine Derivate: Eine sprachlich-exegetische Studie', *ZAW* 28 (1908): 22–41, 110–43; G. Baumann, '"Wissen um Gott" bei Hosea als Urform von Theologie?' *EvT* 15 (1955): 416–25.

[146] H. B. Huffmon, 'The Treaty Background of Hebrew *yāda*', *BASOR* 181 (1966): 31–7.

C Commentary on Hosea

includes matters of morality and moral integrity.[147] This interpretation is followed by Wolff, who sees 'knowledge of God' as 'an ancient formula of priestly-cultic origin'. It means knowledge of YHWH's teachings leading to 'a harmonious community life within Israel'; thus the absence of faithful relationships 'has its roots in contempt for God's will'.[148] Among more recent ommentators the link with ancient Near Eastern treaties has largely fallen from favour and focus, but both other interpretations are drawn on by Dearman (2010), who refers to the 'two nuances' behind the phrase 'knowledge of God': the first is that of a relationship of marriage and physical intimacy, while the second is the expectation that the priests, in particular, possess knowledge of God that they are to share with the people.[149] This helpfully brings the awareness that (1) there is a strong relational element to the term; and (2) that there is also the element of Israel knowing, receiving, and following YHWH's instruction, mediated via the priests.[150]

After the accusation that there is no faithfulness, loyalty, or knowledge of God in the land there follows in 4:2 a catalogue of six actions that are all too present: swearing, lying, murder, stealing, adultery, and bloodshed. Three of these (murder, stealing, adultery) appear to be related to commands in the Decalogue: see 'A Closer Look: Hosea and the Ten Commandments'. The first five 'break out': LXX adds 'in the land', which balances the final line of 4:1 and prepares for the opening line of 4:3.

The act of 'swearing' may relate to the commandment in the Decalogue: 'You shall not make wrongful use of the name of YHWH your God.' Equally, 'lying' could be related to the commandment: 'You shall not bear false witness against your neighbour.' Alternatively it may be that both 'swearing' and 'lying' are being used in a judicial sense of lying under oath. We need not restrict the sense of such words to one particular interpretation, but may allow a breadth of meaning that allows the reader to appropriate the message as they understand it. The translation of *rāṣaḥ* as 'murder' is rightly adopted by most English translations, in contrast to the King James Version (KJV)'s 'killing': it does not include killing in battle,

---

[147] J. L. McKenzie, 'Knowledge of God in Hosea', *JBL* 74 (1955): 22–7.
[148] H. W. Wolff *Hosea* (1974): 67.
[149] J. A. Dearman *Hosea* (2010): 147–8.
[150] See further G. J. Botterweck, '*yāḏa*', *TDOT* 5: 448–81.

78   *Book of Hosea*

or the administration of capital punishment. The verb 'steal' includes both theft of property and kidnapping a person (Exod. 21:16). 'Adultery' concerned primarily the act of sexual intercourse between a man and another man's wife or woman to whom he was betrothed.[151] The verse concludes with the accusation that 'bloodshed follows bloodshed'. Andersen and Freedman propose a very specific meaning to this, namely that it 'probably refers to the shedding of innocent blood by official action, and the crime charged against the nation ... is the formal sacrifice of human beings, in particular children ... so as to meet sacrificial requirements'.[152] However, they offer no justification for their proposal. More likely is that this expression rounds off the accusations of 4:2 by simply lamenting the prevalence of violence and bloodshed in the land.

Macintosh considers that these accusations most likely 'depict the situation during the latter part of the reign of Jeroboam II ... As in the case of Amos, the indictment indicates the hideous realities underlying the apparent prosperity of Jeroboam II's Israel.'[153] Contrariwise, Ben Zvi comments that 'the text does not associate these circumstances with any particular period within the world of the book, nor does it anchor these within the conditions of any period in history or memory'.[154] There is, perhaps, some truth in both perspectives. On the one hand, those who formed the Hosea-text considered that the later years of the northern kingdom leading up to its destruction in 722 were characterised by both the absence of qualities which, they deemed, should have been present in Israel's life (4:1) and the presence of qualities which they felt should not have been so prevalent (4:2). On the other hand, this can hardly be the only time and place in history in which evil ways of living appeared to be widespread. Later readers could quite properly recognise their own society, or societies known to them, in the text that they read. Indeed, contemporary readers in the twenty-first century will do the same.

A Closer Look: Hosea and the Ten Commandments

Three of the words in Hosea 4:2 – murder, stealing and adultery – lead us naturally to think of the commandments of the Decalogue: 'You shall not commit murder. You shall not commit adultery. You shall not steal' (Exod. 20:13–15 = Deut. 5:17–19). This raises the question of the

---

[151] See further H. O. Thompson, 'Adultery', *ADB* 1: 82–7.
[152] F. I. Andersen and D. N. Freedman *Hosea* (1980): 338–9.
[153] A. A. Macintosh *Hosea* (1997): 131.
[154] E. Ben Zvi *Hosea* (2005): 114.

C *Commentary on Hosea* 79

relationship between the two. Is it to be assumed that Hosea 4:2 draws on the Ten Commandments, which were already fixed? Or that Hosea 4:2 contributed to the formation of the Decalogue? Or is the relationship not as straightforward as either of these explanations? We may note, firstly, that the order in Hosea 4:2 differs from that of the Decalogue. However, it is not possible to argue from this that the Decalogue was not fixed by its time. New Testament references to these commandments (Matt. 19:18–19; Mark 10:19; Luke 18:20; Rom. 13:9) have them in varying order, and include commandments from beyond the Decalogue as well as within it: clearly long after the Decalogue was fixed it could be quoted loosely rather than precisely. Hence Macintosh can justifiably assert that the 'free presentation of a number of the Ten Commandments' in Hosea 4:2 'is no evidence that the commandments had not by his time reached a fixed form (*contra* e.g., Wellhausen, Marti)'.[155] However, nor can it be demonstrated that it had reached a fixed form by the eighth century. Scholars hold divergent views as to when the Decalogue was formed. It seems likely that individual commandments circulated in oral form as part of Israel's instructional sayings. It is also possible that sub-collections circulated as small units. In their present form the commandments concerning misuse of the divine name, keeping Sabbath, and honouring of parents speak of YHWH in the third person, as distinct from the majority framed in the second person: they may have constituted a unit which in due course was brought into the Decalogue. The first and second commandments, similarly, may have constituted a group; and, similarly, the commandments from 'You shall not murder' onwards. However, even if – as seems likely – the Ten Commandments had not been formed as a series by the time of Hosea 4:2, it remains true that the two share in the same tradition of condemnation of such practices. This is the best hypothesis with which to work in interpreting the Hosea-text in its first composition in the late eighth century. A different assumption may be made, however, in interpreting the final form of the text in the Second Temple period: by this time the Decalogue was known as a series of Ten Commandments, and thus Hosea 4:2 could be read in the light of them.[156]

---

[155] A. A. Macintosh *Hosea* (1997): 130–1, italics original.
[156] See further J. J. Stamm and M. E. Andrews, *The Ten Commandments in Recent Research* (London: SCM, 1967); A. D. H. Mayes, *Deuteronomy* (NCB; Grand Rapids, MI: Eerdmans/London: Marshall, Morgan & Scott Publ. Ltd, 1979): 162–5; R. F. Collins, 'Ten Commandments', *ABD* 6: 383–7.

80 *Book of Hosea*

Following the accusations of 4:1–2, there comes in 4:3 the resultant verdict: the land itself mourns, its inhabitants languish, and its creatures perish. While NRSV translates the verbs as present tense, grammatically they could be translated as future, and indeed there is merit in doing so as sentence is pronounced. The sentence is that the land/earth will mourn, and those who live in it will languish. Rather than 'mourns', some translate *te'ĕbal* here as 'dries up', this seeming to be more appropriate when the subject is the impersonal 'land'. This raises questions wider than matters of translation. Is 'the land' here purely a poetic metonym for the people, in parallel with 'all who live in it' in the line following? Or does it have an identity of its own? Wolff comments that 'the land, with its plants and animals, exists only for the sake of God's people'.[157] With the rise of environmental concerns since Wolff penned those words, many will find them now quite inadequate. More helpful is Dearman's observation that 'the land itself is depicted as ill, just as the human community is rotten' and that 'there is a close relationship between the flourishing of human community and that of the earth'.[158] Similarly Nogalski comments that the 'creation language drives home the point that breaking God's commands affects all creation negatively'.[159] We may discern a circular pattern, in which the breakdown of community described in 4:2 leads to a lack of care for the land and its wildlife, which in turn leads to a further lowering of human well-being. This may be to see more in the text than the original compilers themselves saw. But our appropriation of the text is not restricted by authorial intention: we bring also the lens of our contemporary concerns.

Along with the mourning of the land and the languishing of its inhabitants comes a perishing of the wild animals, the birds of the air, and even the fish of the sea. NRSV's 'wild animals' is literally the 'beasts of the field', and could refer to domesticated agricultural land or to land inhabited by wild animals.[160] The people's food supply would have been derived from both agricultural produce and the hunting of wild animals, and so would have been affected either way. But the encompassing nature of the description of animals, birds, and fish indicates that it is not merely human interest that is of concern. 'If human beings fail to maintain the proper order of their lives, the entire world of creation suffers.'[161]

---

[157] H. W. Wolff *Hosea* (1974): 69.
[158] J. A. Dearman *Hosea* (2010): 153, 154.
[159] J. D. Nogalski *Hosea–Jonah* (2011): 75. See also M. Deroche, 'The Reversal of Creation in Hosea', *VT* 31 (1981): 400–9.
[160] G. Wallis, 'śādeh', *TDOT* 14: 37–49.
[161] M. A. Sweeney *Twelve Prophets* 1 (2000): 45.

C Commentary on Hosea

This opening unit 4:1–3, therefore, sets out accusations against the people of Israel: there is no faithfulness, loyalty, or knowledge of God in the land, but rather swearing, lying, murder, stealing, adultery, and bloodshed. In consequence YHWH, who has acted as plaintiff in making the accusations, now acts as judge in pronouncing sentence: the land and its inhabitants, both human and animal, will mourn, languish, and perish.

The addressee in 4:1–3 was the people of Israel (4:1). But with judgement pronounced against the people, there come in 4:4–10 exonerating considerations: the people have failed to display knowledge of YHWH because the priests have failed to instruct them in it (4:6). In other ways, too, the priests have let the people down: by their own greed (4:8), and by their unfaithfulness to YHWH (4:10). Consequently people and priests alike are seen as deserving of YHWH's judgement (4:9).

Hosea 4:4 first nullifies the indictment (*rîb*) of 4:1–3 – 'let no one contend and let none accuse' – before reinstating it as a contention with the priests (NRSV's 'contend' and 'contention' are from the same root as *rîb*). It will become evident in 4:9–10 that the charge against the people has not actually been dropped, but 4:4 now directs attention firmly to the priesthood. But who is it that is addressed in these verses? Hosea 4:4–6 are framed in the singular,[162] raising the question of whether a particular priest is being addressed, presumably one holding office at a sanctuary. However, it is more likely that the singular functions as a collective noun.[163] Various suggestions have been made as to which particular group of priests (or individual priest) are being addressed. Wolff considered that the prophet Hosea had close connection to and sympathy with groups of Levites to whom the origins of the book of Deuteronomy could ultimately be traced. In fact, he suggests, Hosea's spiritual home (*geistige Heimat*) was likely among such circles, and his immediate circle of followers was a 'prophetic-Levitic group' which formed an opposition party to the official priests. He considers that members of this circle were also the traditionists responsible for the shaping of 4:4–19.[164] This would make these verses a critique of the official priesthood by Hosea and this prophetic-Levitic opposition group. The individual priest whom Wolff considers is being addressed must be someone in a position of

---

[162] The translation 'with you is my contention, O priest' (4:4b, NRSV) is dependent on a widely adopted emendation of an otherwise difficult Hebrew text. See further H. W. Wolff *Hosea* (1974); J. A. Dearman *Hosea* (2010): 155.

[163] A. A. Macintosh *Hosea* (1997): 136.

[164] H. W. Wolff *Hosea* (1974): 37, 75–6.

82 Book of Hosea

high responsibility, and he proposes the likelihood of it being the priest in charge of one of the leading sanctuaries, such as Bethel. There is thus some parallel with the dispute between the priest Amaziah and the prophet Amos recorded in Amos 7:10–17. Holt disputes the idea of Hosea belonging to an opposition group, but agrees that we can 'infer that Hosea had a thorough and firsthand knowledge of what went on in the temples, and that *he criticizes the cult from within*'.[165] Cook concurs that Hosea's 'lineage roots' are in such circles.[166] However, those who date the Hosea-text to the Second Temple period, or who treat the text in its final form and therefore interpret it in that period, are equally able to find a suitable point of reference. Ben Zvi considers that the singular 'priest' in 4:6 could refer to the post-monarchic high priest and his sons. In that case 'the text conveys on the one level a general condemnation of the priests of old, including those of northern Israel. But on another level, at least by connotation, it also conveys a condemnation of the rightful priests who served in Jerusalem.'[167] Bos, in contrast, locates the context as a tension in the early Persian period between different groups of priests. He considers it at least plausible that the priest condemned in 4:4–10 is the Aaronid high priest at Bethel, and that the condemnation in the text derives from the Zadokite priesthood of Jerusalem promoted by the returnees from Babylon.[168] Trotter's investigation of how the Hosea-text would have been appropriated and read in the early Persian period notes, more generally, that this passage 'would have functioned as a strong warning to the priesthood of the early Persian period that much of the responsibility for the faithfulness of the community to Yahweh rested in their hands'.[169]

Accusation and sentence are closely interwoven in these verses. First it is said that the priest will stumble (4:5): not an offence, but the consequence of the offence. The same verb *kāšal*, 'stumble', is used in 5:5 of both Ephraim and Judah. The line in 5:5 'Judah also stumbles with them' is widely held to have been brought into the text as part of a seventh-century revision (see the commentary *ad loc*), and it is likely that the same is true of the introduction of 'the prophet also shall stumble with you by night' in 4:5. Nowhere else in Hosea are prophets referred to negatively.

---

[165] E. K. Holt, *Prophesying the Past: The Use of Israel's History in the Book of Hosea* (JSOTSup, 194; Sheffield: Sheffield Academic Press, 1995): 111 (italics original).

[166] S. L. Cook, 'The Lineage Roots of Hosea's Yahwism', *Semeia* 87 (1999): 145–61 (147).

[167] E. Ben Zvi *Hosea* (2005): 116.

[168] J. M. Bos *Reconsidering* (2013): 168.

[169] J. M. Trotter *Reading Hosea* (2001): 198.

C Commentary on Hosea 83

It may be that texts such as Jeremiah 2:8, 26; 6:13, which address the issue of false prophets, influenced those who handled the Hosea-text.[170] The Late Pre-exilic Redactional Composition of the Amos-text also comes from this period,[171] and the resonance between Hosea 4:4–6 and Amos 7:10–17 is strong. Following the stumbling of the priest (in the earliest eighth-century form of the text) and of priest and prophet (from the seventh-century version of the text onwards) YHWH announces 'I will destroy your mother.' This may be as harsh as indeed it sounds: in Amos 7:17 the pronouncement of judgement on Amaziah includes – certainly harshly – his wife, sons, and daughters (see the commentary *ad loc*), so it may be that here in Hosea 4:4 reference is to the mother of an individual priest. Andersen and Freedman suggest that 'presumably she exerted an important and baleful influence on the life and career of her son, as was the case with some notorious queen mothers in the history of Israel and Judah (e.g. Jezebel)';[172] clearly a statement from two male commentators! If female voices need to be heard in interpreting Hosea 1–3, so too do they in interpreting a verse such as this. It is, moreover, not necessary to take this line as referring literally to a priest's mother. If, as Macintosh suggests, the singular 'priest' is a collective singular, then the 'mother' may be taken to be the nation as a whole, in the same way as in 2:2–15 [4–17].[173] An advantage of this interpretation is that the destruction of the mother leads naturally into the opening line of 4:6 which makes the accusation that 'my people are destroyed for lack of knowledge'.

Hosea 4:6 makes clear that the people's lack of knowledge of God (4:1) arises because the priests have rejected such knowledge and have 'forgotten the law of your God'. NRSV's translation of *tôrâ* as 'law' is not ideal in this context. A better translation would be 'instruction' or 'teaching'. The word has a wide semantic range. Proverbs 1:8, for example, refers to a mother's *tôrâ*, which NRSV rightly translates as 'teaching'. So here, too, the translation 'instruction' or 'teaching' would be more appropriate. Whatever written law the priests may or may not have had available to them in the

---

[170] So e.g. A. A. Macintosh *Hosea* (1997): 137–40. Additionally, J. Krispenz 'Idolatry, Adultery, Prostitution' (2016): 9–30 (16–17) notes that the line disturbs the verse's literary form.

[171] See Section IV, 'Introduction to Amos' for the composition history of the Amos-text.

[172] F. I. Andersen and D. N. Freedman *Hosea* (1980): 351.

[173] So also J. A. Dearman *Hosea* (2010): 158 writes: 'Reference to the priest's *mother* ... is likely metaphorical and not biological' (italics original). The language remains offensive, nevertheless.

84   *Book of Hosea*

late eighth century when the earliest Hosea-text was formed, it would not have been 'the Torah' as understood in later centuries (although readers in later centuries could and would have read it this way). It is, of course, true in any century that priests and religious leaders bear responsibility for the handing-on and teaching of their religious tradition. Mixed with this accusation is the declaration that because they have rejected knowledge, so YHWH rejects them. There are several occasions in the Hebrew Bible in which YHWH's rejection of someone or of his people follows their rejection of him. In 1 Samuel 15:22–23 Samuel delivers the message of YHWH's rejection of Saul: 'Because you have rejected the word of YHWH, he has also rejected you from being king.' In 2 Kings 17, the Deuteronomistic chapter which describes the fall of the northern kingdom, it is because the nation rejected (NRSV 'despised') YHWH's statutes (17:15) that YHWH rejected them (17:20). In Hosea 4:6 the priests' perceived rejection of YHWH is matched by his rejection of them: their forgetfulness of (i.e. their ignoring of) his *tôrâ* brings the pronouncement that he will forget their children. This could reflect the hereditary nature of the priesthood or, more likely, may be a way of speaking of the priestly family as a whole.

Hosea 4:7–10 switches from the second-person singular of 4:4–6 to third-person plural. While this may indicate separate oral transmission, in the literary text the thematic unity of the passage is evident as the charges against the priests continue into 4:7–8. The accusation that they changed their glory, something given by YHWH, for something shameful and worthless (4:7b) is found also in Jeremiah 2:11 and Psalm 106:20.[174] In 4:8 the word 'sin' (*ḥaṭṭā't*) also means 'sin offering', and it is likely that the *double entendre* is intended. The priests received a portion of the sin offerings brought by the people for their own consumption, so the accusation that they 'feed on the sin of my people' is literal as well as metaphorical. The term 'my people' carries overtones of YHWH's mercy and tenderness (2:1, 23 [3, 25]; 6:11b): hence he is personally affronted by the priests feeding on the people's sin/sin offerings and being greedy for the people's iniquity. We may note that Hosea 4:4–8 does not condemn priesthood or the sacrificial system *per se.* But it very definitely condemns its failure to instruct the people into the knowledge of God and its abuse of privilege and power in exploiting the people's offering of sacrifice for their own greed.

---

[174] MT reads 'I will change their glory', but NRSV's translation follows various ancient readings. See H. W. Wolff *Hosea* (1974): 71.

C Commentary on Hosea

Bridging the Horizons: Priestly Responsibility

All faith traditions have designated religious functionaries or leaders of one kind or another, whether their title be rabbi, priest, minister, imam, or some other. These people have great trust placed in them, and consequently hold great responsibility for the exercise of that trust. When that trust is broken lives are damaged, as is the reputation of the whole faith community. In the twenty-first century numerous allegations of historic child abuse have emerged. The message of Hosea 4:4–10 is clear: faith communities must own up to the sin of their priests or leaders, and ensure that priestly responsibility is exercised with integrity and honesty.

Hosea 4:1–3 constituted YHWH's dispute (*rîb*) with the people, and 4:4–8 with the priests. The two are brought together in 4:9 in what is probably a popular saying incorporated into the unit: 'it shall be like people, like priest'. Both priests and people are held culpable. YHWH's judgement on both priests and people will be the same: he will punish them for their ways and repay them for their deeds. The verb 'punish' (*pāqad*) is frequent in both Hosea (1:4; 2:13 [15]; 4:9, 14; 8:13; 9:9; 12:2 [3]) and Jeremiah (e.g. 9:25; 11:22; 21:14). It is used in Amos 3:2, a verse which reflects the influence of Hosea on the Amos-text. The first punishment in 4:10a is that they will eat but not be satisfied. This kind of punishment in which an apparent blessing fails to lead to the expected positive result is found also in Amos 5:11, Micah 6:14–15, Zephaniah 1:13 (which is probably dependent on Amos 5:11), and as a curse in Deuteronomy 28:30, 38–40. The second punishment is of the same kind, namely that they shall 'prostitute themselves, but not multiply'. Hosea 4:10–11 contain the first occurrences in chapters 4–11 of the root *znh*. The verbal form 'prostitute herself/themselves' or nominal form 'prostitution'[175] is found in 4:10, 11, 12, 13, 14, 15, 18; 5:3, 4; 6:10; 9:1. It has already featured prominently in chapters 1–3. It is thus a *leitmotif* throughout the first two sections of the book (it is absent in chapters 12–14). The language is metaphorical (as in chapters 1–3), portraying the faithlessness of the Israelites in respect of YHWH. This faithlessness has most frequently been understood as Israelite involvement in Canaanite religious practices entailing the offering of sacrifices to Baal and, possibly, cultic prostitution. However, scholars currently hold varying views on the degree to which this

---

[175] For the translation see note 1 in Section II, 'Introduction to Hosea'.

86   *Book of Hosea*

is the case: see 'A Closer Look: Baalism and Canaanite Religion' and, concerning cultic prostitution, the comments below on 4:14.

The reason for the punishments of 4:10 is that they – priests and the people – have forsaken YHWH. The verb *'āzab* is used of forsaking YHWH many times in the book of Jeremiah, sometimes of forsaking him to serve other gods (e.g. 1:16; 5:7, 19), and sometimes in ignoring his laws (e.g. 9:13; the two occur together in 16:11). It is also found in Deuteronomy 28:20; 31:16. In Judges 10:10 the Israelites cry out to YHWH, saying: 'We have sinned against you, because we have forsaken our God and have worshipped the Baals.' While Hosea 4 does not specifically mention Baal worship, it is likely that the activities described in 4:11–19 relate to it. This is confirmed by the last line of 4:10 and first word of 4:11 which, owing to the difficulty of the grammar of the end of 4:10, are generally taken together, and translated as 'to devote themselves to prostitution' (NRSV).[176] The verb used, *šāmar*, has a primary meaning of 'keep', and usage includes the keeping of religious festivals (e.g. Exod. 12:17; 23:15), keeping the Sabbath (e.g. Lev. 26:2; Deut. 5:12), keeping covenant (e.g. 1 Kgs 11:11), and keeping YHWH's commands and statutes (e.g. 1 Kgs 2:3; Amos 2:4). Here, however, what the people keep is none of these: rather they devote themselves to (keep) 'prostitution'.

The verses that follow set out evidence of the people's faithlessness. The accusation is made that 'wine and new wine take away the understanding' which, like the 'like people, like priest' of 4:9, may be a popular proverbial saying taken up and used here. The Hebrew Bible generally has a positive attitude towards wine. Typical is Psalm 104:15, which includes 'wine to gladden the human heart' as one of creation's blessings. It was part of a staple diet, and was among the offerings to be made at the Temple (Deut. 14:22–23; 18:3–4). However, drunkenness was viewed as dangerous, since it led to a lack of control over what one was doing (e.g. Gen. 9:20–21). Here it leads to a lack of 'understanding': the Hebrew *lēb* literally means 'heart', which was viewed as the seat of understanding. This alcohol-induced lack of understanding is part of the people's and priests' participation in the cultic practices described in 4:12–14. As part of these the people 'consult a piece of wood, and their divining rod gives them oracles' (4:12). One is reminded of the mocking invective of passages such as Isaiah 40:19–20; 44:9–20, in which a man takes wood and carves an idol from it, while using other parts

---

[176] Hosea 4:10 ends with an infinitive verb without an object. From LXX onwards the taking of the first word of 4:11 'prostitution' as its object has provided a good solution to this problem. See further H. W. Wolff *Hosea* (1974): 72.

for firewood. Later readers familiar with such a text would naturally read Hosea 4:12 in the light of it. Sustained critiques such as those of Isaiah 44:9–20 and Jeremiah 10:1–16 had not, however, been made in the late eighth century in which the first edition of the Hosea-text was produced, and we cannot be sure of how 4:12–13 might have been understood in that period. In 4:12 the Hebrew word translated by NRSV as 'piece of wood' could equally well be translated 'tree', and the word translated 'divining rod' in NRSV is used elsewhere in the Hebrew Bible to mean the branch of a tree (Jer. 1:11) or a staff (e.g. the staff with which Balaam hits his donkey in Num. 22:27, or that which David took up as he went to fight Goliath in 1 Sam. 17:40). It is not as certain as some commentators and translations suggest that 4:12a necessarily refers to divination techniques.[177] It is possible that 4:12a is simply part of the activities described in 4:13 as taking place on the tops of mountains. These activities take place 'under oak, poplar and terebinth'. On the one hand, oaks were known as mighty, strong trees (Isa. 2:13; Amos 2:9), but are not elsewhere specifically associated with cultic activity. The poplar is mentioned elsewhere only in Genesis 30:37. On the other hand, 'terebinth' (the Hebrew word is elsewhere translated as 'oak') had cultic associations: Jacob buried his family's foreign gods under the oak tree near Shechem (Gen. 35:4).

What took place on the mountain tops and under these trees was sacrifice and the making of offerings. But to whom did the people of eighth-century Israel think they were making sacrifice and offerings? Was this a flagrant rejection of YHWH worship in favour of Baal worship? Was this syncretism, in which it was thought that both YHWH and Baal could be worshipped? Was there an identification (confused or deliberate) of YHWH and Baal, so that people did not realise that there was any distinction to be made? What exactly is the eighth-century text opposing? As Andersen and Freedman state, it 'is not always clear whether Hosea is condemning a false (idolatrous) worship of Yahweh, or an apostate worship of Baal, or even whether the two are identified in the official cult, with Baal used as a title of Yahweh'.[178] The same two verbs are used together in Hosea 11:2, where it is made specific that it was to the Baals that sacrifice was made and to idols

---

[177] J. L. Mays *Hosea* (1969): 73 states that 4:12 'clearly points to some kind of divination' and that there must be reference to 'a technique of rhabdomancy', an assumption reflected in NRSV's translation. Other commentators allow that, while this may be so, an alternative point of reference would be to sacred trees and the practices referred to in 4:13: so G. I. Davies *Hosea* (1993): 124; A. A. Macintosh *Hosea* (1997): 151.

[178] F. I. Andersen and D. N. Freedman *Hosea* (1980): 49.

88 *Book of Hosea*

that offerings (of incense) were made. In the literary context of Hosea 4–11, therefore, we may read 4:13 in the same way. For later generations reading in the light of Deuteronomy and texts influenced by it, the matter is clearer still. Deuteronomy 12:2–3 condemns all cultic sites on mountain heights and hills and under every leafy tree as belonging to the nations who the Israelites were to dispossess. They were therefore to be destroyed, their altars and pillars smashed, their sacred poles and idols to be hewn down. The phrase 'on every high hill and under every spreading tree' became one used to describe the typical location of the kind of cultic activity that Israel was to avoid (1 Kgs 14:23; 2 Kgs 16:4; 17:10; Jer. 2:20; 3:6; Ezek. 6:13). Hosea 4:12–13 are, therefore, an example of how the same words may have been differently heard in different literary contexts and in different periods. Those reading with knowledge of condemnations of idols such as Isaiah 44:9–20, and of Deuteronomy and texts influenced by it, will naturally read Hosea 4:12–13 in the light of them, and therefore, differently from those who would have heard them in the eighth century.

Hosea 4:12 sees the problem as being that priests and people have been led astray by 'a spirit of prostitution'.[179] In 4:10–11 'prostitution' was used in a metaphorical sense of Israel's faithlessness in respect of YHWH. As the accusation continues into 4:13b–14, however, it is literal prostitution which is condemned.[180] Daughters and daughters-in-law 'prostitute themselves' and commit adultery. Nevertheless they will not be punished, since they are led into it by the men – and men of a senior generation, who presumably held power in their families. Wolff saw in these verses a reference to participation in Canaanite bridal rites which, he argued, must have been similar to those described by Herodotus as characteristic Babylonian customs entailing intercourse at the Temple for payment.[181] His proposal seems forced, however, and few commentators now follow him in this.[182] However, it does seem to be the case that this prostitution is linked to cultic centres. The women are described in 4:14b as *zōnôt*, 'prostitutes', and *qədēšôt*, which the revised NRSV translates as 'female attendants'. The pre-2021 NRSV translated this word as 'temple prostitutes'. The term is from the same root as the word 'holy'. Apart from here it is found in Genesis 38:20–22 in the narrative of Judah and Tamar, and in Deuteronomy 23:17 [18], where it is commanded,

---

[179] For the translation see note 1 in the in the 'Introduction to Hosea'.
[180] G. Eidevall *Grapes in the Desert* (1996): 59–60.
[181] H. W. Wolff *Hosea* (1974): 86–7.
[182] G. I. Davies *Hosea* (1992): 125–6 describes H. W. Wolff's view as 'surely an unnatural interpretation'.

C Commentary on Hosea

in the translation of the pre-2021 NRSV, that none 'of the daughters of Israel shall be a temple prostitute', but in the most recent revision that they shall not 'serve in an illicit shrine'. That same verse contains the masculine form of the word, adding that 'none of the sons of Israel shall be a temple prostitute/serve in an illicit shrine'. The masculine form is found also in 1 Kings 14:24; 15:12; 22:46 [47]; 2 Kings 23:7; Job 36:14. In the nineteenth and much of the twentieth century many scholars saw in this term a reference to sacred prostitution. Oden gives the example of Robertson Smith, who wrote that 'the temples of the Semitic deities were thronged with sacred prostitutes'.[183] Countering this view, Oden argues that there is no actual evidence for the practice of sacred prostitution in the ancient Near East, and that evidence for it in the writings of Herodotus, Strabo, and others is neither contemporaneous with supposed Canaanite practices, nor objective. It can, he suggests, be investigated as an *accusation* found in texts such as Hosea 4.14 and Deuteronomy 23.17–18 [18–19], the alleged practice giving grounds for the total rejection and extermination of the Canaanites, but there is no evidence for its actual practice. 'Since', he writes, 'the practice of sacred prostitution is claimed for Israel's neighbors and then denounced in the Hebrew Bible, biblical scholars have generally extended precisely this view.'[184] Subsequently Van der Toorn has argued that, while sexual activity for money may have taken place at or by sanctuaries, it did not hold religious and cultic significance. Rather, he suggests, it was for women to pay debts or fees in relation to vows taken at the sanctuary without the knowledge of, and therefore without the financial support of, their husbands.[185] The arguments of Oden and Van der Toorn find favour with Nogalski.[186] Day, however, has argued that the Hebrew Bible certainly appears to assume the practice, and he notes that the ancient versions support the interpretation of these texts in this way. He notes, too, that some noted Assyriologists accept evidence of the practice of sacred prostitution in the ancient Near East.[187] Adams argues

---

[183] R. A. Oden, *The Bible without Theology* (San Francisco: Harper & Row, 1987): 131–53 (135). The quotation is from W. Robertson Smith, *Lectures on the Religion of the Semites* (New York: Schocken, 1972): 455. This was first published in 1889.

[184] R. A. Oden *Bible without Theology* (1987): 153.

[185] K. Van der Toorn, 'Female Prostitution in Payment of Vows in Ancient Israel', *JBL* 108 (1989): 193–205.

[186] J. D. Nogalski *Hosea–Jonah* (2011): 83.

[187] J. Day, 'Does the Old Testament Refer to Sacred Prostitution and Did it Actually Exist in Ancient Israel?' in C. McCarthy and J. F. Healey (eds.), *Biblical and Near Eastern Essays: Studies in Honour of Kevin J Cathcart* (JSOTSup, 375; London: T&T Clark International, 2004): 2–21; J. Day 'Hosea and the Baal Cult' (2010): 214–15.

that neither sacred prostitution nor even prostitution itself is in view, and that to take the text literally is to misunderstand the metaphorical language by which it speaks of covenant being a marriage. In these verses 'the rebuke is widened to indict female Israelites for their own cultic abominations and to condemn the entire community, including women'.[188] However she fails to refer to or explain the significance of daughters and daughters-in-law not being punished in view of the behaviour of the men. In view of the lack of scholarly consensus, there is wisdom in the comment of Krispenz that the text 'tries to scandalize a behavior, which we do not know well enough'.[189]

Whatever the precise nature of the accusations, the upshot is clear: 'thus a people without understanding comes to ruin' (4:14). The saying is probably a proverb taken up in the text. The verb 'come to ruin' is found in sayings in Proverbs 10:8, 10. The actions of which the priests and people are accused bring ruin in their wake.

Thus far, apart from one line in 4:5, the text of Hosea 4 is that of the earliest, late eighth-century Hosea-text carried forward into subsequent redactional compositions. At this point, however, 4:15 was inserted into the seventh-century, second stage of composition. It takes and adapts Amos 4:4 and 5:5. Jeremias has examined the relationship between the texts of Hosea and Amos, and in considering Hosea 4:15 and 8:14 finds that '[t]hese "Amos-like" verses presuppose fixed compositions in Hosea to which they were added. They presuppose that at least parts of Hosea are already fixed in written form.'[190] Neither Amos 4:4 nor 5:5 are directly copied, but nevertheless the direction of influence is clear. The first line of Hosea 4:15 serves to link the verse to 4:1–14, making explicit that now Judah is being addressed as well as Israel. The purpose of 4:15 is, as Jeremias, states, 'to actualize the prophetic words for people living later than the prophet and living under new circumstances'.[191] The content is adapted to its literary context in the Hosea-text by borrowing from 5:8 and 10:5 the re-naming of Bethel as 'Beth-aven': while Bethel translates as 'house of God', Beth-aven translates as 'house of iniquity', which serves in the Hosea-text to denigrate the site. Bethel had a long pedigree as a sanctuary in Israel. Genesis 28:18–22, generally attributed

---

[188] K. Adams, 'Metaphor and Dissonance: A Reinterpretation of Hosea 4:13–14', *JBL* 127 (2008): 291–305 (303).

[189] J. Krispenz 'Idolatry, Apostasy, Prostitution' (2016): 14.

[190] J. Jeremias, 'The Interrelationship between Amos and Hosea', in J. D. Watts and P. R. House (eds.), *Forming Prophetic Literature: Essays on Isaiah and the Twelve in Honor of John D. W. Watts* (JSOTSup, 235; Sheffield: Sheffield Academic Press, 1996): 171–86 (176).

[191] J. Jeremias 'Interrelationship' (1996): 175.

C Commentary on Hosea

to the Elohistic strand of the Pentateuch,[192] describes Jacob receiving a dream there, naming the place Bethel, meaning 'House of God', and setting up a stone pillar there. This gave ancient legitimisation to Jeroboam's choice of it as the place to which the Israelites should go to offer sacrifice. Gomes argues from an examination of Bethel in the Deuteronomistic History that 'the Bethel sanctuary dominated the landscape of the northern kingdom for over 400 years'.[193] Gilgal, too, was an ancient Israelite sanctuary. Joshua 4:19–20 records it as the first place at which Israel camped after crossing the Jordan, and that Joshua set up twelve stones there as a memorial to the crossing. It is recorded, too, that Samuel visited Bethel, Gilgal, and Mizpah on an annual circuit of visits (1 Sam. 7:16), that Saul was made king at Gilgal (1 Sam. 11:14–15), and that Saul was rejected by YHWH as king there (1 Sam. 15).[194] Gilgal and Bethel were not far from the Israel–Judah border (although the exact location of Gilgal is unknown), and it appears that some Judeans were tempted to go to make use of these old sanctuaries.[195] It is likely that the seventh-century redactional composition of Hosea was produced shortly after the Deuteronomic reform, with its desire to centralise all worship at the one central sanctuary (Deut. 12:1–14). The injunction not to go to Gilgal or Bethel was in harmony with this desire. The literary context of Hosea 4, however, indicates more than that: it is being made clear that these sanctuaries were associated with the practices condemned in 4:1–14.

Additional to the instruction to avoid going to Gilgal and Beth-aven – and not derived from Amos 4:4; 5:5 – is the instruction 'do not swear "as YHWH lives"' (4:15c). It is not readily apparent why such an oath is proscribed. It is used without comment in narrative texts and by Yahwistic prophets in 1 Kings 17:1; 22:14; 2 Kings 2:2. Wolff surmises that because it was, in the prophet's view, Baal who was worshipped at Gilgal and Bethel, therefore to swear in YHWH's name was to do so with deceit;[196] but this seems unlikely.

---

[192] So, for example, G. von Rad, *Genesis* (OTL; London: SCM, 1972): 283.
[193] J. F. Gomes, *The Sanctuary at Bethel and the Configuration of Israelite Worship* (BZAW, 368; Berlin: W. de Gruyter, 2006): 59.
[194] J. M. Bos *Reconsidering* (2013): 96–9 argues that the inclusion of Gilgal may indeed be an allusion to 1 Sam. 11:14–15, and that this indicates a critique of kingship from the late post-monarchic period to which he dates the Hosea-text. Alternatively, he suggests, if the allusion is cultic, 'then the passage ought to be understood as the immigrating Jerusalemite elite's attempt to delegitimize all cult sites that were rivals to the Temple in Jerusalem about to be built or just built', in which case, a late sixth-century dating is appropriate. As at several points in his work, he pleads for a particular interpretation which is not the most natural.
[195] A. A. Macintosh *Hosea* (1997): 163–4.
[196] H. W. Wolff *Hosea* (1974): 90.

92   *Book of Hosea*

Perhaps it is comparable to Jeremiah 5:2 in which people 'say, "As YHWH lives", yet they swear falsely'. Certainty is not possible.

Most commentators take just 4:15, or part of it, to be the sum of what is brought into the text at this point in this seventh-century redaction. It seems more probable, however, that 4:16 should be taken with it. The redactors wish to reinforce the prohibition against going to Gilgal and Bethel by comparing the former inhabitants of Israel to a stubborn heifer. In doing so they take the image of Ephraim as a heifer from Hosea 10:11 and bring it into their own text. The Hebrew words translated by NRSV as 'heifer' are, however, different in the two texts. Hosea 10:11 has *'eǧəlāh* while 4:16 has *pārāh*, this latter term being used also in Amos 4:1 to describe the women of Samaria as 'cows of Bashan'. The redactors who penned Hosea 4:16 drew thematically from 10:11, but they used the term found in Amos 4:1, just a few lines earlier than Amos 4:4 from which Hosea 4:15 drew. Hosea 4:17 introduces the name 'Ephraim' into the text: see 'A Closer Look: "Ephraim" in Hosea'. The verses 4:17–19 may be a resumption of the older, eighth-century literary layer or else the whole of 4:15–19 may have entered the text in the seventh-century redactional composition. I incline towards this latter view, although there are few grounds on which to make the case either way. The introduction of 'Ephraim' serves to pave the way for its use in 5:1–7 and its many subsequent occurrences. Hosea 4:17–19 abounds with textual difficulties, including unexpected female suffixes in 4:18 and 4:19, and in 4:19 a plural 'sacrifices' which is not found elsewhere in the Hebrew Bible and which, from Wellhausen onwards (and as NRSV), has often been emended from *mizzibəhôtām* ('sacrifices') to *mimmizəbbôtām* (altars).[197] Amid the textual confusion, it is evident that it is the accusations of drunkenness and sexual malpractices described earlier in the chapter to which reference is being made. The 'wind' of 4:19 is the Hebrew *rûaḥ*, translated in 4:12 as 'spirit': it is, perhaps, the same spirit of prostitution which has now enveloped the people.

A Closer Look: 'Ephraim' in Hosea

The book of Hosea has a higher number of occurrences of this designation of Israel than any other book 'of the Hebrew Bible. It occurs thirty-six times in Hosea 4–14, compared to thirty-five of the name 'Israel'. In

---

[197] For text-critical details see H. W. Wolff *Hosea* (1974): 72–3; G. I. Davies *Hosea* (1992): 132–5; A. A. Macintosh *Hosea* (1997): 167–74.

C *Commentary on Hosea* 93

several places the two names are found in parallel (5:3, 5; 6:10; 7:1; 10:6; 11:12 [12:1]; 13:1), and they are synonymous throughout the text.[198] In the ancestral traditions of the Bible Ephraim and Manasseh are the two sons of Joseph whom Jacob blessed, placing Ephraim ahead of Manasseh despite him being the younger (Gen. 41:50–52; 48:8–20). The tribe of Ephraim occupied a large part of the hill country in central Israel, and their territory included the ancient sanctuaries of Shiloh, Shechem, and Bethel. Jeroboam I, first king of northern Israel at its separation from Judah, was an Ephraimite (1 Kgs 11:26). It is unsurprising, therefore, that Ephraim's '[t]ribal and national identities coalesce in the prophecies of Hosea'.[199]

Hosea 4 has set out the proceedings of YHWH's indictment (*rîb*) against the Israelites, citing accusations of there being no faithfulness or loyalty, or knowledge of God in the land (4:1); of the prevalence of swearing, lying, murder, stealing, adultery, and bloodshed (4:2); of the priests rejecting knowledge and failing to instruct the people in God's teachings (4:4–6), but rather making profit out of the people (4:8); of priest and people alike forsaking YHWH and being faithless to him through all that went on at their mountain-top sanctuaries (4:11–13); and of the senior men of the land leading their daughters and daughters-in-law into (cultic) prostitution. Negative though this portrayal is, in the late eighth-century first edition of the text it served to explain the actions of YHWH in allowing the destruction of northern Israel and its capital Samaria by the Assyrians in 722. The Hosea-text thus shares with the Amos-text what Barton calls 'a purposeful element of theodicy in the prophetic announcements of judgment'.[200] A century later in the reign of Josiah the introduction of 4:15 served to warn that Judah was in danger of making some of the same mistakes that Israel had made. Sixth- and fifth-century readers and redactors seeking to make sense of the destruction of Jerusalem in 587 and the experience of exile in

---

[198] With the exception of 13:1, on which see the commentary.
[199] L. D. Hawk, 'Ephraim, Ephraimites', *NIDB* 2: 280–3 (283).
[200] J. Barton, 'History and Rhetoric in the Prophets', in M. Warner (ed.), *The Bible as Rhetoric: Studies in Biblical Persuasion and Credibility* (Warwick Studies in Philosophy and Literature; London: Routledge, 1990): 51–64 (52). I use this same quotation in the 'Introduction to Amos'. As I write there, 'The modern reader, schooled in the scientific method of the Enlightenment, may decline to see such disasters as being derived from the actions of God; however, such a view was normal in the ancient world, and … would have helped people to make sense of the defeat and destruction of the northern kingdom at the hands of the Assyrians.'

94   *Book of Hosea*

Babylon would have understood that Judah had failed to heed the warning provided by the example of what happened to Israel in 722, and had been equally faithless to YHWH. Nor were these the sum of the accusations against the Israelites. Priests and people having been accused in Hosea 4, in the very next verse it is priests, people, and king who are addressed in like manner.

Hosea 5:1–7 – Judgement on Priests, People, and King

> 5 Hear this, O priests!
> > Give heed, O house of Israel!
> > Listen, O house of the king!
> > > For the judgement pertains to you;
> > for you have been a snare at Mizpah
> > > and a net spread upon Tabor
> > ² and a pit dug deep in Shittim,
> > > but I will punish all of them.
>
> > ³ I know Ephraim,
> > > and Israel is not hidden from me,
> > for now, O Ephraim, you have prostituted yourself;
> > > Israel is defiled.
> > ⁴ Their deeds do not permit them
> > > to return to their God.
> > For the spirit of prostitution is within them,
> > > and they do not know the LORD.
>
> > ⁵ Israel's pride testifies against him;
> > > Ephraim stumbles in his guilt;
> > > Judah also stumbles with them.
> > ⁶ With their flocks and herds they shall go
> > > to seek the Lord,
> > but they will not find him;
> > > he has withdrawn from them.
> > ⁷ They have dealt faithlessly with the LORD,
> > > for they have borne illegitimate children.
> > > Now the new moon shall devour them along with their fields.

The opening 'Hear this' signifies a new literary section. Thematically 5:1–7 reiterates and expands on elements of chapter 4. Immediately, however, 5:1 introduces a new addressee. The 'house of the king' is now included in the address. The phrase may refer to the royal family or to the wider

C Commentary on Hosea 95

royal establishment. With 'priests' and the 'house of the king' being specific groups within Israel, it is surprising that the middle addressee is the 'house of Israel', especially since it would then entail them being a snare and spreading a net to trap themselves. Most commentators suggest, on the basis of a verse such as Micah 3:1, that it must be representative leaders who are meant.[201] The list of three addressees is matched by reference to three place names in 5:1b–2,[202] giving a neat structure:

> Summons to hear addressed to (a) priests; (b) house of Israel; (c) house of the king;
> Announcement of judgment: 'for the judgment pertains to you';
> Accusations made in respect of actions at (a) Mizpah; (b) Tabor; (c) Shittim;
> Announcement of judgment: 'but I will punish all of them'.

NRSV's 'judgement' translates *mišpāṭ*, which can be translated as 'justice'; hence one could translate, as Wolff does, 'for you are responsible for justice'.[203] In that case the sentence does not constitute an announcement of judgement, but rather an accusation that the priests, leaders of the house of Israel, and royal house have failed to promote and establish justice as they should have. However, in view of the structure of 5:1–2, NRSV's translation is to be preferred. Dearman considers that the breadth of meaning of *mišpāṭ* gives opportunity for 'an ironic pun, a sarcastic double entendre', that is, it means 'something like: "Yes, responsibility for *mišpāṭ* [justice] resides with you and your respective offices, but the *mišpāṭ* [judgement] of YHWH upon you is forthcoming."'[204]

The accusation entails three images which all signify entrapment of the people into unfaithfulness. The snare is a trap primarily for birds (cf. Amos 3:5). The net could be used for large animals such as a lion (cf. Ezek. 19:8). A pit could serve to catch various animals. It is hard to know how much to endow the three places mentioned with interpretative significance. The Mizpah concerned is probably Mizpah in Benjamin, some

---

[201] So *inter alia* H. W. Wolff *Hosea* (1974): 97; A. A. Macintosh *Hosea* (1997) 175–6.

[202] The text of 5:2 is difficult. To translate as 'Shittim' (as does NRSV) requires an emendation adopted by a majority of commentators e.g. H. W. Wolff *Hosea* (1974): 94; J. A. Dearman *Hosea* (2010): 169–70. A dissenting voice is A. A. Macintosh *Hosea* (2007): 178–81, who translates as 'perverse men' cf. NIV's translation: 'The rebels are knee-deep in slaughter.' This entails a re-pointing of the Hebrew, but no consonantal change.

[203] H. W. Wolff *Hosea* (1974): 94

[204] J. A. Dearman *Hosea* (2010): 171.

nine miles north of Jerusalem. It held historical significance as the place where Samuel gathered 'all Israel' (1 Sam. 7:5) and, along with Bethel and Gilgal, was part of an annual circuit made by Samuel each year (1 Sam. 7:16). A tradition in 1 Samuel 10:17–24 associates it with the choosing of Saul as the first king of Israel. It came into renewed prominence after the fall of Jerusalem in 587, when it became the Babylonian centre of administration of the region (2 Kgs 25:23–25; Jer. 40–41) and then, in due course, the centre of Persian administration of the province of Yehud. With regard to Tabor, the narrative of Saul becoming Israel's first king refers to an 'oak of Tabor' near Bethel (1 Sam. 10:3), while the story in Judges 4 of Deborah and Barak coordinating action against Sisera is set on Mount Tabor (Judg. 4:6, 12, 14). Shittim is the region in which, according to Numbers 25:1–4, the Israelites were led into sacrificing to the Baal of Peor. Hosea 9:10 refers to this incident. Bos takes the inclusion of Mizpah as confirmation of a Persian period context for composition and reading of the text. He argues that the stories in 1 Samuel regarding the choice of Saul as king 'were part of an attempt by the Jerusalem elite to undermine the status of the leadership in Mizpah during the early Persian period'. However, he has to acknowledge that '[h]ow the references to Tabor and Shittim may have been read in the early Persian period is … not clear',[205] and it is better to follow the majority view that the text derives from the late eighth century. If there is interpretative significance in the choice of Mizpah, Tabor, and Shittim, it is probably that all had some importance in traditions of Israel's founding and early history.

The conclusion to 5:2 pronounces divine judgement: 'I will punish all of them.' The verb used (*yāsar*) carries a corrective sense. It could be used of parents disciplining a son (Deut. 21:18; Prov. 19:18). Hosea 7:15 uses it of YHWH training Israel's arms as he grew. There is, therefore a fleeting hint that YHWH's punishment may not be the last word, if the nation, its priests, and royal house, will accept correction. It is, if so, no more than a fleeting hint, as in 5:3–7 YHWH's case against Israel continues, developing themes from the previous chapter. The accusation that Israel has 'prostituted yourself' and has a 'spirit of prostitution'[206] (5:3–4) is repeated from 4:10–12. It is now added that her prostituting herself means she is defiled (5:3). This priestly term is one used of an individual who has touched a corpse (Num. 9:6–7) or the carcass of an unclean animal (Lev. 5:2). Hosea 5:3 applies it to Israel's contact with the kinds of activities described in 4:11–19. Hosea 5:4 adds that

---

[205] J. M. Bos *Reconsidering* (2013): 85.
[206] For the translation see note 1 in Section II, 'Introduction to Hosea'.

C Commentary on Hosea

97

the people have become so bound up with such activities that '[t]heir deeds do not permit them to return to their God'. Davies comments that this is 'to be understood not so much as a point of doctrine' but rather as the recognition that, due to their ongoing unfaithful practices, 'they are no longer in a position to recognize that they have done wrong'.[207] The final statement that 'they do not know YHWH' refers back to 4:6. Hosea 5:3–4 has a concentric pattern: the opening and closing lines concern YHWH knowing Ephraim, but Ephraim not knowing YHWH; next in from these lines is the theme of prostitution; and in the centre – and thereby emphasised – is the impossibility of Israel returning to their God.[208]

Hosea 5:4 switches from the first-person divine speech of 5:3 into prophetic speech in which God and YHWH are referred to in the third person. This continues into 5:5–7. As is characteristic of the Hosea-text, accusation and announcement of judgement are interwoven within these verses. Firstly, Israel's pride is said to testify against him. The identical line is found in 7:10. Amos 6:8 also says that YHWH abhors the 'pride of Jacob', which is in parallel to his 'strongholds' that YHWH hates. There the parallelism indicates that Jacob's pride is in his military strongholds and the trust that he places in them. In Hosea 5:5 it is not specified what constitutes Israel's pride, but in parallel with it is the guilt of Ephraim. In the literary context it is to be assumed that Israel's pride and guilt are evident in the accusations of the preceding sections of the text. These cause Ephraim to stumble. The verb used is the same as that in 4:5, linking these verses once more to chapter 4. The statement that 'Judah stumbles with them' is an addition made in the seventh-century redaction of the text in order to make explicit that Judah is being addressed as well as Israel. The consequence of Israel's and Judah's stumbling is that although they go to seek YHWH with their flocks and herds (i.e. with plenty of animals for sacrifice), they will not find him, for 'he has withdrawn from them'. The verb 'withdraw' (ḥālaṣ) is generally used transitively: for example, to remove clothing or shoes (Deut. 25:9–10; Isa. 20:2). However the intransitive use here in 5:6 makes perfect sense: what YHWH withdraws is himself.

The accusations of 5:7a are, firstly, the generalised one that the people have dealt faithlessly with YHWH, as the metaphor of 'prostitution' illustrates (see the comments on 4:10–11); and, secondly, the more specific

---

[207]   G. I. Davies *Hosea* (1992): 142.
[208]   J. Krispenz 'Idolatry, Apostasy, Prostitution' (2016): 22–3.

98   *Book of Hosea*

allegation that 'they have borne illegitimate children'. This accusation, too, may be understood metaphorically: through the people's 'prostitution' a generation is being raised for whom faithlessness in respect of YHWH is the norm. 'Accordingly they are living witnesses to the debilitating syncretism of the cults of Yahweh and of Baal.'[209] The final part of the verse is difficult textually. It literally reads 'A new moon will devour them with their fields.' The sense is probably that 'before the next new moon' or 'before the month is out' the people and their fields will be devoured.[210] Nogalski comments that the translation 'fields' is weak: the word often refers to an allotted portion of land (Num. 18:20; Deut. 18:8; Josh. 14:4; 15:13; 18:7; 19:9). The land which is threatened is land allotted by YHWH.[211]

The legal metaphor of YHWH's *rib* with the people of Israel in chapter 4 (see the comments on 4:1) continues to hover in the background of 5:1–7. Priests, leaders of the people, and the royal house have entrapped the people in 'prostitution' (5:1–4) to the point that the people are now incapable of returning to their God (5:4). Indeed, their pride and guilt in maintaining their faithlessness means that when they do seek YHWH, they will not find him (5:5–7). As with chapter 4, in the earliest, Post-722 Composition of the Hosea-text, these verses will have contributed to explaining why YHWH allowed the destruction of the northern kingdom at the hands of the Assyrians. In the seventh-century redaction it is made clear that its accusations and threats should now be applied to the people of Judah (5:5), who needed, in their turn, to heed the warnings. In due course their failure to do so would be seen as an explanation of the disaster of the destruction of Judah at the hands of the Babylonians in 587.

Hosea 5:8–7:16 – Ephraim's Sickness

> [8] Blow the horn in Gibeah,
>   the trumpet in Ramah.
>   Sound the alarm at Beth-aven;
>   look behind you, Benjamin!
> [9] Ephraim shall become a desolation
>   on the day of punishment;

---

[209]   A. A. Macintosh *Hosea* (2007): 191.
[210]   J. L. Mays *Hosea* (1969): 84–5. A possible alternative is that the new moon festival will prove to be not a time of celebration, but rather the time when the people and their fields are devoured: so J. A. Dearman *Hosea* (2013): 178.
[211]   J. D. Nogalski *Hosea–Jonah* (2011): 88.

C *Commentary on Hosea*

among the tribes of Israel
    I declare what is sure.
[10] The princes of Judah have become
    like those who remove the landmark;
  on them I will pour out
    my wrath like water.
[11] Ephraim is oppressed, crushed in judgement,
    because he was determined to go after vanity.
[12] Therefore I am like maggots to Ephraim
    and like rottenness to the house of Judah.
[13] When Ephraim saw his sickness
    and Judah his wound,
  then Ephraim went to Assyria,
    and sent to the great king.
  But he is not able to cure you
    or heal your wound.
[14] For I will be like a lion to Ephraim
    and like a young lion to the house of Judah.
  I myself will tear and go away;
    I will carry off, and no one shall rescue.
[15] I will return again to my place
    until they acknowledge their guilt and seek my face.
    In their distress they will beg my favour:
6 'Come, let us return to the Lord,
    for it is he who has torn, and he will heal us;
    he has struck down, and he will bind us up.
[2] After two days he will revive us;
    on the third day he will raise us up,
    that we may live before him.
[3] Let us know, let us press on to know the Lord;
    his appearing is as sure as the dawn;
  he will come to us like the showers,
    like the spring rains that water the earth.'
[4] What shall I do with you, O Ephraim?
    What shall I do with you, O Judah?
  Your love is like a morning cloud,
    like the dew that goes away early.
[5] Therefore I have hewn them by the prophets,
    I have killed them by the words of my mouth,
    and my judgement goes forth as the light.
[6] For I desire steadfast love and not sacrifice,
    the knowledge of God rather than burnt offerings.

100   *Book of Hosea*

^{7} But at Adam they transgressed the covenant;
 there they dealt faithlessly with me.
^{8} Gilead is a city of evildoers,
 tracked with blood.
^{9} As robbers lie in wait for someone,
 so the priests are banded together;
 they murder on the road to Shechem;
 they commit a monstrous crime.
^{10} In the house of Israel I have seen a horrible thing;
 Ephraim's prostitution is there; Israel is defiled.

^{11} For you also, O Judah, a harvest is appointed.

When I would restore the fortunes of my people,
7 when I would heal Israel,
 the corruption of Ephraim is revealed,
 and the wicked deeds of Samaria,
 for they deal falsely;
 the thief breaks in,
 and the bandits raid outside.
^{2} But they do not consider
 that I remember all their wickedness.
 Now their deeds surround them;
 they are before my face.
^{3} By their wickedness they make the king glad,
 and the officials by their treachery.
^{4} They are all adulterers;
 they are like a heated oven
 whose baker does not need to stir the fire
 from the kneading of the dough until it is leavened.
^{5} On the day of our king the officials
 became sick with the heat of wine;
 he stretched out his hand with mockers.
^{6} For they are kindled like an oven; their heart burns within them;
 all night their anger smoulders;
 in the morning it blazes like a flaming fire.
^{7} All of them are hot as an oven,
 and they devour their rulers.
 All their kings have fallen;
 none of them calls upon me.
^{8} Ephraim mixes himself with the peoples;
 Ephraim is a cake not turned.
^{9} Foreigners devour his strength,
 but he does not know it;

C Commentary on Hosea

> grey hairs are sprinkled upon him,
> > but he does not know it.
> [10] Israel's pride testifies against him;
> > yet they do not return to the LORD their God
> > or seek him, for all this.
>
> [11] Ephraim has become like a dove,
> > silly and without sense;
> > they call upon Egypt, they go to Assyria.
> [12] As they go, I will cast my net over them;
> > I will bring them down like birds of the air;
> > I will discipline them according to the report made to their assembly.
> [13] Woe to them, for they have strayed from me!
> > Destruction to them, for they have rebelled against me!
> I would redeem them,
> > but they speak lies against me.
>
> [14] They do not cry to me from the heart,
> > but they wail upon their beds;
> they gash themselves for grain and wine;
> > they rebel against me.
> [15] It was I who trained and strengthened their arms,
> > yet they plot evil against me.
> [16] They turn to that which does not profit;
> > they have become like a defective bow;
> their officials shall fall by the sword
> > because of the rage of their tongue.
> So much for their babbling in the land of Egypt.

The imperative 'Blow the horn ...' of 5:8 indicates a new section of text, which is best taken as continuing through to 7:16. While there are separate units within it, these were brought together in the earliest composition of the text on the basis of thematic connections, with only a few lines being added in subsequent redactions.[212] The dominant unifying theme is a critique of seeking to make alliances with Assyria or Egypt, which is interpreted as faithlessness in respect of YHWH and a lack of trust in him (5:13; 7:11, 16). A second, related theme is Israel's sickness and healing (5:13; 6:1–2; 7:1, 5). This significant Hoseanic theme does not recur elsewhere in the text other than in the final unit of chapters 4–11 (11:3) and in the closing chapter (14:4 [5]). The two themes overlap, in that Israel seeks to find healing and

---

[212] See the commentary at 6:5–11.

102   *Book of Hosea*

security through turning to foreign alliances rather than to YHWH, something made explicit in 5:13.

Hosea 5:10, 12, 13 refer to Judah as well as Ephraim. For older commentators who held that the prophet Hosea spoke only to Israel and not to Judah this was problematic, and radical solutions were needed. Harper took the view that in every case an original 'Israel' had been replaced by the name 'Judah' by later redactors.[213] This changed with the publication of an influential essay by Alt in 1919,[214] in which he argued that 5:8–6:6 reflected events of the Syro-Ephraimite War in 734. Behind the text, Alt held, lay the failed attempt of Rezin, king of Syria, and Pekah, king of Israel, to persuade Ahaz, king of Judah, to join an anti-Assyrian coalition. When Syria and Israel marched against Judah, Ahaz appealed to the Assyrian emperor Tiglath-Pileser III for help, leading to Assyrian conquest of Syria and Israel. When Syria and Israel turned northwards to face the emperor of Assyria, Judah invaded Israel from the south. Alt saw five units within 5:8–6:6: the first (5:8–9) referred to Judah's invasion of Israel from the south; the second (5:10) criticised Judah for seeking to annexe land to which they were not entitled; the third (5:11) criticised Israel once more; the fourth (5:12–14) reflected the outcome of it all, in which both Israel and Judah ended up as vassals to Assyria (Alt emended 5:13 to read that 'Ephraim went to Assyria, and the house of Judah to the great king'); and the fifth (5:15–6:6) comprised Hosea's prophetic reflections on the whole unhappy saga. Alt's central hypothesis has been accepted by a majority of scholars, even if particular details are disputed. A challenge to Alt's thesis came from Good, who argued that the blowing of the horn and trumpet in 5:8 refers to cultic rather than to military practice, and that these verses should be seen as having a cultic rather than a military or political point of reference. He suggests that the place names in 5:8 may signify a religious procession through these places to Bethel.[215] His arguments fail to convince, and it is best to agree with Alt's central thesis in respect of 5:8–14.[216]

Hosea 5:8 commands the horn to be blown (*šôpār*) in Gibeah and the trumpet (*ḥăṣōṣərâ*) in Ramah. The *šôpār* was a curved ram's horn. It could be

---

[213] W. R. Harper *Amos and Hosea* (1905): 272.

[214] A. Alt, 'Hosea 5:8–6:6: Ein Krieg und seine Folgen in prophetischer Beleuchtung', *NKZ* 30 (1919): 537–68; reproduced in A. Alt, *Kleine Schriften zur Geschichte des Volkes Israel*, vol. 2 (Munich: Beck, 1953): 163–87.

[215] E. M. Good, 'Hosea 5:8–6:6: An Alternative to Alt', *JBL* 85 (1966): 273–86.

[216] Scholars who do so include G. I. Davies *Hosea* (1992): 148; J. A. Dearman *Hosea* (2013): 179–80; A. A. Macintosh *Hosea* (1997): 195–8; H. W. Wolff *Hosea* (1974): 109, 115.

C Commentary on Hosea 103

sounded to warn of danger or to call to battle (Judg. 3:27; 6:34; 7:8, 16). It could also be blown in the context of a cultic festival (Ps. 81:3 [4]). The *ḥăṣōṣərâ* was a straight metal trumpet. The parallel command to sound the alarm at Beth-aven makes clear that here these instruments are to be blown to warn of danger.[217] The three towns named – Gibeah, Ramah, and Bethel – are all included in the list of towns allotted to Benjamin in Joshua 18:21–28. Gibeah was three miles north of Jerusalem, Ramah five miles north, and Bethel eleven miles north. So assuming that these are the three towns referred to, the verse describes an invasion from Judah northwards through Benjamin towards Israel. Hosea 9:9 and 10:9 refer to the 'days of Gibeah' as a time when Israel sinned. In 5:8, however, it appears to be no more than a geographical reference. Macintosh, noting that Bethel was technically in Ephraim rather than Benjamin, considers that on this occasion (unlike in 4:15 and 10:5) Beth-aven does not refer to Bethel but to a Beth-aven near Ai, in Benjamite territory.[218] However, Sweeney is correct in disagreeing and seeing it as indeed a reference to Bethel here too.[219] NRSV's 'look behind you, Benjamin!' translates a literal 'after you Benjamin'. The same words occur in Judges 5:14. The meaning is uncertain in both places, but NRSV's translation fits the context well. The reason for sounding the alarm is given in 5:9: Ephraim is to experience a day of punishment. The second half of 5:9 underlines to the 'tribes of Israel' (i.e. all the tribes, of both Israel and Judah) that what is declared is irrevocable.

Following the warning of the punishment coming upon Ephraim, 5:10 focuses upon Judah. Specifically it is the 'princes' of Judah who are addressed. The term is found in the Hosea-text in 3:4; 5:10; 7:3, 5, 16; 8:4, 10; 9:15; 13:10. It may be used of military leaders or administrative court officials (e.g. 2 Sam. 3:38; 1 Kgs 4:2). The accusation that they have become 'like those who remove the landmark' reflects the prohibition on individuals moving a boundary marker (Deut. 19:14; Prov. 22:28; 23:10). Here, however, it means the attempt to move a national boundary through invasion. Their actions will cause YHWH to pour out his wrath like water (i.e. in torrents). In 5:11 attention reverts to Ephraim, who is oppressed and crushed in judgement, the reason for which is his going 'after vanity'. A small emendation is required to enable this translation (the Hebrew word does not make sense without it).[220] The vanity concerned is presumably that of having made an

---

[217] See the commentary on 4:15 for the naming of Bethel as Beth-aven, 'House of iniquity'.
[218] A. A. Macintosh *Hosea* (1997): 194–5.
[219] M. A. Sweeney *Twelve Prophets* 1 (2000): 63.
[220] G. I. Davies *Hosea* (1992): 156; H. W. Wolff *Hosea* (1974): 104.

104   *Book of Hosea*

alliance with Syria against Judah. Firstly, however, 5:12 makes clear that
YHWH now speaks to both nations. As Mercutio says in Shakespeare's
Romeo and Juliet, 'A plague on both your houses' – and the plague in Hosea
5:12 is none other than YHWH himself. The noun translated by NRSV as
'maggots' (*'āš*) occurs elsewhere only in Job 4:19; 13:28; 27:18; Psalm 39:11 [12];
Isaiah 50:9; 51:8. In four of these it is linked with garments and translated in
EVV as 'moth'. Some therefore (including NIV) translate thus here.[221] An
alternative view notes that the related verb appears to mean 'waste away'
(Pss. 6:7 [8]; 31:10), and therefore takes the meaning here to be that YHWH
is as a wasting sickness to them.[222] Others again refer to cognate words in
Arabic and translate as 'pus'.[223] An allusion to some kind of disease would
fit the context well in anticipating the references in the next verse (5:13) to
Ephraim's sickness and Judah's wound.

Hosea 5:13 contains the two themes which unify the section 5:8–7:16,
namely the people's sickness and need for healing, and their making of
foreign alliances. Both Israel and Judah are seen as sick and wounded, and
recognise it. In consequence Ephraim went to Assyria to seek help. There is
an imbalance in the verse: with Ephraim and Judah being in parallel in the
opening lines we expect consequential action relating to each, and indeed
5:14 resumes the focus on both nations. Alt emended 5:13 to read: 'Ephraim
went to Assyria, and Judah to the great king.' However he is not widely followed in this, and the text as it stands focuses on Ephraim going to Assyria
and sending to the great king. Commentators seeking to relate each part
of the text to specific historical events suggest that this could refer to the
payment of tribute by Menahem (2 Kgs 15:19–20) or Hoshea (2 Kgs 17:3).[224]
However, it is not necessary to make specific correlation between text and
historical event in order to interpret the text, which simply makes clear that
Assyria and her king will never be a source of healing. The Assyrian king
is described as the great king: the Hebrew *melek yārēb* is found only here
and in 10:6 in the Hebrew Bible, and is sometimes emended by commentators. However it is best taken as a Hebrew rendering of an Akkadian title
for the Assyrian emperor (*šarru rabū*).[225] While Judah is not named in this

---

[221]   G. I. Davies *Hosea* (1992): 156–7; J. A. Dearman *Hosea* (2010): 180, 185; M. A. Sweeney
        Twelve Prophets 1 (2000): 66–7.
[222]   A. A. Macintosh *Hosea* (1997): 207 translates as 'emaciating disease'.
[223]   J. L. Mays *Hosea* (1969): 85; H. W. Wolff *Hosea* (1974): 104, 115.
[224]   A. A. Macintosh *Hosea* (1997): 211; H. W. Wolff *Hosea* (1974): 115.
[225]   A. A. Macintosh *Hosea* (1997): 209, followed by J. A. Dearman *Hosea* (2010): 180. H. M.
        Barstad 'Hosea and the Assyrians' (2013): 107–9 makes an alternative proposal, suggesting

C Commentary on Hosea

verse, her calling on Assyria for help in 734 is recorded in 2 Kings 16:7 and is probably something which would have been remembered for a long time, and therefore assumed. The text makes clear that turning to Assyria will not bring cure and healing to the sickness and wounds that both nations are experiencing as a result of their wars. NRSV's 'cure' translates the Hebrew verb *rāpā'* which is the usual word for 'heal/cure', and that used in 6:1; 7:1; 11:3; 14:4 [5]. It may be that the relatively frequent use of the verb results from a wordplay on the name Ephraim (*'eprayim*) with which it shares its three consonants in reverse order, the two words both occurring in 5:13; 7:1; 11:3.[226] The second verb in 5:13, translated by NRSV as 'heal', is only found here, and is translated as a parallel term on the basis of context.

Assyria cannot heal the people (5:13 says), and it might have been expected that there would follow a statement that it is YHWH who can. Instead, however, 5:14 makes clear that since both nations have turned to Assyria, YHWH will be not a source of healing, but rather will be like a lion hunting them. Because YHWH will be a lion to the people, there will be no one to rescue them. In view of the faithlessness of both Ephraim and Judah, YHWH will be as a disease (5:12) and like a lion (5:14) to them.

Hosea 5:15 is a link verse between 5:8–14 and 6:1–3. The phrase 'I will return to my place' can be read as the lion returning to his lair with his prey. But 'my place' can also be read as a cultic allusion: the place where YHWH's presence is to be found (in Deut. e.g. 12:11 the place where YHWH causes his name to dwell), and thus where the people can seek him. Hence 5:15 represents a change of tenor from 5:12–14, allowing that the people might acknowledge their guilt and seek his face. In contrast to 5:6, where seeking YHWH will not lead to finding him, now there is the possibility that their seeking may lead to finding him. The 'my face' of 5:15 uses the same Hebrew word as 6:2's 'before him'. LXX specifically made 5:15 an introduction to 6:1–3 by adding in the word 'saying' at the end of 5:15, and NRSV's colon at the end of the verse reflects this. As a self-contained unit 5:8–14 would end entirely negatively. But in the literary context of 5:8–7:16, the link verse 5:15 makes it evident that the possibility of turning to YHWH remains.

Older commentaries which take 6:1–3 as a self-contained unit discuss whether this expression of penitence might be an existing liturgical one

---

that, just as in 10:14 'Shalman' is a shortened form of the Assyrian emperor Shalmaneser, so *yārēb* is to be taken as a shortened form of Jeroboam. His suggestion works better for 10:14 than it does here.

[226] So D. F. O'Kennedy, 'Healing as/or Forgiveness? The Use of the Term אפר in the Book of Hosea', *OTE* 14 (2001): 458–74 (469).

attributed to the people, or be modelled on such a liturgical form. They also discuss whether they were spoken by the priests or people in response to Hosea's message or whether, rather, they were words composed by Hosea to indicate the response that YHWH was seeking. In the light of the response in 6:4–6 they discuss, too, whether 6:1–3 constitutes an adequate expression of repentance, or whether it was defective either through being an expression of mere popular piety, influenced by Canaanite religion, or because the words were not matched by the steadfast love and knowledge of God of which 6:6 speaks. These questions do not admit of ready answers, and it is more helpful to focus on the literary context in which 6:1–3 is placed in order to understand their purpose. As noted, 5:15 serves to link 5:8–14 and 6:1–3. Shared vocabulary between 5:13–15 and 6:1–2 (verbs 'tear/torn'; 'heal'; 'return'; and the noun 'face') further strengthens this linkage. It is evident that within the literary flow of the text 6:1–3 is intended to constitute a response to 5:13–14, and thus to 5:8–15 as a whole.

The opening summons invites the people to 'return to YHWH' (6:1). The verb *šûb* (return) is characteristic of the Hosea-text. Indeed, Fabry comments that 'it permeates the message of Hosea like a leitmotif'.[227] It is found twenty-one times in the fourteen chapters of the book, being used of Gomer (2:7 [9]), the people of Ephraim, Israel, and Judah (3:5; 5:4; 6:1; 7:10, 16; 8:13; 9:3; 11:5; 12:6 [7]; 14:1, 2, 7 [2, 3, 8]), and of YHWH (2:9 [11]; 4:9; 5:15; 6:11; 11:9; 12:2, 14 [3, 15]; 14:4 [5]). It is used seven times of the people turning to YHWH or God (3:5; 5:4; 6:1; 7:10; 12:6 [7]; 14:1, 2 [2, 3]), and three times of them returning to Egypt as punishment (8:13; 9:3; 11:5). The contrast in this verse is not between turning to YHWH or Baal, but between turning to YHWH or to the emperor of Assyria who, as 5:13 has pointed out, is not the one ultimately able to help and heal them. The call to return to YHWH acknowledges that it is he who has brought the disasters that have come upon them, and expresses trust that this acknowledgement will lead him now to work for their healing and restoration. Job 5:18 expresses as a generality that 'he wounds, but he binds up; he strikes, but his hands heal': precisely that belief is expressed in Hosea 6:1 in respect of the people's fortunes. The hope expressed in 6:2 is that the people may live not under the tyranny of Assyria or of any foreign power, but 'before him'. Poetically it is hoped that '[a]fter two days he will revive us; on the third day he will raise us up'. NRSV fails to capture a short chiasm. The Hebrew word order is that 'he will

---

[227] H.-J. Fabry, '*šûb*', *TDOT* 14: 461–522 (487).

C Commentary on Hosea

revive us after two days, on the third day he will raise us up'. The form is a graded numerical saying as in the oracles against the nations of Amos 1:3–2:16 ('For three transgressions and for four …': see the commentary *ad loc*) and the poem of Proverbs 30:15–31. The expression 'on the third day' is used frequently to mean 'in/after a short time' (e.g. Gen. 22:4; 2 Kgs 20:5). While Christian readers may be struck by the similarity with Christ being 'raised on the third day in accordance with the scriptures' (1 Cor. 15:4), Hosea 6:2 contains no doctrine of resurrection after death. Rather it means revival of fortunes after disaster. While 1 Corinthians 15:4 may or may not allude fleetingly to Hosea 6:2, if it does it is the only verse in the New Testament to do so. The earliest use of Hosea 6:2 as a specific prediction of Christ's resurrection is by Tertullian.[228]

The call to return to YHWH continues in 6:3 with the characteristic Hoseanic theme of knowing YHWH. The confidence is expressed that if the people press on to know YHWH, then he will appear as the light of dawn after the darkness of night and as refreshing rain watering the ground after a time of drought. The word for YHWH's 'appearing' is used in poetic passages both of YHWH appearing to lead his people in battle (Judg. 5:4; Ps. 68:7 [8]) and of the rising of the sun (Ps. 19:6 [7]). While his appearing 'as the dawn' makes the link with sunrise the stronger, in the context of turning to YHWH rather than to Assyria the link with YHWH leading in battle also finds an echo. The 'showers' are the first showers of autumn, followed in due course by the rains of spring. Mays comments that '[r]ain is the peculiar provenance of Baal in Canaanite theology',[229] and thus 6:3 is an acknowledgement of YHWH as provider of rain rather than Baal. While 5:8–7:16 deals with wars and the people's turning to Assyria rather than with worship of Baal, in the context of the book as a whole such a comment is justifiable.

In its literary context following 5:8–15, Hosea 6:1–3 should be read as words that the people are encouraged to say. In Joel 2:17 words of lamentation are given to the priests, the brevity of those words suggesting that this is a literary device rather than an actual liturgy (see the commentary *ad loc*). The same is true of Hosea 6:1–3: the words represent 'what the people *should* speak'.[230] Lamentations 3:40–41 provides the closest parallel,[231] with

---

[228] See further A. A. Macintosh *Hosea* (1997): 222–3.
[229] J. L. Mays *Hosea* (1969): 96.
[230] J. D. Nogalski *Hosea-Jonah* (2011): 96 (italics original).
[231] G. I. Davies *Hosea* (1992): 151; M. A. Sweeney *Twelve Prophets* 1 (2000): 69.

108 *Book of Hosea*

the words 'let us return to YHWH' being identical in both. In the earliest composition of Hosea in the late eighth century, Hosea 6:1–3 would have been read with the destruction of the northern kingdom in 722 in mind. However, their application is not restricted to any one point in time. As Ben Zvi writes, 'within the world of the book, such a voice and a call are not anchored to any particular circumstances, event, or any group of addressees at a certain occasion'.[232]

Hosea 6:1–3 is one of two calls to repentance in the Hosea-text, the other being 14:1–3 [2–4]. The inclusion of 'Assyria shall not save us' in 14:3 [4] suggests that those who composed and inserted 14:1–3 [2–4] (see the commentary *ad loc*) intended an allusion to 5:13–6:3. They also intended to show a contrast in the outcome of the people's expression of repentance. In the final chapter of the book blessing is finally promised in response to repentance. In chapter 6, in contrast, the following verses 6:4–6 contain no such promise of blessing. In the literary context of the book as a whole it is being shown that the parlous state in which the people find themselves cannot be rectified by one brief expression of turning to YHWH. The book of Amos is unrelenting in its words of judgement right up to the final section 9:7–15. The Hosea-text, in comparison, offers more glimmers of hope along the way (2:14–23 [16–25]; 3:5; 11:8–11). Nevertheless the two texts essentially have in common that only at the end of the literary journey is blessing finally promised. In Hosea 6 the expression of turning to YHWH that the people are to utter does not lead to any instant promise of salvation. It leads, rather, to YHWH holding an internal dialogue with himself as to how he is to deal with Ephraim and Judah.

That the questions attributed to YHWH in Hosea 6:4a are intended to be taken as genuine questions is not to be doubted. While formally addressed to the two nations, they are nevertheless also to be taken as addressed by YHWH to YHWH, as an internal struggle unfolds. Andersen and Freedman capture the sense of internal dialogue well: 'Yahweh's response is not nearly as negative as some exegetes claim. He does not spurn the people's expectations expressed in vv 1–3. What is lacking is a strong affirmation by Yahweh of what he will do.... Is it possible that Yahweh himself does not know what to do?'[233] While Andersen and Freedman relate this internal struggle specifically to 6:4–6, along with several commentators seeing 6:6 as the end of a unit, I wish to suggest that YHWH's internal dialogue be

---

[232] E. Ben Zvi *Hosea* (2005): 135.
[233] F. I. Andersen and D. N. Freedman *Hosea* (1980): 431.

C Commentary on Hosea 109

taken to extend further, to 7:10. Hosea 6:4–6 does not specify that, despite the people's professed repentance in 6:1–3, YHWH will nevertheless act to judge them. Rather 6:4–6 express considerations that make it difficult for YHWH simply to restore the people, as they hoped, but leave open exactly what he will do. The continuing internal dialogue focuses on the many reasons why judgement is deserved, but 6:11b still expresses YHWH's desire to restore the people's fortunes, and only in 7:10 does he finally reach the conclusion that, despite the profession of 6:1–3, Israel is not truly returning to him. Thus there is no announcement of judgement in the whole of 6:4–7:10, despite many reasons given as to why such an announcement would be warranted. Only in the following 7:11–16, which close the section, are accusations joined by announcements of judgement (7:12, 16).

The opening lines of 6:4 portray, as Nogalski writes, 'the anguished cry of the parent of a wayward child'.[234] There is no need to suggest that 'Judah' replaces an original 'Israel'.[235] Hosea 5:8–6:3 concern both Ephraim (Israel) and Judah and, despite the following 6:7–7:16 dealing primarily with the northern kingdom, it is entirely appropriate for 6:4 to refer to both kingdoms. YHWH's agonised cry derives from the suspicion that the repentance which the people of both kingdoms are urged to express in 6:1–3 might be perfectly proper in what it expresses, but lacking reality. Hosea 6:3 had expressed that YHWH's appearing would be as sure as the dawn. The early morning imagery is continued in 6:4 in relation to the people, whose expression of love (*ḥesed*), YHWH fears – indeed knows – will last no longer than the morning mist, which quickly evaporates, and the early morning dew that soon disappears. YHWH desires more than that, and 6:6 enunciates a principle: what he requires is a depth of steadfast love (*ḥesed*) and true knowledge of God, which are worth far more to him than sacrifice and burnt offerings. The tense of 'I desire' gives the sense of this being a timeless truth. The verse relates back to 4:1, where the accusation had been made that there is no faithfulness and loyalty (*ḥesed*), and no knowledge of God in the land (see the comments *ad loc* and 'A Closer Look: Knowledge of and by YHWH'). In 6:6 these qualities are set over against sacrifice and burnt offerings. While in 6:6b NRSV's 'rather than burnt offerings' could be translated as 'more than burnt offerings', in 6:6a the 'and not' specifically uses the negative *lōʾ*, making the contrast between steadfast love (*ḥesed*) and

---

[234] J. D. Nogalski *Hosea–Jonah* (2011): 97.
[235] Contra G. I. Emmerson *Hosea* (1984): 74. She is followed by G. I. Davies *Hosea* (1993): 166.

110   *Book of Hosea*

sacrifice absolute. LeCureux comments that although 'far from unusual in critiquing the cult in prophetic literature, Hosea offers the most complete and most scathing assessment of Israel's present worship situation within the Book of the Twelve'.[236] He notes the frequency with which priests are criticised (4:4, 6, 9; 5:1; 6:9; 10:5), and with which the increase in numbers of altars in Israel is seen as wholly negative (8:11; 10:1–2, 8; 12:11). Similarly sacrifices bring only rejection and destruction (4:13, 19; 6:6; 8:13; 9:4; 11:2; 12:11; 13:2). In many cases the rejection of the priests and their altars and sacrifices relates to the accusation of sacrificing to Baal rather than to YHWH. Here in 6:6, however, that accusation is not made. Rather it is evident that even sacrifices and burnt offering made to YHWH bring no benefit if there is no steadfast love (*ḥesed*) and knowledge (*da'at*) of God. The parallels between 6:6 and 1 Samuel 15:22 are evident. The verb 'desire' in Hosea 6:6 and noun 'delight' in 1 Samuel 15:22 are from the same root, and the words for 'sacrifice' and 'burnt offerings' are the same in both texts. Hosea 6:6 and 1 Samuel 15:22 are apiece with verses such as Isaiah 1:11; Amos 4:4–5; 5:21–24; Micah 6:6–8. The Closer Look section on 'The Prophets, the Cult and Sacrifice' explores this theme further.

In the first composition of the Hosea-text 6:6 followed 6:4 without a break. In the exilic redaction, however, was added 6:5, presumably before 6:6 in order to maintain the sense of climax that 6:6 engenders. While a majority of recent commentators take 6:4–6 as a unit from the earliest literary stage, Yee references several significant older commentators who consider it to have been added, and she herself argues that a Deuteronomistic interest in the role of the prophets is evident here and in other verses in the Hosea-text (12:10, 13 [11, 14]).[237] It may be noted, too, that while 6:4 addresses Ephraim and Judah in the second person, 6:5 switches to the third person; this third-person form continues in 6:7 which, I shall argue, derives from the same exilic hand. Those who take 6:5 to belong to the earliest literary composition have to take the 'prophets' as presumably being figures such as Ahijah of Shiloh, Elijah, Micaiah ben Imlah, and, most recently, Amos, and Hosea himself. A more natural reading from a sixth-century exilic perspective is that those referred to are the eighth- and seventh-century prophets whose words were already being preserved in written tradition. By these prophets, 6:5 states, YHWH has hewn the people. The verb employed is generally used

---

[236]   J. LeCureux, 'Restored Hope? The Function of the Temple, Priest and Cult as Restoration in the Book of the Twelve', *JSOT* 41 (2017): 493–510 (494).

[237]   G. A. Yee *Composition and History* (1987): 175–8.

C Commentary on Hosea

of literal cutting of stone or wood, but is used in a metaphorical sense in the exilic Isaiah 51:9 of YHWH's defeat of the mythological creature Rahab. Its use in Hosea 6:5 of YHWH hewing the people is not found elsewhere. It is also said that YHWH kills by the words of his mouth. It was considered that the prophetic word did not merely announce, but also contributed to the effecting of what was declared: 'my word that goes out from my mouth, it shall not return to me empty, but it shall accomplish that which I purpose and succeed in the thing for which I sent it' (Isa. 55:11). Finally, it is said that 'my judgment goes forth as the light'.[238] NRSV's translation of *mišpāṭ* as judgement rather than the alternative translation 'justice' is appropriate to the context. In the exilic edition of the text this sobering verse leads into the maxim inherited from the earliest layer, which gives as the reason for YHWH's judgement the dearth of steadfast love and knowledge of God, something affirmed by the exilic redactors.

The following verses 6:7–11a may also be taken to derive from exilic redactors, with older material incorporated. Verses 7 and 10 were composed for the exilic redaction of the text, and were placed around earlier, eighth-century material in 6:8–9. Thematically they continue YHWH's internal dialogue that began in 6:4. The dating of 6:7 has been hotly debated, because of the occurrence of the word 'covenant' (*bərît*). An initial question is whether the term refers in this verse to the covenant between YHWH and Israel or, rather, to a treaty, as it does in 10:4 and 12:1 [2]. Despite NRSV's translation there is no definite article to make it 'the covenant', nor, as in 8:1, a first-person suffix to make it 'my covenant'. Nevertheless many do see it as a reference to 'the covenant' between YHWH and Israel, considering that the second half of the verse – 'they dealt faithlessly with me' – strongly suggests it.[239] However, Macintosh considers that the lack of definite article or first-person suffix militates against such a view: it refers, he argues, to the breaking of a treaty between the king and people of Israel by Pekah in his rebellion of 736/735. Noting that some ancient versions translate as 'my covenant', Macintosh cites approvingly the argument of Perlitt that, on the basis of *lectio difficilior*, MT's indefinite form should be accepted.[240] Against

---

[238] NRSV follows a widely adopted minor emendation, which is reflected in LXX and other ancient versions, of moving the consonant *kāp* from the end of one word (judgment) to be the first letter of the next (light).

[239] So, for example, G. I. Davies *Hosea* (1992): 172; J. Day, 'Pre-Deuteronomic Allusions to the Covenant in Hosea and Psalm LXXVII', *VT* 36 (1986): 1–12; H. W. Wolff *Hosea* (1974): 121.

[240] A. A. Macintosh *Hosea* (1997): 238–9, citing L. Perlitt, *Bundestheologie* (WMANT, 36; Neukirchen-Vluyn: Neukirchener-Verlag, 1969): 143.

Perlitt's and Macintosh's position, however, is the argument of Day that the verb *ʿābar* is specifically used of transgressing the covenant between YHWH and Israel in Deuteronomy 17:2; Joshua 7:11, 15; 23:16; Judges 2:20; 2 Kings 18:12; Jeremiah 34:18, and that the same is likely to be true, therefore, in Hosea 6:7.[241] This last argument carries force, and it is best to assume that, as in 8:1, it is the covenant between YHWH and Israel which is referred to here.[242] However, this very fact points towards the exilic origin of this verse (see 'A Closer Look: The Covenant Concept in Scholarly Study'). This origin is confirmed by (1) the continuation of the third-person address of 6:5, which is best taken as also belonging to this redaction; (2) the fact that 6:7b draws on the earlier 5:7a in stating that the people have 'dealt faithlessly' with YHWH; and (3) the recognition that all the verses cited by Day are part of Deuteronomy, the so-called Deuteronomistic History (Joshua–2 Kings), or, in the case of Jeremiah 34:18, to a section of the Jeremiah-text which has undergone a Deuteronomistic redaction. Surprising is the Hebrew text's assertion that the people's transgression of the covenant was 'like Adam', since no covenant with Adam is recorded in the Hebrew Bible: NRSV follows virtually all commentators in emending the preposition to read 'at Adam' and assuming that the name is of the place referred to in Joshua 3:16 rather than to the human Adam of Genesis 2–3. The biblical record contains no known incident of the people's faithless dealing with YHWH at Adam, but that does not prevent a particular incident being in view, albeit one unknown to the modern reader. Similar ignorance on our part must be acknowledged in the following verses 6:8–9. If 6:8 refers to a particular incident, it is one unknown to us. Unusually Gilead is referred to in 6:8 as a city, whereas it generally signifies a region. Some suggest that it may be shorthand for a city such as Ramoth-gilead.[243] The description of it as 'tracked with blood' is non-specific and suggests a characterisation of Gilead rather than reference to a specific incident. The word 'blood' echoes the 'bloodshed upon bloodshed' of 4:2, and this possibly deliberate echo, combined with the non-specific nature of the verse, may indicate that 6:8, too, is a composition of the exilic redactors. The only other reference to Gilead in Hosea is 12:11 [12], which uses the same word *ʾāwen* (iniquity/evil) in relation to Gilead.[244] I argue in the commentary that Hosea 12 is a compilation

---

[241] J. Day 'Pre-Deuteronomic Allusions' (1986): 4.
[242] So also G. Eidevall *Grapes in the Desert* (1996): 105.
[243] So G. I. Davies *Hosea* (1992): 173; J. A. Dearman *Hosea* (2010): 198.
[244] In 6:8 NRSV's 'evildoers' is literally 'men doing evil/iniquity'.

C Commentary on Hosea

of texts made by an exilic redactor,[245] which strengthens the possibility that 6:8 is an exilic composition. The text of 6:9 is unclear. It appears, however, that a gang of priests are accused of murder, most likely of pilgrims on their way to the ancient sanctuary at Shechem. Whatever the precise intention of the original accusation, in the literary context of Hosea 4–11 it adds significantly to the criticism of priests already articulated in 4:4–14. Their actions constitute a 'monstrous crime': the word *zimmâ* is used elsewhere of sexual misdemeanours (e.g. Lev. 18:17; 20:14) and, more appositely in respect of Hosea 6:9, of devising evil plans (e.g. Ps. 26:10; Prov. 24:9; Isa. 32:7).

The previous verses having referred to specific places – Adam, Gilead, the road to Shechem – Hosea 6:10 concludes the unit by widening the scope of accusation to the whole house of Israel, where YHWH has seen a 'horrible thing': the term or closely related terms from the same verbal root are found in Jeremiah 5:30; 18:13; 23:14; 29:17. Mention of Ephraim's prostitution (pre-2021 NRSV: whoredom) links this verse to 5:3, from which the final statement 'Israel is defiled' is also taken *verbatim* (for the significance of the words used see the commentary on 5:3). The borrowing from 5:3 and the link to the Jeremiah-text reinforce the likelihood that this verse rounds off a short unit (6:7–10) introduced into the Exilic Redactional Composition.

In 6:11a there follows a brief saying extending the accusations and the threat of judgement from Israel alone to Judah also. This is almost universally taken by commentators to be an editorial addition. The word 'also' (*gam*) is also used in 4:5 and 5:5, in 5:5 specifically in extending accusations to apply them to Judah also. Those verses were added in the seventh-century redaction of the text. Here in 6:11a the exilic redaction takes the same formula to apply the accusations of 6:7–10 to Judah. The harvest appointed is undoubtedly one of judgement (cf. Jer. 51:33). The destruction of Jerusalem in 587 was seen as such an act of YHWH's judgement in the same way as was the destruction of Samaria in 722. To modern ears the message seems hard, but in fact the realisation that these calamities were not random but were purposed by YHWH allowed hope that appeal to him for mercy could also be made.

A new sub-section begins in 6:11b (6:11b–7:7). The theme of the people's healing (or lack of it) in 7:1 links it with 5:13 and 6:1–2. As noted in the opening remarks to 'Hosea 5:8–7:16: Ephraim's Sickness', this constitutes a unifying theme within the whole section. While 5:8–6:11a concern both Israel and Judah, from 7:1 onwards the focus narrows to consider solely the northern

---

[245] See Section II, 'Guilt and Healing – Hosea 11:12–14:9 [12–14]'.

114   *Book of Hosea*

kingdom. The exilic redactors brought in 6:11b as a link: the phrase 'restore the fortunes' is found in exilic and post-exilic texts to refer to restoration after captivity/exile (Jer. 29:14; Ezek. 16:53; Joel 3:1 [4:1]; Amos 9:14; Zeph. 3:20), so had exilic echoes. However, Judah's captivity is not specifically mentioned, allowing it to be read also as the introduction to 7:1–16's narrower focus on Israel as the exilic redactors allow the earlier text to resume. In the literary context of 5:8–7:16 YHWH's internal struggle which began in 6:4 continues. He longed to restore the fortunes of his people (6:11b) and heal Israel (7:1), but their manifest corruption and wicked deeds prevent him from doing so. The word 'corruption' (*'āwôn*) is a frequent Hoseanic term. It occurs also in 5:5; 8:13; 9:7, 9; 10:10; 12:8 [9]; 13:12; 14:1, 2 [2, 3], most often translated by NRSV as 'iniquity', but also 'guilt' (5:5; 14:2 [3]) or 'offence' (12:8[9]). The word 'wickedness' occurs three times in 7:1–3, in the plural in 7:1 (wicked deeds) and the singular in 7:2 and 7:3. The singular 'thief' (7:1) is a collective noun, derived from the verb 'steal': its use recalls the accusation of 4:2, that stealing was one of the people's wrongdoings. The word 'bandits' is also a collective singular. Hosea 6:2 had expressed the people's hope that they might live before him (YHWH), literally 'before his face'; 7:2 now states that what is before his face are their wicked deeds. In 7:1 Samaria, the capital city, is named for the first time in Hosea, appropriately so in view of it being the likely location of the palace revolts and assassinations which 7:3–7 go on to describe.

The precise meaning of 7:3–7 is elusive. Those commentators seeking to discern particular historical circumstances in the time of the prophet Hosea's ministry struggle to do so. Mays suggests that the king made glad in 7:3 was Hoshea, who took the throne in 733 with the assassination of Pekah. Davies suggests that these verses refer to the revolt of either Pekah or Hoshea. Andersen and Freedman suggest that the 'plural subject throughout is an unidentified group, presumably of priestly background, which schemes against the king and princes of Israel'.[246] A literary approach to the text need not become bogged down in such questions. The piling up of language such as 'wickedness' (7:1, 2, 3), 'their deeds' (7:2), 'treachery' (7:3), 'adulterers'[247] (7:4); 'their anger smoulders' (7:6), 'they devour their rulers' (7:7) indicates that a history of misdeeds and revolts is being described.

---

[246] J. L. Mays *Hosea* (1969): 105; G. I. Davies *Hosea* (1969): 181; F. I. Andersen and D. N. Freedman *Hosea* (1980): 447. For the history of the period see the 'Introduction to Hosea'.

[247] The term here describes the unfaithfulness of those who conspire against a king, cf. Jer. 9:2 [1].

C Commentary on Hosea

The image of the people being like a heated oven (7:4, 6) is not entirely clear, but seems to suggest that as dough rises and grows without needing to be stirred, so the anger and scheming that lead to assassinations and revolts quietly grow until they blaze out (7:6). Whatever the exact circumstances to which the words originally referred, and whatever the precise meaning of the image of the heated oven, from a post-722 perspective the conclusion in 7:7 makes perfect sense: 'All their kings have fallen, none of them calls upon me.' Small wonder that, as YHWH's internal dialogue continues, he finds himself unable to answer the people's expression of penitence (6:1–3), restore their fortunes (6:11b), or heal them (7:1).

The final phrase of 7:7 – 'none of them calls upon me' – both concludes 7:3–7 and prepares the ground for the final verses describing YHWH's internal struggle in 7:8–10. A new but not unrelated image is introduced in 7:8: Ephraim is compared to a cake mixture, seeking help here and there through various alliances with Aram, Egypt, and Assyria. The outcome is not a happy one, however. The word for 'cake' (*'ugâ*) refers to flat round cakes which could be baked quickly (see e.g. 1 Kgs 17:13) but which required turning to avoid burning. Israel is like such a cake which was not turned, and was therefore burned. The various alliances entered into do not, as hoped, lead to his strengthening: rather 'foreigners devour his strength', something which Israel does not recognise (7:9). He fails to recognise, too, that old age has come upon him and that he is in his final years. The grey hairs (7:9) of old age that were a sign of maturity and wisdom are here a sign simply of the advancement of the years. Mays comments that 'the people totter towards death'.[248] As YHWH sees Ephraim's lack of recognition of her condition, his internal dialogue reaches a verdict in 7:10. An accusation of 5:5 is repeated: 'Israel's pride testifies against him.' Despite all the tragic events that unfolded in Israel's final years, they did not return to YHWH, or seek him. The repetition of a sentence from 5:5 and the reference to YHWH in the third person in a passage which is otherwise first-person divine speech leads some commentators to take 7:10 as an addition to the section as originally framed. Others respond, rightly, that if this is so it is an addition which fits into its literary context remarkably well.[249] There is little reason to doubt that it was part of the first, Post-722 Composition of the text. It brings to a climax the whole of YHWH's internal conversation of 6:4–7:10. YHWH has wanted to respond to the people's expression of repentance in 6:1–3

---

[248] J. L. Mays *Hosea* (1969): 109.
[249] So, for example, H. W. Wolff *Hosea* (1974): 126.

116   *Book of Hosea*

by receiving their steadfast love (6:6) and by restoring their fortunes and healing them (6:11b–7:1). However, their faithlessness (6:7, 10), violent ways (6:8–9), wicked deeds (7:1–2), and turning to foreign powers (7:8–9) make this impossible, and 7:10 brings YHWH to his conclusion: for all his goodness to them, he can now only respond to their behaviour in judgement.

With YHWH's mind resolved, 7:11–12 constitutes a judgement oracle, containing the first pronouncement of judgement since 5:9. The summarising accusation of 7:11 contains a fresh image: Ephraim is like a silly dove with no sense, flitting between one foreign power and another, Egypt and Assyria, in their attempt to find safety. Macintosh clarifies that she is silly in the sense of being gullible:[250] these nations will simply take advantage. The phrase 'without sense' is literally 'without heart' (*lēb*), the heart being the seat of understanding. The Hosea-text refers to Egypt in two ways. In some verses it designates the historic land of oppression of Israel's traditions (2:15 [17]; 11:1; 12:9 [10]; 13:4), while in others it means the contemporary world power in parallel with Assyria (7:11; 9:3; 11:5, 11; 12:1 [2]). Here it is this latter sense that is meant. There is, the text indicates, no sense in Israel calling upon Egypt or Assyria for help. So as they go like a silly dove, YHWH will play the role of fowler and spread his net and catch them (7:12). His punishment, however, will have a corrective purpose. NRSV's 'discipline' translates the verb *yāsar*, which is used also in 7:15 and 10:10. Deuteronomy 8:5 uses the same verb of YHWH disciplining Israel as a parent disciplines a child (cf. Prov. 19:18; 29:17). The meaning of the final line of 7:12 is obscure: To what does 'their assembly' refer? The word is used in Judges 20:1–2 of a gathering of chiefs and people to decide how to respond to an atrocity described in Judges 19. Hosea 7:12 could, therefore, refer to some such gathering in the final days of the northern kingdom prior to 722; but one can hardly be sure. Whatever, the precise intention, the verse states the certainty of YHWH's corrective judgement.

There follows in 7:13 a cry of woe. Such a pronouncement can signify a denunciation or a lament. The following verses suggest that the sense of lament is primary. However, both senses may be present: YHWH expresses his sorrow that the people have rebelled against him, knowing that in consequence he will now send his destructive judgement. His sorrow is expressed in his desire is to redeem them. The meaning is equivalent to his desire to heal them expressed in 5:13; 7:1. They, however, speak lies against him.

---

[250] A. A. Macintosh *Hosea* (1997): 274.

C Commentary on Hosea 117

The speaking of lies reflects stock language drawn from psalms of lament (Pss. 4:2 [3]; 5:6 [7]; 58:3 [4]; 62: 4 [5]). YHWH's lament continues into 7:14–16. 'They do not cry to me from the heart' (7:14). This probably refers back to the people's expression of repentance in 6:1–3, to which the whole of 6:4–7:16 is a response. The gashing of themselves (7:14) is found as an Israelite practice in the context of grief (Jer. 16:6; 41:5), but as a means of soliciting an answer to prayer from the deity is found only in 1 Kings 18:28 as one practised by the prophets of Baal, thus providing a fleeting anti-Baalism reference in this section (5:8–7:16) which is otherwise concerned with Israel's reliance on foreign treaties, whereby they rebel against him. Yet, YHWH laments, it was he who had trained and strengthened their arms (7:15). The verb for 'trained' (*yāsar*) is the same as that found in 7:12 of his discipline. Despite this they plot evil, a sentiment which, like the speaking lies of 7:13, is drawn from stock language of lament (Pss. 43:1; 52:2, 4; 109:2). The meaning of the opening line of 7:16 is unclear, and NRSV adopts the most likely general sense, with that which does not profit being the foreign nations to which Israel turned. The people have become like a bow which has lost its tautness and become too slack to be of any use. Their attempts to ally themselves with Egypt will lead to their downfall. The last line of 7:16 is also difficult to translate. Mays and Davies both suggest 'This shall be their derision in the land of Egypt', and Dearman similarly 'This shall be their mockery':[251] in other words, Israel's actions will bring derision/mockery from the very nation to which they turn for help.

The theme of the futility of going to Egypt or Assyria for help and seeking to enter into treaties with them as a means of gaining security has, as noted, been a strong one in the section 5:8–7:16, and the final sentence of it reiterates it once more in respect of Egypt. As 5:13, 6:11b–7:1, 7:10, 7:13, and 7:15 all indicate, YHWH has wanted to be the people's healer, and to provide the safety and security that they seek, but the people have declined to turn to him to receive it. Their expression of repentance in 6:1–3 has proved to be shallow (6:6; 7:14). After a long internal dialogue (6:4–7:10) YHWH concludes that he must allow his judgement against them to be exercised (7:11–16). In the tug of war between YHWH's judgement and his mercy, at this point in the text it is his judgement which must be paramount. Only at the end of chapters 4–11 do these chapters allow that it might be otherwise (11:8–11).

---

[251] J. L. Mays *Hosea* (1969): 110, 113; G. I. Davies *Hosea* (1992): 193; J. A. Dearman *Hosea* (2010): 207, 215.

Bridging the Horizons: Israel's Alliances with Foreign Nations

It is a clear message of the book of Hosea that Israel's making of alliances with foreign nations, principally Egypt or Assyria, represents a failure to trust YHWH for protection and security. Dearman poses a pertinent question in respect of all this: 'Does this make Hosea an isolationist, someone who finds the inevitable compromises of diplomatic relationships reason to reject them?' He responds to his own question by writing that

> This is a possible way to read these expressions and the overall tone of the book, but it is not certain.... Hosea certainly regarded the diplomacy of his day as a compromise of Israel's holy identity and an affront to YHWH's sovereignty over his people. It is not clear that Hosea was opposed *in principle* to the political give-and-take with Egypt and Assyria, but that may have been the case. He is convinced that YHWH has not endorsed the actions and they are thus a betrayal of the covenant between people and Deity.[252]

Perhaps wisely, Dearman does not venture into whether there is any message in this for twenty-first-century readers. Certainly it would be hard to entertain the idea that God opposes international treaties and alliances, which can without doubt be vehicles of stability and peace. In seeking to bring together ancient and contemporary horizons, therefore, we must look to ancient Israel as a religious community rather than as a political entity. Religious believers will wish to hold an absolute loyalty to the God whom they worship and serve. While being willing to work with people of different faiths and religious traditions on issues important to all, they will nevertheless seek to avoid compromising that loyalty and the distinctiveness of their own faith tradition. They will also accept, with Hosea, that while alliances and compromises, both political and religious, have their place in this life, the ultimate bringer of peace and healing for the world will be Almighty God. Hence the lament that 'yet they do not return to the Lord their God, or seek him' (Hos. 7:10) is one which may well be found in their hearts and on their lips, expressed not in anger but in sadness, as is true of YHWH himself in Hosea 5:8–7:16.

---

[252] J. A. Dearman *Hosea* (2010): 209 (italics original).

C Commentary on Hosea

Hosea 8 – Israel Has Forgotten His Maker

8 Set the trumpet to your lips!
  One like a vulture is over the house of the LORD,
 because they have broken my covenant
  and transgressed my law.
² They cry to me,
  'My God, we know you!'
³ Israel has spurned the good;
  the enemy shall pursue him.

⁴ They made kings but not through me;
  they set up princes but without my knowledge.
 With their silver and gold they made idols
  for their own destruction.
⁵ Your calf is rejected, O Samaria.
  My anger burns against them.
 How long will they be incapable of innocence?
⁶ For it is from Israel,
 an artisan made it;
  it is not God.
 The calf of Samaria
  shall be broken to pieces.

⁷ For they sow the wind,
  and they shall reap the whirlwind.
 The standing grain has no heads;
  it shall yield no meal;
 if it were to yield,
  foreigners would devour it.
⁸ Israel is swallowed up;
  now they are among the nations
  as a useless vessel.
⁹ For they have gone up to Assyria,
  a wild ass wandering alone;
  Ephraim has bargained for lovers.
¹⁰ Though they bargain with the nations,
  I will now gather them up.
 They shall soon writhe
  under the burden of kings and princes.

¹¹ When Ephraim multiplied altars to expiate sin,
  they became to him altars for sinning.

120   *Book of Hosea*

^{12} Though I write for him the multitude of my instructions,
     they are regarded as a strange thing.
^{13} Though they offer choice sacrifices,
     though they eat flesh,
     the LORD does not accept them.
  Now he will remember their iniquity
     and punish their sins;
     they shall return to Egypt.
^{14} Israel has forgotten his Maker
     and built palaces,
  and Judah has multiplied fortified cities,
     but I will send a fire upon his cities,
     and it shall devour his strongholds.

The opening imperative of 8:1 indicates a new section of the text, with that of 9:1 similarly indicating a further new section. Thus chapter 8 constitutes a section in itself. While there are smaller units within it, there are varied views among commentators as to where these begin and end, and it is more helpful to treat the section as an entity. The preceding section 5:8–7:16 included an internal dialogue within YHWH himself (6:4–7:10) as to whether he would heal and restore or judge Ephraim. The conclusion in 7:10 is that Israel will not return to him, and the following 7:11–16 brings a clear message of judgement. Chapter 8 continues that message of judgement. The reasons for judgement are various: the breaking of YHWH's covenant and transgressing of his law (8:1b); Israel's spurning of goodness (8:3); their installation of kings and princes with no reference to YHWH (8:4a); their making of idols (8:4b); their worship of a calf-god (8:5–6); going to Assyria for help and protection (8:9); multiplying altars and sinning at them (8:11); regarding YHWH's instructions as strange (8:12); practising iniquity (8:13); the people's forgetting of their Maker and building of palaces and fortified cities (8:14).

It is widely held that 8:14 is an addition to the earliest form of the text. The second half of the verse is the formula found seven times in the series of oracles against the nations in Amos 1–2 and, as argued by Jeremias, presupposes knowledge of the Amos-text.[253] Jeremias considers that it was added, with 4:15, in the century 720–620. However, it was more likely added in the sixth-century redaction, for two reasons. Firstly, it brings Judah into the chapter for the first time, and the oracle against Judah in Amos 2:4–5 was

---

[253]   J. Jeremias 'Interrelationship' (1996): 175–6.

C Commentary on Hosea

itself not added into the Oracles against the Nations (OAN) series in Amos until the Exilic Redactional Composition of the Amos-text.[254] Secondly, the accusation that Israel has 'forgotten his Maker' reflects the exilic language of Second Isaiah (e.g. Isa. 51:13).[255] It is likely that the accusation in 8:6 that 'an artisan made it; it is not God' is also an exilic addition reflecting familiarity with the extended polemic of Isaiah 44:9–20 or similar material.[256] With exilic additions at the end and, probably, in the middle of the chapter, it is unsurprising to find the same in 8:1b. The presence of the concept of YHWH's covenant with Israel in this verse has generated much scholarly discussion. Some hold that it is an eighth-century, pre-Deuteronomic allusion that was subsequently developed more fully in Deuteronomy and writings influenced by it.[257] Others maintain that the reference to it in Hosea 8:1b is an addition made once the concept was already well established, something clearly the case by the exilic period.[258] Inevitably – and quite properly – the views held by particular scholars regarding this verse are enmeshed with their views concerning the emergence of the covenant concept. See 'A Closer Look: The Covenant Concept in Scholarly Research' that follows.

A Closer Look: The Covenant Concept in Scholarly Research

In his book *God and His People: Covenant and Theology in the Old Testament* (1986), Nicholson describes the swings in scholarly opinion regarding how early in Israel's history the concept of a covenant between YHWH and Israel originated and became part of Israel's traditions.[259] Wellhausen considered that this understanding of Israel's relationship with YHWH was a development which did not arise prior

---

[254] See the 'Introduction to Amos' and the commentary on Amos 2:4–5.

[255] So R. Albertz *Israel in Exile* (2003): 231. Alternatively the verse may have been added in the period Jeremias suggests if 8:14a read simply 'Israel has built palaces, and Judah has multiplied fortified cities', the parallelism of which reads well. The further addition linking to Isa. 51:13 would then have been made in the exilic period.

[256] R. Albertz *Israel in Exile* (2003): 231–2.

[257] *Inter alia*, but notably, J. Day 'Pre-Deuteronomic Allusions' (1986): 1–12 has argued for this position.

[258] *Inter alia*, but notably, L. Perlitt *Bundestheologie im Alten Testament* (1969): 146–52. R. Albertz *Israel in Exile* (2003): 231 comments almost in passing that 'since Perlitt … Hos 8:1b has been accepted almost unanimously as a Deuteronomistic interpolation'.

[259] E. W. Nicholson *God and His People* (1986). I have refrained from referencing every author and work referred to in this section in order to avoid a plethora of detailed footnotes. The reader is referred to Nicholson's book.

to the eighth-century prophets. Rather, their preaching contributed to its emergence. This explained the fact that the term *bərît* is not found in the eighth-century prophets as a description of that relationship other than in Hosea 8:1 and 6:7, which he took to be later additions to the text. Those who maintained the antiquity of the covenant concept came up with various explanations for its absence in the eighth-century prophets, such as the suggestion that even though the word *bərît* itself was not present other than in these two verses, nevertheless the concept was implied in the various images of YHWH used (e.g. king, father), or that the concept was so well understood by the eighth century that it did not need reiteration. But, Nicholson, suggests, it was only those who believed on other grounds that the concept was ancient who were persuaded by such suggestions. In the later part of the nineteenth and first part of the twentieth century, Wellhausen's arguments largely held sway. In the middle years of the twentieth century, however, the pendulum swung the other way, and the covenant concept was taken to be ancient, present from the earliest years following Israel's settling in the land. The influences and theories which brought this change about, described by Nicholson, were various. Form criticism, pioneered by Gunkel, entailed the likelihood that ancient, oral traditions were preserved in acts of cultic recitation. Eichrodt's *Theology of the Old Testament*, of which the German first edition was published in 1933, organised his presentation of Old Testament theology entirely around the covenant concept. Max Weber's sociological analysis put forward the idea that Israel was a political community that stood apart from and in contrast to all other nations because of God's concluding of a covenant with them. Alt argued for the antiquity of the patriarchal traditions, including the account in Genesis 15 of YHWH making a covenant with Abraham. Mowinckel had built on Gunkel's work and had developed the idea of a regular ceremony of covenant renewal at Israel's autumn festival (the Feast of Tabernacles), and von Rad traced the origins of this to the early, pre-monarchic period. Perhaps most significant of all, Nicholson suggests, was the compelling and detailed thesis put forward by Noth, that pre-monarchic Israel was constituted in a manner comparable to a Greek amphictyony, a community bound together by a common religion. That religion was founded, Noth argued, on the covenant between YHWH and his people. A further development strengthening the idea of the concept of covenant being early was the publication in 1954 and 1955 of articles by Mendenhall

C Commentary on Hosea

demonstrating, he argued, the similarity between fourteenth-century Hittite treaties and the covenant between YHWH and his people (scholars such as McCarthy argued, in contrast, that later Assyrian and other treaties had as many parallels). For a considerable period of time the view that the concept of a covenant between YHWH and Israel was ancient seemed unassailable. Nevertheless, in the later part of the twentieth century the portrayal of early Israelite society developed by Noth began to be questioned, and in due time the edifice of scholarly work which had been built on his foundations began to show cracks and to crumble. It is currently a minority of scholars (albeit a not insignificant minority) who hold to the view that the covenant concept is ancient. The concept itself was subjected to a searching analysis by Perlitt, who in 1969 published his *Bundestheologie im Alten Testament*, which Nicholson describes as 'the most detailed presentation yet of the view that Israel's covenant traditions are the product of a late period in its history ... in the literature of Deuteronomy and the Deuteronomistic corpus of the seventh and sixth centuries'.[260] This explains its absence from the books of the eighth-century prophets.

The treatment of Hosea 6:7 and 8:1 by commentators is inevitably influenced by their views concerning the antiquity or otherwise of the covenant concept. In turn, interpretation of these verses feeds into ongoing debates concerning the dating of its emergence. This commentary considers that both verses entered the text in the sixth-century exilic redaction, and accepts the premise that the developed expression of the covenant concept found in Deuteronomy and works influenced by it was not earlier than the seventh and sixth centuries. The reader will do well, however, to be aware that there have been varying scholarly opinions held since the 1870s, and that there is currently little scholarly consensus on a range of questions related to the origins and early history of ancient Israel, the dating of relevant texts, and the chronology of the development of the covenant concept.

It may be taken, then, that the earliest, eighth-century text has been expanded in 8:1b, 6, 14 in the exilic redaction. All three expansions add to the range of reasons for judgement that the chapter gives. Hosea 8:14 includes Judah with Israel, and adds the announcement of judgement drawn from Amos 1–2.

---

[260] E. W. Nicholson *God and His People* (1986): 109.

The chapter opens with what is justifiably translated by NRSV as an imperative (the Hebrew lacks a verb, reading simply 'To your lip a trumpet!'). The address could be to the prophet or, more probably, to an imagined sentinel warning of the enemy of 8:3. The sounding of the *šōpār* (NRSV 'trumpet') recalls the *šōpār* (NRSV 'horn') in the opening verse of the preceding section 5:8–7:16, and mention of 'the enemy' in 8:3 echoes the theme of warfare which characterised 5:8–14. If the sentinel looks, 8:1 says, he will see a vulture/eagle over the house of YHWH. By house of YHWH may be meant, on this occasion, not a particular sanctuary, but rather the land of YHWH.[261] The word *nešer* is identified by some as the griffon-vulture, a sinister predator, but in some contexts refers rather to a soaring eagle (e.g. Isa. 40:31).[262] Several biblical passages employ the image of an enemy swooping like a vulture/eagle (Deut. 28:49; Jer. 4:13; 48:40; Lam. 4:19; Hab. 1:8). In the light of impending disaster Israel cries out to YHWH (8:2), a possible fleeting allusion back to 7:14. In the exilic redaction the various reasons for judgement that the chapter will go on to describe are summed up in the accusation 'because they have broken my covenant and transgressed my law' (8:1b). The connecting *ya'an* (because) is a further pointer to the exilic origin of this verse, being found mainly in exilic and later texts (thirty-seven times in Ezekiel; also Isa. 61:1; 65:12; 66:4; Hag. 1:9), although it is not unknown in earlier texts (e.g. Amos 5:11). The parallelism of 'covenant' and 'law' indicates the developed concept of YHWH's covenant with Israel as found in Deuteronomistic literature. In the commentary on 4:6 it was suggested that the word *tôrâ* might be better translated, in that context, as 'instruction' or 'teaching' rather than 'law'; here in 8:1, however, it is clearly the law of YHWH that is meant, which the people are meant to follow as their response to YHWH's making of his covenant with them.

In 8:3 the accusation that Israel has 'spurned the good' is a general one. In Amos 5:14 Israel was urged to 'seek good'; Hosea 8:3 accuses Israel of failing to do so. Consequently an enemy will pursue him. It is understood that this is YHWH's action in judgement. The nation is not named, and Dearman comments that 'it could be Assyria, Egypt or Damascus, all of whom sought to seize and control Israel', while Nogalski comments that 'in the eighth-century literary setting, this enemy can only be understood as Assyria, who will destroy Samaria (the capital of the northern kingdom) and exile the

---

[261] So J. Krispenz 'Idolatry, Apostasy, Prostitution' (2016): 24; A. A. Macintosh *Hosea* (1997): 292; H. W. Wolff *Hosea* (1974): 137.

[262] BDB: 676 notes that it refers 'perhaps not always' to the griffon-vulture.

C Commentary on Hosea

people in 722'.[263] The lack of specification is perhaps deliberate, allowing readers in subsequent centuries to relate the verse to whatever empire or nation was a threat in their time.

The accusations of 8:4 are more specific, but nevertheless allow various possible meanings. The first is that the people made kings with no reference to YHWH. This has three possible interpretations. Firstly, it could refer to the series of coups and assassinations that characterised the later years of the northern kingdom's existence.[264] Secondly, it could imply rejection of the whole northern monarchy, with the southern, Davidic monarchy being considered that approved by YHWH. Thirdly, it could indicate a rejection of kingship *per se*.[265] Dearman is correct in writing that, in regard of the book as a whole, we 'cannot ... know for certain whether Hosea was anti-monarchical in principle ... a monarchist who saw grave problems with the royal administration of his day; or more particularly a northern prophet who preferred the Davidic dynasty'.[266] He himself is disinclined to think that Hosea opposed monarchy in and of itself, and makes the point that the book is critical of priests, but that scholars do not deduce from this that it is against priesthood as an institution.[267] Contrastingly, Machinist evaluates all the references in the text to kingship, and finds it certain that 'Hosea is troubled by more than simply the problem caused by one or two kings. For, as his kingship passages reveal, it is not only individual kings of the North who are going to be punished by Yahweh; it is the entire monarchy, and so the state, that Yahweh is to end because of its crimes.'[268] Linked with the making of kings is that Israel 'set up princes, but without my knowledge' (8:4). The term 'princes' has already been used in 5:10 and 7:3, 5 (where NRSV translates as 'officials'), and the pair 'kings and princes/officials' may be taken to signify the whole apparatus of government.

The accusation flows on into a related accusation in 8:4b–5: the people have made idols of silver and gold, including the royal calf-god. The silver and gold idols of 8:4 could refer to small figurines belonging to families

---

[263] J. A. Dearman *Hosea* (2010): 219; J. D. Nogalski *Hosea–Jonah* (2011): 118.

[264] So H. W. Wolff *Hosea* (1974): 139.

[265] So J. M. Bos *Reconsidering* (2013): 48–53.

[266] J. A. Dearman *Hosea* (2010): 43.

[267] J. A. Dearman *Hosea* (2010): 221. J. M. Bos *Reconsidering* (2013): 168, however, entertains the possibility that the book emanates from the early Persian period Jerusalem priesthood and is opposed to the institution of the priesthood at Bethel.

[268] P. Machinist, 'Hosea and the Ambiguity of Kingship in Ancient Israel', in J. T. Strong and S. V. Tuell (eds.), *Constituting the Community: Studies on the Polity of Ancient Israel in Honor of S. Dean McBride Jr.* (Winona Lake, IN: Eisenbrauns, 2005): 153–81 (174).

126   *Book of Hosea*

and clans within the nation, but the calf-god referred to is undoubtedly that established by Jeroboam I at Bethel (1 Kgs 12:26–30). Its royal instigation and subsequent patronage is what links the accusation of 8:4a with those of 8:4b–5: the political and the religious spheres are not separate. The designation of the calf-god as the calf of Samaria (8:5, 6) is unique. There is no archaeological or literary evidence of a sanctuary with a calf-god having ever existed in Samaria. For example, 1 Kings 16:32 refers to Ahab erecting 'an altar for Baal in the house of Baal, which he built in Samaria', and 2 Kings 10:26–27 refers to its destruction by Jehu, but there is no indication that this contained a calf-god. But with the calf-god at Bethel being effectively the national god of the northern kingdom, and hence of its capital Samaria, the description of it as the calf of Samaria is perfectly appropriate. In setting up the calf-gods at Bethel and Dan, Jeroboam I (or his Deuteronomistic interpreter) proclaimed 'Here are your gods, O Israel, who brought you up out of the land of Egypt' (1 Kgs 12:28), indicating that the calf-god was intended as a focus of Yahwistic worship. It has been much debated whether the bull-calf was intended as a representation of YHWH or as a pedestal on which it was imagined that the deity was seated.[269] Either way, Hosea 8:5 pronounces that it is 'rejected': the verb is the same as that used in 8:3 for the people's spurning of the good. The exilic editors add to the text that it had been made by an artisan, and could not possibly be God.[270] The people's and kings' making of idols causes YHWH's anger (*'ap*) to burn against them (8:5). Hosea uses the word *'ap* here (and in 11:9; 13:11; 14:4 [5]), always with the first-person suffix (my) and in divine speech. The stirring of YHWH's wrath will lead to the destruction of the calf-god (8:6). The Decalogue contains a commandment against the making of idols (Exod. 20:4), and Dearman comments that it is 'likely that Hosea criticizes his contemporaries for something that had been part of Yahwistic worship for some time, namely depicting YHWH in bovine form, but that does not make his criticism innovative'.[271]

Hosea 8:7 uses two proverbial sayings to describe the judgement of YHWH in response to the reasons for judgement of 8:4–6. Both suggest

---

[269] See e.g. Y. H. Chung, *The Sin of the Calf: The Rise of the Bible's Negative Attitude toward the Golden Calf* (LHBOTS, 523; London/New York: Bloomsbury/T&T Clark, 2010): 11–14; J. F. Gomes *Sanctuary at Bethel* (2006): 25–8; J. R. Spencer, 'Golden Calf', ABD 2: 1065–9 (1068).

[270] Other than here the term 'artisan/craftsman' (*ḥārāš*) is found in exilic passages, and notably in the critique of the making of images in Isa. 44:11–13, where it occurs three times in succession (NRSV's 'blacksmith' in 44:12 being 'craftsman of iron' and 'carpenter' of 44:13 being 'craftsman of woods' (see further BDB: 360).

[271] J. A. Dearman *Hosea* (2010): 40.

C Commentary on Hosea

an element of Israel bringing judgement on herself. Forms of the first –
that people reap in accordance with what they sow – are found in Job 4:8;
Proverbs 22:8; and, in the New Testament, in 2 Corinthians 9:6; Galatians
6:7–9. The second contains a rare occurrence of Hebrew rhyme: 'Grain
without head (*semah*) will not produce meal (*qemah*).'[272] The last line of
8:7 – 'if it were to yield, foreigners would devour it' – reads a little strangely,
but has the same logic of 'even if not that, then this' as is found in Amos 5:19.
The description of judgement continues in plainer, direct terms in 8:8: Israel
will be swallowed up (the verb is the same as that of NRSV's 'devour' in the
previous verse) and dispersed among the nations. She will be a 'useless vessel', words used of Coniah in Jeremiah 22:28 and Moab in Jeremiah 48:38.
Hosea 8:9 resumes reasons for judgement which link back to Ephraim's
going to Assyria in 5:13. He is described as a wild ass. The Hebrew *pĕre'* is a
pun on *'eprayim* (Ephraim). In contemporary idiom an ass symbolises stu-
pidity, but the association here should be taken to be with lust, comparable
to Jeremiah 2:24 describing an ass in heat. Israel has lusted after Assyria and
has bargained for (or, it could be translated, 'sold herself for') lovers. The
meaning of 8:10b is unclear; Sweeney sees it as having a sexual innuendo.[273]
What is sure is that it signifies a judgement, as the gathering them up of
8:10a indicates: the same verb is used in Joel 3:2 [4:2] and Zephaniah 3:8 to
describe YHWH's gathering of the nations for judgement.

Hosea 8:11 is thematically linked to 4:7–11. In 4:7 it is the priests whose
sins grow as their numbers increase. In 8:11 the altars at which priests offer
sacrifice are now said to be not places to expiate sin, but to increase sinning.
The Hebrew for NRSV's 'expiate sin' and 'for sinning' is identical, increasing
the irony which NRSV's translation successfully captures. The multiplicity
of altars is condemned also in 10:1, as are places of sacrifice in 4:13. Hosea
8:12 condemns Israel for rejecting the 'multitude of my instructions' that
YHWH wrote for him. What are these instructions/laws that YHWH has
given, and what is the extent of them? It may be the Decalogue that is meant
(see 'A Closer Look: Hosea and the Ten Commandments'). Alternatively the
preposition 'though' could mean 'if' and the assumption not be made that
commandments had actually been written. Dearman translates thus, commenting that the 'essential point seems to be that even if such a collection
existed, Israel would not recognise its authority'.[274] In the spirit of 6:6, the

---

[272] The translation is that of J. L. Mays *Hosea* (1969): 113, 120.
[273] M. A. Sweeney *Twelve Prophets* 1 (2000): 90–1.
[274] J. A. Dearman *Hosea* (2010): 231 (translation 227).

128   *Book of Hosea*

following verse 8:13 states that with YHWH's instructions ignored, sacrifices to him are of no avail: their sacrifices will not be accepted. The declaration is close to that of Amos 5:22 (see the commentary *ad loc*). The concluding announcement of judgement in the earliest, eighth-century text is that YHWH will remember their iniquity and punish their sins (an announcement repeated in 9:9), and they shall return to Egypt. The Egypt to which Ephraim shall return may be, in this verse, the land of slavery remembered in Israel's ancient traditions, or it may be the great power referred to in parallel with Assyria in 7:11. The threat that Israel shall return to Egypt is found also in 9:3 and 11:5, in both of which Egypt and Assyria are in parallel. This suggests that it is the later Egypt, contemporary with Assyria, that is meant. That is not to deny, however, a possible (and possibly deliberate) echo also of the ancient traditions. Readers in later centuries, long after the demise of Assyria, may have found the latter reference to be the stronger.

The exilic redactors added a new ending in 8:14 (see the opening paragraphs of this section on 'Hosea 8 – Israel Has Forgotten His Maker'). Accusations are made that Israel has forgotten his Maker (cf. Isa. 51:13) and built palaces and that Judah has multiplied fortified cities.[275] The verb 'multiplied' links Judah's multiplication of fortified cities to Ephraim's multiplication of altars in 8:11. The addition serves to widen the focus of the whole chapter to include Judah as well as Israel: Judah's guilt led to the destruction of Jerusalem in 587 just as surely as Israel's guilt led to the destruction of Samaria in 722. The judgement announced in 8:14b refers the reader to the Amos-text, from which it is drawn, and thereby invites exilic and post-exilic readers to hear the message of both books if they wish to understand the reasons for YHWH's actions.

Hosea 9:1–9 – 'Do Not Rejoice, O Israel'

9 Do not rejoice, O Israel!
      Do not exult as other nations do,
   for you have prostituted yourself, departing from your God.
      You have loved a prostitute's pay
      on all threshing floors.
² Threshing floor and wine vat shall not feed them,
      and the new wine shall fail them.

---

[275] The word *hēkāl* can mean 'palace' or 'temple'. The parallelism with fortified cities suggests that 'palaces' is the better translation here.

C Commentary on Hosea

³ They shall not remain in the land of the LORD,
   but Ephraim shall return to Egypt,
   and in Assyria they shall eat unclean food.

⁴ They shall not pour drink offerings of wine to the LORD,
   and their sacrifices shall not please him.
Such sacrifices shall be like mourners' bread;
   all who eat of it shall be defiled,
for their bread shall be for their hunger only;
   it shall not come to the house of the LORD.

⁵ What will you do on the day of appointed festival
   and on the day of the festival of the LORD?
⁶ For even if they escape destruction,
   Egypt shall gather them;
   Memphis shall bury them.
Nettles shall possess their precious things of silver;
   thorns shall be in their tents.

⁷ The days of punishment have come;
   the days of recompense have come.
   Israel will cry out,
'The prophet is a fool,
   the man of the spirit is mad!'
Because of your great iniquity,
   your hostility is great.
⁸ The prophet is a sentinel for my God over Ephraim,
yet a hunter's snare is on all his ways
   and hostility in the house of his God.
⁹ They have deeply corrupted themselves
   as in the days of Gibeah;
he will remember their iniquity;
   he will punish their sins.

The imperative of 9:1 indicates a new section of text, which concludes in 9:9. Verses 1, 5, and 7 all contain second-person address while the remainder is in the third person. However it is, in this instance, unnecessary to attribute these verses to different sources or literary layers. Similarly it is not problematic that verses 1 and 7 name Israel while verses 3 and 8 name Ephraim (see 'A Closer Look: "Ephraim" in Hosea'). Apart from one half-verse (9:4b) the whole of 9:1–6 was present in the earliest, late eighth-century composition of the text. To it, 9:7–9 was appended in the seventh century, its conclusion repeating from 8:13b that YHWH will remember their iniquity and punish their sins.

Hosea 9:5 refers to 'the day of the appointed festival' and the 'day of the festival of YHWH'. The references to threshing floors in 9:1–2 suggest that a harvest festival is in view, in particular the Festival of Booths/Tabernacles (Sukkoth), at which the harvests of grapes and olives were gathered. For the duration of the seven-day festival the people were to live in booths/tents. In origin this was probably to make the most of the length of day, but in due course the priestly writer associated it with the people's sojourn in the wilderness after their exodus from Egypt (Lev. 23:39–43). Among commentators seeking to match sections of the text with particular events in the ministry of the prophet, Wolff deduces that Hosea made a prophetic intervention into such a festival. Macintosh considers, rather, that 9:1–7 constitutes the prophet's reflections on the implications of YHWH's sentence of judgement in 8:13.[276] Among those who take a literary approach to the text Bos agrees that the festival of Sukkoth is in view and, in accordance with his late dating of the text, sees the section as dependent on Deuteronomy 16: 13–15 and Leviticus 23:39–43. Ben Zvi acknowledges the allusion to Sukkoth, but does not consider that the reader's response necessarily entails such recognition in order to hold meaning: 'readers may identify the situation in the world of the book as the festival of Sukkoth, but they are certainly not required to do so'.[277]

In the literary setting of Hosea 4–11, the section appears to have been placed deliberately following 8:1–13. Its greater part announces judgement on Israel, but interwoven with such announcements are reasons for them. The section reinforces the themes from earlier parts of chapters 4–11 of Israel's prostitution (9:1 cf. 4:10–16; 5:3–4; 6:10) and of Egypt and Assyria (9:3, 6 cf. 5:8–7:16; 8:9, 13).

The negative imperative of 9:1 reverses the usual expectation of a festival time. Whereas Deuteronomy 16:14 and Leviticus 23:40 invite the people to rejoice, Hosea 9:1 says not to rejoice, nor to exult as other nations do. The reason is nothing to do with Israel's distinctiveness from the nations, but rather indicates that, unlike the nations, Israel stands under YHWH's judgement.[278] The reason is that Israel has prostituted herself (pre-2021 NRSV: played the whore). Within chapters 4–11, this accusation has already been met in 4:10–12 (see the commentary *ad loc*), where it is specified that this prostitution consists of forsaking YHWH (4:10), their God (4:12); and in

---

[276] H. W. Wolff *Hosea* (1974): 151–3; A. A. Macintosh *Hosea* (1997): 335–6.
[277] J. M. Bos *Reconsidering* (2013): 148–52; E. Ben Zvi *Hosea* (2005): 196.
[278] A. A. Macintosh *Hosea* (1997): 337.

C Commentary on Hosea

5:3–4; 6:10. Hosea 9:1 adds the accusation that Israel has loved a prostitute's pay 'on all threshing floors', a term repeated in the next verse. In 2 Samuel 24:18 the prophet Gad instructs David to erect an altar on the threshing floor of Araunah, and in 1 Kings 22:10 the kings of Israel and Judah hold conference in one while prophets prophesy before them. Whether such allusions indicate, as some have argued, that threshing floors could double as places of sacrifice is uncertain, but Hosea 9:4 shows that sacrifice was part of the keeping of the festival. Firstly, however, 9:2 pronounces that threshing floor and wine vat will fail the people, picking up the theme of lack of grain in 8:7 and, in 2:9 [11], YHWH's taking back of grain and wine. The punishment of lack of grain and wine is followed immediately by that of removal from the land. The threat that they shall return to Egypt is repeated from 8:13 (on which see the commentary). The threat of exile to Assyria is a new one. While Assyria has featured as a power to which Israel has mistakenly turned (5:13; 7:11; 8:9), now it is a power which will carry them off. In the foreign land to which they will be taken they will have to eat unclean food, a threat made also to sixth-century Judah in Ezekiel 4:13.

It is probable that 9:4 should also be taken as describing the coming time of punishment: they will not be able to make offerings and sacrifices pleasing to YHWH in a foreign land. 'To be exiled from the land necessarily involves being cut off from the worship of the God of the land. It is thus impossible to offer such worship in a heathen (i.e. unclean) land where other gods hold sway.'[279] That their sacrifices 'shall not please him' is cultic language (e.g. Jer. 6:20; Mal. 3:4). The significance of 'mourners' bread' is that contact with a dead body made one unclean and, by extension, bread eaten during the time of mourning was also unacceptable as an offering (Deut. 26:14). All bread eaten in exile would be deemed, similarly, to defile those who ate it. It would feed them, but could not be offered to YHWH. If the final sentence 'it shall not come near to the house of YHWH' is original to the earliest, late eighth-century composition of the Hosea-text, the 'house of YHWH' must indicate the land as in 8:1 (see the commentary *ad loc*). However the context in 9:4 makes it more likely that the Temple in Jerusalem is meant, in the light of which many commentators take the line to have been added subsequently. Wolff takes it to be an early Judaic addition along with 1:7 and 3:5, verses which were both inserted, he suggests, as hopeful words in respect of Judah;[280] its purpose was to exempt Judah from the judgement described.

---

[279] A. A. Macintosh *Hosea* (1997): 345.
[280] H. W. Wolff *Hosea* (1974): xxxi.

Macintosh takes the whole of 'for their bread ... house of YHWH' to have been added in the sixth-century Babylonian exile of Judah, and sees it as expressing the hope that one day bread will not just be eaten for sustenance but will be offered at a restored Temple in Jerusalem.[281] Macintosh's view is to be preferred. The purpose of the addition was to extend words relating to Israel's exile to Judah's exile in Babylon.

The rhetorical question of 9:5 reinforces the impossibility of keeping a festival of YHWH in a foreign land, and the sense of desperation is enlarged still further in 9:6. Any who fled the Assyrians might well seek refuge in Egypt, as we know that some Judeans did following the destruction of Jerusalem in the sixth century (Jer. 42–43). Were they to do so, Egypt would gather them up not into safety, but into the extensive burial grounds at Memphis. Macintosh calls this 'a meditative expansion of the terse judgment of 8:13b "they shall return to Egypt"'.[282] The translation and meaning of 9:6b are unclear, but that they are words of judgement is not to be doubted. The tents to which judgement will reach could be the booths lived in for seven days at Sukkoth. But the word is also used to refer to houses/homes (e.g. Judg. 19:9).

In the earliest composition, 9:6 was the end of a section, but in the seventh-century redaction 9:7–9 was added as a new conclusion. A number of considerations point to 9:7–9 having entered the text in this redaction. Firstly, NRSV correctly captures the past tense of the verbs in 9:7a: the punishment has already taken place. Secondly, the theme of the rejection of the prophetic message as a reason for judgement (9:7) is one which came into prominence in this period. Williamson writes that 'there emerged the view that the fall of the kingdom was as much due to the rejection of the prophetic word as it was to the offences which gave rise to that word'.[283] This theme is clearly evident in Amos 7:9–17, which has links to this same theme in the Deuteronomistic History (2 Kgs 17:13–18): it was brought into both Amos and Hosea 9:7–9 in their late pre-exilic redactional compositions. Thirdly, the designation of the prophet as a sentinel (*ṣôpeh*) is first found in Jeremiah 6:17, and then in Ezekiel (3:16–21; 33:2–9). Possibly the

---

[281] A. A. Macintosh *Hosea* (1997): 345–6.

[282] A. A. Macintosh *Hosea* (1997): 350.

[283] H. G. M. Williamson, 'The Prophet and the Plumb-Line: A Redaction-Critical Study of Amos 7', *OTS* 26 (1990): 101–21; repr. R. P. Gordon (ed.), *The Place is Too Small for Us: The Israelite Prophets in Recent Scholarship* (SBTS, 5; Winona Lake, IN: Eisenbrauns, 1995): 453–77 (469–70).

C Commentary on Hosea

blowing of the *šôpār* in 8:1 led to the seventh-century redactors introducing this designation into 9:8. Fourthly, there is a loose borrowing of the theme of the hunter (pre-2021 NRSV: fowler) (9:8) from 7:12 and a direct copying of the phrase 'days of Gibeah' (9:9) from 10:9. Fifthly, the closing assertion that 'he will remember their iniquity, he will punish their sins' is a repetition from 8:13b. While the direction of dependence between overlapping themes and direct repetitions is always debatable, the combination of these considerations points to 9:7–9 having entered the text in this period.

The meaning of 9:7 is uncertain. NRSV's 'will cry out' (pre-2021 NRSV: cries) follows LXX rather than MT's 'knows'. The LXX reading entails one different consonant in the Hebrew, reading ר rather than ד, a not infrequent confusion. NRSV's placing of quotation marks around 'The prophet is a fool, the man of the spirit is mad!' follows the interpretation of several commentators who take the words to be uttered by Hosea's opponents; or, if MT is followed, a sarcastic 'Israel knows that the prophet is a fool …' An alternative view is that the words are not a quotation, but constitute an accusation against another prophet who failed to warn of impending disaster.[284] There are places in the Hebrew Bible which show that the view of prophets as madmen was abroad, including the somewhat amusing episode of Jehu's anointing as king by a prophet in 2 Kings 9:11–13: Jehu's companions ask 'Why did that madman come to you?' and then, when told, promptly act on the prophet's words and proclaim Jehu as king. The term 'man of the spirit' (Hos. 9:7) is unusual, but may be taken as equivalent to the more frequent 'man of God' (e.g. 1 Sam. 9:6; 1 Kgs 12:22). The spirit (*rûaḥ*) is associated with prophecy in narratives such as 1 Samuel 10:1–13. For seventh-century readers in Judah the verse reminds them that the words of the prophets are not to be rejected. The final couplet of 9:7 is accusation, referring to Israel's iniquity and hostility. The first term is a frequent one in Hosea (5:5; 8:13; 9:7, 9; 10:10; 12:8 [9]; 13:12; 14:1, 2 [2, 3]), while the second is found only here and in the next verse. The translation and meaning of 9:8 is also difficult. The Hebrew could quite naturally be read as seeing Ephraim as a sentinel, but the word 'prophet' then sits awkwardly. More likely is (as NRSV) that we have the idea of prophet as sentinel. The hunter's snare indicates YHWH's judgement cast over Ephraim. Hosea 9:9 states that the people have corrupted themselves. They have done so as in 'the days of Gibeah'. The reference is to something well known to the ancient readers, very

---

[284] So S. A. Irvine, 'Enmity in the House of God (Hosea 9:7–9)', *JBL* 117 (1998): 645–53 (647–8).

134   *Book of Hosea*

probably the appalling events of the rape and killing of a certain Levite's concubine described in Judges 19–21. The reference is sometimes taken as having anti-monarchic overtones, since Saul's residence as king was there (1 Sam. 10:26; 11:4); if so, the overtones are faint. The section concludes with the repeated statement from 8:13b that YHWH will remember the people's iniquity and punish their sins. Dearman finds the conclusion 'somewhat anticlimactic' because of its repetition,[285] an observation in marked contrast to Wolff's assertion that 9:7–9 represents 'the climax of the disputes' in Hosea 4–11, which is followed by 'a more reflective manner of speech' from 9:10 onwards.[286] Perhaps, however, the two views are not entirely opposite. While the final couplet of 9:9 is somewhat unimaginative, it is evident that 9:1–9 draws from and summarises several themes from earlier in the text. After the textual obscurities of 9:7–8, the meaning of 9:9 is clear: Judean readers looking back to 722 would know that YHWH had indeed remembered the northern kingdom, and had allowed their destruction: it was now for them not to make the same mistakes.

Hosea 9:10–10:15 – Agricultural Similes and Metaphors of Israel

> [10] Like grapes in the wilderness,
>> I found Israel.
>> Like the first fruit on the fig tree,
>>> in its first season,
>>> I saw your ancestors.
>> But they came to Baal-peor
>>> and consecrated themselves to a thing of shame
>>> and became detestable like the thing they loved.
> [11] Ephraim's glory shall fly away like a bird –
>> no birth, no pregnancy, no conception!
> [12] Even if they bring up children,
>> I will bereave them until no one is left.
>> Woe to them indeed
>>> when I depart from them!
> [13] Once I saw Ephraim as a young palm planted in a lovely meadow,
>> but now Ephraim must lead out his children for slaughter.
> [14] Give them, O Lord –
>> what will you give?

---

[285]   J. A. Dearman *Hosea* (2010): 249.
[286]   H. W. Wolff *Hosea* (1974): 161.

C Commentary on Hosea

Give them a miscarrying womb
and dry breasts.
¹⁵ Every evil of theirs began at Gilgal;
there I came to hate them.
Because of the wickedness of their deeds
I will drive them out of my house.
I will love them no more;
all their officials are rebels.
¹⁶ Ephraim is stricken,
their root is dried up,
they shall bear no fruit.
Even though they give birth,
I will kill the cherished offspring of their womb.
¹⁷ Because they have not listened to him,
my God will reject them;
they shall become wanderers among the nations.

10 Israel is a luxuriant vine
that yields its fruit.
The more his fruit increased,
the more altars he built;
as his country improved,
he improved his pillars.
² Their heart is false;
now they must bear their guilt.
The LORD will break down their altars,
and destroy their pillars.

³ For now they will say:
'We have no king,
for we do not fear the LORD,
and a king – what could he do for us?'
⁴ They utter mere words;
with empty oaths they make covenants;
so litigation springs up like poisonous weeds
in the furrows of the field.
⁵ The inhabitants of Samaria tremble
for the calf of Beth-aven.
Its people shall mourn for it,
and its idolatrous priests shall wail over it,
over its glory that has departed from it.
⁶ The thing itself shall be carried to Assyria
as tribute to the great king.

Ephraim shall be put to shame,
  and Israel shall be ashamed of his idol.

7 Samaria's king shall perish
  like a chip on the face of the waters.
8 The high places of Aven, the sin of Israel,
  shall be destroyed.
Thorn and thistle shall grow up
  on their altars.
They shall say to the mountains, 'Cover us',
  and to the hills, 'Fall on us.'

9 Since the days of Gibeah you have sinned, O Israel;
  there they have continued.
  Shall not war overtake them in Gibeah?
10 I will come against the wayward people to punish them,
  and nations shall be gathered against them
  when they are punished for their double iniquity.

11 Ephraim was a trained heifer
  that loved to thresh,
  and I spared her fair neck,
but I will make Ephraim break the ground;
  Judah must plough;
  Jacob must harrow for himself.
12 Sow for yourselves righteousness;
  reap steadfast love;
  break up your fallow ground;
for it is time to seek the LORD,
  that he may come and rain righteousness upon you.

13 You have ploughed wickedness;
  you have reaped injustice;
  you have eaten the fruit of lies.
Because you have trusted in your chariots,
  and in the multitude of your warriors,
14 therefore the tumult of war shall rise against your people,
  and all your fortresses shall be destroyed,
as Shalman destroyed Beth-arbel on the day of battle,
  when mothers were dashed in pieces with their children.
15 Thus it shall be done to you, O Bethel,
  because of your great wickedness.
At dawn the king of Israel
  shall be utterly cut off.

C Commentary on Hosea

Hosea 9:10 opens a section with various agricultural similes and metaphors of Israel: he is like grapes in the wilderness and fruit on a fig tree (9:10); a luxuriant vine (10:1); a trained heifer (10:11). While there are no opening or concluding formulae to define it as a section, the pictorial language distinguishes it from what precedes. The following section which begins in 11:1 is also a simile, of Israel as YHWH's son. Both sections refer back to Israel's election traditions: her time in the wilderness (9:10) and the exodus (11:1). Within 9:10–10:15 are three natural sub-sections, each beginning with reference to 'Israel' (9:10–17; 10:1–8; 10:9–15), and several commentators treat the three separately. However they are closely related, and are best taken together as one literary section. It contains several allusions to earlier portions of the text.

The first simile is that Israel is like grapes in the wilderness and, by implication, that YHWH was like a thirsty traveller delighted to find them. Whether the finding of grapes in a desert is intended to be a miraculous happening or whether the image is of a traveller stumbling on an oasis where grapes might grow is unimportant. What matters is that YHWH the traveller finds delight in them. Paired with this first simile is a second one: Israel is like the first fruit on the fig tree.[287] Isaiah 28:4 describes the pleasure in a 'first-ripe fig before the summer; whoever sees it, eats it up as soon as it comes to hand'. There may be sensual overtones to these images. Song of Songs 2:13 has the lover declare: 'The fig tree puts forth its figs, and the vines are in blossom; they give forth fragrance. Arise, my love, my fair one, and come away.' These similes speak of Israel's past and of an election tradition (also in 2:14–15 [16–17]) of the wilderness as a positive time in her history, when YHWH found delight in her. While the name 'Ephraim' predominates in 9:10–17 (see 'A Closer Look: "Ephraim" in Hosea'), the name 'Israel' is used in 9:10, since the tradition concerned the ancestors of both kingdoms of northern Israel and Judah. Wolff sees here a 'finding' tradition, distinct from and supplementing those of the Pentateuch, in which the wilderness is the key time in YHWH making Israel his people.[288] While such a hypothesis is unnecessary, it is the case that this positive view of the time in the

---

[287] The phrase 'in its first season' is metrically superfluous and absent from LXX. It may have been added by a scribe seeking to expand the sense of freshness of the fruit.

[288] H. W. Wolff *Hosea* (1974): 164. See also G. von Rad, *Old Testament Theology*, vol. 1 (London: SCM, 1975): 177 n. 3, who sees it as 'obviously old but which has been almost completely overlaid by the Exodus tradition which alone became dominant'. Both cite R. Bach, 'Die Erwählung Israels in der Wüste', *Theologische Literaturzeitung* 78 (1953): 67.

138   *Book of Hosea*

wilderness (found elsewhere, specifically, only in Deut. 32:10 and Jer. 2:2[289])
is at odds with the dominant understanding of the Hebrew Bible that the
people constantly murmured, complained, and rebelled in the wilderness.

The blessed time described in 9:10a is, however, short-lived. The ancient
traditions knew too of events concerning Baal-peor. Numbers 25:1–5 tells of
the Israelites joining the Moabites in offering sacrifice to Baal-peor and the
men of Israel having sexual relations with Moabite women. While in Hosea
9:10 Baal-peor is a place name rather than the name of a deity, there seems
little doubt that the same episode is in view.[290] It is not necessary to postulate
that the editors of the earliest Hosea-text had access to the written account
of Numbers 25:1–5. The existence of an oral tradition is sufficient and more
probable.[291] Readers in later centuries, of course, could read and compare
both texts. At Baal-peor, according to Hosea 9:10, the Israelites 'consecrated
themselves to a thing of shame'. The verb *nāzar* ('consecrate/set apart') is
that from which the term 'Nazirite' is derived. Nazirites were people set
apart and consecrated to YHWH (see 'A Closer Look: The Nazirites'), but
here Israel's consecration is to *bōšet* ('a thing of shame'). In Jeremiah 11:13
bōšet is in parallel to Baal, and the word could be used as an alternative
to the name Baal, as in calling Saul's son Ishbaal by the name Ishbosheth
(2 Sam. 2:8 cf. 1 Chron. 8:33; 9:39). Whether or not the god at Baal-peor is
the same Baal as the Canaanite fertility god, within the world of the text the
people's sin is one and the same thing, namely idolatry, sacrificing to Baal,
and immorality. The result is that the people themselves became as detestable as the Baal to whom they sacrifice (cf. Ps. 135:18: 'Those who make them
and all who trust in them shall become like them'). NRSV's 'like the thing
they loved' is better translated 'like him whom they loved', that is, Baal.

While 9:10 describes the past, it is evident from the punishment
announced in 9:11–12 that past and present sin are seen as indistinguish-
able: the detestable ways of the people's ancestors are matched by those of
the present generation. It is said, firstly, that Ephraim's glory shall fly away.

---

[289]   It may also lie behind the imagery of Ezek. 16.

[290]   With the majority of scholars, and contra G. R. Boudreau, 'Hosea and the Pentateuchal
        Tradition: The Case of the Baal of Peor', in M. P. Graham et al. (eds.), *History and
        Interpretation: Essays in Honour of John H. Hayes* (JSOTSup, 173; Sheffield: JSOT Press,
        1993): 121–32, whose argument that it refers to an altogether later, post-settlement epi-
        sode, fails to convince.

[291]   So e.g. E. K. Holt *Prophesying the Past* (1995): 67. As literary text Num. 25:1–5 may itself
        be composite: see I. Kislev, 'P, Source or Redaction: The Evidence of Numbers 25', in T.
        Dozeman, K. Schmid, and B. Schwartz (eds.), *The Pentateuch: International Perspectives
        on Current Research* (Tübingen: Mohr Siebeck, 2011): 387–99.

C Commentary on Hosea

But what is meant by Ephraim's glory? It could mean (1) that his children are his glory, which will be removed with the judgement of 9:11b–12; or (2) that YHWH is Ephraim's glory (cf. Ps. 3:3 [4]), and that since he (not Baal) is the giver of fertility his flying away will lead to the loss of children described in 9:11b–12.[292] Either way, the judgement announced is that there will be no future generations. The pronouncement of 9:11b is absolute: 'no birth, no pregnancy, no conception!' Nevertheless, so as to ensure that there is no room for doubt, 9:12 adds that even if any children were successfully brought up, YHWH will cause them to be lost and their parents bereaved. These are harsh and, indeed, offensive words. It would be easy to suggest that perhaps they were less offensive to ancient than to contemporary ears – but can we be sure that this is so? Those concerned to convey the message of the ancient text to contemporary readers may at this point feel the need to reflect on how to convey the sense of YHWH's absolute abhorrence of wrongdoing in language and images which have the necessary force but which do not offend as grossly as the imagery of these verses. Small wonder that the text adds 'Woe to them indeed' (9:12b), the word 'woe' signifying, as in 7:13, lamentation as much as judgement. The judgement continues into 9:13, the meaning of the first half of which is obscure. NRSV's 'as a young palm' is based on taking the Hebrew ṣôr to be related to the Arabic ṣwr. NIV takes ṣôr to be the Phoenician city of Tyre, translating as 'like Tyre';[293] but it is hard to know why a reference to Tyre should suddenly appear in the text. Whatever the intended meaning of 9:13a, the harsh judgement of 9:11–12 is continued in 9:13b. NRSV's 'slaughter' follows LXX; MT has 'the slayer', which also makes sense and which, it is argued by Macintosh, should be retained on the basis of its greater force.[294] After such harsh judgement, 9:14 interjects a prayer, presumably one attributed to the prophet. But its purpose is not clear. Is it an attempt at prophetic intercession on behalf of the people? Or does it align the prophet with YHWH in abhorrence of the people's idolatry? Is the prophet asking for one particular form of judgement, in the same way that in 2 Samuel 24:11–14 YHWH asks David to choose what form of punishment he and the nation should bear? Whatever the nature of the intercession, the conclusion (9:14b) is the reinforcement of the judgements of 9:11–13.

---

[292] A. A. Macintosh *Hosea* (1997): 365 considers the word to be 'an (early) exegetical gloss' which overloads the meter of the line and is difficult to construe.

[293] See J. K. Kuan, 'Hosea 9:13 and Josephus, *Antiquities* IX, 277–87' *PEQ* 123 (1991): 103–8.

[294] A. A. Macintosh *Hosea* (1997): 371.

140   *Book of Hosea*

Hosea 9:15–17 is structured in parallel to 9:10–14: (1) historical retrospect (9:10, 15a); (2) announcement of judgement entailing no future generations of children (9:11–13; 15b–16); and (3) words of the prophet (9:14; 17). The historical reference point is Gilgal where, 9:15 says, every evil of the Israelites began. Gilgal has already appeared in the Hosea-text at 4:15, and the commentary there notes its associations with Joshua, Samuel, and Saul. However the parallel of 9:15a with 9:10b suggests that a particular incident in which Israel sinned is in view, albeit one unknown to us.[295] There YHWH 'came to hate them'. The verb carries connotations of both emotions and actions. YHWH's hatred of evil deeds (e.g. Deut. 12:31) becomes hatred of those who perpetrate them. The word is used in Deuteronomy 24:3 as grounds for divorce (where it is generally translated 'dislikes'). The people's wicked deeds cause YHWH to drive them 'out of my house', terminology which could also be used in reference to divorce (Deut. 24:1, 3). As in 8:1, the 'house' is more likely YHWH's land than a sanctuary. The judgement includes the 'officials' of the kingdom. The term is found several times in chapters 5–8 (NRSV translates sometimes as 'princes'), but only here in chapters 9–11. As noted in the commentary on 5:10, it can refer to military leaders or to administrative court officials.

The agricultural imagery of 9:10 is resumed in 9:16. Ephraim is 'stricken' (NRSV), perhaps better translated as 'blighted' as a vine or fig tree might be (so NIV; the word is used of grass in Ps. 102:4 [5]). In consequence the root of the plant is dried up and produces no fruit. The lack of fruit becomes a lack of children as 9:16b then resumes the judgement of 9:11b–13. As Andersen and Freedman observe, the verbs 'bereave' (9:12) and 'kill/murder' (9:16) 'cannot be ameliorated'.[296] In 9:17 the 'my God' indicates that the prophet is deemed to speak. Because the people have not listened to YHWH, he will reject them; the verb has already been used of the priests in 4:6 (see the commentary *ad loc*). Consequently he will no longer keep them safe in the land. Rather they will become wanderers among the nations.

Hosea 10:1–2 employs the image of Israel as a vine, an image closely related to that in 9:10 of Israel as grapes. The image is found also in Jeremiah 2:21; and Psalm 80:8–13 [9–14] describes Israel as a vine that YHWH brought out of Egypt.[297] The word 'luxuriant' (10:1) generally has a negative sense,

---

[295] This is not to deny that readers in the post-monarchic period may have seen an anti-monarchic allusion in this verse.

[296] F. I. Andersen and D. N. Freedman *Hosea* (1980): 543.

[297] Similar, too, is the poem of Isa. 5:1–7 portraying Israel as YHWH's vineyard.

C *Commentary on Hosea*   141

and Macintosh translates accordingly as 'damaged'.[298] However NRSV's translation is a long-accepted one and fits the literary context better. It may be, as Ben Zvi suggests, that the text is deliberately ambiguous, offering the reader both meanings.[299] As Israel's prosperity grew, so did the number of his altars. The allusion back to 8:11 is clear. Israel also 'improved his pillars (*maṣṣēbôt*)'. In Genesis 28:18 and Exodus 24:4 there is no condemnation of such pillars. However laws in Exodus 23:24; 34:13 and Deuteronomy 16:22 prohibit them, associating them with practices of the previous inhabitants of the land. Hosea 10:1 clearly disapproves of them. The multiplication of altars and pillars did not reveal devotion to YHWH, but rather their own false hearts (10:2). As noted in the comments on 4:11b, the heart was viewed as the seat of understanding. The word 'false' literally means 'smooth/slippery'. It is used in Psalm 5:9 [10] and Proverbs 28:23 of a flattering tongue. Consequently Israel must bear guilt: the word is used in Hosea primarily in relation to cultic matters (e.g. 4:15). The word entails the bringing of judgement, and YHWH will destroy their altars and pillars.[300]

Grammatically 10:3 is linked to 10:2. However the nature of any thematic connection is unclear. Are the words attributed to the people meant to be words spoken prior to Israel's demise on 722, in which case they are presumably opposing the prophetic message and therefore constitute an accusation? Or are they words which they will utter from their exile, in which case they form part of their punishment? On balance the latter seems more probable: they now have no king, and anyway their kings have proved unable to save them. The middle line – 'for we do not fear YHWH' – is perhaps an acknowledgement made, belatedly, in their exile. Mays follows LXX in taking 10:4 also to be within quotation marks, continuing what the people will say.[301] In MT, however, it reads as prophetic accusation against the people. The 'mere words' and 'empty oaths' may both be associated with the way in which they 'make covenants'. These could be covenants between king and people (2 Sam. 3:21; 5:3) or between nations. NRSV's 'litigation' translates *mišpāṭ*, more generally translated 'justice' or 'judgement'. Amos 6:12 makes the accusation of *mišpāṭ* being turned into poison, and that verse may have

---

[298] A. A. Macintosh *Hosea* (1997): 383–4.

[299] E. Ben Zvi *Hosea* (2005): 207; so also J. D. Nogalski *Hosea–Jonah* (2011): 143–4; M. A. Sweeney *Twelve Prophets* 1 (2000): 103.

[300] NRSV's 'The Lord' is supplied, the text having simply 'he/it'. A. A. Macintosh *Hosea* (1997): 388–90 translates as 'This', meaning the people's false heart and guilt. Most commentators, however, translate as NRSV.

[301] J. L. Mays *Hosea* (1969): 138–40.

142   *Book of Hosea*

influenced the Hosea-text here. While the luxuriant vine of 10:1 might have been expected to produce an abundant harvest of grapes, instead judgement sprouts up like poison (cf. Isa. 5:4). That poison is found in 'the furrows of the field', a phrase that occurs also in 12:11 [12] with reference to Israel's altars becoming like heaps of stones.

In this time of judgement the inhabitants of Samaria are anxious for the calf-god of Bethel (10:5).[302] A god was meant to protect and provide for its people, but now the roles are reversed as the people are anxious for the god! The word 'calf' here is an unusual feminine plural form of the word, and may be meant to signify 'calf-hood', that is, the whole apparatus of the sanctuary at Bethel.[303] Its idolatrous priests will wail for it. The word translated 'idolatrous priests' is found in only two other places (2 Kgs 23:5; Zeph. 1:4) where, as here, the context is of idolatrous worship. The verb 'wail' generally means 'exult', but its semantic range includes the noise of exaltation sometimes being the noise of trembling (Ps. 2:11). The wailing is over the departure of the calf's glory, probably meaning the gold of the calf or the wealth of the whole sanctuary. There exists no historical record of what happened to the calf set up by Jeroboam I at Bethel (1 Kgs 12:26–30), but it is entirely plausible that the prediction of 10:6 that it would be carried to Assyria is correct.[304] As judgement unfolds both king and cult will perish (10:7–8). Amos 7:13 has Amaziah describe Bethel as 'the king's sanctuary', and king and cult were closely intertwined. Gomes comments, regarding Hosea 10:1–8, that '[t]he twin foci of the prophetic attack are the political and cultic establishments, as king and cult were both regarded as guarantors of national security. The cult was also under royal patronage and ensured divine protection for the king and court.'[305] The term 'high places' (*bāmôt*) (10:8) occurs only here in Hosea; 4:13 may be taken to describe what the editors of the text assumed took place at them. 'Aven' may be (as NRSV) a proper name, that is, Bethel (see the commentary on 4:15), or could be translated simply as 'iniquity'. The destroyed altars (cf. 10:2) will become overgrown with thorns and thistles. The words used are different to the briers and thorns which YHWH will allow to grow over his vineyard in Isaiah 5:6, but the imagery

---

[302] See the comments on 4:15 regarding the name 'Beth-aven'.

[303] G. I. Davies *Hosea* (1992): 237; A. A. Macintosh *Hosea* (1997): 399–400.

[304] As noted in the comments on 5:13, H. M. Barstad 'Hosea and the Assyrians' (2013): 107–9 suggests that *yārēb* may be a shortened form of Jeroboam. In that case the meaning would be that the calf became 'tribute from King Jeroboam'. However, it is more natural to see it as being in parallel to 'Assyria', and NRSV's translation should be retained.

[305] J. F. Gomes *The Sanctuary at Bethel* (2006): 163.

C Commentary on Hosea

143

is the same. The final words of 10:8 are picked up and used in Luke 23:30 as Jesus speaks of a forthcoming destruction of Jerusalem.

Between the similes of Israel as vine (10:1–8) and as trained heifer (10:11–15) comes a brief direct prophetic address in 10:9–10. As noted in the comments on 9:9, 'the days of Gibeah' were clearly something well known to the ancient readers, very probably the appalling events of the rape and killing of the Levite's concubine described in Judges 19–21.[306] The accusation made in 10:9 is that Israel has sinned for years, and continues to do so. The significance of Israel's 'double iniquity' in 10:10 is uncertain: possibly it signifies both past (at Gibeah) and present sin. An alternative possibility is that reference is made to a pair of oxen ploughing a double furrow, anticipating 10:12–13. Despite the difficulties, there is no doubting the meaning: that YHWH will punish Israel's sin through gathering peoples against them.

Hosea 10:11 introduces a further metaphor for Israel: she was a trained heifer who loved to thresh. The picture is of a young cow which had not yet been yoked for ploughing. NRSV's 'I spared' her fair neck does not give quite the right sense, which is of YHWH spotting her: Wolff translates 'passed by' and Macintosh, appositely, 'happened upon'.[307] The image is in keeping with YHWH's finding of Israel in the wilderness in 9:10. Eidevall observes, however, that the expression 'focuses on usefulness rather than physical beauty'.[308] As the young cow grows it is expected that it will move on to ploughing up the ground, signifying a response to YHWH's care which Ephraim, Judah, and Jacob are expected to make. The name 'Judah' came into the text in the seventh-century redaction, in preparation for 10:12 which was also brought into the text at this stage.[309] Hosea 10:12 is related to Jeremiah 4:3. The clause 'break up your fallow ground' is identical in both texts, and the image of sowing is in both texts. This could indicate dependence one way or the other, or it could indicate that the two derive from a similar and contemporary milieu. The latter is to be preferred in the light of other considerations which suggest that Hosea 10:12 was not in the earliest composition of Hosea 10:11–13a, and was probably brought in with the

---

[306] It was noted at 9:9 that the reference is sometimes taken as having anti-monarchic overtones, since Saul's residence as king was there (1 Sam. 10:26; 11:4). If so, the overtones are faint.

[307] H. W. Wolff *Hosea* (1974): 179, 185; A. A. Macintosh *Hosea* (1997): 417–8.

[308] G. Eidevall *Grapes in the Desert* (1996): 160.

[309] 'Judah' is seen as an addition or as replacing an original 'Israel' by G. I. Davies *Hosea* (1993): 245–6; A. A. Macintosh *Hosea* (1997): 418–21; J. L. Mays *Hosea* (1969): 144–5; contra H. W. Wolff *Hosea* (1974): 185.

144   *Book of Hosea*

seventh-century redaction. Firstly, Wolff notes its 'multimembered series of imperatives',[310] with the only parallel in Hosea 4–11 being 4:15, which draws from Amos 4:4; 5:5 and belongs to the seventh-century redaction of the text (see the commentary *ad loc*). Secondly, employment of the verb *dāraš* (seek) reflects the influence of Amos 5:4–6, 14–15. It is likely, therefore, that 10:12, too, belongs to the seventh-century redactional composition. Along with the addition in 10:11, its purpose is to admonish the people of Judah to avoid a similar fate as had befallen the northern kingdom in 722 by cultivating righteousness (*ṣədāqâ*) and steadfast love (*ḥesed*), and seeking YHWH. This is the only occurrence of *ṣədāqâ* in Hosea. It can be used of a way of life that human beings or the nation are to seek, or of something that flows from YHWH (see 'A Closer Look: Justice and Righteousness'). The two are not wholly distinct, in that the sowing of righteousness is in parallel with seeking YHWH, who is the giver of righteousness. The term *ḥesed* (variously translated as 'loyalty', 'love', 'steadfast love', 'loving kindness', and 'mercy') is a characteristic Hoseanic term which the seventh-redactors made sure to include (see further the comments on 4:1). If the people of Judah seek YHWH, then he will rain *ṣedeq* upon them; a term closely related to *ṣədāqâ*, and sometimes translated as 'salvation' or 'vindication'.[311]

Hosea 10:13 followed 10:11 in the earliest, late eighth-century text, and made the accusation against Israel that they have ploughed wickedness and reaped injustice. In the seventh-century redaction 10:12 urged the people of Judah to sow righteousness, reap steadfast love, and seek YHWH. However the continuation of the inherited text in 10:13 reveals that the redactors were fearful that Judah would not respond. The language of reaping what you sow has already been met in 8:7 (see the commentary *ad loc*). Here in 10:13 a parallel accusation continues the agricultural imagery: the people have eaten the fruit of lies. The word 'lies' is found also in 11:12 [12:1] which, assuming that it is to be read with 12:1 [2], suggests that it may refer to 'the duplicity shown in dealings with foreign powers'.

---

[310]   H. W. Wolff *Hosea* (1974): 182.
[311]   E.g. Isa. 51:5. NRSV's translation of both terms in Hos. 10:12 as 'righteousness' does not distinguish between the two terms, and indeed the distinction between the two nouns from the same verbal root is not always clear. See B. Johnson, '*ṣādaq*', *TDOT* 12: 239–64 (250–7), who writes that '[a]lthough *ṣedeq* and *ṣədāqâ* are in many instances interchangeable, they cannot really be treated as synonyms: *ṣedeq* evokes the notion of correctness and order, while *ṣədāqâ* emphasises action and activity rather than condition. In this sense *ṣədāqâ* represents *ṣedeq* functionally' (256). The more concrete *ṣədāqâ* can also be found in the plural.

C Commentary on Hosea

However, the same root occurs also in 4:2 and 7:3 (NRSV: treachery).[312] The second half of 10:13 is often taken by those who divide the text into small units as a new saying, since 10:13b–15 constitutes a well-structured judgement oracle. However within a larger literary section 10:13b is in perfectly proper continuation with what precedes it. The people are accused of trusting in their 'chariots' (NRSV). The Hebrew is literally 'your ways', which Macintosh translates as 'policy'.[313] LXX, however, translates as 'chariots', indicating a different Hebrew word. This provides a better parallel to 'warriors' and is preferred by several commentators, and by NRSV. Assyrian records indicate that, at least at certain times, Israel had significant numbers of chariots.[314] In consequence of the people's attitudes and behaviour, the people will experience the tumult of war. Their fortresses will be destroyed 'as Shalman destroyed Beth-arbel on the day of battle'. This incident, clearly well known to the ancient readership, is unknown to us. 'Shalman' may be a shortened form of 'Shalmaneser', in which case it could refer to one of the Assyrian emperors Shalmaneser III, IV, or V, the last of whom destroyed in Samaria in 722 (2 Kgs 17:3). Alternatively, some suggest that it may mean a Moabite king Salamanu, who is named by Tiglath-Pileser III as having paid him tribute. Since Beth-arbel is held by some to be a region in Transjordan, modern Irbid,[315] it is possible that he might have engaged in war or raids against Israel – but we have no evidence of this. Sometimes it is best to own up to our ignorance. Whatever, the particular incident, it was remembered that, horrifically, mothers were dashed in pieces with their children. That dashing of children on rocks did occur is evidenced by 2 Kings 8:12; Psalm 137:9; Isaiah 13:16; Nahum 3:10, but only here in Hosea 10:14 is the dashing of mothers with their children mentioned. The verse picks up the judgement of 9:13, that Ephraim's children would be led out for slaughter. It also anticipates 13:16 [14:1], the final word of judgement in the book, as 9:15 declares 'Thus it shall be done to you' (NRSV) or, more correctly, 'as it was done to you': the verbs are in the perfect tense, and reflect the perspective of those compiling the text after 722. The addressee in 9:15 is Bethel. LXX has, rather, 'Israel'. This gives the correct sense, but for that very reason MT has the stronger

---

[312] G. I. Davies *Hosea* (1992): 247.
[313] A. A. Macintosh *Hosea* (1997): 425.
[314] See J. L. Mays *Hosea* (1969): 147–9; H. W. Wolff *Hosea* (1974): 187. The pre-2021 NRSV translated as 'power'; NIV has 'strength'.
[315] See, *inter alia*, H. M. Barstad 'Hosea and the Assyrians' (2013): 104–5.

claim to being original.[316] The reason for this judgement is because of 'great wickedness': literally 'wickedness of your wickedness', with the repetition of the word reinforcing its gravity. The cutting off of the king of Israel 'at dawn' may mean 'at the very outset of battle'.

The images in 9:10–10:15 of Israel as grapes in the wilderness and first fruit on the fig tree (9:10), as a luxuriant vine (10:1), and as a heifer (10:11), attractive as they sound, in fact present a devastating critique of the people's failure to live as YHWH desired in response to his initiatives towards them, and consequently similarly devastating announcements of his judgement. The prophet Hosea is sometimes presented as a figure less stern than Amos, one whose sense of YHWH's justice and YHWH's mercy are in some kind of tug of war; and, as noted in the commentary, in 6:4–7:10 YHWH himself is portrayed as engaged in an internal dialogue in this respect. In 9:10–10:15, however, as in chapter 8, it is accusation and judgement that dominate – in the earliest, late eighth-century composition entirely so. The seventh-century redaction brought in 10:12, which urges Judah to sow righteousness, reap steadfast love, and seek YHWH so that he may rain his salvation upon them – however, 10:13 expresses pessimism that this would happen. Is there, then, any mercy to be discovered? For this the reader must look to the final unit within chapters 4–11.

Hosea 11:1–11 – Israel, YHWH's Child

11 When Israel was a child, I loved him,
    and out of Egypt I called my son.
² The more I called them,
    the more they went from me;
they kept sacrificing to the Baals
    and offering incense to idols.

³ Yet it was I who taught Ephraim to walk;
    I took them up in my arms,
    but they did not know that I healed them.
⁴ I led them with cords of human kindness,
    with bands of love.
I was to them like those
    who lift infants to their cheeks.
I bent down to them and fed them.

---

[316] F. I. Andersen and D. N. Freedman *Hosea* (1980): 572; A. A. Macintosh *Hosea* (1997): 433; contra H. W. Wolff *Hosea* (1974): 181.

C Commentary on Hosea

⁵ They shall return to the land of Egypt,
and Assyria shall be their king,
because they have refused to return to me.
⁶ The sword rages in their cities,
it consumes their oracle priests
and devours because of their schemes.
⁷ My people are bent on turning away from me.
To the Most High they call,
but he does not raise them up at all.

⁸ How can I give you up, Ephraim?
How can I hand you over, O Israel?
How can I make you like Admah?
How can I treat you like Zeboiim?
My heart recoils within me;
my compassion grows warm and tender.
⁹ I will not execute my fierce anger;
I will not again destroy Ephraim,
for I am God and no mortal,
the Holy One in your midst,
and I will not come in wrath.
¹⁰ They shall go after the LORD,
who roars like a lion;
when he roars,
his children shall come trembling from the west.
¹¹ They shall come trembling like birds from Egypt
and like doves from the land of Assyria,
and I will return them to their homes, says the LORD.

These verses are generally and justifiably held to warrant particular attention, due primarily to their content. The opening verses (11:1–4) present a tender picture of YHWH as a loving parent of his son Israel. However, Israel turns out to be a disobedient son (11:2), in the light of which 11:5–7 announce judgement in terms comparable to earlier sections of the text. There then follows an abrupt change of tone in 11:8–9, as YHWH declares 'How can I give you up?' The passage ends on the positive note of Israel's restoration (11:10–11).[317] In a book which contains many pronouncements

---

[317] In EVV chapter 11 includes 11:12, which in the Hebrew text is 12:1. The concluding 'says YHWH' of 11:11 makes the Hebrew arrangement the more natural, and NRSV's spacing reflects this.

148   *Book of Hosea*

of YHWH's judgement, the presentation of YHWH as a tender parent whose anger and mercy wrestle with each other, with mercy in the end prevailing, is appealing.[318] While 6:4–7:10 has already revealed an internal dialogue within YHWH as to whether or not he should punish his people (see the commentary at 6:4), 11:1–11 does so in a poetic, succinct, and attractive manner. Its importance is strengthened through its position as the concluding unit of chapters 4–11 and by its references back to earlier sections of the text. While the section contains sub-units (11:1–4, 5–7, 8–9, 10–11), it is to be taken and read as one literary unit. Commentators seeking to place material in particular years or periods in the ministry of the prophet Hosea are necessarily tentative in their suggestions, and the literary approach of this commentary does not attempt or need to do so. As Ben Zvi observes, 'Hosea 11 does not require its readers to associate the divine speech with any narrowly defined historical circumstances.… The speech is purposefully devoid of any narrow temporal or historical markers.'[319] The passage has several textual difficulties. The more significant ones are noted below but, as indicated in the Introduction to Hosea, readers wanting more detailed textual comments are referred to the commentaries of Macintosh and Wolff.

In the first, late eighth-century, composition the unit comprised 11:1–9. Several considerations show that 11:10–11 is an expansion of the text created by the compilers of the sixth-century exilic redaction. Firstly, in 11:10a YHWH's roaring like a lion is dependent on Amos 1:2; 3:8. The word used for 'lion' is that most widely used in the Hebrew Bible, including the Amos text (1:2; 3:8, 12; 5:19), while the Hosea-text (5:14; 13:8) uses different words.[320] Secondly, these verses envisage a return home from various places, including 'the west': neither Egypt nor Assyria, the two empires referred to thus far in the text, were in the west, and this additional geographical reference is more akin to exilic and later texts such as Isaiah 49:12. Thirdly, the imagery changes from Israel being YHWH's son to being 'like birds' and 'like doves' (11:11), the latter term being picked up from 7:11. Fourthly, while in 11:1–9 YHWH speaks in the first person, in 11:10–11a he is referred to in the third person. That 11:11b switches back into divine speech is explained by the

---

[318]   J. L. Mays *Hosea* (1969): 151 comments that 'the portrayal of Yahweh as a father caring for his son achieves an explicit tenderness and detail unmatched in the Old Testament'.

[319]   E. Ben Zvi *Hosea* (2005): 238.

[320]   See the commentary on Amos 1:2, which I argue is also exilic, and on Amos 3:8, which I argue was brought into the Amos-text in a seventh-century redactional composition.

C Commentary on Hosea

149

desire of the redactors to complete the verse with the closing 'says YHWH' which, evidently, concluded 11:1–9 in the earlier text.[321]

The opening 11:1 is parallel to the opening verse of the preceding section 9:10–10:15, in that both 9:10 and 11:1 employ images referring back to Israel's election traditions. In 9:10 the image was of Israel as grapes in the wilderness, and the image referred to the wilderness period. Now in 11:1 the image is of YHWH as parent and Israel as his child. It is used in with reference to the tradition of Israel's exodus from Egypt. This parent–child metaphor, like the husband–wife imagery of chapters 1–3, entails the kind of emotional intensity associated with family relationships. The same metaphor is found in Isaiah 1:2–3. Some see the image as a political one: as a king sees himself as father of the nation or an emperor father to his peoples, so YHWH is father to Israel. However, in view of the intensity of the language in the following verses the familial understanding is to be preferred. The word *na'ar* (boy; NRSV: child) can refer to an infant, a weaned child, or a youth: in view of YHWH teaching him to walk (11:3) it appears to be a younger child that is intended here. As parent, YHWH expresses that he loved his son. As noted, in the commentary on 3:1, the verb *'āhēb* (love) is used as an election term in Deuteronomy (e.g. 7:8, 13; 10:15; 23:5 [6]). It has been argued that its usage there derives from the language of ancient Near Eastern vassal treaties.[322] If this is uncertain for Deuteronomy, it is certainly unlikely to be so in Hosea 11, where it is clearly parental love that is meant. The beginnings of this relationship are seen to be in the days of YHWH's deliverance of his people from their slavery in Egypt. This is the only reference to the exodus in Hosea 4–11, but it is referred to in 2:15 [17];[323] 12:9, 13 [10, 14]; 13:4. We cannot know how full or simple a version of the exodus traditions was known at the time

---

[321] That 11:10 is redactional is held by virtually all commentators. Several, however, consider that the original unit was 11:1–9, 11. My view is consonant with that of J. A. Dearman *Hosea* (2010): 293, who writes that it is 'likely that the placement of these two verses is redactional'. That both 11:10 and 11:11 use the verb *ḥārad* (tremble) is, in my view, an argument for seeing them as having been composed together rather than its occurrence in 11:11 being sufficient to prompt the addition of 11:10.

[322] W. L. Moran, 'The Ancient Near Eastern Background of the Love of God in Deuteronomy', *CBQ* 25 (1963): 77–87. Subsequent scholarship has largely accepted Moran's argument. More recently, however, it has been rightly noted that it is not necessary to restrict the semantic range of the verb: it can both be using treaty terminology and have overtones of interpersonal relationships. See further B. T. Arnold, 'The Love-Fear Antinomy in Deuteronomy 5–11', *VT* 61 (2011): 551–69 (552–62).

[323] Hosea 2:15 [17] refers to the time of exodus as 'the days of her youth': the word 'youth' is from the same root as 11:1's *na'ar*, suggesting a deliberate linkage. See the commentary on 2:15 [17].

150   *Book of Hosea*

of the first written composition of Hosea in the late eighth century, but the Hosea-text is evidence that it was known in some form.[324]

YHWH's deliverance of his son Israel is described as him calling his son (11:1). But 11:2 immediately introduces an unhappy contrast. The more YHWH called them, the further they went from him.[325] The verbs have a continuous sense: this behaviour, begun in the past, is ongoing. Their increasing distance from YHWH is evidenced by their sacrificing to Baal and offering incense to idols. The accusation of sacrificing to Baal resumes the accusations of Baal worship in 2: 13, 17 [15, 19]. The accusations also link back to 4:13, where the same verbs 'sacrifice' and 'offering incense' are used (the verb translated 'offering incense' in 11:2 and 2:13 [15] is the same verb translated by NRSV as 'make offerings' in 4:13). This turning away from YHWH is all the more painful for him in view of his parental love for them, as depicted in 11:3–4. These verses portray YHWH as a sentient God who, like a human parent, feels strong emotions in respect of their child.[326] It was he who taught Ephraim to walk,[327] and who took them up in his arms.[328] Despite YHWH's parental care, the people did not acknowledge that it was he who healed them.[329] Use of the verb *rāpā'* (heal) links back to 5:13; 6:1; 7:1 and forward to 14:4 [5]. As noted in the commentary on 5:13, the relatively frequent use of the verb may represent a word play on the name Ephraim (*'eprayim*), the name for Israel which is introduced into 11:1–11 in this verse (see 'A Closer Look: "Ephraim" in Hosea'). Some refer 11:3 to the exodus,[330]

---

[324]   G. I. Davies *Hosea* (1992): 254 draws attention to Ps. 80:8–13, which refer to Israel as a vine which YHWH brought out of Egypt. This psalm appears to have northern Israelite influence (verses 1–2 refer to Israel, Joseph, Ephraim, Benjamin, and Manasseh) and, along with others, Davies sees the exodus holding a special place in early northern Israelite traditions.

[325]   MT has 'from them' rather than NRSV's 'from me'. Along with most commentators, NRSV and other EVV follow LXX.

[326]   It is generally assumed that YHWH speaks as a father. However, G. I. Davies *Hosea* (1993): 254 comments that it is 'commonly assumed that it is as a father that Yahweh is portrayed here, but the images in vv. 3–4 relate to aspects of child-rearing which have traditionally been at least as much the mother's responsibility as the father's. For such a representation of Yahweh cf. Isa 49:15.'

[327]   The verb 'taught to walk' is most probably an unusual form (tiphel conjugation) of the verb *rāgal*, and NRSV's translation is that most widely accepted. For an alternative translation as 'applied myself assiduously' see A. A. Macintosh *Hosea* (1997): 441–3.

[328]   The Hebrew of the second line is barely intelligible, but NRSV translates with the majority of commentators. Translating as 'my arms' rather than MT's 'his arms' goes back to LXX.

[329]   NRSV translates the verb *yāda'* with its usual meaning of 'know'. The sense of knowing meant here is, however, acknowledgement of YHWH (so also in 2:8 [10]).

[330]   E.g. A. A. Macintosh *Hosea* (1997): 444; H. W. Wolff *Hosea* (1974): 199.

C Commentary on Hosea

others to the wandering in the wilderness and the years after entry into the land.[331] O'Kennedy considers that the healing could refer to either of these, or to forgiveness after the sins described in 11:2.[332] It is, however, unnecessary to make such a poetic image allude to any one particular historical circumstance. The power of the text is in the image itself. Nor is it necessary to restrict the meaning of 'healed' to one particular aspect of a verb with a wide semantic range. Descriptions of YHWH's loving actions continue in 11:4: 'I led them with cords of human kindness, with bands of love.' The parental imagery appears to continue. However it may be that the image changes to an agricultural one: the cords and bands could be those that a farmer attaches to an animal, in which case YHWH is depicted as a considerate farmer. NRSV's 'cords of human kindness' is literally 'cords of man/human' which, if the imagery has become agricultural, would signify a farmer's humane treatment of his animals. NRSV's 'who lift infants to their cheeks' entails an emendation from *'ōl* (yoke) to *'ūl* (cheek); the Hebrew therefore favours the agricultural interpretation. However the whole verse is difficult textually, and either interpretation seems possible.[333] What is clear is that the spurning of YHWH's tender kindness expressed in 11:3–4 makes Israel's faithlessness described in 11:2 all the greater.

It is, therefore, not unexpected that there follows an expression of judgement at YHWH's hands. The Hebrew of 11:5 begins with a negative: the opening line actually reads that they shall *not* return to the land of Egypt. NRSV follows several commentators in taking the *lō'* (not) as *lô* and reading it as the object of 'fed' (i.e. 'fed him') in 11:4, a reading found in LXX. Other commentators prefer to keep the *lō'* with 11:5. Even then there are two possible meanings. NIV translates: 'Will they not return to Egypt?' Macintosh, on the other hand, translates: 'He will not return to the land of Egypt, rather it is Assyria who is his king.'[334] All of these options are possible. On balance, NIV's translation has merit, with the 'land of Egypt' symbolising slavery which, in actuality, would be under the Assyrians rather than under Egypt.[335] The earliest composition of the text dates from after the destruction of the

---

[331] J. L. Mays *Hosea* (1969): 154.

[332] D. F. O'Kennedy 'Healing as/or Forgiveness?' (2001): 464.

[333] Those who favour retention of parental imagery into 11:4 include J. P. Kakkanattu, *God's Enduring Love in the Book of Hosea: A Synchronic and Diachronic Analysis of Hosea 11:1– 11* (FAT, 2/14; Tübingen: Mohr Siebeck, 2006): 52–63; H. W. Wolff *Hosea* (1974): 199–200. Those who prefer to see agricultural imagery include J. A. Dearman *Hosea* (2010): 282–5; G. Eidevall *Grapes in the Desert* (1996): 172–4; A. A. Macintosh *Hosea* (1997): 448–9.

[334] A. A. Macintosh *Hosea* (1997): 450.

[335] J. M. Bos *Reconsidering* (2013): 122.

northern kingdom by the Assyrians, and this reading of the text makes good sense from that perspective. The verse picks up the judgement in 8:13 and 9:3 of return to Egypt, but now makes clear that Assyria is the real threat. A further reason for the punishment is given: 'because they have refused to turn to me' (11:5b). The same accusation was made in 7:10, at the conclusion of YHWH's internal struggle with himself in 6:4–7:10 (see the commentary on 6:4). In 11:5 the verb 'return' (*šûb*) begins and ends the verse, and makes the punishment fit the crime: because Israel has refused to return to YHWH, they shall return to Egypt (i.e. slavery under Assyria).[336] The next verse (11:6) describes a military ravaging of the cities, consuming their 'oracle priests': the usage of the Hebrew word is unclear, and alternative possibilities are that it signifies 'idle talk', 'warriors', or perhaps most naturally, the bars of the city gates.[337] Devoured, too, will be the scheming plans of alliances with foreign nations. In 11:7 the people's 'turning away' employs yet again the verb *šûb* (return/turn). In 11:5 the people refuse to return to YHWH, now they are accused of being determined to turn away from him. But to whom or what do they turn? NRSV's 'Most High' translates *'el-'al*, literally 'to what is above', which, some suggest, may be taken to be an equivalent of NRSV's 'Most High'.[338] Others see *'al* as a shortened form of *ba'al* (Baal).[339] The translation of the whole of 11:7b is difficult, but there is no doubting that it completes the judgement that 11:5–7 declares.

The mood changes abruptly, however, in 11:8–9, as the anguished parent – YHWH – cries out, 'How can I give you up, Ephraim? How can I hand you over, O Israel.' Deuteronomy 21:18–21 instructs that the parent of a stubborn and rebellious son should bring him to the elders of the town for punishment, that punishment being death by stoning in order to purge the evil from their midst. YHWH, however, cannot bring himself to act in such a way towards Ephraim/Israel. His parental pity is too strong. How can he treat them like Admah and Zeboiim? These two cities are always associated with Sodom and Gomorrah (Gen. 10:19; 14:2, 8; Deut. 29:23 [22]), the cities of the plain destroyed by YHWH in Genesis 19. There seems no particular reason for Admah and Zeboiim being named rather than the better known Sodom and Gomorrah.[340] But YHWH's heart 'recoils' at the thought of

[336]   On the use of the verb *šûb* (return) in Hosea see the commentary at 6:1.
[337]   See further J. A. Dearman *Hosea* (2010): 276; J. P. Kakkanattu, *God's Enduring Love* (2006): 24–5; A. A. Macintosh *Hosea* (1997): 453.
[338]   J. A. Dearman *Hosea* (2010): 276.
[339]   H. W. Wolff *Hosea* (1974): 192, 201.
[340]   A. A. Macintosh *Hosea* (1997): 462–3.

C Commentary on Hosea

153

doing to Israel as he had done to these cities. The verb is used in Genesis 19:25 and Deuteronomy 29:23 [22] for the overthrow of Sodom and Gomorrah, but here it is YHWH's heart (i.e. his decision to judge Israel) that is overthrown. Hosea 11:9a answers the questions of 11:8a: YHWH's decision is that he will not execute his punishment and destroy Ephraim. NRSV's 'again' is from the verb *šûb* used in 11:5, 7, thus 'I will not return to destroy Ephraim.' There follows an explanatory clause: 'for I am God and no mortal'. A popular interpretation is, as Davies comments, that this 'may be understood to mean that Yahweh as God rises above the human responses of anger and vengeance, and shows mercy instead'.[341] However, in much of Hosea, and in the prophetic corpus as a whole, YHWH as deity reveals his anger and exercises judgement in his divine role, and an interpretation which views these as merely human actions seems unlikely. The closest parallel is in Numbers 23:19, which states that 'God is not a human being, that he should lie, or a mortal, that he should change his mind.' The same sentiment is expressed in 1 Samuel 15:29. The common thread is that YHWH/God will act consistently. In the literary context of Hosea 11:1–11 that divine consistency must surely be the maintenance of the parental love of 11:1–4, and the refusal to allow this to be overcome. The final line declares that YHWH will not come in 'wrath' (NRSV). The Hebrew word is that for 'city', but Jeremiah 15:8 gives evidence of a second word of the same spelling meaning 'anguish', and it is best to assume that Hosea 11:9 uses this same, rare word.[342]

Does 11:8–9 mean that YHWH's judgements, threatened in 11:5–7 – and, in the literary context of Hosea 4–11, of much that has gone before – will now not be executed? Or is it rather that, after judgement has been executed, Israel's restoration will follow, with the promise that at that time YHWH will not execute his fierce anger and destroy Ephraim again? Davies observes that there is 'no doubt that these verses as they are most naturally understood involve the renunciation of some statements made elsewhere in the book (see especially 5:6; 8:5; 13:9, 14)'. But he goes on to prefer the view that 'they speak of the continuation of Israel's relationship with Yahweh through the imminent catastrophe'. He references the idea in 10:10 of YHWH's judgement being disciplinary.[343] He does so, however, in order to align 11:8–9

---

[341] G. I. Davies *Hosea* (1992): 263. A. A. Macintosh *Hosea* (1997): 465 comments that God 'does not, like a man, change his mind or fall prey to the promptings of (even just) anger'.

[342] BDB: 735.

[343] G. I. Davies *Hosea* (1992): 251–4 (251, 253). He could have referred to 7:12, 15 as also revealing disciplinary action: see the commentary on 7:12.

with 11:11, all of which he takes to derive from the prophet Hosea, considering only 11:10 to be a later addition, whereas I have argued that 11:11 is to be taken with 11:10. In the first composition of 11:1–9, the plain meaning of 11:8–9 was that YHWH would not execute his threatened judgement. Even though this was not written until after the fall of the northern kingdom in 722, YHWH's self-questioning in 11:8 and its outcome in 11:9 were allowed to stand, despite 11:9's contradiction of YHWH's previously announced judgement. Hosea 11:8–9, in the first composition, revealed YHWH's internal wrestling in the same way as his internal dialogue contained in 6:4–7:10. There, however, his conclusion was that in the end Israel's refusal to return and seek him (7:10) made judgement inevitable. Here, in contrast, YHWH's warm and tender compassion overturns that verdict. In the context of the text as a whole, neither outcome wins out over the other. Rather, both are allowed to stand, with the reader being left to decide what they understand about YHWH's nature (see 'Bridging the Horizons: The Judgement and Mercy of YHWH').

The exilic addition in 11:10–11 changes the literary context. In the period of Judean exile in Babylon (and of refugees in Egypt, Jer. 42–43), there grew the hope of a return from the various places to which YHWH's people had been exiled or had fled. In a text concerning the northern kingdom, the name 'Assyria' (11:11) was not changed to 'Babylon', which would have jarred on the readers' ears. Nevertheless the exilic and post-exilic hope is of all YHWH's people enjoying a return to the homeland. Sections of Jeremiah 30–31 speak explicitly of a restoration of the fortunes of both Israel and Judah. What is made explicit in Jeremiah 30–31 is present implicitly in Hosea 11:10–11. The people's restoration follows their going after YHWH (11:10a), in contrast to their refusal to seek him in 7:10. They come 'from the west' which, as Nogalski notes, symbolised 'the farthest reaches of civilisation, thus making it a broad promise of the people's return'.[344] In the first (eighth-century) composition of Hosea 4:1–11:9, the assertion that YHWH would not execute his fierce anger followed many prior announcements of judgement, with no reconciliation made between the two. In the exilic redaction Hosea 4:1–11:11 ends with a clear promise that after YHWH's allowing of the destruction of the northern kingdom at the hands of the Assyrians in 722 and of the southern kingdom at the hands of the Babylonians in 587, there will follow, as his people turn to him, a restoration to their homes.

---

[344] J. D. Nogalski *Hosea–Jonah* (2011): 162.

C Commentary on Hosea

The 'says YHWH' of 11:11 closes not just 11:1–11 but the whole section: chapters 4–11. The dominant theme has been of YHWH's threat to judge his people for their perceived wrongdoings. Chapter 4 sets out that YHWH has an indictment against his people. The accusation is made that there is no loyalty or faithfulness in the land, but rather swearing, lying, murder, and bloodshed. Both priests and people are accused of a lack of knowledge of YHWH. Israel's idolatry and sacrificial practices are described as 'prostitution', an accusation found also in 5:1–7, which concludes that the people have 'dealt faithlessly' with YHWH. Hosea 5:8–7:16 contain a sustained critique of the people for seeking to make alliances with Assyria or Egypt, interpreted as another mark of their faithlessness. Both Israel and Judah are held to be guilty in this respect. This section reveals, too, YHWH's desire to heal his people, but his inability to do so because of their constant turning to these foreign nations rather than to him. Chapter 8 continues the theme of Israel's going to Assyria (8:9), and includes, too, a resumption of the accusation of mistaken cultic practices. The accusation is also made that kings were set up without YHWH's approval. In the exilic redaction 8:1 makes clear that these practices represent a breaking of the covenant between YHWH and Israel. Hosea 9:10–10:15 introduces some vivid images of Israel: as grapes in the wilderness (9:10), a luxuriant vine (10:1), and a trained heifer (10:11). All three refer to YHWH's gracious activity on Israel's behalf in the past, providing a further reason why their faithlessness is all the greater. This same dynamic operates in chapter 11: YHWH sees himself as a loving parent who has brought Israel up as his son, only for that son now to turn away from him. Some of the judgements described are harsh, for example, the loss of children (9:11–16). However, there is also a portrayal of the tenderness and mercy which form part of YHWH's nature. He longs to heal and restore his people, but their faithlessness seems not to allow it. Hosea 6:4–7:10 comprises a long internal dialogue, in which YHWH wrestles with himself over what course of action he should take. In the end the verdict is that Israel refuses to return to YHWH, and therefore judgement is pronounced once more. However in 11:1–9 a shorter, more intense internal dialogue concludes with YHWH deciding that he can allow his mercy to override his fierce anger, and that therefore he will not, after all, execute his judgement. In the first, late eighth-century composition the different outcomes of the two descriptions of YHWH's internal wrestlings are not reconciled, but are left in tension.

Readers after Israel's conquest by the Assyrians in 722 will, of course, have looked back at that destruction as being the threatened judgement, and have seen that therefore YHWH did, in the event, allow his judgement to take place. However, 11:8–9 will have left the hope that perhaps even this might not be his final word. Those who produced the text were setting before the people of Judah an object lesson from which they could learn. Given that YHWH could and would execute judgement, but also that he was merciful and did not wish to do so, would they be faithful to YHWH in order to avoid a similar destruction coming to them? The small number of additions made in the seventh century served to relate the text more clearly to Judah as well as to Israel. However, in due course Judah was ravaged by the Babylonians, and Jerusalem destroyed in 587. The Exilic Redactional Composition saw the destruction of Jerusalem in 587 as YHWH's judgement on Judah in the same way that the destruction of Samaria in 722 had been his judgement on Israel. The addition of 11:10–11 by the exilic redactors offered hope of restoration, but now clearly after the judgement of exile had taken place, a pattern which became normative in the books of the pre-exilic prophets.

Bridging the Horizons: The Judgement and Mercy of YHWH

Hosea 11 highlights a question which runs throughout the Hosea-text: How are YHWH's judgement and his mercy related, and can they be reconciled? The dominant themes of the text are of judgements being announced for reasons of Israel's faithlessness. This faithlessness is seen primarily in her engaging in Baal worship, and in her going to Egypt and Assyria for help instead of trusting in YHWH. Yet the text also reveals that YHWH himself regrets his own carrying out of his judgements. He would prefer to see Israel turn to him and be spared (5:15; 6:11b–7:1a). He holds a tender love for his people, expressed in a series of poetic images in 9:10–11:9. He wrestles with himself over what course of action he should take (6:4–7:10; 11:1–9). In the first, late eighth-century composition the verses concerning YHWH's tenderness and mercy (2:14–15 [16–17]; 11:8–9) conclude the otherwise mainly condemnatory material in 1:2–2:15 [17] and 4:1–11:9, and no attempt is made to reconcile the two. In the exilic and post-exilic redactions there emerges the pattern evident in other prophetic texts, that there will be restoration *after* a time of punishment in exile (e.g. Jer. 25 11–12; 29:10). This provided a lens through which post-exilic readers could interpret YHWH's bringing (or certainly allowing) the experience of exile.

C Commentary on Hosea

The question of the relationship between God's mercy and his judgement is one which religious believers today continue to face. It is tempting, first of all perhaps, to assume that a loving God could never judge and exact punishment of those whom he has created. But further thought will recognise that the human cry for justice to be meted out to perpetrators of violent crimes, and to those who abuse, mistreat, and exploit the weak and vulnerable, is a reflection of the divine justice which cannot shrug its shoulders at such wrongdoings, but must indeed act. The ancient credal statement of Exodus 34:6–7 speaks of YHWH as 'a God merciful and gracious, slow to anger, and abounding in steadfast love and faithfulness ... yet by no means clearing the guilty'. Christian tradition looks to the death of Jesus Christ on the Cross as a moment at which, in some way, divine love and divine justice were at one. Examination of theological understandings of the Cross lie beyond the scope of this commentary. As a humble biblical interpreter, however, I venture to suggest that after all the exhaustive labours of biblical scholars and systematic theologians, there remains merit in what is seen in the first composition of the Hosea-text, namely the assertion of the reality of both divine justice and divine love and compassion, with them left as distinct realities held in tension with each other. Such a position will not satisfy our desire for logical tidiness, but may nevertheless be the most honest position to take.

3 Guilt and Healing – Hosea 11:12–14:9 [12–14]

Hosea 11:12–12:14 [12:1–15] – Ephraim, Judah, and Jacob

> ¹² Ephraim has surrounded me with lies
>> and the house of Israel with deceit,
> but Judah still walks with God
>> and is faithful to the Holy One.
> 12 Ephraim herds the wind
>> and pursues the east wind all day long;
> they multiply falsehood and violence;
>> they make a treaty with Assyria,
>> and oil is carried to Egypt.
>
> ² The LORD has an indictment against Judah
>> and will punish Jacob according to his ways
>> and repay him according to his deeds.

158   *Book of Hosea*

³ In the womb he tried to supplant his brother,
     and in his manhood he strove with God.
⁴ He strove with the angel and prevailed;
     he wept and sought his favour;
  he met him at Bethel,
     and there he spoke with him.
⁵ The Lord the God of hosts,
     the Lord is his name!
⁶ But as for you, return to your God;
     hold fast to love and justice,
     and wait continually for your God.
⁷ A trader in whose hands are false balances,
     he loves to oppress.
⁸ Ephraim has said, 'Ah, I am rich;
     I have gained wealth for myself;
  in all of my gain
     no offence has been found in me
     that would be sin.'
⁹ I am the Lord your God
     from the land of Egypt;
  I will make you live in tents again,
     as on the days of the appointed festival.

¹⁰ I spoke to the prophets;
     it was I who multiplied visions,
     and through the prophets I will bring destruction.
¹¹ In Gilead there is iniquity;
     they shall surely come to nothing.
  In Gilgal they sacrifice bulls,
     so their altars shall be like stone heaps
     on the furrows of the field.
¹² Jacob fled to the land of Aram;
     there Israel served for a wife,
     and for a wife he guarded sheep.
¹³ By a prophet the Lord brought Israel up from Egypt,
     and by a prophet he was guarded.
¹⁴ Ephraim has given bitter offence,
     so his Lord will bring his crimes down on him
     and pay him back for his insults.

Hosea 11:12–14:9 [12–14] forms a block of material separate from and additional to chapters 4–11. The main distinguishing feature of chapter 12 is its focus on the ancestral patriarch Jacob (12:3–4, 12 [4–5, 13]). The chapter

C Commentary on Hosea

comprises a series of sayings brought together by a redactor on thematic grounds. 'The thematic unity of Hosea 12 derives more from repetition than from a clear rhetorical structure.'[345] The question arises as to the period in which the redaction of this chapter and, indeed, the block chapters 12–14, was executed. Commentators seeking to attribute most of the text to the prophet Hosea tend to attribute this activity to the later part of the prophet's ministry,[346] or to an early redaction shortly after the fall of Samaria in 722.[347] However, there are grounds for preferring the view derived from literary, redaction-critical studies that this redactional activity took place in a sixth-century exilic setting.[348] While this exilic redaction may have incorporated some earlier sayings, the most natural setting against which to read the whole is the exilic period. Such attributions can only ever be tentative, but a number of considerations taken together form a cumulative case pointing in this direction. These are:

(1) It is evident that chapters 1–11 were completed before 12–14, and that chapters 12–14 explore further themes set out in chapters 4–11.[349] These include the themes of YHWH having an indictment (*rîb*) against his people (12:2 [3] cf. 4:1); of Israel's lies and deceit (11:12 [12:1] cf. 7:3; 10:13); her alliances with Assyria and Egypt (12:1 [2] cf. 7:11; 8:8–10); vocabulary of punishing according to their ways and repaying according to their deeds (12:2 [3] cf. 4:9); the requirement of steadfast love (*ḥesed*) (12:6 [7]; cf. 4:1; 6:6); the iniquity/wickedness of Gilead (12:11 [12] cf. 6:8); references to Gilgal (12:11 [12] cf. 4:15; 9:15); the destruction of altars (12:11 [12] cf. 10:2, 8); the phrase 'on the furrows of the field' 12:11 [12] cf. 10:4).

(2) The statement that 'there he spoke with us' (12:4 [5]) may be read as an 'actualisation' of a kind similar to the exilic Deuteronomy 5:2–3.

(3) The liturgical language of 12:5 [6] reflects language of the exilic period and later in a similar way to the exilic doxologies of Amos 4:13; 5:8–9; 9:5–6.

(4) The plea in 12:6 [7] to 'wait continually for your God' reflects language prominent in the exilic period.

---

[345] J. D. Nogalski *Hosea–Jonah* (2011): 165.

[346] E.g. H. W. Wolff *Hosea* (1974): xxx–xxxi.

[347] E.g. D. R. Daniels *Hosea and Salvation History: The Early Traditions of Israel in the Prophecy of Hosea* (BZAW, 19; Berlin: W. de Gruyter, 1990): 29.

[348] So R. Vielhauer *Das Werden des Buches Hosea* (2007): 178–9.

[349] E. Ben Zvi *Hosea* (2005): 95, 241.

(5) The accusation of 'false balances' (12:7 [8]) shows awareness of Amos 8:5 as well as legal and wisdom traditions.

(6) While in chapters 4–11 the wilderness is a time of blessing (2:14–15 [16–17]; 9:10), in 12:9 [10] it represents judgement.

(7) The reference to the prophets in 12:10 [11], as in 6:5 (see the commentary *ad loc*), reflects an understanding of the prophets more characteristic of the exilic period than of the late eighth century.

(8) 12:13 [14] refers to Moses as a prophet, a theme which arose in a later period.

(9) The statement that Ephraim has given 'bitter offence' (12:14 [15]), more often translated as provoking YHWH to anger, reflects characteristic Deuteronomistic language.

Taken together, these considerations provide a strong case for reading this chapter from the perspective of the Babylonian exile.

I do not include as part of my case that 12:3–4, 12 [4–5, 13] contain reference to ancestral Jacob traditions. While it is likely that these were more widely known by the sixth century than in the eighth century, it is entirely plausible that they could have been known in oral form at the earlier time.

Hosea 11:12–12:2 [12:1–3] contain the names Ephraim, Judah, and Jacob. Ben Zvi is correct in observing that in this period there is a 'merging of conceptual horizons' and that 'the text strongly subsumes Ephraim under the images of Jacob and Israel, and their associated narratives'; and in like manner also 'Judah is conceptually subsumed under Jacob/Israel.' Hence 'divine complaints against Ephraim become relevant to Israel/Jacob, and therefore to Judah'.[350] Similarly Dearman recognises that these verses 'show concern to interpret divine activity in relation to the full covenant community'.[351] Chapters 4–11 acknowledged that YHWH had allowed the devastation of the northern kingdom by the Assyrians in 722 because of the people's faithlessness towards him. The exilic redaction of Hosea 12 invited the Judean exiles to see the Babylonian devastation of Judah and destruction of Jerusalem in the same way, that is, as a consequence of their own faithlessness. Their aim was not to demoralise the people through divine complaints and castigation, despite considering that such castigation was necessary, but rather to offer the explanation that there was divine meaning and purpose in what had happened. That being so, the people might

---

[350] E. Ben Zvi *Hosea* (2005): 247–8.
[351] J. A. Dearman *Hosea* (2010): 295.

C Commentary on Hosea

161

reasonably hope that YHWH still had purposeful intention towards them (as chapter 14 will make clear that he does).

Hosea 11:12–12:2 [12:1–3][352] serve as an introduction both to chapter 12 and to chapters 12–13 as a whole. It may be that the exilic redactor has enlarged an older saying of 11:12a; 12:1 [12:1a, 2] by the addition of 11:12b [12:1b], referring to Judah, so that the exilic form of the text relates to both kingdoms. The hopeful expressions of 11:8–11 are seemingly ignored as 11:12 [12:1] brings an accusation against Ephraim for his lies and deceit. The accusation of lies draws on use of the same word (*kaḥaš*) in 7:3 and 10:13, and the verb from which it is formed in 4:2. In parallel is the accusation of deceit (*mirmâ*): in Hosea the term is found only in this chapter, here and in 12:7 [8]. It is used of Jacob in Genesis 27:35, so provides a fleeting anticipation of verses 3–4 [4–5]. Together the two words symbolise an attitude of faithlessness towards YHWH. The name 'Ephraim' for the northern kingdom is used throughout chapters 4–11, and the exilic redactor maintains this practice. Picture language in 12:1 [2] describes Ephraim's efforts to go his own way as herding the wind and pursuing the east wind. The latter term refers to a scorching, hot wind from the desert (Ezek. 17:10; Jonah 4:8). The emphasis is on the futility of Ephraim's actions. The accusation continues: they multiply falsehood and violence. The term *šōd* ('violence') is used in the earlier literary layers of the text only to refer to Israel's destruction (7:13; 9:6; 10:14), and the exilic redactor's use of the term as an accusation reflects usage elsewhere (e.g. Jer. 6:7; Amos 3:10). It adds a criticism additional to those of lies, deceit, and falsehood, which constitute the primary accusation of these verses. The outworking of these is seen in the final couplet: Ephraim seeks simultaneously to make a treaty with Assyria and to curry favour with Egypt, a theme already met in 7:11 and 8:8–10. He is thereby duplicitous towards both powers, while also failing to trust in YHWH for protection. As noted, from an exilic horizon what is said of Ephraim is true also of Judah, and 11:12b [12:1b] brings in Judah explicitly. The meaning of the half-verse is, however, uncertain. The comparison of NRSV's 'but Judah still walks with God, and is faithful to the Holy One' with NIV's 'and Judah is unruly against God, even against the faithful Holy One' indicates the difficulty of establishing the meaning of the verb apparently used (*rûd*), which means something like 'roam', and could lead to either translation (the conjunction can mean 'but' or 'and').

---

[352] The Hebrew text chapter division is to be preferred over the English text division: 11:12 [12:1] belongs more naturally with chapter 12 than with the preceding verses.

162   *Book of Hosea*

A further complication is the term 'Holy Ones' (plural in the Hebrew) in the final line, generally (but not universally) taken to mean 'The Holy One' (cf. Prov. 9:10).[353] A negative stance towards Judah is more in keeping with the opening statement of 12:2 [3], setting out that YHWH has an indictment (*rîb*) against Judah. In 4:1 the same terminology serves to introduce both chapter 4 and the whole of 4–11 and, as noted, 11:12–12:2 [12:1–3] functions in the same way in introducing both chapter 12 and the whole of 12–14. Those who take this section to be addressed solely to eighth-century northern Israel are compelled to argue that 12:2a [3a] is an addition, or to suggest that 'Judah' has replaced an original 'Israel' (for which there is no textual evidence). However, if it is read as a sixth-century exilic text, such manoeuvres are unnecessary. YHWH having an indictment (*rîb*) against his people draws from 4:1 (see the commentary *ad loc* for the meaning of the term). The assertion that YHWH will punish Jacob according to his ways and repay him according to his deeds (12:2b [3b]) draws its vocabulary from 4:9.

The introduction of the name 'Jacob' allows the redactor to move on to verses 12:3–4 [4–5] which, along with 12:12 [13], concern not Jacob/Israel as a people, but Jacob the ancestor. These verses clearly relate to the Jacob narratives in Genesis.

A Closer Look: Jacob in Hosea 12

The relationship between Hosea 12: 3–4, 12 [4–5, 13] and the Jacob narratives in the Pentateuch has generated much scholarly writing.[354] The following may be noted:

(1) 12:3a [4a] clearly refers to the birth of the twins Esau and Jacob, recounted in Genesis 25:26. In the Genesis text the name 'Jacob'

---

[353] See further G. I. Davies *Hosea* (1992): 270–1; A. A. Macintosh *Hosea* (1997): 473–4; J. D. Nogalski *Hosea-Jonah* (2011): 166; H. W. Wolff *Hosea* (1974): 209–10. There is also a line of interpretation which sees NRSV's 'God' as the Canaanite god El, and 'Holy Ones' as El's royal court: so, for example, R. B. Coote, 'Hosea XII', *VT* 21 (1971): 389–402 (389–90).

[354] Among the literature (additional to the commentaries frequently referred to in this volume) may be mentioned, in chronological order: M. Gertner, 'An Attempt at an Interpretation of Hosea XII', *VT* 10 (1960): 272–84; H. L. Ginsberg, 'Hosea's Ephraim, More Fool than Knave: A New Interpretation of Hosea 12:1–14', *JBL* 80 (1961): 339–47; P. R. Ackroyd, 'Hosea and Jacob', *VT* 13 (1963): 245–59; E. M. Good, 'Hosea and the Jacob Tradition', *VT* 16 (1966): 137–51; R. B. Coote 'Hosea XII' (1971): 389–402; S. L. McKenzie, 'The Jacob Tradition in Hosea', *VT* 36 (1986): 311–22; E. K. Holt *Prophesying the Past* (1995): ch. 2 'Hosea's Jacob': 30–51; R. S. Chalmers, 'Who Is the Real El? A Reconstruction of the Prophet's Polemic in Hosea 12:5a', *CBQ* 68 (2006): 611–30.

C Commentary on Hosea

(*ya'ăqōb*) is a play on the word 'heel' (*'āqēb*). Hosea 12:3a [4a] extends the wordplay: the related verb *'āqab* meaning 'follow at the heel' can have the meaning 'overreach'; hence NRSV's translation as 'supplant'. This may be compared with Genesis 27:36, where Esau complains that Jacob is rightly named because he has 'supplanted' him, using the same verb. Hosea 12:3 [4]'s accusation is literally that in the womb 'he grasped his brother's heel', meaning (as NRSV translates) that even in the womb he sought to supplant his brother. The saying appears to relate to both sections of narrative.

(2) Hosea 12:3b–4a [4b–5a] draws on the account in Genesis 32:22–32 [23–33] of Jacob's wrestling with a man at the ford of the Jabbok. In Genesis 32 Jacob's wrestling is with a man (32:24 [25]), but at dawn it is revealed that he has been striving with God (32:28 [29]). Hosea 12:3b [4b] also has Jacob strive with God, but in 4a [5a] it becomes an angel with whom he strove and prevailed. Several scholars (but by no means all) take the introduction of the angel to be an addition to an original form of the text which referred solely to God.[355] The following line – 'he wept and sought his favour' – is ambiguous. Did Jacob weep and seek the angel's favour, or vice-versa? In Genesis 32 the man asks Jacob to let him go (32:26 [27]), but Jacob asks the man (or God) to tell him his name (32:29 [30]). The line in Hosea 12:4 [5] could refer to either of these. On balance it seems more probable that it is Jacob who weeps and seeks God's/the angel's favour. There is, however, no mention in Genesis 32 of Jacob weeping. Did Hosea or the compiler of the text know of a variant version of Genesis 32 in which Jacob wept? Or is the Hosea-text embellishing the Genesis narrative? Alternatively, Genesis 33:4 tells that Jacob and Esau both wept when they met, and Genesis 32:22–32 [23–33] is the final, climactic part of Jacob's preparation for that meeting. Does Hosea 12:4 [5] take the verb from Genesis 33:4? Yet another suggestion is that Bethel (Hosea 12:4 [5]) was known as a place of weeping: Genesis 35:8 records that when Deborah, Rebekah's nurse died and was buried under the oak tree below Bethel the tree was named 'Oak of weeping'.

---

[355] Those who see the angel as an addition include A. A. Macintosh *Hosea* (1997): 484; H. W. Wolff *Hosea* (1974): 206, 212. Those who do not include J. A. Dearman *Hosea* (2010): 295; M. A. Sweeney *Twelve Prophets* 1 (2000): 122.

(3) In Genesis 32 the wrestling at the stream Jabbok takes place at Peniel, for which 32:30 [31] gives an aetiology. It means 'Face of God', and Jacob gives it that name because he has seen the face of God and lived. Hosea 12:4b [5b], however, sets the incident at Bethel. Accounts of God appearing to Jacob at Bethel are found in Genesis 28:11–22 and 35:6–15, and by naming Bethel the Hosea-text carries an echo of these.

(4) In Hosea 12:12 [13] Jacob flees to the land of Aram. But in Genesis 27:43 it is Haran to which Rebekah tells Jacob to flee. However in Genesis 28:5 Isaac sends Jacob to 'Laban, the son of Bethuel the Aramean'; and Genesis 29:4–5 refers to Haran as the place where Laban lives.

(5) Hosea 12:12 [13] records that Jacob 'served' for a wife. The same verb is used of Jacob serving Laban for Rachel in Genesis 29:15, 18, 20, 25. Hosea 12:12 [13] also states that Jacob 'guarded/kept'. The verb lacks an object, and many commentators and translators (including NRSV) supply the object 'sheep' on the basis of Genesis 30:31, where Jacob says to Laban that he will feed and guard/keep his flock.

There is no reason to doubt that Jacob stories were circulating (probably in oral form) by the eighth century.[356] The presence of both similarities and discrepancies between Hosea and the Pentateuchal narratives indicates that the prophet and those who committed his words to writing knew a variant form of the narratives from those in Genesis, and/or that they have exercised considerable artistic freedom in their telling. The appearances of God to Jacob at Bethel in Genesis 28 and 35 lend credence to the likelihood that the stories were told and preserved at the Bethel sanctuary, making the reference to Bethel in Hosea 12:4b [5b] entirely natural. Gomes suggests that Hosea 12:3–4 [4–5] is a quotation of an old epic poem recited at Bethel;[357] Sweeney and Chalmers suggest that they are liturgical.[358] It is noteworthy that no attempt is made

---

[356] It is noteworthy that J. M. Bos *Reconsidering* (2013): 161, reading Hosea as a Persian period text and seeking to date as much material as possible to it, nevertheless writes: 'Almost certainly tales about Jacob were being told, and maybe even written down, in Israel from a rather early period.'

[357] J. F. Gomes *The Sanctuary at Bethel* (2006): 171.

[358] M. A. Sweeney *Twelve Prophets* 1 (2000): 121; R. S. Chalmers 'Who Is the Real El?' (2006): 624.

C Commentary on Hosea

there to denigrate Bethel in favour of Jerusalem, and this verse does not, therefore, change the name to Beth-aven as in 4:15; 5:8; 10:5. Later redactors have allowed the memory of Bethel as a place at which God appeared to stand.

Hosea 12:3a [4a] states that Jacob tried to 'supplant his brother' (NRSV), the Hebrew literally saying that 'he grasped his brother's heel' (as NIV translates). Genesis 25:26 records as neutral fact that Jacob came out of the womb gripping Esau's heel. Hosea 12:3 [4] interprets this as revealing that Jacob's deception and supplanting of his brother began even in the womb. Reasons of continuity make it natural to take Jacob's striving with God as also being accusatory. This is confirmed by the statement that this striving took place in his 'manhood' (12:3b [4b]). The word used is *'ôn*, used also in 12:8 [9] of the wealth that Ephraim boasts he has gained. It shares consonants with *'āwen*, 'iniquity', which is found in 12:11 [12]. Readers of the text are shown that Israel's current faithlessness towards God matches their ancestor's deceptive behaviour.[359] Some have held that these verses should be read in a positive sense: it is meant that in the womb Jacob overtook his brother, and that this fulfils the divine promise of Genesis 25:23.[360] The striving with God can then also be seen as reflecting Jacob's desire to be close to God. In the literary context of Hosea 12, which begins and ends with clear accusation (11:12–12:1; 12:14 [12:1–2, 15]), the accusatory reading is the more natural. Better still, however, is to recognise the ambiguity of these verses.[361] The character of Jacob in Genesis, similarly, may evoke a range of possible reactions in the reader. His cheating of Esau out of his birthright (Gen. 25:29–34) and his deceit of his aged father Isaac in order to gain his blessing (Gen. 27) reveal Jacob's scheming and dishonest character, and as such invite disapproval. But might some readers find that they also have a sneaking admiration for his cunning? When God appears to Jacob at Bethel on his flight (Gen. 28:10–22), Jacob prays a prayer (28:20–22) which suggests the beginnings of taking God seriously (even though it's a very conditional prayer: *if* God will do several things for him, '*then* YHWH shall be my God'). Jacob's serving Laban for two seven-year periods in order to marry Rachel, whom

---

[359] J. L. Mays *Hosea* (1969): 162.

[360] So, notably, P. R. Ackroyd 'Hosea and Jacob' (1963): 245–59; also J. F. Gomes *The Sanctuary at Bethel* (2006): 174.

[361] G. Eidevall *Grapes in the Desert* (1996): 186–7. He is followed by J. M. Bos *Reconsidering* (2013): 159 and by J. A. Dearman *Hosea* (2010): 294–5.

166   Book of Hosea

he loved (Gen. 29:20) suggests, perhaps, a deepening of his character. The story of Jacob's wrestling at Jabbok (Gen. 32:22–32 [23–33]) admits of no simple interpretation, but his re-naming as Israel (32:28 [29]) suggests, perhaps, a moment of new beginning. All in all, Jacob is a complex, ambiguous being, and the question of whether he is a good or a bad person is too simple a question to put to such a subtle series of narratives. Hosea 12:3–4 [4–5] reflect a similar ambiguity in their meaning.

Hosea 12:4 [5] has a change of subject mid-verse. In the first half of the verse Jacob is the subject. In the final line – 'and there he spoke with us' – clearly God is the subject. The preceding line – 'he met him at Bethel' – could mean either that God met Jacob, in which case the change of subject is from that line, or that Jacob met God, in which case it is not until the final line. The meaning is similar either way. NRSV follows many commentators in changing the Hebrew 'us' of the final line to 'him', in order to maintain continuity with the rest of the verse.[362] The change should be resisted. The line serves to 'actualise' the experience of the past for the present generation, and the 'us' to whom God spoke should be read in its literary context as the current generation of readers.[363] A parallel may be drawn with Deuteronomy 5:3, a verse which belongs to a sixth-century Deuteronomistic layer of text.[364] After reference to the making of the covenant at Horeb, it says: 'Not with our ancestors did YHWH make this covenant, but with us, who are all of us here alive today.' The exilic redactors of Hosea 12 employed a similar technique in this last line of 12:4 [5]. This leads naturally into 12:5 [6], a liturgical/hymnic verse similar to those in Amos 4:13; 5:8–9; 9:5–6. The closest parallels to these hymnic verses are in Job 9:1–12 and Isaiah 40:12, 22–23, and the refrain in Amos 4:13, 5:8–9 and 9:5–6 that 'YHWH is his name' or 'YHWH, the God of hosts is his name' is found predominately in exilic texts in Isaiah (47:4; 48:2; 51:15; 54:5) and Jeremiah (10:16; 31:35–38; 32:18; 46:18; 48:15; 51:15–19, 57). For this and other reasons the Amos verses are widely held to be exilic in origin.[365] Many commentators who take much of Hosea 12 to derive from the eighth century nevertheless take 12:5 [6] to be a later addition.[366] There is

[362]   E.g. H. W. Wolff *Hosea* (1974): 207. LXX lends support to this.
[363]   J. M. Trotter *Reading Hosea* (2001): 209 writes that it 'was not just the ancestor who was found by Yahweh at Bethel, but all the descendants of this eponymous figure ... the present community is identified with the eponymous ancestor'.
[364]   A. D. H. Mayes *Deuteronomy* (1979): 161.
[365]   See further the 'Introduction to Amos' and 'Amos 4:13: The One Who Forms the Mountains and Creates the Winds'.
[366]   So *inter alia* G. I. Davies *Hosea* (1992): 268; H. W. Wolff *Hosea* (1974): 213.

C Commentary on Hosea   167

one difference between this verse and those in Amos, namely that the word for 'name' is not the usual *šēm*. Instead the word that NRSV translates as 'name' is *zēqer*, which carries a sense of YHWH's renown or reputation (cf. Ps. 102:12 [13]). The two words are used in parallel in Psalm 135:13 and, significantly, in Exodus 3:15 where, following the revelation of the divine name, it is said: 'This is my name (*šēm*) for ever, and this my title (*zēqer*) for all generations.' The God who spoke to Jacob at Bethel and who speaks today to the current generation (12:4b [5b]) is no local deity, or merely one of the hosts of gods in the heavenly council: he is none other than YHWH, God of the hosts, whose reputation precedes him.[367]

With YHWH's reputation and majesty declared, the summons of 12:6 to 'return to your God' is entirely appropriate. In 6:1 the people had said (or had been encouraged to say) 'Come, let us return to YHWH.' As noted in the commentary on 6:1, the verb 'return' (*šûb*) is used many times in the Hosea-text. To 6:1 YHWH's response in 6:4–6 was to doubt the sincerity of the words, and to set out that 'I desire steadfast love (*hesed*), not sacrifice' (6:6). The exilic redactor therefore follows his summons to return to God with the summons to hold fast to *hesed* (on the meaning of which see the commentary on 4:1). With *hesed* is linked *mišpāṭ* ('justice'). The only other place in Hosea where these two words come together is 2:19 [21], which is also part of an early post-exilic redaction of the text. Only in these two verses in Hosea does *mišpāṭ* carry the meaning 'justice' rather than its alternative translation 'judgement' (cf. 5:1, 11; 10:4).[368] Its use here is closer to texts such as Amos 5:24 and Isaiah 1:17 than to elsewhere in Hosea. The final line of 12:6 [7] urges the people to 'wait continually for your God'. To 'wait' indicates placing one's hope in God (e.g. Ps. 130:5; Isa. 8:17; 51:5). Neither the verb 'wait' (*qāwâ*) nor the qualifying 'continually' (*tāmîd*) are found in the older literary layers underlying the Hosea-text, but the verb resonates with texts in the exilic Isaiah 40–55 (40:31; 49:23; 51:5).

The continuing text in 12:7–8 [8–9] assumes that the summons is ignored. Ephraim does not place his hope in YHWH, but in his dubious business practices and his wealth. He is described as a 'trader' (NRSV). The word in Hebrew is 'Canaan'. The Phoenician city of Tyre had a particular reputation for its trade (Ezek. 27–28), but it seems that Canaanites generally were held

---

[367] While YHWH's title in Amos 4:13 is 'God of hosts', in Hosea 12:5 [6] it is 'God of *the* hosts'. The addition of the definite article serves to underscore YHWH's supremacy.
[368] G. I. Davies *Hosea* (1992): 277.

168   Book of Hosea

to be merchants.[369] There may be hint of accusation of the Israelites becoming like the former inhabitants of the land,[370] but if so it is less clear and direct than the accusations that follow. Disapproval of the use of false balances (12:7a [8a]) is expressed in both legal and wisdom traditions (Lev. 19:35–36; Deut. 25:13–16; Prov. 11:1; 16:11: 20:10, 23). This same accusation is made in Amos 8:5, a seventh-century re-working of Amos 2:6–7 which brings the accusation into its new formulation of the earlier text.[371] The accusation of Hosea 12:7 [8] is of a kind more representative of the Amos-text than the Hosea-text, and the redactor of Hosea 12 may have been familiar with Amos 8:5. The expression 'false balances' is literally 'balances of deceit', the word 'deceit' (*mirmâ*) being the same word used in 11:12 [12:1]. As noted in the comments on that verse, the word is used, too, of Jacob by Esau in Genesis 27:35. In Hosea 12:7 [8] there may, therefore, be an implicit 'as the ancestor, so the current generation'. Hosea 12:8 [9] contains a play on words in its accusation: Ephraim declares that he has 'found wealth' for himself and that they will not 'find offence' in him. The verbs are the same, and the words for 'wealth' and 'offence' sound very similar.[372] Ephraim protests his innocence despite the false balances or, possibly, his cleverness in nobody being able to find fault with him.

YHWH, however, sees his offence. He describes himself here and in 13:4 as 'YHWH, your God from the land of Egypt'. While this brief self-description may not, in its origin, have been taken from the opening words of the Decalogue (Exod. 20:2; Deut. 5:6), later readers will surely have recognised an association of the two. Within the Hosea-text the formula connects thematically to 11:1. As judgement, YHWH announces that he will make them live in tents again. Ephraim has gained his wealth while settled in the land. YHWH has the power to remove that settled status. As in 9:5 (to which 12:9 [10]) may, fleetingly, allude), the reference to the 'appointed feast/festival' refers, very probably, to the Feast of Sukkoth (see the commentary on 9:5). The threat of 12:9 [10] is that the temporary living in tents that formed part of the festival will become a permanent way of life, as the people are taken back into the wilderness through which they wandered after their exodus from Egypt. It will be noted that the exilic redactor uses the wilderness motif differently from how it is used in 2:14–15 [16–17]; 9:10. There it

---

[369]   Job 41:6 [40:30]; Prov. 31:24; Ezek. 17:4; Zeph. 1:11.
[370]   So J. L. Mays *Hosea* (1969): 166–7.
[371]   See 'Amos 8:4–7: Cheating the Poor and Needy'.
[372]   The translation of 12:8b [9b] is not straightforward, but NRSV gives the likely sense.

C Commentary on Hosea

169

was a time of blessing and of divine favour. Here it is a punishment. Holt differs from most commentators in seeing 12:9 [10], too, as a promise of future blessing, reading the verbs of the next verse as future rather than past, and thus continuing the promise.[373] However, with 12:8 [9] and 12:11 [12] both being condemnatory, it is most straightforward to take 12:9–10 [10–11] in similar vein. More possible is Macintosh's opinion that the 'dwelling in tents is to be construed both in terms of punishment and redemption';[374] although it is punishment which seems to be primarily in view.

The references to Israel's past in 12:9 [10] suggest that the verbs in 12:10 [11] should also be taken to refer to the past rather than translated in the future tense, although either is possible grammatically. The rejection of the prophets becomes an additional reason for judgement. This motif is found also in 2 Kings 17:13–18, part of the exilic Deuteronomistic History. It is reflected, too, in Amos 2:11–12; 7:12–15.[375] All of 2 Kings 17:13, Amos 7:12, and Hosea 12:10 [11] use the term *ḥōzeh* ('seer') or *ḥāzôn* ('vision'), further reinforcing that this verse is at home in the exilic redaction of Hosea 12. YHWH's judgement fits the accusation: through the prophets 'I will bring destruction' – although the translation is, in fact, debatable. There are two verbs *dāmāh*. One means 'be like, resemble', giving (in the Piel) NIV's 'told parables'. The other means 'cease, cause to cease, destroy', giving NRSV's 'bring destruction'. This second verb is found also in Hosea 4:5, 6; 10:7, 15, and in my view has the better claim in 12:10 [11] also.[376] Additionally this verse then links thematically to 6:5, which I have argued also entered the text in the exilic redaction. As noted there, it was considered that the prophetic word did not merely announce, but also contributed to the effecting of what was declared. As in 6:5, so here also.

Both accusation and pronouncement of judgement continue into 12:11 [12], which once again draws on motifs found in chapters 4–11. NRSV's

---

[373] E. K. Holt *Prophesying the Past* (1995): 62–4.

[374] A. A. Macintosh *Hosea* (1997): 501.

[375] Amos 2:11–12 belong to the Exilic Redactional Composition of the Amos-text. Several scholars attribute Amos 7:10–17 to this same redaction. However I argue that it is more likely that it derives from the seventh-century Late Pre-exilic Redactional Composition of Amos, and was thus a precursor of what became a prominent Deuteronomistic motif. For both passages see the commentary *ad loc* and the 'Introduction to Amos'.

[376] BDB: 197–8. Scholars who prefer the meaning 'told parables', or something similar, include F. I. Andersen and D. N. Freedman *Hosea* (1980): 594; A. A. Macintosh *Hosea* (1997): 502; H. W. Wolff *Hosea* (1974): 207. Scholars who prefer 'bring destruction' include J. L. Mays *Hosea* (1969): 166; J. D. Nogalski *Hosea–Jonah* (2011): 170. Scholars who give either translation more or less equal probability include G. I. Davies *Hosea* (1992): 280–1; M. A. Sweeney *Twelve Prophets* 1 (2000): 125.

170

'In Gilead' does not reflect MT, which reads: 'If in Gilead there is iniquity (*'āwen*), they shall surely come to nothing.' The exilic redactor picks up the reference to Gilead in 6:8, which also uses the word *'āwen* of Gilead.[377] It is likely that 6:7–10 have been shaped by the exilic redactor, possibly incorporating older material in 6:8–9 (see the commentary *ad loc*), and 12:11a [12a] makes a cross-reference to it. The second half of the verse refers to Gilgal. It may be that the Hebrew text's opening 'If' of the verse does duty for the second half of the verse too: 'If in Gilgal they sacrifice bulls, so their altars shall be like heaps of stones.'[378] However NRSV's translation is equally possible. Gilgal is referred to in 4:15 and 9:15, the latter of which refers to the evil and wickedness which began there; but this is not picked up on in 12:11 [12]. What is picked up is the theme of altars being destroyed, which is found in 10:2, 8. The implication of 12:11b [12b] is that the sacrificing of bulls at Gilgal was improper, although no explanation is given as to why. Macintosh is correct in noting that Gilgal was nowhere associated with the notorious bull-cult at Bethel and Dan (1 Kgs 12:26–30).[379] Whatever the exact reason, Gilgal, too, is included in the judgement announced, and perhaps included because of the pleasing alliteration in Hebrew of 'Gilead … Gilgal … *gallîm*' ('heap of stones'). Gilgal's altars will become like stone heaps 'on the furrows of the field', a phrase copied from 10:4. The evidence for the exilic redactors' referring to words in chapters 4–11 is once again clear.

Hosea 12:12–13 [13–14] are intended to be read as a contrasting pair. The contrast is in their stated content: Jacob journeyed to Aram in flight from Esau, while Israel journeyed from Egypt because YHWH brought him up from there; Jacob guarded sheep,[380] while Israel was guarded by a prophet (the verb *šāmar*, 'guard/keep', ends both verses). It may be implied, too, that 'Jacob put himself voluntarily under servitude, YHWH took Israel out of servitude.'[381] As noted in the comments on 12:3–4 [4–5], Jacob is an ambiguous character in both the Genesis narratives and in Hosea 12. This ambiguity leaves the reader to supply some interpretations: Does Jacob's servitude for a wife represent his humiliation? Or does it speak, rather, of

---

[377] NRSV's 'evildoers' in 6:8 is literally 'men doing wickedness/iniquity'.
[378] So A. A. Macintosh *Hosea* (1997): 504–6. He is followed by J. A. Dearman *Hosea* (2010): 296. NIV's translation reflects this possibility.
[379] A. A. Macintosh *Hosea* (1997): 506.
[380] As noted in 'A Closer Look: Jacob in Hosea 12'), NRSV follows most commentators in supplying the object 'sheep' on the basis of Gen. 30:31, in order to make sense of the verse. A. A. Macintosh *Hosea* (1997): 508 prefers to read it as 'To a wife he devoted himself.'
[381] E. Ben Zvi *Hosea* (2005): 260.

C Commentary on Hosea

his growing maturity away from dishonesty, brought about by his evident love for Rachel (Gen. 29:20)? Or is it a punishment for his cheating of his brother Esau out of his birthright and his father's blessing? Let the reader decide! For readers in the exilic period Jacob's journey to a foreign land may have spoken to them of their own exile, just as the exodus from Egypt spoke to them of the hope of return to the homeland. This hope would be strengthened by the recollection that Israel's deliverance from Egypt was 'by a prophet' and that the nation had been guarded 'by a prophet' (12:13 [14]). There is no doubt that the reference is to Moses. Deuteronomy 18:15–18 most clearly calls Moses a prophet.[382] Also Numbers 11:25 records that YHWH took some of the spirit that was on Moses and put it on seventy elders, who then prophesied. Other texts indicate that YHWH spoke with Moses face to face in a way superior to that in which he spoke to prophets (Num. 12:6–8; Deut. 34:10–12). Exilic readers would have been strengthened in their hope for return by the memory of Moses the prophet's role in leading the people out of their servitude in Egypt.

The final verse of the chapter returns to YHWH's accusation against Ephraim and his consequent judgement on him. With the opening 11:12–12:2 [12:1–3] it brackets the chapter, and gives the verdict on the indictment (*rîb*) begun in 12:2 [3]. The hiphil of the verb *kāʿas*, translated by NRSV as Ephraim having 'given offence', is characteristic Deuteronomistic vocabulary more usually translated as 'provoking (YHWH) to anger' through worship of other gods (Deut. 4:25; 9:18; 31:29; Judg. 2:12; 1 Kgs 14:9, 15; 16:7, 13, 26, 33; 22:53 [54]; 2 Kgs 17:11, 21:6; 23:19; Jer. 7:18–19; 8:19; 11:17; etc.). Macintosh comments that the verse 'summarises the culpability of the contemporary nation'.[383] Such is the explanation of Ephraim's/Israel's downfall in 722; and for exilic readers, of Judah's downfall in 587.

Hosea 13 [13:1–14:1] – Ephraim's End

13 When Ephraim spoke, there was trembling;
    he was exalted in Israel,
      but he incurred guilt through Baal and died.
² And now they keep on sinning
    and make a cast image for themselves,

---

[382] A. D. H. Mayes *Deuteronomy* (1979): 279–80 argues that these verses are later than Deut. 5:23ff. and 9:9ff., with which they have similarities but also differences. In that case it is by no means clear whether they are earlier or later than Hos. 12:13 [14] as an exilic verse. Either way it remains the case that the reference is to Moses.

[383] A. A. Macintosh *Hosea* (1997): 515.

idols of silver made according to their understanding,
    all of them the work of artisans.
'Sacrifice to these', they say.
    People are kissing calves!
3 Therefore they shall be like the morning mist
    or like the dew that goes away early,
like chaff that swirls from the threshing floor
    or like smoke from a window.

4 Yet I have been the LORD your God
    ever since the land of Egypt;
you know no God but me,
    and besides me there is no saviour.
5 It was I who fed you in the wilderness,
    in the land of drought.
6 When I fed them, they were satisfied;
    they were satisfied, and their heart was proud;
    therefore they forgot me.
7 So I will become like a lion to them;
    like a leopard I will lurk beside the way.
8 I will fall upon them like a bear robbed of her cubs
    and will tear open the covering of their heart;
there I will devour them like a lion,
    as a wild animal would mangle them.

9 I will destroy you, O Israel;
    who can help you?
10 Where now is your king, that he may save you?
    Where in all your cities are your rulers,
of whom you said,
    'Give me a king and rulers'?
11 I gave you a king in my anger,
    and I took him away in my wrath.

12 Ephraim's iniquity is bound up;
    his sin is kept in store.
13 The pangs of childbirth come for him,
    but he is an unwise son,
for at the proper time he does not present himself
    at the mouth of the womb.
14 Shall I ransom them from the power of Sheol?
    Shall I redeem them from Death?
    O Death, where are your plagues?

C Commentary on Hosea

> O Sheol, where is your destruction?
> Compassion is hidden from my eyes.
>
> [15] Although he may flourish among rushes,
>   the east wind shall come, a blast from the LORD,
>   rising from the wilderness,
> and his fountain shall dry up,
>   his spring shall be parched.
> It shall strip his treasury
>   of every precious thing.
> [16] Samaria shall bear her guilt
>   because she has rebelled against her God;
> they shall fall by the sword;
>   their little ones shall be dashed in pieces,
>   and their pregnant women ripped open.

The lack of both concluding formula at 12:14 [15] and introductory formula at 13:1 means that chapters 12 and 13 could be read as one section. However, the accusations of this chapter are different from those of the previous chapter. Furthermore, the verb 'incur guilt/bear guilt' in 13:1 and 13:16 [14:1] bracket the material in chapter 13, suggesting that it is best taken as a section in its own right. Wolff correctly describes chapters 12 and 13 as 'different kerygmatic units which belong together as one transmission complex'.[384] It was argued in the section 'Hosea 11:12–12:14 [12:1–15] – Ephraim, Judah and Jacob' that chapter 12 was an exilic redactional compilation, and the fact that they were transmitted together as one literary complex leads us to expect that chapter 13, too, will be at home in an exilic setting; and so it proves to be. The chapter draws together themes and quotations from earlier parts of the Hosea-text and elsewhere into what Nogalski calls a 'theological collage'. He notes that it 'recaps significant elements of the book's message' and that it 'exhibits a perspective considerably later than most passages elsewhere in Hosea'. Indeed, his heading over chapter 13 is 'Recapping the Message'.[385] This judgement is confirmed by:

(1) 13:1's and 13:16 [14:1]'s theme of 'guilt', drawn from 4:15; 5:15; 10:2;
(2) 13:1's allusion to Baal: the lack of further explanation is because it assumes the reader's familiarity with 2:8, 13 [10, 15]; 9:10; 11:2;
(3) 13:2's 'sinning', picking up 4:7 and 8:11;

---

[384] H. W. Wolff *Hosea* (1974): 224.
[385] J. D. Nogalski *Hosea–Jonah* (2011): 177–80, 186.

(4) 13:2's mention of idols, picking up 4:17; 8:4, 6;

(5) 13:3's expression 'like the morning mist/cloud or the dew that goes away early' being drawn *verbatim* from 6:4;

(6) the theme of 'wilderness' in 13:5, 15 (cf. 2:3 [5]; 2:14 [16]; 9:10);

(7) Israel's forgetfulness of YHWH in 13:6 reflecting her forgetfulness in 2:13 [15]; 4:6 (and the exilic 8:14);

(8) YHWH's actions as a lion (13:7 cf. 5:14);

(9) 13:10's reference to 'your' kings and rulers reflecting 8:4's accusation of making kings and appointing princes without reference to him;

(10) 13:12's 'iniquity' and 'sin' being found as a pair of words also in 4:8; 8:13; 9:9;

(11) the word 'compassion' in 13:14, referring to the word from the same root similarly translated in 11:8;

(12) the cruelty of 13:16 [14:1] reflecting that of 10:14.

Additionally Hosea 13 links to chapter 12 through the expression 'YHWH your God from the land of Egypt' (12:9; 13:4), and through mention of the east wind (12:1 [2]; 13:15).[386]

The opening unit 13:1–3 takes us through past (13:1), present (13:2), and future (13:3) tenses. As in previous chapters, Ephraim is accused. Elsewhere in Hosea the name is used as a synonym for Israel.[387] Here, however, Ephraim is exalted within Israel. Commentators offer various explanations. Mays sees an allusion to the pre-eminence that Jacob accords Ephraim by blessing him ahead of his older brother Manasseh (Gen. 48).[388] Macintosh sees an allusion, rather, to the founding of the northern kingdom and monarchy, since Jeroboam I was an Ephraimite (1 Kgs 11:26; 12:16–20).[389] Wolff takes the reference to be to Mount Ephraim, where the royal residence on Samaria was located.[390] Both Macintosh's and Wolff's views lead to the effective equating of Ephraim and Israel, as in all other parts of the text. The theme of Israel's guilt draws from 4:15; 5:15; 10:2. This was incurred 'through Baal': the lack of any enlargement of the nature of the accusation indicates

---

[386] J. D. Nogalski *Hosea–Jonah* (2011): 178 has a table of 'intertextual features of Hosea 13' which includes other cross-references which are, in my view, less certain. However those set out here are sufficient to make the case. Likely references to texts outside Hosea will be noted in the commentary.

[387] See 'A Closer Look: "Ephraim" in Hosea' page 115.

[388] J. L. Mays *Hosea* (1969): 172.

[389] A. A. Macintosh *Hosea* (1997): 520.

[390] H. W. Wolff *Hosea* (1974): 225.

C Commentary on Hosea

175

that the reader is assumed to be familiar with preceding passages in the text (2:8, 13 [10, 15]; 9:10; 11:2). The final word of the verse gives a consequence: 'and he died'. Is it the death of the northern kingdom at the hand of the Assyrians in 722 that is meant? It is hard to be sure. The whole verse is concise. Dearman comments that 'its terseness paints with a broad brush and almost certainly depends on material elsewhere in Hosea.... It is intended to underscore what has been claimed elsewhere in more detail.'[391] Hosea 13:2 moves from the past into the present: Israel keeps on sinning. The verb picks up 4:7 and 8:11. The accusation of making idols picks up 4:17; 8:4. That of making a cast image (*massēkâ*), however, is a new one. The term is used of the golden calf made by Aaron (Exod. 32:4, 8; Deut. 9:16; Neh. 9:18; Ps. 106:19), and of images of calf-gods made by Jeroboam I at Bethel and Dan (2 Kgs 17:16),[392] as well as of cast images generally (e.g. Deut. 27:15). Hosea 13:2 describes Israel's images and idols as made by 'artisans' (*ḥārāš*). The term is also found in Hosea 8:6 which, it was argued in the commentary, entered the text in the exilic redaction, that is, along with chapters 12–13. It occurs three times in Isaiah 44:11–13 (NRSV's 'blacksmith' in 44:12 being 'craftsman of iron' and 'carpenter' of 44:13 being 'craftsman of woods'). The last part of the verse is difficult to translate and interpret.[393] However, the kissing of calves finds an echo in 1 Kings 19:18, in relation to Baal worship. The descriptions of past misdemeanours in 13:1 and more recent ones in 13:2 lead into a pronouncement of judgement in 13:3. The judgement comprises four similes, each describing something short-lived and impermanent. Dearman describes this verse as 'an exquisite literary formulation'.[394] The first half of the verse with its images of morning mist and early morning dew is taken *verbatim* from 6:4b. There can be no promise of a secure future while Israel's behaviour is as it is.

In contrast to the impermanence to which the making of images and the kissing of calf-gods leads is the reliable generosity of YHWH, set out in 13:4–5. He is 'YHWH your God from the land of Egypt' (on which see

---

[391] J. A. Dearman *Hosea* (2010): 319.

[392] Consideration of the complex relationship between the narratives in Exod. 32 and 1 Kgs 12:26–30 lies beyond the scope of this commentary; standard commentaries on both books may be consulted.

[393] See A. A. Macintosh *Hosea* (1997): 523.

[394] J. A. Dearman *Hosea* (2010): 320. The 'they' to whom the similes refer is most naturally read as being the people. Macintosh, however, takes it to refer to the cast image and idols of 13:2, acknowledging that his is the minority interpretation. See A. A. Macintosh *Hosea* (1997): 525.

176   *Book of Hosea*

the commentary on 12:9 [10]). Hosea 13:4b – 'you know no God but me, and besides me there is no saviour' – clearly reflects the exilic milieu of verses such as Isaiah 43:11; 45:21, but blended with Hoseanic vocabulary of knowing God. As Israel knows God, so in the Hebrew text of 13:5 YHWH states that he knew Israel in the wilderness. LXX and the Peshitta read 'I fed them' rather than 'I knew them', and this reading is followed by several commentators and adopted by NRSV. The arguments either way are finely balanced.[395] Whichever is preferred, the verse indicates that YHWH cared for and provided for his people in the wilderness (cf. 9:10; 11:3). Hosea 13:6, however, contains an unhappy contrast comparable to those of 9:10b and 11:2: once he had fed them, and they were satisfied, in their satisfaction they became proud and forgot him. YHWH's feeding of them could refer to the feeding with manna in the wilderness (Exod. 16) or his bringing them into the land. The forgetting of YHWH picks up the same accusation in 2:13 [15], and contrasts with the many summonses in Deuteronomy to remember (7:18; 8:2, and *passim*). The forgetting that YHWH once fed and satisfied them reflects the warning of Deuteronomy 8:11–20 that when the people are in the land and have their plenty of food, houses, livestock, and silver and gold, then they must not in their arrogance claim that they gained all this by their own power and might, and thereby forget YHWH. Those who take Hosea 13 to go back to the prophet or to an eighth-century formulation assume that this verse influenced the subsequent composition of Deuteronomy.[396] Those (such as this commentary) who take the chapter to be an exilic composition can recognise a theme which came into prominence at that time. The people's pride and forgetfulness of YHWH leads to a pronouncement of judgement, expressed in four images of YHWH as a wild animal: a lion (*šaḥal*), a leopard, a bear robbed of her cubs, and a lion (*lābî'*) (13:7–8). The image of YHWH as a lion picks up 5:14. The rage of a she-bear who loses her cubs reflects a proverbial image (2 Sam. 17:8; Prov. 17:12). The final line of 13:8 indicates the total mangling of the people. Within a few verses (13:4–8) YHWH moves from being protector and provider to being predator. The shepherd becomes the wild animals from whom the shepherd is meant to protect the flock.[397]

---

[395]   J. A. Dearman *Hosea* (2010): 316, 321 and A. A. Macintosh *Hosea* (1997): 528–9 both prefer MT.

[396]   H. W. Wolff *Hosea* (1974): 226.

[397]   G. Eidevall *Grapes in the Desert* (1996): 196–9.

C Commentary on Hosea

The translation of 13:9 is difficult. The Hebrew reads literally: 'He has destroyed you, O Israel, for in me is your help.'[398] Whatever the precise meaning, the general sense of 13:9–10 is clear: Israel has been destroyed, and the kings, rulers, and officials to whom the people looked for protection have utterly failed them. In 13:10 NRSV translates two different Hebrew words as 'rulers': one (*šōpēṭîm*) is found in 7:7, the other (*śārîm*) in 5:10; 7:3, 5, 16; 8:4, 10; 9:15, as well as the post-exilic 3:4.[399] Hosea 13:10 refers to 'your king' and 'your rulers', indicating that YHWH does not consider them to be his appointees, in confirmation of 8:4. As with 8:4, it is open to debate whether 13:10–11 is against monarchy *per se*, or against the monarchy and officials of the northern kingdom but perhaps in favour of the Davidic monarchy, or against particular kings and rulers: see the comments on 8:4. In the exilic literary context of Hosea 13, the first possibility seems most likely. The verses carry an echo of 1 Samuel 8:4–22, in which YHWH, through Samuel, grants the people a king against his better judgement.

Hosea 13:12 recalls the people's iniquity and sin from verses earlier in the book, the two words being paired in 4:8; 8:13; 9:9. Now it is said that they will be bound up and kept in store, that is, for the time of judgement. The verb 'bind up' (*ṣārar*) is used in Isaiah 8:16, where it is a written testimony of the prophet's words which are to be bound up and kept by his disciples. It is not necessary to assume the same of Hosea 13:12, however. Rather, it is YHWH who will not lose the record of their wrongs (cf. Deut. 32:34).

Hosea 13:13 declares Ephraim to be an 'unwise son'. His lack of wisdom is illustrated by the image of a child in the womb refusing to be born at the proper time. We might consider that a son due to be born can hardly be deemed to have moral responsibility. The poetic language, however, is akin to 12:3, where Jacob's supplanting of Esau is traced right back to this same moment. In 13:13 the pangs of childbirth seem to come upon the foetus, rather than the more usual coming on the mother (e.g. Isa. 21:3; Jer. 22:23). It is likely that a child's refusal to be born was a proverbial image of a time of distress (2 Kgs 19:3; cf. Isa. 66:9). Thus in Hosea 13:13 Ephraim brings a time of distress on the nation through his sinful ways.

---

[398] NRSV's translation entails a consonantal emendation of the Hebrew. NIV translates: 'You are destroyed, O Israel, because you are against me, against your helper.' G. I. Davies *Hosea* (1992): 292 suggests a re-pointing of vowels only to give 'I destroyed you, O Israel.' See further A. A. Macintosh *Hosea* (1997): 535–6.

[399] NRSV translates *śārîm* as 'princes' in 3:4; 5:10; 8:4, 10; 'officials' in 7:3, 5, 16; 9:15; 'rulers' in 13:10.

178   *Book of Hosea*

There are various possible meanings of 13:14.[400] Because the Hebrew text does not include punctuation, the first half of the verse could be two questions (as NRSV) or two statements (as NIV). The second part of the verse is more clearly a pair of questions, with an introductory 'where' to each. NIV's translation makes the verse a positive expression of hope for the people being spared the fate of Death and Sheol and, in order to maintain this, the final statement of YHWH not having compassion is taken as the opening statement of the following verse. This is less satisfactory than NRSV's taking the whole verse as four questions. Macintosh proposes that the second half of the verse should be taken as part of the rhetorical questions of the first half, and supplies a connecting phrase between them: 'Shall I redeem them from the hand of Sheol? Shall I ransom them from death, [so that they should say], "so much for your ravages, O Death! so much for your destruction, Sheol!"?'[401] This makes good sense of the verse. The ancient Israelites seem to have been less preoccupied with the world of the dead than the Egyptians and other ancient Near Eastern peoples,[402] but held some awareness of a place known as Sheol. It is rarely described. Isaiah 14:9–10 and Ezekiel 32:21–28 see it as a place to which even great empires and their rulers come in death. It is sometimes in parallel with 'the Pit' (e.g. Ps. 88:3–4 [4–5]). It is a place to be feared (Ps. 18:4–5 [5–6]). On the one hand, a sentiment expressed in Psalms is that the dead are cut off from YHWH's presence, and therefore unable to praise him (Ps. 6:5 [6]; 30:9 [10]; 88:10–12 [11–13]). On the other hand, it can be acknowledged that even Sheol is not beyond YHWH's reach (Ps. 139:8; Amos 9:2). Death and Sheol are found as a pair in Psalm 49:14 [15]; Proverbs 5:5; 7:27, and in Isaiah 28:15, 18, where they are personified as entities with which the people are accused of making a covenant and agreement. In Hosea 13:14b they are also personified, being addressed in the second person. In 13:14a YHWH's question is presumably put to himself, but his internal dialogue is much briefer than the extended one of 6:4–7:10 (on which see the commentary *ad loc*). Should he ransom them from the power of Sheol and redeem them from Death? The verbs 'ransom' (*pādāh*) and 'redeem' (*gā'al*) both connote the buying back of people or possessions. Both can be used of YHWH's actions in ransoming/redeeming from slavery in Egypt or from exile in Babylon (e.g. *pādāh* in Deut. 7:8; 13:5 [6]; Mic. 6:4; Zech. 10:8; *gā'al* in

---

[400]   E. Ben Zvi *Hosea* (2005): 274–5 gives nine possible translations.
[401]   A. A. Macintosh *Hosea* (1997): 546.
[402]   P. Johnstone, 'Sheol', *NIDB* 5: 227.

C Commentary on Hosea

179

Exod. 15:13; Isa. 43:1; 44:22, 23; 48:20; Mic. 4:10[403]). The two verbs are found as a pair also in Jeremiah 31:11. The participle of *gā'al* can function as a noun (*gō'ēl*) meaning 'redeemer' (e.g. Ruth 4:6;[404] Job 19:25). The two terms are thus laden with significance. So should YHWH ransom and redeem his people? In view of their iniquities and sins (13:1–2, 6, 12–13) the answer has to be negative: in contrast to 11:8–9, his compassion will not be displayed, but is hidden even from his own sight. The word 'compassion' (*nōḥam*) occurs only here in the Hebrew Bible, but is from the same root as 'compassion' (*niḥûm*) in 11:8; the contrast is surely deliberate.[405]

The remaining two verses of the chapter (13:15–16 [13:15–14:1])[406] describe the consequent coming judgement. NRSV's translation of Ephraim flourishing 'among rushes' entails reading the Hebrew *'aḥîm* as plural of the rare word *'āḥû* ('rushes'), found elsewhere only in Genesis 41:2, 18; Job 8:11, rather than MT's reading it as plural of *'āḥ* ('brother').[407] More recently, however, scholars have preferred to follow MT's 'among brothers'.[408] The arguments are finely balanced. On the one hand, Ephraim's flourishing among his brothers would make a possible allusion back to 13:1 and his being 'exalted in Israel'. On the other hand, on the principle of *lectio difficilior* 'rushes' is to be preferred, and this reading fits with the imagery of natural phenomena in the lines following. The first such natural phenomenon picks up from 12:1 [2] (on which see the commentary) the coming of a strong east wind, described as a blast from YHWH, who is now executing judgement. Such is the strength and dryness of the wind that the land's water supplies will be dried up. In the final lines of 13:15 the imagery shifts from that of natural disaster to that of military oppressor: the wind becomes the occupying

---

[403] The verb *pādāh* is often (as in NRSV of the verses cited) translated 'redeem' rather than 'ransom'. While confusing for non-Hebraists who may wish to know which verb is used where, this does underline the similar meaning of the two words.

[404] NIV's translation of the word here as 'kinsman-redeemer' is laboured, but helpful.

[405] In 1 Cor. 15:54–55 St Paul cites the LXX of this verse, in combination with the opening line of Isa. 25:8. See further the excursus in J. A. Dearman *Hosea* (2010): 329–31.

[406] The Hebrew text and early versions join 13:16 to chapter 14, with its threats providing the immediate background to the contrasting verses that follow. However some Masoretic versions have a break after it, as does an early Qumran fragment. Considerations of form and content link it with chapter 13, and the division of NRSV and most EVV is to be preferred.

[407] So J. L. Mays *Hosea* (1969): 179, 183; M. A. Sweeney *Twelve Prophets* 1 (2000): 184–5; H. W. Wolff *Hosea* (1974): 222, 228. This reading entails a re-pointing of a vowel. Some also make a consonantal emendation.

[408] So J. A. Dearman *Hosea* (2010): 317; A. A. Macintosh *Hosea* (1997): 552; J. D. Nogalski *Hosea–Jonah* (2011): 186. NIV follows this option.

180 *Book of Hosea*

force that will strip the treasury. Because of her guilt (cf. 4:15; 5:15; 10:2; 13:1), and because she has rebelled against her God (the verb is used only here in Hosea, but is used of Israel's rebellion against YHWH in passages such as Deut. 9:7, 23–24; 31:27; Ps. 78:8; Jer. 5:23), the people shall fall by the sword (cf. 11:6). The final words of punishment reflect those of 10:14, with the difference that there it was mothers who would be dashed to pieces with their children, whereas here it is the little ones who are to be dashed to pieces. A more significant difference, however, is that in 10:14 the action was that of a merciless tyrant, while in 13:16 [14:1] it is YHWH himself who allows it, brings it even. Similarly, the ripping open of pregnant women is found in Amos 1:13 as an accusation made against the Ammonites (see the commentary *ad loc*), and is attested in 2 Kings 8:12; 15:16 as a practice in warfare. But here in Hosea 13:16 it is brought about by YHWH. Hosea 9:11–14 had threatened 'no birth, no pregnancy, no conception'; that Ephraim must 'lead out his children for slaughter'; and 'a miscarrying womb and dry breasts' (see the commentary *ad loc*). Now 13:16 [14:1] adds its final, cruel confirmation of what was already a harsh judgement.

Thus ends a chapter which Dearman describes, fittingly, as containing 'some of the harshest language in the book of Hosea'.[409] Indeed, it is some of the harshest language in the whole prophetic corpus. The Hosea-text contains extremes, from 11:1–9's portrayal of YHWH as a parent tenderly caring for their child through to this. Thankfully the text does not end on this note.

Hosea 14 [14:2–10] – 'I Will Heal Their Disloyalty'

> 14 Return, O Israel, to the LORD your God,
>   for you have stumbled because of your iniquity.
> ² Take words with you
>   and return to the LORD;
> say to him,
>   'Take away all guilt;
> accept that which is good,
>   and we will offer
>   the fruit of our lips.
> ³ Assyria shall not save us;
>   we will not ride upon horses;
> we will say no more, "Our God",

---

[409] J. A. Dearman *Hosea* (2010): 333.

C Commentary on Hosea 181

to the work of our hands.
In you the orphan finds mercy.'

⁴ I will heal their disloyalty;
I will love them freely,
for my anger has turned from them.
⁵ I will be like the dew to Israel;
he shall blossom like the lily;
he shall strike root like the forests of Lebanon.
⁶ His shoots shall spread out;
his beauty shall be like the olive tree
and his fragrance like that of Lebanon.
⁷ They shall again live beneath my shadow;
they shall flourish as a garden;
they shall blossom like the vine;
their fragrance shall be like the wine of Lebanon.
⁸ O Ephraim, what have I to do with idols?
It is I who answer and look after you.
I am like an evergreen cypress;
your fruit comes from me.
⁹ Those who are wise understand these things;
those who are discerning know them.
For the ways of the LORD are right,
and the upright walk in them,
but transgressors stumble in them.

As in sections of Hosea 4–11, a new section is indicated by an imperative (cf. 4:1; 5:1; 5:8; 8:1; 9:1) and by reference to Israel rather than to Ephraim (cf. 4:1; 5:1; 9:1; 10:1; 11:1). In the final form of the text chapters 12–14 comprise a transmission complex distinct from chapters 4–11. It has been argued in the sections on Hosea 12 and Hosea 13 that Hosea 12–13 belong to the exilic redaction of the Hosea-text. It would be a mistake, however, to assume that the same is true of chapter 14 without careful examination of it. The issues are by no means straightforward. Historically, many older scholars saw the positive so-called eschatological passages at the conclusion of both Hosea and Amos to be late additions on grounds of content.[410] Subsequently scholars have been more inclined to note the many links between Hosea 14 and other parts of the text, and to deduce that much of it is derived from the prophet Hosea himself, or from disciples close to him.[411] More recent

---

[410] So, for example, W. R. Harper *Amos and Hosea* (1905): cxxxi–cxxxiii, clix–clxi.
[411] So, for example, H. W. Wolff *Hosea* (1974): 234, who is followed by others.

182 *Book of Hosea*

redaction-critical studies have shed further light on the literary processes behind the text.[412]

It may be noted, firstly, that the phrase in the opening 14:1 [2] 'YHWH your God' is found elsewhere only in 12:9 [10] and 13:4, suggesting that it is, indeed, in close relationship to chapters 12–13. Secondly, however, the chapter exhibits many points of contact with material in chapters 4–11, particularly in 14:1–3 [2–4]. The commentary will draw attention to these. It may be thought, therefore, that Hosea 14 is a late redactional composition setting out a bright future for 'Israel' after the period of Babylonian exile, but one carefully crafted in the light of Hosea 4–11 and 12–13, and deliberately drawing on language and themes from them.[413] To complicate matters further, it is likely that 14:1–3 [2–4] and 14:4–8 [5–9] were not originally composed together. Two considerations suggest different origins. Firstly, 14:1–3 [2–4] addresses Israel in the second person, while in 14:4–8 [5–9] Israel is in the third person. As Davies notes, '[t]he combination of prophetic address to the people with divine speech about the people is unlikely to be original'.[414] Secondly, 14:4–8 [5–9] constitute an unconditional promise of future blessing, while in the preceding 14:1–3 [2–4] repentance is a prior requirement. As Emmerson noted, this 'absence of consistency … suggests that … the salvation saying is not integrally related to the summons to penitence, but rather owes its present position to editorial arrangement'.[415] Vielhauer points out that the suffixes in 14:4 [5] (in English, the pronouns 'their' and 'them') would have no point of reference without the preceding 14:1–3 [2–4], from which he deduces that the plea for repentance is the earlier. He suggests that 14:1–3 [2–4] 'may once have concluded the book of Hosea'.[416]

Following Vielhauer, I consider that 14:1–3 [2–4], with its many links in vocabulary to earlier sections of text, did indeed once conclude the book, in its exilic redaction. This unit was formed together with chapters 12–13. Subsequently, in the post-exilic period, redactors added a further

---

[412] Among several major studies, two articles in English which may be noted are P. A. Kruger, 'Yahweh's Generous Love: Eschatological Expectations in Hosea 14:2–9', *OTE* 1 (1988): 27–48 and R. Vielhauer 'Hosea in the Book of the Twelve' (2012): 55–76.

[413] Some suggest that the redactors may have made use of a pre-existing saying in 14:4–6 [5–7], which is in the singular while the preceding and following verses are in the plural. While this is possible, we can hardly be sure. What is certain is that these words now belong to and fit well in their current literary setting.

[414] G. I. Davies *Hosea* (1992): 300.

[415] G. I. Emmerson *Hosea* (1984): 48.

[416] R. Vielhauer 'Hosea in the Book of the Twelve' (2012): 63.

C Commentary on Hosea

183

composition, with few links of vocabulary to earlier sections of text, but consciously using many images after the manner of those found earlier in the text.

The three-verse call to repentance (14:1–3 [2–4]) is addressed to Israel. As was noted in the comments on 11:12–12:2 [12:1–3], the name does not refer solely to the northern kingdom prior to its destruction in 722 but, in later periods, includes the people of post-monarchic Judah. It is introduced by the imperative 'Return, O Israel, to YHWH your God.' As noted in the commentary on 6:1, the verb *šûb* ('return') is characteristic of the Hosea-text, being found twenty-one times in all. Seven of its occurrences are of the people turning to YHWH or God (3:5; 5:4; 6:1; 7:10; 12:6 [7]; 14:1, 2 [2, 3]). Less usual in 14:1 [2] is the preposition *'ad* used of turning 'to' YHWH. It is used with the same verb five times in Amos 4:6–11, which is part of the exilic redaction of Amos; also in Deuteronomy 4:30; 30:2 (which belong to an exilic layer of the text),[417] Lamentations 3:40, and Joel 2:12. The usage gives a further indication of the exilic provenance of these verses. Israel needs to return to YHWH because they 'have stumbled'. The verb is drawn from 4:5; 5:5. The cause of these disasters was the people's 'iniquity': the word is also drawn from 5:5 (where NRSV translates 'guilt'), and occurs, too, in 4:8; 7:1 (where NRSV translates 'corruption'); 8:13; 9:7, 9; 10:10; 12:8 [9] (where NRSV translates 'offence'); 13:12. The past tense used signifies that the impending disaster threatened in much of the text has now come to pass: Samaria is destroyed (13:16 [14:1]), and so too Jerusalem in 587. In 5:4 the people were unable to return to their God because of their wicked deeds. Now, however, with the judgement having taken place, is the time to do so.

The people are instructed to 'take words with you'. The language is sacrificial, the verb being used in priestly texts (e.g. Exod. 29:19; Lev. 14:12) for the bringing of offerings. Injunctions not to appear before YHWH empty-handed are found in Exodus 23:15; 34:20 and Deuteronomy 16:16. In Hosea 14:2 [3] the offering to be brought is not an animal offering, but words of repentance. The verse expresses a reserve towards cultic sacrifice characteristic of several prophetic texts (see 'A Closer Look: The Prophets, the Cult, and Sacrifice'), but also reflects the fact that in the period after 587 the Jerusalem Temple had been destroyed, and the apparatus of sacrifice was not readily available to those in exile. The words of repentance ask YHWH to 'take away' all guilt; the verb is the same as that translated by NRSV as

---

[417] A. D. H. Mayes *Deuteronomy* (1979): 148–9; 367–9.

'forgive' in 1:6. They ask him to 'accept that which is good', a general expression, the meaning of which need not be narrowed by seeking to give it a particular interpretation. They promise to offer the 'fruit of our lips' (NRSV). The translation entails a frequently adopted emendation (based on LXX), the Hebrew saying 'bulls, our lips'.[418] There follows in 14:3 [4] a list of three stylised expressions of things which the people in their repentance will shun. Firstly, they will no longer look to Assyria for help. By the sixth century, of course, Assyria was no longer a meaningful power: the stylised expression, drawing on earlier parts of the text (5:13; 7:11; 8:9; 12:1 [2]), signifies any foreign power. Secondly, they will 'not ride upon horses'. Horses were a symbol of military might (Deut. 17:16; 1 Kgs 10:26; Isa. 30:16), so thematically there is a link with the accusation made against Ephraim in Hosea 10:13b. They are frequently associated with Egypt, and with trading with Egypt for horses (Deut. 17:16; 1 Kgs 10:28; Isa. 31:3; Ezek. 17:15), so there is a thematic link, too, with the accusation of Ephraim calling on Egypt for help (7:11, 16; 12:1 [2]). Thirdly, they will no longer say 'Our God' to the work of our hands. The assertion links thematically to 4:12; 8:6; 10:5–6; 11:2; 13:2. The expression 'work of our hands' to describe man-made gods suggests Deuteronomistic influence (cf. Deut. 4:28; 2 Kgs 19:18; 22:17; Jer. 25: 6, 7; 32:30; etc.). The final line – 'In you the orphan finds mercy' – is sometimes taken as an addition to the original formulation of the verse. However, it may be read as equivalent to the expression of trust and hope found in some psalms of lament (e.g. Ps. 10:17–18 [18–19]), and there is no need to do so.

The instruction to 'take words' (14:2 [3]) invites a re-visiting of 5:15–6:6. NRSV's colon at the end of 5:15 reflects the view of LXX that 6:1–3 are words of repentance given to the people to say (see the commentary *ad loc*), just as are those in 14:2b–3 [3b–4]. However, YHWH's response to the words of 6:1–3 is to question their depth and sincerity. Taking words was not enough. Rather it is steadfast love (*ḥesed*) and knowledge of God that YHWH seeks (6:6). So will the taking of words in 14:2 [3] effect more than they did in 6:1–3? In the exilic redaction 14:1–3 [2–4] were the final verses of the text, and therefore their effectiveness or otherwise was not spelled out. It was for readers to let their actions match their words, in the hope that YHWH might yet show mercy. Subsequently, in the final, post-exilic revision of the text, 14:4–9 [5–10] were added. In them YHWH speaks in the first person, giving his response.

---

[418] See further G. I. Davies *Hosea* (1992): 302; A. A. Macintosh *Hosea* (1997): 563–5.

C Commentary on Hosea

The opening line of 14:4 [5] resolves the problem expressed in 5:4, that the people's evil deeds have become so all-pervasive that they are unable to turn to their God. YHWH himself will heal their disloyalty, enabling him to bless them once more. It is unusual for the object of healing to be an abstract noun. Elsewhere the word is used of an individual or of the nation, as in Hosea 5:13; 6:1; 7:1; 11:3. 'God wants to indicate that Israel's political sin is a symptom of a more serious sickness. The real problem is the people's broken/disturbed relationship with God that needs to be healed.'[419] The word 'disloyalty/apostasy/faithlessness' (məšûbâ) is frequent in Jeremiah (2:19; 3:22; 5:6; 8:5; 14:7), and Jeremiah 3:22 contains the same promise as Hosea 14:4 [5], that he will heal the people's faithlessness/disloyalty. It is likely that Hosea 14:4 [5] has taken the motif from Jeremiah 3:22.[420] That YHWH will love the people reflects 11:1, 4, and reverses 9:15's statement that 'I will love them no more.' That YHWH will love them 'freely' indicates the generosity of his love. Significantly, despite 14:4 [5] following the call to repentance in the preceding verses, it is not suggested that repentance is a prerequisite for the healing and love that YHWH promises. The promise stands alone and absolute. It reveals a new situation, in which YHWH's anger, which burned against Israel in 8:5, but was not executed in 11:9, has now turned from them.

The promise continues into 14:5–7 [6–8] with a plethora of images, following a feature characteristic of the book as a whole. YHWH will be like the dew to Israel. In 6:4 and 13:3 dew expresses transience, but here in 14:5 [6] it expresses refreshing blessing (cf. Gen. 27:28: Ps. 110:3; 133:3; Prov. 19:12). In judgement YHWH had been as maggots and rottenness (5:12), or like a lion, leopard, or bear hunting (5:14; 13:7–8), but now in blessing he is as dew. The resulting benefits for Israel are described in a series of images of the natural world: blossom like the lily, roots put down like the strong trees of Lebanon,[421] shoots spreading out, sweet-smelling fragrance like that of Lebanon (14:6 [7]) and like the wine of Lebanon (14:7 [8]),[422] flourishing as a

---

[419]   D. F. O'Kennedy 'Healing as/or Forgiveness?' (2001): 465.
[420]   P. A. Kruger 'Yahweh's Generous Love' (1988): 40.
[421]   The Hebrew text has simply 'like Lebanon', but NRSV is justified in adding 'forests of' Lebanon in order to give the sense.
[422]   Two different Hebrew words in 14:6–7 [7–8] are both translated by NRSV as 'fragrance': that in 14:7 [8] literally means 'fame' (and is translated as such by NIV). Lebanon is not noted for its wine elsewhere in the Hebrew Bible. A. A. Macintosh *Hosea* (1997): 574 notes that Ezek. 27:18 mentions wine of Helbon, some way to the south.

186   *Book of Hosea*

garden,[423] blossoming like the vine. The cedars of Lebanon were renowned for their great height and strength (1 Kgs 5:6, 14 [20, 28]; Ps. 104:16; Isa. 2:13). Mention of the vine allows recollection of the picture of Israel as a vine (10:1), although the link is tentative. Some of these images are found also in the Song of Songs: the lily (S. of S. 2:1, 2, 16; 4:5; 5:13; 6:2, 3; 7:2 [3]); Lebanon (S. of S. 3:9; 4:8, 8, 11, 15; 5:15; 7:4 [5]); fragrance (S. of S. 2:13; 4:10, 11: 7:8, 13 [9, 14]); 'dwell beneath my shadow' (S. of S. 2:3); 'blossom like the vine' (S. of S. 6:11; 7:12 [13]); wine (S. of S. 1:2, 4; 5:1; 7:9 [10]). Possibly these overlaps reflect the growing cross-fertilisation of streams of traditions in the post-exilic period.[424] Within these images is the statement of YHWH that the people will live beneath his shadow, an image not far removed from that in some psalms of sheltering under the shadow if YHWH's wings (Pss. 17:8; 36:7 [8]). As noted, while Hosea 14:5–7 [6–8] do not contain the numerous links in vocabulary with earlier parts of the book that are found in 14:1–4 [13:16–14:3], the use of so many images is in keeping with them. Equally, these verses are in keeping with the future blessing of security in the land and fertility promised in Amos 9:14–15, which close a post-exilic concluding section of the Amos-text. The texts of both Hosea and Amos, nominally addressed to the old kingdom of northern Israel, speak in their final form to the Jewish community of the Second Temple period. In both passages the promises are principally those of nature and abundant fertility. Amos 9:11–12, 14 contain also an historical allusion to restoration after exile. More fleetingly, so also does Hosea 14:7 [8]'s 'again': the Hebrew is from the verb *šûb* ('return').

The promise of YHWH's care of Israel continues into 14:8 [9], but with a final warning of the dangers of idols (cf. 4:17; 8:4; 13:2). The precise meaning is uncertain, but the general sense is clear: the people must recognise that the days of worshipping and consulting idols must be over, and are reassured that they do not need them, since YHWH will answer and look after them.[425] Hosea 14:8b [9b] is the only place in the Hebrew Bible where

---

[423]   The Hebrew text has 'they shall make grain live'. The verb is awkward, and most ancient versions support 'they shall flourish'. However, 'as a garden' entails a conjectural emendation. There is merit in retaining 'like the grain' which, while a little strange, then balances 'like the vine' in the line following. See further G. I. Davies *Hosea* (1992): 307.

[424]   For this general development, see O. H. Steck, 'Theological Streams of Tradition', in D. A. Knight (ed.), *Tradition and Theology in the Old Testament* (Philadelphia: Fortress Press, 1977): 183–214.

[425]   NRSV translates the Hebrew of 14:8a [9a], with a change of pronoun: look after 'you' rather than MT's 'him'. LXX translates: 'What has Ephraim to do with idols? It is I who answer and look after him.' This gives a good sense. Others see a dialogue of alternate

C Commentary on Hosea

187

YHWH is said to be like a tree. Trees are more generally associated with Canaanite cultic activities (cf. 4:13). There is, however, no need to do other than take the simile at face value. The evergreen nature of the tree reflects YHWH's unceasing care promised to the people.

When Hosea 14:4–8 [5–9] are read on their own, they constitute an unconditional promise of future overflowing blessing, with only 14:8a [9a] giving a hint that the receiving that blessing entails a rejection of idols. When read in the literary context of the book as a whole, however, readers will naturally and properly recognise an implicit 'as long as you stay faithful to YHWH'. The post-exilic redactors of texts like Hosea and Amos deliberately attached their positive, promise-filled conclusions to texts which had already set out many accusations and warnings, and which showed the justness of YHWH's actions in judging his people.

The final verse 14:9 [10] makes clear that understanding, discernment, and walking in the ways of YHWH are the marks of the wise and the upright. Virtually all commentators, including those whose preference is to date almost all other parts of the text to the time of Hosea, or near to it, take these verses to be exilic or, more probably, post-exilic.[426] It may have belonged with the post-exilic 14:4–8 [5–9] from the outset, or alternatively may have been a subsequent addition to it. All commentators note its closeness to wisdom literature. Yet it uses vocabulary from the Hosea-text ('transgressors' cf. 7:13; 8:1; 'stumble' cf. 4:5; 5:5; 14:1 [2]); and to walk in the ways of YHWH is a characteristic expression of Deuteronomy (8:6; 10:12; 11:22, etc.) and of Psalms (25:4; 51:13 [15]; 81:13 [14], etc.). The wise and discerning will understand 'these things', that is, all the preceding text of the book, and will therefore walk in upright ways. A question rarely asked is why such a verse should be attached to this particular text, and not to texts such as Amos, Micah, and other prophetic books. Perhaps the question is not asked because there is no obvious answer. Was it particularly important for the first book of the Book of the Twelve, or of an earlier Book of the Four,[427] to have such advice attached to it? It may be so. It is the only verse in the book to address individuals, as opposed to the nation, and, whatever

---

lines. Wellhausen emended *'ănî 'ānîtî wa'ăšûnnû* ('I will answer and look after him') to *'ănî 'ānātô wa'ăšērātô* ('I will be his Anat and Asherah') to give a reference to Canaanite deities. There is no textual evidence for such a change, and few recent commentators accept it. Some allow that text may contain a faint allusion to them. See further G. I. Davies *Hosea* (1992): 308; A. A. Macintosh *Hosea* (1997): 576–81.

[426] So *inter alia* A. A. Macintosh *Hosea* (1997): 583; H. W. Wolff *Hosea* (1974): 239.

[427] See the 'Volume Introduction'.

the exact historical reason for it being placed at the end of this book rather than some other, the message is straightforward: those who aspire to be wise will take note of the themes of this book of Hosea. They will endeavour to avoid stumbling, as did the Israelites of old (5:5) and as transgressors still do, avoiding idolatry and reliance on any power other than YHWH, and seeking to walk in his ways alone.

III Book of Joel

A INTRODUCTION TO JOEL

The book of Joel addresses a people facing disaster. The primary disaster described is a locust plague which ravages the land, destroying all crops (1:4–12). It is compared to an invading army in the way in which destruction and havoc is wrought (1:6; 2:4–9), and at some points the description seems to be of an actual army as a separate, additional disaster (2:1–3). Commentators hold different views as to whether a description of a separate disaster (military invasion) is intended in chapter 2 or whether it is a comparison made in describing the invasion of locusts. Other verses seem to describe drought (1:10–12, 16–20). Again, it may be description of yet another separate disaster, woven into that of the locust plague, or it may be taken as part of the description of the one, same disaster. The occurrence of such disaster is seen as a 'day of YHWH' (1:15; 2:1–2, 11). An effect of the disaster is that the priests have nothing to offer in sacrifice (1:9, 13). Faced with such overwhelming disaster, the people as a whole and, within them, the farmers and the priests and elders are urged to turn to YHWH (1:13–14; 2:12–17). In response YHWH will send restoration and blessing (2:18–27). The second half of the book is different, moving into promises of salvation for the Israelites (2:28–32; 3:16–18, 20–21 [3:1–5; 4:16–18, 20–21]) and of judgement on the nations of the world who have oppressed them (3:1–15 [4:1–15]). The judgement on the nations is universal (3:2, 9–15 [4:2, 9–15]), but particular accusation is made against and judgement announced upon 'Tyre and Sidon and the regions of Philistia' (3:4–8 [4:4–8]), and upon Egypt and Edom (3:19 [4:19]).

Historically, scholarship has paid less attention to the book of Joel than to those of Hosea and Amos. In the nineteenth century and first half of the twentieth century there remained a bias, present from Wellhausen onwards, towards the great eighth-century prophetic figures (Amos, Hosea, Isaiah,

Micah), who were seen as the originators of an ethical monotheism which found its pinnacle in their texts. Joel was not seen as comparable. While some early commentators considered that Joel was a pre-exilic prophet, a majority now attributes the book to the post-exilic period, a time which for many years was seen as less important, indeed as somewhat retrograde compared to the glory days of prophecy in the eighth and seventh centuries. In the later part of the twentieth century and into the twenty-first century, however, fresh and positive attention has been paid to the Second Temple period. Additionally, cultic texts are no longer viewed solely through the lens of the critique found in some of the earlier prophets.[1] As noted in the 'Volume Introduction', the book of Joel has become important as, additionally, a number of scholars argue that it occupies a key interpretative position in the Book of the Twelve.

Joel as Literary Text

Joel 1:1 describes the text as the 'word of YHWH that came to Joel son of Pethuel'. In contrast to the headings in Hosea 1:1 and Amos 1:1, no further information is given as to who Joel was, when he lived, where he came from, or the circumstances in which he prophesied. This suggests that the writers of the text had less interest in any historical figure behind the text than in the text itself. As one of the later books of the Hebrew Bible, it contains many citations of and allusions to earlier texts. It draws from liturgical expressions of lament which were, presumably, familiar to the people of the period in which it was promulgated; similar material is known to us from the book of Psalms. It has, with justification, been seen as a literary work drawing on and interpreting scriptural tradition.

Some elements of structure are evident, but not so clearly as to prevent differing scholarly views with regard to where sections begin and end. It is readily apparent that the first part of the book describes disaster, and calls for a turning to YHWH. YHWH is then described as responding by bringing judgement on the nations and salvation to Israel and Zion. The turning point is at 2:18 where, following the summons to the priests to call out to YHWH on the people's behalf, it is said that 'YHWH became jealous for his land, and had pity on his people'; and the remainder of the text contains his response. Some scholars, therefore, see a two-part text with the division at

---

[1] See, for example, L.-S. Tiemeyer (ed.), *Priests and Cults in the Book of the Twelve* (ANEM, 14; Atlanta: SBL Press, 2016).

A Introduction to Joel 191

the end of 2:17.[2] Conversely, the whole first part of the text up to 2:27, including YHWH's response in 2:18–27, is rooted within history, whereas from 2:28 [3:1] onwards the expectation becomes less within history and more in the kind of future global activity of YHWH which would come to characterise apocalyptic literature. Some scholars, therefore, see a two-part text with the division at the end of 2:27.[3] This latter view seems preferable. Firstly, there is in 2:28 a clear introductory formula: 'And it will be that after this' (NRSV translates as simply 'Then afterwards'). A further introductory formula follows in 3:1 [4:1]: 'For then, in those days and at that time.' Secondly, 1:2–20 and 2:1–17 constitute two parallel descriptions of disaster and summons to turn to YHWH, and his response in 2:18–27 addresses both descriptions. Thirdly, as noted, it is from 2:28 [3:1] that the language and imagery becomes less rooted within history and more futuristic and global.

The two parallel descriptions of disaster and summons to turn to YHWH in 1:2–20 and 2:1–17, followed by the divine response in 2:18–27, give a structure to this first part of the text. It is less easy to identify any particular structure within the second half, and indeed Barton takes it to be a 'rather miscellaneous collection of oracles, assembled in no particular order at all'.[4] However, while this may be the impression given by the final form of the text, there are three sections within the second half which appear to be additions to an earlier literary layer, and there is a structure evident within that earlier layer. This leads us to consider the composition history of the text.

The Composition History of the Book of Joel

Some commentators treat the text as a unity, although it is not always clear whether this unity is being seen as original to the text or as a redactional unity. In line with the redaction-critical methodology espoused by this volume (see the 'Volume Introduction'), I consider that the book was compiled in stages. Methodologically it is best to start with the final form of the text, and identify the latest additions to an earlier form at each stage.[5]

---

[2] E. Assis, *The Book of Joel: A Prophet between Calamity and Hope* (LHBOTS, 581; London/New York: Bloomsbury/T&T Clark, 2013): 53; J. Strazicich, *Joel's Use of Scripture and the Scripture's Use of Joel* (Lewiston, NY: Edwin Mellen Press, 1991): 40–7.

[3] So *inter alia* J. Barton, *Joel and Obadiah* (Louisville, KY: Westminster John Knox Press, 2001): 13.

[4] J. Barton *Joel and Obadiah* (2001): 14.

[5] R. P. Knierim, 'Criticism of Literary Features, Form, Tradition and Redaction', in D. A. Knight and G. M. Tucker (eds.), *The Hebrew Bible and its Modern Interpreters* (Philadelphia: Fortress Press, 1985): 123–65 writes that it 'is much more problematic first

Firstly, Redditt has argued, successfully in my view, that 2:28–32 [3:1–5] is a later addition from a party that wished to challenge the hold that a priestly, theocratic party had on the nation by making it clear that the spirit of YHWH was not restricted to a particular priestly class, but that all could prophesy. They saw the division as being between 'everyone who calls on the name of YHWH' (2:32 [3:5]) and those who do not, and in their view this was unrelated to whether someone was a priest or not.[6] His argument revives and develops that of Plöger,[7] and accepts the kind of theory put forward by Plöger, and by Hanson, that there were, in some periods of Second Temple Judaism, visionary proto-apocalyptic factions holding to different hopes for the future from establishment priestly, theocratic views.[8] By placing 2:28–32 [3:1–5] ahead of 3:1–21 [4:1–21], those responsible invited a reading of 3:1–21 [4:1–21] that applied the blessing promised to Judah and Jerusalem as being applicable to (indeed, restricted to) those who joined them in calling upon the name of YHWH. Redditt makes the case, effectively in my view, that 2:28–32 [3:1–5] 'was composed with 1:1–2:27 and 4:1–3, 9–21 in hand'.[9]

Secondly, most scholars accept that 3:4–8 [4:4–8] is an addition to the main part of the chapter, reflecting an incident or period in which Judean people were being sold into slavery. Its insertion at this point reflects the thematic link with the trading of boys and girls in 3:3.

Thirdly, 3:18–21 [4:18–21] are an added conclusion to the book, possibly made as part of the formation of the Book of the Twelve in the Hebrew Bible. Joel 3:18 [4:18] links to Amos 9:13, and the inclusion of Edom in Joel 3: 19 [4:19] links to Obadiah. Before the addition the concluding 3:17 [4:17] makes as good an *inclusio* with 3:1 [4:1] as does 3:20–21 [4:20–21] in the final form.

Prior to these additions, the text of 3:1–3, 9–17 [4:1–3, 9–17] had a coherent thematic unity of YHWH's judgement on the nations and salvation of Judah and Jerusalem. The judgement on the nations is announced in 3:2–3 [4:2–3], and its implementation is described in 3:9–15 [4:9–15]. Structurally the blessing of Judah and Jerusalem frames these verses (3:1, 17 [4:1, 17]).

---

to establish original texts from the present texts and then to identify the later layers than to identify the latest layers first and then to inquire into their pre-history' (156).

[6] P. L. Redditt, 'The Book of Joel and Peripheral Prophecy', *CBQ* 48 (1986): 225–40.

[7] O. Plöger, *Theocracy and Eschatology* (trans. S. Rudman; Oxford: Basil Blackwell, 1968): 97–105.

[8] P. D. Hanson, *The Dawn of Apocalyptic* (Philadelphia: Fortress Press, 1975); P. D. Hanson, *The People Called: the Growth of Community in the Bible* (San Francisco: Harper & Row, 1987): 291–313; O. Plöger *Theocracy and Eschatology* (1968).

[9] P. L. Redditt 'Joel and Peripheral Prophecy' (1986): 231. Redditt's references are to the Hebrew text.

I describe 1:1–2:27; 3:1–3, 9–17 [4:1–3, 9–17] as the 'Eschatological Redactional Composition' of the text. Redditt writes, correctly, that chapter 3 [4] of the book 'gives every indication of having been composed with the first two chapters in hand'.[10] The portion 1:1–2:27 makes a coherent whole, and was at one point a self-contained literary text. It may be described straightforwardly as the 'first composition' of the Joel-text. Thus the text's composition is as follows:

(1) A first composition was made of 1:1–2:27.
(2) In due course the Eschatological Redactional Composition was formed by adding 3:1–3, 9–17 [4:1–3, 9–17] to 1:1–2:27. This was not a random addition, but one deliberately linked to the received text.
(3) Subsequently three separate additions were made: 2:28–32 [3:1–5], 3:4–8 [4:4–8], and 3:18–21 [4:18–21].

Some scholars push further back and claim to discern more than one literary layer behind 1:1–2:27. However, their arguments contain many uncertainties, and are unconvincing.[11] This commentary will therefore comment on the compositional layers here identified.

In terms of dating, there are few historical allusions to assist us. However, there are definite indications that it is entirely a post-exilic work. Firstly, the cult was functioning, and sacrifices were being offered. This points either to the monarchic period or to the Second Temple period. Since pre-exilic prophetic tradition offered some severe critique of cultic activity the latter is more likely.[12] Secondly, there is no mention of any king anywhere in the text, and authority lies with the priests and elders, as was the case in the Persian period.[13] Thirdly, there is no sense of any distinction between Israel and Judah as separate kingdoms: rather 'Zion' (2:1, 15, 23) and 'Israel' (2:27) are both synonymous with 'the land' (1:2, 6; 2:1, 18) and YHWH's

---

[10] P. L. Redditt 'Joel and Peripheral Prophecy' (1986): 226. The phrase 'first two chapters' in the quotation refers to the Hebrew text i.e. 1:1–2:27 in EVV.

[11] See further R. L. Troxel, 'The Fate of Joel in the Redaction of the Twelve', *CBR* 13.2 (2015): 152–74.

[12] See 'A Closer Look: The Prophets, the Cult, and Sacrifice'. J. L. Crenshaw, *Joel: A New Translation with Introduction and Commentary* (AB, 24C; New Haven and London: Yale University Press, 1995): 25 writes that the 'fondness for the cult and external aspects of worship in conjunction with genuine turning to YHWH scarcely resembles anything during the prophetic activity of the eighth- or seventh-century reformers (Amos, Isaiah, Micah, Jeremiah)'.

[13] H. W. Wolff, *Joel and Amos* (trans. W. Janzen, S. D. McBride Jr., and C. A. Muenchow; Hermeneia; Philadelphia: Fortress Press, 1977): 5.

'people' (2:18, 19, 26, 27). This could be so after the destruction of Samaria and the exile of northern Israelites after 722, but is more certainly so in the post-exilic period. Fourthly, it is envisaged that the whole people could be assembled for a fast (1:14; 2:15–16). While there may be poetic exaggeration in this idea, it is likely not to have been deemed ridiculous for such a suggestion to be made. This suggests a population level which is more likely to have appertained in the Second Temple period. Finally, and most significantly, this short text contains over twenty citations of and allusions to earlier biblical texts, the great majority being prophetic texts. The commentary will draw attention to these as they occur.[14] Dependence can, of course, run either way when sayings occur in different texts. However, with this number of inter-biblical quotations, it is likely that from the outset Joel was composed as a literary text incorporating many biblical allusions, and that it is the later text in all but a few instances. Goldingay comments that these quotations 'are so numerous and varied that Joel must be the prophet inspired by them rather than his being the inspiration for these fellow prophets'.[15] The fact that many of the texts quoted are themselves exilic and post-exilic confirms that Joel is a post-exilic text. Noteworthy among the quotations are those relating to the Day of YHWH (1:15; 2:2, 6), a concept which, by Joel's time, had acquired several standard descriptive features reflected in texts such as Isaiah 13:6–9; Ezekiel 30:2; Zephaniah 1:7, 14–16: see the 'Closer Look: The Day of YHWH'.

Can we be more specific than simply saying the 'Second Temple period'? Some argue that a functioning cult suggests a time after that of Haggai and Zechariah (520–518), in which the house of the Lord was restored.[16] Others respond that while Haggai and Zechariah may have achieved restoration of the Temple, sacrifice would have been offered before then. Some note that 2:7–9 refer to the city walls, and argue that this indicates a time after Nehemiah's re-building of the wall in 445.[17] Others comment that while Nehemiah re-built the walls, presumably the ruins of the previous walls were still in place, and that this would be sufficient for the interpretation of 2:7–9.[18]

---

[14]   J. Barton *Joel and Obadiah* (2001): 23 and J. L. Crenshaw, *Joel* (1995): 27–8 both list them in tabular form.

[15]   J. Goldingay, *Hosea–Micah* (BCOT; Grand Rapids, MI: Baker Academic, 2020): 194.

[16]   T. S. Hadjiev, *Joel and Amos* (TOTC, 25; London, IVP, 2020): 5 writes: 'The first part of Joel takes for granted the existence of the Jerusalem temple. This pushes the date of the book after the rebuilding of the temple (515 BC).'

[17]   H. W. Wolff *Joel and Amos* (1977): 5.

[18]   G. Ahlström, *Joel and the Temple Cult of Jerusalem* (Leiden: E. J. Brill, 1971): 18, 114–15.

A Introduction to Joel   195

It is best to begin with the latest portions of text. The late addition 2:28–32 [3:1–5] derives from an anti-establishment, visionary party. Hanson writes that

> the reform efforts of Ezra and Nehemiah seem to have had the effect of usher-ing in a period in which the Judean community dwelt quite securely under the local leadership of its Zadokite priests and the more distant sovereignty of the Persian crown.... Several biblical books are best understood if placed in this period, however, books that seem to indicate that the Zadokite leader-ship and its carefully defined communal structure were not without critics. In the books of Joel, Ruth, and Jonah, we find evidence for the continued activ-ity of circles dedicated to a broadly inclusive vision of the Yahwistic commu-nity that likely arose, at least in part, as a protest against what was deemed an unwarranted exclusivism and narrowness within the mainstream tradition.... Although evidence is lacking within these books that would allow precise dat-ing, it does seem clear that they express a dissident movement within fourth- and third-century Judaism.[19]

This gives a dating of the final form of Joel no earlier than the late part of the fifth century, and quite probably in the fourth century. Precision is difficult, as a feature of the whole Joel-text is that certain motifs have become standard ones not anchored to a particular historical moment. Thus the scattering of YHWH's people in 587 is referred to in 3:2 [4:2]. This does not mean that the text should be dated to the sixth century, but rather this has become a stock description of disaster. Similarly in 3:19–21 [4:19–21] Edom and Egypt are seen as Israel's classic enemies, and we should not look to find a specific historical reason for their inclusion. The one section in which historical references are more spe-cific is 3:4–8 [4:4–8], which addresses 'Tyre and Sidon and the regions of Philistia'. Wolff notes that the Phoenicians and Philistines consti-tuted a political entity in later Persian times, and that Alexander had to break the power of both Tyre and Gaza in 332. Sidon, however, had been destroyed by Artaxerxes III in 343. He considers that a date some while prior to 343 is therefore likely.[20] This makes mention of Greeks (3:6) entirely appropriate, but does not fit well with mention of the Sabeans (3:8), whose influence was diminished by the fourth century. Wolff sug-gests that the Sabeans were recalled simply as a people of the distant

[19]   P. Hanson *The People Called* (1987): 312–13.
[20]   H. W. Wolff *Joel and Amos* (1977): 4–5.

east, and that their mention indicates that the people of Tyre and Sidon and the Philistines would be sold to a far-off people.[21] Redditt argues, in contrast, that the threat to sell to the Sabeans was real and actual, and that therefore these verses derive from the fifth century. On balance, the arguments of Wolff seem the more persuasive (see the commentary on 3:4–8 [4:4–8]). If the addition 3:4–8 [4:4–8] derives from the fourth century (before 343), and 2:28–32 [3:1–5] from the fourth or later part of the fifth century, then 3:1–3, 9–17 must derive from a time earlier than these additions, and 1:1–2:27 be earlier still. Very probably the genesis of the text is in the fifth (or possibly late sixth) century; it may be unwise to be more specific than that.

A different dating has recently been put forward by Assis, who proposes that the text is a unity and addresses the people left in Judah in the exilic period 587–538. He seeks to refute the usual arguments for a later dating. For example, he writes that 'Joel's lack of reference to the monarchy is not proof that he lived in a period when no king reigned, since the topics addressed have no connection to a king.'[22] He sees no evidence of a theocratic leadership, arguing that priests and elders are referred to only in connection with assembling the people and with prayer and fasting. He argues that the offering of sacrifice does not necessarily mean that the Temple had been re-built, and cites Jeremiah 41:5 to show that offerings were still being presented in Judah in these years. References to Edom, Egypt, Tyre, Sidon, and Philistia, he notes correctly, are all entirely appropriate in the exilic period.[23] His thesis is that the people of Judah in these years had come to believe that the events of 587 meant that YHWH had abandoned them. Joel uses the occurrence of a locust plague, he argues, to urge the people to turn to YHWH in their need, and thereby to come to understand that YHWH had not, in fact, abandoned them, but could still be prayed to, and prayed to for political salvation as well as from deliverance from the effects of the locust plague. That YHWH answered their prayer by promising restoration of the land after the locust plague (2:18–27) would help them to believe that YHWH would answer prayer for political salvation too.[24] His thesis is interesting, and his book contains much helpful detailed comment on the text. However, his dating

---

[21] H. W. Wolff *Joel and Amos* (1977): 78–9.
[22] E. Assis *Book of Joel* (2013): 5.
[23] E. Assis *Book of Joel* (2013): 5–10.
[24] E. Assis *Book of Joel* (2013): 190 and *passim*.

A Introduction to Joel

is not persuasive, and his attempts to refute arguments for a post-exilic dating feel, in the end, like special pleading. However, his insight that answered prayer in respect of the locust plague could lead to a confidence that YHWH would answer prayer in respect of the people's political situation is valuable, and provides a plausible explanation for the move in the Eschatological Redactional Composition away from a focus on locusts to a focus on the nations of the world.

It was noted above that Joel 1:1 gives little information about who Joel was and when he lived, and that this indicates that the writers of the text had less interest in any historical figure behind the text than in the text itself. We may now add that the paucity of historical allusions by which to date the text indicates, further, that readers are not being invited to read it against any one particular historical background, but rather as an 'any time' text. Its themes, the compilers believed, were relevant to any period.

Key Themes in the Book of Joel

The first half of the book (1:1–2:17) describes the disaster of a locust plague. Some of it is a literal describing of the effects of a plague of locusts, while some of it draws on stock language used to describe other kinds of disaster, such as military invasion and drought. Faced with such disaster, numerous summons are issued to the people and to groups within the people to wail, lament, put on sackcloth, fast, rend hearts, call a solemn assembly, and pray (1:5, 8, 11, 13, 14; 2:1, 12–13, 15–16, 17). One of the effects of the disaster is that not only is there a shortage of food across the land, but there is also a shortage of food to be offered in grain offerings and drink offerings (1:13; 2:14), so that the sacrifices which were part of the maintenance of the people's relationship with YHWH were threatened. The plea to YHWH is not only for food in the land, but also for food for offerings to be made by the priests. The text is rooted in earlier prophetic tradition through its many quotations of, and allusions to, prophetic texts, and the theme of the Day of YHWH (1:15; 2:1–2, 11). It is also rooted in cultic tradition through its utilisation of the form and language of lament.

A matter of debate among commentators is whether or not the disaster of the locust plague has been sent as a punishment for the people's sins. For those who see it as such, the summons to turn to YHWH is a summons to repentance. Crenshaw, however, noting that nowhere in the text are any sins of the people described or accusations made against them, declines to accept the assumption that the people must have sinned. The summons to turn to YHWH is purely and simply to call for his help in time of trouble.[25] Barton accepts this argument,[26] as does this commentary. Goldingay, similarly, writes that 'in Joel there is no reference to wrongdoing or waywardness that people need to turn from'.[27] To assume that the disaster must be sent in response to sin is to read into the text something found elsewhere in prophetic tradition, but not here. The only verse which might seem to imply criticism is 2:13, with its summons is to 'rend your hearts and not your garments'. Wolff makes much of this verse, arguing that it reveals the sin of empty ritual. It is, however, sufficient to take it as calling for a heartfelt cry to YHWH. Following the descriptions of disaster is YHWH's response (2:18–27), which promises the restoration of fertility in the land. The upshot will be that the people 'shall know that I am in the midst of Israel, and that I, YHWH, am your God and there is no other. And my people shall never again be put to shame' (2:27). This climax to YHWH's response draws on language from Deutero-Isaiah (45: 5–6, 18).

The Eschatological Redactional Composition (1:1–2:27; 3:1–3, 9–17 [4:1–3, 9–17]) shifts the hope of YHWH's intervention into some more distant future time. It may be that it was felt that the promises of 2:19–27 had not been fulfilled or, more probably, that they had been partially fulfilled in the sense of the fertility of the land being restored, but without the consequent acknowledgement of YHWH (2:27) being sufficiently made. Perhaps some – perhaps indeed the ruling elite – felt that all was now well, while those responsible for the addition of 3:1–3, 19–27 [4:1–3, 19–27] considered that Judah's continuing position as a state within the Persian empire should not be considered satisfactory. Hence this redactional composition looks to a day when YHWH will vindicate his people, restore Judah and Jerusalem, and judge the nations of the world who had oppressed her. The additions in 3:4–8 [4:4–8] and 3:18–21 [4:18–21] reinforce this message. The addition of 2:28–32 [3:1–5], which probably derives from a circle of people dissatisfied with the ruling theocratic leadership of the day, introduces two fresh perspectives. Firstly, 2:28–29 [3:1–2] promises that the day is coming when reception of YHWH's spirit will not be restricted to leaders and religious functionaries, but will be poured out

[25] J. L. Crenshaw *Joel* (1995): 40–1.
[26] J. Barton *Joel and Obadiah* (2001): 32, 79–90.
[27] J. Goldingay *Hosea–Micah* (2020): 219.

A Introduction to Joel

on the whole people: young and old, male and female, even slaves, will be included. Secondly, however, 2:30–32 [3:3–5] indicates that this outpouring of the spirit, and the salvation of Mount Zion and Jerusalem, will be on a remnant who call upon the name of YHWH. This introduces a confessional lens through which, in the final form of the text, chapter 3 [4] is to be read.

The theme of the Day of YHWH is present in all the text's literary stages. While Jeremias exaggerates in seeing it as 'the one and only subject of the book of Joel',[28] it is a significant theme through which the compilers of the Eschatological Redactional Composition linked their work to the earlier first composition. In the first half of the text the locust plague is a sign of the nearness of a coming Day of YHWH. Amos 5:20 had declared that this would be a day of darkness, not light, for Israel: this is reinforced in Joel 1:15; 2:1–2, 11. In 2:30–32 [3:3–5] those who call on the name of YHWH will be saved from the Day's dreadful effects. In chapter 3 [4] it is the nations who are to be judged at the Day of YHWH (3:14 [4:14]). The theme is thus used in different ways in different portions of the text, but its presence nevertheless has a unifying effect.

The fact that there is less precision in the dating of the text and its literary layers than with some other biblical texts, owing to there being few historical markers by which to date it, need not demoralise the interpreter. Barton notes, correctly, that 'the book as it stands is not focused on a particular time of crisis',[29] and the fact that the heading in 1:1 contains no chronological information indicates that it is not necessary to relate it to a particular context in order to interpret it and hear it speak. The commentary will, however, recognise that the second part of the text, from 2:28 [3:1] onwards, moves from language which functions within history to language which looks beyond history to a future time in which YHWH will act in a dramatic, universal way in judging the nations of the earth and in restoring and blessing his people Israel. Identification of the first composition (1:1–2:27), the Eschatological Redactional Composition (1:1–2:27; 3:1–3, 9–17 [4:1–3, 9–17]), and additions to the latter in 2:28–32 [3:1–5], 3:4–8 [4:4–8], and 3:18–21 [4:18–21] will inform the exegesis and interpretation of the text.

---

[28] J. Jeremias, 'The function of the Book of Joel for Reading the Twelve', in R. Albertz, J. D. Nogalski, and J. Wöhrle (eds.), *Perspectives on the Formation* (2012): 77–88 (78).

[29] J. Barton *Joel and Obadiah* (2001): 36.

200   *Book of Joel*

B SUGGESTED READINGS ON JOEL

Introductory Works

Hadjiev's *Study Guide* introduces all the main literary issues current in biblical scholarship. Mason's Old Testament Guide still has value. Troxel's article includes a review of recent German scholarship.

Coggins R., 'Joel', *CBR* 2 (2003): 85–103.

Hadjiev T. S., *Joel, Obadiah, Habakkuk, Zephaniah: An Introduction and Study Guide* (T&T Clark Study Guides to the Old Testament; London/ New York: T&T Clark, 2020).

Mason R., *Zephaniah, Habakkuk and Joel* (OTG; Sheffield: JSOT Press, 1994).

Troxel R. L., 'The Fate of Joel in the Redaction of the Twelve', *CBR* 13.2 (2015): 152–74.

Commentaries

Several commentaries have proved helpful in the writing of this commentary, with the greatest influence on it exerted by those of Allen, Barton, Crenshaw, and Wolff.

Allen L. C., *The Books of Joel, Obadiah, Jonah and Micah* (NICOT; Grand Rapids, MI: Eerdmans, 1976).

Barton J., *Joel and Obadiah* (OTL; Louisville, KY: Westminster John Knox Press, 2001).

Bewer J. A., 'Joel', in J. M. Powis Smith, W. H. Ward, and J. A. Bewer, *A Critical and Exegetical Commentary on Micah, Zephaniah, Nahum, Habakkuk, Obadiah and Joel* (ICC; Edinburgh: T&T Clark, 1912): 49–146.

Coggins R., *Joel and Amos* (NCB; Sheffield: Sheffield Academic Press, 2000).

Crenshaw J. L., *Joel: A New Translation with Introduction and Commentary* (AB, 24C; New Haven, CT, and London: Yale University Press, 1995).

Goldingay J., *Hosea–Micah* (BCOT; Grand Rapids, MI: Baker Academic, 2020).

Hadjiev T. S., *Joel and Amos* (TOTC, 25; London: IVP, 2020).

Jeremias J., *Die Profeten Joel, Obadja, Jona, Micha* (Das Alte Testament Deutsch, 24/3; Göttingen: Vandenhoeck & Ruprecht, 2007).

B Suggested Readings on Joel

Nogalski J. D., *The Book of the Twelve: Hosea–Jonah* (Smyth & Helwys Bible Commentary; Macon, GA: Smyth & Helwys, 2011).

Rudolph W., *Joel – Amos – Obadja – Jona* (KAT 13/2; Gütersloh: Gerd Mohn, 1971).

Seitz C. R., *Joel* (International Theological Commentary on the Holy Scripture of Old and New Testaments; London/New York: Bloomsbury/T&T Clark, 2016).

Sweeney M. A., *The Twelve Prophets, vol. 1: Hosea, Joel, Amos, Obadiah, Jonah* (Berit Olam Studies in Hebrew Narrative and Poetry; Collegeville, MN: Liturgical Press, 2000).

Wolff H. W., *Joel and Amos* (trans. W. Janzen, S. D. McBride Jr., and C. A. Muenchow; Hermeneia; Philadelphia: Fortress Press, 1977).

Special Studies

The studies of Assis, Barker, Prinsloo, Redditt, Simkins, Strazicich, Troxel, and Watson are all substantial and valuable. The older works of Ahlström, Bergler, Kapelrud, and Plöger remain worthy of attention.

Ahlström G., *Joel and the Temple Cult of Jerusalem* (Leiden: E. J. Brill, 1971).

Andiñach P. R., 'The Locusts in the Message of Joel', *VT* 42 (1992): 433–41.

Assis E., *The Book of Joel: A Prophet between Calamity and Hope* (LHBOTS, 581; London/New York: Bloomsbury/T&T Clark, 2013).

Barker J., *From the Depths of Despair to the Promise of Presence: A Rhetorical Reading of the Book of Joel* (Siphrut, 11; Winona Lake, IN: Eisenbrauns, 2014).

Bergler S., *Joel als Schriftinterpret* (BEATAJ; Frankfurt: Peter Lang, 1988).

Coggins R., 'Interbiblical Quotations in Joel', in J. Barton and D. J. Reimer (eds.), *After the Exile: Essays in Honour of Rex Mason* (Macon, GA: Mercer University Press, 1996): 75–84.

Cook S. L., *Prophecy and Apocalypticism: The Post-Exilic Social Setting* (Minneapolis: Fortress Press, 1995): 167–209.

Ebach R., 'Joel in the Book of the Twelve', in L.-S. Tiemeyer and J. Wöhrle (eds.), *The Book of the Twelve: Composition, Reception, and Interpretation* (VTSup, 184; Leiden: Brill, 2020): 124–38.

Jeremias J., 'The Function of the Book of Joel for Reading the Twelve', in R. Albertz, J. D. Nogalski, and J. Wöhrle (eds.), *Perspectives on the Formation of the Book of the Twelve* (BZAW, 433; Berlin: de Gruyter, 2012): 77–88.

Kapelrud A. S., *Joel Studies* (Uppsala: Almqvist & Wiksell, 1948).

Kelly J. R., 'Joel, Jonah and the YHWH Creed: Determining the Trajectory of the Literary Influence', *JBL* 132.4 (2013): 805–26.

LeCureux J. T., 'Joel, the Cult, and the Book of the Twelve', in L.-S. Tiemeyer (ed.), *Priests and Cults in the Book of the Twelve* (ANEM, 14; Atlanta, GA: SBL Press, 2016): 65–79.

Nogalski J. D., 'Joel as Literary Anchor in the Book of the Twelve', in J. D. Nogalski and M. A. Sweeney (eds.), *Reading and Hearing the Book of the Twelve* (SBLSymS, 15; Atlanta, GA: SBL Press, 2000): 91–109.

Plöger O., *Theocracy and Eschatology* (Oxford: Basil Blackwell, 1968).

Prinsloo W. S., *The Theology of the Book of Joel* (BZAW, 163; Berlin/New York: W. de Gruyter, 1985).

Redditt P. L., 'The Book of Joel and Peripheral Prophecy', *CBQ* 48 (1986): 225–40.

Rooke D., 'Priests and Profits: Joel and Malachi', in L.-S. Tiemeyer (ed.), *Priests and Cults in the Book of the Twelve* (2016): 81–98.

Simkins R. A., *Yahweh's Activity in History and Nature in the Book of Joel* (Lewiston, NY: Mellen, 1991).

Strazicich J., *Joel's Use of Scripture and the Scripture's Use of Joel* (Leiden/Boston: Brill, 2007).

Troxel R. L., *Joel: Scope, Genre(s), and Meaning* (Critical Studies in the Hebrew Bible, 6; Winona Lake, IN: Eisenbrauns, 2015).

Watson D., 'Divine Attributes in the Book of Joel', *JSOT* 37 (2017): 101–29.

Wöhrle J., 'Joel and the Formation of the Book of the Twelve', *BTB* 40 (2010): 127–37.

C COMMENTARY ON JOEL

1 A Disastrous Plague of Locusts – Joel 1:1–2:27

Joel 1:1 – Heading

1 The word of the LORD that came to Joel son of Pethuel:

The heading is brief. Those of the books of Hosea and Amos, as of several other prophetic texts, contain chronological information, inviting the reading of them with a particular historical context in mind. In the case of Joel no such information is given. Those who produced and handed on the text clearly felt that the events described, of a locust plague and a coming Day of YHWH, did not need to be read in the context of a particular historical setting.

C Commentary on Joel

The name 'Joel' is frequent in the genealogies and other parts of 1 Chronicles, and occurs also in 2 Chronicles 29:12; Ezra 10:43; Nehemiah 11:9. Its only occurrence in pre-exilic narrative is in 1 Samuel 8:2, where Joel is Samuel's first-born son. While, as Barton notes, the genealogies in Chronicles may derive from older material,[30] its prevalence there lends support to a Second Temple dating of the book. The name means 'YHWH is God'. We know nothing about the man after whom the book is named, nor about his father, named as Pethuel, a name found only here in the Hebrew Bible. Some LXX and Syriac MSS translate as 'Bethuel', the name of the father of Rebekah, wife of Isaac in Genesis 22:23; 24:15, 24, 47, 50. As Coggins comments, this is 'likely to be an example of the tendency in much biblical interpretation to link otherwise unknown characters with those about whom some information is available'.[31]

The expression 'the word of the Lord came to' is found in several superscriptions (Jer. 1:2; Ezek. 1:3; Hos. 1:1; Jonah 1:1; Mic. 1:1; Zeph. 1:1; Hag. 1:1; Zech. 1:1) and sometimes at other points in prophetic texts (e.g. Jer. 2:1; 13:3). Over time it evidently became standard, formulaic terminology to use of a prophet and in a prophetic text, and it is used here as a literary device.

Joel 1:2–4 – Hear and Tell

² Hear this, O elders;
    give ear, all inhabitants of the land!
Has such a thing happened in your days
    or in the days of your ancestors?
³ Tell your children of it,
    and let your children tell their children,
    and their children another generation.

⁴ What the cutting locust left,
    the swarming locust has eaten;
what the swarming locust left,
    the hopping locust has eaten;
and what the hopping locust left,
    the destroying locust has eaten.

---

[30] J. Barton *Joel and Obadiah* (2001): 39.
[31] R. Coggins, *Joel and Amos* (NCB; Sheffield: Sheffield Academic Press, 2000): 25.

Commentators discuss whether these verses introduce merely the immediate passage to follow, or the whole first half of the book.[32] In viewing Joel as a literary work, the latter view is to be preferred. They serve to generate in the reader an expectation that what will follow describes an experience which should never be forgotten. The instruction to 'Hear' is found in many prophetic texts (e.g. Isa. 1:2; Hos. 5:1; Mic. 1:2; 3:9).

Those addressed are, firstly, the elders. The term can be used to refer either to a group of leading people within Israel or to those who are older in years.[33] In pre-exilic Israel elders were local leaders who held responsibilities in their tribes and towns (Deut. 21:18–21; 25:7; 1 Kgs 21:8–11). When they came together they were an influential group who could have a role in king-making (1 Sam. 8:4; 2 Sam. 3:17–18; 5:1–3). In the Second Temple period the elders were more significant still. In Ezra 5:5–9; 6:7–14 they are referred to in correspondence between the Persian emperor Darius and the governor of the Persian province of 'Beyond the River' in which was Jerusalem. Ezra 10:8 refers to a proclamation made throughout the land 'by order of the officials and the elders'. However, it may be that in Joel 1:2 it refers to the aged, whose long memories would enable them to pass on their recollection of the events to be described to their children and grandchildren. In 2:16 the term refers to the aged, at the other end of the age-spectrum from children and infants, while in 1:14 it is those who have authority to proclaim a public fast. In both 1:2 and 1:14 the elders are in parallel with 'all the inhabitants of the land'.

The elders and inhabitants of the land are enjoined to pass on to future generations the memory of all that happened. The passing on of tradition from one generation to another is characteristic of the book of Deuteronomy (e.g. 4:9–10; 11:19–21), and the passing on of wisdom from father to son of the book of Proverbs (e.g. 4:1; 7:1, 24). What is to be passed on is the description of the utter devastation of the locust plague, on a scale never seen before, but also the story of the people's calling out to YHWH and his deliverance in response.

---

[32] J. Barton *Joel and Obadiah* (2001): 42 takes them as the introduction to 1:2–20; E. Assis *Book of Joel* (2013): 73 takes them as introducing 1:2–12. The view that they introduce the whole of 1:4–2:27 is held by W. Rudolph, *Joel - Amos - Obadja - Jona* (KAT, 13/2; Gütersloh: Gütersloh Verlagshaus Gerd Mohn, 1971): 23.

[33] Among those who take the term in this verse to leaders of the people are E. Assis *Book of Joel* (2013): 73–4; J. D. Nogalski, *The Book of the Twelve: Hosea–Jonah* (Smyth & Helwys Bible Commentary; Macon, GA: Smyth & Helwys, 2011): 217; H. W. Wolff *Joel and Amos* (1977): 21. Those who take them to be those older in years include J. L. Crenshaw *Joel* (1995): 86; R. Coggins, *Joel and Amos* (2000): 26. Crenshaw translates as 'old timers' (82).

C Commentary on Joel

Joel 1:4 describes the total devastation wrought by a plague of locusts. While the descriptions to follow are in line with descriptions of disaster found in psalms of lament, the portrayal of a plague of locusts bringing total devastation to the land is unique in the Hebrew Bible. In 1 Kings 8:37 Solomon's prayer includes locusts as one among several possible natural disasters which might befall the nation (the others being plague, blight, mildew, or caterpillar), and in Amos 4:9 the devouring of fig trees and olive trees by locusts is one of a series of disasters described in 4:6–11. Here in Joel, however, the locust plague is not one disaster among others. Rather, the whole first half of the book concerns it. It is true that only in 1:4 and 2:25 are locusts specifically referred to, but it is in the light of this opening 1:4 that the rest of the first half of the text is to be read. Some scholars prefer to take the locusts as metaphorical, seeing the real disaster as an invading army. Redditt, for example, writes that 'While certainty is impossible, one may conclude that the reference to locusts in 1:4 is at least as likely to be figurative as it is to be literal.'[34] Similarly Nogalski writes: 'As Joel unfolds, the symbolic nature of these locusts clarifies so that it becomes increasingly possible to identify the locusts as foreign powers who invade the land at YHWH's initiation.'[35] However, the description in 2:4–9 of the locusts being *like* an army of horses and chariots only makes sense if it is something other than an army that is being compared with one.[36] This is a reversal of comparisons made elsewhere in the Hebrew Bible in which the size of armies is compared to a swarm of locusts (Judg. 6:5; 7:12; Jer. 46:23). In those texts armies are compared to locusts. Here in Joel locusts are compared to an invading army. Hence in 1:6 to refer to the locust plague as 'a nation' is entirely appropriately. Barton is correct, too, in observing that, while it seems that what Joel describes is 'overwhelmingly likely to have been a locust plague, the language of invitation to cultic lament is naturally somewhat stylized and may well include details not too closely related to the specifics of what locusts have done: hence, perhaps, the references to drought (1:17) and the pitiful lowing of cattle (1:18)'[37] – and, we may add, to language of military invasion (1:6; 2:2, 4–9). But we may note, too, Assis's proposal that 'the locusts have a double meaning, a literal one and a metaphorical one', and

---

[34] P. L. Redditt, 'Locust', *NIDB* 3: 684–5 (685).
[35] J. D. Nogalski *Hosea–Jonah* (2011): 218–19.
[36] So E. Assis *Book of Joel* (2013): 35–6; J. Barton *Joel and Obadiah* (2001): 44; J. Goldingay *Hosea–Micah* (2020): 217–18.
[37] J. Barton *Joel and Obadiah* (2001): 46.

his thesis that 'the term "locusts" in Joel means both real locusts and, at the same time, is intended to evoke in the reader's mind a political enemy that is represented by locusts'.[38] There are, he suggests, elements of deliberate ambiguity. While it is a locust plague that is described, the consequent call to turn to YHWH for deliverance (1:14; 2:12–13), and the discovery that he hears and responds, is a lesson to be learned for application in many a desperate situation, including that of invasion and conquest by enemies.

The totality of destruction is depicted by the use of four different Hebrew words for 'locust': *gāzām* (cutting locust); *'arbbeh* (swarming locust); *yeleq* (hopping locust); and *ḥāsîl* (destroying locust). It may be that these terms refer not to different species of locust, but to four stages of development of the one species, but we cannot be sure. The first term is found only here and in Amos 4:9.[39] The second is the usual, most frequent designation of locusts, and the one used in the story of the plague of locusts in Egypt in Exodus 10:1–20. The third may designate the youngest locust, just hatched from the egg, while the fourth term may designate the next stage of growth beyond that. However, our knowledge in this respect is limited, and it is, anyway, not the intention of the text to give a lesson in zoology, but rather to pile on the terms in order to convey a sense of the totality of the destruction.

Joel 1:5–14 – Calls to Lament

⁵ Wake up, you drunkards, and weep,
　　and wail, all you wine-drinkers,
　over the sweet wine,
　　for it is cut off from your mouth.
⁶ For a nation has invaded my land,
　　powerful and innumerable;
　its teeth are lions' teeth,
　　and it has the fangs of a lioness.
⁷ It has laid waste my vines
　　and splintered my fig trees;
　it has stripped off their bark and thrown it down;
　　their branches have turned white.

---

[38]　E. Assis *Book of Joel* (2013): 41, 47.

[39]　Hence those who wish to read and comment on the Book of the Twelve as a whole may justifiably see a thematic link between these Joel 1:4 and Amos 4:9, as does M. A. Sweeney, *The Twelve Prophets*, vol. 1 (Berit Olam Studies in Hebrew Narrative and Poetry; Collegeville, MN: Liturgical Press, 2000): 156.

C Commentary on Joel

⁸ Lament like a virgin dressed in sackcloth
for the husband of her youth.
⁹ The grain offering and the drink offering are cut off
from the house of the LORD.
The priests mourn,
the ministers of the LORD.
¹⁰ The fields are devastated,
the ground mourns,
for the grain is destroyed,
the wine dries up,
the oil fails.

¹¹ Be dismayed, you farmers;
wail, you vinedressers,
over the wheat and the barley,
for the crops of the field are ruined.
¹² The vine withers;
the fig tree droops.
Pomegranate, palm, and apple –
all the trees of the field are dried up;
surely, joy withers away
among the people.

¹³ Put on sackcloth and lament, you priests;
wail, you ministers of the altar.
Come, pass the night in sackcloth,
you ministers of my God!
Grain offering and drink offering
are withheld from the house of your God.

¹⁴ Consecrate a fast;
call a solemn assembly.
Gather the elders
and all the inhabitants of the land
to the house of the LORD your God,
and cry out to the LORD.

The description of disaster in much of chapters 1–2 is comparable to complaints and descriptions of tribulations found in communal psalms of lament.[40] Psalms of communal lament address a complaint or cry for help to God in a time of crisis, describing the extreme difficulty of present

---

[40]   G. Ahlström *Joel and the Temple Cult* (1971): 130–1 and *passim*.

208   *Book of Joel*

circumstances (most often their weakness in the face of their enemies). Many also express also hope and trust in YHWH. While the text here in Joel is not itself a liturgy, it draws from liturgical language.

In the light of the ravaging of the land described in 1:4, there follows in 1:5 the first of several imperatives, summoning to lament. It is addressed to 'you drunkards' and 'all you wine-drinkers'. The Hebrew Bible generally has a positive attitude towards wine. Typical is Psalm 104:15, which includes 'wine to gladden the human heart' as one of creation's blessings. It was part of a staple diet, and in Deuteronomy (14:22–23; 18:3–4) is among the offerings to be made at the Temple. Drunkenness, however, was viewed as dangerous, since it led to a lack of control over what one was doing (Gen. 9:20–21; Hos. 4:10). So here in Joel 1:5, drunkenness leads to a lack of awareness of the severity of the disaster, and those under its influence have to be woken up in order to join the nation's need to lament and wail. Crenshaw considers that the terms are not pejorative, and he translates as 'imbibers' rather than 'drunkards'.[41] More frequently, however, the word translated by NRSV as 'drunkard' is pejorative, and he has not been generally followed. Barton argues that the plague must not yet have occurred, as people would surely not need to be woken up if it already had; rather they would already see the plague's appalling consequences.[42] Such a view is too literal and prosaic, however. In the face of the disaster already upon them, the drunkards and wine-drinkers are urged to wake up, weep, and wail. The language is that of lament. Mourning and lament were (and are) expressed audibly and with loud emotion, in contrast to the relative reserve of much contemporary western culture. In the face of the locust plague the drunkards and wine-drinkers were to wake up and wail for the destruction of the vines that would have supplied their future drink.

The swarm of locusts is described as 'a nation' (1:6), that is, an invading army. Proverbs 30:27 uses the same analogy of locusts as an army, which marches in rank. The picture language is further enlarged as their teeth and fangs are described as those of lions and lionesses. The effect of the invasion is the total destruction of the vines and fig trees, which are referred to as 'my vines' and 'my fig trees' (1:7). Who is meant by 'my'? The verse could be taken as words of the waking drunkards coming to their senses, or it could be the prophet referring to his own vines and fig trees. Most probable, however, is that the text has slipped into divine speech, and that it is YHWH

---

[41]   J. L. Crenshaw *Joel* (1995): 82, 94.
[42]   J. Barton *Joel and Obadiah* (2001): 50–1.

C Commentary on Joel

who speaks. As noted in the 'Introduction to Joel', the Joel-text is steeped in biblical allusions, and behind Joel 1:7 lie echoes of the description of the land as YHWH's vineyard (as, for example, in the poem in Isa. 5:1–7).

The second imperative of the section opens 1:8. It is not specified who is addressed. It could, therefore, still be the drunkards and wine-drinkers of 1:5. More likely, however, is that it is a summons to the people as a whole. The form of the verb is unique, but ancient versions and modern commentators alike take it to be a feminine singular imperative. Some have found a problem in a 'virgin' (i.e. a girl not yet married) mourning the husband of her youth. An explanation frequently adduced is that she could have been betrothed, but not yet married when the man died. Deuteronomy 22:23–24 uses the same Hebrew word and refers to a betrothed woman as a wife, which lends support to this possibility. But Coggins is correct to say that perhaps the problem arises from our wish to give 'too precise a reference to poetic language'.[43] Assis draws attention to occurrences of 'virgin Israel' in Jeremiah 18:13; 31:4, 21 [3, 20]; Amos 5:2, and comments that the 'relationship between God and Israel is described in many places through the allegory of the relationship between husband and wife'.[44] Nogalski notes the conceptual links to Hosea 2, where he takes the land to be 'personified as YHWH's unfaithful wife whom he punishes by removing the gifts of grain, wine and oil'.[45] There are links in vocabulary between Joel 1:8 and Hosea 2:15–16 [2:17–18]: it shares the word 'of her youth' (one word in Hebrew); and the word translated by NRSV in Joel 1:8 as 'husband' is the word *baal* used in Hosea 2:16, with NRSV's 'my husband' there being *'îšî*. Those reading and commenting on the Book of the Twelve as a whole are justified in noting the links with the Hosea and Amos texts, but for those treating the book of Joel in itself (as does this commentary) the summons to lament as a betrothed girl whose intended husband has died is entirely fitting within its literary context. Indeed, the fact that the image occurs also in Jeremiah reminds us that the Joel-text is prolific in its borrowing from older texts beyond as well as within the Book of the Twelve.

The cause of lament here is that the grain offerings and drink offerings were not being offered (1:9). The two offerings are not found as a pair before late priestly texts, in some of which they are described as the regular morning and evening offerings (*tāmîd*) to be made (Exod. 29:38–42;

---

[43] R. Coggins *Joel and Amos* (2000): 31.
[44] E. Assis *Book of Joel* (2013): 87.
[45] J. D. Nogalski *Hosea–Jonah* (2011): 221.

Num. 28:3–9; 29:11). This suggests a similar late dating for the Joel-text.[46] Grain and oil were required for the grain offering and wine for the drink offering, but these are precisely what the locust plague rendered unavailable (1:10). The consequential mourning of the priests is not simply because they were entitled to a share of these offerings (Lev. 2:3, 10; Deut. 18:1–5),[47] nor even that their cessation imperilled the people's communion with YHWH. Rather, the maintenance of the cult was linked with maintaining the sustaining of creation. Rooke writes of the priests that 'as the ones who perform the offerings on the altar in the temple they are the ones responsible for maintaining the sacrificial cult with its reciprocal relationship to the created order ... the priests help to ensure the stability of creation, which will in turn mean stable food supplies for the community – a heavy responsibility indeed'.[48] They would also feel a sense of shame that they could not maintain the offerings.[49] They are described as 'ministers of YHWH', but, through no fault of their own they were now unable to fulfil their ministerial duties. In post-exilic texts the term 'ministers' and the verb from which it is derived are used principally of priests and Levites who minister to YHWH in a cultic setting, but there is variation in different texts as to exactly who can make offerings and who can minister in an assisting capacity. Deuteronomy assumes that all priests will be Levites (18:1–8; 21:5). Ezekiel 40:46; 43:19 restrict the offering of sacrifice to the Zadokite descendants of Levi. Numbers 3:5–10 make clear that the Levites are to serve and assist the Aaronic priesthood. In the priestly sections of Exodus the word is used of Aaron and his sons as they perform their priestly duties (Exod. 28:35, 43; 29:30; 35:19). In Chronicles the word is used of both priests and Levites (2 Chron. 8:14; 13:10; 23:6; 31:2, all of which refer to both priests and Levites within the same verse). Here in Joel 1:9 (and in 1:13; 2:17) the term 'ministers of YHWH' refers simply to the priests.[50]

---

[46] So H. W. Wolff *Joel and Amos* (1977): 5, 31 and other commentators. However R. Coggins, *Joel and Amos* (2000): 31 sees this as a weak argument, commenting that 'though we know little of the worship of the first temple, some such offerings must have formed a feature'.

[47] NRSV follows the Hebrew text in taking the verb as an indicative: 'the priests mourn'. Some commentators follow LXX and translate the verb as an imperative addressed to the priests. On balance NRSV is to be preferred.

[48] D. Rooke, 'Priests and Profits: Joel and Malachi', in L.-S. Tiemeyer (ed.) Priests and Cults (2016): 81–98 (84).

[49] R. Simkins, '"Return to Yahweh": Honor and Shame in Joel', *Semeia* 68 (1996): 41–54 (48) draws attention to the shame of the priests in relation to 1:13, 16, but it applies equally in 1:9.

[50] See further K. Engelken, '*šrt*', *TDOT* 15: 503–14.

C Commentary on Joel

Not only do the priests mourn: so, too, does the ground (1:10). There is no problem in non-human objects being described as mourning in a poetic passage such as this (cf. Isa. 3:26, Lam. 2:8, and elsewhere). Some see this verse and 1:11–12 as describing drought rather than the effects of a locust plague. It is possible that the text assumes simultaneous disasters of locust plague and drought, but generally the two do not go together. It is more likely that standard language of disaster is being used to describe the plague of locusts, and there is no need to posit a second and separate disaster.[51]

The third imperative of the section is addressed to the farmers and vine-dressers (1:11–12). The two terms are not frequent in the Hebrew Bible, but occur together also in 2 Chronicles 26:10 and Isaiah 61:5. The first occurs also in Amos 5:16. NRSV's 'Be dismayed' could better be translated 'Be ashamed'. As the priests of 1:9 were unable to fulfil their ministerial duties, so too the farmers were unable to fulfil their agricultural duties, and a similar sense of shame would be felt. The Hebrew contains a wordplay which is impossible to capture in English: the Hebrew for 'be dismayed/ashamed' is *hôbîšû*, while the word used in 1:10 for the wine being dried up is *hôbîš* (and the same verb is used of the trees of the field being dried up in 1:12). The two words sound similar. The effect of the locust plague is that all agricultural produce is devastated and, as the produce of the land withers, so too does the people's joy. Assis comments that 'the physical damage of the land causes parallel damage within the people'.[52] The term for 'people' here is 'sons of men', a phrase used to refer to any human beings rather than specifically to the people of Israel. A natural disaster such as this locust plague can afflict any nation, and is not a consequence of anything specific to the Israelites.

The fourth and final imperative summons of Joel 1 is addressed to the priests. They had already been referred to in 1:9, but now in 1:13–14 words are spoken directly to them. They are called 'ministers of the altar', indicating that it is in their role as cultic functionaries that they are being addressed. They are also called 'ministers of my God'. LXX has simply 'ministers of God', which several commentators see as likely to have been original, with

---

[51] Following E. Assis *Book of Joel* (2013): 90 and R. Simkins, *Yahweh's Activity in History and Nature in the Book of Joel* (Ancient Near Eastern Texts and Studies, 10; Lewiston, NY: Edwin Mellen Press, 1991): 136–8. H. Hurowitz, 'Joel's Locust Plague in Light of Sargon II's Hymn to Nanaya', *JBL* 112 (1993): 597–603 shows that an Akkadian hymn of Sargon II includes a prayer for deliverance from a locust plague in which there is a reference to the orchards being dried up.

[52] E. Assis *Book of Joel* (2013): 95.

MT's version resulting from a copying error. The matter is of no great interpretative significance. As Crenshaw writes, 'At most, Joel uses "my God" to reinforce the authority by which he summons the priests to lamentation.'[53] Equally there does not appear to be any deliberate contrast intended between ministers of 'my God' and the house of 'your God' (1:13) or 'YHWH your God' (1:14). Rather the latter expressions are simply the way in which the Temple is described. In passing we may note that these verses confirm that the text must be dated to a period in which the Temple had been rebuilt and was in use. Assis's attempt to argue that it should be dated to the exilic period and that the site could still be called the 'house of YHWH' even when it did not actually exist is unpersuasive.[54]

The priests are called to put on sackcloth (1:13). To do so was a traditional sign of mourning for the death of an individual (Gen. 37:34; 2 Sam. 3:31). It could also be a sign of repentance and humbling oneself (1 Kgs 21:27–29). It could be a sign of earnestness in prayer (2 Kgs 19:1–2) or in penitence (Jonah 3:5–8). In Jeremiah it is a sign of mourning for calamity afflicting a nation (4:8; 6:26; 49:3; also Isa. 15:3). Here in Joel 1:13 it signifies both lament over the calamity of the locust plague (1:13), and earnestness in crying out to YHWH (1:14). As in 1:9, the calamity includes the fact that the daily grain offering and drink offering cannot be made. Simkins wonders whether there is an implication that the people were wilfully withholding what was needed for the sacrifices because of the food shortages,[55] but it would be reading in too much to see such an accusation in this verse.

The wearing of sackcloth is accompanied by a fast and by the calling of a solemn assembly (1:14). Public fasting of the whole people came to prominence in the post-exilic period (Isa. 58; Zech. 7:1–7; 8:18–19). Fasting, like the wearing of sackcloth, signifies earnestness in crying out to YHWH. Generally a fast would last for a day, and the extension of wearing sackcloth and fasting into the night as well reflects the seriousness of the situation. To keep a solemn assembly (*'ăṣārâ*) entailed the stopping of all daily work in order to engage in religious observance (Lev. 23:36; Num. 29:35; Deut. 16:8). This could be as part of a festival such as Passover (Deut. 16:8) or the Festival of Booths (Lev. 23:36). In Amos 5:21 YHWH declares that he takes no delight in the people's solemn assemblies, and in Isaiah 1:13 that he 'cannot endure solemn assemblies with iniquity'. Here in Joel 1:14, however,

---

[53] J. L. Crenshaw *Joel* (1995): 103.
[54] E. Assis *Book of Joel* (2013): 9.
[55] R. Simkins *Yahweh's Activity* (1991): 145.

C Commentary on Joel

there is no such prophetic critique of them. Rather, with the wearing of sackcloth and fasting, they form part of the desperate crying out to YHWH that is needed. Those to be gathered for the solemn assembly are 'the elders and all the inhabitants of the land'. Here the 'elders' are clearly those who held an office as leading people, rather than those of advanced years (see the comments on 1:2). Leaders and people alike are to join in crying out to YHWH, their God.

A Closer Look: Fasting

In the Hebrew Bible fasting, a total abstinence from food – often accompanied by other physical acts such as wailing, lamentation, tearing one's garments, and putting on sackcloth – was a sign of mourning. So, for example, 1 Samuel 31:12–13 records the inhabitants of Jabesh-gilead burying Saul and his sons, and fasting for seven days. In the following chapter 2 Samuel 1:12 records that David and his men tore their clothes, mourned, wept, and fasted until evening over the death of Saul and his son Jonathan, and for the army and the nation after their defeat at the hands of the Philistines. In 2 Samuel 12:16–23, however, David reverses usual practice by fasting while his and Bathsheba's child was ill, and then ceasing his fast when the child died. When questioned, he answered that he had fasted and wept in the hope that YHWH might be gracious and spare the child, but that now that the child was dead why should he fast? This passage, therefore, links fasting with pleading with God in prayer. In later times this was often linked with penitence and pleading for deliverance and forgiveness. Notably, in Jonah 3:6–10 the king of Nineveh proclaims a fast of all human beings and animals in the city, declaring 'Who knows? God may relent and change his mind; he may turn from his fierce anger so that we do not perish'; and God duly obliges.

In the fifth century Nehemiah wept, mourned, and fasted when he heard news of the dire straits in which the city of Jerusalem found itself (Neh. 1:4). This was an individual fast. A public fast could be declared by a ruler or leader, as in the story of Jonah. It is recorded in 1 Kings 21:9–14 that Queen Jezebel instructed the elders and nobles of the town in which Naboth lived to proclaim a fast, during which they should make false accusations against Naboth. This was therefore a public fast in one locality. Jeremiah 36:6 reveals that there were fast days in the Temple: whether such days were regular in the pre-exilic Jerusalem cult, or whether they were held in times of trouble such as the growing threat of the Babylonians, we cannot know. In the post-exilic period the proclamation of public fasts came into greater prominence. Ezra 8:21–23 tells that Ezra proclaimed a fast, and that he and his whole group fasted and petitioned God to keep them safe on their forthcoming journey. Nehemiah 9:1 records that the whole people of Israel were assembled with fasting, in sackcloth and covered in dust. Isaiah 58:2–7 assumes the practice of corporate fasting. Zechariah 8:19 refers to specific fast days which, the prophetic message indicates, should be viewed as 'seasons of joy and gladness'. Esther 9:30–31 institutes the observance of the Feast of Purim, which includes fasts and lamentations. Joel 1:14; 2:12, 15 are therefore at home in this Second Temple period in which public fasts were regularly held, and they signify the earnestness required in calling out to YHWH in this most desperate of times.[56]

Joel 1:4–14 invites and commands lament and dismay from drunkards and wine-drinkers, the whole nation, the farmers and vine-dressers, and the priests. The call for the elders and all the inhabitants of the land to join in a fast and solemn assembly draws all of these people together in the house of YHWH to join together in crying out to YHWH (1:14). We may note what has not been said thus far. It has not been said that the disaster of the locust plague has been sent by YHWH to punish the people for any sin or wrongdoing. Nor, indeed, has it been said that it has been sent by YHWH at all. If, as is suggested in the comments earlier in this section on 1:7, the 'my' whose vines have been laid waste and fig trees splintered is YHWH himself, then he is in the text as fellow-lamenter with the people, and not as sender of the locusts. The passage reads simply as a description of a natural disaster and its effects. The next verses, however, introduce a new note: this disaster signifies the coming Day of YHWH.

Joel 1:15–20 – The Day of YHWH is Near

> [15] Alas for the day!
>   For the day of the LORD is near,
>   and as destruction from the Almighty it comes.

---

[56] See further D. Lambert, 'Fast, Fasting', *NIDB* 2: 431–4; J. Muddiman, 'Fast, Fasting', *ABD* 2: 773–6.

C *Commentary on Joel*

¹⁶ Is not the food cut off
  before our eyes,
joy and gladness
  from the house of our God?

¹⁷ The seed shrivels under the clods.
  the storehouses are desolate;
the granaries are ruined
  because the grain has withered.
¹⁸ How the animals groan!
  The herds of cattle wander about
because there is no pasture for them;
  even the flocks of sheep are perishing.

¹⁹ To you, O LORD, I cry,
  for fire has devoured
  the pastures of the wilderness,
and flames have burned
  all the trees of the field.
²⁰ Even the wild animals cry to you
  because the watercourses are dried up,
and fire has devoured
  the pastures of the wilderness.

Joel 1:15 brings the introduction of a new theme into the book: the locust plague signifies that a coming Day of YHWH is near. The earliest text in which the phrase 'Day of YHWH' occurs is Amos 5:18–20, in which the people are told not to desire it as a day of light, as presumably they were doing (see the commentary *ad loc*), but that rather it would be a day of darkness for them. Here in Joel, as in Amos 5, it is not a day of blessing for Israel, but a day bringing destruction. In its literary context of Joel 1:4–2:27 the recognition that a Day of YHWH is near forms a continuing part of the lament. The position of 1:15–20 after 1:13–14 invites us to read these verses as the cry to YHWH which 1:13–14 instructs priests, elders, and people to make.

A Closer Look: The Day of YHWH

The phrase 'Day of YHWH' occurs seventeen times in the Hebrew Bible, all except one in prophetic texts (Isa. 2:12; 13:6–9; 22:5; Jer. 46:10; Ezek. 7:10; 13:5; 30:3; Joel 1:15; 2:1–11; 2:31 [3:4]; 3:14 [4:14]; Amos 5:18–20; Obad. 15; Zeph. 1:7–18; Zech. 14:1; Mal. 4:5). It may be a day on which YHWH acts against either Israel (e.g. Joel 2:1–11) or foreign nations (e.g. Isa. 13).

The one non-prophetic occurrence is in Lamentations 2:22. Additionally phrases such as 'day of vengeance' can be associated with it. This volume contains both the earliest occurrence of the phrase (Amos 5:18–20) and one of the fullest descriptions of it (Joel 1:15; 2:1–11). Amos 5:18–20 contains minimal description of what the Day of YHWH entailed: it is a day of darkness, not light, of gloom with no brightness. It is widely surmised that this saying countered a popularly held belief that the Day of YHWH would be a day of blessing for Israel, in which YHWH would defeat her enemies and vindicate her. No chronologically earlier text actually expresses such a belief, but nevertheless it makes best interpretative sense to assume this. However, there has been scholarly disagreement over the setting in which such a positive expression of the Day of YHWH may have been found. The two main proposals are (1) that the concept derived from a cultic setting, which makes good sense of Amos 5:21–24 following 5:18–20; the principal proponent of this view was Mowinckel; and (2) that it derived from traditions associated with warfare in early Israel; the principal proponent of this view was von Rad, who referred to Israel's so-called 'Holy War' traditions.[57] Barton considers that 'there seems little hope of deciding between these two explanations'.[58] However, whatever may have come before Amos 5:18–20 this text sets the tone for the future development of the concept in prophetic literature. The fullest descriptions of the Day of YHWH are found in Isaiah 13, Joel 1:15; 2:1–11, and Zephaniah 1:14–18. The following principal features of the Day of YHWH may be seen in these passages:

(1) YHWH himself is responsible for the Day: it is he who musters an army with which to punish the wicked (Isa. 13:4; Joel 1:15; 2:1–5, 11; in other passages it is a sacrificial feast that YHWH prepares e.g. Zeph. 1:7).
(2) Anguish and panic seize those affected by the Day (Isa. 13:7–8; Joel 2:6).
(3) The Day brings cosmic implications, as creation itself is affected (Isa. 13:10, 13; Joel 2:10).
(4) The result of the Day is utter desolation and destruction (Isa. 13:20–22; Joel 2:3; Zeph. 1:18).

---

[57] See further S. Mowinckel, *He that Cometh: the Messiah Concept in the Old Testament and Later Judaism* (trans. G. W. Anderson; Oxford: Blackwell, 1956); G. von Rad, 'The Origin of the Concept of the Day of Yahweh', *JSS* 4 (1959): 97–108.

[58] J. Barton, *The Theology of the Book of Amos* (Cambridge: Cambridge University Press, 2012): 65.

C Commentary on Joel

> Not every occurrence of the phrase has all these elements associated with it, but it became established prophetic tradition that the Day of YHWH was a threatening day, in which YHWH would act in judgment. Hence Joel 1:15 could say that 'as destruction from the Almighty it comes'. The pronouncement of Amos 5:18–20 that the day would be one of darkness is reiterated in Zephaniah 1:15 and Joel 2:2.

The opening 'Alas' of 1:15 represents the cry that those summoned in 1:14 to gather were to make. The idea that the Day of YHWH was a day of judgement on Israel's enemies was not a foregone conclusion, since Amos 5:18–20 had, centuries earlier, described it as a day of darkness for Israel rather than one of blessing. However the first half of the verse is drawn from Ezekiel 30:2–3, where the Day of YHWH is a 'day of clouds' for the nations. Joel 1:15 also draws from Isaiah 13:6, which reads: 'Wail, for the day of YHWH is near; it will come like destruction from the Almighty', the nation concerned in this passage being Babylon. Joel therefore draws on two passages in which it is foreign nations that are negatively affected by the Day of YHWH. As in Amos 5:18–20, however, here it is Israel that is suffering. The tone, however, is not judgemental. The coming of the Day of YHWH is part of the lament and wailing expressed, rather than an announcement of judgement. Barton is correct in asserting that 'there is no need to read the term in 1:15 as having an "eschatological" sense, if by that we mean the end of the world order: it is simply a day of YHWH's decisive intervention in Israel's affairs', and that we can translate as 'a' rather than 'the' day of YHWH.[59] For readers of the text as subsequently enlarged by the additions of the second part from 2:28 [3:1] onwards, there is the added recognition that the coming Day of YHWH which would affect Israel negatively in 1:15 and 2:1–11, and would lead Israel to cry out to YHWH from their position of need, was in fact a precursor of the great eschatological 'Day of YHWH' when he would judge the nations and bring deliverance to Israel, as described in the second part of the text.

The Hebrew of 1:15b, borrowing directly from Isaiah 13:6, contains an alliteration. The Hebrew for 'destruction' is *šōd*, and for 'Almighty' is *šadday*. Crenshaw attempts to capture the alliteration in translating 'YHWH's day is imminent, dawning like destruction from the Destroyer.'[60]

[59] J. Barton *Joel and Obadiah* (2001): 62.
[60] J. L. Crenshaw *Joel* (1995): 84.

Joel 1:16 links back to 1:9. Food is 'cut off' just as in 1:9 the grain offering and drink offering are 'cut off'. The lack of food in the land meant not only hunger, but also cessation of the sacrifices to YHWH, to whom praise would therefore not be given. Is there an implication here that for his own self-interest, therefore, YHWH would do well to heed the people's cry?[61] The verb 'cut off' also applies to 'joy and gladness': in normal times people gathered at the house of God to celebrate (cf. Deut. 12:5–7), but in this time of devastation, when the sacrifices were not being made, joy and gladness, too, were cut off. This verse portrays the prophet as identifying himself with the people: it is 'our eyes' before which food, and joy and gladness, are cut off.

The translation of the first line of 1:17 is difficult, since three of its words occur only here in the Hebrew Bible. NRSV is representative of most translations in aligning the meaning with the second half of the verse. The last word of 1:18 in the Hebrew text is also surprising: as it stands it means that even the sheep bear guilt. However a small emendation gives the meaning more likely to have been intended, that they are stunned, or 'perishing' as NRSV translates (the pre-2021 NRSV's 'dazed' was, in my view, preferable). While 1:17 continues the earlier description of the parched ground (1:10–12), 1:18 adds a further dimension to the catastrophe, namely the effect on the livestock of the land. There is nothing for them to graze on, and had there been any grain in the storehouses it would certainly have gone to people rather than animals. Like 1:10–12, these verses sound like a description of drought. However, it is once again not necessary to assume that there was a drought as a second disaster distinct from the locust plague. Rather stock language is being employed to emphasise the totality of the destruction at this time of locust plague.

Stock language continues into 1:19–20 (cf. Jer. 9:10 [9]; 14:5–6). The land is so dry that fires break out, devouring trees and pastures. Reference to the 'trees of the field' links back to 1:12. But who is the speaker who cries to YHWH in 1:19? It would be possible to take the whole of 1:15–20 as being the text of the cry that 1:14 instructs the elders and the inhabitants of the land to make, in which case the speaker would be the person voicing the cry on the people's behalf. Alternatively it is the prophet portrayed as identifying himself with the people's sorrow and grief, and crying out with them or on their behalf. In 1:20 the animals, too, cry out, as young ravens are portrayed as doing in Job 38:41. The verb used of the animals crying out is

---

[61] So J. Barton *Joel and Obadiah* (2001): 62.

C Commentary on Joel

the same as that used to describe the panting of a deer in the opening verse of Psalm 42, a psalm of lament.

To cry out to YHWH is to assume that there is some point in doing so. As noted in the concluding comments to 1:5–14, it has not been said that the disaster being experienced is punishment for any sins of the people; and apart from the stock language of the Day of YHWH in 1:15, it has not even been said that YHWH has sent it. Barton considers that it 'is taken for granted that the will of God lies behind natural disaster',[62] and this is correct. However it is an assumption not specifically stated, and an assumption that modern readers, more naturally inclined to think and speak of 'natural disasters', are not required to share. But whatever is assumed in this respect, it will be a natural and proper reaction of religious believers to cry out to God from a position of desperate need, and in so doing to believe that the Lord will hear and be moved by such cries. There may also be times when a whole community of believers or a nation may declare a national day or period of mourning. Joel 1 has urged the participation of priests, elders, farmers, drunkards, and indeed the whole nation in lament and mourning for disaster, and 1:14, 19–20 specifically enjoin a crying out to YHWH. Such cries will not go unnoticed by a merciful God.

Joel 2:1–11 – Proclamation of the Day of YHWH

2 Blow the trumpet in Zion;
> sound the alarm on my holy mountain!
Let all the inhabitants of the land tremble,
> for the day of the LORD is coming, it is near –
² a day of darkness and gloom,
> a day of clouds and thick darkness!
Like blackness spread upon the mountains,
> a great and powerful army comes;
their like has never been from of old,
> nor will be again after them
> in ages to come.

³ Fire devours in front of them,
> and behind them a flame burns.
Before them the land is like the garden of Eden,
> but after them a desolate wilderness,
> and nothing escapes them.

---

[62] J. Barton *Joel and Obadiah* (2001): 64.

^{4} They have the appearance of horses,
  and like war-horses they charge.
^{5} As with the rumbling of chariots,
    they leap on the tops of the mountains,
  like the crackling of a flame of fire
    devouring the stubble,
  like a powerful army
    drawn up for battle.

^{6} Before them peoples are in anguish;
  all faces grow pale.
^{7} Like warriors they charge;
  like soldiers they scale the wall.
  Each keeps to its own course;
    they do not swerve from their paths.
^{8} They do not jostle one another;
    each keeps to its own track;
  they burst through the weapons
    and are not halted.
^{9} They leap upon the city;
    they run upon the walls;
  they climb up into the houses;
    they enter through the windows like a thief.

^{10} The earth quakes before them;
    the heavens tremble.
  The sun and the moon are darkened,
    and the stars withdraw their shining.
^{11} The Lord utters his voice
    at the head of his army;
  how vast is his host!
    Numberless are those who obey his command.
  Truly the day of the Lord is great,
    terrible indeed – who can endure it?

Joel 1:15 introduced the Day of YHWH into the text, and 2:1–11 develops the theme further. It is referred to specifically in 2:1–2 and 2:11, bracketing the material in between, some of which also draws on standard 'Day of YHWH' motifs and terminology. The influence of themes and some phraseology from Zephaniah 1:14–16 and Isaiah 13 is evident.

Commentators hold varying views concerning the nature of the disaster described in 2:1–11. Some, noting that there is no mention of locusts and that much of the passage seems to describe invasion by an enemy army

C Commentary on Joel

rather than a locust plague, see it as a military invasion. The majority of these take it to be some kind of apocalyptic army of YHWH rather than an ordinary, human army. Others, in contrast, note that 2:4–5 compare the invaders to warhorses and chariots and describe them as 'like a powerful army'. The comparison means, they argue, that what is being described must be something different from an army, for how can an army be 'like' an army? They therefore take 2:1–11 to be a further description of a locust plague, now compared to an army. Of these, some see it as a second invasion of locusts, on the basis that 2:25 speaks of 'the years' that the locusts devoured. Others take it to be a continuation of the description of the same locust plague described in chapter 1, in which case the plural 'years' in 2:25 is taken to reflect the severity of the effects of the locust plague, from which the land did not recover in one season.[63] While the perfect tense of the verbs in 1:4–20 describe events that have already happened, the imperfect verbs of chapter 2 can naturally suggest future happenings. However, they need not do so, as Hebrew often oscillates between the two tenses, not least in prophetic texts;[64] and, indeed, 2:10–11 returns to the perfect tense. In commenting on 1:17–20, it was noted that the use of stock language concerning disasters resulted in images describing drought and fire being used of the locust plague. On balance it is best 'to see 2:1–11 as a parallel but heightened description of what has already transpired in 1:4–20'.[65] Coggins writes of the 'range of figurative language' employed, pointing out that it is the locust plague that will be in the minds of readers and hearers of chapter 1 who have read on into chapter 2.[66]

The passage begins with a summons: 'Blow the trumpet in Zion.' The *šôpār* was a curved ram's horn. It could be sounded to warn of danger or to call to battle (Judg. 3:27; 6:34; 7:8, 16). Other prophetic texts in which it is to be sounded as a warning are Hosea 5:8; Jeremiah 4:5; 6:1. Zephaniah 1:16 associated it with the Day of YHWH. But who is addressing whom in the instructions to blow the trumpet and sound the alarm? The reference to

---

[63] J. D. Nogalski *Hosea–Jonah* (2011): 229–33 and H. W. Wolff *Joel and Amos* (1977): 7, 40–3 take it to be an apocalyptic army. J. L. Crenshaw *Joel* (1995): 129 takes it to be a second invasion of locusts, the description of which becomes subsumed by divine warrior language at some points. J. Barton *Joel and Obadiah* (2001): 68–70 takes it to be a continuation of one and the same locust plague, as does E. Assis *Book of Joel* (2013): 122.

[64] J. Barton *Joel and Obadiah* (2001): 69.

[65] T. S. Hadjiev *Joel and Amos* (2020): 30.

[66] R. Coggins, *Joel and Amos* (2000): 39–40 (40). R. Simkins *Yahweh's Activity* (1991): 154–5 argues that to see these verses as still describing locust plague is 'the most natural interpretation'.

'my holy mountain', in parallel with 'Zion' (2:1) indicates that it is YHWH who speaks, certainly in the opening 2:1–2. But by the time we get to 2:11 YHWH is in the third person, and it has become prophetic speech. There is no precise point at which we can say that divine speech ends and prophetic speech begins: rather the one slips seamlessly into the other. The addressee in 2:1 has been conceived variously as the priests (Allen), the city watchman (Barton), the prophet functioning as a sentinel (Crenshaw), or the whole people (Assis).[67] Most naturally it is an imagined sentinel, or the prophet identified as one (as in Ezek. 33:1–9). The Day of YHWH announced by the blowing of the trumpet is a 'day of darkness and gloom, a day of clouds and thick darkness' (Joel 2:2), phrases drawn in their entirety from Zephaniah 1:15. NRSV's 'blackness' (2:2) involves a minor emendation from Hebrew *šaḥar* (dawn) to *šĕḥōr*.[68] In the darkness and gloom YHWH, the divine warrior, assembles his army, a motif prominent in other 'Day of YHWH' passages (cf. Isa. 13:3–5). The scale of the army – 'their like has never been from of old, nor will be again after them in ages to come' – is reminiscent of the description of the locust plague in Egypt in Exodus 10:14. As in 1:19, this is part of the stock language of disaster that the Joel-text employs.

Lost in translation is that Joel 2:3, 2:6, and 2:10 all begin 'Before them', a structural technique which contributes to the coherence of the passage.[69] Joel 2:3 includes two 'before' and 'behind/after' descriptions. Assis points out that the first is spatial, in that fire devours the land before and behind, while the second is chronological, referring to the state of the garden of Eden before and after the disaster.[70] The garden of Eden is found in the books of Genesis (2:8, 10, 15; 3:23; 4:16) and Ezekiel (28:13; 31:9, 16, 18; 36:35); Isaiah 51:3 refers simply to 'Eden'. The occurrence closest to Joel 2:3 is Ezekiel 36:35, which Joel 2:3 reverses: there a desolate land becomes like the garden of Eden (as also in Isa. 51:3); here the garden of Eden becomes a desolate wilderness. The theme of the earth being made desolate relates also to Isaiah 13:9.

---

[67] L. C. Allen, *The Books of Joel, Obadiah, Jonah and Micah* (NICOT; Grand Rapids, MI: Eerdmans, 1976): 67; J. Barton *Joel and Obadiah* (2001): 70; J. L. Crenshaw *Joel* (1995): 117; E. Assis *Book of Joel* (2013): 26–7.

[68] NIV translates: 'Like dawn spreading across the mountains a large and mighty army comes', preserving the Hebrew without emendation, but disturbing the otherwise black tone of the verse.

[69] Technically 'Before it/him' (singular): but assuming that it refers to an army of locusts it is perfectly in order to translate in the plural.

[70] E. Assis *Book of Joel* (2013): 130.

C Commentary on Joel

The description continues with the comparison of the locusts to an army, with horses and chariots (2:4–5). NRSV captures the drama of the description by translating a double occurrence of the word 'sound' as the 'rumbling' of chariots and the 'crackling' of the flame of fire. A similar double occurrence of the same word is found in Isaiah 13:4, where NRSV translates as a 'tumult' on the mountains and an 'uproar' of kingdoms and nations gathering together. Before this army of locusts, all faces 'grow pale' (2:6). The rare word translated thus occurs only here and in Nahum 2:10, so the translation is uncertain. There follows a vivid description of the unstoppable, all-pervasive advance of the locusts (2:7–9). Simkins cites a recorded description of an invasion of locusts in Jerusalem in 1915:

> For three or four days an incessant and unending stream filled the road from side to side, like numberless troops marching on parade.... Up and up the city walls and the castle they climbed to their very heights ... crawling up thick upon the walls and squeezing in through cracks of closed doors or windows, entering the very dwelling rooms. When unable to find an entrance they often scaled the walls to the roofs, and then got into the houses by throwing themselves into the open courts.[71]

Joel 2:4–5 is a powerful poetic description, and it would be over-prosaic to argue, as some do, that these verses prove that the walls of Jerusalem had been re-built and that therefore the text must be dated to after Nehemiah's reconstruction.[72]

The passage concludes by returning to the language of the Day of YHWH. As noted in 'A Closer Look: The Day of YHWH', it is often seen as having a cosmic dimension to it. In Isaiah 13:10 the sun, moon, and stars are affected, as they are here in Joel 2:10, along with the earth quaking and the heavens trembling, as in Isaiah 13:13.[73] The climax in 2:11 sees the locust plague as a divine army, too great to be numbered, led by YHWH himself against his people. Such is the appalling scale of the catastrophe. Zephaniah 1:14 had referred to the 'great day of YHWH' and Joel 2:11 confirms 'Truly the day of YHWH is great.' The influence of Malachi is evident here too: Malachi 4:5

---

[71] R. Simkins, 'God, History and the Natural World in the Book of Joel', *CBQ* 55 (1993): 423–52 (440 n. 22), citing J. D. Whiting, 'Jerusalem's Locust Plague', *National Geographic* 28 (1915): 525–6, 533.

[72] See Section III, 'Introduction to Joel'.

[73] The verb applied to the heavens in Isa. 13:13 is applied to the earth in Joel 2:10, and that applied to the earth in Isa. 13:13 is applied to the heavens in Joel 2:10. With other differences this suggests oral transmission rather than direct literary copying. See further J. L. Crenshaw *Joel* (1995): 126.

[3:23] refers to the 'great and terrible day of YHWH', and Malachi 3:2 asks 'Who can endure the day of his coming?'[74] The words 'vast' and 'numberless' (2:11) are the same words translated by NRSV as 'great and powerful' in 2:2, in both cases referring to YHWH's army. This reinforces that 2:1–2 and 2:11 form an *inclusio* around the verses in between, making this a clearly delineated section of the text.

Crenshaw draws attention to a number of expressions shared between 2:1–11 and chapter 1:[75]

> 'all inhabitants of the land' (1:2; 2:1);
> 'generation' (1:3; 2:2; NRSV's 'in ages to come' in 2:2 is literally 'ages of generation and generation');
> a 'powerful' nation/army (1:6; 2:2, 5, 11; NRSV translates as 'numberless' in 2:11);
> 'the day of YHWH is near'(1:15)/'the day of YHWH is coming, it is near' (1:15; 2:1);
> 'fire has devoured/devours' (1:19, 20; 2:3, 5; the tense in Hebrew is the same in both chapters).

The shared vocabulary and phraseology reinforces that the two chapters are to be taken together as a forceful description of the utterly devastating impact of the locust plague. The locusts appear as a vast, numberless invading army, and the devastation of the land is as total as if fire had swept across it. Joel 2:1–11 complements and completes the preceding description of disaster. The first chapter had called for wailing and lament (1:5, 8, 11, 13) and a crying out to YHWH (1:14, 19) in the face of the disaster. The conclusion of the description of disaster in 2:1–11 is now followed by a call to turn to YHWH, in the hope that he may yet bring restoration and blessing.

Joel 2:12–14 – A Summons to Turn to YHWH

> [12] Yet even now, says the LORD,
>> return to me with all your heart,
> with fasting, with weeping, and with mourning;
> [13] rend your hearts and not your clothing.
> Return to the LORD your God,
>> for he is gracious and merciful,

---

[74] The texts of Malachi and Joel may be dated to a similar period, so it is possible, of course, that both are drawing on the same shared material rather than one influencing the other.

[75] J. L. Crenshaw *Joel* (1995): 130.

C Commentary on Joel

> slow to anger, and abounding in steadfast love,
>   and relenting from punishing.
> ¹⁴ Who knows whether he will not turn and relent
>   and leave a blessing behind him,
> a grain offering and a drink offering
>   for the LORD your God?

Following the description of devastating disaster in 2:1–11 the people are urged to return to YHWH in the hope that he may relent and bring the disaster to an end. While 1:14 called for a fast and for a gathering of the elders and inhabitants of the land at the house of YHWH to cry out to him for help, and 1:19 included a brief 'To you, O Lord, I cry', 2:12–17 constitutes a fuller urging to call on YHWH for deliverance. Its immediate antecedent is the description of disaster in 2:1–11. However, it is also the conclusion and climax to the whole series of laments and summonses of chapters 1–2.

A crucial interpretative issue is the significance of the word 'return' (*šûb*) in 2:12 and 2:13. NRSV gives its usual meaning of 'return'. However it has been argued by some that, because no sins of the people have been referred to or mentioned in the Joel-text, it should here be taken to mean simply 'turn'. In other words, its frequent meaning of repenting of sin is not appropriate here: rather it should be taken to mean turning to YHWH in a time of need. Simkins, Crenshaw, and Barton all take this view. Crenshaw writes: 'Hoping to fill the void left by Joel's silence, modern critics have been less hesitant than he. The charges against his contemporaries range from syncretistic worship to hubris, from emphasis on external ritual to abdication of leadership, from breach of covenant to not being willing to become identified with an impotent deity.'[76] Simkins writes, strongly, that 'Joel himself found no need to specify these sins; nowhere does he accuse the people of infidelity to Yahweh or of breaking covenantal stipulations. This silence about the

---

[76]   J. L. Crenshaw, 'Who Knows What YHWH Will Do? The Character of God in the Book of Joel', in A. B. Beck, A. H. Bartelt, P. R. Raabe, and C. A. Franke (eds.), *Fortunate the Eyes That See* (Grand Rapids, MI: Eerdmans, 1995): 185–96 (189). Crenshaw follows and acknowledges R. Simkins *Yahweh's Activity* (1991): 181–90, and in turn is himself followed and cited by J. Barton *Joel and Obadiah* (2001): 79–80. Each of the possible accusations that scholars put forward, as described by Crenshaw, is indeed readily identifiable in the scholarly literature. So for example: G. Ahlström *Joel and the Temple Cult* (1971): 25–7 argues that the unspoken sins of the people were of worshipping other gods; H. W. Wolff *Joel and Amos* (1975): 49 considers that Joel stands within the prophetic tradition that criticised 'empty ritualism'; P. L. Redditt 'Joel and Peripheral Prophecy' (1986): 235–6 argues that the problem is abdication of leadership by the priests and elders; L. C. Allen *Joel, Obadiah, Jonah and Micah* (1976): 78–9 writes that the 'call to *return* presupposes the covenant relationship' (italics original) and that the people had strayed from it.

people's sins should be taken seriously in interpreting the book.'[77] The argument from the literary context is strong. Linguistically, however, it would constitute a rare usage of the verb *šûb*, and the support provided by verses often adduced to support such an interpretation is not, in reality, all that solid. Barton cites Deuteronomy 30:2 and 2 Kings 23:25 as illustrative of the fact that '*return* often refers not to repentance but to a willingness to hear the word of YHWH'.[78] However, Deuteronomy 30:1–2 speaks of the 'blessings and curses set before you', referring back to the long list of blessings and curses in Deuteronomy 28 and the abandonment of the covenant referred to in 29:25–28: the 'return' of 30:2 thus refers to returning to YHWH after a time of disobedience. Similarly the turning of Josiah to YHWH in 2 Kings 23:24–25 takes place after a long period in which the people of Israel were deemed to have been unfaithful, in not having kept the words of the recently discovered Book of the Law: the aspect of repentance is not, therefore, absent. Better support comes from Isaiah 44:22, which invites the people to 'return to me, for I have redeemed you' (and not 'in order that I may redeem you'). Even this, however, is in the literary context of Isaiah 40–55, which has declared that Jerusalem 'has served her term, that her penalty is paid'. In other words, the invitation to return/turn reflects an acknowledgement of the wrongdoing that had led to the exile from which deliverance is now being announced. We may sum up the situation by agreeing that Joel 2:12–13 does not specify any particular sins that the current generation of people are deemed to have committed which caused YHWH to send a locust plague; but it should also be recognised that history and received tradition led to a belief that neglect of YHWH and his covenant had been frequent in the people's past, and therefore that turning to him in need was inevitably bound up with returning in repentance. Finally in this discussion, we may note that for contemporary readers, the fact that the locust plague is *not* seen by the Joel-text as having been sent by YHWH as punishment for particular sins committed is of great theological importance. As Sweeney writes, 'This in fact reflects the reality of a great deal of suffering in the world for which no cause is ever known or identified.'[79] It is entirely in order for a reader-oriented interpretation of the Joel-text to see it as addressing how the people of God are to behave in a time of suffering for which no apparent cause is evident.

[77] R. Simkins 'God, History and the Natural World' (1993): 446.
[78] J. Barton *Joel and Obadiah* (2001): 77 (italics original).
[79] M. A. Sweeney *The Twelve* Prophets 1 (2000): 165. Similarly T. S. Hadjiev *Joel and Amos* (2020): 13 sees the lack of reason for the disaster as showing 'the mystery of God and the inexplicability of the world'.

C Commentary on Joel

The section begins with divine speech, indicated by 'says YHWH' (2:12). It is a divine invitation to return/turn to him 'with all your heart', a phrase taken from and characteristic of the book of Deuteronomy (cf. 4:29; 6:5; 10:12; 30:2, 10). This should be accompanied by fasting, weeping, and mourning. The words connect to and develop the summons of Joel 1:13–14. The divine speech continues into the first line of 2:13: 'rend your hearts and not your clothing'. As Barton notes, it is widely agreed that the sense is 'tear your hearts as well as your clothes', and 'do not simply engage in external ritual but also lament inwardly'.[80]

The second line of 2:13 reverts to prophetic speech, with YHWH referred to in the third person. Assis takes the change from divine speech to prophetic speech to be a rhetorical device,[81] and indeed it is in no way problematic. The 'your God' appended to 'YHWH' reminds and confirms to the people that they remain his. There follows a version of an ancient credal statement, that YHWH is 'gracious and merciful, slow to anger, and abounding in steadfast love, and relents from punishing'. Its oldest expression is generally held to be Exodus 34:6–7, but it appears in variant forms in Numbers 14:18; Nehemiah 9:17; Psalms 86:15; 103:8; 145:8; Joel 2:13; Jonah 4:2; Nahum 1:3. The closest form to Joel 2:13 is Jonah 4:2. Both texts reverse the order of the first two adjectives ('gracious and merciful' compared to Exod. 34:6's 'merciful and gracious') and omit the quality of 'faithfulness'. More significantly, they omit the whole second half (Exod. 34:7), so that they contain no words about 'forgiving iniquity and transgression and sin', nor about 'visiting the iniquity of the parents upon the children and the children's children, to the third and fourth generation'. Found only in Joel 2:13 and Jonah 4:2 is the closing 'and relenting from punishing'. Other parallels suggest a deliberate linking of the texts of Joel and Jonah. Both Joel 2:14 and Jonah 3:9 add to the formula the words: 'Who knows, he may turn and relent' (NRSV translates the identical first four Hebrew words slightly differently in the two texts, masking their closeness). Both texts include reference to sackcloth and fasting. Kelly has examined the relationship between the two texts, and comments that it 'strains the imagination to posit that such correspondences occur as mere happenstance'.[82] It seems that these two texts were formed in the same *milieu*.[83] Inclusion of

---

[80]   J. Barton *Joel and Obadiah* (2001): 80.

[81]   E. Assis *Book of Joel* (2013): 139.

[82]   J. R. Kelly, 'Joel, Jonah and the YHWH Creed: Determining the Trajectory of the Literary Influence', *JBL* 132.4 (2013): 805–26 (806).

[83]   See further 'A Closer Look: The Destiny of the Nations'.

228   *Book of Joel*

this ancient credal statement underlines that there is point to returning/
turning to YHWH, in that there is the possibility that he may turn and
relent. The verb 'turn' applied to YHWH (2:14) is the same verb used of
the people's turning, and is often used of YHWH's readiness to repent of
proposed actions. So too is the verb used in parallel with it, translated by
NRSV as 'relent' (Hebrew *nḥr*), as found in, for example, the visions of
Amos (7:3, 6). As Nogalski notes, the God of the Hebrew Bible 'is not some
immutable, implacable force devoid of feeling for the people with whom
he has tangled for so long'.[84] He is not unbending, but is willing to respond
and change his mind in response to prayer or repentance. His response,
however, cannot be guaranteed. Thus the 'Who knows whether he will not
turn and relent' – equivalent to the 'perhaps' of Amos 5:15 and Zephaniah
2:3 – is appropriate.[85]

Should YHWH turn and relent, it may be that he will leave behind him a
blessing, a grain offering, and a drink offering (2:14). The word 'behind him'
(one word in Hebrew) is the same as the 'behind it' of 2:3: as the locust plague
leaves behind it a desolate wilderness, so YHWH would, if he responds,
leave a blessing behind him. That blessing would be the restoration of the
offerings referred to in 1:9 and 1:13, the grain offering and the drink offering,
and their restoration would signify the land would itself be restored (see the
commentary on these verses). Verse 14 concludes with YHWH described as
'your God', as in the preceding verse.

Joel 2:15–17 – Let Everyone Assemble and Let the Priests Weep

> [15] Blow the trumpet in Zion;
>   sanctify a fast;
>   call a solemn assembly;
> [16] gather the people.
>   Consecrate the congregation;
>   assemble the aged;
>   gather the children,
>   even infants at the breast.
>   Let the bridegroom leave his room,
>   and the bride her canopy.

---

[84] J. D. Nogalski *Hosea–Jonah* (2011): 241.
[85] See T. Fretheim, 'The Repentance of God: A Key to Evaluating Old Testament God-Talk',
      Horizons of Biblical Theology 10 (1988): 47–70.

C Commentary on Joel

> [17] Between the vestibule and the altar,
>> let the priests, the ministers of the LORD, weep.
>> Let them say, 'Spare your people, O LORD,
>> and do not make your heritage a mockery,
>> a byword among the nations.
>> Why should it be said among the peoples,
>> "Where is their God?"'

Joel 2:15–17 follows naturally on from 2:12–14, despite the Masoretic text containing a marker indicating the close of a section at the end of 2:14. In this final section of preparing to appeal to YHWH for aid in the disaster of the locust plague there is linkage to earlier parts of the book through repetition and allusion, as well as some fresh elements. The imperatives of 2:15–16 continue those of 1:5, 8, 11, 13, 14; 2:1, 12, 13.

The initial call to 'Blow the trumpet in Zion' is a direct repetition from 2:1. There the *šôpār* was to be sounded by a supposed sentinel warning of the approach of an army. Here in 2:15 it is to be blown to summon people to a cultic gathering, as in Psalms 47:5 [6]; 81:3 [4]; 98:6. The following commands repeat those of 1:14 to 'sanctify a fast, call a solemn assembly': see the comments thereon and the accompanying 'A Closer Look: Fasting'. Now, however, there is an additional instruction, namely to sanctify the congregation. The term 'congregation' (2:16) is used in the Second Temple period to refer to the people gathered for worship (2 Chron. 30: 2, 4, 13, 17, 23, 24; Ps. 107:32). The scope of the invitation and summons is widened from 1:14, which called on 'the elders and all the inhabitants of the land'; here the call is to 'the people', to include the aged, the children, even infants at the breast, and bridegrooms and brides. Such is the severity of the disaster that nobody is to be exempted from joining in the fast and the solemn assembly. The word translated as 'aged' is the same as that translated 'elders' in 1:2, 14, but NRSV captures well that here in 2:16 it is those of advanced years who are meant rather than those who held office as an elder. The 'room' which the bridegroom is to leave (2:16) is the dark, inner chamber in which a couple could be alone (Judg. 15:1; 2 Sam. 13:10; 2 Kings 9:2; Song 1:4). The word for the 'canopy' that the bride is to leave is found only here and in Psalm 19:5 [6]. The significance of even bridegroom and bride being summoned is that provision existed for newly-weds to be exempted from military service (Deut. 24:5): however the time was so dire that there could be no exemption from joining the fast and solemn assembly.

Joel 2:17 specifies more precisely where the congregation is to assemble: it is within sight and earshot, it may be assumed, of the space between the vestibule and the altar from where the priests will lead the proceedings. The 'vestibule' is referred to in 1 Kings 6:3, where it is said to measure twenty cubits by ten cubits, and in Ezekiel 8:16, where it is referred to as a room (NRSV translates as 'porch') with a space between it and the altar in which stood about twenty-five men. It is probably to be identified with the place in 1 Kings 8:64 where sacrifices were offered at large, public gatherings. There the priests would be heard by all as they led the people in lamentation. The phrase 'the priests, the ministers of YHWH' picks up the language of 1:9.

The words to be used in the lamentation are given by the prophet. That this is a literary device rather than an actual liturgy is evident from its brevity. The prayer is of a kind found elsewhere in which appeal is made to YHWH to act not just out of compassion for his people, but for the honour of his own reputation: 'do not make your heritage a mockery, a byword among the nations. Why should it be said among the peoples, "Where is their God?"' The language is reminiscent of Psalm 44:9–16 [10–17], but it is passages such as Deuteronomy 9:26–29 and Exodus 32:12 in which appeals to YHWH to act in order to protect his own honour are found. There are also several verses in Ezekiel in which YHWH states that he acts purely and only for the sake of his name (e.g. Ezek. 20:9, 14, 22; 36:21–23; 39:7). It is, therefore, Joel 2:17 suggests, in the interests not only of the people, but of YHWH himself, to hear their lamentation and deliver them from the disaster facing them.

With their repetition of, and allusion to, units in both chapter 1 and chapter 2, these concluding verses draw together the laments and cries expressed in the book thus far. The devastating effect of the locust plague was described in summary form in 1:4. The remainder of 1:5–2:17, with its mixture of descriptive lamentation and imperative calls addressed to various groups, culminating in a call to the whole people, has led up to a climax in 2:15–17. The descriptions have employed stock language of lament, to such a degree that at times the language seems more appropriate to invasion by an army than to locusts; but as a literary work it is to be read, I have argued, as imagery being applied to the plague of locusts. It was also noted, in commenting on 2:14, that to appeal to YHWH carried with it the belief that YHWH's will was not immutable, but that he can and might relent, and deliver the people from this disaster. The verses that follow prove this indeed to be the case.

Joel 2:18–27 – YHWH's Promise of Restoration

¹⁸ Then the LORD became jealous for his land
  and had pity on his people.

C Commentary on Joel

231

¹⁹ In response to his people the LORD said:
  'I am sending you
      grain, wine, and oil,
      and you will be satisfied;
  and I will no more make you
      a mockery among the nations.

²⁰ I will remove the northern army far from you,
      and drive it into a parched and desolate land,
  its front into the eastern sea,
      and its rear into the western sea;
  its stench and foul smell will rise up.'
      Surely he has done great things!

²¹ Do not fear, O soil;
      be glad and rejoice,
      for the LORD has done great things!
²² Do not fear, you animals of the field,
      for the pastures of the wilderness are green;
  the tree bears its fruit;
      the fig tree and vine give their full yield.

²³ O children of Zion, be glad,
      and rejoice in the LORD your God,
  for he has given the early rain for your vindication;
      he has poured down for you abundant rain,
      the early and the later rain, as before.
²⁴ The threshing floors shall be full of grain,
      the vats shall overflow with wine and oil.
²⁵ I will repay you for the years
      that the swarming locust has eaten,
  the hopper, the destroyer, and the cutter,
      my great army, which I sent against you.

²⁶ You shall eat in plenty and be satisfied
      and praise the name of the LORD your God,
      who has dealt wondrously with you.
  And my people shall never again be put to shame.
²⁷ You shall know that I am in the midst of Israel,
      and that I, the LORD, am your God and there is no other.
  And my people shall never again be put to shame.

The opening verses 2:18–19 mark a turning point: after the numerous expressions of lament in 1:2–2:17, the tentative hope of 2:14 that perhaps YHWH might turn and relent proves to be justified. Some who take the whole text

232   *Book of Joel*

to be substantially a literary unity see 2:18 as the beginning of a major new structural section which continues on through the rest of the book.[86] It is preferable, however, to take 2:18–27 as the conclusion to the preceding lament. Several psalms of lament conclude with YHWH hearing the petitioner's or people's cry and answering, and it is likely that such a response was a normal part of cultic and liturgical practice. Thus, for example, in Psalm 12 the lament and plea of verses 1–4 [2–5] are followed in verse 5 [6] by an oracle of YHWH in response. The promises of restoration in Joel 2:18–27 remain firmly within the historical realm, unlike the more eschatological realm which characterises the text hereafter. This reflects the composition history of the text. In its earliest form it would have concluded at 2:27, before later material was added to it.[87]

Joel 2:18–19a are narrative verses which set the scene for words of divine response. NRSV translates the verbs in 2:18–19a in the past tense: just as the locust plague and its disasters had occurred in the past, so too has YHWH's positive response. The narrative assumes, it appears, that the actions commanded in 2:15–17 were carried out. An alternative interpretation would be that 2:18–27 are promissory: if the actions of 2:15–17 are followed, then this is how YHWH will respond.[88] It seems best to read the verbs (with NRSV) in the past tense, and to allow that the reader will assume that there has been a positive response to the call of 2:15–17. The restoration promised is one of agricultural blessing rather than defeat of enemies, confirming that the whole of 1:2–2:11 concerns agricultural rather than military disaster. The blessings promised constitute a reversal of the disaster previously lamented. The majority of reversals link to verses from chapter 1, but the concluding 2:27 links to the conclusion of the plea of the priests and ministers of YHWH in 2:17.

The narrative says that YHWH 'became jealous' for the land. The word is used of the close, exclusive relationship that YHWH has with his people, and also indicates zealous activity on their behalf. In Ezekiel 39:25 it is said

---

[86]   G. Ahlström *Joel and the Temple Cult* (1971): 132; H. W. Wolff *Joel and Amos* (1977): 57.
[87]   See Section III, 'Introduction to Joel'.
[88]   The verbs are in the waw consecutive imperfect form. While this generally has a future meaning, there is also a frequent prophetic perfect usage. J. D. Nogalski *Hosea–Jonah* (2011): 235, 237 expresses a strong preference for taking them as future, but both J. Barton *Joel and Obadiah* (2001): 87 and J. L. Crenshaw *Joel* (1995): 147 are ambivalent on the matter. As Barton comments, 'For the later generations that preserved and transmitted the words of Joel, it did not matter whether the restoration/salvation from impending disaster was recorded as having happened in reality or as being an inevitable consequence of the laments.'

C Commentary on Joel

233

that YHWH will restore the fortunes of Israel and will be jealous of his holy name, and in the light of the mockery of the nations in Joel 2:17 we should take 2:18 to have a similar sense. YHWH also had 'pity' on his people: the word is used in Ezekiel 5:11; 7:4, 9; 8:18; 9:5, 10, where it is part of YHWH's actions against Israel that he will not show pity. In Lamentations 2:2, 17, 21; 3:43 it is lamented that he did not show pity. Here in Joel 2:18 it is used positively: in response to the people's lament after the disaster of the locust plague, YHWH now has pity on them.

That pity is expressed in the promises that YHWH makes in 2:19–20. The first constitutes the most direct reversal of the effects of the locust plague and reverses the losses described in 1:10: he will send the blessings of grain, wine, and oil. The loss of other foods mentioned in 1:11–12 (wheat, barley, figs, pomegranates, dates, and apples) is not specifically reversed in the promise of 2:19, but does not need to be: the restoration of grain, wine, and oil stands for the restoration of fertility generally. These three were basic, staple elements of food and drink, and are frequently found together as signs of YHWH's blessing (e.g. Deut. 7:13; 11:14; 28:51; Hos. 2:8 [10]; in Ps. 104:15 with 'bread' rather than 'grain'). Significant is the added clause 'and you will be satisfied'. In Haggai 1:6 the people are reminded that they ate and drank, but never felt as though they had their fill, and had clothes but were never warm. Joel 2:19, in contrast, specifies that the people will have grain, wine, and oil and will be satisfied. The promise of such blessing will be enlarged in the promises of 2:24 that the threshing floors will be full of grain and the vats overflow with wine and oil, and of 2:26 that 'you shall eat in plenty and be satisfied'. The reversal promised does not include mention of a restoration of the grain offering and drink offering which 1:9 and 1:13 lamented had been cut off and withheld. It would be reading too much into this absence, however, to argue that cultic restoration was not envisaged. Joel 2:19 concludes with an answer to the prayer of the priests and ministers of YHWH in 2:17 by promising that no more will they be made a mockery among the nations.

YHWH's response continues in 2:20 with the promise that he will remove 'the northern army' from the people. The Hebrew is literally 'the northerner': NRSV's translation as 'northern army' gives a more specific interpretation than is warranted. Those who hold that 2:1–11 refer to military invasion rather than to locusts find support for their view in this verse, translating as does NRSV, and pointing out that a locust plague is likely to come from the deserts of the east or south-east rather than from the north. However this is to insist on an over-literal, prosaic approach, and fails to acknowledge the vague and sometimes mythological overtones of the word. Jeremiah 1:13–15; 4:6; 6:1, 22 refer to a mysterious, unidentified 'foe from the north' who will bring disaster. Ezekiel 38:6, 15; 39:2 refer to Gog and Magog and their allies coming from the north. Isaiah 14:13 refers to the mount of assembly in the far north, a notion which appears to have been transferred to Mount Zion in Psalm 48:2 [3]. In an influential article Childs investigated the mythological nature of the foe from the north, writing that the 'book of Joel describes a locust plague … the locust plague, which enters ordinarily from the south, has been described in the language of the enemy-of-the-north tradition'.[89] We may therefore deem that Joel 2:20 is employing mythological imagery to describe the plague of locusts. The text declares that the front of the army of locusts will be driven into the eastern sea (the Dead Sea), and its rear into the western sea (the Mediterranean Sea). Assis suggests that the 'parched and desolate land' into which it is to be driven is in the arid south, thus making all four points of the compass present in this verse, highlighting YHWH's sovereignty over the whole earth.[90] While attractive, this reads more into the text than is justified. The word translated by NRSV as 'foul smell' occurs only here: the parallelism with the preceding 'stench' makes the translation logical. The last line of 2:20 – 'Surely he has done great things' – is surprising. It is the same phrase used in 2:21, and it is possible that it has found its way into 2:20 as the result of dittography. If it is original to 2:20, then its meaning must be that the locust plague has done great, appalling, and terrible things.

There follow in 2:21–24 three imperatives, addressed in ascending order to the soil (2:21), the animals of the field (2:22), and the children of Zion (2:23). Just as much of the vocabulary and phraseology of Joel 1 reflected the influence of cultic psalms of lament, so these verses reflect the influence of psalms of thanksgiving. In 1:10 the ground was described as mourning: here it is called upon not to fear, but to be glad and rejoice (2:21). The biblical injunction to 'Fear not' is widespread, most often addressed to kings (e.g. Isa. 7:4) or to the people (e.g. Isa. 35:4; 41:10, 13; 43:1). Just as it is perfectly appropriate in 1:10 that the ground mourned, so now it is perfectly appropriate that it is urged not to be fearful, but to rejoice. The animals, too, are not to fear (2:22): they will also benefit from the restored fertility

---

[89] B. S. Childs, 'The Enemy from the North and the Chaos Tradition', *JBL* 78 (1959): 187–98 (197).

[90] E. Assis *Book of Joel* (2013): 178–9.

C Commentary on Joel

of the land. In 1:7 the vines were laid waste and the fig trees destroyed: here in 2:22 both fig tree and vine bear their fruit once more. Then in 2:23 the 'children of Zion' are called to 'be glad and rejoice in YHWH your God'. The only other places where the phrase 'children of Zion' is found are Psalm 149:2, with which Joel 2:23 has similarities, and Lamentations 4:2. The reason for Zion's rejoicing is the abundance of rains, in contrast to the drying up and withering of the ground in 1:10–12 and the fire of 1:19–20 and 2:3. The word 'early rain' (*môreh*) is unusual: the usual word is *yôreh*. However, the form *môreh* is found also in Psalm 84:6 [7]. The early rain is given 'for your vindication'. The word 'vindication' is *ṣᵊdāqā*, most often translated as 'righteousness', and this seems preferable here in the light of the following line stating that YHWH has 'poured down for you abundant rain'. Koch has argued that 'righteousness' can be viewed as a fluid poured out on the people in blessing (see further 'A Closer Look: Justice and Righteousness').[91] This sits well alongside the pouring out of rain which, as Allen notes, is itself a sign of covenant blessing.[92] The children of Zion can rejoice because YHWH pours out the rains and the blessing of his righteousness. This verse reverses the drying up of the watercourses in 1:20. The consequence is that, in contrast to the failure of grain of 1:17, the threshing floors are now full of grain, and the vats overflow with wine and oil (2:24). The sense of lavish, overflowing fertility through the blessing of rain is akin to the joy and delight expressed in Psalm 65:9–12.

In the second verse in Joel specifically to refer to the locusts, 2:25 promises that YHWH will repay for the years of destruction wrought by them. The same four terms are used to describe them as in 1:4. Does the plural 'years' mean that there were successive locust plagues over two or more seasons? While not impossible, it is more likely envisaged that the devastation had been so severe that the land took more than one season to recover. It is possible to re-point 'years' (*šānîm*) to 'double' (*šᵊnîm*), making it 'I will repay you double', but it is unnecessary to do so.

The promise of overflowing blessing continues in 2:26. After the time of hunger, the people will now have plenty. This will lead them to praise the name of YHWH. Prinsloo comments that 'Disaster turns to blessing. Yahweh, who wrought the disaster, also wrought this change. But the change is not an end in itself. It must lead to praising Yahweh and confessing him as the one and only God, active in the midst

---

[91]   K. Koch, *The Prophets, vol. 1* (trans. M Kohl; London: SCM, 1982): 58.
[92]   L. C. Allen *Joel, Obadiah, Jonah and Micah* (1976): 93.

of his people.'[93] The people will acknowledge that YHWH is in the midst of Israel, and that there is no other god (2:27). The confession arises not merely because they have full stomachs: rather it is in the light of seeing that their turning to him with fasting, weeping, and mourning (2:12–14), and the holding of the solemn assembly with priestly prayer (2:15–17), has moved YHWH to hear their prayer and answer it. There may be in 2:26–27 an echo of Zephaniah 3:15–17, in which it is twice said that YHWH is 'in your midst'; and Zephaniah 3:11 asserts that 'you shall not be put to shame', comparable to the twice occurring 'you shall never be put to shame' of Joel 2:26–27. The wording is not sufficiently close, however, for literary dependence to be indicated. Conversely, the knowledge by the people that 'I am YHWH, your God and there is no other' does seem to indicate direct knowledge of the exilic Isaiah 45:5, 6, 18. Whereas in Isaiah 45 those in exile in Babylon had yet to see any sign of promises of deliverance being fulfilled, in Joel 2 the knowledge of answered prayer in respect of the locust plague could strengthen the people's belief in YHWH as the one and only god. The repeated promise that 'my people shall never again be put to shame' (2:26–27) reverses the lament of 2:17 that the people, YHWH's heritage, will be a mockery and a byword among the nations. Its double occurrence leads Wolff to take the first occurrence as 'intrusive, erroneously premature'.[94] The double occurrence is, however, not inappropriate as the conclusion to 2:18–27, to the whole first composition of the text, and to the whole first half of the text in its current, final form.

The first composition concluded here. It described and lamented the disaster of the locust plague, drawing in language of lament relating to drought and to invading armies in its vivid descriptions (1:2–2:11). It called for a turning to YHWH and an earnest calling out to him (2:12–17). It has shown that in response YHWH heard, and answered the people's cry by promising to remove the army of locusts (2:20) and restore fertility to the land (2:21–25). The telling of the story serves to strengthen faith that in times of disaster and need, of whatever kind, if the people will turn to YHWH then he will hear and respond. Later hands have then added, from 2:28 onwards, further expressions of the ways in which YHWH will bless his people.

---

[93] W S. Prinsloo, *The Theology of the Book of Joel* (BZAW, 163; Berlin/New York: W. de Gruyter, 1985): 79.

[94] H. W. Wolff *Joel and Amos* (1977): 56.

C Commentary on Joel

2 YHWH's Spirit Poured Out on All Who Call Upon His Name – Joel 2:28–32 [3:1–5]

Joel 2:28–29 [3:1–2] – YHWH's Spirit Poured Out

[28] Then afterward
 I will pour out my spirit on all flesh;
 your sons and your daughters shall prophesy,
  your old men shall dream dreams,
  and your young men shall see visions.
[29] Even on the male and female slaves,
  in those days, I will pour out my spirit.

The section 2:28–32 [3] comprises a significant final redactional addition to the earlier forms of the text. As noted in the 'Introduction to Joel', the first composition was 1:1–2:27. This became the Eschatological Redactional Composition by the addition of 3:1–3, 9–17. While the first composition took an historical perspective in looking back at the disaster of the locust plague, and YHWH's response to the people crying out to him was an historical promise of restored fertility, in 3:1–3, 9–17 the promise and hope expressed for Jerusalem are for the distant future, and the language becomes eschatological rather than historical. The addition 2:28–32 [3] is inserted where it is so that it continues words of promise from the preceding 2:18–27, and it provides a lens through which readers are now invited to read chapter 3 [4].

The section has two sub-units: 2:28–29 and 2:30–32. However, they belong together, with the 'everyone who' of 2:32 reflecting the universality of 'all flesh' in 2:28. The opening 'Then afterwards' of 2:28 is literally 'And it will be after this.' In his study of such transitional formulae De Vries finds this to be one which represents a 'move from a proximate future to a remote future'.[95] Similarly, Hadjiev notes that with this phrase 'we jump forward to an unspecified point in time'.[96] Crenshaw comments that the formula serves to link the passage to the preceding promise of divine compassion in 2:18–27, and that it also serves to 'push the event into the remote – and mythic – future'.[97] Thus the move from an historical outlook to an eschatological outlook is signalled at the outset.

---

[95] S. J. de Vries, *From Old Revelation to New: A Traditio-Historical and Redaction-Critical Study of Temporal Transitions in Prophetic Predication* (Grand Rapids, MI: Eerdmans, 1995): 88.
[96] T. S. Hadjiev *Joel and Amos* (2020): 45.
[97] J. L. Crenshaw *Joel* (1995): 164.

238   *Book of Joel*

There follows a striking promise, indeed one unique in the Hebrew Bible, that YHWH will pour out his spirit (*rûaḥ*) on 'all flesh'. The effect of this outpouring of *rûaḥ* is that all people will be able to receive communications from YHWH through prophecy and the related phenomena of dreams and visions. The link between *rûaḥ* and prophecy is an ancient one. The narrative of 1 Samuel 10:1–13 describes the spirit of YHWH possessing Saul, with the result that he joins a band of prophets and falls into a prophetic frenzy; and 1 Samuel 19:19–24 describes a similar episode affecting both Saul and messengers sent by him. While the eighth- and seventh-century prophets do not generally attribute their ability to prophesy to YHWH's *rûaḥ*, Micah 3:8 declares that, in contrast to other prophets, visionaries, and diviners whose apparently trite words of blessing he deprecates, 'I am filled with power, with the spirit of YHWH, and with justice and might, to declare to Jacob his transgression and to Israel his sin.' An episode pertinent to Joel 2:28–29 is found in Numbers 11:24–30: after some of the spirit that rested on Moses is taken and given to seventy appointed elders, who prophesy in consequence, some unauthorised men, Eldad and Medad, also receive the spirit and prophesy in the camp. Joshua asks Moses to stop them, but Moses replies: 'Are you jealous for my sake? Would that all YHWH's people were prophets, and that YHWH would put his spirit on them' (Num. 11:29). It is reasonable to think that there must be an echo of this episode in Joel 2:28–29. However, the way had also been prepared in passages such as Jeremiah 31:31–34 and Ezekiel 36:26–27. More closely still, in Ezekiel 39:29 YHWH promises that when he restores the people's fortunes and gathers them back from their exile among the nations then 'I will pour out my spirit upon the house of Israel'. Joel 2:28–29, however, goes beyond any of these texts in its comprehensiveness, underlining that *all* members of the nation are to be included in this outpouring of the spirit: male and female, young and old, master and servant. None will be left out. Just as in 2:16 all from the aged to the children were to take part in the solemn assembly seeking YHWH's mercy, so now all are included in the promise. As Redditt writes: 'Charisma would replace office; prophecy would no longer be limited to the elite, but would be poured out on all classes.'[98] The promise is, however, to all within the Judean nation, and not to all across the world. It must be acknowledged that the phrase 'all flesh' more often refers to all humanity (Gen. 6:12; Isa. 40:5, 6; 49:26), or even to all living creatures (Gen. 7:16). Here, however,

---

[98]   P. L. Redditt 'Joel and Peripheral Prophecy' (1986): 232–3.

C Commentary on Joel

the repeated 'your' – your sons, your daughters, your old men, your young men – underlines that it is the people of Judah who are meant.

Prophecy, dreams, and visions are the result of this outpouring of *rûaḥ*. We should avoid seeking to restrict the practice of prophecy to sons and daughters, the receiving of dreams to old men, and the granting of visions to young men. Rather all categories of people will receive revelation from YHWH in all these ways. Prophecy and visions were frequently closely associated: see 'A Closer Look: Seers and Prophets'. Jeremiah 23:25–32 expresses caution about dreams as a medium of divine revelation, associating them with false prophecy. However, in several narrative and legal texts (Gen. 28:10–17; Num. 12:6; Deut. 13:1–5; 1 Sam. 28:6, 15; 1 Kgs 3:5) they are accepted as valid revelation without comment. In Joel 2:28–29 prophecy, dreams, and visions are all viewed positively as YHWH's gifts bestowed with the outpouring of his spirit. The concluding 'in those days, I will pour out my spirit' makes an *inclusio* with the opening 'Then afterwards I will pour out my spirit', once again making clear that the fulfilment of the promise will be at some future, indeterminate eschatological time.

Joel 2:30–32 [3:3–5] – Everyone Who Calls Upon the Name of YHWH Shall Be Saved

> [30] I will show portents in the heavens and on the earth, blood and fire and columns of smoke. [31] The sun shall be turned to darkness and the moon to blood, before the great and terrible day of the LORD comes. [32] Then everyone who calls on the name of the LORD shall be saved, for in Mount Zion and in Jerusalem there shall be those who escape, as the LORD has said, and among the survivors shall be those whom the LORD calls.

NRSV prints 2:30–32 as prose. However, poetic metre is discernible, and there is no reason to separate 2:30–32 [3:3–5] from 2:28–29 [3:1–2] on metrical or any other grounds.[99]

The continuation of what will happen 'afterwards' (2:28) comprises a description of cosmic portents. As noted in 'A Closer Look: The Day of YHWH', such cosmic upheavals are frequently associated with the Day of YHWH. Goldingay comments: 'Whereas the events described in 1:2– 2:17 belonged to *a* day of Yahweh, there is more argument for seeing this moment as *the* day of Yahweh.'[100] The word 'portent' (*môpēt*) signifies 'an

---

[99] So *BHS*; J. L. Crenshaw *Joel* (1995): 163; et al.
[100] J. Goldingay *Hosea–Micah* (2020): 236, italics original.

240   *Book of Joel*

event or object that points beyond itself to remarkable divine intervention'[101] – the divine intervention in this case being the Day of YHWH.
The showing of these portents 'in the heavens and on the earth' highlights
their universality. The language of 'blood and fire and columns of smoke'
draws on battlefield terminology. The description of the darkening of the
sun draws on the language of a solar eclipse; it stands firmly within prophetic tradition (e.g. Isa. 13:10; Ezek. 32:7–8; Amos 8:9). The reddening of
the moon could refer to a lunar eclipse – in literal, scientific terms not possible at the same time as a solar eclipse, but this is not science, it is poetic
language piling up one description of disaster after another. Alternatively,
it could be drawing on the imagery of the preceding verse with the columns
of smoke reflecting the bloodshed of battle. It is unnecessary, however, to
look for precise sources for the imagery employed here, which conveys
the sense of impending disaster perfectly adequately in its own right. Joel
2:30–31 [3:3–4] draws on 2:10, the second half of which is quoted verbatim
in 3:15 [4:15]. In 2:10, in the first composition of the Joel-text, the darkening of sun and moon is part of the Day of YHWH against Israel. Joel 3:15
[4:15], within the Eschatological Redactional Composition, uses this same
imagery in describing the disaster on the nations being judged. In the final
redactional addition, 2:30–31 [3:3–4] draw more loosely on 2:10: both refer
to the earth and the heavens, but with the order reversed; and both refer
to the sun and moon being darkened, but with differing descriptions and
vocabulary. The fact that 3:15 [4:15] does not in any way reflect 2:30–31
[3:3–4] confirms the likelihood that the latter is the later text. The portents
herald the coming of 'the great and terrible day of YHWH' (2:31 [3:4]).
The phrase picks up on 2:11, the relationship of which with Malachi 4:5
[3:23] was noted in the commentary on that verse. Joel 2:31 [3:3] now cites
Malachi 4:5 [3:23]: 'before the great and terrible day of YHWH comes'. The
expression is laden with foreboding.

The final verse of the section (2:32 [3:5]) moves from divine, first-person
speech into third-person commentary, but the change is smooth, and does
not warrant taking this verse to be a separate unit. NRSV's opening 'Then'
is literally 'And it shall be that', implying clear consequence from 2:30–31
[3:3–4]. The verse introduces a limiting with regard to the receiving of the
promised outpouring of the spirit: it will be those who call on the name
of YHWH and those whom YHWH calls. There is no restriction on who
may do so: 'everyone' may call on the name of YHWH, not only priests or

---

[101]   J. Barton *Joel and Obadiah* (2001): 97.

C Commentary on Joel

241

religious functionaries. In that respect the universality of 2:28–29 [3:1–2] is continued. But the writer's expectation is evidently that some will do so and others not, and that it is those who do so for whom there will be an escape. To 'call on the name of YHWH' is to acknowledge YHWH as one's God and express allegiance to him. Thus in the patriarchal narratives Abraham and Isaac call on the name of YHWH where they build an altar to him (Gen. 12:8; 21:33; 26:25). So in Joel 2:32 [3:5] those who escape will be those who express allegiance to YHWH. The expression is also used in 1 Kings 18:24 in Elijah's contest with the prophets of Baal on Mount Carmel, where it means to cry out to one's god to answer prayer and, in that story, to send fire. In Joel 2:32 [3:5] those who escape will undoubtedly cry out to YHWH to answer their prayer for deliverance. The primary sense, however, is that they express their allegiance to him. The verb 'call' makes an *inclusio* in the verse: the opening line has 'those who call on the name of YHWH', while the closing line has 'those whom YHWH calls', these being those on Mount Zion and Jerusalem who escape. Wolff raises the question of who are the survivors whom YHWH calls: Is it possible that the verse intends to include Jews living in the Diaspora as well as those in Jerusalem? Having raised the question, he concludes that this is less likely than the more usual understanding that it is an additional description of those in Jerusalem who escape.[102] The middle line of the verse – 'in Mount Zion and Jerusalem there shall be those who escape' – is a quotation from Obadiah 17. Joel adds 'and Jerusalem', not present in Obadiah 17, but otherwise the wording is identical. Literally the Hebrew says that there will be 'an escape', rather than NRSV's 'those who escape', but NRSV is consistent in translating the same in both verses. This is followed by the words 'as YHWH has said'. This can most straightforwardly be taken to refer to Obadiah 17.[103]

Troxel considers whether 2:32 [3:5] does not, in fact, entail any restriction or division within the people of Jerusalem. It is possible, he suggests, that 'everyone who calls on the name of YHWH' is an additional way of describing all those who live in Mount Zion and Jerusalem, on whom YHWH will pour out his spirit. In that case they are one and the same as the 'all flesh'

---

[102] H. W. Wolff *Joel and Amos* (1977): 68–9.

[103] I consider that Obadiah is an early post-exilic text, and thus earlier than this portion of the Joel-text. Should this not be the case, then it may be that both texts cite an earlier saying, a possibility allowed by J. L. Crenshaw *Joel* (1995): 170. M. Fishbane, *Biblical Interpretation in Ancient Israel* (Oxford: Clarendon Press, 1985): 479 takes it to refer to Isa. 4:2–6, a suggestion to which J. Barton *Joel and Obadiah* (2001): 98 warms, while pointing out, however, that it is not certain that Isa. 4:2–6 is chronologically prior to Joel 2:32 [3:5].

242 *Book of Joel*

of 2:28 [3:1]. Such an interpretation is possible. However, after a linguistic, semantic study of the word *kōl* (all) he concludes that the sense is indeed that this verse 'restricts salvation to those who call upon the name of the Lord'.[104] A thematically similar verse is Zechariah 13:9, where it is made explicit that a third of the people will be left alive: it is this saved third that 'will call on my name'.

In the 'Introduction to Joel', I referred (approvingly) to the argument of Redditt that 2:28–32 [3] is an addition to the text later than 3:1–3, 9–17 [4:1–3, 9–17]. A key argument in favour of this position is that 3:1–21 [4:1–21] promises blessing and salvation to the whole nation, seemingly unaware that anything preceding has indicated otherwise. Redditt argues that the 'pericope 3:1–5 sounds distinctive, even sectarian ... it was composed with 1:1–2:17 and 4:1–3, 19–21 in hand ... 3:5 looks back to 2:14, which it answers, and 3:3 looks ahead to 4:15, which it echoes'.[105] Joel 2:28–32 [3] is a challenge to a settled, theocratic community, Redditt argues. It derives from a group on the periphery of Judean society, not at its centre. This group believed that all could receive the spirit of YHWH and be able to prophesy, not only priests and prophets; but, despairing of what they saw in the nation, they set out their belief that in days to come it would be those who called on the name of YHWH (as they believed that members of their own group did) who would be the ones to receive deliverance.

The Eschatological Redactional Composition which added Joel 3:1–3, 9–17 [4:1–3, 9–17] shifted the perspective of the reader from the historical stance of 1:1–2:27 to the eschatological perspective that would characterise the remainder of the text. Why was such a shift warranted? As discussed in the 'Introduction to Joel', it may have been that the group who introduced this new perspective felt that YHWH's promise in 2:18–27 had not yet materialised, and their strategy for coping with this non-fulfilment was to shift the focus off an immediate, physical promise of blessing and onto a more distant eschatological blessing. The distance of such hopes, however, allowed the leaders of the post-exilic theocratic community to become content to live (with the positions that they held) under Persian rule. The group that added 2:28–32 [3] found this complacent and shallow. This group accepted the eschatological perspective of 3:1–3, 9–17, but added the promise that all members of the community could be filled with the spirit of YHWH,

---

[104] R. L. Troxel, *Joel: Scope, Genre(s), and Meaning* (Critical Studies in the Hebrew Bible, 6; Winona Lake, IN: Eisenbrauns, 2015): 75–8 (78).

[105] P. L. Redditt 'Joel and Peripheral Prophecy' (1986): 231 (references are to the Hebrew text).

C Commentary on Joel

and be able to prophesy and receive dreams and visions. No longer would such inspiration be restricted to priests and prophets. They also challenged the view that all Judahites were to be recipients of future deliverance. Those to be delivered, and to receive YHWH's spirit, would be those who called on the name of YHWH. They thereby summoned others to join them in professing loyalty to YHWH. This provided the lens through which both the preceding and following parts of the Joel-text were now to be read.

Bridging the Horizons: Joel 2:28–32 in the New Testament

In Joel 2:28–29 [3] 'all flesh' receives the gift of YHWH's spirit. It will no longer be restricted to priests, prophets, and leaders, but all will be eligible. As noted in the commentary, however, it is 'all flesh' within Judah that is meant, rather than all humanity. In the New Testament, Peter's speech in Acts 2, with its citation of Joel 2:28–32 [3] in Acts 2:17–21, makes a similar assumption: those gathered in Jerusalem on the day of Pentecost were Jews and proselytes (Acts 2:10), not Gentiles. So when the Holy Spirit is poured out on Gentiles at the conversion of the Roman centurion Cornelius, Peter's circumcised companions 'were astounded that the gift of the Holy Spirit had been poured out even on the Gentiles' (Acts 10:45); and Peter's report to the Church in Jerusalem indicates that he was just as surprised as his companions (Acts 11:15–17). Recognition of the universality of the gift of the Spirit was inextricably linked with recognition that the Gentiles, too, were included in God's salvation. Once the place of Gentiles within the Christian community was established, the way was open for Christian theology to promote the belief that the Holy Spirit was available to all, without exception. Peter's quotation of Joel 2:28–32 [3] ends with the consequential clause that therefore 'everyone who calls on the name of the Lord will be saved' (Acts 2:21). As in Joel, it is those who are loyal to the Lord and now believe in Jesus who are to be included in the promise. The remainder of Joel 2:32 [3:5] is omitted in Acts 2:21, but finds an echo further on in 2:39, where Peter tells the crowd that 'the promise is for you, for your children, and for all who are far away, all whom the Lord our God calls to him'. Joel 2:28–32 [3] also finds its way into St Paul's argument in Romans 10, where he argues that 'there is no distinction between Jew and Greek', but that 'everyone who calls on the name of the Lord will be saved' (Rom. 10:12–13).

244   *Book of Joel*

3 Judgement on the Nations and Blessing on Judah – Joel 3 [4]

Joel 3:1–3 [4:1–3] – Announcement of Judgement on the Nations

> 3 For then, in those days and at that time, when I restore the fortunes of
> Judah and Jerusalem,[2] I will gather all the nations and bring them down
> to the valley of Jehoshaphat, and I will enter into judgment with them
> there, on account of my people and my heritage Israel, because they have
> scattered them among the nations. They have divided my land[3] and cast
> lots for my people and traded boys for prostitutes and sold girls for wine
> and drunk it down.

As argued in the 'Introduction to Joel', 3:1–3, 9–17 [4:1–3, 9–17] were added
to 1:1–2:27 to form the Eschatological Redactional Composition (into
which 2:28–32 [3] was subsequently inserted). Originally, therefore, they
continued on from 2:27, extending YHWH's response of promise of blessing promise in 2:18–27. They move that promise from one of restoration
of the fertility of the land into one of future restoration of the fortunes of
Judah and Jerusalem in times to come. The word 'eschatological' is used
widely in theological writing, often without clear definition. In using the
term of this redactional composition, I do so to mean that the promises
appear to be for a distant future rather than for imminent fulfilment within
history. The locust plague of chapters 1:1–2:27, with its associated devasta-
tions of drought and fire, recedes, and is not mentioned again. The connecting theme is the Day of YHWH. In 1:15 and 2:1–11 the Day of YHWH was
a day of significant action of YHWH within history. In the Eschatological
Redactional Composition it is transformed into a day of final, decisive
action of YHWH in some more distant future. This day will bring blessing
and restoration to Judah, something which, the text makes clear, necessitated and will be accompanied by the judgement on and destruction of
the nations of the world which had oppressed her.[106] Biblical texts of the
Second Temple period express varying expectations regarding the future
of foreign nations in YHWH's plans: some, including the Joel-text, see
them as destined to be destroyed when Israel is finally vindicated, while
others hint that they may be in some way included in Israel's salvation (see
further 'A Closer Look: The Destiny of the Nations'). The restoration is, in

---

[106] J. L. Crenshaw *Joel* (1995): 172–3 comments that the 'only sure way they could stay in
safety was by removing the threat from their powerful oppressors'. H. W. Wolff *Joel and
Amos* (1977): 85 wrote, similarly, that 'Yahweh proves himself to be Israel's God through
his punitive judgment on all oppressors of his people.'

C *Commentary on Joel* 245

the Eschatological Redactional Composition, of the people as a whole. The subsequent addition of 2:28–32 [3] then invited a reading of it in which the salvation would be restricted to those who call upon the name of YHWH (see the comments *ad loc*).

NRSV prints these verses as prose. *Biblia Hebraica Stuttgartensia (BHS)*, however, sets them out as poetry, and many commentators agree.[107] The opening formula 'in those days and at that time' is elsewhere found only in Jeremiah 33:15–16; 50:4, 20. The time will be 'when I restore the fortunes of Judah and Jerusalem'. The expression 'restore the fortunes' is literally 'turn the turning', with the same Hebrew root used twice. It is found several times in the Hebrew Bible (cf. Ezek. 39:25; Amos 9:14; Zeph. 3:20). Behind the phrase lurks, in many instances, the disaster of the destruction of Jerusalem and its Temple, and the carrying off of many people into exile in Babylon, in 587. While its location in Joel makes it refer initially to restoration after the locust plague, this perspective is quickly lost as 3:2 [4:2] refers, rather, to the scattering of 'my heritage Israel' among the nations. This is one of only three instances in Joel of the use of the name 'Israel' (the others being 2:27 and 3:16 [4:16]). It is most likely being used simply as an alternative name for Judah. However, it is possible that its inclusion here was triggered by the opening formula in common with Jeremiah 33:15–16, which states that YHWH will fulfil his promise 'made to the house of Israel and the house of Judah'. In that case there is a fleeting reference to the exile of Israelites after the destruction of Samaria and the northern kingdom in 722 as well as to the exile of Judeans after 587. It is on account of this scattering of his people that YHWH will, one day, gather the nations for judgement. No specific nations are named in the Eschatological Redactional Composition: in the years following 587 'the nations' became a global expression for all those who had oppressed the people of Israel and Judah. The place to which YHWH will bring the nations is the 'valley of Jehoshaphat' (3:2 [4:2]). No such valley is known, and undoubtedly the name 'Jehoshaphat' is chosen because of its meaning, 'YHWH judges'. There is also, very probably, an echo of 2 Chronicles 20:20–26, which records that, in the time of King Jehoshaphat, YHWH had won a battle by causing the enemy forces to fight and destroy one another without Jehoshaphat's forces needing to do other than sing praises. In consequence the location of that battle was named 'valley of Beracah (Blessing)'. The gathering of the nations into a valley signifies that

---

[107] J. Barton *Joel and Obadiah* (2001): 100; J. L. Crenshaw *Joel* (1995): 172; et al. NIV and some other EVV print as poetry.

246 *Book of Joel*

there will be no escape, as there might have been from a hilltop or plateau. There, in a valley with no escape route, YHWH will enter into judgement with the nations who have scattered his people.

The nations stand accused of scattering YHWH's people and dividing the land. More specific accusations follow: they have 'cast lots for my people'. Obadiah 11 makes the accusation that 'foreigners entered his gates and of cast lots for Jerusalem', and Joel 3:3 [4:3] picks up the reference. They are also accused of treating the people of Judah as worthless by selling boy prisoners into slavery, with payment being no more than a night with a prostitute; and of selling girl prisoners for wine. The selling of prisoners of war into slavery was common practice in the ancient Near East, but Joel 3:3 [4:3] condemns the casual way in which it was done for so little price. A similar situation pertains in Amos 2:6, which condemns the transgressors in Israel who 'sell the righteous for silver and the needy for a pair of sandals': while the practice of debt-slavery was legal, it was being abused by selling those whose only sin was poverty for trivial amounts (see the commentary *ad loc*).

In the Eschatological Redactional Composition the passage continued naturally into 3:9 [4:9]. However, a later redactional addition in 3:4–8 [4:4–8], thematically linked to 3:2–3 [4:2–3], delays this continuation in the final form of the text.

Joel 3:4–8 [4:4–8] – Tyre and Sidon and the Regions of Philistia

4 **What are you to me, O Tyre and Sidon, and all the regions of Philistia? Are you paying me back for something? If you are paying me back, I will turn your deeds back upon your own heads swiftly and speedily.**[5] **For you have taken my silver and my gold and have carried my rich treasures into your temples.**[6] **You have sold the people of Judah and Jerusalem to the Greeks, removing them far from their own border.**[7] **But now I will rouse them to leave the places to which you have sold them, and I will turn your deeds back upon your own heads.**[8] **I will sell your sons and your daughters into the hand of the people of Judah, and they will sell them to the Sabeans, to a nation far away, for the** LORD **has spoken.**

That these verses are an addition to the text is indicated, not least, by the fact that the natural connection between 3:1–3 [4:1–3] and 3:9–17 [4:9–17] is broken. Additionally 3:4–8 [4:4–8] address particular nations rather than 'the nations' in general; the selling of the whole people of Judah and Jerusalem is condemned (3:6 [4:6]), rather than of individual boys

C Commentary on Joel

247

and girls (3:3 [4:3]); the section is in prose; and an opening formula 'And also' (omitted by NRSV) indicates a new section.[108] The passage is placed where it is and linked to the earlier text through the thrice occurring verb 'sold/sell' (3:6, 7, 8 [4:6, 7, 8]), which picks up the use of the same verb in 3:3 [4:3], and by the designation of the people as 'Judah and Jerusalem' (3:1, 6 [4:1, 6]).

The naming of specific nations invites and allows consideration of the dating of these verses, and thus of the earlier form of the text without them. However, the matter is not straightforward. Joel 3:4 [4:4] suggests that Tyre and Sidon, the Phoenician cities of the northern coastal region, have been acting together with the Philistines of the southern coastal region. It is known that Tyre and Gaza were allies when conquered by Alexander in 332. Sidon had been destroyed by Artaxerxes III in 343. There is some evidence that the Phoenician cities had been allied with Gaza in the mid-fourth century, before Sidon's destruction. Hence that time, the mid-fourth century prior to 343, is the probable dating of these verses. The Greeks (3:6 [4:6]; literally 'Ionians') could well have been involved in people-trading at this time. Mention of the Sabeans is potentially problematic, since their involvement in slave trade was at its peak in the sixth century and came to an end during the fifth century. A reasonable explanation is that the Sabeans (who may be identified with biblical references to Seba/Sheba) are included as a somewhat exotic Arabian 'nation far away' (3:8 [4:8]). This is confirmed by Jeremiah 6:20 describing Sheba as 'a distant land', and by the visit to Solomon of the exotic and distant 'queen of Sheba' in 1 Kings 10. Alternatively, some date these verses to the sixth or early fifth century, which would make the Sabean reference historical, but a Phoenician–Philistine alliance unlikely. This dating would make better sense of the reference in 3:5 [4:5] to the carrying off of 'my silver and my gold … and my rich treasures' – presumably from the Temple in Jerusalem in 587 – were it not for the fact that generally it is the Babylonians and Edomites who are held responsible for the destruction and looting of the Temple (2 Kgs 25:13; Jer. 51:24, 34; Obad. 11, 13). Indeed, the lack of mention of the Babylonians points away from the sixth century. It is best to take these verses as deriving from the fourth century, before 343.[109]

---

[108] See further J. L. Crenshaw *Joel* (1995): 185–6; H. W. Wolff *Joel and Amos* (1977): 74–5.

[109] The case is well made by H. W. Wolff *Joel and Amos* (1977): 77–8. He is followed by J. Barton *Joel and Obadiah* (2001): 100–1. For different views see E. Assis, 'The Date and Meaning of the Book of Joel', *VT* 61(2011): 163–83; J. M. Myers, 'Some Considerations Bearing on the Dating of Joel', *ZAW* 74 (1962): 177–95.

248   *Book of Joel*

In the opening 3:4 [4:4], YHWH asks Tyre and Sidon and the regions of Philistia: 'Are you paying me back for something?' This is best taken as a rhetorical question, and sarcastic.[110] The real explanation of YHWH's promised actions against them is to be found in 3:5–7 [4:5–7]. Firstly, they are accused of having taken YHWH's silver, gold, and rich treasures into their temples (NRSV) or palaces (NRSV footnote). The word *hêkhāl* can mean 'temple' or 'palace', and the latter seems the better translation in this context. Secondly, they have 'sold the people of Judah and Jerusalem to the Greeks, removing them far from their own border'. This accusation is reminiscent of Amos 1:6, in which Gaza, a leading Philistine town, was accused because they 'carried into exile entire communities, to hand them over to Edom'; and Amos 1:9, in which Tyre is similarly accused 'because they delivered entire communities over to Edom'. These crimes, abhorrent in earlier centuries, continued to be abhorrent in the mid-fourth century. A difference between Amos 1:6, 9 and Joel 3:6 is that Amos 1:6, 9 do not specify that it is Israel who was maltreated in this way, while for Joel 3:6 it is imperative to do so: it is not just the crime against humanity itself that matters here, but that it is being perpetrated against YHWH's own people, the people of Judah and Jerusalem. The judgement to come on Tyre, Sidon, and Philistia will be implemented by YHWH's people, who he will bring back from the places to which they have been sold (3:7–8 [4:7–8]). The Judeans will act as YHWH's agents in punishment by selling them to a distant people, the Sabeans.

The addition 3:4–8 [4:4–8] matches the text to which it was added in seeing Israel's blessing and restoration as necessarily involving judgement on those nations who had wronged her. The difference is that particular political entities are named, while the older 3:1–3, 9–17 [4:1–3, 9–17] – which now resumes – concerns 'the nations' as a whole in a non-specific, and therefore wide, sense.

Joel 3:9–15 [4:9–15] – Judgement Executed

> [9] Proclaim this among the nations:
>   Consecrate yourselves for war;
>   stir up the warriors.
>   Let all the soldiers draw near;
>   let them come up.

---

[110]   J. L. Crenshaw *Joel* (1995): 180.

C Commentary on Joel

249

10 Beat your plowshares into swords,
and your pruning hooks into spears;
let the weakling say, 'I am a warrior.'

11 Come quickly,
all you nations all around;
gather yourselves there.
Bring down your warriors, O LORD.

12 Let the nations rouse themselves
and come up to the valley of Jehoshaphat,
for there I will sit to judge
all the neighbouring nations.

13 Put in the sickle,
for the harvest is ripe.
Go in, tread,
for the winepress is full.
The vats overflow,
for their wickedness is great.

14 Multitudes, multitudes,
in the valley of decision!
For the day of the LORD is near
in the valley of decision.

15 The sun and the moon are darkened,
and the stars withdraw their shining.

Joel 3:9–15 [4:9–15] resume the Eschatological Redactional Composition's description of the Day of YHWH as a day of restoration and blessing for Judah and what was seen as the necessary accompaniment of judgement on the nations (see the opening comments on 'Joel 3:1–3 [4:1–3] – Announcement of Judgement on the Nations'). Key words are found in both 3:1–3 [4:1–3] and 3:9–15 [4:9–15]: 'the nations' (vv. 2, 9, 11, 12); 'gather' (vv. 2, 11); 'valley of Jehoshaphat' (vv. 2, 12); 'enter into judgment/judge' (vv. 2, 12).

The speaker in 3:9–11 [4:9–11] could be the prophet, with a switch to divine speech in 3:12–13 [4:12–13]. More likely, however, it is YHWH who speaks throughout 3:9–13 [4:9–13] (apart from an interjected 'Bring down your warriors, O Lord' in 3:11). But who is being called to proclaim among the nations the need to prepare for war? And in 3:9–10 [4:9–10] is it the nations who are addressed, as is clearly so in 3:11–12 [4:11–12], or is it the Judeans? One view is that Judah is addressed and called to prepare for war

250   *Book of Joel*

in 3:9–10 [4:9–10], with 3:11–12 [4:11–12] then addressed to the nations; 3:13 [4:13] would then be a resumption of address to Judah. In that case the phrase 'among the nations' in 3:9 [4:9] would be a call to Judean exiles to return to Judah to join in the preparations. Alternatively 3:9–10 [4:9–10] are addressed to angelic beings in the heavenly court, who are sent out among the nations to call them to prepare for war, even though the outcome of the war is going to be their destruction. These same angelic beings would then be the ones addressed in 3:13 [4:13], where they are instructed to execute YHWH's judgement on the nations for their wickedness. On balance this second interpretation seems preferable,[111] but the text allows for either.

The nations are summoned to 'consecrate yourselves for war' (3:9 [4:9]). The verb has already been used in 1:14 and 2:15 to refer to sanctifying a fast, and the Eschatological Redactional Composition picks it up to use here. The same expression is found in Jeremiah 6:4, in a passage in which war against Jerusalem is envisaged. Warriors are to be stirred up to draw near for battle: there is possibly an echo of Isaiah 13:3, in which YHWH's 'consecrated ones' (from the same root as 'sanctify') and 'warriors' (the same word as in Joel 3:9 [4:9]) are summoned to execute YHWH's anger. Indeed, echoes of Isaiah 13:3–5 appear to lie behind both 3:9 [4:9] and 3:14 [4:14], and both passages concern the judgement that is part of the Day of YHWH.

There follows in 3:10 [4:10] a reversal of Isaiah 2:4/Micah 4:3. Verses famous for their vision of peace are changed to bring about the exact opposite (the word for 'spear' is different in Joel 3:10 [4:10], but all other vocabulary used is the same). In Isaiah 2:2–4/Micah 4:1–3 the nations stream to Jerusalem in order to be instructed in YHWH's ways and to receive his arbitration. Here in Joel 3:9–12 [4:9–12], they are to come up and be gathered in order to be judged. The place in which they are to be gathered is, as 3:2 [4:2] has already indicated, the valley of Jehoshaphat. There YHWH will take his seat as judge, ready to pronounce sentence on the nations. They are described in 3:12 [4:12] as 'the neighbouring nations', but no restriction is intended: the phrase is the same as that translated in the previous verse as 'nations all around', and refers to all the nations, gathered for judgement. The sentence is then pronounced in 3:13 [4:13]. The angelic beings addressed in 3:9 [4:9] are addressed again, and are instructed to destroy the nations. The language of agriculture is employed: rather than being described as

---

[111]   So *inter alia* J. L. Crenshaw *Joel* (1995): 187–90; J. Goldingay *Hosea–Micah* (2020): 240; T. S. Hadjiev *Joel and Amos* (2020): 51.

C Commentary on Joel

crushed in battle, they are crushed as in the winepress. The language is less vivid and gory than that of Isaiah 63:3–6, but the imagery is the same.

The nations are then described as being gathered in the valley of decision (3:14 [4:14]). The decision is that made by YHWH to judge them: Allen translates as 'Verdict Valley', Goldingay as 'Determination Vale'.[112] The gathering for judgement is described as 'Multitudes, multitudes' – which could equally well be translated 'Tumults, tumults'. The word is found also in Isaiah 13:4, confirming the suggestion above that an echo of Isaiah 13:3–5 lies behind both 3:9 [4:9] and 3:14 [4:14]. Crenshaw draws attention to the onomatopoeia of the Hebrew *hamônim hamônim*, suggesting the sound of a tumultuous gathering of many thousands of people.[113] This tumultuous gathering in Verdict Valley indicates the closeness of the Day of YHWH. The linkage that this theme makes with the first half of the text is made explicit by the repetition of 2:10b in 3:15 [4:15]. There, however, the day was one affecting the people of Judah; here it is applied to the nations in their judgement.

The introductory comments on 'Joel 3:1–3 [4:1–3] – Announcement of Judgement on the Nations' noted the perspective of the Eschatological Redactional Composition that the bringing of blessing and restoration to Judah necessitated an accompanying judgement on and destruction of the nations. While such a perspective is entirely understandable, given the sense of oppression and domination by others that the people of Judah felt they had experienced, contemporary readers may feel that they wish to question this perspective: Does the blessing of YHWH's people in Judah necessarily exclude the blessing of other nations also? Those asking such a question will need to consider perspectives from other biblical texts as well as Joel 3 [4]: see further 'A Closer Look: The Destiny of the Nations'.

Joel 3:16–17 [4:16–17] – YHWH Dwells in Zion

[16] The Lord roars from Zion
  and utters his voice from Jerusalem,
  and the heavens and the earth shake.
  But the Lord is a refuge for his people,
  a stronghold for the people of Israel.

---

[112] L. C. Allen *Joel, Obadiah, Jonah and Micah* (1976): 116–17; J. Goldingay *Hosea–Micah* (2020): 234, 241.
[113] J. L. Crenshaw *Joel* (1995): 192.

252   *Book of Joel*

> [17] So you shall know that I, the Lord your God,
>   dwell in Zion, my holy mountain.
> And Jerusalem shall be holy,
>   and strangers shall never again pass through it.

These two sayings are brought together at the conclusion of the Eschatological Redactional Composition to confirm the blessing of Judah and Jerusalem promised in 3:1 [4:1], and they form an *inclusio* with it around the accompanying judgement of the nations which has occupied 3:2–15 [4:2–15].

There is no problem in YHWH appearing to have moved from the valley of Jehoshaphat to Zion/Jerusalem. Rather, yet once more the Joel-text is citing earlier texts and appropriating earlier themes. Joel 3:16a [4:16a] is identical to Amos 1:2a. In the 'Commentary on Amos' I argue that Amos 1:2 entered the Amos-text in its Exilic Redactional Composition. I therefore concur with Nogalski that 'even though Amos 1:2 plays a redactional role in its own book, it was probably already in place by the time of the composition of Joel'.[114] The fact that the two verses are a mere seven verses apart in the Hebrew text suggests strongly that redactional processes within the Book of the Twelve have been at work, and lend support to the view of several scholars that the placing of the book of Joel before Amos is not accidental.[115] A variant form of the saying is found in Jeremiah 25:30a. This would also have been available to the redactors of Joel; but it is the Amos form that is followed, in order to make the link clear.

Joel 3:16–17 [4:16–17] appropriates pre-exilic traditions associated with Zion, which see it as YHWH's dwelling place. It is from Zion that YHWH speaks, rules, judges, and protects (see 'A Closer Look: Zion'). As YHWH roars from Zion, the heavens and the earth shake (3:16 [4:16]). The language picks up 2:10: while the order of 'earth' and 'heavens' is reversed, and 3:16 [4:16] employs one verb for both rather than each having related verbs in 2:10, the link is unmistakeable. The shaking of the heavens and the earth signifies the drama of the events of the Day of YHWH, which would include both the judging of the nations and the blessing of Judah. In language reminiscent of the Zion psalms, YHWH declares that he is a refuge and a stronghold for his people. The term 'refuge' (*maḥaseh*) is found in several psalms, including at the head of Psalm 46, one of the psalms of Zion (Ps. 46:1 [2]). The term 'stronghold' (*māʿôz*) is also found in psalms such as 27:1. The only other verse in which the two occur together is Isaiah 25:4

---

[114] J. D. Nogalski *Hosea–Jonah* (2011): 249.
[115] See further the 'Volume Introduction'.

C Commentary on Joel

253

in which, as in Joel 3 [4], interwoven passages concerning YHWH's judgement of the nations and blessing of Israel are also to be found. The people are called the 'people of Israel'. As noted in the comments on 3:2 [4:2], this is one of only three places in which the Joel-text uses the name 'Israel': it is used as an alternative name for Judah, which is now the remaining and continuing Israel.

The upshot of YHWH's blessing of the people is twofold. Firstly, the people acknowledge YHWH as God, and that he dwells in Zion (3:17a [4:17a]). The priests' prayer in 2:17 that YHWH's heritage should not be a mockery and byword among the nations had been answered in the promise of 2:27 that the people would know that YHWH was in the midst of his people, and that the people would know that he is their God, and there is no other. They would never again be put to shame. Now Joel 3:17 [4:17] reinforces that the promise, probably seen as not yet fulfilled, would be fulfilled at the future time of the Day of YHWH. Secondly, Jerusalem herself would be kept holy. The designation of Jerusalem as holy is found also in Isaiah 52:1. In both verses, that holiness is linked to the absence and banning of foreigners: 'for the uncircumcised and the unclean shall enter you no more' (Isa. 52:1); 'and strangers shall never again pass through it' (Joel 3:17 [4:17]). In both verses the 'no more' and 'never again' is a reference back to the destruction of Jerusalem by the Babylonians in 587, which was a recent event when Isaiah 52:1 was penned, but the memory of which was never forgotten.

The Eschatological Redactional Composition originally ended at this point. Subsequently the addition of 3:18–21 [4:18–21] brought the text to the final form that we now have.

Joel 3:18–21 [4:18–21] – Judah, Edom, and Egypt

[18] In that day
    the mountains shall drip sweet wine,
        the hills shall flow with milk,
    and all the streambeds of Judah
        shall flow with water;
    a fountain shall come forth from the house of the LORD
        and water the Wadi Shittim.

[19] Egypt shall become a desolation
        and Edom a desolate wilderness,
    because of the violence done to the people of Judah,
        in whose land they have shed innocent blood.

254   *Book of Joel*

²⁰ But Judah shall be inhabited forever
    and Jerusalem to all generations.
²¹ I will avenge their blood, and I will not clear the guilty,
    for the Lᴏʀᴅ dwells in Zion.

While 3:18 [4:18] and 3:19–21[4:19–21] are separate sayings, they are brought
together in this addition to the Eschatological Redactional Composition.
The opening link-formula 'In that day' encompasses both sayings.

Joel 3:18a [4:18a] is a variant form of the same saying in Amos 9:13b.
The main difference between the two versions is that in Joel 3:18a [4:18a]
the hills are said to flow with milk, which is not mentioned in Amos 9:13b;
and there are other minor differences. This suggests that direct literary
dependence is unlikely. More probable is that both texts include a saying in current circulation. It was noted in the commentary on 3:16 [4:16]
that its occurrence seven verses before the nearly identical Amos 1:2 lent
credence to the view that the placing of Joel before Amos in the Hebrew
text was deliberate and of redactional significance in the formation of the
Book of the Twelve. The overlap between Joel 3:18 [4:18] and Amos 9:13
strengthens this view. The abundant fertility described in Joel 3:18 [4:18]
contrasts with the loss of fertility described in 1:4–12, in language more
extravagant than that of the restoration promised in 2:19–26. The sweet
wine that 1:5 described as lacking is restored, the cattle of 1:18 no longer
wander about dazed, but produce milk, and the dry watercourses of 1:20
flow with water. The picture of rich fertility includes a fountain flowing
out of the house of YHWH. This recalls the vision of water flowing from
the promised Temple in Ezekiel 47:1–12. Essentially the same idea is found
in Zechariah 14:8. The blessing of abundant fertility is a gift of YHWH.
The promise is that it will water the Wadi Shittim. No such valley is known
(and the Shittim of Joshua 2:1; 3:1 is east of Jordan). It could be translated
as 'valley of the acacias'.[116] Whatever its exact intended point of reference,
it serves to indicate that the fountain flowing from the house of YHWH
would water a wide area.

Joel 3:19 [4:19] contrasts this fertile blessing with the fate of Egypt and
Edom. Just as 3:4–8 [4:4–8] differed from the Eschatological Redactional
Composition to which it was added by addressing particular nations rather
than 'the nations' in general, so too 3:19 [4:19] focuses on these two countries. However, while 3:4–8 [4:4–8] appears to concern particular historical

---

[116]   G. Ahlström *Joel and the Temple Cult* (1971): 92–4.

C Commentary on Joel

activities of the nations concerned, it is less clear that 3:19 [4:19] does so. Some hold that the reference to both Egypt and Edom having spilled blood within the land of Judah points to a particular episode with regard to Egypt, namely the campaign of Ptolemy Sater against Jerusalem in 312.[117] More probably, however, Egypt and Edom are selected as two archetypal nations that have mistreated Judah over the centuries, with particular incidents becoming legendary in Judean memory. The actions of Edom in rejoicing at the fall of Jerusalem in 587 were never forgotten (Ps. 137:7; Lam. 4:21–22; Obad. 10–14), and provide sufficient justification for its inclusion. With less certainty but with definite plausibility, the killing of King Josiah by Pharaoh Neco at Megiddo in 609 was something remembered for years afterwards, certainly in Deuteronomistic circles (2 Kgs 23: 29–30). Egypt and Edom, 3:19 [4:19] says, will receive the opposite of the blessing and fertility promised to Judah in the preceding verse. Because they had done violence to the people of Judah, in whose land they have shed innocent blood, they will experience the desolation of their own lands.

Joel 3:20 [4:20] reverts to Judah and Jerusalem, promising that they will be inhabited for ever (in contrast to the opposite promise made in respect of Babylon in Isa. 13:20, where it is said that Babylon 'will never again be inhabited or lived in for all generations'). The translation of the final verse 3:21 [4:21] is uncertain. A footnote in NRSV gives the literal translation, namely that 'I will hold innocent their blood that I have not held innocent', which makes little sense. Its translation in the main text entails an emendation of the first verb (one that appears to be supported by LXX and Syriac Peshitta) which gives the reasonable sense that YHWH will not clear the guilt of Egypt and Edom, but will avenge the blood of Judah that they had shed. Thus Judah and Jerusalem will be blessed, and the nations of Egypt and Edom punished. For, as the last line of the text states, 'YHWH dwells in Zion', from where he will execute his justice. The premise of the whole of Joel 3 [4], that YHWH's blessing of Judah and Jerusalem necessarily entailed judgement on the nations, is worked out, in this addition, specifically in the case of two of Judah's arch-enemies, Egypt and Edom.

The final form of the Joel-text thus concludes with the assertion that YHWH dwells in Zion, and that from there he will, at some future time, bring abundant fertility and blessing to Judah (3:18, 20 [4:18, 20]) and judge those who have done violence to Judah. Ultimately the book brings hope to God's people after times of trial and difficulty, hope derived from the belief

---

[117] So M. Treves, 'The Date of Joel', *VT* 7 (1957): 149–56 (154).

that in the Day of YHWH he will act to bless his people and judge those who have wronged them. The blessing of Judah is upon the nation as a whole in the Eschatological Redactional Composition. It may be recalled, however, that the latest addition to the Joel-text of 2:28–32 [3] restricted the salvation promised to those who call on the name of YHWH (see the commentary *ad loc*), providing a lens through which the whole of chapter 3 [4] was to be read: YHWH's salvation is offered to all, but it is those who call on the name of YHWH who are able to receive it.

A Closer Look: The Destiny of the Nations

Brueggemann writes that

> Israel did not live its life or practice its faith in a socio-political vacuum. From beginning to end, Israel lived among nations who, in varying ways, decisively impinge upon Israel's life. On the one hand, Israel had to work out its relations to the nations, which was not obvious in light of Israel's peculiar theological identity. On the other hand, Israel had to articulate how the nations were related to Yahweh.[118]

From the eighth century onwards Israel had to face the reality of powerful empires which dominated much of their known world. In 722 the Assyrians destroyed the northern kingdom, carrying off most of the population into exile and settling people into the land from other parts of their empire (2 Kgs 17). Isaiah 10:5–6 saw Assyria as 'the rod of my anger' used to punish Israel for her sins, but with the verses following (10:7–14) announcing judgement on Assyria for her actions. Similarly, Jeremiah saw the Babylonians as YHWH's agents in judging Judah for her sins (Jer. 38:17–23); but subsequent to the Babylonian destruction of Jerusalem in 587, Jeremiah 50–51 announces judgement on Babylon for her actions. Other nations addressed in the prophetic books include Edom, Moab, Ammon, Philistia, Syria/Aram, Tyre, and Egypt.

Beyond references to particular nations, there arose in the Second Temple period varied eschatological expectations concerning the future of 'the nations' as a generalised category. Pre-exilic Zion traditions had already referred to 'the nations' in such a generalised sense. For example, Psalm 96, one of the so-called enthronement psalms, urges that YHWH's

---

[118] W. Brueggemann, *Theology of the Old Testament: Testimony, Dispute, Advocacy* (Minneapolis: Fortress Press, 1997): 492.

C Commentary on Joel

glory be declared 'among the nations', and that it should be said among the nations: 'YHWH is king!' As ruler and king, YHWH will judge the earth and its peoples with equity and truth (Ps. 96:10b, 13). Psalm 47, another enthronement psalm, asserts that 'God is king over the nations; God sits on his holy throne' (Ps. 47:8 [9]). In Psalm 2, a royal psalm, YHWH's rule makes it futile for the nations to plot against him and his anointed one (Ps. 2:1–2). In Psalm 46, a Zion psalm, the nations are in uproar as YHWH utters his voice (Ps. 46: 6 [7]), and YHWH declares that he will be exalted 'among the nations' (Ps. 46: 10 [11]). In this psalm one of the reasons for YHWH's exaltation is that 'he makes wars to cease to the end of the earth; he breaks the bow and shatters the spear; he burns the shields with fire' (Ps. 46:9 [10]).[119] Thematically this links to the vision of Zion/Jerusalem in Isaiah 2:2–4/Micah 4:1–3, in which the nations stream to the mountain of YHWH's house to receive his instruction and his arbitration between peoples, with the result that 'nation shall not lift up sword against nation, neither shall they learn war any more' (Isa. 2:4/Mic. 4:3).[120] That such Zion traditions were still recalled and utilised in the period of the composition of the Eschatological Composition of Joel, and additions to it, is evident (Joel 2:32; 3:16, 21 [3:5; 4:16, 21]). Additionally, when Israel was disobedient YHWH's punishment was to give them 'into the hands of the nations' (Ps. 106:41) and scatter them 'among the nations' (Ps. 44:11 [12]; Ezek. 11:16); and therefore it was from 'the nations' that YHWH's people would be recalled (Jer. 29:14; Ezek. 36:24; 37:21).

Exilic hopes for the future and eschatological expectations which grew from them develop earlier traditions concerning the nations in varying directions. In Joel 3 [4] the expectation is that Judah will be restored and blessed, and the nations destroyed in YHWH's judgement. But other scenarios are envisaged elsewhere. Some prophetic texts envisage other nations experiencing restoration after destruction in the same way as

---

[119] The so-called enthronement psalms, royal psalms, and psalms of Zion have all been widely held to have been part of the pre-exilic Jerusalem cult. See J. Day, 'How Many Pre-Exilic Psalms Are There?' in J. Day (ed.), *In Search of Pre-Exilic Israel* (JSOTSup, 406; London/New York: T&T Clark International, 2004): 225–50.

[120] Varying views are held concerning the origin and dating of Isa. 2:2–4/Mic. 4:1–3, and of the relationship between the two passages. R. E. Clements, *Isaiah 1–39* (NCB; Grand Rapids, MI/London: Eerdmans/Marshall, Morgan & Scott, 1980): 40 writes that 'we must ascribe the prophecy to a time after the destruction of Jerusalem in 587 ... the early post-exilic period, probably the early fifth century, is most likely'.

Judah: for example, Ezekiel 29:13–16 promises that after being made a desolation, YHWH will gather the Egyptians from the peoples among whom they were scattered, and will restore the fortunes of Egypt, and the Egyptians will know that YHWH is God. Similarly, Isaiah 23:17–18 promises the restoration of Tyre after a period of seventy years (the same period of time that Jeremiah 29:10 says that Judah will be in exile). In this case Tyre will re-commence her trade, but rather than hoarding her profits, she will use them to supply abundant food and clothing 'for those who live in the presence of YHWH' (Isa. 23:18). Isaiah 60:3–7, similarly, envisages the wealth of the nations being brought to a restored Israel. Then there are some passages which envisage the salvation of the nations. Zechariah 2:11 [15] sees a future time in which 'many nations shall join themselves to YHWH on that day, and shall be my people'. Zechariah 8:22–23 says: 'Many people and strong nations shall come to seek the Lord of hosts in Jerusalem, and to entreat the favour of the Lord … ten men from nations of every language shall take hold of a Jew, grasping his garment and saying, "Let us go with you, for we have heard that God is with you."' The focus is still on Zion, but the nations may join the Jews in going there to entreat YHWH. Different again is Isaiah 19:18–25. Verse 18 declares that five cities in Egypt will speak the language of Canaan and will swear allegiance to the Lord of hosts. The next verse announces that there will be an altar to YHWH in Egypt, and a pillar to YHWH at its border (19:19). YHWH will make himself known to the Egyptians (19:21). There will be a highway from Egypt to Assyria, and 'Israel will be the third with Egypt and Assyria, a blessing in the midst of the earth, whom YHWH has blessed, saying, "Blessed be Egypt my people, and Assyria the work of my hands, and Israel my heritage"' (19:24–25).

We may also note the book of Jonah, which tells a story in which Nineveh, the capital city of Assyria, repents of its sin in sackcloth and ashes, and in consequence is spared the judgement which YHWH had threatened. This is to the chagrin of the Israelite prophet, who had sought to evade the call to go to Nineveh precisely because he knew YHWH to be 'a gracious God and merciful, slow to anger, and abounding in steadfast love, and ready to relent from punishing' (Jonah 4:2), and was therefore fearful that YHWH might forgive even the Assyrians. Many commentators hold that, as the story mocks Jonah, so it also mocks the view that YHWH would spare only Israel and not foreign nations. The closing sentence of the story certainly fits such an interpretation, saying

C *Commentary on Joel*   259

of YHWH: 'Should I not be concerned about Nineveh, that great city, in which there are more than a hundred and twenty thousand people who do not know their right hand from their left, and also many animals?' (4:11). There are parallels with the book of Joel: in the proclamation of a fast (Jonah 3:5; Joel 2:15); in the 'Who knows whether God/YHWH might relent?' (Jonah 3:9; Joel 2:14); in the form of the ancient credal formula derived from Exodus 34:6–7: as noted in the commentary on Joel 2:13, that verse and Jonah 4:2 are closer to each other in the form of the saying than to any other version of it. The difference is that Joel is concerned with Judah, while Jonah is concerned with Nineveh: in Jonah, YHWH acts with regard to Nineveh in just the same way that he acts with regard to Judah in Joel.

Thus the perspective of Joel 3, that the nations will be destroyed, is one among a range of futures for the nations envisaged in the Hebrew Bible. That awareness will help contemporary readers who might struggle with the biblical perspective if it was solely that of the Joel-text. As it is, the reader encounters a range of perspectives, indicating that the biblical tradition overall is at ease with including such a range, and with declining to prefer any one of them as more 'correct' than another.[121]

---

[121] See further: D. L. Christensen, 'Nations', *ABD* 4: 1037–49; T. L. Donaldson, 'Nations', *NIDB* 4: 231–8; W. Brueggemann *Theology of the Old Testament* (1997): 492–527; and in this volume 'A Closer Look: Oracles against the Nations'.

IV Book of Amos

A INTRODUCTION TO AMOS

The book of Amos is often recognised as 'an important source for the claim that ancient Israel's classical prophets had a fundamental concern with social justice'.[1] This recognition makes it appealing to those concerned with issues of social justice in the world today. Its importance is, in fact, most often expressed negatively as a condemnation of social *in*justice, and the book presents the presence of such injustice in Israel as a primary reason why Israel's God, YHWH, announces judgement on his people.

The announcement of divine judgement, and the reasons for it, makes up the greater part of the text. Often YHWH speaks in the first person, his words prefixed by the messenger formula 'Thus says YHWH',[2] or concluded with a formulae such as 'says YHWH' at the end of a saying. The manifestations of judgement announced upon Israel range from destruction by an enemy (3:11), through exile (4:3; 6:7; 7:17) and natural disaster (4:6–11), to wailing and lamentation (5:16–17; 8.10), while in the case of the foreign nations condemned in chapters 1–2 there is the refrain 'So I will send a fire' (1:4, 7, 10, 12, 14; 2:2, 5). The reasons for judgement on Israel include oppression of the poor by the rich (2:6–8; 4:1; 5:11; 8:4–6), violence and robbery (3:10), perverting justice (5:7, 10), and excessive luxury of living while neglecting the perceived parlous state of the nation (6:6). The many announcements of judgement are relieved only by calls in chapter 5 to 'Seek me and live' (5:4), 'Seek the Lord and live' (5:6), 'Seek good and not evil' (5:14), and by the promises in 9:11–15 of restoration after judgement. Most of the text is oracular in form, with the notable exception of some hymnic verses which punctuate the text in 4:13; 5:8–9; 9:5–6.

[1] A. G. Auld, *Amos* (OTG; Sheffield: JSOT Press, 1986): 9.
[2] See the commentary on 1:3. The formula is found in 1:3, 6, 9, 11, 13; 2:1, 4, 6; 3:12; 5:3, 4, 16.

A Introduction to Amos

The majority of the book contains words directed at the northern kingdom of Israel. The breakaway of the northern kingdom from Davidic rule at the end of the reign of Solomon is described in 1 Kings 12, and subsequent chapters tell the stories of the two kingdoms, up to 2 Kings 17, which describes the demise of the northern kingdom and destruction of its northern capital city Samaria at the hands of the Assyrians in 722 BCE. The text dates the ministry of Amos to the closing years of Israel as a kingdom (see the comments on 'Amos 1:1 – Heading'). The primarily northern focus to the text should not, however, blind us to its significance for the southern kingdom of Judah (to which there is reference in 2:4–5 and 6:1) and for the 'Israel' which emerged from Judah's exile in Babylon in the sixth century. As a literary work, the text belongs not to the eighth-century kingdom of Israel, but in its earliest form to the southern kingdom of Judah in the late eighth century, and in its final form to the post-exilic community of the late sixth or early fifth century.

Amos as Literary Text

This last observation leads into consideration of the book of Amos as literary text. It is readily apparent, even to the casual reader, that it exhibits clear elements of structure. It is evident, firstly, that there are two major blocks of material each of which constitutes a series. In chapters 1–2 there is a series of Oracles against the Nations (henceforth abbreviated to OAN) which culminates in a brief oracle against Judah (2:4–5) and a longer, climactic oracle against Israel (2:6–16). Near the end of the book, in chapters 7–9, there is a series of visions, beginning in 7:1 and extending to 9:4. This series of five visions in 7:1–3, 4–6, 7–9; 8.1–3; 9:1–4 is broken by a narrative episode in 7:10–17 and by judgement oracles in 8:3–14, indicating the likelihood that both may have entered the text subsequent to an earlier literary edition of the text in which the series was unbroken.[3] Alert to the possibility

---

[3] Some scholars consider that 9:1–4 should not be seen as part of this series. So, for example J. L. Mays, *Amos: A Commentary* (OTL; London: SCM, 1969): 152; G. Eidevall, *Amos* (AYB, 24G; New Haven, CT: Yale University Press, 2017): 224–6. However, it has been well argued by, among others, H. Gese, 'Komposition bei Amos', in J. A. Emerton (ed.), *Congress Volume, Vienna 1980* (VTSup, 32; Leiden: Brill, 1981): 74–95 that 9:1–4 should be included as the fifth vision in the series. This position is supported by T. S. Hadjiev, *The Composition and Redaction of the Book of Amos* (BZAW, 93; Berlin: W. de Gruyter, 2009): 62–8; G. R. Hamborg, *Still Selling the Righteous: A Redaction-Critical Investigation into Reasons for Judgment in Amos 2:6-16* (LHBOTS, 555; London: T&T Clark, 2012): 50–2; J. Jeremias, *The Book of Amos* (OTL; Louisville, KY: Westminster John Knox Press, 1998): 154–5, S. M. Paul, *Amos* (Hermeneia; Philadelphia: Fortress Press, 1991): 223.

262   *Book of Amos*

of series in the text, it is then no surprise to observe the presence of other, shorter series of sayings, as in the series of questions in 3:3–8, and the series of YHWH's actions in 4:6–11 each ending with the refrain 'yet you did not return to me, says YHWH'.

The two major series of OAN and visions come at the beginning and towards the end of the book. Between them, in chapters 3–6, are found words of Amos, and of YHWH speaking through Amos. These are in two roughly equal parts: chapters 3–4, introduced by the words 'Hear this word that YHWH has spoken against you, O people of Israel', and chapters 5–6, introduced by the words 'Hear this word that I take up over you in lamentation, O house of Israel.' This suggests strongly that the composition of the book is far from random: it is carefully structured. This is confirmed by recognition of a different, complementary organisational pattern also at work. At the centre of the book is 5:1–17, which has a chiastic structure (see the commentary *ad loc*). Around it are accusations relating to the cult in 4:4–5 and 5:18–27, and around them accusations against the rich and powerful in Samaria in 3:9–4:3 and 6:1–14. These extend the chiastic structure significantly. All in all, the evidence of intentional literary activity is overwhelming.

The question arises: Is this literary activity a feature of redactional activity? Or is it original to the earliest, first composition?[4] These questions, of course, presuppose that there was such a literary development, a view with which some scholars disagree. Some argue that the text is a product of the Second Temple period, and that if there was any pre-history of compositional development, it is now impossible to reconstruct it. Thus Coggins interprets the final form of the text in a Second Temple setting, writing that 'even if we assume that there is more ancient material now incorporated into the book, it is misleading to suppose that the particular thrust of such material can be recovered from an essentially later composition'.[5] Linville also takes a final form approach to the text, which 'should be seen as the property of the latter half of the Persian period'. He remains 'open to the idea that it contains many passages of a more ancient provenance',[6] but does not explore what these might be in view of his choice of a final form

---

[4]   See the 'Volume Introduction' for the redaction-critical methodology being employed here.

[5]   R. J. Coggins, *Joel and Amos* (NCB; Sheffield: Sheffield Academic Press, 2000): 76.

[6]   J. R. Linville, *Amos and the Cosmic Imagination* (SOTSMS; Aldershot: Ashgate Publishing Company, 2008): 8.

interpretation. It is a valid interpretative choice to comment solely on the final form of the text. It is not, however, a necessary choice, and Linville's openness to the view that the text contains older material is more helpful than Coggins's apparent despair at the possibility of ever identifying it. In opposite vein, the recent commentary of Carroll R. sees the text 'as a literary creation that goes back largely to the prophet himself', with just a small amount of material 'added shortly after the conclusion of his ministry and possibly under his influence'.[7] He finds redaction-critical proposals too uncertain for his liking, considers that 'the material in the book historically can be placed credibly within the first half of the eighth century BC', and takes the book's thematic coherence and literary art as an argument favouring its original unity.[8] His proposal, however, is no more certain than those of scholars who recognise a process of compositional development; and while the earliest compositional layer does indeed preserve material relating to the eighth century, the text also contains material better related to later periods.

The redaction-critical methodology that this volume espouses draws on scholarly arguments about which a significant measure of consensus is established and evident among scholars such as Wolff and Jeremias, and in the more recent studies of Hadjiev and Hamborg.[9]

Hadjiev gives cogent reasons why it is beyond reasonable doubt that the earliest form of the text was made before the post-exilic period. Firstly, he notes, 'the description of punishment is far too general and does not seem to reflect the experience of later times … exile is only *one* of the aspects of the coming calamity and the earthquake threats are difficult to understand in the context of a post-exilic attempt to make sense theologically of the Babylonian advance and the destruction of Judah'. Secondly, the nations referred to in the OAN, and the climax of the series being the kingdom of Israel as distinct from Judah point to an eighth-century setting. Thirdly, the small amount of hope-filled material compared to the 'unbalanced stress on Israel's sin and punishment' points away from a post-exilic setting for most of the book.[10] These and other indications of a pre-exilic origin and

---

[7]   M. D. Carroll R., *The Book of Amos* (NICOT; Grand Rapids, MI: Eerdmans, 2020): 52.

[8]   M. D. Carroll R. *Amos* (2020): 46–52 (51).

[9]   H. W. Wolff, *Joel and Amos* (Hermeneia; Philadelphia: Fortress Press, 1977); J. Jeremias *Amos* (1998). T. S. Hadjiev *Composition and Redaction* (2009); G. R. Hamborg *Still Selling the Righteous* (2012). The analysis of G. Eidevall *Amos* (2017) has much in common with these scholars, but also some differing positions from them.

[10]   T. S. Hadjiev *Composition and Redaction* (2009): 12–14.

development of the text encourage the interpreter to look behind the final form into likely earlier compositions which underlie it.

The Composition History of the Book of Amos

Wolff's seminal commentary posited a six-stage process of formation of the book of Amos. He envisaged three eighth-century layers: 'Words of Amos from Tekoa', the vision cycles, and other words from an 'Old School of Amos'. There was then a seventh-century 'Bethel-exposition' during the reign of Josiah, which included the hymnic verses 4:13; 5:8–9; 9:5–6. Subsequently there was a Deuteronomistic redaction, and a post-exilic redaction which included the words of promise of restoration in 9:11–15.[11] This substantial commentary has remained influential. However, many are not persuaded that there was a 'Bethel-exposition' of the seventh century, nor that it is possible to separate out three different eighth-century strands.

While Wolff identified words of the prophet Amos and subsequent literary layers, Jeremias focuses primarily on the literary text. He considers that there were two significant editions of the text: a first edition, produced soon after the fall of Samaria and the northern kingdom in 722, and a second edition produced after the fall of Jerusalem in 587 in the exilic or early post-exilic period. He considers that the first edition gained some additions about a century after its original formation, in the age of Jeremiah in the seventh century, and that the second edition gained the closing 9:7–15, and a few other small additions, in the post-exilic period. He comments that this 'growth of the book over many centuries reflects the high estimation it enjoyed even in the biblical period itself, as well as the lively engagement it elicited'.[12] Eidevall adopts a similar position, but with the difference that he dates the whole of chapters 7–9 to the exilic and post-exilic periods.[13] My own position is closest to that of Jeremias.[14]

As noted in the discussion of redaction-critical methodology in the 'Volume Introduction', the further back in time and the greater the number of compositional layers that are proposed, the greater the humility that is needed in putting forward proposals for the identification of such layers. As Knierim writes: 'It is much more problematic first to establish original

[11] H. W. Wolff *Joel and Amos* (1977): 106–13.
[12] J. Jeremias *Amos* (1998): 5–9 (9).
[13] G. Eidevall *Amos* (2017): 22–3.
[14] G. R. Hamborg *Still Selling the Righteous* (2012).

A *Introduction to Amos* 265

texts from the present texts and then to identify the later layers than to identify the latest layers first and then to inquire into their pre-history.'[15] It is best, therefore, to work backwards from the final form to the earlier layers. In the case of the book of Amos, it is possible to identify four compositional layers (including the final form). Having first of all identified the likely outlines of these, it will then be possible to describe their literary and theological features.

The latest literary layer – which I refer to as the Post-exilic Redactional Composition – is the final form of the text as we now have it. The verses in it that were most clearly added to an earlier text are those of the second half of chapter 9, about which there has been longstanding scholarly agreement that they were added to the book in the post-exilic period. Wellhausen famously described 9:13–15 as 'roses and lavender instead of blood and iron',[16] and subsequent commentators have quoted his words with regard to the whole of 9:11–15. The thematic contrast between these closing verses and the rest of the book is an obvious and significant pointer to them coming from a later time than the main part of the text. Additionally, the reference to 'the booth of David that is fallen' (9:11) refers most naturally to the destroyed city of Jerusalem. Where there is variation of scholarly opinion is regarding the point in the text at which this post-exilic addition begins. Virtually all see it as including 9:11–15. Many commentators also draw attention to the qualification of the destruction announced in 9:8, 'except that I will not utterly destroy the house of Jacob', and take that to belong to it too. Others take the whole of 9:7–15 to have been absent from the previous redactional composition. This last position is, in fact, the most probable, in view of the strong argument presented by Koch that 9:5–6 concluded the text before this time.[17] Other than this closing section, however, there are only a few phrases of text which were not part of the preceding compositional layer (see the commentary on 2:7; 5:22; 6:5).

The Exilic Redactional Composition was a more substantial revision of its predecessor. There are two main strands of material which

---

[15] R.P. Knierim, 'Criticism of Literary Features, Form, Tradition and Redaction', in D. A. Knight and G. M. Tucker (eds.), *The Hebrew Bible and its Modern Interpreters* (Philadelphia: Fortress Press, 1985): 123–65 (156).

[16] In German 'Rosen und Lavendel statt Blut und Eisen': J. Wellhausen, *Skizzen und Vorarbeiten, Fünftes Heft: Die kleinen Propheten Übersetzt, mit Noten* (2nd ed.; Berlin: Georg Reimer, 1892): 94.

[17] K. Koch, 'Die Rolle der hymnischen Abschnitte des Amos-buches', *ZAW* 86 (1974): 504–37 (525–30).

entered the text in this composition. Firstly, there are verses related to Deuteronomistic tradition. An influential article by Schmidt identified Deuteronomistic additions in 1:1 and 3:1; the oracles against Tyre, Edom, and Judah in 1:9–10, 1:11–12; 2:4–5; the expansion of 2:6–16 in 2:10–12; the addition of 3:7 in the series 3:3–8; and 5:26.[18] Many scholars have accepted his argument, as does this commentary. Other material which may be associated with these Deuteronomistic additions is found in 8:8–14, with its sections introduced by the late formulae 'On that day' (8:9, 13) and 'The time is surely coming when ...' (8:11). The second strand of new material in this Exilic Redactional Composition is of a liturgical nature, evident in the doxologies 4:13, 5:8–9; 9:5–6 and in the series of sayings in 4:6–11 with its repeated 'yet you did not return to me'. The language of the doxologies is different from most of the Amos-text, and has its closest linguistic and theological parallels in Job 9:1–12 and Isaiah 40:12, 22–23. Scholars generally date Isaiah 40–55 to the exilic period, and the book of Job to the exilic or post-exilic period, so there is good reason to date Amos 4:13; 5:8–9; and 9:5–6 to this period too. The exilic editors placed these verses at structurally significant points: 4:13 ends the first half of the 'Words of Amos' in chapters 3–6; 5:8–9 comes at the very centre of the chiastic verses 5:1–17, at the centre of the book; and 9:5–6 forms the conclusion. Ahead of 4:13 is 4:6–12, which Jeremias describes as an exilic penitential liturgy.[19] The closest parallels to these verses are found within Leviticus 26, Deuteronomy 28, and 1 Kings 8:33–37, all of which are generally dated to the exilic period.[20] The commentary will note some other additions made in the redaction (see on 1:1, 2; 3:1b, 13–14; 5:6, 13, 25–26; 7:9, 16). Eidevall attributes the visions series of chapters 7–9 to this redaction. Noting the similarity of some aspects of the vision reports to Jeremiah 1:11–14; 24:1–5, he deduces that in these chapters 'Amos ... is not pictured as an uncompromising prophet of doom.... He is instead portrayed as a prophet like Moses, or even more to the point, as a

---

[18] W. H. Schmidt, 'Die deuteronomistische Redaktion des Amosbuches: Zu der theologischen Unterschieden zwischen dem Prophetenwort und seinem Sammler', *ZAW* 77 (1965): 168–93.

[19] J. Jeremias *Amos* (1998): 8, 67.

[20] R. Albertz, *Israel in Exile: The History and Literature of the Sixth Century BCE* (Studies in Biblical Literature, 3; Atlanta, GA: SBL, 2003): 227 considers that we should identify two distinct literary layers here: an early exilic composition which introduced 4:6–13 and the doxologies, and a subsequent later exilic composition which introduced the Deuteronomistic material. However it is hard to demonstrate that the liturgical strand is specifically 'early exilic', and the view of Jeremias that we should take this as one composition with these two strands of new material is to be preferred.

A Introduction to Amos 267

prophet like Jeremiah.'[21] However, the account in 7:10–17 appears to interrupt the series of visions, and since this account is itself from this period or earlier, an earlier dating of the series is to be preferred.

Going further back, the preceding Late Pre-exilic Redactional Composition of the last quarter of the seventh century has less, but still significant, new material. Notable is the inclusion of the narrative episode of 7:10–17, with 7:9 as a connecting verse. These verses bring into the text that rejection of the prophetic message constituted a reason for judgement additional to those already described in the earlier, first composition. Evidently those who produced this redactional composition felt that the people of Judah in their own day were in danger of making the same mistakes that the people of northern Israel had made a century before. Also significant is the entry of 8:3–7, between the fourth and fifth visions. These verses heighten the tension before the fifth and final vision. They also link the visions series back to the OAN series by providing a reinterpretation of 2:6–8. The commentary will note that 3:8 and 6:9–10 came into the text in this redactional composition, as well as additions in 2:8.

This brings us to the earliest written form of the text, the Post-722 Composition. This was formed with a clear structure from the outset, comprising:

> Superscription: 1:1
> Series of five OAN: 1:3–8, 13–15; 2:1–3, 6–9, 13–16
> Words addressed to the people of Israel: 3:1–4:5 (minus some later material)
> Words addressed to the house of Israel: 5:1–6:14 (minus some later material)
> Series of five visions: 7:1–8; 8:1–2; 9:1–4

This structure was present in this earliest, first composition of the text and, while partially disturbed by subsequent additions, remains evident in the final form of the text.

Some scholars believe that a first literary composition was made before the destruction of Samaria in 722, perhaps after an earthquake that was seen as a fulfilment of Amos's words. Indeed, Hadjiev goes further in arguing that there were originally two pre-722 scrolls containing Amos-material, a 'Repentance Scroll' containing words now found in 4:1–6:7, and a 'Polemical Scroll' comprising the five OAN and the five visions. These, he suggests, were combined in the seventh century.[22] While this is an attractive

---

[21]   G. Eidevall *Amos* (2017): 23.
[22]   T. S. Hadjiev *Composition and Redaction* (2009): 183–209.

268   *Book of Amos*

suggestion, it is doubtful whether there is enough evidence in the text to support it. As noted, the further back in time and number of literary layers proposed, the more tentative the proposals become, and I find Hadjiev's proposals unconvincing.[23]

Key Themes in the Book of Amos

The Post-722 Composition contains some strong theological themes. Central is the judgement of YHWH upon Israel, and upon the nations in chapters 1–2. The judgement on the nations is described as a sending of devouring and destroying fire (1:4, etc.). With regard to Israel, the final units of the OAN and visions series (2:13–16; 9:1–4) interweave descriptions of punishment by earthquake and by defeat in battle. Punishment by earthquake is also found in 3:15; 6:11; and by military defeat in 4:2b–3; 5:3; 6:14. Punishment by exile is found in 1:6, 15; 5:5, 27; 6:7. The theme of the destruction of houses appears in 3:15; 5:11; 6:11. The dominant reason for judgement, expressed in many units, is the mistreatment and exploitation of the poor by the rich and powerful. The text takes it as self-evident that such behaviours were 'wrong'. In the earliest literary layer this is not reinforced by reference to any of Israel's legal or sapiential traditions.

While this sounds a harsh message, it gave an explanation of why the Assyrians had destroyed the northern kingdom. It was not, as many might have been tempted to believe, because the Assyrian gods were more powerful than YHWH. Nor was it because YHWH was no longer taking any interest in his people. Rather, Israel's wrongdoing over many years had caused YHWH to allow this calamity. There is, as Barton puts it, 'a purposeful element of theodicy in the prophetic announcements of judgment'.[24] The modern reader, schooled in the scientific method of the Enlightenment, may decline to see such disasters as derived from the actions of God; however, such a view was normal in the ancient world, and the Post-722 Composition of Amos would have helped people to make sense of the defeat and destruction of the northern kingdom at the hands of the Assyrians.

The announcement of judgement seems categorical in some verses. Most notably, 8:2 states that 'The end has come upon my people Israel', and

---

[23]   See my evaluation of Hadjiev's work in G. R. Hamborg *Still Selling the Righteous* (2012): 41–4.

[24]   J. Barton, 'History and Rhetoric in the Prophets', in M. Warner (ed.), *The Bible as Rhetoric: Studies in Biblical Persuasion and Credibility* (Warwick Studies in Philosophy and Literature; London: Routledge, 1990): 51–64 (52).

A Introduction to Amos

reinforces the verdict of verses such as 2:13–16; 3:15; 4:2–3; 6:14. Yet there is an apparently contrasting theme in 5:4, namely the invitation to 'Seek me and live', on which 5:14–15 expands: 'Seek good and not evil, that you may live.... Hate evil and love good, and establish justice in the gate. It may be that the Lord will be gracious to the remnant of Joseph.' Commentators have handled this contrast in various ways. Some have concluded that the invitations to 'seek' must belong to a later literary layer.[25] However, this is argued on the basis of content alone, and this one single criterion should not be deemed sufficient to warrant such a conclusion. Others imagine that there must have been progression in Amos's own ministry: initially he hoped for repentance and spoke words of invitation, but as he failed to see any response, and the third and fourth visions of categorical judgement (7:7–8; 8:1–2) were given to him, his message became one of unconditional judgement.[26] The problem here is that the text itself gives no evidence for such development, and we would have expected it to do so were it the case. Yet others recognise that the apparently unconditional announcements of judgement may, in reality, carry an unspoken, implicit 'unless you repent'. Thus Tromp writes that 'his announcements of judgment are meant to be conditional: they show the direction which the course of events is necessarily taking unless the audience changes its ways drastically'.[27] Similarly Hadjiev writes that 'the "unconditional" prophecies of doom could have functioned as implicit calls for repentance'.[28] There is without doubt some truth in this last approach. There is, however, merit in letting the tension remain unresolved; or rather, explained by the setting in which this first edition of the Amos-text was made, namely in the southern kingdom of Judah shortly after the fall of the northern kingdom in 722. The categorical announcements of judgement had been fulfilled. They therefore gave clear evidence to the post-722 readers that YHWH had brought the destruction of the northern kingdom. But those same readers needed themselves to hear the summons to 'seek me' and to 'seek good and not evil', lest Judah in turn should suffer a similar fate at YHWH's hand.

---

[25] So R. B. Coote, *Amos among the Prophets* (Philadelphia: Fortress Press, 1981); also J. Lust, 'Remarks on the Redaction of Amos V 4–6, 14–15*', in A. S. Van der Woude (ed.), *Remembering All the Way: A Collection of Old Testament Studies Published on the Occasion of the Fortieth Anniversary of the Oudtestamentisch Werkgeselschap in Nederland* (Leiden: E. J. Brill, 1981): 129–54.

[26] So F. I. Andersen and D. N. Freedman, *Amos: A New Translation with Introduction and Commentary* (AB, 24A; New York: Doubleday, 1989).

[27] N. J. Tromp, 'Amos V 1–17: Towards a Stylistic and Rhetorical Analysis', *OTS* 23 (1984): 56–83 (72).

[28] T. S. Hadjiev *Composition and Redaction* (2009): 21.

Chapters 5 and 6, in which the invitations to 'seek' occur, also include the pair of words 'justice' and 'righteousness' (5:7, 24; 6:12; simply 'justice' in 5:15). They provide a further thematic element of this Post-722 Composition. The meaning and significance of these terms will be discussed in the commentary.

The seventh-century Late Pre-exilic Redactional Composition brings a significant new theme into the text with the addition of 7:9–17. A further reason for YHWH's judgement is the rejection of the prophetic word. If the very word which was intended to bring a change of heart is instead rejected, there is yet more reason for YHWH's judgement. These verses also introduce the term 'prophet' (*nābî'*), and the verb 'prophesy' (*nb'*), as does 3:8 which is also introduced into the text in this redactional composition. This redactional composition also added 8:3–7 into the text. These verses reinterpret the earlier 2:6–7, and in the process introduce yet another reason for judgement, namely practices contrary to Israel's legal and wisdom traditions: the use of false measures, weights, and balances is prohibited in Deuteronomy 25:13–15, and verses such as Proverbs 20:23 declare them to be 'an abomination to the Lord'.

The Exilic Redactional Composition of the sixth century makes clear that, just as YHWH had allowed the destruction of the northern kingdom by the Assyrians as an act of his judgement, so now he had allowed the destruction of Jerusalem and the conquest of the kingdom of Judah by the Babylonians as a similar act of judgement. The introduction of the oracle against Judah into the OAN series (2:4–5) made this explicit. These verses give as the reason for YHWH's judgement that 'they have rejected the law of the Lord, and have not kept his statutes, but they have been led astray by the same lies after which their ancestors walked'. These constitute reasons for judgement not found in the earlier compositions. This redactional composition also refers to the exodus from Egypt, the forty years in the wilderness, and the possession of the land (2:10; 3:1; 5:25), indicating a growing understanding of these as 'saving acts' of YHWH in the light of which the people should respond by living in accord with YHWH's will. Scholars debate at what point the concept of a 'covenant' between YHWH and his people was formulated and became widely accepted.[29] Within the book of Amos it is fair to say that even though the term *bərît* is not found other than in 1:9, the concept is nascent in this Exilic Redactional Composition.

---

[29] See 'A Closer Look: The Covenant in Scholarly Research'.

A *Introduction to Amos* 271

Amos 2:11–12 builds on the theme introduced into the Late Pre-exilic Redactional Composition of the rejection of the prophetic word as a reason for judgement. While 7:13 shows Amaziah telling Amos not to prophesy at Bethel ever again, 2:11–12 generalise this theme to a widespread rejection of the prophets and nazirites who had been sent by YHWH.

The hymnic verses which entered the text in this composition (4:3; 5:8–9; 9:5–6) portray YHWH as not only the director of history and of the destiny of nations, as the earlier compositions assume, but also as director of creation itself. He forms the mountains and creates the wind (4:13); he turns darkness into morning and darkens the day into night (5:8). They show YHWH to be both Creator and Judge. YHWH as Creator 'makes destruction flash out against the strong, so that destruction comes upon the fortress' (5:9). His power in creation is also evident in the liturgical series 4:6–12, in which actions such as the withholding of rain (4:7) and striking with blight and mildew (4:9) are seen as endeavours to turn the people to call on YHWH. These endeavours fail, leading to the conclusion that the people must be ready 'to meet your God, O Israel' (4:12) – the God who ominously 'makes the morning darkness' (4:13). If there had been separate prophetic and liturgical, priestly circles in pre-exilic Judah, these verses are evidence of some coming together and mutual influence in the years in exile and beyond.

The most significant addition to the text in the Post-exilic Redactional Composition is the closing section 9:7–15. Hitherto the people have been addressed as a whole, but within these verses distinctions are made: while the eyes of YHWH are upon the 'sinful kingdom', nevertheless 'I will not utterly destroy the house of Jacob, says the Lord' (9:8); and those who will die by the sword are not the whole people but 'the sinners of my people' (9:10). This represents a move towards the kind of individual responsibility described in a chapter such as Ezekiel 18 (see also Deut. 24:16, and cf. Deut. 7:9–10; 29:16–21 [29: 15–20]). The verses 9:11–15 then describe blessings for the future, which in 9:13–15 include the blessing of abundant fertility in the land. These verses reverse some of the previous judgements. For example, 5:2 had declared that maiden Israel is 'fallen, no more to rise … with no one to raise her up'; 9:11 then declares that 'On that day I will raise up the booth of David that is fallen.' The verbs for 'rise/raise' and 'fallen' are the same in both verses. Similarly 9:14 reverses 5:11.

It is noteworthy that the promises of hope are saved until the end of the book. The judgements announced and the reasons for them are allowed to stand as they are and be heard first of all. There is an implication that these promises of blessing carry the warning: 'as long as you do not lapse back into the old, sinful ways described in this book'.

The commentary will take account of the four literary contexts outlined, in line with the view expressed in the 'Volume Introduction' that there is interpretative meaning in all the stages of composition which can plausibly be identified. At most points in the book of Amos the beginning and ending of sections is clear, and the commentary follows them.

B SUGGESTED READINGS ON AMOS

Introductory Works

The 2002 commentary of Carroll R. surveys literature up to its publication date, with his 2019 review article bringing his survey up to date. Houston's Phoenix Guide is particularly helpful in introducing recent approaches to the text, and argues some particular positions of its own. Auld's older volume retains value. Barton's volume is written in his ever-lucid style and is invaluable.

Auld A. G., *Amos* (OTG; Sheffield: JSOT Press, 1986).
Barton J., *The Theology of the Book of Amos* (Cambridge: Cambridge University Press, 2012).
Carroll R., M. D., *Amos – The Prophet and His Oracles* (Louisville, KY: Westminster John Knox Press, 2002).
Carroll R., M. D., 'Twenty Years of Amos Research', *CBR* 18 (2019): 32–58.
Houston W. J., *Amos: Justice and Violence* (Phoenix Guides to the Old Testament, 26; Sheffield: Sheffield Phoenix Press, 2015).

Commentaries

The commentary of H. W. Wolff (1977) is a seminal work which subsequent commentators cannot ignore, whether or not they agree with his approach. That of Jeremias (1998) is the commentary closest to my own approach: I consider it unsurpassed. Paul's and Carroll R.'s commentaries both consider that the great majority of the text contains words of the prophet Amos, and both contain a wealth of detailed comment. Coggins's and Linville's volumes both comment on the final form of the text.

Andersen F. I. and D. N. Freedman, *Amos: A New Translation with Introduction and Commentary* (AB, 24A; New York: Doubleday, 1989).

B Suggested Readings on Amos

Carroll R., M. D., *The Book of Amos* (NICOT; Grand Rapids, MI: Eerdmans, 2020).

Coggins R. J., *Joel and Amos* (NCB; Sheffield: Sheffield Academic Press, 2000).

Cripps R. S., *A Critical and Exegetical Commentary on the Book of Amos* (2nd ed., London: SPCK, 1955).

Eidevall G., *Amos* (AYB, 24G; New Haven, CT: Yale University Press, 2017).

Goldingay J., *Hosea–Micah* (BCOT; Grand Rapids, MI: Baker Academic, 2020).

Hadjiev T. S., *Joel and Amos* (TOTC, 25; London: IVP, 2020).

Harper W. R., *A Critical and Exegetical Commentary on Amos and Hosea* (ICC; Edinburgh: T&T Clark, 1905).

Jeremias J., *The Book of Amos: A Commentary* (trans. D. W. Stott; Louisville, KY: Westminster John Knox Press, 1998).

Linville J. R., *Amos and the Cosmic Imagination* (SOTSMS; Aldershot: Ashgate Publishing Company, 2008).

Mays J. L., *Amos: A Commentary* (OTL; London: SCM, 1969).

Nogalski J. D., *The Book of the Twelve: Hosea–Jonah* (Smyth & Helwys Bible Commentary; Macon, GA: Smyth & Helwys, 2011).

Paul S M., *Amos* (Hermeneia; Philadelphia: Fortress Press, 1991).

Rudolph W., *Joel–Amos–Obadja–Jona* (KAT, 13/2; Gütersloh: Gütersloher Verlagshaus, 1971).

Soggin J. A., *The Prophet Amos: A Translation and Commentary* (trans. J. Bowden; London: SCM, 1987).

Sweeney M. A., *The Twelve Prophets, vol. 1: Hosea, Joel, Amos, Obadiah, Jonah* (Berit Olam Studies in Hebrew Narrative and Poetry; Collegeville, MN: Liturgical Press, 2000).

Wolff H. W., *Joel and Amos* (trans. W. Janzen, S. D. McBride Jr., and C. A. Muenchow; Hermeneia; Philadelphia: Fortress Press, 1977).

Special Studies

The volumes of Barstad, Carroll R., Coote, Crenshaw, Hagedorn and Mein, Hadjiev, Hamborg, Möller, and Radine are all substantive studies. Out of a myriad of articles on Amos, those included address particular issues of importance.

Ackroyd P R., 'A Judgment Narrative between Kings and Chronicles? An Approach to Amos 7.9-17', in G. W. Coats and B. O. Long (eds.), *Canon and Authority: Essays in Old Testament Religion and Theology*

(Philadelphia: Fortress Press, 1977): 71–87; repr. P. R. Ackroyd, *Studies in the Religious Tradition of the Old Testament* (London: SCM, 1987): 196–208.

Asen B., 'No, Yes and Perhaps in Amos and the Yahwist', *VT* 43 (1993): 433–41.

Barré M., 'The Meaning of *l' 'šybnw* in Amos 1.3–2.6', *JBL* 105 (1986): 611–31.

Barstad H. M., *The Religious Polemics of Amos* (VTSup, 34; Leiden: E. J. Brill, 1984).

Barstad H. M., 'Can Prophetic Texts Be Dated? Amos 1–2 as an Example', in L. L. Grabbe (ed.), *Ahab Agonistes: The Rise and Fall of the Omri Dynasty* (London: T&T Clark, 2007): 21–40.

Barton J., *Amos's Oracles against the Nation: A Study of Amos 1.3–2.5* (SOTSMS, 6; Cambridge: Cambridge University Press, 1980).

Brettler M. Z., 'Redaction, History, and Redaction-History of Amos in Recent Scholarship', in B. E. Kelle and M. B. Moore (eds.), *Israel's Prophets and Israel's Past: Essays on the Relationship of Prophetic Texts and Israelite History on Honor of John H Hayes* (LHBOTS, 446; New York: T&T Clark, 2006): 103–12.

Carroll R., M. D., *Contexts for Amos: Prophetic Poetics in Latin American Perspective* (JSOTSup, 132; Sheffield: JSOT Press, 1992).

Coote R. B., *Amos among the Prophets* (Philadelphia: Fortress Press, 1981).

Crenshaw J. L., *Hymnic Affirmation of Divine Justice: The Doxologies of Amos and Related Texts in the Old Testament* (SBLDS, 24; Missouri: Scholars Press, 1975).

Davies P. R., 'Amos, Man and Book', in B. E. Kelle and M. B. Moore (eds.), *Israel's Prophets and Israel's Past* (2006): 113–31.

Davies P. R., 'Why Do We Know About Amos?' in D. V. Edelman and E. Ben Zvi (eds.), *The Production of Prophecy: Constructing Prophecy and Prophets in Yehud* (Bible World; London: Equinox Publishing Ltd, 2009): 55–72.

Eidevall G., 'A Farewell to the Anticultic Prophet: Attitudes to the Cult in the Book of Amos', in L.-S. Tiemeyer (ed.), *Priests and Cults in the Book of the Twelve* (ANEM, 14; Atlanta, GA: SBL Press, 2016): 99–114.

Gese H., 'Komposition bei Amos', in J. A. Emerton (ed.), *Congress Volume, Vienna, 1980* (VTSup, 32; Leiden: E. J. Brill, 1981): 74–95.

Hadjiev T. S., *The Composition and Redaction of the Book of Amos* (BZAW, 393; Berlin: W. de Gruyter, 2009).

Hagedorn A. C. and A. Mein (eds.), *Aspects of Amos: Exegesis and Interpretation* (LHBOTS, 536; New York/London: T&T Clark, 2011).

B *Suggested Readings on Amos*

Hamborg G R., *Still Selling the Righteous: A Redaction-Critical Investigation into Reasons for Judgment in Amos 2:6-16* (LHBOTS, 555; New York/London: T&T Clark, 2012).

Houston W. J., *Contending for Justice: Ideologies and Theologies of Social Justice in the Old Testament* (LHBOTS, 428; London: T&T Clark, 2006): 52–73.

Jeremias J., 'Amos 3–6: From the Oral Word to the Text', in G. M. Tucker, D. L. Petersen, and R. R. Wilson (eds.), *Canon, Theology and Old Testament Interpretation: Essays in Honor of Brevard S. Childs* (Philadelphia: Fortress Press, 1988): 217–29.

Jeremias J., *Hosea und Amos: Studien zur den Anfängen des Dodekapropheton* (FAT, 13; Tübingen: J. C. B. Mohr, 1995).

Jeremias J., 'The Interrelationship between Amos and Hosea', in J. W. Watts and P. R. House (eds.), *Forming Prophetic Literature: Essays on Isaiah and the Twelve in Honor of John D. W. Watts* (JSOTSup, 235; Sheffield: Sheffield Academic Press, 1996): 171–86.

Kapelrud A, S. *Central Ideas in Amos* (Oslo: Universitetsforlaget, 1961).

Knierim R. P., '"I will not cause it to return" in Amos 1 and 2', in G. Coats and B. Long (eds.), *Canon and Authority in Old Testament Religion and Theology* (Philadelphia: Fortress Press, 1977): 163–75.

Linville J.R., 'What Does "It" Mean? Interpretation at the Point of No Return in Amos 1–2', *Biblical Interpretation* 8.4 (2000): 400–24.

McConville J. G., '"How Can Jacob Stand? He is So Small!" (Amos 7.2): The Prophetic Word and the Re-Imagining of Israel', in B. E. Kelle and M. B. Moore (eds.), *Israel's Prophets and Israel's Past* (2006): 132–51.

Möller K., *A Prophet in Debate: The Rhetoric of Persuasion in the Book of Amos* (JSOTSup, 372; London: Sheffield Academic Press, 2002).

Park A. W., *The Book of Amos as Composed and Read in Antiquity* (SBL; New York: Peter Lang, 2001).

Radine J., *The Book of Amos in Emergent Judah* (FAT, 2/45; Tübingen: Mohr Siebeck, 2010).

Rottzoll D. U., *Studien zur Redaktion und Komposition des Amosbuchs* (BZAW, 243; Berlin: W. de Gruyter, 1996).

Schmidt W. H., 'Die deuteronomistische Redaktion des Amosbuches. Zu den theologischen Unterschieden zwischen dem Prophetenwort und seinem Sammler', *ZAW* 77 (1965): 168–93.

Waard J. de, 'The Chiastic Structure of Amos V.1–17', *VT* 27 (1977): 170–7.

Williamson H. G. M., 'The Prophet and the Plumb-Line: A Redaction-Critical Study of Amos 7', *OTS* 26 (1990): 101–21.

276   *Book of Amos*

C COMMENTARY ON AMOS

1 A Series of Oracles against the Nations – Amos 1–2

Amos 1:1 – Heading

> 1 **The words of Amos, who was among the shepherds of Tekoa, which he**
> **saw concerning Israel in the days of King Uzziah of Judah and in the days**
> **of King Jeroboam son of Joash of Israel, two years before the earthquake.**

The book is introduced as the words of Amos, who was among the shepherds of Tekoa. Tekoa was a Judean village to the south of Jerusalem, and 7:12 confirms that Amos was from Judah. The word translated as 'shepherds' is the plural of *nōqēd*, which is not the usual Hebrew word for 'shepherd'. It occurs only here and in 2 Kings 3:4, where it is said of Mesha king of Moab that he was a *nōqēd* – translated by NRSV in that verse as 'sheep-breeder'. The latter translation, or possibly 'sheep-farmer', would fit well with 7:14, where Amos describes himself as 'a herdsman and a dresser of sycamore trees'.

The verse contains two relative clauses, making an overloaded sentence and indicating expansion from an originally simpler form. The heading to the first composition was probably: 'The words of Amos from Tekoa which he saw concerning Israel two years before the earthquake.' The chronological note referring to the kings of Judah and Israel is a characteristically Deuteronomistic dating formula, and was added in the exilic period. At first reading, it is strange that the second relative clause describes Amos as seeing words: one would expect someone to hear words and see visions, not to see words. The book, of course, contains both prophetic words and visions. More importantly, however, the verb here for 'seeing' is *ḥāzāh*. This is not the word used for everyday seeing, but is regularly used of prophetic words and visions (cf. the almost identical Isa. 2:1). Nouns from the same root include 'seer' and 'vision'. See further 'A Closer Look: Seers and Prophets'.

The heading dates the ministry of Amos to 'two years before the earthquake'. This would give a precise date if we knew the year in which the earthquake occurred! (I sometimes ask students if they can remember the year of the 'Boxing Day tsunami' which devastated countries bordering the Pacific and Indian oceans: most struggle to be sure, and I would guess that in a further forty years few will know). Clearly it was a major, catastrophic, and memorable occurrence. It is also referred to in Zechariah 14:5. However, this verse's knowledge of it may derive Amos 1:1, and therefore not be independent corroboration. Several commentators (e.g. Mays, Wolff, Paul) refer to the 1950s and 60s excavations of the archaeologist Yadin at Hazor,

C Commentary on Amos

from which Yadin deduced that there was a significant earthquake around the year 760. If this was the earthquake referred to, then Amos's ministry would have been around 762.[30] However, Yadin may have deduced his dating of the earthquake to 760 with the help of Amos 1:1, in which case we have a circular argument.[31] Houston suggests that Isaiah 2:12–17; 5:25; and 9:10 [9] may also refer to this earthquake, and cites more recent archaeological discussion which points to an earthquake in the mid-eighth century.[32] This earthquake may have been seen as a fulfilment of some of the words of Amos, ensuring that any transcriptions made were not lost or destroyed. This phrase indicates that Amos's ministry was brief and focused, in contrast to those whose ministries spanned several years.

In the Exilic Redactional Composition, a chronological note relating Amos's ministry to the reigns of the kings of Judah and Israel has been added. This Deuteronomistic addition cross-references the Amos-text to the so-called Deuteronomistic History (Joshua–2 Kings). Uzziah reigned from 783 to 742, and Jeroboam II from 786 to 746, giving a period of 783–746 within which the earthquake and Amos's ministry took place. The Deuteronomistic historian describes Jeroboam's reign in 2 Kings 14:23–29, condemning Jeroboam for doing 'evil in the sight of YHWH'. Reference is also made to his successful restoration of a border, and of the restoration to Israel of the cities of Damascus and Hamath. This success in military and political terms is often taken as an indication of a prosperous reign. However, Houston argues that success in taking back territory does not necessarily imply economic prosperity, and suggests that times of military activity can also be times of economic stringency, in which the poor suffer the most.[33]

Amos 1:2 – YHWH Roars from Zion

[2] And he said:
The Lord roars from Zion,
   and utters his voice from Jerusalem;
the pastures of the shepherds wither,
   and the top of
Carmel dries up.

---

[30] J. L. Mays *Amos* (1969): 20; S. M. Paul *Amos* (1991): 35; H. W. Wolff *Joel and Amos* (1977): 124.
[31] G. Eidevall *Amos* (2017): 6, 96.
[32] W. J. Houston, *Amos: Justice and Violence* (Phoenix Guides to the Old Testament, 26; Sheffield: Sheffield Phoenix Press, 2015).
[33] W. J. Houston *Amos: Justice and Violence* (2015): 53–4.

278   *Book of Amos*

The initial 'And he said' makes 1:2 a word of Amos that 'YHWH roars from Zion'. The verse stands at the head of the text indicating that it should all be seen as deriving from YHWH. In fact, Amos is mentioned only in 1:1 and 7:10–17. In all other parts of the text the words stand alone as those of YHWH.

The place of origin of YHWH's roaring is Zion/Jerusalem. Just as Amos is from the southern village of Tekoa, so YHWH speaks from the capital city of the southern kingdom of Judah, where in due course the first text of Amos would be written. The roar reaches to Mount Carmel, in the north of the northern kingdom of Israel. The Jewish historian Josephus suggests that in this period of the divided monarchy Carmel may have formed the boundary between Tyre and Israel. This verse therefore indicates that the voice of YHWH speaks, and his judgement extends, over the whole of the kingdom of Israel. That YHWH roars rather than whispers or merely speaks alerts the reader to the forceful nature of the words to come in the text.

This introductory verse draws from other verses in the Amos-text, signalling some of what is to come. The series of questions in 3:3–8 ends: 'The lion has roared; who will not fear? The Lord God has spoken; who can but prophesy?' The characteristic parallelism of Hebrew poetry links YHWH's speaking with the roaring of a lion, and 1:2 makes it explicit that it is YHWH who roars. The inclusion of the 'top of Carmel' links it with 9:3, the final vision in which YHWH's judgement is seen as being executed. Jeremias comments that 'during this period Mount Carmel, with its dense forests, together with Bashan (cf. Amos 4:1), Lebanon, or the plain of Sharon, stands representatively for the most fertile regions of Palestine'.[34] Finally, the verb 'wither' ('*ābhal*) links it with 9:5, where NRSV's 'mourn' is the same word in Hebrew. This last verse formed the conclusion (9:5–6) of the Amos-text in the Exilic Redactional Composition, and it is likely that 1:2 was incorporated into the text at this point too.

As discussed in the 'Volume Introduction', Amos 1:2a is virtually identical to Joel 3:16a [4:16a]. In the Hebrew Bible, in which Amos follows Joel, they are only a few verses apart (the LXX order is different). It is unlikely that this is accidental. It is probably part of the process by which the first part of the Book of the Twelve was compiled and edited. This same half-verse is found yet again in Jeremiah 25:30, although here 'from Zion' and 'from Jerusalem' have been replaced by 'from on high' and 'from his holy habitation': we may surmise, perhaps, that the change was made in the exilic

[34] J. Jeremias *Amos* (1998): 14.

C Commentary on Amos

period in which Zion/Jerusalem had been destroyed. The common Amos 1:2a and Joel 3:16a remind the reader that Amos is part of the Book of the Twelve; and the editors of Jeremiah link that text with Amos, confirming that both are to be recognised as part of the prophetic corpus.

A Closer Look: Zion

The etymology and origin of the term 'Zion' are uncertain. It occurs a hundred and fifty-two times in the Hebrew Bible, of which ninety-three are in prophetic texts (forty-six in Isaiah), and thirty-seven in the Psalms. Its earliest mention is in 2 Samuel 5.7, where it is recounted that 'David took the stronghold of Zion, which is now the city of David' (and one possible etymology, on the basis of an Arabic parallel, is that it once meant 'hilltop ridge' or 'fortress'). While it may originally have referred to a particular part of Jerusalem, its most prevalent use is as a synonym for the city. In some passages it refers to the Temple. Scholars describe some psalms as 'Zion Psalms': notably 46, 48, and 76 (some also include 84, 87, 122, and 132, or earlier, subsequently expanded, versions of them). In the exilic Psalm 137 Israel's tormentors mock saying 'Sing us one of the songs of Zion.' YHWH dwells in Zion (Pss. 9:11; 76:2; Isa. 8:18). He blesses from Zion (Pss. 128:5; 134:3). He rules and judges from Zion (Ps. 2:6). From Zion his law/instruction (*tôrâ*) goes forth (Isa. 2:3/Mic. 4:2). His rule from Zion is not only over the nation of Israel, but over all the nations of the world (Ps. 46:5–6). In the exilic period, Zion's restoration is longed for, and safe return there is promised in Isaiah 51:11, so that YHWH will once again reign there (Isa. 52:7). Jerusalem's inhabitants can be referred to as the 'Daughter of Zion' (twenty-two times e.g. Isa. 1:8; only once plural 'daughters of Zion', in Song 3:11; once only 'sons of Zion', in Lam. 4:2).

In the poetic parallelism of Amos 1:2, 'Zion' and 'Jerusalem' are clearly one and the same, and it is the place from which YHWH's judgement is pronounced.

Amos 1:3–2:3 – Oracles against Foreign Nations

³ Thus says the Lord:
   For three transgressions of Damascus,
       and for four, I will not revoke the punishment;,
   because they have threshed Gilead
       with threshing-sledges of iron.

⁴ So I will send a fire on the house of Hazael,
and it shall devour the strongholds of Ben-hadad.
⁵ I will break the gate-bars of Damascus
and cut off the inhabitants from the Valley of Aven,
and the one who holds the sceptre from Beth-eden,
and the people of Aram shall go into exile to Kir,
says the Lord.

⁶ Thus says the Lord:
For three transgressions of Gaza,
and for four, I will not revoke the punishment,
because they carried into exile entire communities,
to hand them over to Edom.
⁷ So I will send a fire on the wall of Gaza,
fire that shall devour its strongholds.
⁸ I will cut off the inhabitants from Ashdod
and the one who holds the sceptre from Ashkelon;
I will turn my hand against Ekron,
and the remnant of the Philistines shall perish,
says the Lord God.

⁹ Thus says the Lord
For three transgressions of Tyre,
and for four, I will not revoke the punishment,
because they delivered entire communities over to Edom,
and did not remember the covenant of kinship.
¹⁰ So I will send a fire on the wall of Tyre,
fire that shall devour its strongholds.

¹¹ Thus says the Lord:
For three transgressions of Edom,
and for four, I will not revoke the punishment,
because he pursued his brother with the sword
and cast off all pity;
he maintained his anger perpetually
and kept his wrath for ever.
¹² So I will send a fire on Teman,
and it shall devour the strongholds of Bozrah.

¹³ Thus says the Lord:
For three transgressions of the Ammonites,
and for four, I will not revoke the punishment,
because they have ripped open pregnant women in Gilead
in order to enlarge their territory.

C Commentary on Amos

281

> [14] So I will kindle a fire against the wall of Rabbah,
>> and it shall devour its strongholds,
> with shouting on the day of battle,
>> with a storm on the day of the whirlwind;
> [15] then their king shall go into exile,
>> he and his officials together,
> says the Lord.

> 2 Thus says the Lord:
> For three transgressions of Moab,
>> and for four, I will not revoke the punishment,
> because he burned to lime
>> the bones of the king of Edom.
> [2] So I will send a fire on Moab,
>> and it shall devour the strongholds of Kerioth,
> and Moab shall die amid uproar,
>> amid shouting and the sound of the trumpet;
> [3] I will cut off the ruler from its midst,
>> and will kill all its officials with him,
> says the Lord.

Amos 1:2 alerted the reader to expect forceful words of judgement. Such words are first directed not at Israel, but towards other nations. The climax to the series is the oracle against Israel in 2:6–16, and the whole series is for Israel's hearing. This is not to say that the OAN lack theological value in themselves: far from it. But it is to say that Israel was in no position to join in the criticism and judgement voiced towards other nations when her own house needed to be put in order.

The climaxing of the series of OAN with the oracle against Israel introduces us to a characteristic feature of the Amos-text, namely that there are several places in which rhetorical force is achieved by building an expectation and then suddenly and climactically reversing it. This OAN series is the most notable. Some question whether, in fact, much should be made of this element of surprise, since a text written down for reading and re-reading necessarily becomes familiar, and therefore not a surprise at all. However, as one who has studied the Amos-text over many years, I still feel the force of this rhetorical strategy, and I see no reason to doubt that ancient readers would have done so. Barton summarises this rhetorical strategy well:

> It is clear that the culmination of the sequence in an oracle against Israel itself is a deliberate part of the structure. The audience has to be imagined applauding after each oracle against a foreign nation.... This is the kind of thing an

audience would expect from a prophet. The oracle against Israel is meant to wipe the smile off their faces, as YHWH turns from judgment on their enemies to judgment in themselves.[35]

As Goldingay puts it: the OAN 'lull the Ephraimites into a sense of false security before kicking them in the teeth'.[36] Theologically the OAN recognise and express that the judgement of YHWH is not limited to his own people, but that other nations too are accountable to him. Each oracle indicts the nation concerned of having committed 'transgressions'. The word 'transgression' (*pešaʿ*) may be used to refer to offences against individuals, political rebellion against rulers, and sin against God. The question arises of the basis of judgement against non-Israelite nations. In some of the other OAN collections in the prophetic books it is because a nation has acted wrongfully against Israel that YHWH will judge them (e.g. Ezek. 25:12–14), and a minority of commentators has tried to interpret Amos 1:3–2:3 in the same way. Others have noted that most of the nations addressed in these oracles were once part of the Davidic empire, and have suggested that they are being judged for their rebellion in no longer being subject to Israel. Some have held that an Israelite covenant between YHWH and his people existed which was extended to other nations, so that their offence was in the breaking of a covenant. Others, again, have wondered whether there were formal agreements about the behaviour of nations in war – a kind of ancient Geneva Convention. More likely than any of these suggestions, however, is that Amos viewed certain kinds of atrocity and appalling actions in war as simply and inherently 'wrong' in moral terms. Once again, Barton expresses this well:

> The prophet speaks as though there was almost a kind of self-evidence about the moral norm contravened by the nations.... It looks as if people in Israel had certain beliefs about what it was acceptable to do even in wartime, which they thought other nations ought to accept too. That would make ancient Israelite society very like many other societies, both ancient and modern, in which most people have a more or less vague sense that certain things are outrageous.[37]

The OAN follow a set structure, although with two variant patterns. Three oracles that entered the text in the Exilic Redactional Composition (1:9–10; 1:11–12; 2:4–5) are slightly different from those belonging to the

---

[35] J. Barton, *Theology of the Book of Amos* (Cambridge: Cambridge University Press, 2012): 57.
[36] J. Goldingay, *Hosea–Micah* (BCOT; Grand Rapids, MI: Baker Academic, 2020): 257. Goldingay uses the term 'Ephraim' as his preferred designation of northern Israel.
[37] J. Barton *Theology of the Book of Amos* (2012): 59.

C Commentary on Amos

earliest Post-722 Composition (1:3–5; 1:6–8; 1:13–15; 2:1–3). The structure of those in the Post-722 Composition is as follows:

(1) The so-called 'Messenger Formula': 'Thus says YHWH'.
(2) A graded numerical sequence introduces a summary announcement of judgement: 'For three transgressions of Xxx and for four, I will not revoke the punishment.'
(3) A reason for the announcement of judgement is given, beginning simply 'because …' (*'al*).
(4) Judgement is announced, in each case beginning 'So I will send a fire on … and it shall devour the strongholds of Yyy.' The description of the judgement then continues in words specific to each oracle.
(5) A closing formula: 'says YHWH'.

The oracles of exilic origin (1:9–10; 1:11–12; 2:4–5) follow essentially the same pattern, but differ from it in three respects. Firstly, the reason for judgement (element 3) is longer, with two reasons given rather than one. Secondly, the announcement of judgement (element 4) is shorter, with no continuation beyond the 'I will send a fire' which will 'devour its strongholds', and thus nothing specific to that nation. Thirdly, the closing formula is absent. Additionally it may be noted that the first half of the reason for judgement in 1:9 is adapted from that in 1:6. There is no such repetition elsewhere in the series.

Before proceeding to comment on each of the OAN separately, it will be helpful to comment on those features that are common to them all.

Thus Says YHWH (1:3, 6, 9, 11, 13; 2:1, 4, 6)

This formula, found in several prophetic texts, is frequent in Amos. As well as its occurrences in the OAN it is found also in 3:11, 12; 5:3, 4, 16; 7:17. It is widely referred to as the 'Messenger Formula'.[38] This phrase, taken from usage in a range of settings, is used in prophetic texts to convey the sense that the prophets were to be seen as messengers of YHWH. An example of its secular usage is found in Genesis 32:3–5,[39] where we read that Jacob sent messengers ahead of him to his brother Esau, instructing them: 'Thus shall you say to my lord Esau: Thus says your servant Jacob', and the message

---

[38] Among several works which treat this formula, a classic treatment is C. Westermann, *Basic Forms of Prophetic Speech* (trans. H. C. White; Cambridge/Louisville, KY: Lutterworth Press/Westminster/John Knox Press, 1991): 98–128.

[39] The translator of Westermann's work uses the term 'profane' (C. Westermann *Basic Forms* (1991): 93) rather than 'secular': the latter seems more helpful, however.

284   *Book of Amos*

then follows. Or again, in 2 Kings 18:28–29: 'Then the Rabshekah stood and called out in a loud voice in the language of Judah: "Hear the word of the great king, the king of Assyria! Thus says the king"', and again the message follows. Westermann deduces from the parallels with secular usage that the 'prophet, as a messenger of God who delivers God's word, understands himself as the bearer of a message',[40] that is, a divine message from YHWH. As Jeremias writes, 'in prophetic contexts it serves to legitimize the prophets' divine commission before their listeners'.[41] In written prophetic texts it became a formulaic introduction to a unit. However, the sense that the words that follow carry divine authority persists.

For Three Transgressions of XXX and for Four (1:3, 6, 9, 11, 13; 2:1, 4, 6)
Graded numerical sayings are characteristic of wisdom literature. For example, Proverbs 30:21–23 begins: 'Under three things the earth trembles; under four it cannot bear up' (cf. Prov. 6:16–19; 30:15–16, 18–19, 29–31; Job 5:19–26; 33:14–15). Wolff instances this as one of several links that he sees between the Amos-text and Israel's wisdom tradition, and he argues that the prophet Amos was steeped in the traditions of ancient Israelite clan wisdom.[42] The degree to which this is so is debatable. However, the parallels help us to see that the formula used here is an entirely natural one. Equivalent idioms in English would be 'For transgression after transgression' or 'For one transgression after another'.

I Will Not Revoke the Punishment (1:3, 6, 9, 11, 13; 2:1, 4, 6)
Translation sometimes necessitates interpretation. The Hebrew literally says 'I will not cause it to return', without specifying to what the 'it' refers. NRSV's translation follows the most frequently adopted solution, namely that it refers to the coming punishment (so Jeremias, Mays, Paul). Other possibilities that have been suggested are: the announcement of punishment, as distinct from the punishment itself (Wolff); the 'Day of YHWH' (Maag); YHWH's anger (Harper, Knierim, Coote); the roar of YHWH referred to in 1:2 (Andersen and Freedman).[43] Jeremias rightly notes, with regard to

---

[40]   C. Westermann *Basic Forms* (1991): 93.
[41]   J. Jeremias *Amos* (1998): 21.
[42]   H. W. Wolff, *Amos the Prophet: The Man and His Background* (Philadelphia: Fortress Press, 1973).
[43]   The works referred to here are: F. I. Andersen and D. N. Freedman *Amos* (1989): 234–5; R. B. Coote *Amos among the Prophets* (1981): 115; W. R. Harper, *A Critical and Exegetical Commentary on Amos and Hosea* (ICC: Edinburgh, T&T Clark, 1905): 16; J. Jeremias *Amos*

C Commentary on Amos

Wolff's distinction, that the question of whether the 'it' refers to the punishment or to the announcement of that punishment is of little consequence. NRSV's translation is entirely proper, and the most likely meaning. It is possible that the lack of precise referent is deliberate. Paul refers to this as a 'rhetorical device of frightening and suspense-ridden anticipation',[44] and indeed this unspecified judgement feels more ominous than one that is defined. The deliberate openness in the text allows future readers and hearers of the text to interpret it in terms relevant to their contemporary situation.[45]

'So I Will Send A Fire ... and It Shall Devour the Strongholds' (1:4, 7, 10, 12, 14; 2:2, 5)

The destruction of cities and walls by burning with fire was a normal part of warfare in the world of the ancient Near East. Wolff refers to the Assyrian emperor Shalmaneser III's description of his conquest of Hamath, in which he records that 'I threw fire into his palaces.'[46] In these OAN, YHWH becomes the enemy of each nation or city as he brings his judgement upon them. The term 'strongholds' occurs mainly in the prophetic books, especially Amos and Jeremiah. Out of thirty-four occurrences in the Hebrew Bible, eleven occur in Amos, six of them in the OAN series. It carries the implication of fine and well-fortified buildings, which nevertheless will not stand before the judgement of YHWH. As Wolff notes: 'Even the fortified wall will not withstand the divine pyrotechnics.'[47]

The Order and Historical Setting of the OAN

Apart from the Israel oracle coming at the end, and the Judah oracle before it in the Exilic Redactional Composition, it is difficult to discern any particular pattern or purpose in the order of the oracles. This is true whether one looks at the final form of the series of eight, or at the five oracles which constituted the series in the first, Post-722, Composition.[48] It may be noted, however, that the nations addressed are all neighbours of Israel. As a series, these OAN predict

---

(1998): 22; R. P. Knierim, '"I will not cause it to return" in Amos 1 and 2', in G. W. Coats and B. O. Long (eds.), *Canon and Authority in Old Testament Religion and Theology* (Philadelphia: Fortress Press, 1977): 163–75; V. Maag, *Text, Wortschatz und Begriffswelt des Buches Amos* (Leiden: E. J. Brill, 1951): 240, 245–57; J. L. Mays *Amos* (1969): 24; S. M. Paul *Amos* (1991): 46.

[44] S. M. Paul *Amos* (1991): 47.

[45] G. R. Hamborg *Still Selling the Righteous* (2012): 200–1.

[46] H. W. Wolff *Joel and Amos* (1977): 155.

[47] H. W. Wolff *Joel and Amos* (1977): 158.

[48] A. Bentzen, 'The Ritual Background of Amos 1:2–2:16', *OTS* 8 (1950): 85–99 seemed to provide a promising line of enquiry by comparing these OAN to Egyptian execration

286   *Book of Amos*

disaster for the whole region, including Israel. In the late 760s in which 1:1 sets the ministry of Amos, the imminent rise of the Assyrian empire may or may not have been evident. By the time of the first written composition of the Amos-text after 722, however, the Assyrian empire was the dominant power ruling the whole region. The five oracles of the Post-722 Composition reflect this historical setting, while the three exilic oracles (against Tyre, Edom, Judah) reflect the sixth-century period of Babylonian dominance. Recognition of these historical settings aids understanding of the text. However, for readers of later centuries understanding of historical context may be of less importance than understanding the nature of the accusations that YHWH makes against nations, and the judgements threatened in consequence.

Amos 1:3–5: Oracle against Damascus/Aram

The opening line addresses the city of Damascus, but 1:5 indicates that as the capital city of Aram, it stands for the whole nation, both ruler and people. Aram was to the north-east of Israel, its southern border being with Gilead, that part of Israel east of the river Jordan.

Two kings of Aram are referred to in 1:4: Hazael and Ben-hadad. Hazael ruled in the second half of the ninth century, some three quarters of a century ahead of when 1:1 sets the ministry of Amos. There was frequent war with Israel and Judah during his reign, and it appears from 2 Kings 10:32–33; 12:17–18; 13.3–4, 22–25 that Hazael had the upper hand for much of the time. There are three Aramean kings named Ben-hadad in the biblical tradition. The second of these was murdered by Hazael (2 Kgs 8:7–15), and Hazael became king in his stead. The next king after Hazael was his son, also named Ben-hadad (2 Kgs 13:3, 24), into whose reign wars with Israel continued.[49] It is likely that tensions and wars between Aram and Israel continued on into the eighth century, even though we do not have an account of them in the Hebrew Bible. Wolff finds it 'quite improbable that Amos, in the oracle against Aram, would refer to events which had taken place at least two generations earlier'.[50] Paul takes the names to be dynastic, and suggests that 'Amos is not referring to two retrospective Aramean kings but rather to two dynastic titles for the

texts of the eighteenth century BCE. However, over time scholars have not been persuaded by this suggestion. Others have suggested varying geographical patterns, none of which are convincing.

[49]   Both 'Hazael' and 'Ben-hadad' seem to have been frequent Aramean names ('Ben-hadad' sometimes in the form 'Bar-hadad'), and there may well have been others than those referred to in the Hebrew Bible.

[50]   H. W. Wolff *Joel and Amos* (1977): 150.

C Commentary on Amos

kingdom of Aram per se',[51] thus also allowing the likelihood that this oracle is not referring solely and specifically to ninth-century incidents.

The accusation in 1:3b that 'they have threshed Gilead with threshing-sledges of iron' need not be taken to refer to any one particular occasion. Wars both ancient and modern generate much cruelty.[52] It is noteworthy that although there had been frequent war between Aram and Israel, the accusation is not that the Arameans had mistreated YHWH's people. It is the cruel and barbaric nature of their actions that is condemned, actions which no doubt had been employed by the Arameans against other enemies besides the people of Gilead. The text considers that there were limits to the kind of behaviour considered acceptable, even in times of war. Judgement is announced using the formulaic sending of fire by YHWH, which will devour the strongholds of Ben-hadad. It continues with YHWH promising to 'break the gate-bars of Damascus'. The city gates would have been secured with bars, but these will be no defence. YHWH also promises to 'cut off the inhabitants from the Valley of Aven, and the one who holds the sceptre from Beth-eden'. The Hebrew word for 'inhabitants' is singular, literally 'the one who dwells' or 'the one who sits', meaning 'the one who sits on the throne', that is, the king. This parallels 'the one who holds the sceptre' in the following line. However LXX and other ancient versions translate as the plural 'inhabitants'. The place names here are highly symbolic. The word 'Aven' means 'wickedness' or 'iniquity'. Some commentators translate 'Valley of Aven' as 'Sin Valley'. Similarly, Beth-eden may be translated as 'House of Pleasure' or 'House of Delight'.[53] The location of these places is of less interest to later readers than their symbolic meanings.

The final element of punishment is that 'the people of Aram shall go into exile in Kir'. It was known Assyrian practice to exile whole populations and re-settle them elsewhere, as 2 Kings 17:5–6, 24 records with regard to the treatment of Israel in 722. Such is the fate announced for the Arameans. Particularly poignant is that their exile is to be to Kir. In 9:7 we read that the Arameans were brought up from Kir by YHWH in the same way that the Israelites were brought up from Egypt. This punishment is therefore exile to the region from which, historically, they had come.

---

[51] S. M. Paul *Amos* (1991): 50.

[52] M. D. Carroll R. *Amos* (2012): 140 comments that 'this is a figurative expression for ruthlessness'.

[53] J. Jeremias *Amos* (1998): 17; J. R. Linville *Amos and the Cosmic Imagination* (2008): 47; H. W. Wolff *Joel and Amos* (1977): 129, 156.

288 Book of Amos

Amos 1:6–8: Oracle against Gaza/the Philistines

While Gaza is named in the opening line of this oracle, the Philistine cities of Ashdod, Ashkelon, and Ekron are included in 1:8, and the oracle deals with the Philistines as a whole. Lacking is the city of Gath. Some date this oracle to after 711, on the basis that Gath was destroyed by the Assyrian emperor Sargon in that year. Others have noted that there were times when Gath seemed to belong to Judah or was subject to the Syrians rather than belonging to the Philistines. However, the cities of Gaza, Ashdod, Ashkelon, and Ekron are also included without Gath in Jeremiah 25:20, Zephaniah 2:4, and Zechariah 9:5–7, suggesting that the four cities without Gath were widely deemed to refer to the Philistines as a whole. It not necessary to think otherwise in Amos 1:6–8.

The accusation against the Philistines is that 'they carried into exile entire communities, to hand them over to Edom'. The Hebrew of the first clause is literally 'because they exiled a whole exile': the repetition of the root gives a strong emphasis to the action. This refers to carrying off the entire population of a village or settlement. The purpose was, it may be assumed, to sell them to Edom as slaves. It is not specified whether or not the settlements concerned were Israelite. If they were, it is not the reason given for the Philistines' guilt, which lies in their mistreatment of human beings, who were being regarded as no more than economic commodities. Jeremias sees here also an allusion to the greed of the Edomites, who he suggests needed slaves in order to expand their copper industry.[54]

The announcement of judgement on the Philistines is similar to that announced on the Arameans in the preceding oracle. Different is the closing half-verse which states that 'I will turn my hand against Ekron, and the remnant of the Philistines shall perish.' Wolff notes that YHWH's 'hand' denotes his overwhelming strength.[55] The final statement declares that any remnant which looks as though it might survive will, in fact, perish. This punishment might seem to be even more severe than the punishing of the Arameans by exile. However, it is unlikely that there is any intention in the text to contrast the two in severity: in both cases, the punishment is utter disaster.[56]

---

[54] J. Jeremias *Amos* (1998): 27; so also S. M. Paul *Amos* (1991): 57.

[55] H. W. Wolff *Joel and Amos* (1977): 158.

[56] M. D. Carroll R. *Amos* (2020): 153 considers the meaning to be that a Philistine remnant will survive, despite suffering 'comprehensive loss'. This seems a less natural reading of the words.

C Commentary on Amos 289

Amos 1:9–10: Oracle against Tyre

While the two preceding oracles were part of the series of five in the first, Post-722 Composition of the Amos-text, there now come two which entered the text in the Exilic Redactional Composition. The city-state addressed in 1:9–10 is Tyre, which in exilic times was a major trading power (Ezek. 26–28). The accusation against Tyre is repeated from that against the Philistines in 1:6, with slight differences in wording. This repetition is one of the considerations which point to this oracle being later than the original series. The fact that Tyre and Edom are not geographically adjacent and are unlikely to have had trading relationships has led some commentators to suggest that 'Edom' should be read as 'Aram', with just one consonantal change in Hebrew from ד to ר being needed. However there is no textual evidence for this. The continuation of the accusation introduces a phrase found nowhere else in the Hebrew Bible: the 'covenant of brothers (NRSV: kinship)' which Tyre has ignored. Some commentators (e.g. Carroll R.) relate this to the treaty between Solomon and King Hiram of Tyre in 1 Kings 5:1–12 [15–26], and indeed in 1 Kings 9:13 Hiram calls Solomon 'my brother'. Others, however (e.g. Barton, Wolff) relate it to brotherly dealings between Edom and Israel, whose ancestors Esau and Jacob were literal, physical brothers in the patriarchal narratives.[57] Either is possible; but perhaps the second is more likely, since the following oracle states that Edom 'pursued his brother with the sword' (1:11), which is likely to refer to the behaviour of the Edomites at the fall of Jerusalem in 587 (cf. Ps. 137:7). As well as the sense found in the previous oracle that to carry off a whole community and sell them as slaves was an appalling wrong, here there is a further dimension to the accusation, in that the wrong involved related nations.

As noted in the discussion of the structure of these oracles, while the accusation is longer than in the previous oracle, the announcement is correspondingly shorter. It includes only the formulaic sending of 'fire that shall devour its strongholds', with no elaboration.

Amos 1:11–12: Oracle against Edom

The exilic Psalm 137:7 recalls how on 'the day of Jerusalem's fall' Edom celebrated. The Edomites are portrayed as urging the Babylonians on, saying 'Tear it down! Tear it down!' Obadiah 11–14, also from the exilic or early post-exilic period, describes the same happening, with Israel described as

---

[57] M. D. Carroll R. *Amos* (2020): 157; J. Barton *Theology of the Book of Amos* (2012): 108; H. W. Wolff *Joel and Amos* (1997): 159.

'your brother' over whom Edom gloated. It adds, further, that they caught Israelite fugitives and handed them over to the Babylonians. Again, Ezekiel 35:5 accuses Edom: 'you cherished an ancient enmity, and gave over the people of Israel to the power of the sword at the time of their calamity'. Such passages indicate the depth of betrayal that the Israelites felt in respect of Edom in their time of exile and in the wake of the destruction of Jerusalem in 587. The patriarchal narratives tell of the ancestors of the two nations, Esau and Jacob, being brothers. Hence the accusation in this oracle can state that Edom 'pursued his brother'. Historical relationships between the two nations, however, included many times of strife, and the enmity of Edom towards Israel was not something new in 587. The downfall of Edom is announced also in Joel 3:19 [4:19], which is the preceding chapter of Hebrew text, providing a link between the two texts which is noted by those exploring how the Book of the Twelve is read as a whole.

The accusation in this oracle is the longest in the series: 'he pursued his brother with the sword and cast off all pity; he maintained his anger perpetually, and kept his wrath for ever'. The meaning of various of the Hebrew terms here is debated. NRSV has 'cast off all pity'. The word for 'pity' or compassion is also the word for 'womb', and in Judges 5:30 is used to mean a girl. On the basis of this Paul translates here 'destroyed his womenfolk'. He is followed by Linville.[58] This is possible. Most commentators, however, prefer the usual translation adopted by NRSV.[59] In the line following, NRSV has 'his anger' as the object of the verb, as in some of the ancient versions. However the Hebrew has it as the subject: 'his anger tore perpetually'. While awkward, the sense of this is clear enough without any change being warranted. The same applies in the clause following, which in Hebrew reads that 'his wrath kept (i.e. continued) for ever'. Overall the accusation is that the Edomites have behaved without any pity or compassion, and have given free rein to anger. Additionally they have taken no account of the supposed brotherly links between the two nations. The punishment announced is that YHWH will send fire on Teman, which will devour the strongholds of Bozrah. While Teman and Bozrah were cities, they can also refer to the two main regions which made up the territory of Edom (Bozrah in the north, Teman in the south).[60] In other words, the destruction will affect the whole country.

---

[58] S. M. Paul *Amos* (1991): 43, 64–5; J. R. Linville *Amos and the Cosmic Imagination* (2008): 55.
[59] J. Jeremias *Amos* (1998): 18; H. W. Wolff *Joel and Amos* (1977): 130.
[60] J. L. Mays *Amos* (1969): 35; S. M. Paul *Amos* (1991): 67.

C Commentary on Amos

The atrocities described in these two exilic oracles reflect immediate and recent events, and in this respect differ from the oracles present in the earlier, Post-722 Composition, where this is less evidently the case. It is, of course, the same YHWH who continues to abhor such atrocities, and whose word of judgement continues to be present against those who perpetrate them.

Amos 1:13–15: Oracle against the Ammonites

The series present in the Post-722 Composition resumes with an oracle against the Ammonites. The first oracle of the series was against Damascus/Aram, which was to the north of that part of Israel east of Jordan known as Gilead. Ammon is to the south and east of Gilead, and over the years there were regular border disputes and conflicts between them. The accusation is that 'they have ripped open pregnant women in Gilead in order to enlarge their territory'. The verb used for 'rip open' is the same as that used of bears and wild animals ripping open their prey (2 Kgs 2:24; Hos. 13:8). This horrific practice is known in the Hebrew Bible (2 Kgs 8:12; 15:16). It is also attested in an Assyrian description of the might of the emperor Tiglath-Pileser I, of whom it was boasted that he 'shredded to pieces the body of the pregnant, he pierced the body of the weak'.[61] The aim was probably twofold: to terrorise, and to reduce the population of the next generation of a neighbouring enemy. The message of YHWH declares his abhorrence of the practice, and judgement is announced in consequence. Verse 14 departs from the usual formula in one respect: while all the other oracles say that YHWH will 'send' fire, in this one alone it is said that he will 'kindle' a fire. The same verb is used in relation to the Ammonites in Jeremiah 49:2 and to Damascus in Jeremiah 49:27 (which quotes Amos 1:4 but using this verb from 1:14). Wolff suggests that a scribe copying the Amos-text has introduced the verb under the influence of Jeremiah 49.[62] This is possible. However, there is no reason why the original form could not have had this variation.[63] The fire will be on the wall of Rabbah, the capital city of Ammon. The name 'Rabbah' simply means 'Great', and 2 Samuel 12:26 calls it 'Rabbah of the Ammonites' to distinguish it from other great cities. The description of the judgement entails warfare ('with shouting on the day of battle') and storm phenomena ('with a storm on the day of the whirlwind'). NRSV's 'shouting' is a somewhat feeble

---

[61] Cited in H. W. Wolff *Joel and Amos* (1977): 161.
[62] H. W. Wolff *Joel and Amos* (1977): 161.
[63] S. M. Paul *Amos* (1991): 69.

292   *Book of Amos*

translation: 'fanfare' or 'war-cry' are alternative, rather more dramatic, translations. It is the shout of an attacking army, as used in, for example, the story of Joshua's attack on Jericho (Josh. 6:5, 20; cf. 1 Sam. 4:5–6; Ezek. 21:22 [27]). The language of storm draws on theophanic traditions of YHWH appearing in or riding on the storm (cf. Ps. 83:15 [16]; Isa. 29:6). Von Rad identified such traditions as belonging to an ancient 'Holy War' tradition, which, he considered, the prophets took up and adapted in their prophetic messages.[64] The upshot is that the Ammonites' king and his officials will go into exile (1:15). This verse is reproduced, with some variation, in Jeremiah 49:3, for which some textual traditions have the name of the Ammonite god Milcom in place of 'their king'.

Amos 2:1–3: Oracle against Moab

This oracle is noteworthy because it is made explicit that the transgression was not against Israel, but was nevertheless a transgression against YHWH. In most of the previous oracles, while it is the sheer horror and outrage of the actions described that warrants YHWH's judgement, it has been at least possible and in some cases evident that Israel has been affected by the transgressions. Thus the door has been left open to an interpretation that sees 'action against Israel' as the cause of YHWH's anger. In this final oracle against a foreign nation, however, that door is closed. The transgression was specifically an atrocity suffered by Edom. The atrocity is that Moab 'burned to lime the bones of the king of Edom'. This constituted an outrage of disrespect to a dead king: any corpse, and especially a royal corpse, should be given a proper burial, even if it was an enemy's corpse. Some commentators have found this to be insufficiently outrageous to warrant YHWH's judgement, and have therefore speculated that burning to lime was in order to then use that lime in whitewash on stones (cf. Deut. 27:2, 4) or on houses.[65] This would constitute even greater irreverence and disrespect. Others wonder whether a sacrifice of the bones to a demon lies behind this verse. However, for most peoples in most cultures in most centuries, respectful burial of the dead has been something assumed to be a right and proper action, and denial of that opportunity has been considered an outrage. The description of this action as an outrageous transgression is entirely proper.

---

[64] G. von Rad, *Holy War in Ancient Israel* (Grand Rapids, MI: Eerdmans, 1991).
[65] So S. M. Paul *Amos* (1991): 72, who cites the ancient Targum tradition that Moab 'burnt the bones of the king of Edom and whitewashed [with] them his house like with plaster/lime'.

C Commentary on Amos
293

Once again, fire will be sent on the offending nation, Moab, and on the strongholds of Kerioth. The Mesha Stone (discovered in 1868, and now in the Louvre) refers to Kerioth as the location of a shrine to the Moabite god Chemosh,[66] so it was an important place for the Moabites. The expansion of the description of judgement in 2:2b draws on the same kind of warfare terminology as 1:14b. Again there is the sound of the war-cry (NRSV: shouting), and additionally the sound of the trumpet (*šôpār*) with which battle was engaged. The oracle concludes with the announcement of the cutting off of Moab's ruler: the word *šōpēṭ* is that used of Israel's raised-up leaders in the book of Judges, and may be translated 'ruler' or 'prince'. This may refer to a regent rather than a king, or else simply be an equivalent to 'king'. The officials of the land will die with him.

While it is barely possible to discern any geographical patten to the order of the OAN in Amos 1:3–2:3, some literary pattern is evident in those of the Post-722 Composition (Damascus/Aram, Gaza/the Philistines, the Ammonites, Moab), particularly in the announcements of judgement. Firstly, the first two oracles form a pair, in both of which the ones punished are 'the one who dwells/sits' (i.e. on the throne) and 'the one who holds the sceptre'. The third and fourth oracles form a second pair, both drawing on warfare terminology to describe the punishment. In a different pairing, the first and third are paired, in that the punishment is exile, while in the second and fourth the punishment is death. This suggests a careful work of composition. Furthermore, with the oracle against in Israel in 2:6–16, this series of five OAN matches the series of five visions in the Post-722 Composition (7:1–3; 7:4–6; 7:7–8; 8:1–2; 9:1–4), where again the first four units are grouped as two pairs (see the commentary *ad loc*). With such clear evidence of intentional literary structuring, we may look, too, for some strong and coherent theological themes. In 1:3–2:3 it is made evident that YHWH's authority was not bounded by national borders: peoples and kings of foreign nations were answerable to him and accountable for their actions, as well as the people of Israel. It is made evident, too, that there were forms of human behaviour so morally outrageous and appalling that there did not need to be any written code of law to say so; and none such are referred to in the text. Furthermore, engagement in warfare did not bring exemption from responsibility: even in war, there were limits to be set by simple human decency. Actions such as uncontrolled cruelty in war (1:3), carrying off whole communities to sell into slavery (1:6), ripping open pregnant women (1:13), and failing to respect

---

[66] *ANET*: 320.

294 *Book of Amos*

the dead by giving proper burial (2:1) were all abhorrent to YHWH, and by extension should be so to human beings too. The pair of exilic oracles (1:9–12) accepts and assumes these perspectives, and introduces the idea that past 'brotherhood' constitutes an additional reason why judgement is deserved.

If the series of oracles ended here, it would have given the comfort to Israel that blame lay with others. Instead, however, the series continues with oracles against Judah and Israel.

Bridging the Horizons: Atrocities and War Crimes

The oracles against Damascus, the Ammonites, and (probably) Moab describe atrocities committed in war. There was no international agreement outlawing such practices, but Amos sees them, nevertheless, as utterly abhorrent, evidently 'wrong' in the eyes of any decent individual or nation, and deserving of YHWH's judgement. In the contemporary world, in contrast, the Geneva Convention sets out standards of behaviour to which many countries have agreed. The OAN of Amos 1–2 and the Geneva Convention have in common that they see the committing of atrocities in war as immoral and simply 'wrong' without appeal to any particular religious tradition. Amos 1–2, of course, assumes one, but the basis on which the atrocities described are condemned is a sense of moral outrage which can be owned and shared, in the contemporary world, by people of any faith or none.

The oracle against Gaza/the Philistines (1:6–8) condemns the carrying into exile of entire communities. This was probably the taking into slavery of a whole village community, quite possibly on more than one occasion. It would be comforting if we could imagine that such inhumane practices belonged solely to an ancient, distant world, and not to the twenty-first century CE. Such is not, however, the case. Modern slavery, and the capture and sale of individuals and groups for sex trafficking, is all too modern a problem. Now, as in the ancient world, it remains as abhorrent and deserving of punishment.

The OAN of Amos 1–2 see the judgement on nations who commit war crimes and atrocities as coming directly from the actions of YHWH, who will cause them, in turn to be taken into exile, or their rulers to be 'cut off'. Modern readers, schooled in Enlightenment thinking, will less readily see the direct action of God in political upheavals. However, the belief that such practices should not go unpunished remains. That belief

C Commentary on Amos

is now worked out through the International Court of Justice (ICJ), the principal judicial arm of the United Nations, as well as though the adoption by various nations of a War Crimes Act. Those who stand within the Judaeo-Christian tradition will be able to see the work of the ICJ and related bodies as reflecting, in some way, the nature of a God of justice.

A Closer Look: Oracles against the Nations

Scholars of the nineteenth and first half of the twentieth centuries, keen to uphold the portrayal of the pre-exilic prophets as original and creative purveyors of an ethical monotheism, often regarded the OAN as something of an embarrassment. They saw them as an expression of an Israelite nationalism that denounced foreign nations, and deemed this incompatible with their elevated understanding of the character of the prophets. Hence Pfeiffer wrote: 'Although such anathemas against the heathen were inaugurated by Amos ... they reflect on the whole not the moral indignation of the great pre-exilic prophets, but rather the nationalism of the "false prophets" and of the later Jews chafing for centuries under alien rule.'[67] Or again, the *Interpreter's Bible* (*IB*) commentator on Zephaniah stated: 'None of these make important contributions to the history of religious thought or to an understanding of the divine will.'[68]

More recent scholarship has recognised that, when read in their literary contexts, they form an integral part of the prophetic corpus, and are not devoid of theological insight. Significant collections of OAN are found in the books of Isaiah (much of chapters 13–23), Jeremiah (46–51), and Ezekiel (25–32). In Ezekiel they are part of an overarching structure to the book: chapters 1–24 are principally words of judgement on Judah, chapters 25–32 are OAN, and chapters 33–48 are principally words of hope for the future. There is a similar pattern in the Isaiah-text, in that chapters 1–12 are principally words of judgement on Judah; chapters 13–23 are mainly OAN; and chapters 40–66 are words of hope for the future. However in this case chapters 24–39 following the OAN contain a mixture of further words of judgement on Judah and on 'the nations'. The LXX of Jeremiah follows the same pattern in placing the OAN in the

---

[67] R. H. Pfeiffer, *Introduction to the Old Testament* (3rd ed.; New York: Harper & Brothers, 1941): 443.

[68] C. L. Taylor, Jr., 'The Book of Zephaniah', *IB*, vol. 6: 1007–34 (1013).

296   *Book of Amos*

middle of the book, following 25:13a. It has been well argued that the LXX
is based on a different Hebrew textual tradition from that of MT and is
not a late, inferior deviation from it.[69] It appears that the compilers of
these texts saw YHWH's judgement on the nations as part of the process
of transition from judging to blessing his people.

Nor should the OAN be seen purely and simply as a form of salvation
of prophecy for Israel. This was expressed, for example, by Westermann.
Having noted that in terms of formal structure there is no difference
between the OAN and judgement oracles against Israel, he nevertheless
considers that they must be 'bracketed out' because of their content and
that 'they belong in the line of salvation-speeches because they imply
salvation for Israel'.[70] This is the case in some OAN deriving from the
period following the destruction of Jerusalem in 587, but not in others.
In many, the pride of a nation is given as a reason for judgement: the
pride of Moab (Isa. 16:6; Jer. 48:29; Zeph. 2:9–10); Tyre and Sidon's pride
in their wealth (Isa. 23:1–12; Ezek. 28:2–5). Some OAN give no reason
for judgement. We have, therefore, look to their literary and historical
context to see if this gives any indication of why YHWH condemns these
nations. None of the Isaiah oracles against the Philistines (14:28–32),
Damascus (17:1–3), and Egypt (19:1–15) contain any reasons for judgement. In terms of historical context, if these date from the eighth century in which Isaiah's ministry is set, then all these nations, along with
Moab and Tyre against whom the accusation of pride is made, and along
with Israel and Judah, would have been at risk of being conquered by the
growing, dominant power of the Assyrian empire. The prediction of their
downfall functions, therefore, as an assertion of Assyrian dominance,
and confirms what is stated in Isaiah 10:5, that Assyria is 'the rod of my
(= YHWH's) anger'. Far from functioning as salvation-prophecy for
Israel, these nations and Israel will suffer the same fate.[71] Similarly, in
Jeremiah, oracles against Egypt (46:13–24), Kedar (49:28–33), and Elam
(49:34–38) are all without reasons for judgement; and 46:12 points to the

---

[69] See, for example, J. Janzen, *Studies in the Text of Jeremiah* (Harvard Semitic Monographs,
6; Cambridge, MA: Harvard University Press, 1973): 29–30. T. Fretheim, *Jeremiah* (Smyth
& Helwys Bible Commentary; Macon, GA: Smyth & Helwys, 2002): 577 comments that
the position of these oracles in LXX 'is commonly considered to have been their original
placement in the book'.

[70] C. Westermann *Basic Forms* (1991): 204–5.

[71] G. R. Hamborg, 'Reasons for Judgement in the Oracles against the Nations of the Prophet
Isaiah', *VT* 31 (1981): 145–59.

C Commentary on Amos

dominance of the Babylonian empire in the late seventh and early sixth centuries as the reason for their downfall. These nations would all end up dominated by the Babylonians, as would also be true of Judah.

Amid the many chapters in the prophetic books containing OAN, Amos 1–2 stands alone as giving acts of cruelty and atrocity as reasons for judgement, with it not being the case that these were necessarily committed against Israel. If some were, the text does not highlight this, but rather highlights the atrocity itself. For those aware of and concerned about the committing of acts of atrocity in the twenty-first century CE, it is this that makes Amos 1–2 significant and appealing chapters of the Hebrew Bible.

Amos 2:4–16 – Oracles against Judah and Israel

⁴ Thus says the Lord:
For three transgressions of Judah,
   and for four, I will not revoke the punishment,
because they have rejected the instruction of the Lord,
   and have not kept his statutes,
but they have been led astray by the same lies
   after which their ancestors walked.
⁵ So I will send a fire on Judah,
   and it shall devour the strongholds of Jerusalem.

⁶ Thus says the Lord:
For three transgressions of Israel,
   and for four, I will not revoke the punishment,
because they sell the righteous for silver
   and the needy for a pair of sandals –
⁷ they who trample the head of the poor into the dust of the earth
   and push the afflicted out of the way;
father and son go in to the same young woman,
   so that my holy name is profaned;
⁸ they lay themselves down beside every altar
   on garments taken in pledge;
and in the house of their God they drink
   wine bought with fines they imposed.
⁹ Yet I destroyed the Amorite before them,
   whose height was like the height of cedars
   and who was as strong as oaks;
I destroyed his fruit above
   and his roots beneath.

298   *Book of Amos*

¹⁰ Also I brought you up out of the land of Egypt
    and led you for forty years in the wilderness,
    to possess the land of the Amorite.
¹¹ And I raised up some of your children to be prophets
    and some of your youths to be nazirites.
    Is it not indeed so, O people of Israel?
  says the Lord.
¹² But you made the nazirites drink wine
    and commanded the prophets
    saying, 'You shall not prophesy.'
¹³ So, I will press you down in your place,
    just as a cart presses down
    when it is full of sheaves.
¹⁴ Flight shall perish from the swift,
    and the strong shall not retain their strength,
    nor shall the mighty save their lives;
¹⁵ those who handle the bow shall not stand,
    and those who are swift of foot shall not save themselves,
    nor shall those who ride horses save their lives;
¹⁶ and those who are stout of heart among the mighty
    shall flee away naked on that day,
  says the Lord.

After oracles in 1:3–2:3 addressed to foreign nations, the series reaches its climax in the oracle against Israel in 2:6–16. In the earliest, Post-722 Composition this followed immediately from that addressed to Moab (2:1–3). In the Exilic Redactional Composition the oracle addressed to Judah in 2:4–5 was inserted. It has a purpose in its own right in addressing people in exile in Babylon, as well as providing a different precursor to 2:6–16.

Amos 2:4–5: Oracle against Judah
The accusation against Judah is quite different to the accusations made against foreign nations, which concerned war crimes and acts of atrocity. In this oracle Judah is not accused of wronging or harming human beings, but of rejecting and neglecting YHWH. The verb for 'reject' (*mā'as*) is used in the Hebrew Bible both for people's rejection of YHWH, and for YHWH's rejection of people. In Hosea 4:6 both senses are found together: 'because you have rejected knowledge, I reject you from being a priest to me'. Similarly, 2 Kings 17:15–20 contains both uses: 'They rejected (NRSV: despised) his statutes.... They went after false idols ... YHWH rejected all the descendants of Israel.' These verses explaining the downfall of the northern kingdom in 722, and adding in Judah's disobedience (v. 19), are heavily Deuteronomistic

C Commentary on Amos

in style. The overlap in vocabulary with Amos 2:4–5 confirms the view that this oracle bears marks of exilic Deuteronomistic influence. The themes and vocabulary of rejection of the law of YHWH and failure to keep his statutes are characteristically Deuteronomistic. The 'instruction' of YHWH translates *tôrâ*, which the pre-2021 NRSV translated as 'law'. Either translation is possible. It is in parallel with YHWH's 'statutes' (*ḥuqqîm*), and it is perhaps preferable to take the *tôrâ* to refer to the Deuteronomic corpus of law and the *ḥuqqîm* to the individual precepts within the corpus. The law and statutes of Deuteronomic tradition would have been well known in Judah by the late seventh and early sixth century. Amos 2:4–5 states, however, that having them and knowing of them was not enough: they had to be kept.

The text continues with the accusation that 'they have been led astray by the same lies after which their ancestors walked'. The word 'lies' is the one word in the verse which is less characteristically Deuteronomistic. More characteristic is that they 'went after idols' (cf. 2 Kgs 17:15). However the occurrence of this one less usual word amid much characteristically Deuteronomistic terminology does not undermine the recognition of Deuteronomistic influence.

The punishment meted out to Judah is the formulaic sending of fire, which will devour the strongholds of Jerusalem, with no further elaboration. However, in the wake of 587, no elaboration was needed. Readers and hearers would know that the burning down of the city had already taken place. Harsh though this judgement sounds, it allowed recognition of the possibility that the destruction of Jerusalem did not need to be seen as a random, purposeless event, nor as evidence of YHWH's weakness compared to the gods of the Babylonians, but that YHWH himself had purposed it. This recognition had the potential to make sense of the disaster as one brought by YHWH, who might, therefore, not have ended his dealings with his people.

Amos 2:1–16: Oracle against Israel

This unit is the climax of the OAN series of Amos 1:3–2:16. It is also the first unit of the Amos-text to be directed at the kingdom of Israel. This makes it significant, and it is unsurprising that later editions of the text made additions to it. The most significant of these is the addition of 2:10–12 in the Exilic Redactional Composition, with some phrases also being added in 2:8 in the Late Pre-exilic Redactional Composition and in 2:7 in the Post-exilic Redactional Composition.[72]

---

[72] See the 'Introduction to Amos' for explanation of these literary layers.

The oracle begins with the same formulation as the preceding units: 'For three transgressions of Israel and for four, I will not revoke the punishment.' Thereafter the structure of the oracle diverges, with both accusation and announcement of judgement being longer. Far from being able to point the finger at the transgressions of other nations from a position of innocence, Israel herself is accused of serious transgressions within the nation's life. The accusation begins 'because they sell the righteous for silver and the needy for a pair of sandals' (2:6b). Verse 7 then begins with a Hebrew participle: 'they who trample ...'. The verbs convey a sense of ongoing, continued actions rather than a few particular occurrences. Those wronged are the righteous and the needy (2:6b) and the poor and afflicted (2:7). The word 'righteous' (*ṣaddîq*) can be translated 'righteous' or 'innocent', the latter sense being appropriate when referring to someone found to be in the right in a legal dispute. Some commentators have held that this verse refers to the corruption of those responsible for administering justice: by taking bribes they sell the innocent. This is a possible interpretation. More likely, however, is that this verse refers to the practice of debt-slavery: when someone was unable to pay their debts, they or a member of their family could be sold into servitude to work off the unpaid debt. A legal provision, however, was being used (the text indicates) in an extreme, harsh, and uncaring manner, with no concern for the misery caused to the indebted individual and family, whose only sin was to be poor. On this interpretation NRSV's translation as 'righteous' is correct. Whichever is the case, the accusation is that people are being sold. The verb here (*mākar*) is used for the selling of land, of property, of possessions, and of people into servitude. We may not deduce from this accusation that the institution of debt servitude was itself being condemned. As Pleins writes: 'Becoming a debt slave was permitted in Israel as a way to pay off one's financial obligations.'[73] Theoretically it provided a way out of debt. The story of Elisha and the widow in 2 Kings 4:1–7 accepts the practice without comment, and Exodus 21:2–11 and Deuteronomy 15:12–18 seek to regulate, but not abolish it. However, it was clearly easy for unfeeling and powerful people to exploit the system. The text continues with the accusation that the needy were being sold for a pair of sandals. References to the pulling off of sandals in Deuteronomy 25:9–10 (when a man refuses to fulfil his duty of perpetuating his brother's line by marrying his widow) and in Ruth 4:7 (to confirm a transaction) have led some commentators to link

---

[73] J. D. Pleins, *The Social Visions of the Hebrew Bible* (Louisville, KY: Westminster John Knox, 2001): 369.

C *Commentary on Amos*   301

Amos 2:6b with such customs. However it is difficult to do so, and Genesis 14:23, which refers to Abram saying to the king of Sodom that he would not take 'a thread or even a thong of a sandal' from him, points in a different direction: the righteous and needy were being sold into slavery over trivial debts, and for little profit. In contemporary English we would say that they were being sold for a pittance.

The next verse (2:7a) makes the accusation that the poor were being trampled into the dust of the earth and the afflicted pushed out of the way. The most natural meaning of this is that the powerful, alongside their economic strength, were using physical force against the weak. The verb for pushing the afflicted out of the way is also used in 5:12 in the context of denying justice to the poor in a legal dispute, but it is not necessary to import that meaning into this passage. Amos 2:7b then states that 'father and son go into the same young woman'. The verb 'go into' (*hālakh*) is not generally used of sexual intercourse, but that meaning seems inescapable here. The significance of the term 'young woman' (which the pre-2021 NRSV translated as 'girl') has occasioned much discussion. The term used can refer to one betrothed, or to a concubine, or to female attendants or handmaids. It may refer to a slave girl, but not necessarily so. It may mean simply a girl of marriageable age. While the accusation concerns sexual acts, Coggins suggests that 'it is more likely that the concern is with the exploitation of the woman rather than with the sexual act in itself ... the young woman is to be seen as a victim of oppression';[74] and this is certainly in keeping with the other elements of the accusation in this unit. In the Post-exilic Redactional Composition the original form of 2:7b has been expanded with the phrase 'to profane my holy name'. The vocabulary of profaning the name of YHWH is dependent on the language of Ezekiel (20:39; 36:20–22) and the so-called Holiness Code (Lev. 20:3; 22:2, 32).

The accusation continues in 2:8: 'they lay themselves down on garments taken in pledge ... they drink wine bought with fines they imposed'. The first accusation appears to relate to Exodus 22:26–27 [25–26], which reads: 'If you take your neighbour's cloak in pawn, you shall restore it before the sun goes down; for it may be your neighbour's only clothing to use as cover: in what else shall that person sleep?' While Exodus 22:26 [25] refers to the neighbour's cloak, and Amos 2:8 to 'garments', the same verb *ḥābal* is used (which NRSV translates 'take in pawn' in Exod. 22:26 and 'take in pledge' in Amos 2:8). Similar but slightly different is Deuteronomy

---

[74]   R. J. Coggins *Joel and Amos* (2000): 103.

24:12: 'If the person is poor, you shall not sleep in the garment given you as the pledge.' The verses in Exodus fall within the so-called 'Book of the Covenant', which at one time scholars dated early in Israel's history, possibly even to the pre-monarchic period. Few scholars would now defend such an early dating, however, and it is likely that the compiling of the so-called Book of the Covenant and the Post-722 Composition of the Amos-text were roughly contemporaneous. Most probably Amos 2:8a is a loose citing of an orally transmitted injunction which also found its way into the Book of the Covenant.[75] Exodus 22:25–27 and Deuteronomy 24:6, 10–13 seek to place limits on the perfectly legal practice of taking items of property in pawn, in order to mitigate the effect on those who were poor and destitute. Deuteronomy 24:6 prohibits the taking of a millstone because it was essential to the making of bread and thus to life itself. Exodus 22:26 and Deuteronomy 24:12–13 stipulate that a garment taken in pawn should be returned for the poor person to sleep in at night. While it is difficult to imagine a garment being taken in pledge each day and returned each night, the intention of the injunctions – to mitigate hardship – is clear. What Amos 2:8 describes is the keeping overnight of garments taken in pledge, causing undue hardship. In the second half of the verse the drinking of wine bought with fines imposed conveys an equal unscrupulousness. While we don't know precisely how fines were imposed and to whom they were paid, it is likely that they were for restitution or compensation of some kind (Deut. 22:19). Amos suggests that those taking them, however, were callous people whose high-life way of living disregarded any concern for what was a proper use of fines paid.

The phrases 'beside every altar' and 'in the house of their God' were added in the Late Pre-exilic Redactional Composition. The earlier form of the text dealt purely and simply with the mistreatment of the poor by the rich and powerful. The additions bring in an additional focus of condemnation: it might reasonably be thought that those associated with the sanctuaries – 'the clergy', we would say today – might have a concern for the poor. But in practice it turns out that they are complicit in the malpractices of the selfish wealthy. Not only are garments taken in pledge being kept overnight, they are being used to lie on as people drink wine bought with fines in the very places which signified the presence of God. These additions reflect thematic influence from the Hosea-text, of which condemnations of sanctuaries and their priests are characteristic (Hos. 8:11–13; 10:1–2).

[75]   G. R. Hamborg *Still Selling the Righteous* (2012): 131–50.

C Commentary on Amos

The accusations of 2:6–8, therefore, concern the maltreatment of the righteous, the needy, the poor, and the afflicted by those who were powerful and wealthy. Houston describes what he calls the 'mechanisms of oppression' in the world in which the Amos-text was formed: it was all too often a function of patronage, in which a small number of wealthy individuals act as patrons and protectors of ordinary citizens.[76] Others have seen it as a function of landlord–tenant farmer relationships (rent capitalism).[77] Like many social systems, these could work perfectly well for all concerned, or they could be abused by the powerful to the detriment of the weak. It is noteworthy, however, that the text refrains from defining more specifically who these oppressors were: they are simply 'they'. Coote describes them as 'the secure, the strong, the well-to-do, the well-housed and well-fed, the authorities, the holders of power and privilege – in short, the ruling elite of Israel's agrarian society'.[78] This lack of precision and openness invites the reader to relate these accusations to those in positions of power, wealth, and influence in their own society who misuse what they have to oppress or mistreat those who are weak, and at the bottom of society.

Furthermore, just as the oppressors are not clearly specified, neither are their victims. The four terms 'righteous', 'needy', 'poor', and 'afflicted' reappear variously in 4:1; 5:11; 5:12; and 8:4–6. Attempts have been made to specify to whom in society each term refers. Giles writes that '[t]he "poor" own property, while the "needy" may or may not'.[79] Such distinctions are hard to argue, however, and certainly within the Amos-text text the terms seem to be used interchangeably.[80] It is also the case that the meaning of terms can take on a different significance as time moves on. These terms may well have held different connotations in the later centuries of the Exilic and Post-exilic Redactional Compositions than in the earlier, late eighth-century text. It has been well argued that in later centuries these terms come to mean those of pious religious character, rather than necessarily those who were materially poor. This is especially true of the term *'ănāwîm*, translated by

[76] W. J. Houston *Amos: Justice and Violence* (2015): 62–5.
[77] B. Lang, 'The Social Organisation of Peasant Poverty in Biblical Israel', in B. Lang, *Monotheism and the Prophetic Minority* (SWBA, 1; Sheffield: Almond Press, 1983): 114–27.
[78] R. B. Coote *Amos among the Prophets* (1981): 16.
[79] T. Giles, 'דל and אביון: The Poor and Needy in the Book of Amos', *BRT* 1 (1991): 12–20 (16).
[80] So W. J. Houston *Amos: Justice and Violence* (2015): 33; W. J. Houston, *Contending for Justice: Ideologies of Social Justice in the Old Testament* (LHBOTS, 428; London: T&T Clark International, 2006): 62.

NRSV in this passage as 'afflicted', and elsewhere as 'humble' or 'meek' (in Num. 12:3 Moses is described as 'humble', using this word).[81]

The text continues with a different kind of reason for judgement in 2:9. Here YHWH reminds the Israelites of his past action on their behalf in destroying the Amorites so that they could possess the land. The verb 'destroyed' and the term 'Amorite' are both frequent in Deuteronomistic literature, but both are also found in other strands of the Hebrew Bible, including the so-called Elohistic strand. Contrary to the view of some scholars, there are insufficient grounds to date this verse (unlike 2:10–12) to the exilic period. It should be taken to be part of the earliest Post-722 Composition of the text.[82] It is, as Hadjiev notes, 'well integrated into its present context and seems to be presupposed by the later addition in vv 10–12'. The height of the Amorite is described as being like the height of tall cedar trees and as strong as mighty oak trees. The former inhabitants of the land are often depicted in the Bible as having been large and tall. They are variously described as the Nephilim, the descendants of Anak (Num. 13:33), the Anakim (Deut. 1:28; 9:2), the Rephaim, Emim, and Zamzummim (Deut. 2:10–12, 20–21). Only here in Amos 2:9 is it said of the Amorite. Despite their height and strength, their destruction will be complete, from top (his fruit above) to bottom (his roots beneath). This verse provides a transition from the reasons for judgement given in 2:6–8 and the announcement of that judgement in 2:13–16 by showing that the offences of 2:6–8 are not simply against human beings, but also against YHWH himself.

Theologically the destruction of a people so that YHWH's people could possess the land raises huge difficulties for the modern interpreter. Certainly it may not be used by any nation or group of people to justify the driving out of another in the name of God. Within the literary context of Amos, it has become a formulaic element of the recited memory of past deliverance, and religious believers naturally and easily read it without for one moment imagining that it gives such license.

In the Post-722 Composition 2:9 led straight into the announcement of judgement in 2:13–16. However, in the sixth-century exilic expansion of the text, 2:10–12 was brought in to reinforce and expand the theme of 2:9. There are several pointers to these verses belonging to this later redaction.

---

[81]   See further S. R. Driver, 'Poor', in J. Hastings (ed.), *A Dictionary of the Bible, vol. 4* (Edinburgh: T&T Clark, 1902): 19–20; S. Gillingham, 'The Poor in the Psalms', *ET* 100 (1988–1989): 15–19; G. R. Hamborg *Still Selling the Righteous* (2012): 168–91.

[82]   T. S. Hadjiev *Composition and Redaction* (2009): 52; contra R. B. Coote *Amos among the Prophets* (1981): 71–2.

C Commentary on Amos

Firstly, there is a shift in address from 'they' in 2:6–9 to 'you' in 2:10–12. Secondly, the exodus from Egypt and forty years of wilderness wandering (2:10) were chronologically earlier than the destruction of the Amorites and occupation of the land (2:9), and it is unlikely that a single composed text would have placed the destruction of the Amorite at the beginning. Thirdly, scholars have increasingly recognised that there is insufficient textual evidence to demonstrate widespread knowledge of a cycle of tradition comprising 'exodus – wilderness – entry into the land' as early as the eighth century. Fourthly, the clause 'and I led you in the wilderness for forty years' appears verbatim in Deuteronomy 29:5 [4], a verse in a section of Deuteronomy generally held to belong to an exilic Deuteronomistic edition of Deuteronomy.[83] Fifthly, the theme of rejection of the prophets and their words as constituting a further reason for judgement is more characteristic of the later period. A counter-argument sometimes offered is that the verb for 'brought you up' (2:10) is not the one favoured by Deuteronomy, but is found in other, supposedly earlier, texts. I have examined this in detail elsewhere, and have shown that many of the verses cited as earlier are in fact not so, and that the verb used in Amos 2:10 is used in other exilic passages.[84]

The callous treatment of the poor described in 2:6–8 is here portrayed as all the more offensive in the light of YHWH's favour towards his people in bringing them up out of the land of Egypt and into the land that they came to occupy. This brings a more theological rationale into the reasons for judgement: not only are the actions of verses 6–8 naturally and evidently somehow 'wrong', they also ignore or even forget the past saving actions of YHWH on the people's behalf. Furthermore, verses 2:11–12 introduces yet further reasons for judgement: prophets and nazirites, sent by YHWH, have not been listened to, but have been rejected. In 2 Kings 17:13–15, another exilic passage describing the downfall of the northern kingdom of Israel, it is stated that YHWH had 'warned Israel and Judah by every prophet and every seer' that they should turn from their evil ways, but that they had not done so. Amos 2:11–12 expresses the same view: 'But you made the nazirites drink wine, and commanded the prophets, saying, "You shall not prophesy."' The narrative of the rejection of Amos's words by the priest Amaziah had already been brought into the text in the seventh-century Late Pre-Exilic Redactional Composition in 7:10–17, and the exilic 2:10–12 now indicates a wider rejection of the words of nazirites and prophets as a reason for judgement.

---

[83] A. D. H. Mayes, *Deuteronomy* (OTL; London: SCM, 1979): 46.
[84] G. R. Hamborg *Still Selling the Righteous* (2012): 151–67.

A Closer Look: The Nazirites

References to nazirites in the Hebrew Bible are few. The root from which the word is formed means to 'set apart'. The story of the birth of Samson in Judges 13 contains the instruction to his mother that she is not to drink wine or strong drink during her pregnancy, and that when the child is born 'no razor is to come on his head, for the boy shall be a nazirite to God from birth' (13:5). Similarly, in the story of his betrayal by Delilah, Samson reveals that 'a razor has never come upon my head; for I have been a nazirite to God from my mother's womb' (16:17). It appears that Samuel, too, was dedicated to YHWH as a nazirite from his birth. The Hebrew text of Hannah's prayer to YHWH in 1 Samuel 1:11 says that 'I will give him to YHWH all the days of his life, and no razor shall ever touch his head', and 1:15 alludes to Hannah's own abstinence from wine and strong drink. In 1 Samuel 1:22 NRSV follows a reading found in LXX and a Qumran scroll: 'I will set him before you as a nazirite until the day of his death. He shall drink neither wine nor intoxicants, and no razor shall touch his head.' Numbers 6:9–12, a priestly text generally dated to the post-exilic period, describes the custom of a nazirite vow being taken for a period of time.

Amos 2:11–12 indicates that someone could be called to be a nazirite as a young person just as someone could be called to be a prophet. The feature of their way of life on which 2:12 focuses is their abstinence from drinking wine. The exilic Amos-text makes clear that the nazirites and the prophets were both groups of people through whom YHWH had warned his people, but to no avail.

After the setting out of reasons for judgement, 2:13–16 describes YHWH's actions. In the Post-722 Composition, 2:13 followed 2:9. The message conveyed was that as YHWH has destroyed the Amorites before them, so now he will turn his attention to the Israelites. The meaning of 2:13 is uncertain. It is clearly an action of YHWH, who speaks in the first person, but his action can be interpreted differently, depending on how the imagery is understood and how the rare verb used is to be translated. The image may be of a cart so laden with sheaves that it sinks and gets stuck in the ground, in which case the action of YHWH is of pushing it into the ground. Alternatively it may be that YHWH breaks open the ground as in an earthquake, causing the cart to sink into the earth. Gese has argued, in the view

C Commentary on Amos

of many convincingly so, that the latter is to be preferred.[85] Earthquake is also the likely expression of YHWH's judgement in 3:15 and 6:11 which, with 2:13, account for the editors who placed 1:1 as the heading of the book seeing 'the earthquake' as a fulfilment of Amos's words. In the face of the earthquake even the fastest and fittest will be unable to escape. As the description of the fastest and fittest unfolds in verses 14–16, however, it begins to sound more like military defeat than earthquake. This adds to the uncertainty of precisely what form of judgement is being described. Lack of certainty in this regard, however, does not detract from the sense of impending doom, and it may be a deliberate rhetorical strategy: 'This undefined judgment is even more ominous than one defined; and the deliberate openness in the text allows future readers to interpret it in terms relevant to their contemporary situation.'[86]

The additions made to this important unit in each of the redactional compositions all hold interpretative significance. In the Post-722 Composition the reasons for judgement on Israel in 2:6–8 are comparable to those on the foreign nations in 1:3–2:3. The actions of the wealthy, powerful men of Israel in selling the righteous for silver and trampling on the afflicted, in exploiting weak and vulnerable girls, on misusing garments taken in pledge and fines imposed on the poor, were simply abhorrent, offensive, and wrong. No elaborate theology was necessary for this to be recognised. Those accused are simply 'they', leaving a deliberate openness in the text as to whom precisely the accusations refer. In the seventh-century Late Pre-exilic Redactional Composition additions in 2:8 specify that offences are taking place 'beside every altar' and 'in the house of their God'. The implication is that the priests were complicit in this mistreatment of the weak by the powerful. A further reason for judgement in the Post-722 Composition is found in 2:9: the immoral actions of the wealthy indicated a forgetfulness of the saving actions on YHWH on their behalf in the past. This is elaborated in 2:10–12, brought into the text in the Exilic Redactional Composition, which also specifies as further reasons for judgement that they had ignored the prophets and nazirites sent by YHWH. Also in this redaction, the preceding oracle against Judah had brought into the text rejection of the law of YHWH and not keeping his statutes as reasons for judgement, and the oracle against Israel is now heard in the light of this too. Finally, the Post-exilic

---

[85] H. Gese, 'Kleine Beiträge zum Verständnis des Amosbuches', *VT* 12 (1962): 417–38. So also G. Eidevall *Amos* (2017): 118–19; J. Jeremias *Amos* (1998): 42–3.

[86] G. R. Hamborg *Still Selling the Righteous* (2012): 200–1.

308   *Book of Amos*

Redactional Composition, reflecting familiarity with verses in Ezekiel and
the Holiness Code, brings in the profanation of YHWH's name caused by
the exploitation of women as a further reason for judgement (2:7). Thus the
earliest form of the text is content simply to declare YHWH's judgement
because of actions by the wealthy and powerful against the weak and vulnerable which are simply 'wrong', while subsequent additions strengthen
the theological basis of that assertion.

The various literary layers allow a fruitful reading and hearing of the text
in the twenty-first century CE. Those of no religious or theological persuasion, but with any kind of social conscience, will find the declaration that
the exploitation and mistreatment of the poor and weak by the wealthy and
strong is simply abhorrent and wrong. This will resonate with their social
conscience. Those who stand within the Judaeo-Christian tradition will
recognise, additionally, that the theological themes of neglect of YHWH's
saving actions on behalf of his people, neglect of his word delivered by his
messengers, and profanation of YHWH's name constitute additional, powerful reasons for judgement.

2 Words of YHWH to Israel – Amos 3–4

Amos 3:1–2 – 'You Only Have I Known'

> 3 Hear this word that the Lord has spoken against you, O people of Israel,
>   against the whole family that I brought up out of the land of Egypt:
> ² You only have I known
>   of all the families of the earth;
> therefore I will punish you
>   for all your iniquities.

Amos 3:1–2 forms a hinge between the OAN of Amos 1–2 and the prophetic
sayings of Amos 3–6. The reference to the special relationship that YHWH
has with Israel, as distinct from other nations, casts an eye backwards to the
OAN, but more significantly introduces what is to come. While the OAN
series of 1:3–2:16 and the visions series in 7:1–9:6 comprise blocks of material which hold together, chapters 3–6 comprise smaller units. The opening 'Hear this word that YHWH has spoken against you' of 3:1, introducing
chapters 3–4, has a parallel in the 'Hear this word that I take up against you'
of 5:1, which introduces chapters 5–6. These introductory formulae mark
out the two halves of this middle block of the book. The phrase 'against the
whole family that I brought up out of the land of Egypt' was not present

C Commentary on Amos

in the earliest Post-722 Composition, but entered the text in the Exilic Redactional Composition. This is indicated by (1) YHWH speaking in the first person, while the preceding clause speaks of him in the third person; and (2) the fact that it is clearly an expansion of the original short 'against you'. The reference to having 'brought you up out of the land of Egypt' links it to 2:10, which also entered the text in this composition. Its purpose is to ensure that 3:2, originally addressed to the northern kingdom, is now seen to have been applied to the whole people of Israel, including Judah.

The vocabulary of 3:2 has links with the Hosea-text. It contains three key words which are quite unusual in Amos, but are frequent in Hosea.[87] The verb 'know' with YHWH as subject is found only here in Amos, but is used in Hosea 5:3 and 13:5 to indicate a special relationship. While too much play has sometimes been made of the use of the verb in verses such as Genesis 4:1 to indicate the closeness of sexual union as a parallel for the closeness of the union of YHWH with his people (see 'A Closer Look: Knowledge of and by YHWH'), undoubtedly it conveys a sense of special relationship. The verb for 'punish' (*pāqad*) is found in Hosea 1:4; 2:13 [15]; 4:9, 14; 8:13; 9:9; 12:2 [3]. As Jeremias comments, 'Few verbs can be as typical for Hosea's message as this one.'[88] Similarly the word for 'iniquities' is found in Hosea 4:8; 5:5; 7:1; 8:13; 9:7, 9; 12:8 [9]; 13:12; 14:1–2 [2–3]. Clearly those who crafted Amos 3:2 as literary text did so under the conscious influence of Hosea, with the intention that their readers take note of both texts. Israel is, according to this verse, uniquely known of 'all the families of the earth'. The only other verses in the Hebrew Bible to employ this phrase are Genesis 12:3, in which YHWH promises Abram that in him 'all the families of the earth' will be blessed, and Genesis 28:14, in which he makes the same promise to Jacob. Both Amos 3:2 and the verses in Genesis place the special relationship with Israel within a global setting.

The commentary on Amos 1:3–2:16 described the rhetorical strategy, found a number of times in the Amos-text, of building an expectation and then suddenly reversing it. That same strategy is employed in 3:2. To be assured that 'you only have I known of all the families of the earth' leads to an expectation that words of positive promise are to follow. Instead, however, the expectation is reversed: 'therefore I will punish you for all your iniquities'. YHWH's special relationship with his people is all the more reason why his judgement

---

[87] See J. Jeremias, 'The Interrelationship between Amos and Hosea', in J. W. Watts and P. R. House (eds.), *Forming Prophetic Literature: Essays on Isaiah and the Twelve in Honor of John D. W. Watts* (JSOTSup, 235; Sheffield: Sheffield Academic Press, 1996): 171–98 (182–3).

[88] J. Jeremias 'Interrelationship' (1996): 182.

on them is warranted, for the reasons already described in 2:6–16, and for those which will be set out in chapters 3–6. Is there a tension here with Amos 9:7, which denies any such special relationship? Barton sees the two as contradictory: 9:7 denies that there ever was any such special relationship, while 3:2 accepts that there was, but seeks to prevent the wrong conclusion that Israel would therefore be excused her sin. Houston's treatment of these verses is nuanced: while formally they contradict each other, they have the same rhetorical aim and effect, namely to deny to Israel any sense of privilege and protection on the basis of a belief in such a special relationship.[89] Rhetorical aim and effect override the requirements of logical consistency.

These introductory verses have set the scene for the prophetic oracles of judgement to come. Before they begin, however, a series of questions seeks to justify the basis of authority on which the forthcoming words of judgement will be given.

Amos 3:3–8 – YHWH Has Spoken: Who Can But Prophesy?

3 Do two walk together
    unless they have made an appointment?
4 Does a lion roar in the forest
    when it has no prey?
Does a young lion cry out from its den
    if it has caught nothing?
5 Does a bird fall into a snare on the earth
    when there is no trap for it?
Does a snare spring up from the ground
    when it has taken nothing?
6 Is a trumpet blown in a city,
    and the people are not afraid?
Does disaster befall a city
    unless the Lord has done it?
7 Surely the Lord God does nothing,
    without revealing his secret
    to his servants the prophets.
8 The lion has roared;
    who will not fear?
The Lord God has spoken;
    who can but prophesy?

---

[89]   J. Barton *Theology of the Book of Amos* (2012): 71–2; W. J. Houston *Amos: Justice and Violence* (2015): 44.

C Commentary on Amos

These verses constitute a clever series of rhetorical questions. From an opening apparently harmless question, those following become increasingly ominous, until a climax is reached which speaks of disaster sent by YHWH in 3:6 and a compulsion to prophesy in 3:8.

The series underwent development during the composition history of the text. There is widespread agreement that 3:7 was not part of the original series. It entered it in the Exilic Redactional Composition under Deuteronomistic influence. The reasons for this are (1) it interrupts the series of questions with a statement which is only loosely connected to it; and (2) the language and interest is characteristically Deuteronomistic: passages in Kings and passages in Jeremiah displaying Deuteronomistic influence refer to 'his/my servants the prophets' (cf. 2 Kgs 17:13, 23; 21:10; 24:2; Jer. 7:25; 26:5; 35:15; 44:4). More disputed is whether the original series ended at 3:6 or included 3:8. I have argued elsewhere that the series in the earliest, Post-722 Composition comprised 3:3-6.[90] There is every reason to see 3:6 as the original climax. The question 'Does disaster befall a city, unless YHWH has done it?' glances backwards to the destruction of cities announced in the OAN of chapters 1:3-2:3, and also points forwards to what will be announced in the immediately following oracle with regard to the city of Samaria (3:9-11). Its climactic character is further evident in the change of interrogative from the Hebrew *hă* in 3:3-5 to the more intensive *'im* in 3:6. This final question is in accord with the central thrust of this earliest textual layer, in which the announcement of YHWH's judgement is paramount. A century later, in the time of Josiah, the Late Pre-exilic Redactional Composition brought in 3:8 as a new climax. It was a skilful addition, with the roaring lion picking up the imagery of 3:4, while thematically it prepared the ground for 7:14-15, which also entered the text in this redactional composition. The exilic 1:2 then drew on 3:8 in its formulation.

The opening 3:3 is unique in being a single question, in contrast to those in 3:4-6 which are all paired: in the remote Israelite or Judean countryside, 'Do two people walk together unless they have made an appointment?'[91] Is there a hint here that the two who walk together are YHWH and Amos, as some suggest? The text does not indicate this: the question and those that follow it are literal rather than allegorical. However, texts engage us at many

---

[90] G. R. Hamborg *Still Selling the Righteous* (2012): 67-70.
[91] S. M. Paul *Amos* (1991): 104, 109-10 argues that the question does not imply an arrangement deliberately made, and translates 'Do two walk together without having met?' However the verb more frequently implies an appointment, and his is a minority view.

levels, and readers are at liberty to see such an additional layer of meaning if it strikes them so. This opening question is followed by two pairs of questions relating to the capture of animals. The words for 'lion' and 'young lion' in 3:4 are different nouns in the Hebrew, but the focus is less on any contrast between the two as in the contrast between the before and after of capturing prey. Before the capture a lion is silent, stalking quietly in the hope of not being seen or heard, while after the capture there is the noise of triumphant devouring. The questions of 3:5 have generated scholarly discussion as to what is meant and consequently how they should be translated. NRSV follows the literal Hebrew, which leaves the problem of why a bird should fall into a snare on the ground. The words for 'snare' and 'trap' are found together many times in the Hebrew Bible (Josh. 23:13; Ps. 141:9; Isa. 8:14), and it is likely that a two-part weapon of some kind is meant. Wolff translates the first noun as 'wooden missile', commenting that it 'must be some sort of throwing stick.... There is evidence that the boomerang and the throwing stick were common weapons in the ancient Near East.' Mays refers to 'a hunter's throw-net'. Paul, in contrast, translates it as 'bait' which entices a bird into a trap.[92] We cannot be sure. But the significance of the rhetorical question is clear: Can a bird be caught in a trap if no trap has been set? The first question of 3:6 then sounds more ominous: 'Is a trumpet blown in a city, and the people are not afraid?' Cities would have had watchmen on the city walls watching out for enemies, and the trumpet would be sounded to warn of danger or to muster fighting men. In due course some prophets saw themselves as watchmen, warning of YHWH's judgement (cf. most notably Ezek. 3:16–17; 33:1–9), but that parallel is not drawn here. Rather the final question reveals the climax towards which the series of questions has moved: 'Does disaster befall a city, unless YHWH has done it?' The first literary layer of the Amos-text was formed in the wake of the destruction of Samaria in 722. These verses express that this had been no random event, but that YHWH caused it. The words to come in Amos 3–6 will explain why. It is implied here that the audience doubted that YHWH would act against them in judgement and, as Gitay writes, 'Amos's main concern is the recognition that God reveals himself not only in matters of success but also in terms of sin and punishment.'[93] The series of rhetorical questions makes

---

[92] H. W. Wolff *Joel and Amos* (1977): 180, 185; J. L. Mays *Amos* (1969): 61; S. M. Paul *Amos* (1991): 104, 110–11.

[93] Y. Gitay, 'A Study of Amos's Art of Speech: A Rhetorical Analysis of Amos 3:1–15', *CBQ* 42 (1980): 293–309 (296).

C *Commentary on Amos*   313

the case that YHWH had indeed acted in judgement a compelling one: the reader is left with little choice but to assent.

A century later the Late Pre-exilic Redactional Composition added 3:8 to the series of questions. It uses the imagery of a lion's roar (from 3:4) to describe how YHWH has spoken: And if YHWH has spoken, who can but prophesy? This new climax to the series of questions makes a different proposition compelling: the historical Amos is seen as having had a compulsion to deliver his words of judgement on Israel,[94] and the people of Judah a century later needed to take these words seriously as being as relevant to them too. When the Exilic Redactional Composition subsequently brought 1:2 into the text, it drew from the two halves of 3:8, thus portraying YHWH himself as a roaring lion. This portrayal now stands over the whole book. The words 'prophesy' and 'prophet' are not found in the Post-722 Composition, but they appear in the Late Pre-exilic Redactional Composition here and in 7:10–17.

The Exilic Redactional Composition added 3:7. Rhetorically, this delayed proceeding immediately from 3:6 to 3:8, heightening the tension leading up to the final pair of questions. The verse also enunciates the belief that YHWH's judgement was not unforeseen, but that he had made his mind known to 'his servants the prophets'. Other Deuteronomistic verses state that warnings had been given by the prophets, and had been ignored, in respect of the destruction both of Samaria (2 Kgs 17:13–14) and Jerusalem (2 Kgs 24:2; Jer. 7:25–26; 35:15–16; 44:4–5). Amos 3:7 is in keeping with these. The climax of the series in 3:8 is even more powerful in consequence.

The Post-exilic Redactional Composition did not make any further changes or additions to these verses. However, a final form reading of the text can lead to yet another perspective on it. Linville envisages the text being read aloud among an ancient scholarly guild of the Second Temple period, which he calls (with admitted mischief) the 'Dead Prophets Society'. The reading invites the audience into the world of the text. A majority of commentators sees the audience as being those compelled to acknowledge the validity of YHWH's actions in judgement (3:6) and the justification for the message of judgement being spoken (3:8). Linville suggests, however, that an equally valid reader response is to hear the call to prophesy of 3:8, along with the following 'proclaim' of 3:9, as addressed not to Amos, but 'to no one in particular'. He takes the words as possible 'triggers for the readers' imagination, so that they can find themselves following in Amos' footsteps,

---

[94] As W. J. Houston *Amos: Justice and Violence* (2015): 26 writes: 'Clearly 3:3–8 is a reply to people who are questioning Amos's authority.'

314   *Book of Amos*

if not playing the role of Amos itself'.[95] Such a reading should not displace
the more widely accepted interpretation of the series of questions providing
justification for the actions of YHWH and the words of Amos announcing
it, but as an additional interpretative possibility it is suggestive.

Amos 3:9–11 – Summon the Witnesses

> [9] Proclaim to the strongholds in Ashdod
>   and to the strongholds in the land of Egypt,
>   and say, 'Assemble yourselves on Mount Samaria,
>   and see what great tumults are within it
>   and what oppressions are in its midst.'
> [10] They do not know how to do right, says the Lord,
>   those who store up violence and robbery in their strongholds.
> [11] Therefore, thus says the Lord God:
>   An adversary shall surround the land,
>   and strip you of your defence,
>   and your strongholds shall be plundered.

It is not specified who is being addressed by the instruction to 'Proclaim' in
3:9. It may be assumed, however, that the literary arrangement of the text
is significant at this point: perhaps the one who accepts the call of 3:8 to
prophesy is the one who will now answer the call to 'proclaim'. In the earliest Post-722 Composition, which did not include 3:7–8, the link between
3:3–6 and 3:9–11 was the theme of disaster befalling a city, and 3:6 established the principle that such disaster would have been brought by YHWH.
Now 3:9–11 specifies that the principle is to be worked out in respect of the
city of Samaria. These verses are the first of three units (3:9–11; 3:12–15; 4:1–3)
which focus on Samaria. The theme of oppression in 3:9 and 4:1 opens and
closes this group of oracular sayings.

The opening verse summons people in the strongholds of Ashdod and
Egypt to come to act as witnesses to what they see going on in Samaria.
LXX has 'Assyria' rather than 'Ashdod'. The Hebrew text is more likely to be
original: given that Assyria and Egypt are often found as a pair of two great
world powers, a change from 'Ashdod' to 'Assyria' is understandable, while
a change the other way round would be hard to explain. The inhabitants of
Ashdod had themselves already been portrayed as undergoing the punishment of YHWH (1:8), so there is some irony in them now being asked to be

[95]   J. R. Linville, 'Amos among the "Dead Prophets Society"', *JSOT* 90 (2000): 55–77 (76).

C Commentary on Amos

witnesses to the wrongdoings of the inhabitants of Samaria. NRSV translates a plural 'mountains of Samaria' as a singular 'Mount Samaria', noting in a footnote that it has done so. The singular is found in 4:1 and 6:1, but there is no reason to accommodate 3:9 to them.

The invitation in 3:9 is to the 'strongholds' of Ashdod and Egypt, and 3:10 refers to the violence and robbery in their 'strongholds'. In 3:11 it is then the 'strongholds' of Samaria which will be plundered. As noted in the commentary on the OAN, out of thirty-four occurrences of this word in the Hebrew Bible, eleven – nearly a third – occur in the book of Amos. The term implies fortified buildings, which were seen as a source of pride and strength. Those in Ashdod and Egypt are invited, imaginatively, to come to see the great tumults and oppressions going on in Samaria. What is imagined is a court scene, in which YHWH is about to pronounce judgement on the accused in Samaria, and those from Ashdod and Egypt are to be witnesses to the justification for YHWH's sentence. The Deuteronomic lawcode states that a conviction is not to be made and the death sentence not administered on the basis of the evidence of one witness: there must always be at least two (Deut. 17:6; 19:15). So here witnesses from two foreign nations are summoned. What they see are 'tumults' and 'oppressions'. The first term often denotes confusion and panic arising from divine judgement, or from the panic caused by YHWH when throwing his enemies into confusion (1 Sam. 5:9). But it can, more generally, mean disturbances or confusion in civic life, and that is the sense here. The meaning of the word 'oppressions' is well described by Paul: it designates 'the manifold "oppression" of the downtrodden masses, at whose expense the upper class increases its ill-gotten gains'.[96] Amos 2:6–8 has already made concrete what is here described in an abstract way, and passages such as 4:1–3; 5:10–12; 6:1–7 will describe such 'oppressions' further. The accusation continues: 'They do not know how to do right, those who store up violence and robbery.' Again, 2:6–8 has already described the kinds of actions which justify the use of such terms. In Ezekiel 45:9 'violence and robbery' is contrasted with 'justice and righteousness', a pair also found in Amos 5:7, 24; 6:12. The wealthy are not accused of storing up riches, but they are accused of storing up the violence and oppressions by which their riches are gained. The 'Therefore' of 3:11 marks the transition from reasons for judgement to its announcement. The punishment fits the crime: as the wealthy Samaritans have stored up violence and oppression in their strongholds, so now their

---

[96] S. M. Paul *Amos* (1991): 117.

316 *Book of Amos*

strongholds will provide no defence. They will themselves be plundered by an enemy. The enemy is not named, but those reading the text after the downfall of Samaria in 722 will have taken it to have been the Assyrians, described in Isaiah 10:5 as 'the rod of my anger'. It will have been the perceived fulfilment of words such as these which first led to the formation of a written text preserving them, with the intention and hope that present and future generations might avoid the evils of a past generation.

Amos 3:12–15 – Warn the Wealthy

¹² Thus says the Lord: As the shepherd rescues from the mouth of the lion two legs or a piece of an ear, so shall the people of Israel who live in Samaria be rescued, with the corner of a couch and part of a bed.
¹³ Hear and testify against the house of Jacob,
    says the Lord God, the God of hosts:
¹⁴ On the day I punish Israel for its transgressions,
    I will punish the altars of Bethel,
and the horns of the altar shall be cut off
    and fall to the ground.
¹⁵ I will tear down the winter house as well as the summer house,
    and the houses of ivory shall perish,
and the great houses shall come to an end,
    says the Lord.

It is likely that 3:12, 15 formed one saying in the earliest Post-722 Composition, and that 3:13–14 were inserted in the Exilic Redactional Composition. The pointers to this are (1) the expression 'house of Jacob' is only found elsewhere in the Amos-text as a designation of Israel in the post-exilic 9:8b (see the commentary *ad loc*); (2) the verb 'testify' in 3:13 is used in the sense of 'warn', a sense most characteristic of Deuteronomistic usage and in the work of the Chronicler (cf. 2 Kgs 17:13; Neh. 9:34); (3) the phrase 'the Lord YHWH God of hosts' is an expanded, later form of the earlier simple 'YHWH' of 3:12 and 3:15, and its insertion into the middle of a saying rather than at the end is characteristic of a later period from the exile onwards; (4) the reference to Bethel is out of place in this group of sayings concerning Samaria; and in both occurrences of 'Bethel' in the Post-722 Composition (4:4; 5:5), it is in a pair with Gilgal, not on its own; and (5) the expression 'on the day I punish …' (3:14) is only found elsewhere in exilic texts (cf. Jer. 27:22).[97]

---

[97]   G. R. Hamborg *Still Selling the Righteous* (2012): 72–3; J. Jeremias *Amos* (1998): 59–63.

C Commentary on Amos

The original saying 3:12, 15 appears, in formal terms, to be entirely an announcement of judgement, with no separate accusation or reasons for judgement given. However, its content indicates the reasons for judgement in the very act of pronouncing it. The text of the last part 3:12 is confused, but it contains the words for 'bed' and 'couch', and is of a piece with 6:4 in its condemnation of the level of luxury in which the wealthy of Samaria lived, with no concern for those struggling to survive materially. Verse 15 then speaks of the winter house, the summer house, houses of ivory, and the great houses (the last of these could equally well be translated as the 'many houses'). It is not to be doubted that wealthy Israelites might have had summer and winter dwellings: Judges 3:20 refers (probably) to the cool roof-chamber of Ehud's summer dwelling, while Jeremiah 36:22 refers to King Jehoiakim's winter apartment, and 1 Kings 22:39 tells of an ivory house built by King Ahab. There is nothing inherently wrong with owning and living in more than one property; but there is if an expanding property empire entails others living in poverty. Isaiah 5:8–10 is more explicit, and provides a commentary on these verses: 'Ah, you who join house to house, who add field to field, until there is room for no one but you.... Surely many houses shall be desolate, large and beautiful houses, without inhabitant.'

Amos 3:12 is best understood as being in the nature of a dispute, with the hearers imagined as people who believed that there would be a deliverance for the people. The text sarcastically asserts that yes, there will be a deliverance: in the same way that a shepherd seeking to deliver a sheep from the jaws of a lion might come away with a pair of legs or the piece of an ear! Exodus 22:13 states that the remains of a domestic animal mangled by wild beasts may be brought as evidence that the person looking after it hasn't, in fact, stolen it, but that it really has been killed. So if there are survivors delivered from the coming destruction, they will only serve to show that the nation has, essentially, been mauled to death. The image of a devouring lion makes a link back to 3:4 and, when 3:8 and 1:2 entered the text in due course, to them also, making a possible allegorical interpretation in which the lion YHWH destroys the sheep, Israel.

The exilic addition 3:13–14 asks the readers to 'Hear, and warn the house of Jacob' of coming judgement. The warning is that Israel will be punished for their transgressions. The exilic editors drew the verb 'punish' from 3:3, and the word 'transgressions' from the OAN series, thereby linking these verses into the wider Amos-text. An element of that judgement is that the 'horns of the altar shall be cut off'. The horns of the altar provided a place of sanctuary. Hence 1 Kings 1:50–52 describe Adonijah clinging to the horns of

318   *Book of Amos*

the altar until Solomon will swear that he will not take his life if he leaves, and his plea is successful. In contrast, Solomon fails to respect the principle of sanctuary for Joab, and orders his death nevertheless (1 Kgs 2:28–34). The threat in Amos 3:14 is that the horns of the altar will be cut off, so there will be no sanctuary for the house of Jacob. The altar concerned is that at Bethel. By the time of this exilic section of text, Bethel was associated with what had become the archetypal 'sin of Jeroboam' in setting up altars at Bethel and Dan. The narrative in 1 Kings 12:26–33 describes his actions in doing so, noting that 'this thing became a sin' (v. 30). Amos 3:14 is at one with the perspective of the Deuteronomistic History of 1 and 2 Kings in seeing the sanctuary at Bethel as having been a place of sin for the people of Israel. Within the Amos-text, it also prepares the reader for the dispute between Amos and Amaziah, the priest at Bethel, in 7:10–17.

Amos 3:9–11 and 3:12–15 both, therefore, announce and warn of impending judgement on the people of Israel, for reasons of the tumults, oppressions, violence, and robbery of 3:9–10 and the luxurious but unconcerned lifestyle of the wealthy described in 3:12, 15. A third unit in 4:1–3 now completes a trio of units concerning Samaria.

Amos 4:1–3 – The Cows of Bashan

> 4 Hear this word, you cows of Bashan
>   who are on Mount Samaria,
>   who oppress the poor, who crush the needy,
>   who say to their husbands, 'Bring something to drink!'
> ² The Lord God has sworn by his holiness:
>   The time is surely coming upon you
>   when they shall take you away with hooks,
>   even the last of you with fishhooks.
> ³ Through breaches in the wall you shall leave,
>   each one straight ahead;
>   and you shall be flung out into Harmon,
>   says the Lord.

The third saying concerning Samaria has remained unexpanded from its inclusion in the earliest Post-722 Composition to the final form of the text. It is addressed to the 'cows of Bashan who are on Mount Samaria'. In contemporary English usage, this sounds like a deliberate insult. However, it is unclear whether or not it would have been taken this way in the ancient world. The region of Bashan was known as a fertile one, and Psalm 22:12

C Commentary on Amos

[13] refers to 'strong bulls of Bashan'. It may be, therefore, that 'cows of Bashan' refers to the power and influence of those being addressed. Most commentators take those addressed to be the wealthy women of Samaria. Some, however, argue that if the 'bulls of Bashan' of Psalm 22 refer to strong soldiers, then here in Amos 4:1 the 'cows of Bashan' are soldiers or leading men of Samaria being mocked as weak, as supposedly mighty men behaving like women. This would explain nicely why some forms of words in these verses are masculine when feminine would be expected ('Hear' and 'their' husbands in 4:1, 'upon you' and 'take you away' with hooks in 4:2 are all in masculine form). It would also explain the word translated by NRSV as 'husbands'. The usual word for 'husband' is ba'al, whereas here we have 'ādôn, a term often used together with 'YHWH', but also of kings, masters, and military leaders. In that case the translation would be 'masters' or 'officers' rather than 'husbands'. Either interpretation is possible, with the usual understanding of an address to the wealthy women of Samaria perhaps being the more probable.[98] If this is so, then it is their husbands who are weak, and seemingly ordered around by their wives. The reason given in 4:1 for their judgement is that they oppress the poor and crush the weak. This accusation is of a piece with that of 2:6–7, the commentary on which refers to the significance of the terms 'poor' and 'needy'. Additionally they demand that their husbands bring them drink. This is one of three verses in the Amos-text which refer to the consumption of alcoholic drink (the others being 2:8 and 6:6). Abundance of wine is seen in the Hebrew Bible as one of YHWH's blessings to his people (cf. Ps. 104:15; Joel 3:18 [4:18]), and no Jewish celebration is complete without wine. What is condemned in these verses in Amos is not the drinking of wine, but a way of living that exploits the poor and weak while feasting and drinking with no concern for their plight.

The announcement of judgement begins strongly with YHWH swearing by his holiness that the time of judgement is coming. A similar oath formula is found in Amos 6:8 and 8:7. It serves to underline that YHWH will not go back on his intention to punish. The announcement continues: 'The time is surely coming upon you when ...' Some phrases similar to this one are found principally in later literary strands of the Hebrew Bible, but de Vries's comprehensive overview of such formulae states that 'the distinctively

---

[98] T. S. Hadjiev *Composition and Redaction* (2009): 146–7 discusses the question of the masculine forms, seeing them as reflecting grammatical peculiarities of the Hebrew language. His conclusion is that it is best to take these verses as 'criticizing the women of Samaria's aristocracy'; similarly G. Eidevall *Amos* (2017): 136.

320   *Book of Amos*

styled occurrence in Amos 4:2 is unquestionably original'.[99] What would
happen when the time came is, however, unclear to us, as the meaning of
the two words 'hooks' and 'fishhooks' is obscure. Similarly, if 'Harmon' in
4:3 is a place name, as NRSV takes it to be, it is one which is not referred
to elsewhere and whose location is unknown.[100] Amid the lack of clarity
as to the precise nature of the coming judgement, however, one point is
clear: judgement is coming, most probably in the form of exile, and all are
included in it.

A feminist critique of these verses will justifiably ask whether the text displays an anti-women bias at this point. Sanderson writes of the Amos-text
that 'the book as a whole has only fuelled the fires of misogynistic interpretation', with 1:13 being the sole verse that shows, she suggests, any sympathy
to women.[101] With regard to Amos 4:1–3, we may note that while it is the
leading women of Samaria who are addressed, similar accusation is made
against the leading men in 6:1.

Amos 4:4–5 – 'Come – and Transgress'

> ⁴ Come to Bethel – and transgress;
>   to Gilgal – and multiply transgression;
>   bring your sacrifices every morning,
>   your tithes every three days;
> ⁵ bring a thank offering of leavened bread
>   and proclaim freewill offerings, publish them;
>   for so you love to do, O people of Israel!
>   says the Lord God.

Following the three units concerning Samaria in 3:1–4:3, the section 4:4–13
is introduced by a focus on the shrines at Bethel and Gilgal. Amos 4:6–13
entered the text in the Exilic Redactional Composition. In the earliest Post-
722 Composition, therefore, 4:4–5 stood alone as a short saying, as its closing 'says the Lord YHWH' indicates. Thematically it is close to 5:21–24. It is

---

[99] S. J. de Vries, *From Old Revelation to New: A Traditio-Historical and Redaction-Critical Study of Temporal Transitions in Prophetic Predication* (Grand Rapids, MI: Eerdmans, 1995): 77.

[100] The commentaries of Andersen and Freedman, Jeremias, Paul, Wolff, and others refer to the ancient versions and discuss the translation issues of 4:2–3 *ad loc.*

[101] J. E. Sanderson, 'Amos', in C. A. Newsom and S. H. Ringe (eds.), *The Women's Bible Commentary* (London: SPCK, 1992): 205–7 (206). J. R. Linville *Amos and the Cosmic Imagination* (2008): 83 cites this same quotation.

C Commentary on Amos

a mocking parody of a priestly summons to come to the sanctuary to offer sacrifice and be blessed by YHWH. Rather than the people being invited to Bethel and Gilgal to sacrifice and be blessed, they are invited to come to transgress and be judged.

Deuteronomy 12 famously sets out that YHWH should be worshipped and sacrifices offered only at the one place where he would cause his name to dwell, referring to Jerusalem. In the light of this, a post-Deuteronomic reading entails a condemnation of the sanctuaries at Bethel and Gilgal *per se*. The Post-722 Composition, however, pre-dates this seventh-century Deuteronomic injunction, and condemns not the offering of sacrifice at these places themselves, but rather (as Amos 5:21–24 makes more explicit) the continual offering of sacrifice and worship alongside continuing, unchecked injustice built into Israelite society. Bethel was one of the two shrines established by Jeroboam I. The narrative in 1 Kings 12:26–29 includes mention of the golden calves that Jeroboam had made for the shrines at Bethel and Dan, at the southern and northern extremities of his kingdom. In Hosea 8:4–6 this is the sin that is rejected, but that is not the focus of Amos 4:4–5. Bethel had a long pedigree as a sanctuary in Israel. Genesis 28:18–22, generally attributed to the Elohistic strand of the Pentateuch,[102] describes Jacob receiving a dream there, naming the place Bethel, meaning 'House of God', and setting up a stone pillar there. This gave ancient legitimisation to Jeroboam's choice of it as the place to which the Israelites should go to offer sacrifice. Gomes argues from an examination of Bethel in the Deuteronomistic History that 'the Bethel sanctuary dominated the landscape of the northern kingdom for over 400 years'.[103] Gilgal, too, was an ancient Israelite sanctuary. Joshua 4:19–20 records it as the place at which Israel first camped after crossing the Jordan, and that Joshua set up twelve stones as a memorial to the crossing. It is recorded, too, that Samuel went to Bethel, Gilgal, and Mizpah on an annual circuit of visits (1 Sam. 7:16); that Saul was made king at Gilgal (1 Sam. 11:14–15); and that Saul was rejected by YHWH as king there (1 Sam. 15).

Amos 4:4–5 refer to various sacrifices and offerings. The morning sacrifices (*zebaḥ*) of 4:4 were part of daily ritual, which may also have been offered on the first day of a pilgrim's arrival at the sanctuary. The tithe (*ma'ăśēr*), the offering of a tenth of one's annual income, is referred to in

---

[102] G. von Rad, *Genesis* (OTL; London: SCM, 1972): 283.
[103] J. F. Gomes, *The Sanctuary at Bethel and the Configuration of Israelite Worship* (BZAW, 368; Berlin: W. de Gruyter, 2006): 59.

322   *Book of Amos*

Deuteronomy 14:22–29. Mayes takes 14:22 to be an old, pre-Deuteronomic law, which 14:23–29 then enlarges.[104] The thank offering (*tôdâ*) and freewill offering (*nədābâ*) were particular forms of additional sacrifice. The text assumes knowledge of all of these, and that they were practised. However, the closing line of 4:5 is biting in how it sees their purpose: 'for so you love to do, O people of Israel'. The people assumed that YHWH desired these sacrifices and would be pleased by them, but 4:5 indicates that while they may bring pleasure to the people, they bring no pleasure to YHWH. Amos 5:21–22 makes this explicit: 'I hate, I despise your festivals, and I take no delight in your solemn assemblies. Even though you offer me your burnt offerings and grain offerings, I will not accept them; and the offerings of well-being of your fatted animals I will not look upon.' This raises a much-discussed question: Are Amos 4:4–5 and 5:21–24, and some other passages in prophetic texts, against sacrifice *per se*, or is the accusation one of neglect of the poor, and of righteousness and justice, while the sacrifices continue to be offered? See 'A Closer Look: The Prophets, the Cult, and Sacrifice'.

Amos 4:6–12 – 'Yet You Did Not Return to Me'

> [6] I gave you cleanness of teeth in all your cities
> and lack of bread in all your places,
> yet you did not return to me,
> says the Lord.
> [7] And I also withheld the rain from you
> when there were still three months to the harvest;
> I would send rain on one city
> and send no rain on another city;
> one field would be rained upon,
> and the field on which it did not rain withered;
> [8] so two or three towns wandered to one town
> to drink water and were not satisfied;
> yet you did not return to me,
> says the Lord.
> [9] I struck you with blight and mildew;
> I laid waste your gardens and your vineyards;
> the locust devoured your fig trees and your olive trees;
> yet you did not return to me,
> says the Lord.

---

[104] A. D. H. Mayes *Deuteronomy* (1979): 244–6.

C Commentary on Amos

323

¹⁰ I sent among you a pestilence after the manner of Egypt;
   I killed your young men with the sword;
I carried away your horses;
   and I made the stench of your camp go up into your nostrils;
yet you did not return to me,
says the Lord.

¹¹ I overthrew some of you
   as when God overthrew Sodom and Gomorrah,
   and you were like a brand snatched from the fire;
yet you did not return to me,
says the Lord.
¹² Therefore, thus I will do to you, O Israel;
   because I will do this to you,
   prepare to meet your God, O Israel!

The exilic 4:6–13 begins with a deliberate contrast with the ending of the earlier 4:4–5,[105] which had referred to the offering of sacrifice as something that 'you love to do, O people of Israel'. This is now contrasted with the voice of YHWH declaring 'But I …' (literally: 'And also I …'). There follows a structured series of sayings depicting the kinds of disasters that the offering of sacrifices (4:4–5) was meant to avert. Each description ends with the words 'yet you did not return to me, says YHWH'. This immediately raises a question: How is it that the people were to see the disasters described as actions of YHWH calling them to repentance? As Mays writes, 'The cogency of reciting this narrative as a record of Israel's failure to respond to Yahweh presupposes that Amos had a basis for recognizing the blows as the personal overtures of Yahweh, and that the people should have recognized them as such and responded.'[106] The basis for such recognition is found in comparing 4:6–11 with verses in Leviticus 26, Deuteronomy 28, and 1 Kings 8 which contain similar descriptions of disaster. All the verses concerned are widely held to be exilic or post-exilic.[107] Amos 4:6–11 describe the disasters of lack of bread,

---

[105] For 4:6–13 see Section IV, 'Introduction to Amos'.
[106] J. L. Mays *Amos* (1969): 79.
[107] Leviticus 26 is the last chapter of the so-called Holiness Code. Its relationship to the rest of Leviticus is viewed variously in current scholarship, but few would propose a pre-exilic dating: see L. R. Bailey, *Leviticus–Numbers* (Smyth & Helwys Bible Commentary; Macon, GA: Smyth & Helwys, 2005): 201–2. A. D. H. Mayes *Deuteronomy* (1979): 349–51 sees Deut. 28 as a chapter with more than one layer of expansion: all the verses with parallels to Amos 4:6–11 are exilic. Amos 4:6–11 has the closest parallels to 1 Kgs 8:33–37, but the latter cannot be dated before the exile: see V. Fritz, *1 and 2 Kings: A Continental Commentary* (trans. A. Hagedorn; Minneapolis: Fortress, 2003): 96–9; B. O. Long, *1 Kings* (FOTL, 9; Grand Rapids, MI: Eerdmans, 1984): 103–4.

324   *Book of Amos*

lack of rain, blight and mildew, locusts, plague, and defeat in battle, and these same disasters are found in Leviticus 26, Deuteronomy 28, and 1 Kings 8. Leviticus 26:23, 27 envisage the possibility that despite such disasters the people may still not turn back to YHWH, as Amos 4:6–11 declares to be the case. In 1 Kings 8, at the prayer of Solomon set at the dedication of the Temple, Solomon prays that when such disasters lead the people to 'pray towards this place, confess your name, and turn from their sins, because you punish them, then hear in heaven, and forgive the sins of your servants' (8:35–36); and 8:46–50 indicates that the place from which the people will be praying is in captivity in a foreign land. There is sufficient variation in wording and order that there is unlikely to be textual dependence across these texts and with Amos 4:6–11, but it is evident that they all emerge from the same cultural and literary milieu and chronological setting, one which saw such disasters as warnings designed to lead to repentance. It is unlikely that the disasters described in these verses refer to specific, dateable happenings. Rather they comprise the kinds of typical disaster that could and did strike at various times.

The first disaster is 'cleanness of teeth' and lack of bread. As Nogalski writes, 'Far from a dentist's dream, clean teeth in the ancient world would have been unthinkable as long as there was food.'[108] This is followed in 4:7–8 by lack of rain. The absence of rain for three months before harvest time would mean that the entire crop would fail. The lack of rain affects some areas, but not all, resulting in movements of people in search of provision. The third disaster is that of loss of crops (4:9). The first cause of this is 'blight and mildew'. These two words are frequently found together (Deut. 28:22; 1 Kgs 8:37 = 2 Chron. 6:28; Hag. 2:17). The second cause is the devouring of fig and olive trees by locusts. For readers of the Book of the Twelve, Joel 1–2 had provided a vivid description of the destruction that locusts cause. Amos 4:10 then contains two disasters. The first is that of plague, which is described as 'after the manner of Egypt'. The reference is to the narrative in Exodus 9, in which plagues are sent first on the Egyptian livestock (9:2–7) and then on Pharaoh and the Egyptian people and officials (9:14). Now, however, it is the Israelites who will be the victims of plague. The remainder of the verse describes disaster in battle. Young men will die by the sword, their horses will be captured,[109] and there will be a stench of unburied bodies. The final disaster, that of being overthrown 'as when God overthrew Sodom and Gomorrah', has no parallel in

---

[108] J. D. Nogalski, *Hosea–Jonah* (Smyth & Helwys Bible Commentary; Macon, GA: Smyth & Helwys, 2011): 302.
[109] The translation here is uncertain, but NRSV's is as likely as any.

C Commentary on Amos

any of Leviticus 26, Deuteronomy 28, or 1 Kings 8, although Leviticus 26:30–33 describes a general overthrowing and destruction of the land. The same reference is found in other texts which reflect the destruction of Jerusalem in 587 (Deut. 29:23 [22]; Isa. 13:19; Jer. 49:18; 50:40). Those who survived the disaster would be 'like a brand snatched from the fire'.

These verses assume a theological framework of belief which accepted that YHWH would send disaster either to punish or to warn, something with which contemporary readers (including religious believers) will struggle. No less problematic, however, is to accept the total randomness of such disasters, and the consequent positing of a God who does not care enough to intervene in his world. How might the contemporary reader proceed? It is possible to ask whether there might be something that God is saying through adverse circumstances, disasters included, even if the answer may sometimes be negative. Amos 4:6–11 gives a positive answer: YHWH had been using these disasters to call his people to repentance. However, they had failed to respond, so now face the judgement that the book of Amos describes. These verses would help those in the exilic period, who looked back at the destruction first of Samaria in 722 and then, more recently, of Jerusalem in 587, to see the justness of YHWH's actions, and thereby, at the very least, that he was not disinterested in them. That interest in them would, in due course, be the basis of a hope for the future.

Firstly, however, there was need to hear the concluding 4:12. This enigmatic verse contains an apparent repetition: 'Thus I will do to you … because I will do this to you.' But it is unclear what 'thus' and 'this' are. Some commentators assume possible textual corruption.[110] Others argue that the verse refers to something which would have been self-evident to the ancient readers, but which is obscure to us.[111] More satisfying is the suggestion of Paul that it speaks of 'a culminating catastrophe, which resounds even the more intimidating and terrifying because of its indefinite and unspecified nature'.[112] This would make it of a piece with the equally enigmatic 'I will not cause it to return' of chapters 1–2, the unspecified nature of which made the threatened judgement feel even more ominous (see the commentary *ad loc*). In view of this, there is no doubt that the meeting with God for which the people are told to prepare will be a meeting for judgement.[113]

---

[110] J. L. Mays *Amos* (1969): 81.
[111] H. W. Wolff *Joel and Amos* (1977): 215.
[112] S. M. Paul *Amos* (1991): 149.
[113] In an influential article Brueggemann argued that the instruction to 'prepare to meet your God' was an invitation to last-minute repentance in the context of a covenant-renewal

326   *Book of Amos*

Amos 4:13 – The One Who Forms the Mountains and Creates the Winds

[13] For lo, the one who forms the mountains, creates the wind,
   reveals his thoughts to mortals,
makes the morning darkness,
   and treads on the heights of the earth –
   the Lord, the God of hosts, is his name!

As noted in the 'Introduction to Amos', Amos 4:13; 5:8–9; 9:5–6 are different from most of the Amos-text. They have their closest parallels in Job 9:1–12 and Isaiah 40:12, 22–23. These parallels are linguistic (for example, the use of participles here and in verses such as Job 9:5–10) and thematic, in the portrayal of YHWH exercising authority over creation. The refrain in 4:13; 5:8–9; and 9:5–6 that 'YHWH is his name' or 'YHWH, the God of hosts is his name' is found predominately in exilic texts in Isaiah (47:4; 48:2; 51:15; 54:5) and Jeremiah (10:16; 31:35; 32:18; 46:18; 48:15; 51:15–19, 57). These hymnic verses were brought into the Exilic Redactional Composition at key points in the text – in this case, at the end of a significant series of sayings and of the first half of the words of YHWH spoken through Amos – to create an added theological dimension to the text which recognises that the one announcing judgement on Israel was one and the same God who acted in creation.[114] YHWH is described here as the one who forms the mountains, creates the wind, and makes the morning darkness. The three verbs *yāṣar*, *bārā'*, and *'āśâ* are found together in the same order in Isaiah 45:7 and in a different order in Isaiah 43:7; 45:18. The first two are also found together in Isaiah 43:1. It is only in these chapters and in Amos 4:13 that these two verbs are found together. In Jeremiah 18:3–6 the word 'potter' is from the verb *yāṣar*, that is, 'the one who forms', and the verb *'āśâ* is used of his activity in shaping a pot from the clay. The verb *yāṣar* is also used of YHWH forming man from the dust of the ground in Genesis 2:7, while the verb *bārā'* is that used in the priestly account of creation in Genesis 1:1.

---

ceremony. However, the likelihood of this is rightly rejected by J. L. Mays *Amos* (1969): 82; S. M. Paul *Amos* (1991): 214. Brueggemann correctly notes the overlap in vocabulary with Exod. 19:11, 15, 17, but, as J. Jeremias *Amos* (1998): 75 n. 26 writes, he 'is too quick to interpret them liturgically'.

[114] A full exploration of these hymnic verses, attributing them to the exilic period, is J. L. Crenshaw, *Hymnic Affirmation of Divine Justice: The Doxologies of Amos and Related Texts in the Old Testament* (SBL Dissertation Series, 24; Missouri: Scholars Press, 1975). T. S. Hadjiev *Composition and Redaction* (2009) 136–9, 198–200 is a minority voice in arguing that these verses were present in the earlier layers of the text. See my refutation of his arguments in G. R. Hamborg *Still Selling the Righteous* (2012): 80–1.

C Commentary on Amos

There is a chiastic arrangement in this verse, before the final line. The physical forming of mountains of the first clause and treading the heights of the earth of the final clause constitute its outside, with the less physical creating of the wind and making the morning darkness forming an inner layer. The central line states that YHWH reveals his thoughts. There is, however, some ambiguity as to whether 'his thoughts' refers to the thoughts and plans of YHWH, or to the uncovering of the evil thoughts of human beings. On balance the sense of the verse in context makes the first option more probable.[115] The translation of 'makes the morning darkness' is also ambiguous. The Hebrew contains no prepositions, and could mean that YHWH brings morning from the darkness.[116] However, NRSV's translation is that adopted by the majority of commentators. The 'heights of the earth' on which YHWH treads may be a reference to Bethel, on which he now treads in judgement.

The series of warnings in 4:6–11 portrayed YHWH using actions in creation to try to lead his people to turn to him, but failing to find a response. As the one who forms the mountains and creates the wind, YHWH now turns his creative power on bringing judgement, by turning any hope of dawn and deliverance into darkness and trouble. The exilic introduction of 4:6–13 adds to the theological basis of the judgement announced in the preceding, earlier 3:1–4:5, and heightens the sense of impending disaster. The 'word that YHWH has spoken against you' (3:1) is now seen to comprise not only prophetic words of accusation and announcement of judgement, but also divine action in creation itself. The verse concludes not just the preceding 4:6–12, but the whole of Amos 3–4. The message is clear: while evil was being perpetuated with no turning to YHWH, there could be no escape from his justice.

3 Words of Amos to Israel – Amos 5–6

Amos 5:1–17 – Lament for a Fallen Nation

> 5 Hear this word that I take up over you in lamentation, O house of Israel:
> ² Fallen, no more to rise,
>   is maiden Israel;
> forsaken on her land,
>   with no one to raise her up.

---

[115] M. D. Carroll R. *Amos* (2020): 286; H. W. Wolff *Joel and Amos* (1977): 223–4.
[116] S. M. Paul *Amos* (1991):137 translates 'turns blackness into glimmering dawn'.

3 For thus says the Lord God:
The city that marched out a thousand
shall have a hundred left,
and that which marched out a hundred
shall have ten left.

4 For thus says the Lord to the house of Israel:
Seek me and live,
5 but do not seek Bethel,
and do not enter into Gilgal
or cross over to Beer-sheba,
for Gilgal shall surely go into exile,
and Bethel shall come to nothing.
6 Seek the Lord and live,
or he will break out against the house of Joseph like fire,
and it will devour Bethel, with no one to quench it.

7 Ah, you that turn justice to wormwood
and bring righteousness to the ground!
8 The one who made the Pleiades and Orion
and turns deep darkness into the morning
and darkens the day into night,
who calls for the waters of the sea
and pours them out on the surface of the earth,
the Lord is his name,
9 who makes destruction flash out against the strong,
so that destruction comes upon the fortress.

10 They hate the one who reproves in the gate,
and they abhor the one who speaks the truth.
11 Therefore, because you trample on the poor
and take from them levies of grain,
you have built houses of hewn stone,
but you shall not live in them;
you have planted pleasant vineyards,
but you shall not drink their wine.
12 For I know how many are your transgressions
and how great are your sins –
you who afflict the righteous, who take a bribe
and push aside the needy in the gate.
13 Therefore the prudent will keep silent in such a time,
for it is an evil time.

14 Seek good and not evil,
that you may live,

C Commentary on Amos

and so the Lord, the God of hosts, will be with you,
    just as you have said.
[15] Hate evil and love good,
    and establish justice in the gate;
it may be that the Lord, the God of hosts,
    will be gracious to the remnant of Joseph.

[16] Therefore thus says the Lord, the God of hosts, the Lord:
In all the squares there shall be wailing,
    and in all the streets they shall say, 'Alas! Alas!'
They shall call the farmers to mourning
    and those skilled in lamentation, to wailing;
[17] in all the vineyards there shall be wailing,
    for I will pass through the midst of you,
says the Lord.

The second half of the sayings in chapters 3–6 are introduced by the words: 'Hear this word that I take up against you.' They form a parallel with the opening words of the first half in 3:1. These introductory formulae mark out the two halves of the middle section of the book. Amos 5:1 conveys that it is the prophet who speaks.

Amos 5:1–17 has a chiastic structure and is at the centre of a wider chiastic pattern within the text: around it are accusations relating to the cult in 4:4–5 and 5:18–27, and around them accusations against the rich and powerful in Samaria in 3:9–4:3 and 6:1–14. This gives 5:1–17 a significant position in the text. Amid unrelenting accusations and announcements of judgement in the text, these verses, uniquely, contain invitations to 'Seek me and live' (5:4), 'Seek YHWH and live' (5:6), and 'Seek good and not evil, that you may live' (5:14). The structural considerations suggest that readers are being invited to pay particular attention to these verses.

Credit to recognition of the chiastic structure of 5:1–17 is generally given to De Waard, whose influential article in 1977 outlined it as:[117]

    A 1–3
        B 4–6
            C 7
                D 8a–8c
                    E 8d (YHWH is his name)
                D' 9
            C' 10–12 (13)
        B' 14–15
    A' 16–17

---

[117] J. De Waard, 'The Chiastic Structure of Amos V.1–17', *VT* 27 (1977): 170–7.

330   *Book of Amos*

Prior to recognition of this structure commentators had struggled with the order of verses, to the point of rearranging them. Hence Wolff describes these verses as 'so curiously linked with one another … and so difficult to understand in their mutuality', and he follows some older commentators in linking 5:7 with 5:10–12 and suggesting that its present position is due to 'a copyist's error'.[118] De Waard's recognition of this chiastic structure has been widely supported, and obviates any need for such rearrangements. This structure was present in the earliest composition of the text.[119] The one verse which does not fit naturally into it is 5:13 (which de Waard brackets in his outline): it is likely that this belongs to a later literary layer. Verse 6 also belongs to a later layer (see the comments later in this section). As noted in the 'Introduction to Amos', the hymnic verses 4:13; 5:8–9; and 9:5–6 all entered the text in the Exilic Redactional Composition. The structure in the Post-722 Composition was thus:

> A 1–3
>   B 4–5
>   C 7, 10–12
>   B' 14–15
> A' 16–17

The unit opens and closes with laments (5:1–3, 16–17). The lament, or mourning song, (*qînâ*) was a grief-filled poem or song used at someone's death, as epitomised by David's lament over Saul and Jonathan (2 Sam. 1:17–27). Jeremiah 9:17–18 calls for the 'mourning women … skilled women' to come to raise a lament, just as Amos 5:16 refers to 'those skilled in lamentation'. This was part of ancient Israelite funerary rites. Jeremiah 9:17–19 is, like Amos 5:1–3, a prophetic announcement of Israel's funeral. Similarly Ezekiel 26:17–18 raises a lament over Tyre, and Ezekiel 32:2 over Egypt. The lament in Amos 5:2 is for 'maiden Israel' (NRSV translates the same words as 'virgin Israel' in Jer. 18:13; 31:4, 21). Grief is always the greater when it is felt that a life has ended before its time, and such is the case in the death of a young girl who did not live to be married and have children. There is no healer or medicine to raise her up (Amos 5:2). Israel's time is to be cut short, and even YHWH will not raise her up this time, as the next verse makes clear by combining the lamentation with an announcement of

---

[118] H. W. Wolff *Joel and Amos* (1977): 231, 233.
[119] G. Eidevall *Amos* (2017): 152; G. R. Hamborg *Still Selling the Righteous* (2012): 83; J. Jeremias *Amos* (1998): 85.

C Commentary on Amos

judgement by defeat in battle. Military units will be, literally, decimated. The survival of a hundred out of a thousand or ten out of a hundred is not to be taken as offering hope of a remnant preserved, but rather as describing the totality of defeat (as in 3:12 the rescuing of two legs or a piece of an ear of an animal eaten by a lion). The description of Israel's funeral is expanded in 5:16–17. There will be wailing in the square and streets, with cries of 'Alas! Alas!' The word will come in 5:18 and 6:1 to introduce new units.[120] The farmers, too, are called to mourning, and there will be wailing in their vineyards (5:17). While in 5:1–3 the judgement is military defeat, 5:17 has wailing in the vineyards, the destruction of which will result in the loss of the wine and oil that they would have produced. This is caused by the direct action of the judging presence of YHWH: 'for I will pass through the midst of you, says YHWH' (5:17).

The reasons for the judgement are found in 5:7–12, at the centre of the chiastic pattern. Between the reasons for judgement and its announcement, however, come words of invitation in 5:4–6, 14–15 to 'seek me', 'seek YHWH', and 'seek good and not evil', with the hope that 'it may be that YHWH, the God of hosts, will be gracious to the remnant of Joseph'. As Jeremias writes, '[t]his can only mean that one might, by following the summons, sunder the connection between sin and death'.[121] Perhaps the funeral is not inevitable. In the context of the unrelenting words of judgement in the book as a whole, the hope is slight. But it is there.[122] For readers of the text looking back at the destruction of northern Israel by the Assyrians in 722, the invitations would clearly be heard as words to them to seek YHWH in order to avoid a similar fate befalling them. The invitations to 'seek' present in the earliest, Post-722 Composition were expanded in the Exilic Redactional Composition by the addition of 'or cross over to Beer-sheba' in 5:5, and by the addition of 5:6. These additions do not disturb the chiastic pattern of the whole.

The first, brief invitation is to 'Seek me and live' (5:4). The verb 'seek' (*dāraš*) can be used in an everyday sense of looking for an object or a person, but its use in a theological sense is more prevalent in the Hebrew

---

[120] In 5:16 the Hebrew is *hô* rather than *hôy*, despite the latter being more often used as an interjection. There seems to be no significance in the difference. In 5:18 and 6:1 the more frequent *hôy* is used.

[121] J. Jeremias *Amos* (1998): 85.

[122] In a noteworthy article R. Smend, 'Das Nein des Amos', *EvT* 23 (1963) 404–23 argued that 8:2's 'The end has come upon my people Israel' summed up the defining message of Amos. With regard to the thematic tension between this dominant theme and the verses here see the 'Introduction to Amos' and the comments that follow.

Bible overall. In narrative texts it is used of enquiring of YHWH in making a decision or to know something, generally through a prophet or human intermediary (Gen. 25:22; Exod. 18:15; 1 Sam. 9:9). In other texts, including psalms and prophetic texts, to seek YHWH appears to be to cultivate a right attitude towards him and towards right living, and such is the case here. The summons is to seek YHWH and live, in contrast to the preceding funerary verses. The brief opening summons is immediately followed by the instruction *not* to go to Bethel or Gilgal to do so. The commentary on Amos 4:4–5 describes the significance of Bethel and Gilgal as ancient northern sanctuaries (see the comments *ad loc*), and those verses describe YHWH's non-acceptance of the offerings and sacrifices made there. Now their fate is described: Gilgal shall go into exile, and Bethel shall come to nothing. The fate of Gilgal is described using a vivid alliteration, which is impossible to capture in English: *haggilgāl gālōh yigleh*. Having instructed the people not to see YHWH in Bethel or Gilgal, 5:4–5 do not specify a particular place where he is to be sought. In particular, the text does not say to go to Jerusalem, as if northern sanctuaries were being condemned while the southern capital was deemed to be acceptable. Rather, to seek YHWH appears to be to do with inner attitude. This is developed in 5:14–15 which, within the same earliest literary layer, unpack what is meant. To seek YHWH is to seek good and not evil; to hate evil, and to establish justice. If the people seek good and not evil, they may live, and YHWH will indeed be with them, as they claim he is. The summons to 'hate evil and love good' continues with the injunction to 'establish justice in the gate'. This picks up the accusation of 5:10, indicating that 5:14–15 builds on both 5:4–5 and 5:7, 10. The significance of the 'gate' as the place where justice was administered is explored in 'A Closer Look: Justice in the Gate'. The promise in 5:15 is cautious: perhaps YHWH will be gracious to the remnant of Joseph. The tribes of Joseph were northern tribes, so the name could be used to describe the northern kingdom. The 'remnant of Joseph' could refer to a kingdom already ravaged but not yet destroyed by the Assyrians, or to those who remained in the land after its conquest by the Assyrians in 722. The latter seems more probable. Readers in Judah, where the first written composition of the Amos-text was made, would clearly recognise that despite the reference to 'remnant of Joseph' it was they, too, who needed to seek good and hate evil, hate evil and love good, and establish justice in the gate, if they were to avoid a similar catastrophe in their own country.

C Commentary on Amos

A Closer Look: Justice in the Gate

We know little about the administration of justice in early Israel, but it appears that disputes were brought to a group of elders at the gate (Deut. 17:2–5; 21:19; 22:15, 24; 25:7). In 2 Samuel 15:2–4 Absalom seeks to undermine the authority of King David and boost his own by placing himself near the gate and intercepting those bringing a lawsuit for the king to judge. In Ruth 4:1–11 Boaz ensures that the elders at the gate hear Ruth's next of kin say that he does not wish to buy the field of Naomi and the hand of Ruth in marriage, and that they declare themselves to be witnesses to Boaz's consequent right to do so. Job 29:7 describes how Job used to go out to the city gate and take his place in the square, presumably as one of the respected elders of the city. The references in Amos 5:10–12, 15 to justice in the gate confirm the fleeting picture that these texts give us, of justice being administered and disputes settled by a group of elders assembled at the gate. The accusation of Amos 5 is that the practice was being abused through blatant lies and bribery.

The Exilic Redactional Composition expanded these words of invitation. That 5:6 is later than 5:4–5 is indicated by the different, stronger punishment of Bethel: fire will devour Bethel, rather than it merely coming to nothing. Additionally, while 5:4–5 deals with Bethel and Gilgal, the latter is not included in 5:6. This verse looked back to the record of Josiah's destruction of Bethel in 2 Kings 23:15.[123] A further addition was made in 5:5. As well as not seeking YHWH in Bethel or Gilgal, neither should the people 'cross over to Beer-sheba'. Beer-sheba was in the southern part of Judah, and texts referring to the days of the united kingdom could describe its extent as being 'from Dan to Beer-sheba' (Judg. 20:1; 1 Sam. 3:20; 2 Sam. 3:10). Amos 8:14, also part of the exilic layer of the text, indicates that Beer-sheba was a sanctuary whose practices made it one that the inhabitants of Judah should avoid, just as the Israelites had been told to avoid Bethel and Gilgal.

In the centre of the chiastic 5:1–17 come, in the earliest Post-722 Composition, the reasons for judgement, which are set out in 5:7, 10–12. NRSV begins 'Ah', following several commentators in adding a Hebrew

---

[123] G. R. Hamborg *Still Selling the Righteous* (2012): 84–5; J. Jeremias *Amos* (1998): 8, 89; H. W. Wolff *Joel and Amos* (1977): 111, 240.

hōy, as is found in 5:18 and 6:1. The addition makes better grammar, but is unnecessary: the verse reads perfectly well as an exclamatory cry without it. The accusation is that justice has been turned to wormwood, and righteousness has been brought to the ground. Wormwood was a bitter plant, frequently used to describe the bitterness of disaster (Jer. 9:15; 23:15; Lam. 3:15, 19). Justice and righteousness are found as a pair again in 6:12, where it is said that the people have turned justice into poison and righteousness into wormwood. The two words are also paired in 5:24, and 'justice' occurs again in 5:15. While it is commonplace to refer to Amos as a prophet or a text condemning social injustice and, by extension, calling for justice, these are the only places in which the word 'justice' occurs. Elsewhere oppression and wrongdoings are described which can validly be seen as expressions of injustice, but the term itself is used less in the text than it is by commentators on the text. Nevertheless, with 5:1–17 being the structurally central unit of the text, and with 5:7, 10–12 being the centre of the chiasm (in the Post-722 Composition), the words take on great significance. Their meaning is explored in 'A Closer Look: Justice and Righteousness'. Amos 5:7 having expressed the summary accusation of lack of justice and righteousness, 5:10–12 gives concrete examples of how this lack is seen: the people administering justice at the gate are hated for it, those who speak the truth (presumably either as litigants or as witnesses) are abhorred (5:10), and bribery is prevalent (5:12). Those who suffer the consequences are, as ever, the poor and needy (5:11–12). In verse 12 the *ṣaddīq* are afflicted: NRSV translates 'righteous', as in 2:6, but here in 5: 12 it could equally well, perhaps better, be translated 'innocent', since it is a legal setting which is envisaged. In contrast to 2:6–8, here in 5:10–12 the actions of those oppressing the poor and needy are clearly against Israel's legal and wisdom traditions (Exod. 20:16; 23:8; Prov. 17:23). The accusations of 5:7, 10–12 contain hints of judgement too: those who have built themselves fine houses of hewn stone will not get to live in them, and those who have planted large vineyards will not get to drink the wine made from their grapes. This kind of punishment in which an apparent blessing fails to lead to the expected positive result is found also in Hosea 4:10a and in Micah 6:14–15, and as a curse in Deuteronomy 28:30, 38–40. It appears, too, in Zephaniah 1:13, which Amos 5:11 appears to have influenced. At some point was added 5:13, asserting that in such an evil time the wisest course of action is to keep quiet. The lack of reference to any specific time invites readers to consider the degree to which their own day might be so described.

C Commentary on Amos

A Closer Look: Justice and Righteousness

Wolff notes that the words 'justice' (*mišpāṭ*) and 'righteousness' (*ṣədāqâ*) do not occur as a pair in Israel's legal collections, but do in Proverbs (e.g. 16:8; 21:3).[124] They also occur in other prophetic texts, especially Isaiah (e.g. 1:21, 27; 5:7; 9:7 [6]; 33:5). Both words can be variously interpreted. They can be understood as legal terms, signifying the opposite of the abuse of justice described in verses such as Amos 5:10, 12. Thus Harper writes: 'The very institutions which were intended to secure justice produce injustice … Righteousness, here meaning civil justice, is personified, and represented as an individual thrown down.'[125] Alternatively, they can be understood as ethical values and as a way of life that human beings should practise and promote. Weinfeld writes: 'If we look at exactly what it was that the prophets opposed, we see that the main wrongdoing is not the perversion of the judicial process, but oppression perpetrated by the rich landowners and ruling circles, who control the socio-economic order.' He adds: "Our interpretation of 'justice and righteousness" does not exclude the juridical sense of the expression … Our contention, however, is that "justice and righteousness" is not a concept that belongs to the jurisdiction alone.'[126] They may also be seen as divine attributes conveying blessing. In this case the accusation in 5:7 and 6.12 is that these divine blessings have been misused and perverted. Berquist writes with regard to Amos 5:21–24 that 'justice and righteousness seem to be attributes or activities of the deity, rather than the result of human accomplishment'.[127] Berquist also draws attention to the imagery of flowing water as providing a key to the unlocking of the significance of the terms, and in this is close to Koch, who writes that 'When we look at them closely they resemble a *fluid*. They pour out healingly like a river over the people (5:24).'[128] He links the reception of these divine qualities to cultic activity. Jeremias writes: 'These are entities already given by

---

[124] H. W. Wolff *Joel and Amos* (1977): 245. Deut. 16:18 instructs that judges and officials shall render *mišppaṭ-ṣedeq*, which may be translated as 'right judgement' (NRSV: 'just decisions').

[125] W. R. Harper *Amos and Hosea* (1905): 119.

[126] M. Weinfeld, *Social Justice in Ancient Israel and in the Ancient Near East* (Jerusalem: Magnes Press, 1995): 36, 44.

[127] J. L. Berquist, 'Dangerous Waters of Justice and Righteousness: Amos 5.18–27', *BTB* 13 (1993): 54–63 (60).

[128] K. Koch, *The Prophets*, vol. 1 (trans. M Kohl; London: SCM, 1982): 58 (italics original).

336   *Book of Amos*

God, as it were internally established qualities which Israel itself cannot create; it can, however, certainly corrupt them.'[129] There is considerable merit in this last understanding of the terms. While the explicit cultic link proposed by Koch is not certain, it is certainly the case that the relevant texts in Amos can be read appropriately in this way. A helpful bringing together of these possible understandings is provided by Houston. He writes that 'they refer to God's just ordering of the world, and in the human realm to just and generous social and political relationships, or what we would call social justice, and the legal, political and religious means by which they may be ensured'.[130] Amos 5:7, 10–12 spells out that the flow of God's gifts of justice and righteousness, his just ordering of the world, and the consequent intended establishing of just and generous relationships were being blocked by the exploitative greed of the powerful, and their illegal actions in the administration of justice.

Amos 5:7, 10–12 were originally the centre of the chiastic 5:1–17. In the Exilic Redactional Composition, however, 5:8–9 were brought into the text as a new centre. As noted in the 'Introduction to Amos', the hymnic verses 4:13; 5:8–9; 9:5–6 have been inserted at structurally significant points in the text, in this case at its very centre. YHWH had already been introduced in 4:13 as the one who makes the morning darkness. Here in 5:8 he is described as exercising power to turn the darkness of night into day, but also then, in judgement, to darken the day into night. He can threaten to undo the order of creation by pouring the chaotic waters of the sea on to the land. He who has the power to sustain or undo creation itself, as he chooses, is the same one who, 5:9 says, will bring destruction to the powerful who oppress the poor and needy.

Theologically, 5:1–17 introduces the concepts of 'justice and righteousness' into the Amos-text, concepts whose ideals are being betrayed by the injustice and oppression described through the greater part of the book. They also raise the question of how YHWH who announces judgement through the overwhelmingly greater part of the text can, nevertheless, summon the people to seek him and live, seek good and not evil, hate evil and love good, and establish justice in the gate. Those composing and reading the text after 722 knew that it was too late for the people of northern Israel. It was now essential that the people of Judah did not go the same way, but instead sought YHWH.

[129]   J. Jeremias *Amos* (1998): 90.
[130]   W. J. Houston *Amos: Justice and Violence* (2015): 35–6.

C *Commentary on Amos*

337

Amos 5:18–20 – 'Alas for You Who Desire the Day of YHWH'

[18] Woe to you who desire the day of the Lord!
  Why do you want the day of the Lord?
 It is darkness, not light,
[19] as if someone fled from a lion
  and was met by a bear
 or went into the house and rested a hand against the wall
  and was bitten by a snake.
[20] Is not the day of the Lord darkness, not light,
  and gloom with no brightness in it?

Jeremias draws attention to the parallel structures of 5:18–27 and 6:1–14. Each begins with a woe-cry directed against excessive self-confidence (5:18–20; 6:1–7). This is followed by a description of behaviour that YHWH hates (5:21; 6:8). There follows a question put to Israel (5:25; 6:12). Each ends with a pronouncement of judgement (5:27; 6:14).[131] We are reminded that the Amos-text is a carefully constructed literary work, something further confirmed by the opening 'Alas/Woe' of 5:18 linking to the cry of the mourners in 5:16.

Amos 5:18–20 was present in the earliest Post-722 Composition of the text, and remained unchanged in subsequent redactional compositions. In the Post-722 Composition it represents the earliest example of a prophetic woe oracle, and the earliest occurrence of the theme of the Day of YHWH. The literary form and possible origins of the woe oracle are explored in 'A Closer Look: Woe Oracles'. Those addressed are they 'who desire the Day of YHWH'. While the phrase 'Day of YHWH' is not used in the Hebrew Bible chronologically prior to this unit, the only meaningful way to interpret the unit is that it aims to counter a prevailing popular view that the Day of YHWH would be a day of blessing, in which YHWH would defeat Israel's foes and establish her supremacy. Just as the OAN series and other passages in Amos reverse expectations and understandings (see 'Words of YHWH to Israel – 3–4'), so here the positive expectation of the Day of YHWH is reversed. First a question is put: Why do you want the Day of YHWH? Contrary to expectation, it will not be a day of light, but a day of darkness. The point is made twice: briefly in 5:18 and more fully in 5:20. In between, 5:19 makes clear that there will be no escaping the visitation of YHWH, and any appearance of respite will prove to be illusory.

---

[131] J. Jeremias *Amos* (1998): 98–9.

338   *Book of Amos*

While eighth-century BCE readers will have heard the message in these terms, readers in subsequent centuries will have been familiar with a developed set of assumptions of what the Day of YHWH entailed (see 'A Closer Look: The Day of YHWH'). More specifically, those reading the Book of the Twelve in MT will have known from reading Joel 1:15–2:11 that the Day of YHWH was to be one of calamity. They would have known that it would be 'a day of darkness and gloom, a day of clouds and thick darkness' (Joel 2:2). Nevertheless, as Linville acknowledges in his commentary on the final form of the text, 'The rhetoric of 5:18–20 plays off a common belief, or at least a belief easily ascribed to anonymous others, that God will one day provide limitless bounty for Israel.'[132] Furthermore, while some Day of YHWH passages are directed at Israel, others are directed at foreign nations, so there may have been those who hoped that in their day it would be foreigners who would feel its effects rather than themselves. The element of surprise would not have been as acute for later readers as for eighth-century readers, but the words may nevertheless have been just as discomforting. It can be a perennial danger for religious believers to imagine that words of judgement are for people other than themselves.

A Closer Look: Woe Oracles

Amos 5:18 and 6:1 both begin 'Woe to ...'. The pre-2021 NRSV translated as 'Alas for ...'. The Hebrew *hôy* can be translated either way. As noted in the commentary on 5:7, some scholars consider that this verse also originally began in the same way. Westermann counts thirty-six occurrences of *hôy* in the 'prophetic cry of woe' in the Hebrew Bible: twenty-five against Israel and eleven against foreign nations.[133] Many are in series, as in Isaiah 5:8–24; 28–31; Habakkuk 2:6–20. The introductory *hôy* (Woe/Alas) is most often followed by a participle which specifies who is being addressed. There is generally then an accusation and announcement of judgement. On the one hand, Westermann saw these sayings as a variant form of the prophetic judgement oracle. He related them to treaty curses such as are found in Deuteronomy 27, and saw them as derived from them. On the other hand, Gerstenberger saw, rather, a relationship with wisdom sayings. He recognises that 'wisdom'

---

[132] J. R. Linville *Amos and the Cosmic Imagination* (2008): 115.
[133] C. Westermann *Basic Forms* (1991): 191.

C *Commentary on Amos*

can refer to sophisticated literary writings or to popular, local clan wisdom, and concludes that 'the woe-form in its original shape came out of the popular ethos'.[134] Its link with laments for the dead is evident in a text such as 1 Kings 13:30, but it is also used in a wider sense as a cry of despair (e.g. 2 Kgs 6:5). In prophetic texts from Amos onwards the woe oracles are mostly invective against the people.

Amos 5:21–27 – 'Let Justice Roll Down like Waters'

[21] I hate, I despise your festivals,
    and I take no delight in your solemn assemblies.
[22] Even though you offer me your burnt offerings and grain offerings,
    I will not accept them,
  and the offerings of well-being of your fatted animals
    I will not look upon.
[23] Take away from me the noise of your songs;
    I will not listen to the melody of your harps.
[24] But let justice roll down like water
    and righteousness like an ever-flowing stream.
[25] Did you bring to me sacrifices and offerings the forty years in the wilderness, O house of Israel? [26] You shall take up Sakkuth your king and Kaiwan your star-god, your images that you made for yourselves; [27] therefore I will take you into exile beyond Damascus, says the Lord, whose name is the God of hosts.

While 5:18–20 and 5:21–27 were probably originally independent units, from the earliest Post-722 Composition they have been placed together. There is no opening formula in 5:24, and it is intended that it be read as a natural follow-on to the Day of YHWH being a day of darkness, not light. The closing 5:27 is an announcement of judgement with an expanded closing formula (says YHWH, whose name is the God of hosts). Verses 21–24 function as the accompanying accusation, but are unusual in containing both accusation and instruction. Into this oracle as found in the Post-722 Composition, the Exilic Redactional Composition has inserted 5:25–26.

The opening 5:21–23 lists three related areas of Israel's worshipping life that YHWH will no longer accept: their festivals, their offerings, and their songs of praise. The description of these as 'your' festivals, assemblies,

---

[134]   E. Gerstenberger, 'The Woe-Oracles of the Prophets', *JBL* 81 (1962): 249–63 (258).

offerings, and songs underlines that YHWH does not currently regard them as his. The same strategy is used in 4:4–5. YHWH says, first of all: 'I hate, I despise your festivals and take no delight in your solemn assemblies (5:21).' In Deuteronomy it is practices of the former inhabitants of the land that YHWH characteristically hates (Deut. 12:31; 16:22). Now it is Israel's own practices that he despises. The word 'festival' (*ḥag*) is used in the lists of festivals in Exodus 23:14–17; 34:22 and Deuteronomy 16:10–16 to refer to the three major Israelite festivals: the Feast of Unleavened Bread, the Feast of Weeks, and the Feast of Booths/Tabernacles. The term 'solemn assembly' (*'ăṣārâ*) refers to festive holidays. For the theological import of the text, less important than the precise festivals and solemn assemblies to which reference is made are the verbs used of them: that YHWH hates and despises them. The following verse 5:22 declares that YHWH will not accept the offerings that the people bring. Three offerings are referred to: the burnt offering (*'olâ*), the grain offering (*minḥâ*), and the offering of well-being (*šelem*). Again, less important theologically than identifying precisely what sacrifices and offerings were made in various periods are the verbs employed: YHWH will not accept or look upon them. Finally, YHWH instructs that 'the noise of your songs' be removed, and declares that he will 'not listen to the melody of your harps'. The record in 1 Chronicles 15:16–24 of the appointment of musicians by King David reflects the Second Temple period, but there is no reason to doubt that music played a part in pre-exilic worship too (2 Sam. 6:12–19; 1 Kgs 1:39–40). Again, however, the text declares that this brings YHWH no pleasure. The reason becomes apparent in 5:24: what delights YHWH is neither sacrifices and offerings nor songs and music, but the practice of justice and righteousness. 'A Closer Look: Justice and Righteousness' explores the meaning of these terms, and views positively the suggestion of Koch that these are qualities given by YHWH, to be received by the people through their participation in cultic activity. They could roll down and flow from YHWH to the people and lead to a just ordering of society. But while the people declined to practise justice and righteousness, YHWH would take no pleasure in all the cultic activity going on. Amos 5:24 makes clear that the people had the remedy to hand, if they chose to take it.

These verses, along with 4:4–5, raise the question of whether the prophets and the books containing their words were against cultic activity *per se*, or whether, rather, it was the mismatch between sacrifice and offerings on the one hand and lack of justice being practised on the other.

C Commentary on Amos

A Closer Look: The Prophets, the Cult, and Sacrifice

Amos 4:4–5 implies that YHWH has little interest in the offering of sacrifice, and that it is 'you' (the people) who love it rather than him. Amos 5:21–24 then makes explicit that YHWH hates and despises their religious festivals. LeCureux writes of these verses: 'A more complete, clear and total rejection of every aspect of the cult is difficult to find in prophetic literature.'[135] Other passages in the prophetic books contain similar sayings. Hosea 6:6 declares that 'I desire steadfast love and not sacrifice, the knowledge of God rather than burnt offerings.' Meanwhile, 1 Samuel 15:22 has Samuel declare: 'Has YHWH as great delight in burnt offerings and sacrifices, as in obedience to the voice of YHWH? Surely, to obey is better than sacrifice, and to heed than the fat of rams.' Isaiah 1:11 asks: 'What to me is the multitude of your sacrifices? says YHWH; I have had enough of burnt offerings of rams and the fat of fed beasts; I do not delight in the blood of bulls, or of lambs, or of goats.' The verses following refer to the bringing of offerings as futile, to incense being an abomination to YHWH, and to the festivals being burdensome to YHWH (1:13–14). Micah 6:6–7 asks 'With what shall I come before YHWH, and bow myself down before God on high? Shall I come before him with burnt offerings, with calves a year old? Will YHWH be pleased with thousands of rams, with tens of thousands of rivers of oil?' The subsequent 6:8 indicates that these are rhetorical questions expecting the answer 'No'. Some take such passages to mean that the eighth-century prophets whose words lie behind such texts were against the practice of sacrifice in principle, and that they point towards an internal religion which did not need external rituals. Others consider it unlikely that a religion without ritual could have been envisaged. They take them to mean that the sacrifices and tithes are empty and meaningless while there is no justice and righteousness, no steadfast love and kindness in human relationships, but not that they are inherently wrong. This fits with the rebuke of Jesus: 'Woe to you, scribes and Pharisees, hypocrites! For you tithe mint, dill and cumin, and have neglected the weightier matters of the law: justice and mercy and faith. It is these you ought to have practised without neglecting the others' (Matt. 23:23). Barton offers a characteristically

---

[135] J. LeCureux, 'Restored Hope? The Function of the Temple, Priest and Cult as Restoration in the Book of the Twelve', *JSOT* 41 (2017): 493–510 (501).

342   *Book of Amos*

lucid discussion of this issue, in which he writes that 'Amos sets his face against cultic religion', but also concludes: 'What the preexilic prophets at least seem to oppose is the offering of physical objects – animal carcasses and cereals – at YHWH's shrines as though these were *substitutes* for behaving rightly towards other people.'[136]

The debate is often left at that point. However it is important that we go further in recognising that these anti-ritual sayings became and are now part of the literary and theological tradition. LeCureux explores the place of these texts in the Second Temple period and in the Book of the Twelve, arguing that Hosea–Micah show no desire to see the sacrificial system and priests reinstated (in contrast to Haggai–Malachi).[137] Interpretation from within the tradition leads to the acknowledgement that while worship and ritual form a natural response to God, there is always the danger that they become ends in themselves. No pleasure is brought to God if worship and ritual are not matched by the practice of justice and righteousness (Amos) and by steadfast love and knowledge of God (Hosea). In other words, religion and ethics are inextricably bound together. This link between religion and ethics is often assumed to be something natural and obvious, but in the ancient world this was not so. Sacrifice was about propitiating the deity, seeking divine blessing or guidance, or maintaining ritual purity. These were separate arenas from matters of human behaviour. It is to biblical tradition, and especially to the eighth-century prophets and the texts incorporating their words, that we largely owe our now natural assumption that worship of God and right relationships in human behaviour belong together.

Incorporated into the text by the editors is then a rhetorical question: 'Did you bring to me sacrifices in the wilderness?' – and clearly the answer expected is 'No'. This is surprising in historical terms, since the Pentateuchal narratives give the contrary impression. It is likely that the editors sought to make a link with the Hosea-text, which is strongly negative towards the multiplication of altars and sacrifice (cf. Hos. 8:11–13). The preference for a religion of the heart which did not rely on sacrifice is then found in Deuteronomy and in texts influenced by subsequent Deuteronomistic tradition, including Jeremiah 7:21–23, which is the only other passage to say that sacrifices were not offered in the wilderness. The reference in Amos 5:25

[136]   J. Barton *Theology of the Book of Amos* (2012): 84–92 (91, 92, italics original).
[137]   J. LeCureux 'Restored Hope?' (2017).

C Commentary on Amos

to the forty years in the wilderness appears to have been added in the Exilic Redactional Composition, linking it to the exilic 2:10, and this redaction also brought 5:26 into the text. This verse and 8:14 are the only verses in the Amos-text in which the accusation is of turning to false gods, rather than the dominant accusation of social injustice. Sakkuth and Kaiwan were astral deities in Assyrian and Babylonian cults. They may have been introduced into northern Israel by the Assyrians after 722, and would definitely have been known to the Judean exiles in Babylon after 587.[138] In both the earliest Post-722 Composition and the Exilic Redactional Composition the unit ends with the declaration of judgement: the people will be taken into exile 'beyond Damascus'. Possibly in the 760s when Amos spoke, the reference might have been non-specific. From 722 onwards, however, all readers would have understood that it was the Assyrians who were meant. The declaration is the conclusion to 5:18–27 as a composite, but now single, unit.

Bridging the Horizons: Martin Luther King Jr.

Amos 5:24 seems to have been a favourite Bible verse of Dr Martin Luther King, albeit frequently in paraphrased form. Ackerman has documented several occasions in which King uses the verse in speeches, the most famous being his 'I have a dream' speech in Washington on 28 August 1963.[139] In it comes the sentence: 'We will not be satisfied until justice rolls down like waters and righteousness like a mighty stream.' As Ackerman notes, the (somewhat dubious) translation 'mighty stream' is found in the King James Bible translation of the verse. However, that version also translated *mišpāt* as 'judgement' rather than the more accurate 'justice' as found in all more recent versions. Thus King's translation is not derived from any one English translation, but is his own version drawing on mixed translations. Rhetorical effectiveness outweighed scholarly accuracy of translation. In his 'Letter from Birmingham Jail' (dated 16 April 1963) he acknowledges the eighth-century prophets as one of the sources of inspiration for his civil rights work: 'Just as the prophets of the eighth century B.C. left their villages and carried their "thus saith

---

[138] NRSV's naming of deities entails re-pointing the Hebrew words, which are *sikkût* and *kiyûn*. The vowels have probably been used to associate the words with the word *šiqqûs* (abomination). NIV follows an alternative understanding in translating as 'the pedestal of your idols, the star of your god'. In support of NRSV's understanding see, *inter alia*, M. D. Carroll R. *Amos* (2020): 349–53.

[139] S. Ackerman, 'Amos 5:18–24', *Interpretation* 57 (2003): 190–3.

344   *Book of Amos*

the Lord" far beyond the boundaries of their home towns … so I am
compelled to carry the gospel of freedom beyond my own home town.'[140]
King found that the theme of justice in the books of the eighth-century
prophets inspired him. Many other individuals have found the same.
Recent scholarly study has focused more on the text than on the prophets
as individuals, but the power of the theme remains undiminished.

*Amos 6:1–14 – 'Alas to Those Who Live in Luxury But Are Not
Grieved over the Ruin of Joseph'*

6 Woe to those who are at ease in Zion
    and for those who feel secure on Mount Samaria,
the notables of the first of the nations,
    to whom the house of Israel resorts!
² Cross over to Calneh and see;
    from there go to Hamath the great;
    then go down to Gath of the Philistines.
Are you better than these kingdoms?
    Or is your territory greater than their territory,
³ you that put far away the evil day
    and bring near a reign of violence?

⁴ Woe to those who lie on beds of ivory
    and lounge on their couches
and eat lambs from the flock
    and calves from the stall,
⁵ who sing idle songs to the sound of the harp
    and like David improvise on instruments of music,
⁶ who drink wine from bowls
    and anoint themselves with the finest oils
    but are not grieved over the ruin of Joseph!
⁷ Therefore they shall now be the first to go into exile,
    and the revelry of the loungers shall pass away.

⁸ The Lord God has sworn by himself
(says the Lord, the God of hosts):
I abhor the pride of Jacob
    and hate his strongholds,
    and I will deliver up the city and all that is in it.

---

[140]   Martin Luther King Jr., *Why We Can't Wait* (New York: New American Library of World
Literature, Inc., 1964): 77.

C Commentary on Amos

9 If ten people remain in one house, they shall die. [10] And if a relative, one who burns it, takes up the body to bring it out of the house, and shall say to someone in the innermost parts of the house, 'Is anyone else with you?' the answer will come, 'No'. Then the relative shall say, 'Hush! We must not mention the name of the Lord.'

[11] For the Lord commands,
 and he will shatter the great house to bits
 and the little house to pieces.
[12] Do horses run on rocky crags?
 Does one plough the sea with oxen?
But you have turned justice into poison
 and the fruit of righteousness into wormwood,
[13] you who rejoice in Lo-debar,
 who say, 'Have we not by our own strength
 taken Karnaim for ourselves?'
[14] Indeed, I am raising up against you a nation,
 O house of Israel, says the Lord, the God of hosts,
and they shall oppress you from Lebo-hamath
 to the Wadi Arabah.

While 6:1–7 reads like a coherent unit, it may be felt that verses 8–14 contain a number of sayings that the compilers placed in this final section of 'words of Amos' simply because they had not been fitted in elsewhere. If this is so – and it may be – they have nevertheless fitted them well into the structure of the text. As noted in 'Amos 5:18–20 – "Alas for You Who Desire the Day of YHWH"' and 'Amos 5:21–27 – "Let Justice Roll Down like Waters"', there is a parallel pattern between 5:18–27 and 6:1–14 (woe oracle, description of behaviour that YHWH hates, question, pronouncement of judgement). Additionally 6:1–14 rounds off the whole of chapters 3–6, by resuming the focus on Samaria which had characterised 3:9–4:3.

It is probable that all of 6:1–14 was present in the earliest Post-722 Composition with the exception of 6:9–10, which are almost universally considered to be later. Not all commentators agree. Some find the presence of 'Zion' in 6:1 problematic, considering that Amos only spoke to the northern kingdom of Israel. They therefore take the first part of 6:1 to be largely an expansion, translating simply 'Woe to those who feel secure on Mount Samaria.'[141] However, this destroys the poetic metre of the verse. While we cannot be sure what oral saying of Amos may lie behind it, the written text

---

[141] So H. W. Wolff *Joel and Amos* (1977): 269–70.

was a Judean one from the outset. It is therefore unsurprising to find Zion addressed. Some take 6:2 to be an insertion, as it disturbs the pattern of the woe oracle of 6:1–3, and moves from third-person participles in 6:1 to imperatives in 6:2.[142] Again, while it is possible that an oral saying of Amos may have comprised 6:1, 3, it is unlikely that the literary text ever existed without 6:2. Calneh and Hamath were conquered by the Assyrian emperor Tiglath-Pileser III in 738, and Gath probably in his campaign against Philistia in 734. The inclusion of 6:2 in the Post-722 Composition is therefore entirely appropriate.[143] Finally, the phrase 'but are not grieved over the ruin of Joseph' in 6:6 is taken by some to be an addition, on the grounds that it is extra-metrical, and probably assumes the disaster of 722. Again, while it is possible that an oral saying existed without this line, it is unlikely that the literary text ever did. Verses 9–10, conversely, may well have entered the text in the seventh-century Late Pre-exilic Redactional Composition. There is an opening secondary linkage (omitted by NRSV), 'and it shall be that'; YHWH is referred to in the third person, rather than in the first person of 6:8; and they are in prose, while the surrounding verses are poetic. Jeremias describes them as commentary on 6:8 and anticipation of 6:11.[144]

Amos 6:1–7 is a powerful critique of those who lived in unashamed luxury. If, as some hold, the phrase 'but are not grieved over the ruin of Joseph' in 6:6b is not original to the text, then originally it is the luxurious lifestyle itself which is condemned. However, if 6:6b is original, those who live such a luxurious lifestyle are condemned all the more because they have no care or concern for the nation's well-being. The first verse makes clear to a Judean readership that Zion, their capital, is no better than the now-destroyed capital of northern Israel, Samaria. The opening 'Woe to …' (pre-2021 NRSV: 'Alas for …') identifies it as a woe oracle (see 'A Closer Look: Woe Oracles'). The accusation of 6:1–3 is that the wealthy are living lives of complacency and ease. The 'notables' are presumably the governing upper classes. In their complacency they mentally defer any warning of 'the evil day' (6:3), equivalent to the Day of YHWH of 5:18–20, to some distant future time. Instead they bring near a reign of 'violence' (*ḥāmās*), a word already used in the accusation of 3:10. They are warned against their complacency by the comparison of Israel with Calneh, Hamath, and Gath. If cities such as these could fall to the Assyrians, why should the notables of Zion

---

[142] So, again, H. W. Wolff *Joel and Amos* (1977): 274–5.
[143] G. Eidevall *Amos* (2017): 173; G. R. Hamborg *Still Selling the Righteous* (2012): 88–9.
[144] J. Jeremias *Amos* (1998): 92.

C Commentary on Amos

and Samaria consider that they would be safe? The meaning of 6:2 is somewhat unclear. The Hebrew of the last line actually reads: 'Or is their territory greater than your territory?' NRSV follows an emendation made by many scholars. Mays, however, considers that the unchanged Hebrew is a quotation put on the lips of the complacent upper classes ('Let our countrymen travel to Calneh, Hamath and Gath, and observe that none of these countries is so large as Judah and Israel'), while Linville takes 6:2 to be expressing the equality of these nations and Israel.[145] Verse 4 resumes the participles of 6:1 (NRSV makes this clear by adding a 'Woe to/Alas for' which is not present in the Hebrew text). The focus now is not on mere complacency, but on extravagant displays of luxurious lifestyle. 'Beds of ivory' are not referred to elsewhere, but this verse has a clear, deliberate echo of 3:12, 15. The feasting and lounging is accompanied by music,[146] drinking wine from bowls, and anointing themselves with the finest oils. It must be remembered that the Hebrew Bible is not against music, wine, or precious oils. Indeed, they are celebrated as gifts of YHWH (e.g. Ps. 104:15). What is described in Amos 6 is held to be wrong, however, for various reasons. The 'bowls' from which they drink were quite probably those used in a cultic setting, in which case there was gross irreverence.[147] Their very size also indicates a level of excess unrelated to the healthy enjoyment of wine that Psalm 104:15 describes. And overarching it all is the complacency which is in no way troubled by the 'ruin of Joseph' (6:6).[148] Following six verses of accusation, 6:7 announces judgement. These rich upper classes will be the first to go into exile. This is the third occurrence in 6:1–7 of the word 'first', which literally translates as 'head'. In 6:1 it is the notables of the 'first' of the nations who are accused. In 6:6 they anoint themselves with the finest (= first of) oils. Now, with great irony, they will be the 'first' to go into exile: the judgement fits the accusation. At that time their revelry will come to an end. The word 'revelry' (*marzēaḥ*) occurs only here and in Jeremiah 16:5, where it refers to a funeral feast (NIV translates 'Do not enter a house where there is a funeral meal'). However, it is found in Ugaritic and other texts, where it denotes 'a

---

[145] J. L. Mays *Amos* (1969): 115; J. R. Linville *Amos and the Cosmic Imagination* (2008): 121.

[146] A post-exilic addition is 'like David' (one word in Hebrew), in accord with the Chronicler's portrayal of David as musician *par excellence* (e.g. 1 Chron. 23:5; 2 Chron. 29:27). While the principal addition in the Post-exilic Redactional Composition is 9:7–15, other minor additions such as this indicate that the whole Amos-text continued to be valued.

[147] J. Jeremias *Amos* (1998): 113.

[148] Israel is referred to by the name 'Joseph' as in 5:15: see the commentary on that verse.

348   *Book of Amos*

religio-cultic institution the purpose of which is to seek and achieve communion with a patron deity.… The central ritual of the cultic fellowship was therefore a cultic meal.'[149] Barstad assembled a wide range of Akkadian and Ugaritic texts containing the word, and demonstrated that such feasts were widespread.[150] He also argued that, since the Ugaritic texts often entailed the presence of the god El at such feasts, the condemnation of the meal in Amos 6:4–7 is 'for its connections with non-Yahwistic deities rather than for its immorality'.[151] This is a dubious assertion. McLaughlin conducted a thorough examination of occurrences of the term, and considered that Amos 6:7 opposes 'lifestyle at the expense of, and with indifference to, the poor'.[152] An important implication of the occurrences of the term in Jeremiah 16:5, and in the Ugaritic and Akkadian texts, is that these feasts were not private affairs in the homes of wealthy people, and invisible to others. On the contrary, they were both public and religious. This public display of wealth and luxury with no concern for the 'ruin of Joseph' is what is condemned.

Amos 6:8 is, in its literary context, an effective additional conclusion to 6:1–7. YHWH's swearing by himself picks up 4:2, in which he swore by his holiness: the oath conveys a certainty about a judgement which will not be revoked. The reference to Israel's 'strongholds' links back to 3:9–11, in which it occurs four times (as well as occurrences in the OAN: 1:4, 7, 14; 2:2). Introduced into the text is the enigmatic 6:9–10, of which the precise meaning is unclear, but the general intention apparent. Unclear is what is meant by 'a relative, one who burns it'.[153] The second of the two Hebrew words here only occurs in this text, and the translation as 'one who burns' is based on its closeness to the verb for 'burn'. However cremation was not widely practised, and the translation is not wholly satisfactory. Paul translates 'embalmer' on the basis of the closeness of the word to the word for 'resin' in Rabbinic Hebrew.[154] We cannot be sure. Unclear, too, is the meaning of the second half of the verse. What is clear is that 6:10 is similar to 5:3 in asserting that even if there appear to be a few survivors, this will indicate less the hope of a remnant than the totality of judgement.

---

[149] H.-J. Fabry, '*marzēaḥ*', *TDOT* 9: 11.

[150] H. M. Barstad, *The Religious Polemics of Amos* (VTSup, 34; Leiden: E. J. Brill, 1984): 128–42.

[151] H. M. Barstad *Religious Polemics* (1984): 141.

[152] J. McLaughlin, *The Marzēaḥ in the Prophetic Literature* (VTSup, 86; Leiden: E. J. Brill, 2002): 107.

[153] The pre-2021 NRSV replaced the suffix 'it' with 'the dead', on the basis of the reference following it to 'the body'.

[154] S. M. Paul *Amos* (1991): 215–16.

C Commentary on Amos

Amos 6:11 intensifies the judgement of 3:15. There it is said that the 'great houses' will come to an end. Here both great and little houses will be shattered to pieces. Like 5:25, 6:12 then asks rhetorical questions. The Hebrew of 6:12 reads 'Does one plough with oxen?' – to which the answer is 'yes'! However, a widely accepted emendation is to put a space between two consonants, making two words which translate as NRSV. The answer to both rhetorical questions is then negative, leading to the accusation that Israel has done something equally preposterous in turning YHWH's gift of justice into poison and of righteousness into wormwood. The accusation is a reiteration of 5:7, differently phrased (see the commentary *ad loc* and 'A Closer Look: Justice and Righteousness').

Verse 13 addresses the boasting complacency of the powerful. That Jeroboam II's reign contained notable military successes is noted in 2 Kings 14:23–29. The naming of Lo-debar and Karnaim could refer to specific military successes, or the names may have been chosen for symbolic reasons. Lo-debar is a place referred to in 2 Samuel 9:4–5; 17:27, but here in Amos 6:13 it is pointed as 'Lo-dabar', literally meaning 'no-thing'. Karnaim literally means 'horns', symbolic of strength. The boast is that they have taken strong cities. But 6:14 destroys all complacency: YHWH is raising up a nation against them. Just as the location of exile in 5:12 was not named, so here the nation is not named. However, readers of the text from 722 onwards would have taken it to be the Assyrians. This nation will oppress the Israelites 'from Lebo-Hamath to the Wadi Arabah' (6:14). The border 'from Lebo-Hamath as far as the Sea of the Arabah' is referred to in 2 Kings 14:25 as that which Jeroboam II restored. The entire land will be oppressed. The message is blunt: the complacency of those who indulge in feasting and revelry with no concern for the poor and for the welfare of the nation, and who turn justice into poison and righteousness into wormwood, will have that complacency shattered when YHWH acts against them. Contemporary readers may wonder whether military actions can be taken as acts of God in this way, but may well share something of the divine outrage against the complacent wealthy who have no concern for the poor and needy or for the good of the nation as a whole.

Amos 6:14 concludes not just its immediate unit, but the whole section chapters 3–6. While not as closely structured as the OAN series of 1:3–2:16, nor the visions series in 7:1–9:4, the section is nevertheless carefully crafted both structurally and thematically. In its final form it begins by specifying that the words to come apply to 'the whole family that I brought up out of the land of Egypt' (3:1), that is, both kingdoms of Israel and Judah, and 6:1

350   Book of Amos

addresses those at ease in the capital cities of both. While the words are mainly addressed to northern Israel, the text was composed, read, and heard in Judah, whose people were expected to see the implicit warnings to them. After 3:1–8's defence of the compulsion to prophesy, the units in 3:9–4:3 address, principally, those who live in the political capital of northern Israel, Samaria, as does 6:1–14. Accusations against the powerful are made concerning their oppression, violence, and robbery (3:9–11; 4:1), their trampling on the poor (5:11), their careless feasting, and wealthy and luxurious lifestyle (6:1–7), and their corruption of justice and righteousness (6:12). Within these come units where the focus is principally on Bethel, the religious centre of the kingdom (4:4–5:27). Here hollowness of worship (4:4–5; 5:18–27) is condemned if there is no justice and righteousness (5:7, 24). Throughout the section complacency is attacked: the failure to heed YHWH's attempts to call to repentance (4:6–13); the belief that the Day of YHWH would bring light and blessing (5:18–20); the trust in cult and sacrifice (4:4–5; 5:18–27); the feasting and revelry which considers that all is well, despite the ruin of Joseph (6:1–7). Yet also, centrally placed, are invitations to seek YHWH and live (5:4–6, 14–15). It may be too late for the people of Israel after their destruction by the Assyrians in 722, but there is still time for the people of Judah, if they will heed the words recorded.

4   A Series of Visions – Amos 7:1–9:6

Amos 7:1–9 – 'This is What the Lord YHWH Showed Me'

> 7 This is what the Lord God showed me: he was forming locusts at the time the latter growth began to sprout (it was the latter growth after the king's mowings). ² When they had finished eating the grass of the land, I said,
> 'O Lord God, forgive, I beg you!
>   How can Jacob stand?
>   He is so small!'
> ³ The Lord relented concerning this;
>   'It shall not be', said the Lord.

> ⁴ This is what the Lord God showed me: the Lord God was calling for judgment by fire, and it devoured the great deep and was eating up the land. ⁵ Then I said,
> 'O Lord God, cease, I beg you!
>   How can Jacob stand?
>   He is so small!'

C *Commentary on Amos*

6 The Lord relented concerning this;
  'This also shall not be', said the Lord God.

7 This is what he showed me: the Lord was standing beside a wall built with
  a plumb line, with a plumb line in his hand. 8 And the Lord said to me,
  'Amos, what do you see?' And I said, 'A plumb line.' Then the Lord said,
  'See, I am setting a plumb line
    in the midst of my people Israel;
    I will spare them no longer;
9 the high places of Isaac shall be made desolate,
    and the sanctuaries of Israel shall be laid waste,
    and I will rise against the house of Jeroboam with the sword.'

Amos 7:1–9:6 contains a series of visions. Many commentators accept
that in the earliest written text 7:1–8; 8:1–2; 9.1–4 stood alone as a series of
five visions. Some scholars see the fifth vision as separate from the series
(see the 'Introduction to Amos'). Certainly the first four visions contain a
progression from the first pair to the second pair, with the latter declaring
that YHWH will no longer hold back his judgement. However, the real climax is in the execution of that judgement seen in the fifth vision in 9:1–4.
Furthermore, as noted in the 'Introduction to Amos', the series of OAN in
chapters 1–2 and the visions series in chapters 7–9 surround the words of
Amos in chapters 3–6. The two series are matched in literary structure: in
the earliest composition they both comprise a series of five units, of which
the fifth is similar to, but also different in form from, the preceding four.
This clearly intentional structure makes a powerful literary context for the
middle chapters. Jeremias is persuasive in showing that the placing of the
visions series after the 'words of Amos' is significant. It serves to

> show Amos' readers how he changed from the messenger of divine patience
> to the messenger of relentless judgment; put differently, they serve to legiti-
> mize the prophetic message of judgment against Israel.... The most likely
> explanation for their position at the end of the book is that according to
> the logic of the book itself, Israel's enormous sin must first be presented (in
> chaps. 2–6) before Yahweh's inaccessibility to prophetic intercession and
> thus Amos' own new function can be presented.[155]

Such is the importance of the visions that it is unsurprising that later editions expanded the series. Between the third and fourth visions has been
inserted the narrative episode 7:10–17 (with 7:9 as a connecting verse). This

---

[155] J. Jeremias *Amos* (1998): 126.

explicates further the reasons why the time for intercession was now over. Most probably it entered the text in the seventh-century Late Pre-exilic Redactional Composition (see the commentary *ad loc*). Material has also been added between the fourth and fifth visions, the multiple connecting phrases suggesting that this has been done in stages. Probably 8:4–7 were added in the Late Pre-exilic Redactional Composition, with 8:3 as a connecting verse, and 8:8–14 in stages within the Exilic Redactional Composition (again, see the commentary later in this section). The effect of added verses between 8:1–2 and 9:1–4 is to introduce increased suspense before the final vision with its description of judgement being seen to take place. The Exilic Redactional Composition also added 9:5–6 as a new conclusion to the text.

The first four visions all begin 'This is what the Lord YHWH showed me'[156] (the opening of the third vision in 7:7 has 'he' rather than 'the Lord YHWH', who in the words immediately following is what is seen in this vision). Visions were a natural part of biblical prophetic experience, and vision reports are a regular feature in prophetic texts (see 'A Closer Look: Seers and Prophets').

The first two visions have an identical structure:

(1) Introductory formula: 'This is what the Lord YHWH showed me' (7:1a, 4a).
(2) Content of the vision (7:1b, 4b).
(3) Amos intercedes (7:2, 5).
(4) YHWH relents of his intention (7:3, 6).

The third and fourth visions also have a structure identical to one another, but different from the first two:

(1) Introductory formula: 'This is what he/the Lord YHWH showed me' (7:7a; 8:1a).
(2) Content of the vision (7:7b; 8:1b).
(3) Question and answer (7:8a; 8:2a).
(4) Explanation of the vision, which is an announcement of judgment (7:8b; 8:2b).
(5) Additional description of judgment (7:9; 8:3).[157]

---

[156] The Hebrew text has *'ădōnāy* (Lord) followed by the divine name (YHWH). NRSV translates as 'the Lord God'. NIV translates as 'the Sovereign Lord'.

[157] As noted, neither 7:9 nor 8:3 was present in the Post-722 Composition.

C Commentary on Amos

Repetition was a means of reinforcing the certitude of something. As Joseph says about Pharaoh's dream, 'the doubling of the dream means that the thing is fixed by God' (Gen. 41:32). So here, the sequence of two visions in which Amos successfully intercedes, followed by two visions in which no intercession is possible, underlines that there had been a time when intercession was possible but that it no longer was: the judgements announced in chapters 3–6 were definite.

In the first vision (7:1–3) Amos sees YHWH forming a plague of locusts. The Hebrew term for 'locusts' is rare, occurring just here and in Nahum 3:17, but is one of a range of terms for 'locust' found in the Hebrew Bible.[158] The root from which it is derived suggests that it means a large swarm of locusts; or Paul suggests that it refers to the larva stage, directly after hatching.[159] This swarm is being prepared as the 'latter growth' begins to sprout. The word for 'latter growth' only occurs here, but is related to the term in Hosea 6:3 and elsewhere for the spring rains. It may be the rarity of the word which has caused an explanatory note to be added which is now part of the text: 'it was the latter growth after the king's mowings', implying that the king had a right to a share of the early crop. Whatever the uncertainties of detail, the meaning is clear: a locust plague was about to be released. Such a plague would be devastating, as Joel 1:4–10 describes – and readers of the Book of the Twelve, reading Amos after Joel, will have read that description. In the vision that he sees, Amos cries out in intercession for YHWH to forgive. The prophet does not, in his intercession, seek to deny the justice of how he sees YHWH acting, but he pleads for Jacob (Israel) to be forgiven: for 'how can Jacob stand? He is so small!' While proclamation was the primary function of a prophet, intercession was another. In response to the prophet's intercession, YHWH relents, and declares 'It shall not be.'

The second vision (7:4–6) matches the first: YHWH calls for 'judgment by fire' to consume the land.[160] The sending of fire was the standard refrain of punishment in the OAN series of chapters 1–2. Now YHWH calls fire down upon Israel too. This fire will consume the 'great deep'. This was the cosmic sea which, in ancient Near Eastern belief, lay under the earth and generated

---

[158] P. L. Redditt, 'Locust', *NIDB* 3: 684–5.
[159] S. M. Paul *Amos* (1991): 227, with a footnote citing E. Hammershaimb, *The Book of Amos: A Commentary* (Berlin: Schocken Books, 1970): 108.
[160] The translation 'judgment by fire' is difficult. The Hebrew literally means 'to contend by fire'. The pre-2021 NRSV translated as 'shower of fire', following an attractive and widely accepted emendation proposed by D. R. Hillers, 'Amos 7:4 and Ancient Parallels', *CBQ* 26 (1964): 221–5.

354   *Book of Amos*

the rivers and springs which water the land, and without which the earth would dry up (Gen. 7:11; Job 38:16; Ps. 37:6[7]; Ezek. 31:4). The burning up of this would lead to there being no water to irrigate the land. The word translated here by NRSV as 'land' is not the usual word, but one which means something like 'portion of land' or 'territory'. Again the prophet intercedes, calling on YHWH to cease, appealing once more to his compassion: 'How can Jacob stand? He is so small!' Once again, YHWH relents and declares 'It shall not be.'

The intercessory pleas of these two visions appeal solely to YHWH's compassion, and those pleas succeed. These visions reveal that, while most of the Amos-text brings a message of unrelenting judgement, there had presumably been a time in the prophet's ministry when he considered the possibility that YHWH's judgement could be averted. If so, the third and fourth visions dispel that possibility.

A Closer Look: The Prophets as Intercessors

Prophets held a mediating role between God and human beings. Primarily this entailed speaking the word of YHWH. However, it also entailed intercession and prayer on the people's behalf. In 1 Samuel 12:23 Samuel declares: 'far be it from me that I should sin against YHWH by ceasing to pray for you'. In Exodus 32:9–14 Moses is seen as a prophetic figure in successfully interceding with YHWH to avert his wrath from consuming the people (and cf. Deut. 5:22–33 and 18:15–22). Contrastingly, in Ezekiel 9:8–10 Ezekiel's plea that YHWH not destroy the people is overruled. In Jeremiah 7:16; 11:14; 14:11–12 YHWH prohibits Jeremiah from interceding: 'do not pray for this people, do not raise a cry or prayer on their behalf, and do not intercede with me, for I will not hear you' (7:16). Had not YHWH so commanded, we may assume that Jeremiah would have done so. Intercession only makes sense if the person to whom intercession is made is, on occasion, willing to change their mind. The Hebrew Bible is clear that YHWH is such a God who can and does change his mind, and is sometimes willing to relent of his intended actions. He is not an immutable, inscrutable God before whom intercession has no point. YHWH can forgive in response to intercession or repentance. Amos's intercession in the first two visions (7:1–6) is successful. In the remaining visions, however, YHWH pre-empts Amos, allowing no opportunity for intercession.

C *Commentary on Amos*

In the third vision, what is shown to the prophet is YHWH himself standing beside a wall. Four times in Amos 7:7–8 comes the word *'ănāk*, a word which appears nowhere else in the Hebrew Bible. NRSV follows longstanding practice in translating as 'plumb line'. This gives a pleasing meaning to the unit: a plumb line would show a wall to be out of true, and Israel was being judged because she had not been true to YHWH. However, it has been convincingly shown that a more probable translation, based on Akkadian *annaku*, is 'tin'.[161] The regret is that the intended meaning is less clear. Tin is a soft metal, and Paul suggests that this may signify Israel's weakness.[162] Jeremias suggests that since tin was often used with bronze to make an alloy for weapons, this is a threat that YHWH is now armed as Israel's enemy.[163] A further possible and attractive line of interpretation is that a wordplay is intended. Such is definitely the case in 8:1–2 (see the commentary *ad loc*), with which 7:7–8 is directly parallel. It has been suggested that *'ănāk* is similar in sound to *'ānāḥâh*, meaning 'mourning', and that the meaning is that YHWH is placing mourning into Israel's midst;[164] or that it sounds like *'ānōkî*, meaning 'I', a wordplay for which Jeremias finds an Akkadian parallel. In that case YHWH would be setting himself among the people to judge them.[165] Sweeney allows the possibility of either wordplay suggested, preferring that of *'ānāḥâh* (mourning).[166]

This latter suggestion is plausible. Whereas in the first two visions Amos successfully interceded for the holding back of the actions seen in the visions, in 7:8 YHWH prevents any such opportunity. 'Amos, what do you see?' asks YHWH. In reply, Amos pronounces "*'ănāk*', perhaps, as discussed, seeing tin. YHWH then makes a pun in saying 'yes, and I am setting mourning in the midst of my people'. This is completely in accord with the parallel vision in 8:1–2. Novick goes further in arguing that in replying "*'ănāk*' Amos is unwittingly YHWH's instrument in placing mourning in

---

[161] B. Landsberger, 'Tin and Lead: The Adventures of Two Vocables', *JNES* 24 (1965): 285–96. S. M. Paul *Amos* (1991): 233–5 states that the usual translation 'must now be discarded' (234). Most recent commentators agree: G. Eidevall *Amos* (2017): 198; J. Jeremias *Amos* (1998): 130–3; J. D. Nogalski *Hosea-Jonah* (2011): 339. Holding to the translation 'plumb-line' is H. G. M. Williamson, 'The Prophet and the Plumb-Line: A Redaction-Critical Study of Amos 7', *OTS* 26 (1990): 101–21, who is followed by T. S. Hadjiev, *Joel and Amos* (TOTC, 25; London: IVP, 2020): 165–6.

[162] S. M. Paul *Amos* (1991): 234–5.

[163] J. Jeremias *Amos* (1998): 131.

[164] J. D. Nogalski *Hosea-Jonah* (2011): 339.

[165] J. Jeremias *Amos* (1998): 133.

[166] M. A. Sweeney, *The Twelve Prophets*, vol. 1 (Berit Olam Studies in Hebrew Narrative and Poetry; Collegeville, MN: Liturgical Press, 2000): 254–5.

356   *Book of Amos*

Israel. The prophetic word had power not just to announce a judgement but to implement it, and Novick sees YHWH as causing Amos to do just that in the third and fourth visions.[167] In the final line of 7:8 YHWH declares 'I will spare them no longer' (pre-2021 NRSV: 'I will never again pass them by'). Chillingly, the presence of YHWH brings not blessing, but judgement, in the light of the many reasons for judgement that the text has given in 2:6–16 and chapters 3–6.

In the Post-722 Composition the text proceeded straight to the fourth vision after 7:8. However a century later (see 'Amos 7:10–17 – "O Seer, Go, Flee"') the Late Pre-exilic Redactional Composition introduced the narrative episode concerning Amaziah, with 7:9 as a link verse. The 'high places' to which 7:9 refers were places of worship which, in Josiah's seventh-century reform, were viewed as idolatrous and therefore destroyed (2 Kgs 23:8–20), which took place in the same period in which this redactional composition was formed. There are echoes of Hosea here (Hos. 10:8). As discussed in the 'Volume Introduction', it is likely that the two texts were read together and influenced each other from early on after 722. The high places are here called the 'high places of Isaac': the name indicates the southern kingdom of Judah, and reminds Judean readers that, while Amos the prophet addressed Israel, they also now need to heed the text's message. The verse then links to 7:10–17 by referring to Jeroboam. It is credible that this verse seeks to nuance (some would say, correct) 7:11, which predicts that Jeroboam will die by the sword. In fact, 2 Kings 14:29 records that 'Jeroboam slept with his ancestors', that is, died a natural death. However his son Zechariah, who reigned after him, was 'struck down' (2 Kgs 15:10). YHWH's rising against the 'house of Jeroboam' allows Zechariah's death to be seen as the fulfilment of the threat. While 7:9 is now joined to 7:7–8 and concludes the third vision, its purpose in linking to the narrative following is evident.

Amos 7:10–17 – 'O Seer, Go, Flee'

> [10] Then Amaziah, the priest of Bethel, sent to King Jeroboam of Israel, saying, 'Amos has conspired against you in the very centre of the house of Israel; the land is not able to bear all his words. [11] For thus Amos has said,
> "Jeroboam shall die by the sword,
>   and Israel must go into exile
>   away from his land."'

---

[167] T. Novick, 'Duping the Prophet', *JSOT* 33 (2008): 115–28.

C *Commentary on Amos* 357

[12] And Amaziah said to Amos, 'O seer, go, flee away to the land of Judah, earn your bread there, and prophesy there, [13] but never again prophesy at Bethel, for it is the king's sanctuary, and it is a temple of the kingdom.'
[14] Then Amos answered Amaziah, 'I am no prophet, nor a prophet's son; but I am a herdsman, and a dresser of sycamore trees, [15] and the Lord took me from following the flock, and the Lord said to me, 'Go, prophesy to my people Israel.'
[16] 'Now therefore hear the word of the Lord.
You say, "Do not prophesy against Israel,
    and do not preach against the house of Isaac."
[17] Therefore, thus says the Lord:
Your wife shall become a prostitute in the city,
    and your sons and your daughters shall fall by the sword,
    and your land shall be parcelled out by line;
you yourself shall die in an unclean land,
    and Israel shall surely go into exile away from its land.'

Many scholarly words have been written on this one narrative episode in the book. In large measure this reflects the historical concerns of older commentators keen to find biographical details of Amos the prophet, and a description of his call to prophesy. The episode provides little of this, such that we are forced to the conclusion that this was not its purpose. Wolff puts it well:

> Anyone who suspects that we have here a fragment from a biography of Amos must explain the lack of information at the beginning concerning the circumstances of Amos's appearance at Bethel, to say nothing of the fact that there is likewise missing at the end any report of the decision made by the royal court on the basis of the message from Bethel and of the course of action taken by Amos after his eviction by Amaziah.[168]

Consequently, as Hadjiev notes, 'students of the text have begun increasingly to recognise that whatever historical information lies behind 7:10–17 its main purpose is not to convey biographical information about the prophet'.[169] More fruitful is to explore the literary purpose of these verses and of their position in the visions series.[170] Overlapping vocabulary

---

[168]   H. W. Wolff *Joel and Amos* (1977): 308.
[169]   T. S. Hadjiev *Composition and Redaction* (2009): 82.
[170]   Two articles significant in forwarding this approach were P. R. Ackroyd, 'A Judgment Narrative between Kings and Chronicles? An Approach to Amos 7:9–17', in G. W. Coats and B. O. Long (eds.), *Canon and Authority* (1977): 71–87; repr. P. R. Ackroyd, *Studies in the Religious Tradition of the Old Testament* (London: SCM, 1987): 196–208; and H. G. M. Williamson 'The Prophet and the Plumb-Line' (1990).

between these verses and the third and fourth visions suggests that the narrative has been composed specifically to fit into its present literary context:[171] 'midst/very centre' (same Hebrew word) in 7:8 and 7:10; 'never again' (7:8, 13 and 8:2); 'my people Israel' (7:15 and 8:2); and, within 7:10–17, the repeated 'Israel must/shall surely go into exile' (7:11, 17). Additionally both Ackroyd and Williamson identify vocabulary found within the books of Kings. A noteworthy literary link is the root 'conspire/conspiracy', which occurs in Amos 7.10 in the words of Amaziah about Amos. It is used in several parts of the so-called Deuteronomistic History, not least in 2 Kings 9–15, which cover the dynasty of Jehu who, it is said, 'conspired' against Joram (2 Kgs 10.9). Jeroboam II was the penultimate king of the Jehu dynasty, his son Zechariah being the last king, against whom Shallum 'conspired' (2 Kgs 15.10). Evidently this unit has links with the Deuteronomistic History, and consequently some scholars consider that 7:10–17 was an exilic addition to the Amos-text. However, it is not characteristically Deuteronomistic in style, and it is more likely that this unit has influenced subsequent Deuteronomistic thought.[172] The theme which may have fed from this Amos 7:10–17 into Deuteronomistic thought is that the rejection of the prophetic word constitutes a reason for judgement additional to other reasons given. This is clear, not least, in 2 Kings 17, the chapter which describes the fall of Samaria and the destruction of the northern kingdom in 722:

> YHWH warned Israel and Judah by every prophet and every seer, saying, 'Turn from your evil ways and keep my statutes, in accordance with all the law that I commanded your ancestors and that I sent by my servants the prophets.' They would not listen, but were stubborn…. Therefore YHWH was very angry with Israel and removed them from out of his sight. (2 Kgs 17:13–18)

A further link with this chapter is that 'YHWH warned Israel and Judah by every prophet and every seer' (2 Kgs 17:13): both terms occur together in Amos 7:12–15. This theme, that the rejection of the prophetic word is a reason for judgement, is not present in the Post-722 Composition of the Amos-text, but is brought in with this narrative unit which, in turn,

---

[171] This is not to deny the possibility that there was an older oral tradition concerning an encounter between Amos and Amaziah at Bethel. Indeed, the fact that 7:11 predicts the violent death of Jeroboam when history showed that he died peaceably makes it likely. However, the close literary links with the visions suggest that only with its insertion into the Amos-text was this composed in literary form.

[172] T. S. Hadjiev *Composition and Redaction* (2009): 83–8; G. R. Hamborg *Still Selling the Righteous* (2012): 55–7; J. Jeremias *Amos* (1998).

influenced subsequent Deuteronomistic thought. It is well placed between the third and fourth visions: it gives additional reason why YHWH is justified in saying that the end has come and that 'I will never again pass them by' (7:8; 8:2).

The encounter opens with Amaziah being described as the priest of Bethel. Bethel was the major religious site of the northern kingdom, and it is likely that both the sanctuary and its official were maintained by the king and accountable to him (in 7:13 Amaziah calls it 'the king's sanctuary'). So Amaziah sends a message to Jeroboam II. We cannot know whether Amos saw himself as conspiring against the king, but such is Amaziah's interpretation of Amos's words. No doubt both Jeroboam and Amaziah knew their history: that Jeroboam's great-grandfather Jehu had come to the throne in a bloody coup, in the instigation of which the prophet Elisha had played a part (2 Kgs 9:1–14). With Jehu having conspired against the then-king Joram, it was not impossible that someone might conspire against Jeroboam, and that, once again, a prophet might have a role in this – or so Amaziah feared, anyway. His message states that the house of Israel was unable to bear Amos's words, indicating that he accepted that the prophetic word held power and could be part of bringing Israel down. He then gives a summary of how he understands Amos's message (7:11). His words do not reflect a specific saying of Amos from elsewhere in the text, and whether Amaziah was attempting a genuinely honest summary or whether he put his own slant on it, we cannot know. Part of his summary, that Israel will go into exile, picks up on Amos's words as recorded, but nowhere elsewhere in the text does Amos prophesy that Jeroboam shall die by the sword. The narrative continues as though Amaziah did not wait for a response from Jeroboam, but immediately tells Amos to flee to Judah, whence he came (7:12–13). Bethel was over thirty miles from Samaria, so Amaziah did not feel the need to wait two or three days for a response: he would have been used to acting with royal authority delegated to him. While Amaziah's words could be taken as an instruction or command, they are generally and more naturally taken as giving Amos an opportunity to take a safe route out of the danger that he is in if he remains.

Amaziah addresses Amos as 'Seer', and tells him not to 'prophesy' again at Bethel. Amos, in turn, responds that he is (or was, see later in this section) not a 'prophet'. In this passage the terms 'seer' and 'prophet' appear to be interchangeable, and the verb 'prophesy' can be used of both equally. The translation of the Hebrew of Amos's words in 7:14–15 requires a judgement to be made on their interpretation. Hebrew does not need to include the

360   *Book of Amos*

verb 'to be', so it literally says: 'Not a prophet I, and not the son of a prophet, but a shepherd I, and one dressing sycamore trees.' Hence NRSV's translation of 'I *am* no prophet ... but I *am* a herdsman' is accurate, but equally possible is NIV's translation: 'I *was* no prophet ... but I *was* a herdsman.' Amos could have meant (1) that he used not to be a prophet, but now he is; (2) that he does not in fact consider himself to be a prophet even now, merely a herdsman called at this time to prophesy; or (3) that he is a prophet, but not a professional one paid to be on duty at a sanctuary. The interpretation and translation adopted depends not just on considerations internal to this unit, but to wider understandings of the office and function of a prophet.[173] As well as not being (or not having been) a prophet, Amos states that neither is/was he 'a prophet's son': in the books of Kings the 'sons of the prophets' constitute a prophetic company (e.g. 1 Kgs 20:35; 2 Kgs 2:3; 4:1, 38). Amos is saying that he does not belong to any such company. Rather he is a herdsman. The Hebrew word for 'herdsman' (*bōqēr*) occurs only here, but is presumably from the same root as that for cattle (*bāqār*) and therefore correctly translated by NRSV. The word for 'dresser' of sycamore trees also occurs only in this verse. Despite uncertainty regarding the precise meaning of these words, it is evident that Amos describes himself as being in the business of farming (and thus there is no conflict with the description of Amos in 1:1 as shepherd/sheep-breeder). His answer to Amaziah sets out his credentials for prophesying. He had not been brought up as, nor had chosen to be, a prophet. Rather YHWH had taken him and had said 'Go, prophesy.' His response in a specific situation lies behind the generalised 3:8, which also entered the text in the seventh-century Late Pre-exilic Redactional Composition (see the commentary *ad loc*).

There follows an individual judgement oracle on Amaziah. The accusation (7:16) is that he has sought to prevent Amos from prophesying and preaching. The judgement (7:17) affects not just Amaziah, but his family too. Amaziah himself will die, and Israel will surely go into exile. It is harsh to modern ears to hear of all the members of a family suffering such punishment for something that does not flow from their personal actions. A moderating reading can helpfully see the final line as an interpretative key: Israel will go into exile, and Amaziah's family are caught up in the kinds of things that happen to a people defeated in battle and carried into exile.

---

[173] While all commentaries address this, S. M. Paul *Amos* (1991): 243–7 gives a helpful overview of opinions. His conclusion is that 'If an unambiguous solution were available, the problem would have been resolved ages ago' (247).

C Commentary on Amos

There is no concluding 'says YHWH' or other such formula, as the final line referring to the surety of Israel's exile also leads straight into the fourth vision that now follows.

A Closer Look: Seers and Prophets

Amos 7:12–15 raises a question of terminology. Amaziah addresses Amos as 'seer', telling him to go and 'prophesy' elsewhere. Amos responds that he is/was not a 'prophet'. The term 'seer' is *ḥōzeh*, from the same root as the word 'vision', *ḥāzāh*. The term 'prophet' is *nabî*. In 2 Kings 17:13 and Isaiah 29:10 the two terms are found in parallel, and it is unlikely that any distinction between them is intended. Prophets frequently saw visions, and seers were assumed to prophesy. The interchangeability of the terms is evident in several passages. The story of the boy Samuel is introduced in 1 Samuel 3:1 by saying that the 'word of YHWH was rare in those days; visions were not widespread'. In the narrative Samuel then sees YHWH standing before him and hears him speak. The consequence is that all Israel recognised Samuel as a 'trustworthy *nabî* of YHWH' (1 Sam. 3:20). Some prophetic texts are headed 'the vision of ...' (Isa. 1:1; Obad. 1; Nahum 1:1). Amos 1:1 declares the text to be 'the words of Amos ... which he *saw*' (italics added). In Numbers 24:4, 16 Balaam's oracles are described as 'the oracle of one who hears the words of God and sees the vision of the Almighty'. In 2 Samuel 24:11 Gad is referred to as David's *ḥōzeh*. Further, 2 Chronicles 29:25 refers to 'Gad the king's *ḥōzeh* and the prophet Nathan', and the two are clearly in parallel. Lamentations 2:9 laments that Zion's prophets (plural of *nabî*) obtain no vision (*ḥāzôn*). Pedersen and Wilson both argue that *nabî* was the preferred term in northern Israel and *ḥōzeh* in Judah; beyond the exilic period, however, the traditions and usage merged.[174] Another term for 'seer' is *rō'eh*. It is found in parallel to *nabî* in Isaiah 30:10. In 1 Samuel 9:9 it is said, in a late editorial comment, that 'the one who is now called a *nabî* was formerly called a *rō'eh*'. Lindblom comments concerning the terms *ḥōzeh* and *rō'eh* that it 'is impossible to establish any distinction between them'.[175] It seems that from the period of the monarchy onwards there was no clear distinction between seers and prophets. The narrative of Amos 7:12–15 therefore makes perfect sense.

---

[174] D. L. Pedersen, *The Roles of Israel's Prophets* (JSOTSup, 17; Sheffield: JSOT Press, 1981); R. R. Wilson, *Prophecy and Society in Ancient Israel* (Philadelphia: Fortress Press, 1980).

[175] J. Lindblom, *Prophecy in Ancient Israel* (Oxford: Basil Blackwell, 1965): 90.

362 *Book of Amos*

Amos 8:1–3 – The Basket of Summer Fruit

> 8 This is what the Lord God showed me: a basket of summer fruit. ² He said,
>   'Amos, what do you see?' And I said, 'A basket of summer fruit.' Then the
>   Lord said to me,
> 'The end has come upon my people Israel;
>   I will spare them no longer.
> ³ The songs of the temple shall become wailings on that day',
>   says the Lord God;
>   'the dead bodies shall be many,
>   cast out in every place. Be silent!'

This vision is the second half of the second pair of visions, and is directly parallel to 7:7–9. Again, Amos is shown something, this time a basket of summer fruit, and again YHWH asks: 'What do you see?' Amos answers: 'A basket of summer fruit', to which YHWH responds 'Indeed, the end has come upon my people Israel.' This is a famous pun. The Hebrew for 'summer fruit' is *qayiṣ*, and for 'end' is *qēṣ*, words which sound similar. The vision of the summer fruit is in fact a vision of the end of Israel. NIV seeks to capture the pun by translating 'a basket of ripe fruit … the time is ripe for my people Israel'. As in the third vision, YHWH causes Amos to announce the judgement by answering YHWH's question.[176] The judgement in this fourth vision has a ring of finality to it: 'The end has come … I will spare them no longer' (pre-2021 NRSV: 'I will never again pass them by'), the final clause being repeated from 7:8. Amos 8:2 has been seen as a summary of the message of Amos.[177] Such a view fails to balance it with the 'Seek' invitations in 5:4, 6, 14. But at this point the message is clear: while YHWH had allowed Amos to intercede in the first two visions, now he allows no such opportunity. Rather he leads Amos to announce: 'The end has come upon my people Israel.' The books of Kings have earlier prophets announcing the end of a king's reign (e.g. 1 Kgs 14:10–11; 16:1–4; 21:20–24), but Amos announces the end of the nation itself.

To these two verses which comprised the fourth vision in the earliest Post-722 Composition has now been added 8:3, which, like 7:9, is a link verse to the verses following, added in the seventh-century Late Pre-exilic Redactional Composition. It adds description to the coming judgement. The first half draws on 5:1–2, 16–17 in declaring that there will be wailing in

---

[176] T. Novick 'Duping the Prophet' (2008).
[177] Notably and influentially R. Smend 'Das Nein des Amos' (1963).

C *Commentary on Amos*   363

that day. The joyful songs of praise in the temple will become the wailing of lament.[178] The second half reinforces 6:10 (also brought into the text in this redactional composition) with its description of many dead bodies, and its ending with the same interjection from 6:10: 'Hush!/Be silent' (NRSV translating the same Hebrew word differently in the two verses).

Thus far 7:1–8:3 has given no reasons for judgement other than the rejection of Amos's message by Amaziah. Its place in the text as a whole is such that it assumes the reader knows what the reasons are from 2:6–6:14, and in the eighth-century Post-722 Composition that is taken to be sufficient. Jeremias describes the logic of this as being that 'Israel's enormous sin must first be presented (in chaps. 2–6) before Yahweh's inaccessibility to prophetic intercession and thus Amos' own new function become comprehensible.'[179] The Late Pre-exilic Redactional Composition updated the text to be heard in seventh-century Judah, adding reasons for judgement in 8:4–7. The Exilic Redactional Composition enlarged yet further on the judgement itself in 8:8–14. Just as the addition of 7:9–17 created suspense before the fourth vision, so these verses create yet further suspense before the fifth and final vision in 9:1–4.

Amos 8:4–7 – *Cheating the Poor and Needy*

> [4] Hear this, you who trample on the needy,
>   and bring to ruin the poor of the land,
> [5] saying, 'When will the new moon be over
>   so that we may sell grain,
> and the Sabbath,
>   so that we may offer wheat for sale?
> We will make the ephah small and the shekel heavier,
>   and practise deceit with false balances,
> [6] buying the poor for silver
>   and the needy for a pair of sandals
>   and selling the sweepings of the wheat.'
> [7] The Lord has sworn by the pride of Jacob:
> Surely I will never forget any of their deeds.

Amos 8:4–6 re-works 2:6–7, and re-focuses them to address people in seventh-century Judah. The unit is addressed to 'you that trample on the

---

[178] The word 'temple' can also mean 'palace', in which case it is the celebratory music of the palace to which this half-verse refers.

[179] J. Jeremias *Amos* (1998): 126.

364   *Book of Amos*

needy': the wording is close to that of 2:7. The second clause, 'and bring to ruin the poor of the land', is not from 2:6–7, but is thematically similar. The following verse 8:5, however, brings in accusations not made in 2:6–7. Firstly, those accused are impatient and greedy businessmen who cannot wait for the new moon and Sabbath to be over so that they can start trading again. Because Israel followed a lunar calendar the new moon was sometimes used simply as chronology, as in, for example, Exodus 19:1: 'At the third new moon after the Israelites had gone out of the land of Egypt.' But it was also a religious festival. In 1 Samuel 20:5, 18, 24 this is referred to in passing in the narrative concerning David and Jonathan. Psalm 81:3 [4] refers to it as 'our festal day'. It was a suitable day on which to go to consult a man of God (2 Kgs 4:23). It is found as a pair with 'Sabbath' in three other texts: 2 Kings 4:23, Isaiah 1:13, and Hosea 2:11 [13]. The Isaiah and Hosea texts are pre-exilic, and the Kings text preserves pre-exilic narrative, strengthening the view that Amos 8:4–7 is a seventh-century rather than an exilic addition to the text.[180] Sabbath, too, was an ancient institution.[181] Both versions of the Decalogue contain the positive commandment to remember the Sabbath, although with different motivational reasons given (Exod. 20:8–11; Deut. 5:12–15). Amos 8:5 reflects a strong distaste for these businessmen who had no religious feeling for the new moon and Sabbath, and who regarded them simply as wasted trading days. Their actions in this respect were not against any law, however. In the second half of the verse, in contrast, their actions were more suspect: 'We will make the ephah small and the shekel great, and practice deceit with false balances.' The ephah was a unit of measure of grain. The shekel was a unit of weight (later, from the post-exilic period, it meant a coin). These traders in seventh-century Judah tampered with the measures, something firmly disapproved of in both legal and wisdom traditions (Lev. 19:35–36; Deut. 25:13–16; Prov. 11:1; 16:11; 20:10, 23). These are specific accusations of actions deemed both immoral and illegal. Amos 8:6 then resumes drawing on 2:6–7, with a difference. There the accusation was that 'they sell the righteous for silver and the needy for a pair of sandals'. Here it is that they are 'buying the poor for silver and the needy for a pair of sandals'. No particular significance need be attached to the changing of the terms 'righteous' and 'poor' to 'poor' and 'needy'. However, the changing of the verb from 'sell' to 'buy' is significant. In 2:6

---

[180]   Contra T. S. Hadjiev *Composition and Redaction* (2009): 108, and with G. R. Hamborg *Still Selling the Righteous* (2012): 59–60; J. Jeremias *Amos* (1998): 7, 145.
[181]   G. F. Hasel, 'Sabbath', *ABD* 5: 849–56; A. Schuele, 'Sabbath', *NIDB* 5: 3–10.

C *Commentary on Amos* 365

the reference was to the powerful creditor selling the poor into debt-slavery for trivial debts (see the commentary *ad loc*). In 8:6 it is those who do the buying of such people who are accused of trading not just in goods, but in human beings. The final line adds that they are also 'selling the sweepings of the wheat', again indicating dishonest practices. These verses take the generalised accusations of 2:6–8 and apply them to dishonest business practices a century later in Judah. The interpreter and preacher will feel that this process of re-application to a different time and place is one which needs to be continued into the present day.

After setting out reasons for judgement, 8:7 then declares that YHWH will not forget their deeds, something made doubly sure by his swearing by the pride of Jacob. This draws on 6:8, where YHWH has sworn by himself and declared that he abhors the pride of Jacob. It is strange in 8:7, however, that it is the pride of Jacob, abhorred in 6:8, by which he now swears. It may be that there is a note of sarcasm: just as the pride of Jacob is clearly never going to change, so it is certain that YHWH will never forget their deeds.[182] This concise announcement of judgement was enlarged in the Exilic Redactional Composition by the addition of a series of sayings in 8:8–14.

Amos 8:8–14 – *The Time of Judgement is Coming*

⁸ Shall not the land tremble on this account,
    and everyone mourn who lives in it,
and all of it rise like the Nile,
    and be tossed about and sink again, like the Nile of Egypt?
⁹ On that day, says the Lord God,
    I will make the sun go down at noon,
    and darken the earth in broad daylight.
¹⁰ I will turn your feasts into mourning
    and all your songs into lamentation;
I will bring sackcloth on all loins
    and baldness on every head;
I will make it like the mourning for an only son,
    and the end of it like a bitter day.
¹¹ The time is surely coming, says the Lord God,
    when I will send a famine on the land,
not a famine of bread or a thirst for water,
    but of hearing the words of the Lord.

---

[182] M. D. Carroll R. *Amos* (2020): 454–6; H. W. Wolff *Joel and Amos* (1977): 328.

366   *Book of Amos*

^{12} They shall wander from sea to sea
        and from north to east;
    they shall run to and fro, seeking the word of the Lord,
        but they shall not find it.
^{13} On that day the beautiful young women and the young men
        shall faint for thirst.
^{14} Those who swear by Ashimah of Samaria
        and say, 'As your god lives, O Dan',
    and, 'As the way of Beer-sheba lives' –
        they shall fall, and never rise again.

Introductory connecting formulae like 'on that day' (8:9), 'the time is surely coming' (8:11), and 'in that day' (8:13) are typical of the exilic period and later, confirming that all these verses entered the text in the Exilic Redactional Composition. Amos 8:8 functions as a transitional verse. Its imagery is of an earthquake, thus linking both back to 2:13 (see the commentary *ad loc*), 3:15, and 6:11, and also forward to 9:1. The mourning picks up the theme of 5:16–17 and also anticipates 8:10. The second half of 8:8 and of 9:5 are virtually identical, bracketing the exilic section 8:8–9:6: thus even if, as many hold, 8:9–10, 8:11–12, and 8:13–14 came into the text in stages, in their final form they are meant to be read as one section. It is not clear to what the 'on this account' of 8:8 refers. It could refer to YHWH's oath in 8:7 or, more probably, to the wrongdoings that the text thus far has described. The linking of human sin and the breakdown of creation is found also in texts such as Hosea 4:3; Jeremiah 3:3; 12:4; 23:10.[183]

The following verses enlarging the description of YHWH's judgement employ a range of imagery and themes. The 'day' in the opening line of 8:9 is the day of judgement on Israel in 2:16 and 8:3, where the same phrase is used. It also refers back to the Day of YHWH in 5:18–20, with the description of the sun going down at noon and the earth darkening, enlarging on the description there of the Day of YHWH as a day of darkness. It was believed that creation was held in place by YHWH's sustaining power: now he allows an element of breakdown of creation as his judgement takes place. This brief cosmic dimension to his judgement is quickly brought back to a theme already set out in 5:16–17: in Israel there will be mourning and wailing on that day. The wearing of sackcloth and shaving of the head were both

---

[183] For a treatment of this theme linking to contemporary environmental concerns see H. Marlow, *Biblical Prophets and Contemporary Environmental Ethics* (Oxford: Oxford University Press, 2009).

C Commentary on Amos

marks of mourning, and the grief will be as intense as for the loss of an only son. Verses 11–12 then describe a famine of the hearing the words of YHWH. The practice of going to a prophet to enquire of YHWH is seen in 1 Samuel 28:6; 2 Samuel 21:1; 1 Kings 22:5; and elsewhere: the judgement here is that no answer will be given. Essentially the same judgement is made in Hosea 5:6. These verses also display familiarity with Deuteronomy 8:3's assertion that 'one does not live by bread alone, but by every word that comes from the mouth of YHWH'. The judgement is appropriate after the rejection of the prophetic word expressed by Amaziah in 7:10–17: the word of YHWH has been rejected, and the consequence is that it will no longer be available to be heard. Finally, verses 13–14 say that even Israel's youth will faint for thirst (picking up the same word used in 8:11). Those addressed in 8:14 are addressed in accusatory fashion, but the translation and interpretation are disputed. NRSV's 'Ashimah of' Samaria is based on a frequently followed change of vocalisation from MT, which literally reads 'the guilt of' Samaria,[184] with no mention of a deity. Ashimah was a god mentioned in 2 Kings 17:30 as having been brought into the land that had been northern Israel by the people of Hamath who were forcibly settled there by the Assyrians after 722, and it is possible that a pun is intended: the swearing by this foreign deity causes guilt. Dan had been a sanctuary established by Jeroboam I, along with Bethel, when northern Israel separated from Judah (1 Kgs 12:26–30). The status of this sanctuary by the time of the exilic Amos 8:14 is uncertain, but a later Hellenistic inscription refers to 'the god of Dan', suggesting that there was some kind of shrine in use at Dan over an extended period of time.[185] The 'way' (*derek*) of Beer-sheba could refer to northerners making pilgrimage to the southern Beer-sheba. Alternatively, some note a possible Ugaritic cognate *drkt*, 'power', and take 'power of Beer-sheba' also to be the name of a deity. Thus it is possible that this verse contains three references to deities, amounting to a condemnation of Israel for this reason. The inclusion of Beer-sheba, a southern sanctuary, would remind Judean readers that, while the text is nominally addressed to northern Israel, they too needed to hear its accusation. The verse alludes also to Hosea 4:15 and its condemnation of the worship of false gods.

Whatever exactly is meant, the final line draws on 5:2 in its climax of these verses which enlarge on the announcement of judgement: 'they shall fall, and never rise again'.

---

[184] Emending *'ašmat* to *'ăšimat*.
[185] J. Jeremias *Amos* (1998): 153.

368   *Book of Amos*

Amos 9:1–6 – Judgement Executed

9 I saw the Lord standing beside the altar, and he said:
  Strike the capitals until the thresholds shake
    and shatter them on the heads of all the people,
  and those who are left I will kill with the sword;
    not one of them shall flee away,
    not one of them shall escape.
² Though they dig into Sheol,
    from there shall my hand take them;
  though they climb up to heaven,
    from there I will bring them down.
³ Though they hide themselves on the top of Carmel,
    from there I will search out and take them;
  and though they hide from my sight at the bottom of the sea,
    there I will command the serpent, and it shall bite them.
⁴ And though they go into captivity in front of their enemies,
    there I will command the sword, and it shall kill them;
  and I will fix my eyes on them
    for harm and not for good.

⁵ The Lord, God of hosts,
  he who touches the earth and it melts,
    and all who live in it mourn,
  and all of it rises like the Nile,
    and sinks again, like the Nile of Egypt,
⁶ who builds his upper chambers in the heavens,
    and founds his vault upon the earth,
  who calls for the waters of the sea,
    and pours them out upon the surface of the earth –
  the Lord is his name.

In the earliest, Post-722 Composition, 9:1–4 followed 8:1–2 and was the fifth and final vision of the series and the conclusion of the Amos-text. In the seventh century the judgement oracle 8:4–7 was added, with connecting verse 8:3, making a pause before the final vision and end of the text. Then, in the sixth-century exilic revision, 8:8–14 enlarged on the description of judgement before the final vision, and 9:5–6 was added as a new conclusion to the text.

Amos 9:1–4 is a sobering conclusion to the visions series. It is made clear that the judgement announced in the third and fourth visions (7:7–8; 8:1–2) is absolute, and cannot be stopped. It begins not with Amos being shown

C Commentary on Amos

something by YHWH as in the first four visions, but by him seeing the Lord himself. The Hebrew 'Lord' in 9:1 is *'ădōnāy*, the master.[186] The altar on or beside which he stands is not named, but in the light of all that has gone before in the text must be Bethel, Israel's main sanctuary. However, the lack of naming it has a positive purpose: it becomes representative of a judgement which could befall any sanctuary in any place and time. The Lord commands: 'Strike the capital.' Who is commanded? Is it Amos? Is it angels or heavenly beings? Or is it meant to be vague, as if a passive 'Let the capitals be struck'? Whatever exactly is meant, it is clear that the effect is the destruction of the sanctuary, and all in it. The language suggests an earthquake. Furthermore, this moment symbolises the end not just of Bethel, but of the nation. And there will be no escape. The second half of 9:1 mirrors 2:14–16, in which, equally, none escape. In the light of the apparent totality of destruction in 9:1, it may seem surprising that in 9:2–4 there are still those trying to flee and hide. However we should not read these verses as strictly chronological, but as piling on descriptions of the Lord's actions. The parallels between 9:2–3 and Psalm 139:7–12 have often been noted. Some may try to hide in Sheol, the shadowy pit of the dead. Some psalms suggest the absence of YHWH from Sheol, or at any rate that the dead cannot praise YHWH or call on him from there (Pss. 6:5 [6]; 88:3–7 [4–8]; 115:17; Isa. 38:18), but other texts indicate that his reach extends there (1 Sam. 2:6; Ps. 49:14–15 [15–16]; Prov. 15:11). Amos 9:2–3 and Psalm 139:7–12 assume the latter. Others might try to hide in heaven. Others might try to hide on Mount Carmel, a fertile region with dense undergrowth. Yet others might try to hide in the depths of the sea, but even there YHWH could send his serpent (pre-2021 NRSV: sea-serpent). Various biblical passages refer to a large creature inhabiting the sea, sometimes referred to as Leviathan (cf. Job 41:1–2; Ps. 74:14; Isa. 27:1). While the Israelites were wary of the sea, viewing it as chaotic, it was not out of YHWH's reach and control. Finally, 9:4 states that even if some are taken into captivity, even then the sword – already used in 9:1 – will catch up with them. The upshot is that wherever people try to hide, YHWH will find them and, because of all the sin and injustice described in the Amos-text, he will give his attention to them in judgement.

In the Post-722 Composition, the text ended here. But the Exilic Redactional Composition added a new ending in 9:5–6. For discussion of

---

[186] See note 156, Section IV, for the use of this term in conjunction with the divine name in the series of visions.

the nature of the hymnic verses 4:13; 5:8–9; 9:5–6, see the 'Introduction to Amos' and 'Amos 4:13 – The One Who Forms the Mountains and Creates the Winds'. Theologically they strengthen the actions of YHWH by portraying him not just as the God of Israel, but the God of all creation, making his actions in judgement all the more terrifying. The God who creates can also melt the earth. Even the great river Nile in Egypt is affected, and the chaotic waters of the sea are poured out in destruction. The one who does this, the final clause declares, is the one whose name is YHWH.

Looking back at 7:1–9:6 as a whole, we may see the development within its compositional history. The earliest, Post-722 Composition (7:1–8; 8:1–2; 9:1–4) with its uninterrupted series of five visions shows, firstly, YHWH's judgement being averted through intercession, and then its inevitability, and finally its execution. No reasons for judgement are given, these being found in the oracles of the preceding chapters. A hundred years later the Late Pre-exilic Redactional Composition brought in 7:9–17, with the rejection of the prophetic word as an added reason for judgement; and 8:3–7, in which the continued trampling on the poor by the wealthy and the dishonest practices evident in seventh-century Judah provide yet further grounds. Finally the sixth-century Exilic Redactional Composition brought in 8:8–14, with further descriptions of YHWH's judgement ahead of the final vision; and 9:5–6 which, like 5:8–9 show the judge to be not just the God of Israel, but the God of all creation.

Post-Enlightenment readers will find the descriptions of destruction by YHWH as punishment for sin alien to their natural way of thinking. However, this was a natural belief in the centuries in which Amos spoke and in which the text was formed. Lest we be left simply with a sense of God's harshness, it is worth recalling the function that the text held for Judean readers after the fall of Samaria in 722 and in exile in Babylon in the sixth century. These disasters might have led people to consider that the gods of the Assyrians and Babylonians were greater and more powerful than YHWH. The text counters this by showing that YHWH had allowed, indeed intended, them. The closing words of 9:6, that he would fix his eyes on them for harm and not for good, were terrifying, but less so than the possibility that he would not turn his eyes on them at all, but would simply abandon them forever. The one who turned his eyes on them was at least maintaining his interest in them, so there was the hope that perhaps in the future his interest might once again become a kindly one. In the period after the years of exile in Babylon, this hope was indeed expressed, through the addition of the closing section that follows.

C Commentary on Amos 371

5 The Future: Judgement and Blessing – Amos 9:7–15

Amos 9:7–10 – The Future: Judgement – But Not on All

> [7] Are you not like the Cushites to me,
>> O people of Israel? says the Lord.
>> Did I not bring Israel up from the land of Egypt
>>> and the Philistines from Caphtor and the Arameans from Kir?
> [8] The eyes of the Lord God are upon the sinful kingdom,
>> and I will destroy it from the face of the earth
>> – except that I will not utterly destroy the house of Jacob,
> says the Lord.
> [9] For lo, I will command
>> and shake the house of Israel among all the nations
> as one shakes with a sieve
>> but no pebble shall fall to the ground.
> [10] All the sinners of my people shall die by the sword,
>> who say, 'Evil shall not overtake or meet us.'

The whole of 9:7–15 was added to the text in the post-exilic period, the Exilic Redactional Composition having concluded with 9:5–6.[187] This includes 9:7, which many commentators seeking to delineate 'genuine' sayings of the prophet Amos frequently attribute to him.[188] It may be that 9:7 was a saying of Amos still in oral circulation, but only brought into the text in its post-exilic redaction.[189] Alternatively it may be a later composition dependent on 2:10 and 3:1.[190] It is evident that 9:7–10 are closely related to 9:1–4, and it appears that they constitute what Wolff describes as 'the literary distillate of later discussions concerning the fifth vision'.[191] The vocabulary used indicates this: YHWH's 'eyes' (9:4, 8); his command (9:3, 4, 9); 'the sword' (9:4, 10); harm/evil (9.4, 10; the Hebrew word is the same in both verses). The use of 'Jacob' in 9:8 reflects 7:2, 5.

Amos 9:7 addresses the objection that YHWH would surely not destroy his people in judgement, because he had made them his own special people all those years ago in bringing them up from the land of Egypt. The first half of the verse simply negates any sense that Israel was special to YHWH: 'Are you not like the Cushites to me?' The Cushites lived in what is now southern

---

[187] See Section IV, 'Introduction to Amos'.
[188] W. R. Harper *Amos and Hosea* (1905): 191–3; J. L. Mays *Amos* (1969): 156–9; S. M. Paul *Amos* (1991): 282–4.
[189] J. Jeremias *Amos* (1998): 162–3.
[190] G. R. Hamborg *Still Selling the Righteous* (2012): 93–4.
[191] H. W. Wolff *Joel and Amos* (1977): 345.

372   *Book of Amos*

Egypt and Sudan. The pre-2021 NRSV used the translation 'Ethiopians' rather than 'Cushites': LXX translated as *aithiopia*, and several English versions translate thus. The revised NRSV's retention of the Hebrew 'Cushites' seems preferable. To the Israelites the Cushites were a remote and distant people. So in 9:7a YHWH indicates that far from Israelites being a special people to him, they are now remote and distant to him in view of their sins.[192] The second half of 9:7 imagines the view being expressed that 'surely YHWH brought Israel up from the land of Egypt'. There have already been several points in the text where it has appeared to agree with a view supposedly held, only for a different consequence then to be expressed than that expected. The whole OAN series employs this strategy when it turns its attention to Judah and then Israel, and it is found also in 3:2; 4:4–5; 5:18–20 (see the commentary *ad loc*). Here in 9:7 the strategy is employed a final time: yes, YHWH did indeed bring Israel up from the land of Egypt – and the Philistines from Caphtor and the Arameans from Kir. In just a few words the usual significance drawn from the exodus from Egypt, that Israel was YHWH's special people, is undermined, as the claim to Israel's specialness is completely relativised. In strict logical terms 9:7b contradicts 3:2's affirmation that 'You only have I known of all the families of the earth.' However, the consequence drawn there is not, as was presumably usually asserted, that therefore they would be specially blessed, but that therefore they would be punished for their iniquities. In different ways 3:2 and 9:7 both prevent any sense of false security on Israel's part on the basis of them being YHWH's special people. The question arises as to whether 9:7 is seriously asserting, theologically, that YHWH never had considered that he had any special relationship with Israel. Barton explores this in writing that, if so, the theology being expressed 'may be called the *non-election of Israel*. Amos did not merely draw out unpalatable conclusions from Israel's special status, but actually denied it altogether.'[193] Such a denial would be almost unique in the Hebrew Bible. However, it would be a mistake to draw a doctrinal assertion from this verse. The aim is to challenge complacency, not to re-write theology. In these verses which discuss the judgement of 9:1–4, this verse upholds it.

The two nations whose migrations are described, the Philistines and the Arameans, are those addressed in the first of the two OAN in 1:3–8. Thus

---

[192]   So *inter alia* M. D. Carroll R. *Amos* (2020): 496–7. There have been interpretations suggesting that the Cushites were chosen for comparison because of the darkness of their skin (cf. Jer. 13:23). The text does not indicate this, and such interpretations appear to reveal a subconscious racism.

[193]   J. Barton *Theology of the Book of Amos* (2012): 74 (italics original).

C Commentary on Amos 373

9:7, in the final section of the text, reminds the reader to read it as a whole. Kir, from which 9:7 says the Arameans had come, was the place to which 1:6 says they will go into exile. It is thus equivalent to saying that Israel would be sent back to Egypt. Kir is also referred to in Isaiah 22:6, but its location is unknown. The Philistines are said to have come from Caphtor, generally identified with Crete.[194]

The discussion of 9:1–4 continues in 9:8–10. Verse 9:8a reiterates what has been said in various ways in the text as a whole, that YHWH will destroy the kingdom of Israel. The verb used is the same as that used in 2:9 of YHWH destroying the Amorites when he brought Israel into the land. YHWH will treat the Israelites as he had the Amorites. YHWH destroying 'from the face of the earth' is a quotation from 1 Kings 13:34, where the phrase is used of the house of Jeroboam I, first king of northern Israel. This assertion of 9:8a is then contradicted by 9:8b–10, when for the first time in the text it is declared that the judgement will not be total: YHWH will not 'utterly destroy the house of Jacob',[195] but it will be only the 'sinners of my people' who are destroyed. This is enlarged in 9:9–10, with their picture of YHWH shaking the house of Israel as in a sieve.[196] The stones retained in the sieve are those to whom the destruction will apply. These verses are part of a line of thought which emerged in the exilic and post-exilic periods, that YHWH would not deal solely with the nation as a corporate entity but with groups and individuals within it. Barton cites Ezekiel 9:4 as an example: judgement is to come, but a cherub is instructed to place a mark on the foreheads of those to be spared because they sigh and groan over the abominations that YHWH hates.[197] This emerging thinking began to sever what had hitherto been the assumed identification of Israel as the people of God and Israel as the nation settled in the land. Paul puts is succinctly: 'the *nation* of Israel ... shall be destroyed, but the *people* of Israel shall not be totally eradicated'.[198] Similarly Jeremias writes that these verses want 'to avoid the misunderstanding that

---

[194] H. W. Wolff *Joel and Amos* (1977): 347–8 cites Jer. 47:4, which refers to Caphtor as an island; and the Philistines being called Cretans (Cherethites) in Ezek. 25:16; Zeph. 2:5.

[195] P. R. Davies, 'Why Do We Know about Amos?' in D. V. Edelman and E. Ben Zvi (eds.), *The Production of Prophecy: Constructing Prophecy and Prophets in Yehud* (London: Equinox Publishing Ltd, 2009): 55–72 notes that the name 'Jacob' originally referred to northern Israel, but at some point after 722, and certainly by the sixth and fifth centuries, meant Judah.

[196] It is clear that 9:9–10 are meant to be read with 9:8, and it is strange that NRSV makes a paragraph break between 9:8 and 9:9. I have removed this in my printing of the text.

[197] J. Barton *Theology of the Book of Amos* (2012): 123.

[198] S. M. Paul *Amos* (1991): 285 (italics original).

374   *Book of Amos*

the existence of the people of God as such ceases along with the state'.[199]
These verses are written from the perspective of those who have survived
the Babylonian exile and have been able to return to the land which was
then under Persian rule. They now needed to establish what it meant for
'Israel' to be the people of God, and one clear principle was that they should
seek to avoid the sinful ways of life that had led to YHWH's judgement.

Amos 9:11–15 – Blessing and Security

[11] On that day I will raise up
    the booth of David that is fallen
and repair its breaches
    and raise up its ruins,
    and rebuild it as in the days of old,
[12] in order that they may possess the remnant of Edom
    and all the nations who are called by my name,
    says the Lord who does this.

[13] The time is surely coming, says the Lord,
    when the one who ploughs shall catch up with the one who reaps,
    and the treader of grapes with the one who sows the seed;
the mountains shall drip sweet wine,
    and all the hills shall flow with it.
[14] I will restore the fortunes of my people Israel,
    and they shall rebuild the ruined cities and inhabit them;
they shall plant vineyards and drink their wine,
    and they shall make gardens and eat their fruit.
[15] I will plant them upon their land,
    and they shall never again be plucked up
    out of the land that I have given them,
    says the Lord your God.

Within Amos 9:11–15, verses 12–13 link the Amos-text to the books of Joel
and Obadiah, which precede and follow Amos in the MT order of the Book
of the Twelve. Jeremias argues that, while 9:11, 14–15 are early post-exilic,
9:12–13 were added at a later stage in which the Book of the Twelve was
being formed.[200] This is eminently plausible. Nevertheless 9:11–15 reads well
as a whole and is best commented on as a unit.

---

[199] J. Jeremias *Amos* (1998): 165.
[200] J. Jeremias *Amos* (1998): 162. He is followed by J. D. Nogalski *Hosea–Jonah* (2011): 355.

C Commentary on Amos

375

Opening formulae in these verses are drawn from 8:9–14. The 'On that day' of 9:11 is the identical opening phrase of 8:9 and 8:13; the opening 'The time is coming' of 9:13 is drawn from 8:11. As noted in the commentary on these verses, such formulae are typical of the exilic period and later. The promise of 9:11 concerns the 'booth of David'. This most naturally refers to the destruction of Jerusalem in 587. A booth was a temporary structure which could easily collapse, but which could then be re-built. The kingdom of David had collapsed in the events of 587, but the promise here is that YHWH will raise it up. In 5:2 it had been declared that maiden Israel had 'fallen, no more to rise'. Now, however, the same verbs are used to declare that YHWH will 'raise up the booth of David that is fallen'.

The following verse, 9:12, adds that when the booth of David is restored and fully repaired, the people will possess the remnant of Edom. In King David's time Edom had been part of enlarged Israelite territory, and this verse looks back to that time. In 587, however, the Edomites had apparently rejoiced over the fall of Jerusalem, and consequently earned the bitterness towards their actions expressed in Psalm 137:7; Jeremiah 49:17–22; Lamentations 4:21–22; Ezekiel 25:12–15; and the book of Obadiah. The phrase 'remnant of Edom' suggests that at the time when this verse was written Edom had already suffered a measure of destruction. Jeremias refers this to losses suffered through the incursion of Arab tribes in the early fifth century BCE.[201]

The promise of 9:13 is an almost miraculous level of fertility: the crops to be harvested and the grapes to be picked will be so abundant that the harvesting will still be going on when the next sowing is due. The second half of the verse is close to Joel 3:18 [4:18], linking the two texts in the Book of the Twelve. In Amos 4:7–9 the loss of harvest had been part of the litany of disasters sent in an attempt to lead the people to call upon YHWH, which implies the belief that neglect of YHWH led to poor harvests. Now, however, 9:13 asserts that YHWH will bring fertility and prosperity in abundance. This blessing of abundance is linked simply to the promise of YHWH.

The final verses 9:14–15 are less 'miraculous', but assert confidently that the judgements meted out earlier in the text will be reversed. In the OAN series in chapters 1–2, including the oracles against Judah and Israel, YHWH had declared that he would 'not revoke the punishment', literally 'I will not cause it to return' (see the commentary *ad loc*). Now, however, he will 'restore' (the same Hebrew verb) the fortunes of his people Israel. The

---

[201] J. Jeremias *Amos* (1998): 167.

remainder of 9:14 is a reversal of 5:11. Whereas the judgement of 5:11 was that the people would not live in the houses that they had built nor drink the wine from their vineyards, now they will re-build the city and live in the houses that they have built, and drink the wine from the vineyards that they have planted. In 9:15 the promise that they shall 'never again' be plucked up may be intended as a contrasting echo of 7:8 and 8:2, where YHWH declares that he will 'never again' pass them by, that is, let them escape judgement. This final verse gives great assurance of security for the future: never again will the people be taken from the land that YHWH himself has given them.

It may be wondered what significance 9:11–15 has within the Amos-text as a whole. Does it undermine, completely or in part, all that has gone before? After all the announcements of judgement and the reasons given for them, does a 'happy ending' mean that they no longer apply and can now be safely discounted? It seems unlikely that this was ever the intention. What is remarkable is that all that has gone before has been allowed to stand as it is, with minimal insertions in the final Post-exilic Redactional Composition. It cannot be gainsaid that the promises of 9:11–15 are unconditional. Yet their literary context, following all that has gone before, suggests implied conditions. As I have written elsewhere:

> It is entirely likely that readers of the unconditional announcement of future blessing in 9.11–15 were ... capable of assuming, and, indeed, likely to assume, an unspoken 'unless you lapse into the unjust and exploitative ways of life that brought about YHWH's previous judgments'. It is significant that the unconditional promise of blessing is attached to the Amos-text, and is clearly meant to be read in the light of it ... and that includes readers of the Post-exilic Redactional Composition of the Amos-text.[202]

In the final form of the text the challenge to practise justice remains strong, and in the time of promised future blessing it is undiminished.

---

[202] G. R. Hamborg *Still Selling the Righteous* (2012): 247.

Author Index

Ackerman, S., 343
Ackroyd, P. R., 162, 165, 273, 357–8
Adams, K., 89
Ahlström, G., 194, 201, 207, 225, 232, 254
Albertz, R., 6, 10, 11, 13, 14, 57, 69, 121, 266
Allen, L. C., 200, 222, 225, 235, 251
Alt, A., 31, 102, 104, 122
Andersen, F. I., 18, 28, 30, 35, 37, 38, 42, 48, 64, 67, 78, 83, 87, 108, 114, 140, 146, 169, 269, 272, 284, 320
Andiñach, P. R., 201
Andrews, M. E., 79
Angel, H., 33, 44
Arnold, B. T., 149
Asen, B., 274
Assis, E., 191, 196–7, 201, 205, 209, 211–2, 221–2, 227, 234, 247
Auld, A. G., 259, 272

Bach, R., 137
Bailey, L. R., 323
Barker, J., 201
Barré, M., 274
Barstad, H. M., 24, 31, 104, 142, 145, 273–4, 348
Barton, J., 3, 10, 12, 15, 93, 190–1, 194, 198–200, 203–5, 208, 216–9, 221, 222, 225–7, 232, 240, 241, 245, 247, 268, 272, 274, 281–2, 289, 310, 341, 372–3
Baumann, G., 39, 76
Ben Zvi, E., 10, 12, 14, 18, 23–4, 29–30, 37, 46, 49, 60, 65, 78, 82, 108, 130, 141, 148, 159–60, 170, 178
Bentzen, A., 285
Bergler, S., 201

Berquist, J. L., 335
Bewer, J. A., 200
Birch, B., 30
Bird, P., 33, 39
Bos, J. M., 23, 31, 35, 37, 46, 69, 82, 91, 96, 125, 130, 151, 164–5
Boshoff, W., 33, 39
Botterweck, G. J., 77
Boudreau, G. R., 138
Bowman, C. D., 39
Brettler, M. Z., 274
Brueggemann, W., 256, 259, 325
Buss, M. J., 19, 31

Carroll R, M. D., 2, 263, 272–4, 287–9, 327, 343, 365, 372
Chalmers, R. S., 31, 162, 164
Childs, B. S., 2–3, 234
Christensen, D. L., 259
Chung, Y. H., 31–2, 126
Clements, R. E., 12, 257
Clines, D. J. A., 34, 57
Coggins, R. J., 15, 200–1, 203–4, 209–10, 221, 262, 272–3, 301
Collins, J. J., 6
Collins, R. F., 79
Collins, T., 13
Cook, S. L., 82, 201
Coote, R. B., 162, 269, 273–4, 284, 303–4
Crenshaw, J. L., 193–4, 197–8, 200, 204, 208, 212, 217, 221–5, 232, 237, 239, 241, 244–5, 247–8, 250, 251, 273–4, 326
Cripps, R. S., 273
Cuffey, K. H., 10

377

Author Index

378

Daniels, D. R., 31–2, 159
Davies, G. I., 17, 19, 28, 30, 38, 41, 44, 47, 61, 64,
 67, 75, 87–8, 92, 97, 102–4, 107, 109, 111–2, 114,
 117, 142–3, 145, 150, 153, 162, 166–7, 169, 177,
 182, 184, 186–7
Davies, P. R., 5, 274, 373
Day, J., 24, 32, 56, 89, 111–2, 121, 257
Day, P. L., 32, 39
Dearman, J. A., 19, 21, 30, 38, 46–7, 52, 54–7, 61,
 64, 77, 80–1, 83, 95, 98, 102, 104, 112, 117–18,
 124–7, 134, 149, 151–2, 160, 163, 165, 170,
 175–6, 179–80
Donaldson, T. L., 259
Driver, S. R., 304

Ebach, R., 201
Edelman, D., 5
Eichrodt, W., 122
Eidevall, G., 19, 31–2, 88, 112, 143, 151, 165, 176,
 261, 263–4, 266, 273–4, 277, 307, 319, 330,
 346, 355
Emmerson, G. I., 21, 32, 65, 109, 182
Engelken, K., 210

Fabry, H.-J., 106, 348
Fishbane, M., 241
Floyd, M. H., 12
Fontaine, C. R., 34, 39
Freedman, D. N., 18, 28, 30, 35, 37–8, 42, 48, 64,
 67, 78, 83, 87, 108, 114, 140, 146, 169, 269, 272,
 284, 320
Fretheim, T., 228, 296
Fritz, V., 323

Gerstenberger, E., 338
Gertner, M., 162
Gese, H., 261, 274, 306
Giles, T., 303
Gillingham, S., 304
Ginsberg, H. L., 162
Gitay, Y., 312
Goldingay, J., 19, 30, 32, 74, 194, 198, 200, 205,
 239, 250–1, 273, 282
Gomes, J. F., 91, 126, 142, 164–5, 321
Good, E. M., 102, 162
Graetz, N., 34, 39
Gunkel, H., 122

Hadjiev, T. S., 34, 44, 194, 200, 221, 226, 237,
 250, 261, 263–4, 267–9, 273–4, 277, 304, 319,
 326, 355, 357–8, 364

Hagedorn, A. C., 273, 274
Hamborg, G. R., 4, 261, 264, 268, 273, 275, 285,
 296, 302, 304–5, 307, 311, 316, 326, 330, 333,
 346, 358, 364, 371, 376
Hammershaimb, E., 353
Hanson, P. D., 192, 195
Harper, W. R., 2, 18, 28, 31, 57, 65, 102, 181, 273,
 284, 335, 371
Hasel, G. F., 364
Hawk, L. D., 93
Hillers, D. R., 353
Holt, E. K., 31, 32, 82, 138, 162, 169
House, P. R., 6, 8, 13–14
Houston, W. J., 272, 275, 277, 303, 310, 313, 336
Huffmon, H. B., 76
Hurowitz, H., 211

Irvine, S. A., 133

Jeremias, J., 10–11, 31–2, 90, 120–1, 199–201,
 261, 263–4, 266, 272–3, 275, 278, 284, 287–8,
 290, 307, 309, 316, 320, 326, 330–1, 333, 335,
 337, 346–7, 351, 355, 358, 363–4, 367, 371,
 373–5
Johnson, B., 144
Johnstone, P., 178
Jones, B. A., 13

Kakkanattu, J. P., 31–2, 151–2
Kapelrud, A. S., 201, 275
Keefe, A., 34
Kelle, B. E., 18, 20, 30, 34
Kelly, J. R., 202, 227
King Jr., M. L., 343–4
Kislev, I., 138
Knierim, R. P., 191, 264, 275, 284
Koch, K., 43, 235, 265, 335–6, 340
Krispenz, J., 32, 41, 83, 90, 97, 124
Kruger, P. A., 182, 185
Kuan, J. K., 139

Lambert, D., 214
Landsberger, B., 355
Lang, B., 303
Laurin, R. B., 12
LeCureux, J., 15, 110, 202, 341–2
Leuchter, M., 24, 33
Leveen, A., 13
Lindblom, J., 361
Linville, J. R., 5, 262–3, 272–3, 275, 287, 290, 313,
 320, 338, 347

Author Index

Long, B. O., 323
Lust, J., 269

Maag, V., 284
Machinist, P., 33, 125
Macintosh, A. A., 17, 19, 21, 28, 31, 35, 38, 44–6,
  52–3, 64–5, 78–9, 81, 83, 87, 91–2, 95, 98,
  102–4, 107, 111–2, 116, 124, 130–2, 138–9,
  141–3, 145–6, 148, 150–3, 162–3, 169–71, 175–9,
  184–5, 187
Marlow, H., 366
Mason, R., 200
Mayes, A. D. H., 79, 166, 171, 183, 305, 322, 323
Mays, J. L., 16, 18–19, 28, 31, 35, 38, 44, 46–8,
  64–5, 69, 87, 98, 104, 107, 114–15, 117, 127, 141,
  143, 145, 148, 151, 165, 168–9, 174, 179, 261, 273,
  276, 284, 290, 312, 323, 325–6, 347, 371
McCarthy, D. J., 123
McConville, J. G., 275
McKeating, H., 76
McKenzie, J. L., 76
McKenzie, S. L., 162
McLaughlin, J., 348
Mein, A., 273, 274
Melugin, R. F., 13
Mendenhall, G. E., 122
Meyers, C., 3, 47
Möller, K., 273, 275
Moon, J., 34, 44
Moran, W. L., 149
Mowinckel, S., 122, 216
Myers, J. M., 247

Nicholson, E. W., 121–3
Nissinen, M., 31, 33
Nogalski, J. D., 6–11, 13–15, 31, 64, 67, 71, 74, 80,
  89, 98, 107, 109, 124, 141, 154, 159, 162, 169,
  173–4, 179, 201–2, 204–5, 209, 221, 228, 232,
  252, 273, 324, 355, 374
Noth, M., 122–3
Novick, T., 355, 362

O'Kennedy, D. F., 33, 105, 151, 185
Oden, R. A., 89

Park, A. W., 275
Paul, S. M., 261, 272–3, 276, 284–6, 288, 290–2,
  311–2, 315, 320, 325–7, 348, 353, 355, 358, 371, 373
Pede, D. E., 14
Pedersen, D. L., 361
Perlitt, L., 111, 121, 123

Pfeiffer, R. H., 295
Pleins, J. D., 300
Plöger, O., 192, 201–2
Prinsloo, W. S., 201–2, 235

Rad, G. von, 91, 122, 137, 216, 292, 321
Radine, J., 273, 275
Redditt, P. L., 14, 192–3, 196, 201–2, 205, 225,
  238, 242, 353
Ringgren, H., 74
Robertson Smith, W., 89
Römer, T., 14
Rooke, D., 202, 210
Rottzoll, D. U., 275
Routledge, R., 31, 34
Rudnig-Zelt, S., 22, 31, 33
Rudolph, W., 31, 201, 204, 273

Sanderson, J. E., 320
Scaiola, E. & D., 14
Schart, A., 4, 6, 9, 10, 13–15
Schmidt, W. H., 266, 275
Schmitt, J. J., 43
Schuele, A., 364
Seitz, C. R., 11, 201
Seow, C. L., 18
Setel, T. D., 34, 39, 41, 71
Sherwood, Y., 34, 38–9, 42, 67, 70
Simkins, R. A., 201–2, 210–2, 221, 223, 225
Smend, R., 331, 362
Soggin, J. A., 273
Stamm, J. J., 79
Steck, O. H., 186
Stone, L. G., 13
Strazicich, J., 191, 201–2
Sweeney, M. A., 3–4, 6, 9, 13–15, 31, 33, 51, 61, 64,
  75, 80, 103–4, 107, 127, 141, 163–4, 169, 179,
  201, 206, 226, 273, 355

Taylor Jr., C. R., 295
Thelle, R. I., 34, 43, 70
Thompson, H. O., 78
Tiemeyer, L.-S., 190
Treves, M., 255
Tromp, N. J., 269
Trotter, J. M., 33, 59, 69, 82, 166
Troxel, R. L., 193, 200–2, 241

Van der Toorn, K., 56, 89
Vielhauer, R., 22, 31, 33, 66, 159, 181–2
Vries, S. J. De, 13, 46, 237, 320

Waard, J. de, 275, 329–30
Wallis, G., 80
Watson, D., 201–2
Watts, J. W., 14
Weber, M., 122
Weinfeld, M., 335
Wellhausen, J., 2, 16, 79, 92, 121–2, 187, 189, 265
Werse, N. R., 14, 65
Westermann, C., 19, 74, 283–4, 296, 338
Whiting, J. D., 223
Williamson, H. G. M., 132, 275, 355, 357–8
Wilson, R. R., 361
Wöhrle, J., 6, 10, 14–15, 202

Wolff, H. W., 19–21, 24–5, 28, 31, 38, 40, 42, 45–6, 52, 61, 64–5, 67, 77, 80–1, 84, 86, 88, 91–2, 95, 102–4, 111, 115, 124–5, 130, 131, 134, 137, 143–6, 148, 150–2, 159, 162–3, 166, 169, 173–4, 176, 179, 181, 187, 193–6, 198, 200–1, 204, 210, 221, 225, 232, 236, 241, 244, 247, 263–4, 272–3, 276–7, 284–91, 312, 320, 325, 327, 330, 333, 335, 357, 365, 371, 373

Yee, G. A., 22, 33, 70, 110

Zobel, H.-J, 75

Scripture Index

References are to English versions

HEBREW BIBLE
Genesis
1:1, 326
1:30, 61
2–3, 112
2:7, 326
2:8, 222
2:10, 222
2:15, 222
3:23, 222
4, 76
4:1, 76, 309
4:16, 222
4:17, 76
4:19, 41
4:25, 76
6:12, 238
7:11, 354
7:16, 238
9:2, 61
9:9–10, 26, 61
9:20–21, 86, 208
10:19, 152
12:3, 309
12:8, 241
13:7–8, 74
14:2, 152
14:8, 152
14:23, 301
15, 122
19, 152
19:25, 153
21:33, 241
22:4, 107
22:17, 48
22:23, 203

24:15, 203
24:24, 203
24:47, 203
24:50, 203
25:22, 332
25:23, 165
25:26, 162, 165
25:29–34, 165
26:20–22, 74
26:25, 241
27, 165
27:28, 185
27:35, 161, 168
27:36, 163
27:43, 164
28, 164
28:5, 164
28:10–22, 165
28:10–17, 239
28:11–22, 164
28:14, 309
28:18–22, 90, 321
28:18, 141
28:20–22, 165
29:4–5, 164
29:15, 164
29:18, 164
29:20, 164, 166, 171
29:25, 164
30:31, 164, 170
30:37, 87
31:19, 68
31:34–35, 68
32, 163
32:3–5, 283
32:12, 48

381

Scripture Index

Genesis (cont.)
32:22–32, 166
32:24, 163
32:26, 163
32:28, 163, 166
32:29, 163
32:30, 164
33:4, 163
35, 164
35:4, 87
35:6–15, 164
35:8, 163
37:34, 212
38:14–15, 52
38:20–22, 88
40:14, 75
41:2, 179
41:18, 179
41:32, 353
41:50–52, 93
47:29, 75
48, 174
48:8–20, 93

Exodus
3:14, 47
3:15, 167
6:7, 47
9, 324
9:2–7, 324
9:14, 324
10:1–20, 206
10:14, 222
12:17, 86
15:13, 75, 179
16, 176
17:2, 74
17:7, 74
18:15–22, 354
18:15, 332
18:21, 74
19:1, 364
19:11, 325
19:15, 325
19:17, 325
20:2, 168
20:4, 126
20:8–11, 364
20:13–15, 78
20:16, 334
21:2–11, 300

21:6, 62
21:10, 53
21:16, 78
21:22, 61
21:32, 67
22:13, 317
22:16, 57
22:25–27, 302
22:26–27, 301
22:26, 301–2
23:2–3, 74
23:6, 74
23:8, 334
23:14–17, 340
23:15, 86, 183
23:24, 141
24:4, 141
28:4, 68
28:12, 68
28:15, 68
28:25–28, 68
28:35, 210
28:43, 210
29:19, 183
29:30, 210
29:38–42, 209
32, 175
32:4, 175
32:8, 175
32:9–14, 354
32:12, 230
34:6–7, 8, 75, 157, 227, 259
34:6, 46, 227
34:7, 227
34:13, 141
34:16, 41
34:20, 183
34:22, 340
35:19, 210

Leviticus
2:10, 210
2:3, 210
5:2, 96
14:12, 183
18:17, 113
19:35–36, 168, 364
20:3, 301
20:10, 71
20:14, 41, 113
20:17, 41

Scripture Index

20:21, 41
22:2, 301
22:32, 301
23:36, 212
23:39–43
23:40, 130
26, 266, 323–5
26:2, 86
26:23, 324
26:27, 324
26:30–33, 325
27:4, 67

Numbers

3:5–10, 210
6:9–12, 306
9:6–7, 96
11:24–30, 238
11:25, 171
11:29, 238
12:3, 304
12:6–8, 171
12:6, 239
13:8, 37
13:16, 37
13:33, 304
14:4, 49
14:18, 227
18:20, 98
22:27, 87
23:19, 153
24:4, 361
24:16, 361
25:1–5, 138
25:1–4, 96
25:3, 56
28:3–9, 210
29:11, 210
29:35, 212

Deuteronomy

1:28, 304
2:10–12, 304
2:20–21, 304
4:9–10, 204
4:25, 171
4:28, 184
4:29, 227
4:30, 183
5:2–3, 159
5:3, 166
5:6, 168

5:12–15, 364
5:12, 86
5:17–19, 78
5:22–33, 354
5:23ff., 171
6:5, 227
6:12–14, 55
7:1–6, 55
7:8, 66, 149, 178
7:9–10, 271
7:13, 54, 66, 149, 233
7:18, 176
8:2, 176
8:3, 367
8:5, 116
8:6, 187
8:11–20, 176
8:19, 55
9:2, 304
9:7, 180
9:9ff., 171
9:16, 175
9:18, 171
9:23–24, 180
9:26–29, 230
10:12, 187, 227
10:15, 66, 149
11:14, 54, 233
11:19–21, 204
11:22, 187
12, 321
12:1–14, 91
12:2–3, 88
12:2–7, 55
12:5–7, 218
12:11, 105
12:31, 140, 340
13:1–5, 239
13:5, 178
14:22–29, 322
14:22–23, 86, 208
14:22, 322
14:23–29, 322
15:12–18, 300
16:8, 212
16:10–16, 340
16:13–15, 130
16:14, 130
16:16, 183
16:18, 335

384 Scripture Index

Deuteronomy (cont.)
16:22, 141, 340
17:2–5, 333
17:2, 112
17:6, 315
17:16, 184
18:1–8, 210
18:1–5, 210
18:3–4, 86, 208
18:8, 98
18:15–18, 171
19:14, 103
19:15, 315
19:17, 74
21:5, 74, 210
21:18–21, 152, 204
21:18, 96
21:19, 333
22:15, 333
22:19, 302
22:22, 71
22:23–24, 62, 209
22:24, 333
23:5, 66, 149
23:17–18, 89
23:17, 88
24:1, 140
24:3, 140
24:4, 61
24:5, 229
24:6, 302
24:10–13, 302
24:12–13, 302
24:12, 302
24:16, 271
25:7, 204, 333
25:9–10, 97, 300
25:13–16, 168, 270, 364
26:14, 131
27, 338
27:2, 292
27:4, 292
27:15, 175
28, 226, 266, 323–5
28:20, 86
28:22, 324
28:30, 85, 334
28:38–40, 85, 334
28:49, 124

28:51, 54, 233
29:5, 305
29:16–21, 271
29:23, 152, 325
29:25–28, 226
30:1–10, 69
30:1–2, 226
30:2, 183, 226–7
30:10, 227
31:16, 86
31:18, 66
31:20, 66
31:27, 180
31:29, 171
32:10, 58, 138
32:34, 177
34:10–12, 171
Joshua
2:1, 254
2:12, 75
3:1, 254
3:16, 112
4:19–20, 91, 321
6:5, 292
6:20, 292
7, 58
7:11, 112
7:15, 112
7:25, 58
7:26, 58
14:4, 98
15:13, 98
18:7, 98
18:21–28, 103
19:9, 98
23:13, 312
24:12, 47
Judges
2:11–13, 55
2:12, 171
2:20, 112
3:3, 56
3:7, 55
3:20, 317
3:27, 103, 221
4:6, 96
4:12, 96
4:14, 96
5:4, 107

Scripture Index

385

5:14, 103
5:30, 290
6:5, 205
6:33, 45
6:34, 103, 221
7:8, 103, 221
7:12, 205
7:16, 103, 221
8:27, 68
8:33, 56
10:10, 86
11:8, 49
11:25, 74
12:2, 74
13, 306
13:5, 306
14:15, 57
15:1, 229
16:5, 57
16:17, 306
17:5, 68
18:14, 68
18:17–18, 68
18:20, 68
19–21, 134, 143
19, 116
19:9, 132
20:1–2, 116
20:1, 333

Ruth
4:1–11, 333
4:6, 179
4:7, 300

1 Samuel
1:11, 306
1:15, 306
1:22, 306
2:6, 369
3:1, 361
3:20, 333, 361
4:5–6, 292
5:9, 315
5:24, 364
7:5, 96
7:6–7, 49
7:9, 63
7:16, 91, 96, 321
8:2, 203
8:4–22, 177

8:4, 204
9:6, 133
9:9, 332, 361
10:1–13, 133, 238
10:3, 96
10:17–24, 96
10:26, 134, 143
11:14–15, 91, 321
11:4, 134, 143
12:23, 354
15, 91, 321
15:10, 35
15:17–18, 49
15:22–23, 84
15:22, 110, 341
15:23, 68
15:29, 153
17:40, 87
19:19–24, 238
20:5, 364
20:8, 75
20:18, 364
23:8–12, 68
25:40, 41
28:6, 239, 367
28:15, 239
29:1, 45
29:11, 45
31:12–13, 213

2 Samuel
1:12, 213
1:17–27, 330
2:8, 138
3:10, 333
3:17–18, 204
3:21, 141
3:31, 212
3:38, 68, 103
5:1–3, 204
5:3, 141
5 :7, 279
6:12–19, 340
6:19, 66
7:4, 35
9:4–5, 349
12:16–23, 213
12:26, 291
13:10, 229
15:2–4, 74, 333

Scripture Index

2 *Samuel* (cont.)
17:8, 176
17:27, 349
21:1, 367
24:11–14, 139
24:11, 361
24:18, 131

1 *Kings*
1:39–40, 340
1:50–52, 317
2:3, 86
2:28–34, 318
3:5, 239
4:2, 68, 103
5:1–12, 289
5:6, 186
5:14, 186
6:3, 230
8, 323–5
8:33–37, 266, 323
8:35–36, 324
8:37, 205, 324
8:46–50, 69, 324
8:64, 230
9:13, 289
10, 247
10:26, 184
10:28, 184
11:11, 86
11:26, 37, 93, 174
12, 1, 17, 261
12:2, 37
12:16–20, 174
12:22, 133
12:26–29, 321
12:26–33, 318
12:26–30, 126, 142, 170, 175, 367
12:30, 318
13:30, 339
13:34, 373
14:9, 171
14:10–11, 362
14:15, 171
14:23, 88
14:24, 89
15:12, 89
16:1–4, 362
16:7, 171
16:13, 171
16:26, 171

16:31–33, 56
16:32, 126
16:33, 171
17:1, 91
17:2, 35
17:13, 115
18:17–40, 55
18:24, 241
18:28, 117
18:37, 63
19:18, 175
20:35, 360
21:1–16, 45
21:1, 45
21:8–11, 204
21:9–14, 213
21:20–24, 362
21:27–29, 212
22:5, 367
22:10, 131
22:14, 91
22:39, 317
22:46, 89
22:51–53, 56
22:53, 171

2 *Kings*
2:2, 91
2:3, 360
2:24, 291
3:2, 56
3:4, 276
4:1–7, 300
4:1, 360
4:23, 54, 364
4:38, 360
6:5, 339
8:7–15, 286
8:12, 145, 180, 291
9–15, 358
9–10, 45
9, 45
9:1–13, 45
9:1–14, 359
9:2, 229
9:11–13, 133
10:9, 358
10:26–27, 126
10:32–33, 286
12:17–18, 286
13:3, 286

Scripture Index

13:22–25, 286
13:24, 286
14:23–29, 277, 349
14:25, 349
14:29, 356
15, 17, 36
15:10, 358
15:16, 180, 291
15:19–20, 104
16:4, 88
16:7, 105
17, 17, 84, 256, 261, 358
17:3, 104, 145
17:5–6, 287
17:10, 88
17:11, 171
17:13–18, 132, 169, 358
17:13–15, 305
17:13–14, 313
17:13, 169, 311, 316, 358, 361
17:15, 84, 299
17:15–20, 298
17:16, 175
17:19, 298
17:20, 84
17:23, 311
17:24, 287
17:30, 367
18:12, 112
18:28–29, 284
18:31, 55
19:1–2, 212
19:3, 177
19:18, 184
20:3, 75
20:5, 107
21:6, 171
21:10, 311
22:17, 184
23:4–5, 56
23:5, 142
23:7, 89
23:8–20, 356
23:15, 333
23:19, 171
23:24–25, 226
23:24, 68
23:25, 226
23:29–30, 255
24:2, 311, 313

25:13, 247
25:23–25, 96
1 Chronicles
8:33, 138
9:39, 138
15:16–24, 340
23:5, 347
2 Chronicles
6:28, 324
8:14, 210
13:10, 210
20:20–26, 245
23:6, 210
26:10, 211
29:12, 203
29:25, 361
29:27, 347
30:2, 229
30:4, 229
30:13, 229
30:17, 229
30:23, 229
30:24, 229
31:2, 210
Ezra
5:5–9, 204
6:7–14, 204
8:21–23, 214
10:8, 204
10:43, 203
Nehemiah
1:4, 213
9:1, 214
9:17, 227
9:18, 175
9:34, 316
11:9, 203
Esther
9:30–31, 214
Job
4:8, 127
4:19, 104
5:18, 106
5:19–26, 284
8:11, 179
9:1–12, 166, 266, 326
9:3, 74
9:5–10, 326
13:19, 74
13:28, 104

388   *Scripture Index*

Job (cont.)
  19:25, 179
  23:6, 74
  27:18, 104
  29:7, 333
  33:14–15, 284
  36:14, 89
  38:16, 354
  38:41, 218
  40:2, 74
  41:1–2, 369
  41:6, 168
Psalms
  2, 257
  2:1–2, 257
  2:6, 279
  2:11, 142
  3:3, 139
  3:4, 63
  4:2, 117
  5:6, 117
  5:9, 141
  6:5, 178, 369
  6:7, 104
  9:11, 279
  10:17–18, 184
  12, 232
  12:1–4, 232
  12:5, 232
  17:8, 186
  18:4–5, 178
  19:5, 229
  19:6, 107
  19:9, 75
  22:12, 318
  25:4, 187
  26:10, 113
  27:1, 252
  30:9, 178
  31:10, 104
  34:4, 63
  36:6, 186, 354
  39:11, 104
  43:1, 117
  44:11, 257
  44:9–16, 230
  46, 252, 257, 279
  46:1, 252
  46:5–6, 279
  46:6, 257

  46:9, 257
  46:10, 257
  47, 257
  47:5, 229
  47:8, 257
  48, 279
  48:2, 234
  49:14–15, 369
  49:14, 178
  51:13, 187
  52:2, 117
  52:4, 117
  58:3, 117
  62: 4, 117
  65:9–12, 235
  68:7, 107
  74:14, 369
  76, 279
  76:2, 279
  78:8, 180
  80:1–2, 150
  80:8–13, 140, 150
  81:3, 103, 229, 364
  81:13, 187
  83:15, 292
  84, 279
  84:6, 235
  85:10, 75
  86:15, 227
  87, 279
  88:3–7, 369
  88:3–4, 178
  88:10–12, 178
  96, 256
  96:10b, 257
  96:13, 257
  98:6, 229
  102:4, 140
  102:9, 53
  102:12, 167
  103:13, 46
  103:8, 227
  104:15, 54, 86, 208, 233, 319, 347
  104:16, 186
  106:19, 175
  106:20, 84
  106:41, 257
  107:32, 229
  109:2, 117
  110:3, 185

Scripture Index

389

115:17, 369
118:5, 63
118:21, 63
122, 279
128:5, 279
130:5, 167
132, 279
133:3, 185
134:3, 279
135:13, 167
135:18, 138
137, 279
137:7, 255, 289, 375
137:9, 145
139:7–12, 369
139:8, 178
141:9, 312
145:8, 227
149:2, 235

Proverbs
1:8, 83
3:8, 53
4:1, 204
5:5, 178
6:16–19, 284
7:1, 204
7:24, 204
7:27, 178
9:10, 162
10:8, 90
10:10, 90
11:1, 168, 364
15:11, 369
15:18, 74
16:8, 335
16:11, 168, 364
17:12, 176
17:14, 74
17:23, 334
19:12, 185
19:18, 96, 116
20:10, 168, 364
20:23, 168, 270, 364
21:3, 62, 335
22:8, 127
22:28, 103
23:10, 103
24:9, 113
28:23, 141
29:17, 116

30:15–31, 107
30:15–16, 284
30:18–19, 284
30:21–23, 284
30:27, 208
30:29–31, 284
31:24, 168

Song of Songs
1:2, 186
1:4, 186, 229
2:1, 186
2:2, 186
2:3, 186
2:11, 186
2:13, 137, 186
2:16, 186
3:9, 186
3:11, 279
4:5, 186
4:8, 186
4:10, 186
4:11, 186
4:15, 186
5:1, 186
5:13, 186
5:15, 186
5:16, 66
6:2, 186
6:3, 186
6:11, 186
7:2, 186
7:3, 186
7:8, 186
7:9, 186
7:12, 186
7:13, 186

Isaiah
1–12, 295
1:1, 361
1:2–3, 149
1:2, 204
1:8, 279
1:11, 110, 341
1:13–14, 341
1:13, 54, 212, 364
1:17, 167
1:21, 26, 62, 335
1:27, 62, 335
2:1, 276
2:2–4, 250, 257

Scripture Index

Isaiah (cont.)

2:3, 279
2:4, 250, 257
2:12–17, 277
2:12, 215
2:13, 87, 186
3:26, 211
5:1–7, 140, 209
5:4, 142
5:5, 53
5:6, 142
5:7, 62, 335
5:8–24, 338
5:8–10, 317
5:25, 277
7:3, 46
7:4, 234
8:3–4, 46
8:14, 312
8:16, 177
8:17, 167
8:18, 279
9:7, 62, 335
9:10, 277
10:5–19, 45
10:5–6, 256
10:5, 296, 316
10:7–14, 256
11:12–13, 48
13–23, 295
13, 215, 216, 220
13:3–5, 250–1
13:3–5, 222
13:3, 250
13:4, 216, 223, 251
13:6–9, 194, 215
13:6, 217
13:7–8, 216
13:9, 222
13:10, 216, 223, 240
13:13, 216, 223
13:16, 145
13:19, 325
13:20–22, 216
13:20, 255
14:9–10, 178
14:13, 234
14:28–32, 295
15:3, 212

16:6, 295
16:13–14, 3
17:1–3, 295
19:1–15, 295
19:18–25, 258
19:18, 258
19:19, 258
20:2–4, 42
20:2, 97
21:3, 177
22:5, 215
22:6, 373
23:1–12, 295
23:17–18, 258
23:18, 258
24–39, 295
25:4, 252
27:1, 369
28–31, 338
28:4, 137
28:15, 178
28:18, 178
29:6, 292
29:10, 361
30:10, 361
30:16, 184
31:3, 184
32:7, 113
33:5, 62, 335
35:4, 234
36:16, 55
38:18, 369
40–66, 295
40–55, 167, 226, 266
40:5, 238
40:6, 238
40:12, 166, 266, 326
40:19–20, 86
40:22–23, 166, 266, 326
40:31, 124, 167
41:10, 234
41:13, 234
43:1, 179, 234, 326
43:7, 326
43:11, 176
44:9–20, 25, 86, 88, 121
44:11–13, 126, 175
44:12, 126, 175
44:13, 126, 175

Scripture Index

44:22, 179, 226
44:23, 179
45, 236
45:5–6, 198
45:5, 236
45:6, 236
45:7, 326
45:18, 198, 236, 326
45:21, 176
47:4, 166, 326
48:2, 166, 326
48:20, 179
49:12, 148
49:15, 150
49:23, 167
49:26, 238
50:9, 104
51:2, 48
51:3, 222
51:5, 144, 167
51:8, 104
51:9, 111
51:11, 279
51:13, 121, 128
51:15, 166, 326
52:1, 253
52:7, 279
54:5, 166, 326
55:11, 111
58, 212
58:2–7, 214
60:3–7, 258
61:1, 124
61:5, 211
65:12, 124
66:4, 124
66:9, 177
Jeremiah
1:1, 35
1:2, 203
1:11–14, 266
1:11, 87
1:13–15, 234
1:16, 86
2:1, 203
2:2, 58, 75, 138
2:8, 25, 55, 83
2:11, 84
2:19, 185

2:20, 88
2:21, 140
2:23, 55
2:24, 127
2:26, 25, 83
3:3, 52, 366
3:6, 88
3:18, 48
3:20, 66
3:22, 185
4:3, 143
4:5, 221
4:6, 234
4:8, 212
4:13, 124
4:30, 52
5:2, 92
5:6, 185
5:7, 86
5:19, 86
5:23, 180
5:30, 113
6:1, 221, 234
6:4, 250
6:7, 161
6:13, 25, 83
6:17, 132
6:20, 131, 247
6:22, 234
6:26, 212
7:9, 55
7:16, 354
7:18–19, 171
7:18, 66
7:20, 66
7:21–23, 342
7:25–26, 313
7:25, 311
8:5, 185
8:19, 171
9:2, 114
9:10, 218
9:13, 86
9:15, 334
9:17–19, 330
9:17–18, 330
9:25, 85
10:1–16, 87
10:16, 166, 326

Jeremiah (cont.)
11:13, 138
11:14, 354
11:17, 171
11:22, 45, 85
12:4, 366
13:3, 203
14:5–6, 218
14:7, 185
14:11–12, 354
15:8, 153
16:5, 347–8
16:6, 117
16:11, 86
18:3–6, 326
18:13, 113, 209, 330
19:1–13, 41
20:7, 57
21:14, 45, 85
22:23, 177
22:28, 127
23:10, 366
23:14, 113
23:15, 334
23:25–32, 239
24:1–5, 266
25:6, 184
25:7, 184
25:11–12, 156
25:13a, 295
25:20, 288
25:30, 278
25:30a, 252
26:5, 311
27:22, 316
29:10, 156, 258
29:14, 114, 257
29:17, 113
30–31, 154
30:4, 68
30:9, 68
31:4, 209, 330
31:11, 179
31:21, 209, 330
31:27–34, 48
31:31–34, 238
31:35–38, 166
31:35, 326
32:18, 166, 326
32:30, 184

33:15–16, 245
34:18, 112
35:15, 311
35:15–16, 313
36:6, 213
36:22, 317
38:17–23, 256
40–41, 96
41:5, 117, 196
42–43, 132, 154
44:4–5, 313
44:4, 311
44:15–19, 66
44:15–22, 57
44:24–30, 66
46–51, 295
46:10, 215
46:12, 295
46:13–24, 295
46:18, 166, 326
46:23, 205
47:4, 373
48:15, 166, 326
48:29, 295
48:38, 127
48:40, 124
49, 291
49:2, 291
49:3, 212, 292
49:17–22, 375
49:18, 325
49:27, 291
49:28–33, 295
49:34–38, 295
49:35, 46
50–51, 256
50:4, 245
50:20, 245
50:40, 325
51:15–19, 166, 326
51:24, 247
51:33, 113
51:34, 247
51:57, 166, 326
Lamentations
2:2, 233
2:8, 211
2:9, 361
2:17, 233
2:21, 233

Scripture Index

2:22, 216
3:15, 334
3:19, 334
3:40–41, 107
3:40, 183
3:43, 233
4:2, 235, 279
4:19, 124
4:21–22, 255, 375

Ezekiel

1–24, 295
1:3, 203
3:16–21, 132
3:16–17, 312
4:4–8, 42
4:13, 131
5:11, 233
6:13, 88
7:4, 233
7:9, 233
7:10, 215
8:16, 230
8:18, 233
9:4, 373
9:5, 233
9:8–10, 354
9:10, 233
11:16, 257
13:5, 215
16, 138
16:8–14, 52
16:53, 114
17:4, 168
17:10, 161
17:15, 184
18, 271
19:8, 95
20:9, 230
20:14, 230
20:22, 230
20:39, 301
21:21, 68
21:22, 292
23:40, 52
25–32, 295
25:12–15, 375
25:12–14, 282
25:16, 373
26–28, 289
26:17–18, 330

27–28, 167
27:18, 185
28:2–5, 295
28:13, 222
29:13–16, 258
30:2–3, 217
30:2, 194
30:3, 215
31:4, 354
31:9, 222
31:16, 222
31:18, 222
32:2, 330
32:7–8, 240
32:21–28, 178
33–48, 295
33:1–9, 222, 312
33:2–9, 132
34:23–24, 69
34:25–28, 26, 61
35:5, 290
36:20–22, 301
36:21–23, 230
36:24, 257
36:35, 222
36:26–27, 238
37:15–23, 48
37:21, 49, 257
37:24–25, 69
38:6, 234
38:15, 234
38:20, 61
39:2, 234
39:7, 230
39:25, 232, 245
39:29, 238
40:46, 210
43:19, 210
45:9, 315
47:1–12, 254

Hosea

1–3, 16, 19, 20, 22, 25–6, 29, 35, 37–40, 42–4,
    48–9, 58, 64, 70–1, 76, 83, 85, 149
1–2, 60, 62, 64, 66
1, 40, 44, 64
1:1, 1, 16–7, 21, 25, 36, 40, 190, 203
1:2–2:15, 28, 156
1:2–2:1, 19, 40
1:2–9, 47–8, 64
1:2–8, 38, 40

Scripture Index

Hosea (cont.)

1:2, 16, 27, 38–42, 47, 66
1:3, 44, 64
1:4–9, 471:6, 46, 62–3
1:4, 27, 44–7, 49, 60, 63, 70, 85, 309
1:5, 46, 60–1
1:6, 27, 44, 60, 70, 184
1:7, 17, 20, 46, 60–1, 131
1:8–9, 47
1:9, 44, 46, 63, 70
1:10–2:1, 26, 29, 44, 46–8
1:10–11, 49
1:10, 47–8
1:11, 17, 47–8, 60, 69
2, 40, 47, 49, 66, 209
2:1, 38, 47, 49, 60, 62–3, 84
2:2–15, 19, 51, 57, 83
2:2–13, 27, 40, 47, 64
2:2, 16, 41, 47, 49, 51, 66–7, 70
2:3–13, 44
2:3–4, 39
2:3, 53, 54, 58, 70, 174
2:3a, 51
2:3b, 51
2:4, 16, 41, 53, 60, 70
2:5, 16, 41, 54, 70
2:5a, 53
2:5b, 53
2:6–7, 53, 70
2:6, 53, 57, 67, 69
2:7, 106
2:8–13, 53
2:8, 7, 27, 40, 43, 53–5, 60, 70, 150, 173–5, 233
2:9–10, 70
2:9, 8, 53–4, 63, 70, 106, 131, 373
2:10, 53–4
2:11–12, 70
2:11, 54, 364
2:12–13, 70
2:12, 8, 54, 58, 63, 227
2:13, 27, 40, 43, 45, 53, 55–6, 60, 85, 150, 173–6, 309
2:14–23, 48, 57, 108
2:14–16, 58
2:14–15, 28–9, 40, 48, 55, 57–8, 137, 156, 160, 168
2:14, 53, 57–8, 69, 174
2:15–16, 209
2:15, 58, 116, 149
2:16–23, 26, 60, 64

2:16–20, 19, 40, 59
2:16–17, 40, 43, 60
2:16, 55, 59–61, 63, 209
2:17, 55, 59, 150
2:18, 26, 29, 46, 59–61
2:18a, 60
2:18b, 60
2:19–20, 26, 29, 59, 60, 62–3, 167
2:20, 60, 62–4, 75–6
2:21ff., 16
2:21–23, 19, 40
2:21–22, 26, 63
2:22, 8, 29, 44, 60
2:23, 29, 49, 64, 84
3, 26, 40, 60, 64–6, 70
3:1–5, 19, 38
3:1–4, 65
3:1–2, 65
3:1, 16, 27, 39, 41, 44, 64–6, 70, 149
3:2, 66
3:3–4, 65
3:3, 16, 41, 65, 67, 69, 70
3:4, 65, 67–9
3:5, 19, 20, 27, 29, 44, 48, 49, 65, 76–9, 106, 108, 131, 183
4–14, 19–20, 25, 29, 39–40, 43, 62, 71, 92
4–11, 19, 20, 22, 25–6, 37, 44, 48, 55, 58, 73, 85, 88, 101, 113, 117, 130, 144, 146, 148–9, 153, 155, 158–62, 169–70, 181–2
4:1–11:11, 73, 154
4:1–11:9, 28, 154, 156
4–9, 22
4, 26, 52, 73, 86, 90, 91, 93–4, 97–8, 155, 162
4:1–14, 90–1
4:1–9, 73
4:1–3, 73–4, 81, 85
4:1–2, 74, 80
4:1, 19, 27, 60, 62, 74–7, 81, 83, 93, 98, 109, 144, 159, 162, 167, 181
4:2, 28, 41, 45, 74–5, 78–80, 93, 112, 114, 145, 161
4:3, 27, 77, 80, 366
4:4–19, 81
4:4–14, 113
4:4–10, 27, 81–2, 85
4:4–8, 84–5
4:4–6, 28, 75, 81, 83–4, 93
4:4, 81, 83, 110
4:4b, 81
4:5, 25, 82, 90, 97, 113, 169, 183, 187

Scripture Index

4:6, 55, 63, 76, 81–3, 97, 110, 124, 140, 169, 174, 298
4:7–11, 127
4:7–10, 84
4:7–8, 84
4:7, 127, 173–5
4:7b, 84
4:8, 28, 81, 84, 93, 174, 177, 183, 309
4:9–10, 81
4:9, 45, 81, 85, 86, 106, 110, 159, 162, 309
4:10–16, 130
4:10–15, 40–1
4:10–14, 27
4:10–12, 96, 130
4:10–11, 85, 88, 97
4:10, 16, 81, 85–6, 130, 208
4:10a, 85, 334
4:11–19, 86, 96
4:11–13, 93
4:11, 16, 28, 85–6
4:11b, 141
4:12–14, 86
4:12–13, 28, 43, 87, 88
4:12, 16, 85–8, 92, 130, 184
4:12a, 87
4:13–14, 41, 68
4:13, 16, 85, 87–8, 110, 127, 142, 150, 187
4:13b–14, 28, 88
4:14, 16, 45, 85–6, 89–90, 309
4:14b, 88
4:15–19, 92
4:15, 10, 16, 17, 26, 28, 85, 90, 92–3, 103, 120, 140–4, 159, 165, 170, 173–4, 180, 367
4:15c, 91
4:16, 16, 92
4:17–19, 92
4:17–18, 43
4:17, 92, 174–5, 186
4:18, 41, 85, 92
4:19, 92, 110
5–8, 140
5–7, 22
5:1–7, 26, 92, 94, 98, 155
5:1–4, 98
5:1–2, 95–6
5:1, 19, 62, 73–4, 94, 110, 167, 181, 204
5:1b–2, 95
5:3–7, 96
5:3–4, 40, 96, 130–1
5:3, 16, 27, 41, 63, 76, 85, 93, 96–7, 113, 309

5:4, 16, 41, 85, 96–8, 106, 183, 185
5:5–7, 97–8
5:5, 17, 25, 28, 82, 93, 97, 98, 113–15, 133, 183, 187, 309
5:6–7, 27
5:6, 54, 102, 153, 367
5:7a, 97, 112
5:8–7:16, 26, 104–5, 107, 113–14, 117–18, 120, 124, 130, 155, 179–80, 184–6
5:8–6:6, 163–4
5:8–6:3, 109
5:8–15, 106–7
5:8–14, 102, 105–6, 124
5:8–9, 102
5:8, 19, 90, 101–3, 165, 181, 221
5:9, 27, 103, 116
5:10, 68, 102–3, 125, 140, 177
5:11, 102–3, 167
5:12–14, 17, 102, 105
5:12, 16, 102, 104–5, 185
5:13–6:3, 108
5:13–15, 106
5:13–14, 106
5:13, 16, 27, 43, 101–2, 113, 116–17, 127, 131, 150, 184–5
5:14, 16, 104–5, 148, 174, 176, 185
5:15–6:6, 102, 184
5:15, 54, 105–6, 156, 173–4, 180, 184
6, 108
6:1–3, 35, 105–9, 115, 117, 184
6:1–2, 101, 106, 113
6:1, 54, 105–6, 150, 152, 167, 183, 185
6:2, 105, 106, 114
6:3, 107, 109, 353
6:4–7:16, 117
6:4–7:10, 26, 57, 109, 115, 117, 120, 146, 148, 152, 154, 178
6:4–6, 28, 106, 108–10, 167
6:4, 16, 17, 62, 109–11, 114, 148, 152, 174, 185
6:4a, 108
6:4b, 175
6:5–11, 101
6:5, 25, 62, 110, 112, 160, 169
6:6, 62–3, 68, 76, 106, 108–10, 116–17, 127, 159, 167, 184, 341
6:6a, 109
6:6b, 109
6:7–7:16, 109
6:7–11a, 111
6:7–10, 25, 113, 170

Hosea (cont.)

6:7, 25, 110–2, 116, 122–3
6:7b, 112
6:8–9, 25, 111–12, 116, 170
6:8, 112, 159, 170
6:9, 110, 113
6:10, 16, 27, 40–1, 85, 93, 111, 113, 116, 130, 131, 155–6
6:11, 17, 106
6:11a, 25, 113
6:11b–7:7, 113
6:11b–7:1, 116–7
6:11b–7:1a, 156
6:11b, 84, 109, 113–5
7:1–16, 114
7:1–4, 28
7:1–3, 114
7:1–2, 116
7:1, 16, 93, 101, 105, 113–16, 150, 183, 185, 309
7:2, 114
7:3–7, 68, 114–15
7:3, 68, 103, 114, 125, 145, 159, 161, 177
7:4, 114
7:5–7, 28
7:5, 68, 101, 103, 125, 177
7:6, 114
7:7, 114, 177
7:8–10, 115
7:8–9, 116
7:8, 16, 115
7:9, 115
7:10–16, 27
7:10, 28, 68, 97, 106, 109, 115, 117–18, 120, 152–4, 183
7:11–16, 109, 117, 120
7:11–12, 116
7:11f., 16
7:11, 43, 101, 116, 128, 131, 148, 159, 161, 184
7:12, 16, 109, 116–17, 133, 153
7:13, 116–17
7:13, 27, 139, 161, 187
7:14–16, 117
7:14, 117, 124
7:15, 96, 116–7, 153
7:16, 43, 68, 101, 103, 106, 109, 117, 177, 184
8, 25, 26, 120, 146, 155
8:1–13, 130
8:1, 19, 25, 29, 111–12, 120, 122–4, 131–3, 140, 155, 181, 187
8:1b, 120–1, 123, 124

8:2, 63, 76, 124
8:3, 27–8, 120, 124, 126
8:4–6, 126, 321
8:4, 28, 68, 103, 125, 174–5, 177, 186
8:4a, 120, 126
8:4b–5, 125, 126
8:4b, 29, 120
8:5–6, 27, 120
8:5, 126, 153, 185
8:6, 121, 123, 126, 174–5, 184
8:6a, 25
8:7, 126, 131, 144
8:8–10, 159, 161
8:8, 27, 127
8:9, 27, 120, 127, 130–1, 155, 184
8:10, 68, 103, 177
8:10a, 127
8:10b, 127
8:11–13, 302, 342
8:11, 28, 110, 120, 127–8, 141, 173–5
8:12, 28, 120, 127
8:13, 27, 45, 68, 85, 106, 110, 114, 120, 128, 130–1, 133, 152, 174, 177, 183, 309
8:13b, 129, 133, 134
8:14, 10, 17, 25, 29, 90, 120, 123, 128, 174
8:14a, 121
8:14b, 128
9–11, 140
9:1–9, 26, 134
9:1–7, 130
9:1–6, 129
9:1–2, 130
9:1, 16, 19, 40–1, 55, 85, 120, 129–31, 181
9:2, 27, 131
9:3, 27, 69, 106, 116, 128–30, 152
9:4, 20, 68, 110, 131
9:4b, 25, 129
9:5, 129, 132, 168
9:6, 132, 161
9:6b, 132
9:7–9, 26, 28, 129, 132, 134
9:7–8, 134
9:7, 114, 129, 132–3, 183, 309
9:7a, 132
9:8, 129, 133
9:9, 45, 85, 103, 114, 129, 133–4, 143, 174, 177, 183, 309
9:10–11:9, 156
9:10–10:15, 19, 26, 137, 146, 149, 155
9:10–17, 137

Scripture Index 397

9:10–14, 140
9:10, 16, 19, 27, 40, 55, 58, 96, 137–40, 143, 146,
    149, 155, 160, 168, 173–6
9:10a, 138
9:10b, 140, 176
9:11–16, 155
9:11–14, 180
9:11–13, 139
9:11–12, 138–9
9:11b–13, 140
9:11b–12, 139
9:11b, 139
9:12, 27, 139, 140
9:12b, 139
9:13, 139, 145
9:13a, 139
9:13b, 139
9:14, 139–40
9:14b, 139
9:15–17, 140
9:15, 27, 66, 68, 103, 140, 145, 159, 170, 177, 185
9:15a, 140
9:15b–16, 140
9:16, 140
9:17, 27, 140
10:1–8, 137, 142–3
10:1–2, 27, 68, 110, 140, 302
10:1, 16, 20, 28, 127, 137, 140–2, 146, 155,
    181, 186
10:2, 141–2, 159, 170, 173–4, 180
10:3, 141
10:4, 62, 111, 141, 159, 167, 170
10:5–6, 184
10:5, 27, 90, 103, 110, 142, 165
10:6, 93
10:7–8, 142
10:7, 169
10:8, 110, 142–3, 159, 170, 356
10:9–15, 137
10:9–10, 143
10:9, 103, 133, 143
10:10, 114, 116, 133, 143, 153, 183
10:11–15, 143
10:11–13a, 143
10:11, 16, 17, 20, 92, 137, 143–4, 146, 155
10:11b, 26, 28
10:12–13, 143
10:12, 26, 28, 62, 143–4, 146
10:13–15, 28
10:13, 28, 144–6, 159, 161

10:13b–15, 145
10:13b, 145, 184
10:14, 104, 145, 161, 174, 180
10:15, 169
11, 26, 148, 149, 155–6
11:1–11, 20, 148, 150, 153, 155
11:1–9, 20, 25, 58, 76, 148, 154–6, 180
11:1–4, 147–8, 153
11:1, 16, 58, 66, 116, 137, 149–50, 168, 181, 185
11:2, 27, 40, 55, 87, 110, 147, 150–1, 173,
    175–6, 184
11:3–4, 150–1
11:3, 16, 101, 105, 149–50, 176, 185
11:4, 151, 185
11:5–7, 147–8, 152–3
11:5, 27, 69, 106, 116, 128, 151–3
11:5b, 152
11:6, 152, 180
11:7, 28, 152–3
11:7b, 152
11:8–11, 19, 48, 108, 117, 161
11:8–9, 26, 28–9, 48, 57, 62, 147, 152–3, 156, 179
11:8, 154, 174, 179
11:8a, 153
11:9, 106, 126, 153–4, 185
11:9a, 153
11:10–11, 25, 147–8, 154, 156
11:10–11a, 148
11:10, 149, 154
11:10a, 148, 154
11:11, 55, 116, 147–9, 154–5
11:11b, 148
11:12–14:9, 20, 158
11:12–14:4, 26
11:12–14:3, 25
11:12–12:2, 160, 162, 171, 183
11:12–12:1, 165
11:12, 17, 29, 93, 144, 147, 159, 161, 168
11:12a, 161
11:12b, 161
12–14, 19, 20, 22, 25, 44, 48, 85, 159, 162, 181
12–13, 161, 175, 181–2
12, 29, 112, 158–60, 162, 165–6, 168–70, 173–4
12:1, 29, 43, 111, 116, 144, 159, 161, 174, 179, 184
12:2–12, 20
12:2, 17, 45, 85, 106, 159, 162, 171, 309
12:2a, 162
12:2b, 162
12:3–4, 158, 160–2, 164–6, 170
12:3, 163, 165, 177

Scripture Index

Hosea (cont.)
12:3a, 162, 165
12:3b–4a, 163
12:3b, 163, 165
12:4, 159, 163, 166
12:4a, 163
12:4b, 164, 167
12:5, 159, 166–7
12:6, 62, 106, 159, 167, 183
12:7–8, 29, 167
12:7, 160–1, 168
12:7a, 168
12:8, 114, 133, 165, 168–9, 183, 309
12:8b, 168
12:9–10, 169
12:9, 116, 149, 160, 168–9, 174, 176, 182
12:10, 25, 110, 160, 169
12:11, 68, 110, 112, 142, 159, 165, 169
12:11a, 170
12:11b, 170
12:12–13, 170
12:12, 158, 160, 162, 164
12:13–13:6, 20
12:13, 25, 110, 149, 160
12:14, 106, 160, 165, 173
13, 173–4, 176, 177, 179
13:1–3, 174
13:1–2, 43, 179
13:1, 40, 55, 93, 173–5, 179–80
13:2, 68, 110, 173–5, 184, 186
13:3, 16, 53, 174–5, 185
13:4–8, 176
13:4–6, 29
13:4–5, 175
13:4, 63, 76, 116, 149, 168, 174, 182
13:4b, 176
13:5–8, 16
13:5, 16, 40, 76, 174, 176, 309
13:6, 174, 176, 179
13:7–8, 29, 176, 185
13:7f., 16
13:7, 174
13:8, 148, 176, 291
13:9–10, 177
13:9, 153, 177
13:10–11, 29, 177
13:10, 68, 103, 174, 177
13:11, 126
13:12–13, 179
13:12, 114, 133, 174, 177, 183, 309

13:13, 16, 177
13:14, 153, 174, 178
13:14a, 178
13:14b, 178
13:15–16, 179
13:15, 29, 174, 179
13:16, 20, 29, 145, 173–4, 179–80, 183
14, 161, 179, 181
14:1–9, 20
14:1–4, 186
14:1–3, 29, 108, 182
14:1–2, 309
14:1, 20, 106, 114, 133, 182–3, 187
14:2, 106, 114, 133, 183–4
14:2b–3, 35, 184
14:3, 26, 63, 108, 184
14:4–9, 19, 25–6, 48, 184
14:4–8, 29, 60, 182, 187
14:4–6, 182
14:4, 1, 16, 29, 66, 101, 105, 106, 126, 150, 182, 185
14:5–7, 16, 185–6
14:5, 16, 185
14:6–7, 185
14:6, 185
14:7, 8, 106, 185–6
14:8, 16, 26, 63, 186
14:8a, 187
14:8b, 186
14:9, 21, 25, 29, 187

Joel
1–2, 27, 207, 225, 289–91, 324
1:1–2:27, 192–3, 196, 198–9, 237, 242, 244
1:1–2:17, 197
1, 211, 219, 221, 224, 230, 232, 234
1:1, 35, 190, 197, 199
1:2–2:17, 231, 239
1:2–2:11, 232, 236
1:2–20, 191, 204
1:2–12, 204
1:2, 74, 193, 204, 213, 224, 229
1:3, 224
1:4–2:27, 204, 215
1:4–20, 221
1:4–14, 214, 219
1:4–12, 189, 254
1:4–10, 353
1:4, 205, 206, 208, 230, 235
1:5–2:17, 230
1:5, 197, 208–9, 224, 229, 254

Scripture Index

1:6, 189, 193, 205, 208, 224
1:7, 208, 214, 235
1:8, 197, 209, 224, 229
1:9, 189, 209–12, 218, 228, 230, 233
1:10–12, 189, 218, 235
1:10, 54, 210–1, 233–4, 314, 336
1:11–12, 211, 233, 315–6
1:11, 197, 224, 229
1:12, 211, 218
1:13–14, 189, 211, 215, 227
1:13, 189, 197, 210, 212, 224, 228–9, 233
1:14, 194, 197, 204, 206, 212, 214, 217–9, 224–5, 229, 250
1:15–2:11, 338
1:15–20, 215, 218
1:15, 189, 194, 197, 199, 215–7, 219, 220
1:15b, 217
1:16–20, 189
1:16, 210, 218
1:17–20, 221
1:17, 205, 218, 235
1:18, 205, 218, 254
1:19–20, 218–9, 235
1:19, 218, 222, 224–5
1:20, 218, 224, 235, 254
2, 189, 221, 230, 236
2:1–17, 191
2:1–11, 215–7, 220–1, 224–5, 233, 244
2:1–5, 216
2:1–3, 189
2:1–2, 189, 197, 199, 220, 222, 224
2:1, 193, 197, 222, 224, 229
2:2, 194, 205, 217, 222, 224, 338
2:3, 216, 222, 224, 228, 235
2:4–9, 189, 205
2:4–5, 221, 223
2:5, 224
2:6, 194, 216, 222–3
2:7–9, 194, 223
2:10–11, 221
2:10, 216, 222–3, 240, 252
2:10b, 2512:11, 223–4
2:11, 189, 197, 199, 216, 220, 222, 224, 240
2:12–17, 8, 189, 225, 236
2:12–14, 229, 236
2:12–13, 197, 206, 226
2:12, 183, 214, 225, 229
2:13, 8, 198, 225, 227, 229, 259
2:14, 197, 227–9, 230–1, 242, 259
2:15–17, 229–30, 232, 236

2:15–16, 194, 197, 229
2:15, 193, 214, 229, 250, 259
2:16, 204, 229, 238
2:17, 107, 191, 197, 210, 229–30, 232–3, 236, 253
2:18–27, 189, 191, 196, 198, 232, 236–7, 242, 244
2:18–19, 231
2:18–19a, 232
2:18, 190, 193, 194, 232–3
2:19–27, 198
2:19–26, 254
2:19–20, 233
2:19, 54, 194, 233
2:20, 233, 234, 236
2:21–25, 236
2:21–24, 234
2:21, 234
2:22, 234
2:23, 193, 234
2:24, 233, 235
2:25, 205, 221, 235
2:26–27, 236
2:26, 8, 194, 233, 235
2:27, 191, 193–4, 198, 232, 236, 245, 253
2:28–32, 189, 192–3, 195–6, 198–9, 237, 242–5, 256
2:28–29, 198, 237–9, 241, 243
2:28, 191, 236–7
2:28, 199, 217, 239, 242
2:30–32, 199, 237, 239
2:30–31, 240
2:31, 215, 240
2:32, 192, 237, 240–1, 243, 257
3, 193, 199, 237, 251, 253, 255–7, 259
3:1–21, 192, 242
3:1–15, 189
3:1–3, 192–3, 196, 198–9, 237, 242, 244, 246, 248, 249, 251
3:1, 114, 191–2, 247, 252
3:2–15, 252
3:2–3, 192, 246
3:2, 127, 189, 195, 245, 249–50, 253
3:3, 192, 246–8
3:4–8, 189, 192–3, 195, 198–9, 246, 248, 254
3:5–7, 248
3:5, 247
3:6, 195, 246, 247, 248
3:7–8, 248
3:7, 247
3:8, 195, 247
3:9–21, 192

Joel (cont.)

3:9–17, 192, 196, 198–9, 237, 242, 244, 246
3:9–15, 189, 192, 249
3:9–13, 249
3:9–12, 250
3:9–11, 249
3:9–10, 249
3:9, 246, 249–51
3:10, 250
3:11–12, 249
3:11, 249
3:12–13, 249
3:12, 249, 250
3:13, 250
3:14, 199, 215, 250–1
3:15, 240, 251
3:16–18, 189
3:16–17, 252
3:16, 7, 245, 252, 254, 257
3:16a, 252, 278
3:17, 192, 253
3:17a, 253
3:18–21, 192–3, 198–9, 253
3:18, 7, 192, 254–5, 319, 375
3:18a, 254
3:19–27, 198
3:19–21, 195, 242, 254
3:19, 189, 192, 254, 290
3:20–21, 189, 192
3:20, 255
3:21, 8, 255, 257

Amos

1–2, 11, 25, 120, 123, 260–1, 268, 294, 297, 308, 325, 351, 353, 375
1, 36–7, 252, 266–7
1:1, 1, 17, 190, 261, 276, 278, 286, 307, 360–1
1:2, 7, 148, 252, 254, 266, 278, 279, 281, 284, 311, 313, 317
1:2a, 252, 278
1:3–2:16, 74, 107, 299, 308–9, 337, 349
1:3–2:3, 282, 293, 298, 307, 311
1:3–8, 267, 372
1:3–5, 283
1:3, 260, 293
1:3b, 287
1:4, 260, 268, 286, 291, 348
1:5, 286
1:6–8, 283, 288, 294
1:6, 248, 260, 268, 283, 289, 293, 373
1:7, 260, 348
1:8, 288, 314

1:9–12, 294
1:9–10, 266, 282–3, 289
1:9, 248, 260, 270, 283
1:10, 260
1:11–12, 266, 282–3
1:11, 260, 289
1:12, 260
1:13–15, 267, 283
1:13, 260, 293, 320
1:14, 180, 260, 291, 348
1:14b, 293
1:15, 268, 292
2–6, 351, 363
2:1–3, 267, 283, 298
2:1, 260, 294
2:2, 260, 348
2:2b, 293
2:4–5, 120, 261, 266, 270, 282–3, 298–9
2:4, 86, 260
2:5, 260
2:6–6:14, 363
2:6–16, 74, 261, 266, 281, 293, 298, 310, 356
2:6–9, 267, 305
2:6–8, 260, 267, 303–5, 307, 315, 334, 365
2:6–7, 168, 270, 319, 363, 364
2:6, 246, 260, 334
2:6b, 300–1
2:7, 265, 299, 308, 364
2:7a, 301
2:7b, 301
2:8, 267, 299, 301–2, 307, 319
2:8a, 302
2:9, 87, 304–7
2:10–12, 266, 299, 304–5, 307
2:10, 270, 305, 309, 343, 371
2:11–12, 169, 271, 305–6
2:12, 306
2:13–16, 267–9, 304, 306
2:13, 306, 366
2:14–16, 307, 369
2:16, 366
3–6, 262, 266, 308, 310, 312, 329, 345, 349, 351, 356
3–4, 262, 308, 327
3:1–4:5, 267, 327
3:1–4:3, 320
3:1–8, 350
3:1–2, 308, 337
3:1, 19, 74, 266, 270, 308, 327, 329, 371
3:1b, 266
3:2, 11, 85, 309–10, 372

Scripture Index

3:3–8, 262, 266, 278
3:3–6, 311, 314
3:3–5, 311
3:3, 311, 317
3:4–6, 311
3:4, 311–3, 317
3:5, 95, 312
3:6, 311, 312–14
3:7–8, 314
3:7, 266, 311, 313
3:8, 148, 267, 270, 311, 313–14, 317
3:9–4:3, 262, 329, 345, 350
3:9–11, 311, 314, 318, 348, 350
3:9–10, 318
3:9, 313–15
3:10, 161, 260, 315, 346
3:11, 260, 283, 315
3:12–15, 314, 318
3:12, 148, 260, 283, 316–18, 331, 337, 347
3:13–14, 266, 316, 317
3:13, 74, 316
3:14, 316–8
3:15, 268–9, 307, 316–18, 347, 349, 366
4:1–6:7, 267
4:1–3, 314–15, 318, 320
4:1, 19, 74, 92, 260, 278, 303, 314, 319, 350
4:2–3, 269, 320
4:2, 319–20, 348
4:2b–3, 268
4:3, 260, 271, 320
4:4–5:27, 350
4:4–13, 320
4:4–5, 110, 262, 321, 320–3, 329, 332, 337, 340, 350, 372
4:4, 10, 26, 90, 91, 144, 316, 321
4:5, 322
4:6–13, 266, 320, 323, 327, 350
4:6–12, 266, 271, 327
4:6–11, 183, 205, 260, 262, 266, 323, 325, 327
4:7–9, 375
4:7–8, 324
4:7, 271
4:9, 205, 206, 271, 324
4:10, 324
4:12, 271, 325
4:13, 159, 166–7, 260, 264, 266, 326, 330, 336, 370
5:1–6:14, 267
5, 215, 260, 270, 333
5:1–17, 262, 266, 329, 333–4, 336
5:1–3, 330–1
5:1–2, 362

5:1, 19, 74, 308, 329
5:2, 209, 271, 330, 367, 375
5:3, 260, 268, 283, 348
5:4–15, 144
5:4–6, 26, 144, 331, 350
5:4–5, 332, 333
5:4, 260, 269, 283, 329, 331, 362
5:5–6, 262, 308
5:5, 26, 90, 91, 144, 268, 316, 333
5:6, 260, 266, 329–30, 333, 362
5:7–12, 331
5:7, 26, 62, 260, 270, 315, 330, 332–6, 338, 349–50
5:8–9, 159, 166, 260, 264, 266, 271, 326, 370
5:8, 271, 330, 336
5:9, 271, 336
5:10–12, 315, 330, 333–4, 336
5:10, 260, 332, 334–5
5:11–12, 334
5:11, 85, 124, 260, 268, 271, 303, 334, 350, 376
5:12, 301, 303, 334–5, 349
5:13, 104–6, 266, 330, 334
5:14–15, 26, 269, 331–2, 350
5:14, 124, 260, 329, 362
5:15, 228, 270, 332–4, 347
5:16–17, 260, 330, 362, 366
5:16, 211, 260, 283, 330, 331, 337
5:17, 331
5:18–27, 262, 329, 337, 343, 345, 350
5:18–20, 7, 216–7, 337–9, 346, 350, 366, 372
5:18, 331, 334, 337–8
5:19, 127, 148, 337
5:20, 199, 337
5:21–27, 339
5:21–24, 110, 216, 320–2, 335, 339–41
5:21–23, 54, 339
5:21–22, 322
5:21, 212, 337, 340
5:22, 128, 265, 340
5:24, 167, 270, 315, 334–5, 339, 340, 343, 350
5:25–26, 266, 339
5:25, 270, 337, 342, 349
5:26, 266, 343
5:27, 268, 337, 339
6, 270, 347
6:1–14, 262, 329, 337, 345, 350
6:1–7, 315, 337, 345–8, 350
6:1–3, 346
6:1, 261, 315, 320, 331, 334, 338, 345–7, 349
6:2, 346–7
6:3, 346

Scripture Index

Amos (cont.)

6:4–7, 348
6:4, 317, 347
6:5, 265
6:6, 260, 319, 346, 347
6:6b, 346
6:7, 260, 268, 347–8
6:8–14, 345
6:9–10, 267, 345, 346, 348
6:10, 348, 363
6:11, 268, 307, 346, 349, 366
6:8, 97, 319, 337, 346, 348, 365
6:12, 26, 62, 141, 270, 315, 334–5, 337, 349–50
6:13, 349
6:14, 268–9, 337, 349
7:1–9:6, 308, 351, 370
7:1–9:4, 349
7:1–8:3, 363
7:1–8, 267, 351, 370
7:1–6, 354
7:1–3, 261, 293, 353
7:1, 261
7:1a, 352
7:1b, 352
7:2, 352, 371
7:3, 228, 352
7:4–6, 261, 293, 353
7:4a, 352
7:4b, 352
7:5, 352, 371
7:6, 228, 352
7:7–9, 261, 264, 266, 351, 362
7:7–8, 355–6, 358–9
7:7, 352
7:7a, 352
7:7b, 352
7:8, 355, 356, 358–9, 362, 376
7:8a, 352
7:8b, 352
7:9–17, 132, 270, 363, 370
7:9, 11, 266, 267, 351, 356, 362
7:10–17, 82–3, 169, 261, 267, 270, 278, 305, 313, 318, 351, 356–8, 358, 367
7:10, 358
7:11, 356, 358–9
7:12–15, 169, 358, 361
7:12–13, 359
7:12, 169, 276
7:13, 142, 271, 358–9
7:14–15, 311, 359

7:14, 276
7:15, 358
7:16, 266, 360
7:17, 83, 260, 283, 358, 360
8.1–3, 261
8:1–2, 267, 269, 293, 351–2, 355, 368–70
8:1a, 352
8:1b, 352
8:2, 268, 331, 358–9, 362, 376
8:2a, 352
8:2b, 352
8:3–14, 261
8:3–7, 267, 270, 370
8:3, 352, 362, 366, 368
8:4–7, 168, 352, 363–4, 368
8:4–6, 260, 303, 363
8:4, 74
8:5, 54, 160, 168, 364
8:6, 364
8:7, 319, 365–6
8:8–9:6, 366
8:8–14, 266, 352, 363, 365, 368, 370
8:8, 366
8:9–14, 375
8:9–10, 366
8:9, 240, 266, 366, 375
8.10, 260, 366
8:11–12, 366–7
8:11, 266, 366–7, 375
8:13–14, 366–7
8:13, 266, 366, 375
8:14, 10, 333, 343, 367
9, 265
9:1–4, 261, 267–8, 293, 351–2, 363, 368, 370–3
9:1, 366, 369
9:2–4, 369
9:2–3, 369
9:2, 178
9:3, 278, 371
9:4, 261, 369, 371
9:5–6, 159, 166, 260, 264–6, 271, 278, 326, 330, 336, 352, 368–71
9:5, 278, 366
9:6, 370
9:7–15, 108, 264–5, 271, 347, 371
9:7–10, 371
9:7, 287, 310, 371–3
9:7a, 372
9:7b, 372
9:8–10, 373
9:8, 265, 271, 371, 373

Scripture Index

9:8a, 373
9:8b, 316
9:9–10, 373
9:9, 371, 373
9:10, 271, 371
9:11–15, 25, 260, 264–5, 271, 374, 376
9:11–12, 186
9:11, 265, 271, 374
9:12–13, 374
9:12, 375
9:13–15, 265, 271
9:13, 7, 192, 254, 375
9:13b, 254
9:14–15, 186, 374–5
9:14, 114, 186, 245, 271, 376
9:15, 376

Obadiah
1, 361
10–14, 255
11–14, 289
11, 246, 247
13, 247
15, 215
17, 241

Jonah
1:1, 203
3:5–8, 212
3:5, 259
3:6–10, 213
3:9, 227, 259
4
4:2, 8, 161, 258–9, 277

Micah
1:1, 35, 203
1:2, 74, 204
3:1, 74, 95
3:9, 74, 204
4:1–3, 250, 257
4:2, 279
4:3, 250, 257
4:4, 55
4:10, 179
6:1, 74
6:2, 74
6:4, 178
6:6–8, 110
6:6–7, 341
6:8, 341
6:9, 74
6:14–15, 85, 334
7:18–20, 8, 25

Nahum
1:1, 361
1:3, 8, 227
2:10, 223
3:10, 145
3:17, 353

Habakkuk
1:8, 124
2:6–20, 338

Zephaniah
1, 7
1:1, 35, 203
1:4, 142
1:7–18, 215
1:7, 194, 216
1:11, 168
1:13, 85, 334
1:14–18, 216
1:14–16, 194, 220
1:14, 223
1:15, 217, 222
1:16, 221
1:18, 216
2:3, 228
2:4, 288
2:5, 373
2:9–10, 295
3:8, 127
3:11, 236
3:14–21, 25
3:15–17, 236
3:20, 114, 245

Haggai
1:1, 203
1:6, 233
1:9, 124
2:17, 324

Zechariah
1–8, 8
1:1, 203
1:17, 66
2:11, 258
7:1–7, 212
8:18–19, 212
8:19, 214
8:22–23, 258
9–14, 8
9:5–7, 288
10:2, 68
10:8, 178
11:15, 66

Zechariah (cont.)
13:9, 242
14:1, 215
14:5, 276
14:8, 254
Malachi
2:6–9, 76
3:2, 224
3:4, 131
4:5, 215, 223, 240

APOCRYPHA
Sirach
44–49, 6
49:10, 6, 8

NEW TESTAMENT
Matthew
19:18–19, 79
23:23, 341
Mark
10:19, 79

Luke
18:20, 79
23:30, 143
Acts
2, 243
2:10, 243
2:17–21, 243
2:21, 243
2:39, 243
10:45, 243
11:15–17, 243
Romans
10:12–13, 243
10, 243
13:9, 79
1 Corinthians
15:4, 107
15:54–5, 179
2 Corinthians
9:6, 127
Galatians
6:7–9, 127

Subject Index

Abraham/Abram, 6, 48, 122, 241, 301, 309
Achan, 58
Achor, 58
Ahab, 45, 126, 317
Amaziah, 82–3, 142, 271, 305, 318, 356–60, 363, 367
Ammi. *See* Lo-Ammi
Ammon/Ammonites, 180, 256, 291–4
Amorite(s), 304–6, 373
Amos, 1–2, 5, 17, 36, 82, 110, 146, 189, 261–2, 264, 266–7, 269, 271, 276–8, 282, 284, 286, 294–5, 302, 305, 307, 311–14, 318, 323, 326, 334, 342–3, 345–6, 351–63, 368–72
Amos, book of, 1, 4–12, 19, 24–6, 35–6, 53, 74, 76, 78, 83, 85, 90, 93, 108, 120, 128, 132, 148, 166–9, 181, 183, 186–7, 189, 202, 209, 228, 252, 254, 260–1, 264–72, 277–9, 281, 283–6, 289, 291, 299, 302–4, 306, 309, 312, 315–20, 325–6, 332, 336–7, 339, 342–3, 353–4, 358, 368, 369, 374, 376
Aram/Arameans, 115, 164, 170, 256, 286–9, 291, 293, 372–3
Assyria/Assyrians, 17, 21, 24, 27, 36, 45–6, 49, 93, 98, 101–2, 104–8, 115–18, 120, 123–4, 127–8, 130–2, 142, 145, 148, 151–2, 154–6, 159–61, 175, 184, 256, 258, 261, 268, 270, 284–8, 291, 296, 314, 331–2, 343, 346, 349–50, 367, 370

Baal/Baalism, 1, 24, 27, 39–40, 43, 53–8, 60–1, 85–7, 91, 96, 98, 106–7, 110, 117, 126, 138–9, 150, 152, 156, 173–5, 209, 241
  Baal-berith, 56
  Baal-Hermon, 56
  Baal-peor, 55–6, 138

Babylon/Babylonians, 46, 82, 88, 96, 98, 154, 156, 160, 178, 214, 217, 247, 253, 255–6, 263, 270, 286, 289–90, 297–9, 343, 370
Babylonian Exile, 1, 22, 49, 57, 69, 94, 132, 154, 160, 178, 182, 236, 245, 261, 370, 374
Babylonian Talmud, 6
  Baba Batra, 6–8
Bashan, 92, 278, 318–19
Beer-sheba, 331, 333, 367
Bethel, 5, 23–4, 27, 82, 90–3, 96, 102–3, 125–6, 142, 145, 163–7, 170, 175, 264, 271, 316, 318, 320–1, 327, 332–3, 350, 357–9, 367, 369
Book of the Covenant, 302
Book of the Four, 10, 13, 35, 187
Book of the Twelve, 1, 6–11, 13, 35, 39, 74, 110, 187, 190, 192, 206, 209, 252, 254, 278–9, 290, 324, 338, 342, 353, 374–5
booths, festival of, 130, 132, 212, 340
burnt offering. *See* Offering(s)

Canaan, Canaanite(s), 55–6, 85, 88–9, 106, 107, 138, 162, 167, 187, 258
Chroniclers, books of, 203, 210
covenant, 25–6, 29, 60–1, 75, 86, 90, 111–12, 118, 120–4, 141, 155, 160, 166, 178, 225–6, 235, 270, 282, 289
cultic prostitution. *See* prostitute/prostitution

David, 17, 29, 49, 65, 68, 75, 87, 131, 139, 213, 265, 271, 279, 330, 333, 340, 347, 361, 364, 375
Davidic, 69, 125, 177, 261, 282
Day of YHWH, 7, 189, 194, 197, 199, 202, 214–17, 219–24, 239–40, 244, 249–53, 256, 284, 337–9, 345–6, 350, 366
Decalogue, 77–9, 126–7, 168, 364, *See also* Ten Commandments

405

406 Subject Index

Deuteronomic, 57, 121, 299, 315, 321–2
  Deuteronomic Reform, 23, 91
Deuteronomistic, 22, 25, 35, 47, 57, 66, 84, 91,
  110, 112, 121, 123–4, 126, 160, 166, 169, 171,
  184, 255, 264, 266, 276, 277, 298–9, 304–5,
  311, 313, 316, 318, 342, 358–9
  Deuteronomistic History, 55, 112, 132, 169,
  277, 321, 358
Deuteronomy, book of, 23, 25, 27, 55, 66, 81, 88,
  112, 121, 123, 149, 176, 187, 204, 208, 210,
  227, 305, 340, 342
drink offering. See offering(s)

Edom, 189, 192, 195–6, 248, 254–6, 266, 286,
  288–90, 292, 375
  Edomites, 247, 288–90, 375
Egypt, 16, 20, 27, 49, 58–9, 101, 106, 115–18, 124,
  126, 128, 130–2, 140, 148–9, 150–2, 154–6,
  159, 161, 168, 170–1, 174–5, 178, 184, 189,
  195–6, 206, 222, 254–6, 258, 270, 287, 296,
  305, 308–9, 314–15, 324, 330, 349, 364, 370–3
  Egyptians, 178, 258
Elijah, 5–6, 110, 241
Elisha, 5, 45, 300, 359
Enoch, 6, 76
Ephod, 67–8
Esau, 162–3, 165, 168, 170–1, 177, 283, 289–90
Exodus (from Egypt), 20, 58–9, 130, 137, 149–50,
  168, 171, 270, 305, 372
Exodus, book of, 210, 302
Ezekiel, 6–7, 42, 354
Ezekiel, book of, 6, 35, 53, 60, 124, 222, 230, 295,
  301, 308
Ezra, 195, 214

faithfulness, 27, 29, 60, 62–4, 69, 74–5, 77, 81–2,
  93, 109, 155, 157, 227
faithless/faithlessness, 39, 43, 47–8, 52, 85–6,
  88, 93–4, 98, 101, 105, 111–12, 116, 151, 155–6,
  160–1, 165, 185
fast/fasting, 2, 8, 194, 196–7, 204, 212–14, 225,
  227, 229, 236, 250, 259
final Form, 3–4, 18–9, 22–3, 25, 30, 35, 37, 48, 79,
  82, 181, 186, 191–2, 195, 199, 236, 246, 253,
  255, 261–5, 267, 272, 285, 313, 318, 338, 349,
  366, 376
freewill offering. See offering(s)

Gaza, 195, 247–8, 288, 293–4
Genesis, book of, 60, 162–5, 170, 222, 309

Gibeah, 102–3, 133, 143
Gilead, 112–13, 159, 170, 286–7, 291
Gilgal, 24, 91–2, 96, 140, 159, 170, 316, 320–1,
  332–3
Gomer, 41–4, 46–8, 51, 62, 64, 70, 106
grain offering. See offering(s)
Greeks, 195, 247–8

Habakkuk, book of, 9
Haggai, 194
Haggai, book of, 7–9, 35, 342
Heal/Healing, 1, 26, 29, 101, 104–6, 113–18, 120,
  150–1, 155, 185
Hezekiah, 17, 36, 75
Holiness Code, 301, 308, 323
Hosea, 1–2, 5, 17, 18, 20–4, 28, 36–8, 40–52,
  64–5, 69–70, 81–2, 87, 102, 106, 110, 114, 118,
  125–6, 130, 133, 146, 148, 154, 159, 163, 181,
  187, 189
Hosea, book of, 1, 4–12, 16–21, 23–4, 30, 35, 39,
  41, 45, 52, 54–5, 62, 65, 68–70, 73, 75–6,
  78–9, 82–5, 87, 90–3, 97–8, 103, 106, 108,
  110, 112, 114, 116, 118, 131, 133, 138, 140–2,
  144, 148, 150, 153, 156–7, 161, 163–4, 167–8,
  172–5, 180–3, 186–9, 202, 209, 302, 309,
  342, 356, 364
Hoshea, 17, 37, 104, 114

idolatry, 1, 28, 52, 68, 138–9, 155, 188
injustice, 28, 144, 260, 321, 334–6, 369
  social injustice, 343
Isaac, 164–5, 203, 241, 356
Isaiah, 2, 6, 41, 46, 189, 296
Isaiah, book of, 6–7, 9, 35, 166, 279, 295–6, 335, 364
  Second Isaiah, 121

Jacob, 6, 20, 29, 68, 87, 91, 93, 97, 143, 158, 160–8,
  170–1, 173–4, 177, 238, 265, 271, 283, 289–90,
  309, 316–18, 321, 353–4, 365, 371, 373
Jehu, 45, 126, 133, 358–9
Jeremiah, 21, 41, 256, 264, 267, 354
Jeremiah, book of, 6–7, 35, 45, 53, 55, 66, 85–6, 112,
  113, 166, 193, 209, 212, 279, 285, 295–6, 311, 326
Jeroboam I, 37, 91, 93, 126, 142, 174–5, 318, 321,
  367, 373
Jeroboam II, 1, 17, 36–7, 45, 78, 277, 349, 356, 358–9
Jerome, 7
Jerusalem, 5, 7–8, 23–4, 26, 29, 44, 46, 82, 93, 96,
  103, 113, 128, 131–2, 143, 156, 160, 165, 183, 192,
  198–9, 204, 213, 223, 226, 237, 241, 243–8,

Subject Index 407

250, 252–3, 255–8, 264–5, 270, 276, 278–9, 289–90, 296, 299, 313, 321, 325, 332, 375

Jezebel, 45, 83, 213

Jezreel, 44–7, 49, 51, 60, 63

Job, 74, 333

Job, book of, 18, 74, 266

Joel, 190, 196–7, 225

Joel, book of, 1–2, 4–9, 11–12, 35, 189–90, 193–5, 198–9, 202–6, 208–9, 209–10, 212, 215, 217, 222, 225–7, 234–5, 237, 240–5, 252–9, 278, 353, 374

Jonah, 258

Jonah, book of, 9, 35, 195, 213, 227, 258–9

Joram, 45, 358–9

Joseph, 75, 93, 269, 331–2, 346–8, 350, 353

Josephus, 278

Joshua, 37, 58, 91, 238, 292, 321

Joshua, book of, 6, 55, 112, 140, 277

Josiah, 22–3, 93, 226, 255, 264, 311, 333, 356

Judges, book of, 6, 293

justice, 26, 29, 62–3, 75, 95, 111, 141, 144, 146, 157, 167, 235, 238, 255, 260, 269–70, 295, 300–1, 315, 322, 327, 332–6, 340–5, 349–50, 353, 376

Social Justice, 260

Kings, books of, 6, 17, 35, 55–6, 112, 277, 311, 318, 358, 360, 362, 364

Lo-ammi, 47–9, 63

Ammi, 49, 51

locust(s), 2, 8, 189, 196–7, 199, 202, 204–6, 208, 210–12, 214–15, 218, 220–4, 226, 228–30, 232–7, 244–5, 324, 353

Lo-ruhamah, 46–7, 49, 60, 63

Ruhamah, 49, 51, 60

Malachi, book of, 6, 8–9, 35, 223–4, 342

Mercy, 1, 26, 28–9, 57–60, 62–4, 75, 84, 113, 117, 144, 146, 148, 153–7, 184, 238, 341

messenger formula, 260, 283

Micah, 2, 190

Micah, book of, 7–10, 35, 74, 76, 187, 342

Minor Prophets. *See* Book of the Twelve

Mizpah, 23, 91, 95–6, 321

Moab/Moabites, 127, 138, 145, 256, 276, 292–4, 296, 298

Moses, 25, 37, 58, 74, 160, 171, 238, 266, 304, 354

Nahum, book of, 8–9

Nazirite(s), 138, 271, 305–6, 307

Nehemiah, 194, 213, 223

New Moon, 54, 98, 364

Noah, 6

Obadiah, book of, 9, 192, 241, 374–5

offering(s), 86–8, 131, 150, 183, 196, 197, 208–10, 321, 332, 339–40

burnt offering, 109–10, 322, 340, 341

drink offering, 197, 209–10, 212, 218, 228, 233

freewill offering, 322

grain offering, 197, 209, 212, 218, 228, 233, 322, 340

offering of well-being, 322, 340

sin offering, 84

thank offering, 322

Omri, 45

Oracles against the Nations (OAN), 74, 107, 120–1, 261, 263, 267–8, 270, 281–3, 285, 293–7, 299, 308, 311, 315, 317, 337, 348–9, 351, 353, 372, 375

Pentateuch/Pentateuchal, 3, 58, 61, 68, 91, 137, 162, 164, 321, 342

Philistia/Philistine(s), 57, 189, 195–6, 213, 246–8, 256, 288–9, 293–4, 296, 346, 372–3

Phoenicia/Phoenician(s), 139, 167, 195, 247

Priest(s), 26–8, 68, 73, 75, 77, 81–6, 88, 90, 93–6, 98, 106–7, 110, 113, 125, 127, 140, 142, 152, 155, 189, 190, 192–3, 195–7, 210–12, 214–15, 219, 222, 229–30, 232–3, 240, 242–3, 253, 298, 302, 305, 307, 318, 342, 359

prostitute/prostitution, 16, 27–8, 38–42, 44, 48, 52–3, 64, 67, 71, 85–6, 88–90, 92–3, 96–8, 113, 130–1, 155, 246

cultic prostitution, 85–6, 93

sacred prostitution, 55–6, 89–90

temple prostitute, 67, 88–9

Proverbs, book of, 204, 335

Psalms, book of, 178, 187, 190, 279

Rahab, 75, 111

Ramoth-gilead, 112

redaction criticism/redaction-critical method, 3–4, 12, 22, 24, 30–1, 37, 39–40, 159, 182, 191, 262–3, 264

righteousness, 26, 29, 62–3, 144, 146, 235, 270, 315, 322, 334–6, 340–3, 349–50

Ruhamah. *See* Lo-ruhamah

Ruth, book of, 195

Subject Index

Sabbath, 54, 79, 86, 364
Sabeans, 195–6, 247–8
sacred prostitution. *See* prostitute/prostitution
sacrifice, 1, 27–8, 55, 67–8, 78, 84–5, 87, 91–2, 97,
    109–10, 127–8, 131, 138, 150, 167, 170, 183,
    189, 193–4, 196–7, 210, 212, 218, 230, 292,
    321–3, 332, 340–2, 350
Samaria, 5, 17, 21, 23–4, 26, 29, 43, 45, 46, 92, 93,
    113–14, 124, 126, 128, 142, 145, 156, 159, 174,
    183, 194, 245, 261, 262, 264, 267, 312–16,
    318–20, 325, 329, 345–7, 350, 358–9, 367, 370
Samuel, 84, 91, 96, 140, 177, 203, 306, 321, 341,
    354, 361
Samuel, books of, 6, 96
Saul, 68, 84, 91, 96, 134, 138, 140, 143, 213, 238,
    321, 330
Second Isaiah, 121, *See also* Isaiah, book of
Second Temple. *See* Temple
Septuagint (LXX), 2, 9, 35, 67, 77, 86, 105, 111,
    133, 137, 139, 141, 145, 150–1, 166, 176, 179,
    184, 186, 203, 210–11, 255, 278, 287, 295–6,
    306, 314, 372
Sex/Sexual, 39, 56, 61, 67, 70, 76, 78, 89, 92, 113,
    127, 138, 294, 301, 309
Shittim, 95–6
    Wadi Shittim, 254
Sidon, 189, 195–6, 247–8, 296
sin offering. *See* offering(s)
Sirach, book of, 6
social injustice. *See* injustice
social justice. *See* justice
Sodom, 301
Sodom and Gomorrah, 152–3, 324
Solomon, 1, 205, 247, 261, 289, 318, 324
Song of Songs, book of, 186
steadfast love, 29, 60, 62–3, 68, 75, 106, 109–11,
    116, 144, 146, 157, 159, 167, 184, 227, 258, 341–2

Sukkoth, 130, 132, 168
Syria/Syrians, 102, 104, 256, 288

Tabor, 95–6
Tekoa, 5, 17, 264, 276, 278
Temple, 5, 8, 22, 67, 82, 86, 88–9, 91, 131–2, 183,
    194, 196, 208, 210, 212–13, 245, 247–8, 254,
    279, 324, 363
    Second Temple, 22, 25, 79, 82, 186, 190,
        192–4, 203–4, 214, 229, 244, 256, 262, 313,
        340, 342
temple prostitute. *See* prostitute/prostitution
Ten Commandments, 77–9, 127, *See also*
    Decalogue
teraphim, 67–8
thank offering. *See* offering(s)
theodicy, 8, 93, 268
Torah, 7, 29, 76, 84
Tyre, 139, 167, 189, 195–6, 247–8, 256, 258, 266,
    278, 286, 289, 296, 330

Ugarit/Ugaritic, 55–6, 347–8, 367
unfaithfulness, 1, 8, 27, 40, 81, 95, 114

whore/whoredom, 16, 41, 52–3, 113, 130, *See also*
    prostitute/prostitution
wilderness, 20, 28, 40, 53, 58–9, 69, 130, 137–8,
    143, 146, 149, 151, 155, 160, 168, 174, 176, 222,
    228, 270, 305, 342–3
wisdom literature/traditions, 160, 168, 187, 270,
    284, 334, 339, 364

Zechariah, 17, 36, 45, 194, 356, 358
Zechariah, book of, 7, 9, 35
Zephaniah, book of, 7–9, 10, 35, 295
Zion, 7, 190, 193, 199, 221–2, 229, 234–5, 241,
    252–3, 255–8, 278–9, 345–6, 361

Printed in the United States
by Baker & Taylor Publisher Services